Making Sense of Society

Edited by
Ian
Marsh

# Making Sense of Society

## An Introduction to Sociology

Longman
London and New York

Addison Wesley Longman Limited
Edinburgh Gate
Harlow, Essex CM20 2JE, England
*and Associated Companies throughout the world.*

*Published in the United States of America*
*by Addison Wesley Longman Publishing Company, New York*



First published 1996

ISBN 0 582 22895 6 PPR

**British Library Cataloguing-in-Publication Data**

A catalogue record for this book is
available from the British Library

**Library of Congress Cataloging-in-Publication Data**

A catalogue record for this book is
available from the Library of Congress

Set by 30 in 11¼/12pt Perpetua
Produced by Longman Singapore Publishers (Pte) Ltd.
Printed in Singapore

# Contents

# Contributors

Ian Marsh *Liverpool Hope University College*
Mike Keating *Liverpool Hope University College*
Anne Eyre *Westminster College, Oxford*
Janet McKenzie *Anglia Polytechnic University, Cambridge*
Rosie Campbell *Liverpool Hope University College*
Tony Finnegan *Liverpool Hope University College*
Ian McIntosh *University of Stirling*
Mike Kilroe *Liverpool Hope University College*
Dawn Jones *Liverpool Hope University College*
Laurence Sidorczuk *Liverpool Hope University College*

# Preface

*Making Sense of Society* provides a general introduction to sociology for undergraduate students. It is aimed, particularly, at students following introductory sociology courses in higher education. For some students the first year undergraduate course provides their only formal study of sociology; for others it serves as a basis for their further study. Also, some students come to their first year courses having studied A Level or Access courses in sociology, while others have studied no sociology previously. Indeed one of the reasons why we feel a new textbook is needed at this level is because of the diversity of background knowledge of sociology among students starting their higher education courses.

In the brave new world of mass education and dwindling resources the textbook is here to stay and we hope that this one will become a useful addition. Large numbers and higher staff–student ratios are placing increasing pressure on teachers in higher education. In emphasizing an interactive approach to learning we have tried to produce a book that will, in part at least, remove the burden of everything coming from the teacher and allow students to become active participants in the learning process.

*Making Sense of Society* provides a general overview of the major substantive areas in sociology. Although each chapter is self-contained the book is organized around three main themes – Making Sense of Society, which looks at the ways in which sociologists collect and interpret their data (Chapter 1 to 3); Social Structure, which emphasizes the social and economic influences on life chances and lifestyles (Chapter 4 to 9); and Socialization and Social Control, which examines the ways in which our lives are governed by culture and the means by which we receive this culture (Chapters 10 to 14).

Within reason we have aimed to provide some consistency of structure across the book, thus certain features are included in each chapter:

*Questions* to encourage reflection and discussion. The sorts of questions asked vary – some ask students for gut reactions to an issue, others require more thought and analysis.

*Boxed sections* that highlight case studies, specific examples of research, international perspectives, definitions, terminology and biographies of key writers.

*Summaries* of the main points and issues covered.

*Further reading* suggestions.

Each chapter concludes with two *Activities* that could form the basis of fuller classroom or seminar examination and discussion.

## Acknowledgements

This book has been a collaborative endeavour between, in the first instance, sociology lecturers at Liverpool Hope University College (formerly Liverpool Institute of Higher Education) and Longman. We have had tremendous support from a number of people at Longman – although we do not wish to take all the blame for the high turnover there. In particular we would like to thank Charlie Carman for her help at the start of the project, Chris Harrison who has been there throughout, Christine Firth for her meticulous attention to detail and, most of all, Sarah Caro whose commitment, encouragement and hassling (in the nicest possible way) have seen us through the last two years.

It is conventional for writers to thank the various family members, friends, colleagues and academic influences who have helped and inspired them. However with ten writers contributing to this book such a list would be excessive – and anyway we'd be bound to forget some key influence. We would, though, like to thank Graham White who while Head of Department at Liverpool brought most of the contributors to this book together and Barbara Davies and Sue Marsh who helped produce the typescript for the less word processor adept writers.

Ian Marsh
Mike Keating
January 1996

Chapter 1

# Sociological understanding and common sense

**Chapter outline:** Introduction • The image of sociology • The sociological perspective • The sociological perspective in practice • The origins of sociology • Culture and socialization • The power of culture • Summary • Further reading • Activities

## Learning objectives

When you have studied this chapter you should be able to address these key questions:

- What is sociology?
- What are its origins as a discipline?
- What kinds of explanations does sociology offer for social and personal behaviour?
- What is culture and how does it affect social and personal behaviour?

## Introduction

I am always somewhat surprised when college students estimate that 30% of the population of the United States is Jewish (actually, the figure is close to 1.9%); that 40% of all Americans are black (actually the figure for those who regard themselves as black or African American is more like 12%); that 60% of our population is Catholic (actually, the figure is 20% maximum); that 40% of our elders are in nursing homes (the figure is more like 4%).

Where does this misinformation about our society come from? Why can't Americans get their social facts straight? Part of the answer is that all of us are socialised with unrepresentative samples of social reality. Inevitably, we learn to view the world from our own biased and limited slice of experience. We tend to apply what we see every day to what we don't see every day. (Levin 1993: 44)

There is no reason to suppose that students (or non-students for that matter) in other countries would be any better informed about the 'social geography' of their own societies. Most of us were brought up in areas that could be characterized as predominantly middle or working class and that have predominantly white or ethnic minority populations. Most of us still mix mainly with people from similar class and ethnic backgrounds. Most of us grew up with people of a similar age and will still have as our closest friends people of a similar age. While there are many exceptions to these generalizations, modern, large-scale societies have almost invariably organized themselves by separating their schools and neighbourhoods by race, class, religion and age. It is not surprising that our knowledge of the social facts and geography of our own societies is so inaccurate.

How would you describe the social geography of the area in which you were brought up (consider class, ethnicity, age, religion)?

Name an area that could be described as predominantly (a) ageing; (b) black; (c) Catholic; (d) Jewish; (e) middle class; (f) Muslim; (g) Protestant; (h) white; (i) working class.

**Case Study**

### The Kray twins: local heroes?

The Krays were an old-fashioned East End family – tight, self-sufficient and devoted to each other. The name was Austrian, and the twins had Irish, Romany and Jewish blood. The centre of their world was to remain the tiny terrace house at 178 Vallance Road where they grew up and where their Aunt May and their maternal grandparents still lived. The area was badly bombed in the war; before that it was one of the poorest parts of the entire East End and a breeding ground for criminals. It was Bill Sykes's home ground, 'The Rookeries' of Dickens were once just down the road, and Jack the Ripper murdered one of his last victims round the corner in Hanbury Street.

The house, 178 Vallance Road, was tiny, the second in a row of four blank-faced Victorian terraced cottages. There was no bathroom, the lavatory was in the yard at the back, and day and night the house shook as the Liverpool Street trains roared past

*(box continued)*

*(box continued)*

the bedroom windows. For Violet none of this mattered. Her parents were just around the corner; so was her sister, Rose. Her other sister, May, was next door but one, and her brother, John Lee, kept the café across the street.

And old Grandfather Lee, who still kept his famous left hook in trim, punching a mattress hung up in the yard. He would sit with the twins for hours in his special chair by the fire. . . . And sometimes the old man would talk about the other heroes of the old East End, its criminals. Spud Murphy of Hoxton who killed two men in a spieler in Whitechapel and who shouted to the police that he'd bring a machine-gun and finish everyone off before he was caught; Martin and Baker, two Bethnal Green men who took the nine o'clock walk after shooting three policemen at Carlisle. And for the old man, Jack the Ripper's murders were still a local happening. (Adapted from Pearson 1972: 12–27)

**Ronnie Kray's funeral**

The East End of London accorded one of its most infamous sons the equivalent of a state funeral yesterday. Crowds big enough to gladden the heart of an emperor turned out to shower the last journey of Ronnie Kray with tribute, and to greet his handcuffed twin brother Reggie as though he were a conquering hero. . . .

**Fig 1.1** The funeral of Ronnie Kray from *The Times* 30.3.95. (Photograph by Adrian Brooks, courtesy of Times Newspapers Ltd.)

*(box continued)*

*(box continued)*

The Kray twins, who long ago assumed the status of folk heroes, were each serving 30 years for different murders. Ronnie, the elder of the two by 45 minutes, died of a heart attack in Broadmoor two weeks ago aged 61; Reggie was let out of Maidstone for the day under heavy guard. (*The Times* 30 March 1995: 1)

**Questions**

**Does social background offer a 'complete explanation' for the Krays' criminal behaviour? What other factors might have played a part?**

**Why do you think the Krays have become 'folk heroes'?**

Sociology provides us with a more accurate picture of the social geography of the society we live in. It offers particular and exciting ways of understanding ourselves, other people and the social world. It examines the social facts and forces that affect us all. It helps us to make sense of the changes that occur around us all of the time; changes such as the effect of new technologies on everyday life; the variations in employment patterns as factories open or close; the influence on education, health and other services of economic and political philosophies and policies. In view of the insights into social life that sociology provides, it might seem strange that it is not a subject that is taught to all children as a matter of course. Before looking at what sociology is and how it has developed, we shall consider briefly its 'image'.

## The image of sociology

In the mid-1960s Peter Berger published a very readable introduction to the study of sociology which began by informing us that 'There are very few jokes about sociologists'. He explained that this was probably due to their low profile in 'the popular imagination' (Berger 1967a). However, much has changed since then and sociology has a far higher public profile largely due to its inclusion in the school curriculum, its status as a degree-bearing discipline and the regular appearance of its experts on television and radio documentaries. As a result the sociologist no longer escapes humorous mud slinging at the professions. Whether it is at the hands of Malcolm Bradbury (*The History Man*), Ben Elton (*The Young Ones*) or simple throw-away comments about the number of sociologists it takes to change a light-bulb, the jokes have not been particularly flattering and tend to rely on crude and predictable stereotypes.

Dr Christopher Pole made use of the BBC's *Punters* programme (Radio 4, 8 August 1991) to defend the professional and academic status of sociology and to broadcast his objections to the ridicule that sociology often attracts from the media. In the studio debate that followed, Roger Scruton (Professor of Aesthetics at Birkbeck College) castigated the study of sociology as 'an endless quest for knowledge about trivia'. Among other things he complained that sociology was intellectually sloppy, politically biased and morally corrupting. 'This subject', he said, 'has concentrated on those areas of enquiry which are interesting to someone with a socialist agenda; obsessed with class, with domination, with hierarchy and exploitation. . . . all those old ghastly nineteenth century ideas. All this amounts to a case to be answered by the sociological establishment.'

Dr Pole was joined in the studio by Professor of Sociology Jennifer Platt, who argued that such misconceptions informed much of the bad press received by sociology and the public ignorance and distrust surrounding it. Dr Pole advocated its continued study on the grounds that it encouraged inquiry, demanded intellectual precision and asked awkward questions:

**In any kind of sociology it is absolutely essential to question what we are doing and what we are being told . . . what we are studying and from which perspective. That is the very essence of the discipline; that is why I do sociology because I want to investigate, because I want to work at various different perspectives.**

As this was precisely the reason for Professor Scruton's disenchantment it is hardly surprising that he remained unconvinced. He concluded by warning the audience:

**There are certain matters which should not be pried into . . . least of all by half-baked lefties from universities. . . . Because of this relentless questioning of human institutions and human realities it may be inappropriate for young people to study it.**

Such views are no doubt shared by some politicians, journalists and members of the public but sociology is also an increasingly popular subject in schools and colleges throughout the western world. Despite the attacks on its academic credentials, educational status and practical worth, sociology has survived to establish itself not only as a separate discipline but also as an integral part of education in general. As the Higginson Report (DES 1988) pointed out

**A free society depends for its strength on the ability of individual members to make sense of their surroundings and to think for themselves. (quoted in McNeill 1990)**

Sociology is regarded as an essential part of professional training courses for teachers, social workers and people who work within the National Health Service and the criminal justice system. In the United States and in continental Europe trained sociologists are employed as consultants in areas such as industrial relations; it is clear that having a degree in the subject is no barrier to future career prospects. The Conservative Cabinet minister Virginia Bottomley has a degree in the subject while Ralph Dahrendorf, formerly Professor of Sociology and director of the London School of Economics, was elevated to the House of Lords for his contribution to public life.

Finally, it is worth asking whether the study of any subject should have to be justified in purely vocational terms, such as preparing people for specific occupational positions. Sociology retains its popularity with young and old alike because it asks questions about the very things that directly affect our lives. It has an immediate relevance which other subjects cannot boast and provides insights into the workings of the world we inhabit. Although he was writing in the 1960s, Peter Berger explained that sociology could be viewed as 'an individual pastime' because it transformed the meaning of those familiar things we all take for granted:

> **The fascination of sociology lies in the fact that its perspective makes us see in a new light the very world in which we have lived all our lives.**
>
> *(Berger 1967a: 32–3)*

Q What did you think sociology was about before you started to study the subject?

How would you have described a sociologist?

Has this initial impression of sociology and sociologists changed?

If so, how?

Why do you think some people – including politicians and journalists – might feel threatened by a subject which encourages the questioning of 'human institutions and human realities'?

## The sociological perspective

We have already heard sociology dismissed as 'an endless quest for knowledge about trivia' and it is often criticized as being nothing more than 'common sense'. On the other hand we find the subject being attacked as 'too theoretical' or obsessed with statistics. If aspects of social life, like poverty, child abuse, crime and educational failure, can be regarded as 'trivia' then the first complaint must be true but it is doubtful whether you would be reading this book if you agreed with it. The apparent contradictions between the view of sociology as common sense and the counter-objection (from many students) that it is too complex in its approach to everyday life can be resolved. Although sociology deals with everyday life and common sense, that does not mean that it limits itself to explanations which simply depend upon feelings of what makes sense. Such opinions would rely upon what Bauman (1990) has called 'a personalised world-view' and should be distinguished from a sociological perspective. Sociology and sociologists have a very strong relationship with common sense in that the object of study is often the common-sense view of social reality held by members of society. It is in the way that they study the experience of ordinary people's daily lives, the questions they ask and the concepts that they use which distinguishes sociologists from other people and disciplines.

The theories and methods used by sociologists are the concern of Chapters 2 and 3 but we should note that in studying people going about their everyday lives, sociologists employ a scientific and theoretical perspective which seeks to establish some kind of factual picture of what is going on. This sociological perspective relies upon rigorous procedures and is informed by rational argument, criticism and existing knowledge. In this sense sociology is a combination of common sense, statistical inquiry and social theory and provides a distinct, but partial, view of what is going on:

> **Sociology as an approach to understanding the world, can be differentiated from other approaches in that it attempts to be scientific, that is to produce empirically warranted and verifiable statements about the social world and is basically distinguished by its distinctive assumptions, concepts, questions, methods and answers.**
>
> *(Cuff et al. 1990: 9)*

**Q** What common-sense assumptions do you have about (a) yourself; (b) your country and community; (c) your family?

What evidence is there for these assumptions?

Can you test them?

How widely shared are they?

In the writings of Berger (1967a) and C W Mills (1970) and more recent contributions from Bauman (1990) and Kingdom (1991), we get a very strong notion of what sociology is, often as a result of stressing what it is not. They make clear that sociology is an antidote to personal and subjective observations and a complete rejection of explanations that are grounded in naturalistic or individualistic assumptions about 'human nature'. The emphasis is quite clearly upon the individual as a social animal within the context of a social environment. As this emphasis challenges popular and sometimes deeply held notions of human nature and individual responsibility it is not surprising that sociology meets with a certain amount of resistance. Anticipating what has become known as the 'structure versus agency debate', C W Mills pointed out in his introduction to *The Sociological Imagination* (1970) that the primary role of the sociologist is to reveal the complex relationship between the individual and society:

**The sociological imagination enables us to grasp history and biography and the relations between the two within society. That is its task and its promise. To recognise this task and this promise is the mark of the classic social analyst. . . . No social study that does not come back to the problem of biography, of history, and of their intersections within a society, has completed its intellectual journey.**

*(Mills 1970: 12)*

Mills demonstrates that by unifying biography and history we are forced to place our own individual experiences and attitudes in the context of social structure and that societies themselves are not unique but have to be placed within an historical context.

Thus we have to go beyond personal experience and common sense for answers to our questions. The most vivid example can be seen in Mills's distinction between 'personal troubles' and 'public issues'. Whether we are looking at unemployment, war, divorce or the problems of urban living, there are aspects of our lives over which we have some control – 'personal troubles' for which we bear some responsibility and to which we can offer some private solution. However, there are other conditions that offer no such remedy because the troubles that we experience (no matter how personally) are beyond our control; they have historical and structural causes and as such represent 'public issues' which can be changed only by large-scale economic developments or social reform.

Writing twenty years later Zygmunt Bauman reiterates the importance of Mills's early insights into the crucial relationship between history, society and biography:

**Deeply immersed in our daily routines, though, we hardly ever pause to think about the meaning of what we have gone through: even less often have we the opportunity to compare our private experience with the fate of others, to see the social in the individual, the general in the particular, this is precisely what sociologists can do for us. We would expect them to show us how our individual biographies intertwine with the history we share with fellow human beings.**

*(Bauman 1990, quoted in Giddens 1992: 8)*

In western societies where the cult of the individual and the notion of voluntary action are crucial aspects of our cultural history, and the coverage of politics is often reduced to the antics of personalities rather than their policies, it is not surprising to hear prime ministers proclaiming that 'there is no such thing as society' (Margaret Thatcher) or referring to 'the classless society' (John Major) as if it were a matter of agreed fact. In such a climate sociology must struggle to assert the concepts upon which its perspective is based; if it does not it will disappear among the clamour of those whom John Kingdom (1991) has called 'the new individualists'.

**Q** What do you think Margaret Thatcher meant when she proclaimed 'there is no such thing as society'? What are the broader (a) moral (b) political (c) sociological implications of such a statement?

## The sociological perspective in practice

### Sociology as an empirical enterprise

Sociology has had to fight to establish itself as a social science. Using the principles of the scientific method established by the natural sciences, sociologists have developed methods of data collection which enable them to claim that sociological knowledge is as reliable as that found in any other sphere of the social sciences. This does not mean that sociology can produce infallible laws of the human universe (many natural sciences have failed to do this) but it can endeavour to follow the rules of the scientific method to establish verifiable data and valid correlations which may be used to confirm or deny an hypothesis (or create a new one). In essence sociologists demand that theoretical positions are tested against evidence and that this evidence is gathered by the most logical method in an objective manner and interpreted in an impartial way. The application of the scientific method to sociology is examined in Chapter 3. In general terms, the use of the scientific approach enables social researchers to establish two things.

First, through observation and measurement a statistical record of how things are can be compiled, much in the tradition of social accountancy discussed later in this chapter (pp. 17–18). Such statistics are based upon and confirm the assumption that social life is largely routine, predictable and unconscious. William James recognized the importance of this when writing about habitual behaviour over 100 years ago:

> **Habit is . . . the enormous fly-wheel of society, its most precious conservative agent. . . . It keeps the fisherman and the deck hand at sea through the winter; it holds the miner in the darkness, and nails the countryman to his log cabin and his lonely farm through all the months of snow.** *(James 1890: 143)*

We normally take for granted the 'patterned regularity' of social life because we are steeped in the familiarity bred by habit. On a superficial level these patterns may simply be descriptions of how people normally behave within their culture, perhaps dressing in 'appropriate' manner for different occasions, such as interviews or funerals. On another level it may be noticed that some forms of behaviour are exclusive, for example the majority of people do not enter higher education, while patterns may also emerge which change over time, such as the rise in the recorded levels of crime.

Second, the compilation of data allows us to identify possible correlations between the patterns of behaviour so that we begin to notice that certain patterns of behaviour are more commonly discovered among particular groups of people. Some social groups are less likely to pass exams than others, people who live in urban areas may be more prone to burglary than those who inhabit the suburbs or the countryside and the children most likely to be found anywhere but school in termtime come from backgrounds where education is not highly valued. This does not mean that sociology can predict exactly who will fail their exams, get burgled or bunk off from school, but it can make 'tendency statements' about the likelihood of the correlations reproducing themselves.

## Sociology as explanation

Social correlations need to be explained and the emphasis in sociology is upon social conditions rather than biological, psychological or genetic factors. This is not to deny that we are, as a species, the product of millions of years of biological evolution or that individual differences call for psychological explanation. However, sociologists resist any generalization which suggests that behaviour can be reduced to biological explanations alone. Not only do such claims have very powerful ideological connotations, but also they fly in the face of the clear evidence linking behaviour to social circumstances and cultural experience. The power of culture and the importance of the learning experience are examined later (pp. 23–7), but the areas we have used so far as examples are clear cases where social circumstances are an essential part of any explanation; educational failure, crime, truancy and mental breakdown are all issues that call for sociological illumination.

In the popular imagination, pure evil may still be the most appropriate explanation for senseless crime, madness may be conveniently dismissed as a disease of the mind and some individuals are simply ineducable. Sociology teaches us that educational success is related to gender and class, that recorded crime is largely committed by juveniles, that black people are more likely than whites to be diagnosed as schizophrenic by British and North American psychiatrists and that the number of British children truanting from school is currently running at about 30,000 per year and in some parts of inner-city London the rate is as high as 40 per cent. It is not surprising that when things happen to us (which we were not expecting) we take it personally or blame it on chance. However, if we are aware of the way in which the odds are stacked the element of chance is drastically reduced: your failure to pass your exams is something you share with a lot of other people, your house was the third to be burgled in your street that week and your children have discovered that the classmates who still attend your local community comprehensive school are now regarded as deviant.

**Q** Think of some of the key events in your own life. To what extent was their outcome affected by (a) social factors (where you live, what school you went to); (b) biological factors (your gender, race); (c) psychological factors (your intelligence and personality)? How easy it is to distinguish between these different factors?

In this section we have talked of the sociological perspective as if it were a uniform and standardized body of concepts, theories and findings. This would give the impression of a discipline free from criticism and internal division and it would be wholly incorrect. One of the main difficulties that students of this subject experience is the failure of sociologists to agree with one another and the diversity of opinion that exists within it. Without exaggerating these differences, there are obvious disagreements over methodological procedures and theoretical perspectives which provide the conceptual backdrop to what sociology is all about and which are explored in Chapters 2 and 3.

Furthermore, there is political disagreement over the value and neutrality of sociology. Apart from the criticisms of philosophers who have argued that sociology cannot logically fit into the scientific frame of reference, there are complaints from within the discipline itself that sociology's claim to be an objective science is undone by its actual behaviour in the real world of research and theoretical activity. Radical and Marxist critics like Gouldner (1971, 1975) have complained that much sociology has developed into a tame form of social surveillance on behalf of the most powerful groups in society, into 'cow sociology' – a domesticated animal to be watered and fed in return for regular milking. On the other hand Professor David Marsland has joined forces with Roger Scruton in his attack on the left-wing political bias which he claims is the overriding characteristic of current sociology.

Whatever its shortcomings, sociology is a rewarding area of study; it offers the opportunity to ask questions, to consider different perspectives to evaluate evidence and to reflect on those attitudes previously thought of as 'common sense'. As a result we begin to see ourselves and the social world we inhabit in a different way. As an echo of Berger's claim that the first wisdom of sociology is that 'things are not what they seem', Bauman has summarized the position brilliantly:

**When repeated often enough, things tend to become familiar, and familiar things are self-explanatory; they present no problems and arouse no curiosity. . . . Familiarity is the staunchest enemy of inquisitiveness and criticism – and thus also of innovation and the courage to change. In an encounter with that familiar world ruled by habits and reciprocally reasserting beliefs, sociology acts as a meddlesome and often irritating stranger. It disturbs the comfortingly quiet way of life by asking questions no one among the 'locals' remembers being asked, let alone answered. Such questions make evident things into puzzles: they defamiliarize the familiar. Suddenly, the daily way of life must come under scrutiny. It now appears to be just one of the possible ways, not the one and only, not the 'natural' way of life.**

*(Bauman 1990, quoted in Giddens 1992: 11)*

## The origins of sociology

Sociology is generally regarded (by western sociologists) as a western academic pursuit. However, as Ritzer has acknowledged, 'scholars were doing sociology long ago and in other parts of the world' (Ritzer 1992: 8). Abdel Rahman Ibn-Khaldun, for example, was active in sociological research and teaching at Cairo University 500 years before its emergence as an academic discipline in Europe. This section, therefore, should be seen as an introduction to.the foundations of western sociology.

**Case Study**

### Abdel Rahman Ibn-Khaldun (1332–1406)

Ibn-Khaldun was born in Tunis, North Africa, in 1332. He was schooled in the Koran, mathematics and history and followed a career in politics, serving in a variety of positions in Tunis, Morocco, Spain and Algeria. After his 'political career', he undertook an intensive five-year period of study and writing and became a lecturer at the centre of Islamic Study at the Al-Azhar Mosque University in Cairo. By his death in 1406, Ibn-Khaldun had produced a number of studies that shared many ideas and themes with contemporary sociology. He believed in the scientific study of society, empirical research and the importance of locating the causes of social phenomena. He examined social institutions (in the political and economic spheres, for example) and was interested in comparing primitive and modern societies. (Adapted from Ritzer 1992: 8)

The intellectual roots of sociology stretch beyond the activists of the nineteenth century to the political and social philosophers of classical Greece, the social contract theories of Hobbes, Locke and Rousseau and the Enlightenment of eighteenth-century Europe. In their attempts to understand human nature and harness their insights to a vision of social improvement, the early writers discussed issues and employed concepts that were clearly sociological in nature:

> **In the writings of Aristotle, Plato, Hobbes, Locke and Rousseau there are numerous sociological themes relating to problems of social differentiation, inequality, social conflict and social cohesion, the development of the division of labour and private property – but this does not make these theorists sociologists.**
>
> *(Swingewood 1991: 9–10)*

Swingewood makes an important distinction between the early writers who focus attention upon 'human nature as the basis of human society' and the writers of the Enlightenment, who emphasized the importance of social structure and social laws. He suggests that it was not until the Enlightenment of the eighteenth century that 'a peculiarly invigorating mixture of political philosophy, history, political economy and sociology' laid the basis for looking at the world in a new way.

The laws governing these historical and social processes were no longer deferred to as the hidden hand of God working mysteriously behind the scenes. Rather the dynamics of social order and historical change were seen as open to human inquiry – hidden truths that could be revealed by rational speculation and scientific study.

**Q** What differences might there be between a society in which historical and social processes are seen as the 'hand of God' and one in which they are open to rational human inquiry? Can you think of societies in which the two views coexist?

## Social theory in Europe and America

European sociology has its recent origins in the intellectual aspirations and social upheavals of the nineteenth century; its foundation as a discipline is usually attributed to Auguste Comte (1798–1857). Comte invented the name 'sociology' and also the term 'positivism'. He established the Positivist Society in 1848 and saw positivism as the search for order and progress in the social world. He felt that a science based on experimentation and open to testing was the only valid form of human knowledge and, in the face of a great deal of academic prejudice, devoted himself to the establishing of sociology as the study of social facts. A year after Comte's death Emile Durkheim (1858–1917) was born; he continued the fight for sociology to be recognized by the academic community as 'the science of institutions, their genesis and their functioning'.

At the same time British sociology developed from the theoretical work of political economists like Adam Smith (1723–90) and the idea of social evolution advocated by Herbert Spencer (1820–1903). However, the major contribution of the early British sociologists was to be found in social research and the belief that social science could solve the social problems of industrial society through statistical analysis and social reform. Some early sociologists had to masquerade as anthropologists or botanists to achieve academic positions but by 1903 the Sociological Society of London had been founded and in 1907 the London School of Economics and Political Science established the first Department of Sociology. Liverpool University created a new School of Social Science in the same year although the emphasis was upon social administration and social work training. Loss of direction, internal divisions and traditional academic resistance within the universities meant that the formal progress of sociology in Britain was very slow. While the USA could boast 169 institutions teaching sociology as early as 1901, British universities were tardy in recognizing the claim of sociology and it was not until the 1950s that interest in the subject was revived. By the 1960s there were no more than forty sociologists in the whole of the UK and only twelve degree courses on offer (Abrams 1968; Kent 1981).

Meanwhile in Germany, the establishment of sociology as a discipline met with similar opposition from academics who rejected Marxism as nothing more than a political philosophy but also refused to take seriously the efforts of Max Weber (1864–1920) and Georg Simmel (1858–1918), who founded the German Sociological Society in 1910. Both did achieve academic posts but Weber was dogged by depression and poor health while Simmel found that academic prejudice against his ideas was compounded by the anti-semitism that was so deeply rooted in German culture. Both writers probably achieved greater respect in the less prejudiced atmosphere of North American universities.

By contrast, in the USA sociology developed alongside the new universities of the late nineteenth century and as a result was treated with the same respect given to any other academic profession. The first sociology department was founded at the University of Kansas in 1889 and the famous centre of American sociology was established at Chicago in 1892.

**Q** Why do you think sociology was more readily accepted in the USA than in Britain and continental Europe?

Do you think these reasons are still applicable today?

## The emergence of sociology

The emergence of sociology as a moral science cannot simply be accounted for by identifying its intellectual ancestry. To understand why these ideas flourished in recent history it is necessary to place them within the context of the economic, social and political upheavals of the eighteenth and nineteenth centuries. In other words the historical emergence of sociology needs to be treated sociologically. The work of the early sociologists has to be seen as a product of their direct experience, as middle-class intellectuals, of an age characterized by social change. We shall examine this age of transition to try and make sense of the social forces which shaped the interests, priorities and ideas of the major social theorists and researchers of early western sociology.

Societies which had remained relatively static for centuries now found themselves embroiled in the dramatic transformation from feudalism to capitalism. Just as the religious and political certainties of Absolutist monarchies were shaken by the critical attacks of the Enlightenment, so the traditional practices and social relationships of rural life gave way to the new demands of the industrial and political revolutions of the period. The shift from the traditional occupations of cottage industry and agricultural production to the new skills and practices of the factory system saw massive migrations of rural populations to the centres of industrial production and the rise of the 'industrial classes'. While the new middle classes were closely associated with the radical ideas of the Enlightenment and the French Revolution, the working classes were more clearly linked to the social crisis epitomized by urban poverty, crime and poor health and to the new forms of political unrest like Chartism, trade unionism and socialism.

As Nisbet (1970) has pointed out, many of the terms that we now use in everyday discourse (e.g. industry, ideology, bureaucracy, capitalism, crisis) take their modern meaning from the attempts by nineteenth-century social commentators to make some sense of 'the collapse of the old regime under the blows of industrialism and revolutionary democracy'. The main features of these industrial and political upheavals can be summarized as: the industrial revolution; the spirit of capitalism; mass society and urban life; political change; and the crisis of the modern mind. We shall look briefly at each of these features.

### *The industrial revolution*

Through the industrial revolution, technology and the factory system transformed people's relationship to the work process, society and one another. Industrial production as a concept and a practice was not new; Colin Spencer (1986) tells us that the Romans were so keen on fish sauce that liquamen factories were to be found all over the Roman Empire where catches of sprats and anchovies were salted, fermented and bottled on a grand scale. What was new in the eighteenth and nineteenth centuries was the transformation of working methods to a system of factory production.

This new mode of production linked to the individualism and enterprise of capitalism not only uncorked 'productive energies' previously repressed and created wealth on a scale hitherto unimagined but also led to economic and social changes that were regretted by conservative and socialist thinkers alike. In particular the shift from the family to the factory as the unit of production and the 'degradation of labour' through the destruction of craft skills, the emergence of a specialized division of labour and an emphasis upon a 'time-oriented' work discipline are seen at the root of a general decline in status and moral condition for the labourer. Such working practices and conditions not only encouraged feelings of alienation and exploitation but also provided an ideal environment for solidarity and resistance. Not surprisingly the world of work is a crucial area of social investigation for all the early writers; this tradition was continued by empirical researchers in the field of industrial relations.

### *The spirit of capitalism*

Despite being a contemporary phenomenon that has clear links with the industrial revolution, capitalism is not synonymous with it. The principles of enterprise and profit characterize early trading practices and money-lending as well as the agricultural revolution of eighteenth-century Britain. In 'post-industrial' societies the shift from manufacture towards service industries is still underpinned by the ethics of capitalism while in socialist countries it has been claimed that industrialism is a necessary feature of any post-capitalist revolution and a force for public good.

Nevertheless, capitalism was inextricably bound up with the revolution in production and the industrialization of western societies. Materialism, commercial enterprise and possessive individualism replaced what Nisbet (1970) calls 'the superior values of Christian-feudal society'. The economics of the free market and *laissez-faire* attitudes towards the obligations of employers and the rights of the workforce replaced romantic notions of *noblesse oblige* with the 'cash nexus'. The emphasis on money as the basis for relationships between people was mirrored in the relationship with the land. As the importance of landholding declined in the face of share-ownership in large-scale industrial enterprises the allegiance that people had to their roots (in moral communities) was destroyed. While this idea of the link between people and the land might have been romanticized, it formed the backdrop to much of the writings about loss of community; it has been reflected in the feelings of isolation and loneliness that seem to be widely experienced in modern, urban society.

Despite the characteristics of individualism and freedom, capitalism also contained contradictory elements that threatened its survival; these included the development of social classes, the intensification of class conflict and the irrational elements of a free-market economy. In the view of Karl Marx such a system was based upon exploitation, alienated labour and political force.

Early sociological theorists differed widely over the nature, development and impact of capitalism (Chapter 2 looks at differing analyses of capitalism offered by the founding writers of sociology). They were, however, clearly aware that anyone trying to make sense of industrial society had to take account of its emergence as the dominant western economic system.

**Q** **Despite frequent predictions of the imminent demise of capitalism it is still the dominant political and economic paradigm in much of the western world. Which of its characteristics do you think make it so attractive and so resilient as a system?**

### *Mass society and urban life*

Urbanism is also closely linked with the industrial revolution but, like capitalism, it is a separate social phenomenon. The concept of city living has a proud history that predates the industrial revolution by centuries. The city-states of Greece and Rome as well as the ancient civilizations of Africa, Asia and South America all celebrated their cultural and economic achievements in urban centres dedicated to art, politics and learning. Without over-romanticizing ancient and medieval city life, it was the industrial revolution that transformed the quality and meaning of urban living.

New cities dedicated to trade and industry emerged across Europe and North America in the nineteenth and twentieth centuries. Sprawling and unplanned, these new centres of economic activity and mass living grew at an alarming rate. They became battery farms for the production of labour for factory work and brought with them the social problems of poverty, overcrowding, poor health and political riot which have been associated with inner-city living ever since. Nisbet highlights the concern with social issues created by modern urban life:

> **It is . . . the city that forms the context of most sociological propositions relating to disorganisation, alienation, and mental isolation – all stigmata of loss of community membership.** *(Nisbet 1970: 28)*

**Fig 1.2** The social problems associated with inner-city living often have the biggest impact on children, with poor health and educational provision and a lack of leisure facilities: Chaucer House, Lambeth, London. (Photograph by Chris Bryan, courtesy of Robert Harding Picture Library Ltd.)

### *Political change*

The new modes of thought, the changes in social relationships and the emphasis upon individualism which have already been mentioned went hand in hand with the struggle for democracy. Nisbet (1970) has called this struggle 'the first great ideological revolution in western history' and it started with the bloody and momentous events in France and North America at the end of the eighteenth century, continued throughout the nineteenth century and fuelled the civil rights movements of the mid-twentieth century. According to the concept of liberal democracy, the values of freedom and liberty were enshrined in the utilitarian principle of 'the greatest happiness of the greatest number' which along with the growth of the secular state became almost synonymous with mass society.

In this new world the rights of the individual and the power of the state challenged the traditional authority of the Christian Church, the monarchy and the guilds. Even the patriarchal family came under attack from those calling for equality in marriage, changes in divorce law and the protection of children. The traditional authority of the family and the Church was further undermined by the transfer of education to state control, where its provision rapidly became a sign of democratic civilization and a matter of legal obligation. The idea of equality (also bequeathed by the French Revolution) led to political aspirations of a different kind. Whereas liberty and freedom were the watchwords of liberal democracy, the egalitarianism of the French Revolution led directly to socialism as an expression of working-class political resistance. The growth of the trade union movement in Britain and syndicalism in France, the flourishing radical press and the writings of Marx and Engels as well as the activities of the English Chartists and Parisian Communards, all indicate the extent to which revolution, once started, could not be contained by constitutional monarchs and electoral reform.

### *The crisis of the modern mind*

The emergence of science and the decline of religion come together to create what Asa Briggs (1967) has called 'the crisis of the modern mind'. The one does not necessarily exclude the other but the popularity and prestige of scientific discovery was clearly seen as a threat to religious authority. Science not only offered different types of explanations for the workings of the natural world but also provided the tools for its conquest and exploitation. The discoveries of archaeologists and astronomers had long since struck at the heart of biblical truth while Darwin's view of the origins of the human race was at the centre of a growing conflict between science and religion. The emergence of this dual phenomenon is clearly reflected in the concern and attitudes of the early sociologists. The decline of religion attracted much attention and examination of the social significance of religion permeates the theoretical work of Durkheim, Weber and, to a lesser extent, Marx. Meanwhile, the early theoretical models of Spencer and Comte attempt to mimic the mechanical, organic and evolutionary relationships discovered by physics and biology. Even the political manifesto of Marx and Engels was based upon the principles of 'scientific socialism'. We have a curious mixture of overlapping themes here; some sociologists were clearly inspired by religion, others thought that sociology was a new religion based upon the assumptions of scientific discovery, while a small group felt that sociological inquiry was a useful way of investigating religious belief and established the study of religion as a distinct area of sociology.

All of these changes came together to create a dynamic and sometimes chaotic environment into which the early sociologists were born. Many of their ideas were products of the changes to which they were witness and the major areas of sociological inquiry were more or less established during this period. The themes of religion, urbanism, capitalist development and political stability became essential areas of sociological speculation while the issues of poverty, crime, industrial relations and family life have retained their place as objects of social inquiry ever since. This connection between the discipline and its historical origins was clearly reflected in both sociological theory and social research.

Confronted with a rapidly changing, fragmented and rootless mass society the early theorists developed their systematic critiques of the modern world. Whether it is Comte anguishing over the collapse of authority or Durkheim looking for a new moral order there is a strong conservative element in much sociological theory. This may be contrasted with Marx's celebration of social conflict as an inevitable consequence of class society and Weber's more pessimistic view of the eventual rationalization of society and the replacement of 'magic' with the 'iron cage' of bureaucratic order. Many of these perspectives are dealt with more fully later but the crucial point is that without the momentous social and political events of the post-Enlightenment there would have been no great social crisis to observe, there would have been no middle-class intellectuals to recount it and there would have been no social theory.

**Q** List those aspects of sociological theory and study which you see as inherently conservative and those which are inherently radical. How applicable are they to academic study in general rather than just sociology in particular?

## Social research in Britain

If anything, social research was even more clearly linked to the social changes that were taking place than was social theorizing. The social problems which were related to urban living, particularly those that threatened the established order of society such as crime and political unrest, commanded the attention of early researchers. In the USA, Chicago had become an experimental laboratory in urban survival while in Britain cities like London, Manchester and Liverpool attracted empirical social scientists like flies buzzing round a dung heap.

In Raymond Kent's (1981) history of empirical sociology, the British research movement is divided into two camps – the social accountants and the social explorers.

### *The social accountants*

The purpose of collecting statistical data, according to McCulloch (1825), was 'to describe the condition of a particular country at a particular period'. Using survey techniques and official records a statistical history of Britain can be traced back to the Domesday Book of 1086. Social surveys of Scotland (John Sinclair 1791–99) and England (Sir Frederick Eden 1797) as well as demographic compilations dating back to John Graunt's account of mortality in 1662 demonstrate that the desire for empirical information was nothing new.

In the nineteenth century, however, the demand for useful statistics was not only a consequence of the popularity of the social sciences but also the desire of the political elite to know what was going on in a rapidly changing world. The obsession with statistics developed in the USA and Germany but most obviously in

Britain where the government started its own ten-yearly Census in 1801 and maintained an official statistical record of the state of the nation in the 'Blue Books' of the period. Statistical societies were established and attracted social reformers; the Statistical Society of London was, according to Kent (1981), 'almost . . . a branch of government' in its pursuit of politically useful 'state-istics'.

As a result the emphasis of the social accountants was not simply upon the state of society but on those areas of society that posed a political or moral threat to its survival. Studies of the condition of the working classes in general and social issues in particular dominate a twenty-year period after the founding of the first statistical societies in the early 1830s. Then, as now, much attention was paid to the phenomenon of rising crime and much effort was spent on teasing out the patterns of crime and their possible causes. Although the Reverend John Clay (1839) identified moral variables such as 'drunkenness, idleness, bad company, weak intellect and temptation' as the keys to understanding criminal behaviour, Plint's *Crime in England* (published in 1851) has a far more sociological feel to it as he played down the notion of urban decadence and emphasized economic inequality, class position and age as the crucial factors. Similar attention was given to politically sensitive areas such as education, strikes and health, all of which attracted the attention of political economists and social reformers.

By the 1850s 'social accountancy' was on the decline but it had established the importance and usefulness of social statistics for those who felt threatened by movements they only dimly understood and needed to control. The early use of social statistics can therefore be seen as an attempt by those with economic and political power to chart those areas of the social world which were largely unknown to them, to identify potential trouble spots and to generate ideas for social reform that targeted the habits of the poor rather than the economic system of the day.

Case Study

### Statistics held to account

Members of the various statistical societies were mostly middle-class men who were professionals, industrialists or members of the establishment, and they espoused policies of free trade and economic laissez-faire. They were suspicious of the factory reformers and preferred to see the towns rather than the factories as the major source of social ills. To them it was urbanisation and the physical environment that it produced that determined the habits and character of the people; making surveys of their actual condition was the obvious first step to be taken towards its improvement. The goal, however, was not the formation of a welfare state, but the creation of an environment that would foster a thrifty and virtuous working class. (Kent 1981: 31–2)

### Questions

**In what ways are social statistics still used today to justify particular economic and political views and interests? Give some examples.**

*The social explorers*

The accumulation of statistics was gradually overtaken by social anthropologists who derived their inspiration and approach from the tradition of the industrial novel and who analysed in depth the condition of the industrial working class. They were more concerned with identifying the structural context of social problems than simply blaming poverty on the fecklessness of the poor.

**[Social exploration] is the discovery of the unknown and presupposes a rigid class structure in which a representative of the social class consciously sets out to explore, analyse and report upon the life of another class lower on the social scale. It tells the story of one person's journey into alien culture and offers the detailed results of his findings. . . . The data that emerges from social exploration are typically qualitative, often emotive, frequently narrative and utilise the imagery of exploration primarily to draw attention to the inequalities in society and to force upon the reader an awareness of his social blindness.** *(Kent 1981: 37)*

One of the earliest examples of this approach was Engels' study of Manchester which marks a reaction against the purely empirical collection of facts found in the work of the statistical societies. Engels' family were wealthy textile manufacturers who owned a factory in Manchester where he was sent in 1842; while there he wrote his famous account of the *Condition of the Working Class in England* (1845). In it he attempted to describe the conditions of the working population of the day, although his accounts are very much based upon personal observation. Mayhew's (1949) later study of the London poor may be seen as a more structured attempt to create a natural history of the urban underclass because he was more concerned to record the attitudes and beliefs of the people he was studying in his endeavour 'to collect facts, and to register opinions'. As a result of such studies the criminal and anti-social behaviour of the urban working class became more understandable as part of a subcultural reaction to harsh economic circumstances.

The journalistic and polemical approach of Engels and Mayhew was followed by the less critical but more thorough efforts of Charles Booth. The wealthy owner of a Liverpool shipping company and member of the London Statistical Society, Booth attempted to weld together the various techniques of social research used by his predecessors to study the problem of poverty. Observation, systematic interviews and official statistics were all employed in his survey of London poverty. Booth's (1889) massive survey was published in seventeen volumes and provides a detailed account of social conditions at the end of the nineteenth century. He used sampling techniques and preceded his twenty-year project with a 'pilot study' of London's East End. His investigations were based on a subsistence definition of poverty: if income fell below a certain level a family could be classified as 'poor' and if significantly below this level 'very poor'. Booth found that 35 per cent of people in East London were poor and 12.5 per cent very poor. His work attempted to examine poverty on a formal, impersonal level rather than on an anecdotal basis, which explains its importance as a pioneering piece of empirical sociological research.

Social explorers continued to use statistical analysis to probe 'darkest Britain' in the twentieth century. The Mass Observation studies of Tom Harrison and Charles Madge used another economic depression as an excuse to investigate the important events and hidden 'tribes' of England in the 1930s (Harrison and Madge 1986). The Mass Observation organization aimed to conduct surveys of the population and to report the results as widely as possible. The founders believed that social science should not be purely academic and attempted 'to marry social anthropology to journalism in the interests of revealing Britain to its inhabitants'. The movement involved a network of observers in different parts of the country making observations on how they and other people spent their daily lives. The results provided a very full picture of social change in Britain before and during the Second World War. Initially Mass Observation tended to be associated with left-wing politics; however, it ended by stimulating the growth of 'market research and public opinion polling . . . rather than social investigation proper' (Mitchell 1968: 210).

**Q** Suggest how (a) social accountants and (b) social explorers would go about studying changing family patterns and the role of religion in society.

## Culture and socialization

In this section we shall define the key concepts of culture and socialization. The application of these concepts is then explored by assessing the power of culture through cultural diversity and deprivation.

### Culture

**Q** What does the term 'culture' mean to you?

What activities would you describe as 'cultural'?

The activities which we associate with 'culture' tend to include traditional arts such as ballet, literature and painting. Trips to the theatre, art gallery and opera house are seen as examples of cultural involvement (and often recalled by resentful members of school outings). This view of 'culture' is only one definition of the term. It is what Matthew Arnold (1963) called 'the best that has been known and said in the world' and concentrates on the intellectual aspects of a civilization. The subjective and elitist nature of this definition has been questioned in the second half of the twentieth century.

However, there is another sense in which the concept of culture can be used. Sociologists prefer a much broader, less subjective and impartial definition that refers to the values, customs and acceptable modes of behaviour that characterize a society or social groups within a society. Culture, then, refers to the non-biological aspects of human societies – to the values, customs and modes of behaviour that are learned and internalized by people rather than being genetically transmitted from one generation to the next.

This general notion of culture is directly related to social behaviour through the moral goals of a society (its *values*), the status positions of its members (*social roles*) and the specific rules of conduct related to society's values and roles which are known as *norms*. In other words, those general values that society holds in high esteem are reflected in the norms governing our everyday attitudes and behaviour.

A key figure in the sociological analysis of culture and in the development of communication and cultural studies has been Raymond Williams (e.g. 1958). His work has highlighted the two concepts of culture introduced above – the emphasis on the whole way of life of a society or social group and the more specialized if more common view of culture as artistic and intellectual activities. In line with his socialist beliefs, Williams developed and examined the notion of 'cultural materialism', arguing that cultural practices have to be seen as forms of material production.

**Case Study**

### Behavioural etiquette: a Victorian guide

In 1866 Edward Turner Esq compiled *The Young Man's Companion*, a written record of the sort of advice aspiring young gentlemen might require. It was aimed at 'the very numerous class of young men in this country, whose education may have been neglected early in life, and who only require a thorough initiatory elementary knowledge to greatly advance their prospects in the world'. Great value was clearly placed upon polite behaviour in the successful performance of the role of gentlemen. It is an indication of the extent to which these standards are open to cultural change that the book was reprinted a century later as a joke. Among the hints to be found in the chapter on 'Accomplishments and Graces' we are warned against the social disgrace of enjoying a good laugh:

> Frequent and loud laughter is the characteristic of folly and ill manners. It is the manner in which the mob express their silly joy at silly things. (Turner 1965: 19)

And later, in his advice on table manners, Turner recommends behaviour that in any other circumstances would be seen as rudeness:

> If you are dining in company with high bred people and there is any article of food on the table, which you know to be very expensive, you should not treat it as such but effect to presume that such a thing is quite common at *that* table, and help yourself and others with entire freedom. . . . Avoid, also, that most vulgar habit which prevails among half-bred country people, of abstaining from taking the last piece on a dish. It amounts almost to an insult to your host, to do anything which shows that you fear that the vacancy cannot be supplied, and that there is likely to be a scarcity.
>
> (Turner 1965: 35)

## Socialization

The emphasis upon culture, rather than biological instinct, as the key to understanding human behaviour implies that learning plays an essential part in creating social beings. In sociology the term given to the process by which we learn the norms, values and roles approved by our society is socialization. The survival of children into adulthood and the future of culture itself depend upon society's successful organization of this process.

Unless a society is to rely for its survival on the fear induced by the armed police forces or other agencies of control, socialization is the key to social cohesion and cultural endurance. The rules and customs governing normal social interaction must become internalized by the members of society in such a way that they become part of the individual's view of the world and of themselves without the individual feeling brain washed. As Berger (1967a) makes clear, this balancing act can work only if it is achieved by stealth on the part of society and through acceptance on behalf of the individual.

**Society not only controls our movements, but shapes our identity, our thought and our emotions. The structures of society become the structures of our own consciousness. Society does not stop on the surface of our skins. Society penetrates us as much as it envelopes us. Our bondage to society is not so much established by conquest as by collusion.** ***(Berger 1967a: 140)***

Gradually, as part of the process of 'growing up', individuals absorb the standards and expectations of society so unconsciously that they become transformed into social beings almost without noticing it. The requirements, rules and standards of society have become part of their own identity, motives and desires so imperceptibly that they are experienced as natural and unique although they are clearly social and uniform.

Individuals begin at an early age to become aware of the existence of others and to take this knowledge into account as they form their own identities. Society may not be capable of survival without its members' conformity but equally individuals cannot develop clear ideas of who they are without some level of social interaction.

Q Norms of conduct are often learned from an early age and unconsciously absorbed so that they become part of our 'taken-for-granted' assumptions about appropriate social behaviour.

List as many norms of conduct as you can.

How do these norms differ for different social groups – consider differences between (a) young and old; (b) women and men; (c) poor and rich?

The cases which we mention later in this chapter of children who were deprived of such social interaction in their formative years are clear evidence of the crucial role played by the socialization process in the structuring of identity and the development of the individual.

Charles Cooley, one of the founders of the symbolic interactionist perspective in sociology (see pp. 72–3), examined the development of self-consciousness and maintained that consciousness in general and the self-concept in particular can be understood only in the context of an individual's interaction with society. He called this concept the 'looking-glass self' and argued that it developed on two levels of the socialization process involving primary and secondary groups.

Primary groups are based on intimate relationships and face-to-face interaction; they are crucial in establishing early codes of conduct as well as self-perception, both of which forge the link between an individual and society. The family is the clearest example of a primary group and it is here that the most basic rules of culturally acceptable behaviour are established. Parents, says Erich Fromm (1960),

**in their own personalities . . . represent the social character of their society or class. They transmit to the child what we may call the psychological atmosphere or the spirit of a society just by being as they are – namely representatives of this very spirit. The family thus may be considered to be the psychological agent of society.**

*(Fromm 1960, quoted in Meighan et al. 1979: 129)*

Secondary groups are less intimate and more formal organizations which do not provide the intimate and personal interaction of primary groups. These groups are often our first contact with society in general; as such they not only reinforce the lessons learned within primary groups but also introduce us to new standards of behaviour which are universally agreed upon in society at large. These standards are often represented by individuals whose roles symbolize the wider values of society. The school is a good example of a secondary group as here we begin to learn that we are not unique individuals at the centre of the universe but members of a wider society which will judge us by its rules and standards rather than our own. It has often been pointed out that after being the big fish in the little pond of family life children experience school as a microcosm of society within which they pick up the skills, values and tricks that will enable them to get by in the adult worlds of work, leisure and the social security system. In the view of Talcott Parsons (1959), the school classroom can be seen as a miniature social system:

**The school is an agency through which individual personalities are trained to be motivationally and technically adequate to the performance of adult roles . . . the socialisation function may be summed up as the development in individuals of the commitments and capacities which are essential prerequisites of their future role performance.**

*(Parsons 1959, quoted in Miliband 1969: 215)*

The major agencies of socialization are covered in detail in later chapters where we look at the contribution of the family, the school, religion and the mass media to the reproduction of culture as it is handed on from one generation to the next. Here we shall look at the way in which the concept of culture has been applied by anthropologists, psychologists and sociologists in their attempts to identify its significance for individuals as well as society.

Who are the key people involved in the socialization of children at the following ages: (a) 0–4 years; (b) 5–10 years; (c) 11–15 years; (d) 16–21 years?

## The power of culture

### Cultural diversity

How would you feel about being offered dog meat for breakfast? What would be your reaction to a professor giving a lecture wearing nothing but a loin cloth? Would you be surprised to find people of your grandparents' generation using cocaine? Whether we look at fashion, food or leisure activities, anthropology and history reveal a wide range of cultural diversity over all forms of behaviour and belief that suggests that human activity cannot be reduced to simple biological or social models which have been fixed for eternity. What is regarded as normal and acceptable behaviour by one society or cultural group may be punished as a crime elsewhere. As Matza (1969) reminds us, 'one man's deviation is another's custom' and it is clear that cultural standards are relative to time, place and social position.

### *Women's work and men's work*

The diversity of sex roles is often used as an example of the power of cultural conditioning and regularly quoted as evidence against conventional explanations for the differences between the sexes. In her analysis of women's work, Ann Oakley (1974a) argues that 'roles in traditional non-industrialised societies are often defined to some extent by sex status' but goes on to emphasize that there is no simple or universal rule for the division of labour by sex. Instead, we find that the rules regarding sex-appropriate tasks vary enormously from one culture to another. To demonstrate this argument she contrasts two African societies – the Mbuti pygmies of the northern Congo and the Lele from the south.

**Case Study**

#### Two African societies: Mbuti and Lele

The Mbuti are a hunter-gatherer people who 'have no rules for the division of labour by sex'. Although there are some very loose practices of 'women's work' and 'men's work' these are not related to general types of activities but to specific tasks (men gather honey, women gather vegetables) while the most important task of hunting is carried out by men and women together. Child care is also shared but is carried out by the middle-aged men and women or by the older boys and girls. There is no division by sex between the worlds of domestic labour and economic production.

The Lele practise a very rigid division of labour by sex although again it does not distinguish between the worlds of domestic activity and public production nor do women have an unequal status to men because of the nature of the work they carry out. The division of labour and of life in general is geographical. The men inhabit the forest and cultivate raffia but are excluded from the grasslands where the women cultivate the groundnut, collect firewood and tend the fishponds. Segregation also affects village life where men and women keep to different parts of the village and enjoy segregated leisure and mealtimes. As Oakley points out, the main point here is not simply the massive cultural difference in sex-specific behaviour between two geographical neighbours but the general similarity between them when it comes to distinguishing between the domestic world and the economic:

> The situation among the Lele (and among the Mbuti) is the same as that in the majority of traditional African societies: the work done by the women is essential to the economic survival of the society. Despite the ritual allocation of some tasks to men and some to women, men's work and women's work are equal in status and importance . . . the separation between home and work is not a feature of human society as such but of industrialised society specifically. (Oakley 1974a: 13)

### *Love and marriage*

The importance of culture is also obvious when we consider the relationship between men and women in their pursuit of one another. Courtship, marriage and sexual activity reveal patterns of normal behaviour which are anything but universal despite the fact that the desires and emotions involved are powerful natural drives genetically transmitted to ensure the survival of the species.

From a western perspective, the notions of free choice, romantic love and jealousy may lead to the conclusion that monogamy is a natural response to the questions of courtship, marriage and sexual reproduction. However, the briefest review of other cultures or our own history demonstrates how relative such arrangements are.

Arranged marriages are often associated with the Hindu religion, but this practice is widespread, often touching on cultures where we would least expect to find it. Until the First World War (1914–18) the use of 'dynastic marriage' for political purposes was a crucial aspect of European history. For centuries it was regarded as normal practice for royal marriages to act as a form of international diplomacy to maintain bonds of alliance and peace between states, nations and cultures (Baignent *et al.* 1986). Marriages were also arranged between wealthy families in order to increase their wealth, status or family honour.

Some marriages are still arranged in Japan, where the question of marriage partner is regarded as so important, especially for family honour, that it cannot be left to the romantic preferences of the daughter. A 'go-between' is employed to discover likely partners with good prospects from families of honourable status and background. This is as much an issue of parental concern for the daughter as it is a matter of family honour because the bride changes family membership on her wedding day and belongs to her husband's family thereafter. To signify this 'death' in her parents' eyes on her wedding day, she wears white, the Japanese symbol of mourning. In Chinese communities some arranged marriages are known as 'ghost weddings', which make sense when placed in the context of a culture where a belief in the power of the spirit world still survives.

---

**Recently, the *China Daily News* carried a report on July 14 1982. According to this Taiwanese newspaper, a 42-year-old man married his wife's sister who had died twenty years previously at the age of eight. The importunate spirit had visited her mother several times, saying that she wanted to marry her sister's husband. With the consent of the sister, a classical traditional wedding ceremony was held at which the living wife served as a maid of honour. On the night of the marriage ceremony, the man had to sleep alone so that the spirit of the dead woman could come to him and the marriage would be spiritually consummated. From that time onwards, the man had a double duty to his two wives and owed ritual duties to the ghost wife.**

***(Bloomfield 1983: 81–5)***

---

Even if love and marriage do not necessarily go together, we might be tempted to assume that love and sex do. In 'dynastic marriages' it was not expected that the marriage would be fulfilling but 'courtly love' provided the opportunity for satisfaction outside of marriage. The well-publicized indiscretions of the British Royal Family in the 1990s suggest that such arrangements are still tolerated. However, in

West Africa Nigel Barley's (1986) discussion of adultery with a Dowayo elder reveals that even simple rules regarding sexual attraction are by no means universal:

> **All Dowayos, male and female, were to report on the appointed day and vote. It is the Chief's responsibility to ensure a good turn-out and Mayo humbly accepted this as his lot while Zuuldibo sat in the shade calling out instructions to those doing the work. I sat with him and we had a long discussion on the finer points of adultery. 'Take Mariyo,' he said. 'People always tried to say she was sleeping with my younger brother, but you saw how upset she was when he was ill. That showed there was nothing between them.' For Dowayos sex and affection were so separate that one disproved the other. I nodded wisely in agreement; there was no point in trying to explain that there was another way of looking at it.** *(Barley 1986: 135)*

### *Monogamy and polygamy*

The practice of adultery has meaning only within societies that practise monogamous courtship and marriage. In such cultures the breaking of these rules can provide the grounds for divorce, justifiable homicide and punishment by the criminal justice system. However, in other cultures the practice of having more than one partner is not only tolerated but also institutionalized in polygamous marriage.

Among the Nyinba people of north-west Nepal the western notion of romantic love is thought of as selfish and greedy and the inevitable cause of sorrow. Instead they practise fraternal polyandry whereby the wife is shared by the brothers of the family she marries into. Such marriages are often arranged but even when they are based on the sexual attraction of the bride for one particular brother she must still become the wife of the others, spending her wedding night with the eldest brother irrespective of her preference. For the purposes of family stability it is also important that the wife shows no favouritism to any individual brother and that she demonstrates this impartiality by bearing at least one child for each man. Strict penalties are maintained for anyone caught 'fooling around' outside of the marriage.

A more commonly practised version of polygamy is polygamous marriage, which allows a man to have several wives. Despite being against the teachings of the Bible and the laws of their societies, Mormon fundamentalists still believe that it is a sacred duty for a man to take several brides even though the Mormon Church rejected the practice in 1890.

**Case Study**

#### Safe passage to the Celestial Kingdom

As Carys Bowen-Jones (1992) has described, girls in the Mormon community are 'turned in' to the Priesthood leader once they reach 15 years of age and he 'places' them with an appropriate husband. It does not matter that the husband may already have a wife. Women are expected to share their husband and become 'wife sisters'. This arrangement has been sanctioned by the Mormon belief in 'plural marriage' and fear of social contamination.

*(box continued)*

*(box continued)*

Fundamentalist Mormons see polygamy as a sacred duty. They believe a polygamous lifestyle on earth will ensure their safe passage into a Celestial Kingdom after death, where every worthy male will be given a world of his own to people with his extended family. . . . A woman's exaltation after death depends on the number of children she produces, and many women here remain in a state of almost constant pregnancy from their late teens to their late thirties. . . . Contact with outsiders – or Gentiles as they're known here – is vigorously discouraged by the church elders, especially among the women. . . . The self-imposed social isolation of Colorado City, and of the neighbouring town of Hildale, which houses another 1,500 polygamists, is undoubtedly one of the main reasons why such a lifestyle has endured here for 60 years.

(Bowen-Jones 1992: 60)

**Questions**

**Our discussion of cultural diversity has looked at sex roles and love and marriage. Describe the extent of cultural diversity in the areas of (a) fashion; (b) child-rearing; (c) recreational drug use. (Consider diversity over time and from place to place.)**

## Culture and development

The importance of socialization and in particular the quality of the cultural experiences of children in the early years of the socialization process are crucial for physical, intellectual, emotional and social development.

This point is clearly demonstrated if we look at what happens when children are deprived of these cultural experiences. The cases that we shall look at illustrate different degrees of exclusion from culture and include examples where children have been partially deprived of what a culture has to offer as well as those extreme cases of children who have grown up beyond the frontiers of human civilization.

### *Feral children*

The legends of Romulus and Remus, Mowgli and Tarzan have etched into the minds of many of us distorted and romantic images of children reared in the wild by animals. According to legend these children come to little harm, retain their human characteristics and develop strong identities to become singing and dancing role models of the silver screen. The reality could not be more fantastic or further from the picture portrayed by *Greystoke* and *The Jungle Book*. Since the fourteenth century over fifty-three recorded cases have been found of feral children, including the Irish sheep-child, the Lithuanian bear-child and the Salzburg sow-girl. Other unlikely parents include wolves, baboons, leopards and an Indian panther (Malson and Itard 1972: 80–2). Some of these cases may be 'the stuff of myth rather than experiences' (Maclean 1977) but Armen (1974) recorded the behaviour of a boy reared by gazelles in the Sahara; as Armen made no attempt to capture and return the child to 'civilization' it is difficult to know how long the child managed to survive in the wild by reliance on those skills learned from gazelles.

In the case studies we can see not only how important early socialization is but also the extent to which it may be changed by later exposure to human contact.

Case Study

### Kamala and Amala: the wolf girls of Midnapore

In late September 1920, the Reverend Singh responded to appeals for help from local villagers in Bengal. They were being terrorized by ghosts in the form of 'man-beasts' and the Reverend Singh set up a hide from which to observe and destroy the creatures. At first, he tells us in his journal, he saw three wolves followed by two cubs but was then astonished by the apparition that followed:

> Close after the cubs, came the 'ghost' – a hideous looking being, hand, foot and body like a human being; but the head was a big ball of something covering the shoulders and the upper portion of the bust leaving only a sharp contour of the face visible. Close at its heels there came another awful creature exactly like the first, but smaller in size. Their eyes were bright and piercing, unlike human eyes. . . .
>
> The first ghost appeared on the ground up to its bust, and placing its elbows on the edge of the hole, looked this side and that side and jumped out. It looked all round the place from the mouth of the hole before it leaped out to follow the cubs. It was followed by another tiny ghost of the same kind, behaving in the same manner. Both of them ran on all fours. (Maclean 1977: 60–1)

The children and wolf cubs were protected by the mother, who was quickly killed by the archers in the hunting party. The offspring were then trapped in sheets and taken into captivity where the Reverend Singh hoped that he could return the feral children to the fold of God's love and human kindness in the safety of his orphanage.

His account of this struggle to civilize the wolf-children has been diligently researched by Charles Maclean, who reveals how far from recognizable human beings these children had become as a result of their bizarre upbringing. From the start both girls behaved more like wild animals than human children. They appeared frightened by daylight and slept naked on the floor during the middle of the day. They howled at night and shared the eating habits of dogs; they ate carrion as well as raw flesh and gobbled cockroaches, lizards and mice alive. They ran on all fours and relied heavily upon sense of smell, showing a clear preference for the company of dogs over the friendship of other humans. They snarled and growled in fear when approached and even attacked the orphanage children who dared to get too close.

After three months the Reverend Singh had to record in his diary that the children had made no progress. They did not laugh or smile and continued in their nocturnal and anti-social habits. He was forced to conclude:

> They had cultivated the animal nature and condition of life almost to perfection in the animal world . . . if they were to grow in humanity, they would have to fight with their fixed animal character, formed during those years with the wolves in their care and in the jungle i.e. the whole animal environment. Theirs was not a free growth as is the case of a human child of that age. . . . it was hampered growth, consequently very, very slow in all its progress.

Gradually, however, the new environment began to work its changes. Over the next seven months, Mrs Singh's belief that 'love was the key' produced small signs of adaptation to human society. Amala, in particular, showed signs of intelligence and initiative

*(box continued)*

*(box continued)*

and learned to recognize the names of food and drink. Vegetables were still refused but the children learned to use their hands when eating and drinking and began to play games when food was the reward. A year later they had mastered the skill of sleeping in a bed.

In September 1921, Amala died as the result of illness and the Reverend Singh claims that her 'sister' showed remorse and even cried over the body. Kamala now began to show signs of learning basic skills by copying other children. In June 1923, she stood for the first time and eventually learned to walk upright and moved into the girls' dormitory. By the time of her death in 1929, Kamala had showed the definite effects of her socialization in the orphanage. She had grown afraid of the dark, learned to sit at a table and came to prefer the friendship of other children. She understood language and developed a basic vocabulary of over thirty words, through her combinations of which she demonstrated a basic grasp of a self-concept. She proved to be pretty hopeless at household tasks but did show signs of recognizing the difference between right and wrong to the extent that the Reverend Singh decided that this 'sweet and obedient child' deserved to celebrate New Year's Day 1925 by being baptized.

### *Extreme deprivation*

In this case above contact with human beings had been replaced by influences from other animals so that the children had learned different survival skills through the processes of imprinting, identification and imitation. We now turn our attention to examples of human beings who have experienced extreme isolation and deprivation, usually as a result of being abandoned and whose development is retarded rather than different. Again many of these stories have excited the literary imagination. Alexander Selkirk abandoned as a castaway on a desert island in 1704 became the inspiration for Defoe's Robinson Crusoe; Swift based Gulliver's meeting with the Yahoos on his own encounter with Peter of Hanover in 1726. The true story of John Merrick is now famous as the legend of the Elephant Man; Helen Keller's story has become widely known through her own books and the film of her life.

Case Study

#### Anna and Isabella

In the USA in the 1940s two girls were separately discovered who had been living in almost total isolation from human contact. In both cases the girls were illegitimate and had been hidden away to protect the family's honour. They were discovered at around the same stage of development (6 years); both were provided with supplementary care and special education. In the more extreme case, Anna had survived with the barest minimum of human contact. Apart from being fed enough to keep alive she was given no love or attention nor any opportunity to develop physically through exploration or movement but left instead on filthy bedding in the attic in clothes that were rarely changed. Not surprisingly, Anna had failed to develop physically and appeared to be deaf and blind. She was apathetic, expressionless and incapable of coordination and communication. In his report on the case Kingsley Davis summarized the situation:

*(box continued)*

*(box continued)*

> Here, then, was a human organism which had missed nearly six years of socialisation. Her condition shows how little her purely biological resources, when acting alone, could contribute to making her a complete person. (Davis 1949: 205)

After four years of care and attention in a special school, Anna managed to learn to walk, to repeat words and try to carry on conversations, and to keep herself and her clothes clean. She discovered the worlds of play and colour and had begun to develop intellectually and emotionally before she died at the age of 10.

Isabelle had the meagre advantage of being in regular contact with her mother, a deaf-mute who had been incarcerated with her in a darkened room by Isabelle's grandfather. Although she had learned to communicate with her mother through a personal system of gesture, Isabelle was severely retarded physically and intellectually. She was fearful of strangers and reacted violently towards men. However, the specialist attention of doctors and psychologists enabled Isabelle to recapture the lost years of her early life through 'a systematic and skilful programme of training'. Isabelle's response to this intense socialization process was as rapid as it is remarkable and clearly demonstrates the essential role played by the environment and education in the stages of child development.

> The task seemed hopeless at first, but gradually she began to respond. After the first few hurdles had at last been overcome, a curious thing happened. She went through the usual stages of learning characteristics of the years from one to six not only in proper succession but far more rapidly than normal. In a little over two months after her first vocalisation she was putting sentences together. Nine months after that she could identify words and sentences on the printed page, could write well, could add to ten and could retell a story after hearing it. Seven months beyond this point she had a vocabulary of 1500–2000 words and was asking complicated questions. Starting from an educational level of between one and three years, she had reached a normal level by the time she was eight and a half years old. In short, she covered in two years the stages of learning that ordinarily require six. She eventually entered school where she participated in all school activities as normally as other children. (Davis 1949: 206–7)

Thirty years after the discovery of Anna and Isabelle, another well-known case came to light. For most of her 13 years Genie had been imprisoned in a darkened room of her father's house where she was either tied up or caged. Her isolation appears to have been relieved only by interruptions for food and punishment. If she made a noise her father would respond with growls and barks and often beat her with a stick.

When she finally escaped with the help of her mother, Genie was found to be malnourished, incontinent and barely able to walk. She appeared to be almost blind, salivated constantly and could not speak. Like Isabelle she reacted violently to challenging situations and would urinate and masturbate in public. Under the guidance of a psychologist, Susan Curtiss, Genie learned to dress, eat correctly and use a toilet but she had probably spent too many years of her bleak early life in isolation to ever catch up on her lost childhood; she never developed her ability with language beyond that of a 4 year old although her IQ score improved from 38 to 74 in the space of six years. Many important questions raised by this case remain unanswered due to Genie's father committing suicide and her mother bringing the support programme to an end with a court case in which she sued the Children's Hospital for damages (Pines 1981).

As David Skuse (1984) has pointed out, the value of these studies is not simply that they demonstrate the importance of nurture over nature or of the environment over inheritance but that we çan go too far in the direction of 'super environmentalism' and imagine that behaviour is fixed by experience as opposed to genetic blueprints.

---

**Extreme deprivation in early childhood is a condition of great theoretical and practical importance. . . . Most human characteristics, with the possible exception of language . . . are virtually resistant to obliteration by even the most dire early environments. On removal to a favourable situation, the remarkable and rapid progress made by those with good potential seems allied to the total experience of living in a stimulating home and forming emotional bonds to a caring adult.**

***(Skuse 1984: 571–2)***

---

Q

The 'nature/nurture' debate as to how much we are influenced by our environment and how much we are the product of our biological and genetic inheritance has been long and fiercely argued. In what ways might a sociological perspective add to this debate? How could you use the case studies above to illustrate your argument?

### *Cultural deprivation and social opportunity*

In the early studies of crime during the 1920s and 1930s and in the first attempts to understand educational failure, social scientists focused upon the role played by cultural deprivation in the creation of deviance and under-achievement. The term was not restricted to intellectual and educational activity but referred to a broader concept which implied a culturally determined notion of desirable standards of material and social existence from which some individuals and families may be excluded. Such circumstances would be synonymous with poverty or poor housing, and the term is often used interchangeably with concepts such as 'underprivileged', 'disadvantaged', 'lower class' and, more recently, 'underclass' (Jencks 1993). 'Poor family conditions' have been offered since the end of the nineteenth century as a possible explanation for anti-social and criminal behaviour.

#### *Crime and delinquency*

During the early part of the twentieth century the idea that delinquency could be related to deprivation took root. Juvenile courts began to require reports on the 'home surroundings' of young offenders and in 1927 a Home Office committee accepted the view of many reformers that delinquent children were themselves victims:

---

**There is little or no difference in character and needs between the neglected and the delinquent child. It is often mere accident whether he is brought before the court because he is wandering or beyond control or because he has committed some offence. Neglect leads to delinquency.**

***(Home Office 1927: 111, cited in Pachman 1981)***

---

A series of reports between the 1940s and 1960s saw the emphasis shift away from evil and depravity towards the concept of deprivation and 'the lack of satisfactory family life' in the search for an understanding of rising juvenile crime. The social investigations of researchers such as J B Mays (1954) and Norman Tutt (1974) confirmed the relationship between delinquency and cultural deprivation.

In his summary of Sprott's (1954) work on lower-class families and 'Delinquent Subculture', Tutt paints a despairing picture of the criminal family type:

**The . . . families lived in an atmosphere of squalor, possessions were untidy and uncared for, and individual ownership was not prized. The families' leisure was largely taken up with gambling. Irregular sexual unions were frequent and openly discussed. . . . Minor acts of physical aggression – mothers clouting children, siblings fighting – were frequent. Parents tended to quarrel openly and violently; the father left the responsibility of bringing up the children entirely to the mother. Children were given pocket money at random to spend as they liked. . . . Neither were they encouraged to use their leisure time constructively.**

*(Tutt 1974: 25)*

*Educational failure*

Alongside the concern with juvenile crime, and often overlapping with it, was the attempt by social researchers and politicians to understand educational failure in an age when educational opportunity was, in theory, a right for all children. Cyril Burt (1925) was one of the first researchers to confront the issue and, although his emphasis was upon the inherited nature of intelligence, his ideas on selective education, based upon the notorious '11 plus' examination, were partly justified as a device for rescuing able working-class children from homes blighted by poverty and educational deprivation.

In the 1950s and 1960s the work of Riessman (1962) in the USA and Douglas (1964) in Britain firmly established the idea that the educational underachievement of children from poor backgrounds was, in part, a result of cultural deprivation. Government investigations such as the Plowden Report in 1967 clearly identified parental attitudes towards education and the lack of educational resources in the home as the key to school performance.

During the 1980s the right of liberal reformers to monopolize the concept of cultural deprivation has been challenged from the political right. Beneath the concern to identify the social causes of crime and failure there has always been a hint of moral superiority. It took only a change in the political climate for these feelings to manifest themselves in a way which seeks to 'blame the victims' rather than help them.

Charles Murray, a fellow of the American Enterprise Institute, has argued that welfare dependency and single motherhood have become part of a culture that threatens to destroy family life, social morality and the rule of law.

**Children learn how to be responsible adults by watching what responsible adults do. The absence of such examples for boys seems especially dangerous. The violence and social chaos in America's inner cities tells us how a generation of males behave when about half of them grow to adolescence without a constraining sense of what it means to be an adult male.** *(quoted in Sunday Times 10 May 1992)*

According to Murray unruly males may be the problem but it is their mothers who are to blame. If the subculture of deprivation is to be broken the answer is to stop tinkering with educational reform and eradicate the system of benefit that encourages such attitudes. Murray argued that by refusing benefits to single parents, the values surrounding marriage, family and proper child care will be resurrected. This less obvious aspect of the cultural deprivation argument is increasingly dominating the debates over moral decline, truancy and the rise in juvenile crime.

**Summary**

- Sociology helps us make sense of the world we live in. It asks questions about and seeks answers for the things that directly affect our lives. In studying people and the societies that they live in, sociology relies on rigorous procedures and is informed by rational argument and existing knowledge.
- There is no uniform and all-embracing sociological perspective. Sociologists disagree over research procedures (methodologies) and theoretical perspectives; these different approaches and positions emerged as the subject of sociology developed.
- Modern (western) sociology is generally seen as originating from the economic, social and political upheavals and revolutions of the nineteenth century, in particular, as a result of developments such as the industrial revolution and the move to the factory system of production; urbanization; the growth of capitalism; and the wider acceptance of liberal democracy and the support for the rights of individuals.
- Culture and socialization are two key concepts used in sociology. Culture is used to refer to the values, customs and styles of behaviour of a society or social group and socialization to the process by which people learn the norms, values and roles approved in their society. Socialization depends on social interaction and without this individuals could not develop as social beings.
- The importance of these concepts is shown if we look at individuals who have been deprived of socialization and of cultural experiences – children brought up in the wild or shut away and ignored by their families and having no contact with other humans.
- Sociologists have utilized the concept of cultural deprivation to explain patterns of social behaviour such as differences in criminal behaviour or educational attainment between different social groups.

## Further reading

Bauman, Z (1990) *Thinking Sociologically*, Oxford: Blackwell.
An up-to-date and 'theoretical' introduction to sociology that discusses in some depth the relationship between sociology and common sense.
Berger, P L (1967) *Invitation to Sociology: A Humanistic Perspective*, Harmondsworth:
Mills, C W (1970) *The Sociological Imagination*, Harmondsworth: Penguin. Given that this is an introductory chapter, there are no particular substantive studies that provide an overview of the area. However, the introductory books by Peter Berger and C Wright Mills have had a tremendous impact and been an important influence on many people currently working in sociology. They are still well worth reading; perhaps more than any other introductory studies they capture the excitement and challenge of studying the human world.

Levin, J (1993) *Sociological Snapshots*, Newbury Park, CA: Pine Forge.
This series of essays tries to relate the familiar, common-sense world of our everyday experiences to the more abstract sociological interpretation and theorizing. The first two sections, on culture and socialization, are particularly relevant to this introductory chapter.

Nisbet, R A (1970) *The Sociological Tradition*, London: Heinemann Educational.
In this classic introduction to the history of sociology, Nisbet focuses on the period between 1830 and 1900 which saw the emergence of modern sociology. He sets the development of sociology in its political and economic context, in particular highlighting the importance of the 'two revolutions' – the industrial revolution of the late eighteenth/early nineteenth century and the political revolution that started in France in 1789 – on nineteenth-century thought.

## Activities

### ■ Activity 1 Sky burials

**Steve Mair describes a burial ceremony in Tibet and demonstrates how the disposal of the dead is dealt with in a radically different manner from the way it is dealt with in contemporary western society.**

#### Fly away Peter

**During a six-week visit to Tibet, Steve Mair set off from Llasa early one morning to attempt to witness one of the world's most startling spectacles. Photographs were forbidden. And unnecessary.**

It was six-thirty on a cold Tibetan morning and still pitch black when, stumbling and yawning, we set off out of town towards the nearby hills. . . .

Previously I'd had no intention of trying to see a sky burial since, although what I'd heard about this custom fascinated me, I thought that to intrude on other people's grief was obscene, to say the least. Joe had felt the same, and besides we had been told that we would not be welcome there and had even heard stories about rocks being thrown at Westerners who did try to go. This turned out to be true, but it was Westerners who had tried, stupidly, to take photographs of the burial after being warned not to do so.

However, two days before, we'd met a New Zealander who said she'd been to see a burial that morning, and that no hostility had been shown to her. Also, and most importantly, she said that there were no family of the deceased present during the ritual. So that was it, that there were no relatives present was the deciding factor (they apparently arrive later, after it's over, just to see that the job has been done and their loved ones properly dispatched). Joe and I both made up our minds to try to witness a burial before leaving Lhasa.

Now here we were, on a hill outside Lhasa, standing in the Tibetan pre-dawn chill with the man by the fire silently stropping his butcher's blade. For a few moments it was quite eerie as we stood gazing at the two covered bodies until finally, in sign language, we asked if we could stay. They asked if we had cameras. We assured them we didn't. They warned us again we should not take photographs, we said we understood, and then after a little discussion they motioned us to sit.

We sat for half an hour in almost total silence, trying to imagine the ceremony, while the Tibetans continued to smoke and drink tea and from time to time produce more large knives to be sharpened. . . .

By now it was quite light and we'd been joined by three other Westerners, who had obviously had the same idea, and an old Buddhist monk carrying a large prayer flag, who had come down from the monastery on the opposite side of the hill to preside over the burial. First the monk made himself comfortable in a makeshift altar behind us, and then commenced a soft, rhythmic chanting while setting up a gentle staccato beat on a goatskin drum and blowing down a conch-like trumpet. . . .

After he'd been praying for ten minutes or so and with the crisp morning air filled with these strange mystical sounds as well as the sweet smell of burning juniper bushes that one of the workmen had lit all around us, the sun suddenly appeared over the hills to the east instantly bathing the whole tableau in warmth and light. At this point seven of the workmen finished their tea, put out their cigarettes, donned grubby and bloodstained overalls, and set off towards the large rock that was thirty feet in front of us. At last the ceremony began.

Five of the workmen sat down behind the bodies, facing us, while the remaining two drew the large knives from their belts and threw the covers off the bodies. One of the bodies was of a plump female, perhaps in her forties, while the other was that of a skinny, old man. Mercifully they were lying face down so we couldn't see their faces. This was just as well since I think by now most of us had begun to feel a little queasy: I certainly had.

For most of the time we watched the 'butcher' who was working on the woman. He began by making a cut from the nape of the neck down to the buttocks and then on down the back of each leg up to the heel. He pulled off the skin from the back in two pieces and threw them to the ground with a loud slap. At this point the squeamishness left me as the red meat and white fat of the body was revealed: it was just like Smithfields, a side of beef waiting to be cut up. From then on, I watched in total fascination.

As he proceeded to cut up the torso, the knife pierced the gut, and the blood and juices flooded out over the rock and down its side. He chopped off the limbs and removed the bones, which he tossed in turn to the five men sitting down. They were crushers and, using large stone hammers, they began to reduce the bones to a fine powder. . . .

Although we all sat and watched this strange spectacle in silence and awe, I came to realise they were just ordinary workmen doing a difficult and messy job. They could have been a gang of tarmac layers in the north of England. . . .

After half an hour all that was left of the bodies were the heads. These were first scalped, cutting off all the hair, and then the skin peeled off to leave just the bare skulls. They placed the skulls in one of the shallow grooves that dotted the rock and smashed them open with a large stone. After tipping out the two halves of the brain they tossed the pieces to the crushers to do their job.

After 40 minutes the work was complete and both bodies had been reduced to a small, unrecognisable rubble-heap of flesh and powdered bone mixed with tsampa, the coarse flour made from barley that is the Tibetans' staple diet. By that time a dozen or more vultures had gathered on the slope at the side of the rock and were silently waiting. As the two butchers wiped the blades on their overalls and made their way back to the fire one of the crushers picked up a piece of flesh and tossed it amongst the birds.

It was as if a dinner gong had sounded. A cacophony of screeches erupted from the previously silent birds and suddenly the sky overhead turned black as 60 to 70 of the largest vultures I've ever seen (I'd seen quite a few in India) descended on to the slope by the rock. . . .

For a few seconds they milled around on the slope until one of the throng finally flew up on to the rock and began feeding. This seemed to be the signal as all at once the rest of the birds jumped, hopped, and flew on to the rock which became at once a brown, seething unidentifiable mass as, with wings folded and heads down, they began tearing at the food. The noise was terrible as they greedily devoured the remains, squawking and squabbling over the larger pieces, but after 10 minutes or so they had finished. . . .

The 'burial' was over. It had taken less than one hour from beginning to end, and there was not a morsel of food left on the rock, just a few dark stains.

By now the men had removed their overalls and were smoking and drinking tea again as they cleaned and packed away their tools. Myself, Joe, and the three other Westerners rose stiffly to our feet (we had sat virtually without moving for over an hour), thanked the Tibetans, who now showed little interest in us, and started back down the hill, still in total silence, each of us trying to assess what we had just seen.

In a land where wood is scarce and at a premium, and the ground is as hard as rock, and where the Buddhist beliefs of the people proclaim the continuity of all life (birth, death, and rebirth) they had developed this unusual method of disposing of their dead. We had experienced no feelings of disgust or horror, merely a sense of wonderment, and also privilege, at having been allowed to witness this unique Tibetan custom.

On the way back to town I finally asked Joe what he had thought of it all. 'Bloody incredible,' he said, 'there's no need for photographs at all, it's something I'll remember for the rest of my life.' I totally agreed. (*Guardian* 18 October 1986)

### Questions

What aspects of the sky burials are very different from your own notions of a 'decent burial'?

What similarities are there between the Tibetan burial rituals and those practised in contemporary Britain?

What possible explanations might there be for the type of burial ceremony described by Mair?

How does Mair's account illustrate the relationship of culture to history and economic necessity?

## ■ Activity 2 How sociological is your imagination?

Take out your notebook, sharpen your pencil, discard your most cherished cultural assumptions and suspend good old common sense. You are an outsider and your job is to observe and describe what you see around you.

Choose one type of activity (preferably one which you are not familiar with) and simply record your observations. This may be as simple as observing people in a cafeteria or pub (Who are they? Where do they sit? What do they do?) or it may involve you in an anthropological pursuit of the exotic and the bizarre: a night at the wrestling, an evening at the opera or an afternoon spent watching football or playing bingo (Who are the punters? What do they wear? How do they behave?).

Using your newly found sociological imagination, how do you interpret your observations? Do any patterns emerge? Do any hypotheses suggest themselves? What problems have you encountered in your search for new sociological truths?

### Notes for students

This activity is intended to help you understand the process all observers go through in making sense of the world around them. We all use information previously learned to make sense of the situations, and we pick up clues from those we're watching or interacting with. No two people will therefore make sense in exactly the same way. The point of this exercise is to make you aware of what sociologists do when they 'explain behaviour', to raise the issues of subjectivity, value and interpretation. Whether or not you have studied sociology previously, it is hoped you will be stimulated into thinking differently about the world around you, questioning behaviour which might have been 'taken for granted'.

1 First you must select your observation. Think through some possible choices. Religious and cultural events lend themselves well to this activity and you may find that local newspapers contain some helpful ideas.
2 You need to decide how you are going to record your observation. Will you keep notes in a book (obviously or unobtrusively)? Will you trust to your memory and write up your impression as soon as possible? Will you use a tape recorder/still camera/video? There's no right way in this activity: think about the pros and cons of each recording method.
3 After the observation, note the following. How long did the observation last? Did you know if the participants were typical? (How would you decide this?) Did anyone explain what they were doing? Were there written instructions (e.g. church prayer book – how much sense did that make?) Did you make your own sense of what you saw?
4 Let your imagination generate explanations: you're allowed to present competing explanations for what you think you saw and should select the most likely account from your standpoint, explaining in terms of further logical arguments or theories.

### Outline

A suggested outline for the written part of the assignment is as follows:

1 **Introduction** Observation chosen: Where? When? Why?
2 **Method** How the observation was recorded – pros and cons. Did you remain 'non-participant' or did you participate? What were the effects of this? In retrospect would you change the way you did the activity?
3 **Explanations** This section should describe your observation – clues picked up both orally and visually from the participants should be highlighted. You should go beyond pure description and attempt imaginative explanations in order to generate hypotheses about the social behaviour you observed. Factors which may help you in considering explanations and gaining a sociological understanding of what you are observing might include the following: Does there appear to be a shared set of values and rules among the group? Is there a certain social etiquette that must be

maintained? What social characteristics strike you about the group? Are they all male? All female? Predominantly older people? Why? What do the participants appear to get out of the interaction? Escape, pleasure, social contact, sense of identity, etc.

4 **Reflexive account** In this section you reflect on your own role in this observation: if you'd been a different type of person would you have made another interpretation? It is in this section that you raise issues of objectivity/subjectivity, value and interpretation. You need to account for your own role in the process of understanding, i.e. the interpretation you made of the situation. Are you male/female, white/black, disabled/able bodied, young/mature, middle class/working class? Do you hold certain religious, moral or political beliefs? How did these factors shape your interpretation and also actually shape the behaviour of the people involved in the interaction?

5 **Conclusion** How useful did you find this exercise?

Chapter 2

# Sociological theories

**Chapter outline:** Introduction • Classical sociological theories • Durkheim and consensus • Marx and conflict • Weber and meaning • Contemporary sociological theories • Interpretive sociology • Symbolic interactionism • Ethnomethodology and the rules of everyday life • Feminist theories • The Frankfurt School and critical theory • Structuralism • Post-structuralism • Post-modernism • Summary • Further reading • Activities

## Learning objectives

When you have studied this chapter you should be able to address these key questions:

- What are the major theoretical perspectives in sociology?
- How have the writings of Durkheim, Marx and Weber influenced the development of sociological theories?
- How have the established sociological theories been criticized by feminism and other more recent theorizing?

## Introduction

To be sure, theory is useful. But without warmth of heart and without love it bruises the very ones it claims to save. (Gide 1952)

Sociological theory deals with the 'big questions' which we all ask ourselves from time to time. Questions such as: Who are we? Is there a reason for the way we are? How do our lives fit in with the wider society? Who has power and influence over us? Why do some people live in poverty?

Studying theory can and should be an exciting enterprise. However, many people, including students, are suspicious of theory and are keen to extol the virtues of being 'down to earth' and practical. This distinction between practice and theory is not a clearcut one: most of our practical actions and decisions are influenced by the theoretical assumptions we hold. The decision to buy flowers for one's mother on Mother's Day, for instance, might be based on an assumption that males and females have different tastes that reflect their different personalities.

**Q** List the kinds of 'theoretical assumptions' that (a) teachers make about their pupils' attitudes to school work; (b) employers make about what motivates their employees; (c) influenced your decision to study sociology.

This chapter explains the development of the major theoretical approaches in sociology and looks at the work of some of the founders of modern sociology and at their continuing influence. The first section of the chapter will focus on the lives, ideas and work of the three thinkers who have had the greatest influence on modern sociology – Emile Durkheim, Karl Marx and Max Weber. While not exact contemporaries, all three were born in the nineteenth century and developed theories that responded to the economic, political and social changes of that century – the rapid industrialization of Europe and North America and the effects of capitalism on western society. It is important to bear in mind that the origins of sociological theorizing were profoundly political. When Durkheim, Marx and Weber tried to understand nineteenth-century industrialization they did not do it just out of intellectual interest or academic indulgence, they aimed to explore the effects of these changes on the shape and quality of social life – and to consider how the changes might (or might not) improve this quality of life. Indeed the development of early, 'classic' sociology can be seen as an attempt to answer the question 'What is industrial society?' Durkheim, Marx, Weber and other early theorists tried to explain how industrial society had come about, what held it together and what kept pulling it apart.

While sociological explanations and theories might be relatively recent, the questions that interest sociology have been considered by thinkers throughout history. What is new is the modern science of society. The roots of modern sociology can be found in the Enlightenment of the seventeenth century and the social revolutions of the eighteenth century. The scientific discoveries of the Enlightenment helped to transform the social order, with secular knowledge (based on reason and science) replacing sacred tradition. The revolutions in North America, France and England resulted from social movements based on notions of human rights; these revolutions advocated democracy rather than autocracy. As our account of the origins of sociology demonstrated (pp. 10–11) the world from which sociology emerged was characterized by rapid and often frightening change. The industrial revolution, for instance, brought unprecedented productivity at the same time as increased poverty, congested cities, high unemployment and miserable living conditions.

## Sociological perspectives

Although there are other, and earlier, writers whose work is important to sociology, Durkheim, Marx and Weber are generally reckoned to be the key figures in the development of sociological theory. Their work and ideas have been developed by later writers into particular schools of thought or perspectives with their own analytical styles and interpretations. While you may be puzzled by the diversity of theoretical approaches or perspectives, it is important to realize that there is no agreed theoretical standpoint in sociology. Giddens (1993a) suggests that this lack of agreement is due to the nature of the subject itself: sociology is about people and their behaviour and it is a highly complex task to study this. The lack of one overall theoretical approach should not be taken as a sign of weakness but rather an indication of the vitality of sociology. Human behaviour is complicated and it is unrealistic to expect a single unified theoretical perspective to cover all aspects of it. Although there is a diversity of theoretical approaches, there is also a good deal of overlap between them. All sociological theories have in common an emphasis on the ways in which human behaviour and belief are the products of social influences; indeed this distinguishes sociology from other approaches to human behaviour.

**Q** **It is not just sociology that is characterized by theoretical disagreement. Consider the different subjects you have studied or are studying. What different and contradictory approaches or explanations have you come across in these subjects?**

**Which subjects appear to have a unified theoretical stance? Why do you think this might be?**

In introducing the sociological perspective in Chapter 1, alternative explanations of human behaviour were considered. Until relatively recently (the nineteenth century) interest in social aspects of behaviour had been very limited; non-social approaches to human behaviour were predominant. In reflecting on this lack of interest in the social aspects of human existence, Jones (1993) highlights two important non-sociological explanations of human behaviour – *naturalistic explanations* and *individualistic explanations*.

The naturalistic explanation suggests that human behaviour is the product of inherited disposition; humans, like animals, are programmed by nature. This style of explanation is common enough. For instance, it is sometimes argued that it is 'natural' for women and men to fall in love, marry and live in a small family unit (and, therefore, it is 'unnatural' not to want to do this). However, there are many variations to the supposedly 'natural' family practice in both western, industrial societies and non-industrial societies.

The individualistic explanation sees human behaviour as a result of the psychological make-up of individuals. Criminals, for instance, are people with certain kinds of personalities, maybe lacking a sense of right or wrong. Again, wider study casts doubt on these explanations. The bulk of people who are convicted of crime are male, young and from working-class backgrounds: is it feasible to believe that criminal personalities are concentrated in such groupings? And if class is important, why are working-class women under-represented among the criminal population?

These examples help to illustrate the importance of social influences on human behaviour. Where the particular sociological theories and approaches differ is in their emphasis on what these social influences are and how they can be explained.

## Classical sociological theories

### Durkheim and consensus

Although there is no definitive version of the history of western sociology, there is a general agreement that it was born in nineteenth-century France, as a consequence of changes in French society brought about by the democratic revolution of 1789 (see pp. 15–16). The two French writers who did most to 'create' the subject were Auguste Comte, who helped establish the idea of the study of society as a project and who gave the subject its name, and Emile Durkheim, who gave sociology its academic credibility and influence. Durkheim devoted his life to establishing sociology as a distinctive and accepted field of study by building a professional sociology in France. He established university departments to train students in the theories and methods of this new science and edited and directed the publication of a journal which was the leading light of the new sociological movement – *L'Année Sociologique*. As well as this organizing role, Durkheim is best known as an author. His four major studies have given him a key position in sociology:

- *The Division of Labour in Society*, 1893
- *The Rules of Sociological Method*, 1895
- *Suicide: A Study in Sociology*, 1897
- *The Elementary Forms of the Religious Life*, 1912.

**Case Study**

**Emile Durkheim (1858–1917)**

Durkheim's life spanned a period of great change in French and European history. Durkheim grew up in the aftermath of the French defeat by Prussia in the war of 1870–71, while the final years of his life were overshadowed by the outbreak of the First World War in 1914. Durkheim was the son of a rabbi and was brought up in an orthodox Jewish family. He was expected to follow in his father's footsteps and become a rabbi, but 'conversion' to Catholicism and then to agnosticism in his youth led him into an academic life. Durkheim was a brilliant student; he studied at the Ecole Normale Supérieure, Paris, where his interests in social and political philosophy developed. His political views matured while he was studying in Paris; he seems to have been pro-democracy and social reform in the face of the reactionary views of the monarchists and Catholic right. However, Durkheim tended to remain aloof from day-to-day political life preferring to study and debate politics in terms of general theoretical

*(box continued)*

*(box continued)*

principles. After graduating, Durkheim taught philosophy in several schools between 1882 and 1885. He then spent a year in Germany where he was deeply impressed by German advances in social science and psychology. The articles he wrote on these developments helped him to get a post as lecturer in social science and education at the University of Bordeaux in 1887 – the first social science post at a French university. It was while at Bordeaux that Durkheim produced his major works; the first three books listed above were written during this period of his life. By 1902 Durkheim's academic reputation was established and he moved to Paris as Professor of Education and Social Science at the Sorbonne where he remained until his death.

## Durkheim's work

In attempting to answer the question 'What is industrial society?', Durkheim focused on the moral basis of social order and stability – the moral basis of what he termed social solidarity. Durkheim believed that social order was based on a core of shared values. This belief is a key aspect of the functionalist approach in sociology that Durkheim helped establish.

Durkheim argued that without the regulation of society, individuals would attempt to satisfy their own desires and wishes without regard to their fellows. This societal regulation or constraint had to be based on a shared set of values. Thus a working society necessitated the individuals within it accepting these common values. Durkheim called this common set of values the collective conscience. This term is a little ambiguous in that the French word 'conscience' means both 'consciousness' and 'conscience'. However, Durkheim defined the collective conscience as 'the totality of beliefs and sentiments common to average citizens of the same society'.

Q

What common, generally held values make up the 'collective conscience' of modern society?

Which of these values do you use to guide your everyday life?

Which of these values are used by (a) your family; (b) your friends; (c) your teachers?

Durkheim suggested that while we as individuals may think we choose to behave in certain ways, in reality the choices are made for us. The kinds of possibilities of thought and experience available to us are not invented by us individually, they are learned. Durkheim uses religion to illustrate this point. Our religious beliefs and practices are learned; they were in existence before us and if we had been born in another society or age it is likely we would hold quite different beliefs and follow different religious practices. Although self-evident, this point is fundamental to the consensus approach in sociology and is illustrated by Durkheim's comment:

**When I fulfil my obligations as brother, husband or citizen I perform duties which are defined externally to myself and my acts, in law and custom. Even if they conform to my own sentiments and I feel their reality subjectively . . . I merely inherited them through my education. . . . The church member finds the beliefs and practices of his religious life made at birth, their existence prior to him implies their existence outside himself.** ***(Durkheim 1964: 1–2)***

For Durkheim, then, the achievement of social life among people, the existence of social order and social solidarity, is ensured by collective standards of behaviour and values. However, while social solidarity is crucial for the existence of society, the specific type or form it takes is not fixed and changes with the changing forms of society. In his first major work, *The Division of Labour in Society*, Durkheim examines the changes in the form of social solidarity from early, pre-modern societies to complex, modern ones.

## *The Division of Labour* and forms of social solidarity

One of the major academic issues which Durkheim focused on was the significance of the rise of individualism in modern, industrial society. *The Division of Labour in Society* attempts to demonstrate how the rise of individualism exemplifies the emergence of a new type of social order – an order that will increasingly transcend traditional forms of society.

Durkheim argues that the function of the division of labour in modern society is the social integration of individuals, which is achieved through their fulfilling a range of complementary roles and tasks. The theme of the study is the relationship between individuals and the collectivity. The question or problem that Durkheim tackles is 'How can a multiplicity of individuals make up a society?' or 'How can a consensus – the basic condition of social existence – be achieved?'

Durkheim addresses this question by distinguishing between two forms of social solidarity – mechanical and organic solidarity. He argues that the basis of social solidarity in pre-industrial, small-scale societies is different from that in modern, industrial society; the former he termed *mechanical solidarity*, the latter *organic solidarity*.

**Definition**

### Mechanical solidarity

A solidarity of resemblance. Individuals are essentially alike: they feel the same emotions and hold the same things sacred. Individuals are not differentiated in the sense that there is little job specialization. This type of solidarity has existed throughout most of human history; archaic, pre-literate societies were characterized by it. In such situations collective feelings predominate, property tends to be communally owned and the discipline of the small community and of tradition is dominant.

### Organic solidarity

Consensus comes, essentially, from differentiation between individuals. With the increasing range of functions and tasks in modern complex societies comes an increasing differentiation between individuals. Individuals are more interdependent: because people engage in different activities and ways of life they are very dependent on others and this dependence leads to the development of networks of solidarity. In these situations, social order does not rest on uniformity but rather on individuals pursuing different but complementary functions. This differentiation releases and encourages individualism and individual talent. In the face of this society needs a strong moral force and consensus to hold it together and to ensure interdependence. In spite of individuals being unlike one another (in terms of their occupations, for instance) they need to get on together in order for social life to work.

In defining and describing the different forms of solidarity, Durkheim is talking in general and abstract terms. He was not suggesting that there is a simplistic and rigid divide between mechanical and organic solidarity: societies do not necessarily exhibit either mechanical or organic solidarity. Societies with a highly developed organic solidarity will still need to have common beliefs; all societies have to have some common set of assumptions about the world. So the collective conscience is vital in all societies; without it there would just be disintegration into a collection of mutually antagonistic individuals. However, the collective conscience varies in extent and force from one society to another. Where mechanical solidarity is predominant it embraces virtually all of the individual conscience; in modern, differentiated societies characterized by organic solidarity the scope for individuality is greater – people have greater freedom to follow their own preferences.

**Definition**

### Anomie

Durkheim also referred to 'abnormal' forms of the division of labour. In the context of modern societies, characterized by organic solidarity, the lack of a general and strong consensus that encouraged interdependence between people would lead to a situation of anomie. Durkheim felt that this was likely to be a particular problem in modern, developed societies that were experiencing rapid social upheaval, such as becoming industrialized. In small-scale societies, characterized by mechanical solidarity, it is easier for a general consensus to be upheld.

Anomie was initially used by Durkheim to refer to situations where there was substantial disagreement over the appropriate norms and values for governing social behaviour. It occurred when aspects of a society were inadequately regulated. However, anomie can be applied in an individual as well as a social context. Durkheim's analysis of suicide is the most famous illustration of this application of anomie. One of the four categories of suicide that Durkheim highlighted was 'anomic suicide': without the regulation of norms to define appropriate behaviour, life becomes aimless and the individual is more prone to commit suicide; as a society becomes more anomic in times of economic upheaval, such as periods of depression or boom, the suicide rate tends to increase.

Durkheim also found a link between divorce and suicide in that divorced men are particularly prone to suicide. He suggested that 'conjugal anomie' and the consequent greater likelihood of suicide occurred when the regulation of marriage was undermined. Here too anomie is a weakening of the established normative framework.

### Questions

How relevant do you think the concept of anomie is today?

Do you think it helps to explain the growing number of teenage male suicides?

## Functionalism: Durkheim's approach developed

Emile Durkheim is generally regarded as the principal figure in the establishment of the sociological perspective of functionalism. In explaining social solidarity and the division of labour, Durkheim adapted the arguments of the Victorian sociologist Herbert Spencer that societies evolve according to the basic laws of natural selection, survival and adaptation. Thus they can be most easily understood and analysed if they are compared to biological organisms. Durkheim suggested that societies or social systems work like organic systems: they are made up of structures of cultural rules (established practices and beliefs, for instance) and people are expected to conform to them. The organic analogy is used by Durkheim and others as a way of getting to grips with the very abstract nature of sociological theory. The comparison of society with a living organism, such as a human being or a plant, provides a model for interpreting human behaviour.

Although by no means original, this analogy is central to Durkheim's work and to the functionalist perspective. From this perspective, the institutions of society – the kinds of educational arrangements and family forms it has, for instance – are analogous to the parts of an organism, such as the parts of a body. It is quite commonplace for the history of societies to be explained in terms of the human life cycle. Like individuals, societies tend to start as small units and get bigger and, sometimes, to wither away; the history of the Roman Empire, for instance, could be described by such a model. Thus the analogy can be used in describing the development of societies: studies of the USA regularly refer to the 'birth of a nation'. In the development of sociological theory this approach has been associated with the work of Herbert Spencer, who looked at the evolution of societies and compared them with individual organisms.

Another way in which the model of the organic analogy has been used is in comparing the structure of organisms with societies. As parts of the body, the heart or liver, for instance, are understood in terms of the function they perform, so social institutions, such as families or schools, have to be understood in terms of their

**Definition**

### The organic analogy and the functioning of society

**The classic exponents of this application of the organic analogy have been anthropologists who have studied other societies 'in the field'. As the British anthropologist Radcliffe-Brown puts it:**

> The life of an organism is conceived as the functioning of its structure. . . . If we consider any recurrent part of the life process such as digestion, respiration etc, its function is the part it plays in the contribution to the life of the organism as a whole.

**Applying this analogy he goes on:**

> The social life of a community is here defined as the functioning of the social structure. The function of any recurrent activity, such as the punishment of crime or a funeral ceremony, is the part it plays in the social life as a whole and therefore the contribution it makes to structural continuity. (Radcliffe-Brown 1952: 179–80)

functions for maintaining society. In order to understand how the body works the various parts have to be examined in relation to one another. If one part was examined in isolation it would not tell us how life was maintained: scrutiny of the heart or liver by themselves would not tell us how the human body 'worked'. Similarly, any part of social life, any social institution, has to be understood in terms of the way it functions to maintain the whole social structure.

The term 'function', then, is used to refer to the contribution an institution makes to the maintenance and survival of the wider social system. In determining the functions of the various institutions or parts of society, the functionalist approach assumes that there are certain basic requirements which must be met for the society to exist and survive; these requirements or needs are called *functional prerequisites*. Examples of these might include reproduction, systems of communication and agreed standards of behaviour.

Given that the parts of society are interconnected and interrelated, each part will affect all the other parts and for the system to survive there will have to be compatibility between the parts. Functionalists generally argue that this integration is based on value-consensus – essentially an agreement by members of society over values and standards. In western society, for instance, materialism is widely valued. Hence the economic system is geared to producing a wide range of consumer goods; the economic system is backed up by the value placed on materialism by the family, the mass media, the education system and so on. The rest of this section will look at how Durkheim's functionalist approach has been applied in the study of specific areas of society. In particular, we shall examine the functionalist approaches to the study of religion and crime.

**Q** The functionalist analysis of any area or institution of society starts by asking what function does it perform for the maintenance of that society.

What do you think are the functions of the following institutions: (a) the family; (b) the mass media; (c) the education system?

## Functionalism and religion

The functionalist analysis of religion stresses how and to what extent religious beliefs and practices contribute to meeting the needs (or prerequisites) of society. Durkheim's study *The Elementary Forms of the Religious Life* describes how religion provides the basis of the collective conscience – the shared values and ideas – of a society. Religion, therefore, expresses and fulfils a social need and promotes social solidarity and cohesion: in other words it binds people together.

Durkheim's ideas on the role of religion were based on anthropological material on the religion of the Australian aborigines, which he called 'totemism'. This term referred to the fact that each group of aborigines, each clan, had a sacred symbol or totem that they worshipped. The totem functioned both as a symbol of god and of the society and in worshipping it the aborigines were, in effect, worshipping society.

Perhaps the most influential part of Durkheim's theory is the definition of religion by its functions, and the emphasis on religious rites, the collective acts of worship, rather than on what is actually believed. As Durkheim put it:

**The most barbarous and the most fantastic rites and the strangest myths translate some human need, some aspect of life. . . . The reasons with which the faithful justify them may be, and generally are, erroneous . . . [but] In reality there are no religions which are false. All are true in their own fashion; all answer, though in different ways, to the given conditions of human existence.**

*(Durkheim 1976: 14–15)*

Q

To what extent do you think we can talk about religions being true or false?

What functions can religious practices, such as acts of worship, provide for (a) individuals and (b) society as a whole?

The religious rites of the aborigines were seen as a sort of ritual mechanism for reinforcing social integration. Although the aborigines who came together to perform a rain dance have, as far as they are concerned, come together with the purpose of producing rain, Durkheim suggests that this is largely irrelevant. The important point is that they have come together to perform a collective activity which binds them together and which reaffirms commitment to the group's values and norms.

Thus Durkheim is interested in how religion binds people to society; religion is seen as giving 'sacred authority to society's rules and values'. Functionalists writing since Durkheim have extended his analysis of primitive religions to all religion and have argued that religion of some form is a necessary integrating force in all societies. From this point of view the focus is not on the content of different religions – whether they be Protestant, Catholic or Hinduism, for instance – but the fact that they all form similar integrative functions.

Case Study

## The role of religion

**The role of religion in binding people together is regularly stressed by contemporary religious leaders. For example, the Archbishop of Canterbury, in response to criticisms about the Christian Church's lack of moral guidance to young people made after the trial of two 10-year-old boys found guilty of the murder of 2-year-old toddler James Bulger in 1993, commented that:**

Somehow we need to recover a sense of belonging to one society. Let us move away from the Do It Yourself morality that has been going on, with everyone doing what is right or wrong in their own eyes. It is not too late to return to a sense of purpose, to a sense of shared values based on the Christian tradition.

(quoted in *Guardian* 29 November 1993)

## Question

**Can you think of any other examples of how religion or religious leaders in the contemporary world have attempted to promote a sense of belonging to society?**

The importance attached to religion as an integrating force raises the question of what happens when religion declines in importance in society. A response to this has been to emphasize that the functions of religion are still fulfilled by present-day equivalents of religion, such as nationalism or socialism, for example, where political figures become deified and 'worshipped'.

The functionalist approach suggests that religion, in one form or another, is a necessary feature of society. A major problem with this approach is that in modern societies several religions coexist, regulating and integrating their followers differently; thus religious pluralism will tend to work against social cohesion. This criticism implies that Durkheim's analysis of religion is perhaps more appropriate to small-scale, simpler societies. A second important problem is that functionalism focuses on the integrative functions of religion – the provision of shared values and so on – and tends to ignore the effect of religion as a force for division and disharmony in society. There are numerous societies divided over religious dogma and belief and such divisions can be so deep rooted as to lead to bitter and violent conflict, as a glance at both British and world news will soon reveal.

## Functionalism and crime

**Crime is present . . . in all societies of all types. There is no society that is not confronted with the problem of criminality. . . . To classify crime among the phenomena of normal sociology is not to say merely that it is an inevitable, although regrettable phenomenon . . . it is to affirm that it is a factor in public health, an integral part of all healthy societies.** ***(Durkheim 1964: 65–7)***

As with other areas of functionalist analysis, the importance of shared values and norms is central to the explanation of crime. Crime consists of behaviour that breaks or departs from the shared values and norms of society. The functionalist approach, as developed by Durkheim, focuses on the functions performed by the various institutions and parts of society – in particular, the function they perform in the promotion and maintenance of social unity and cohesion. This classic functionalist approach can be applied to crime as to other areas of society. Given that crime is behaviour that breaks rules, it might seem odd to talk about its functions. However, functionalists argue that crime is necessary and indeed useful for society; certainly it has to be controlled but it still has positive functions.

Put simply, the functionalist argument is that crime is universal, in that it exists, to some extent at least, in all known societies. Furthermore, as it is normal it must also be functional. And it is functional in that it helps to sustain conformity and stability. The fact that some individuals commit acts which break rules is accompanied by a sense of outrage which reinforces, for the majority, the support of those rules. When someone commits a particularly horrible crime, such as child murder, people often feel closer together through sharing their collective outrage. Through bringing people closer together crime can have the effect of contributing to social cohesion. Thus the presence of the criminal allows the rest of society to draw together and reaffirm their values: it strengthens the society or social group. The definition of behaviour as 'criminal' helps social cohesion by distinguishing between those who follow the laws and those who do not and by establishing a boundary between what is seen as acceptable and unacceptable behaviour.

Of course, it is not the criminal actions themselves that draw people together; rather it is the publicizing and punishing of crime that does this. The reaction to and punishment of crime is of central importance. The public trial of law-breakers and the media obsession with publicizing crime and criminal trials help to clarify the boundaries of acceptable behaviour. The reaction to and the punishment of crime does not always correspond with the extent of social harm done by the particular criminal action. It does though, according to Durkheim, express the strength of common values and standards. The extent of harm done by an act of violence against a child, for instance, may be slight compared to the number of people harmed by a company ignoring pollution or industrial safety laws. However, the reaction against the child murderer will be far stronger than against the offending company. The reaction to crime is essentially emotional rather than rational and the demand for punishment seems to demonstrate a desire to see the offender suffer pain – evidenced by the angry crowds outside courtrooms at particularly horrific murder trials. These kinds of responses can be best understood if crime is seen as an action that offends widely against strongly held norms and values. Durkheim argued that for there to be social cohesion and agreement people need to be able to react against those who depart from the shared rules and values and that crime creates this opportunity. (See pp. 541–3 for a fuller discussion of Durkheim's analysis of the punishment of crime.)

## Marx and conflict

Karl Marx, like Durkheim, was concerned with the broad questions of what held societies together and how societies change over time. And, as with functionalism, Marxism is a structural theoretical perspective: it concentrates on the structure of society and explains individual actions in terms of the social structure in which they are located. Both functionalism and Marxism stress the crucial and pervasive influence of society. However, in contrast to functionalism, Marx's writings emphasized conflict in society.

**Case Study**

### Karl Marx (1818–83)

Marx was born in Trier, Rhineland, where his father was a lawyer. He grew up in an atmosphere of sympathy for the ideas of the Enlightenment and the French Revolution. In 1835 he became a student at Berlin University, where his political ideas became more radical. As a student, Marx was influenced by the philosophy of Hegel and his followers, who were critical of the religion and politics of the Prussian state, where Berlin was situated. After university, Marx became a journalist (rather than his professed ambition of becoming a university lecturer), writing articles on social and political problems for a Cologne radical paper which earned him some notoriety.

In 1843 Marx moved to Paris, where he was introduced to the ideas of socialism and communism and where he met Frederick Engels, who became his lifelong friend and co-writer. During this period Marx studied economics and came across the theories of

*(box continued)*

*(box continued)*

**classic economists such as Adam Smith and Ricard. This interest in economics shaped Marx's belief that political power is closely linked to economic power; Marx's political views cannot be separated from his historical analysis of the development of capitalist society.**

**After a brief spell in Germany, during the revolution of 1848, Marx moved to London and exile there in 1849. For the rest of his life Marx devoted his time to two major tasks; first, building a revolutionary workers' party, and second, producing a detailed analysis of the capitalist socio-economic system. These two tasks were connected in that Marx believed that an understanding of the theory of capitalism and its problems was a necessary prerequisite to enable its political overthrow. The quote on Marx's grave in Highgate Cemetery, London, illustrates his commitment to political action: 'The philosophers have only interpreted the world in various ways; the point is to change it'. Marx never finished his life work, his study *Economics* which was to cover all aspects of capitalist society. *Das Kapital* (1867–95), perhaps his most famous work, was intended as only a part of this wider project.**

## Marx's work

For Marx the way that people live is, in many ways, a consequence of the arrangements they make for survival, and the methods of producing and distributing food will to some extent determine lifestyle, religious belief, custom and so on. Marx starts his analysis of society and history at this point, that the most obvious and vital fact of life is the need to survive by finding food and shelter. The one constant universal factor in human existence is the system that people devise for maintaining existence and this system will influence all else they do. Thus subsistence is basic to all societies and how it is achieved affects their whole structure and organization.

## Marx's analysis of society

For Marx, there are two essential components of a society: first, the *economic base* or *substructure* (also called the infrastructure in some texts) that provides the material needs of life, and second, the *superstructure*, basically the rest of society including the family, the education system, ideas and beliefs, the legal system and the political system. This division distinguishes between the material and the non-material world. The material world (the economic base) comes first and determines the non-material, because without it the non-material (the superstructure) would not be possible. The economic base is itself composed of the *forces of production* and the *relations of production*. The forces (or means) of production include factories, machinery, raw materials and technology. The relations of production refer to how people relate to one another at work, in particular to the relations that owners and employers have with those who work for them.

The superstructure is the non-material but essentially it reflects the economic base. For example, the education system and the legal system protect and support the basic values of the economic structure of society. In contemporary western society they support the capitalist economic system or base.

## The development of capitalism: historical materialism

Marx was a prolific writer and in his work there are different emphases, hence the difficulty of interpreting Marx and the existence of various different interpretations. However, it is probably fair to say that the essence of Marx's work was to explain the nature and form of modern society, in particular to explain the evolution of capitalism and how it would lead eventually to a communist system.

Conflicts around the system of production, and especially in the relations of production, between workers and owners, were seen by Marx as the essential factors of modern society. These conflicts reveal the nature of capitalist societies and demonstrate how there will have to be a new system of social organization. Marx asserts that capitalism is a necessary stage prior to the establishment of communism in all modern societies (just as feudalism was a necessary forerunner to capitalism). This emphasis on conflict highlights the vital role of social classes in Marx's theory of social change. In all societies that have existed so far (apart from those characterized by early forms of communism – what Marx termed 'primitive' communism) there has been a broad division into two classes, one of which exploits the other. The struggle between these two class groupings (loosely the ruling and ruled classes) leads to societies moving from one form of economic system to another. Thus the role of social class and class struggle is a key element of Marx's analysis of society.

Marx's theory of social change, his theory of historic development, is called *historical materialism*. For Marx, social structures are not created randomly, there is a clear pattern to the way societies in different parts of the world and at different periods of history have organized the production of material goods. According to Marx, throughout history societies have exhibited one of five modes of production which, in chronological order, are Primitive Communist, Ancient, Feudal, Capitalist and Communist. Each of these forms of society leads inevitably to the next. The importance of conflicts of production to Marx's historical analysis is demonstrated in his account of the ways in which societies move from one mode of production to another.

## The emergence of capitalism from feudalism

Marx described feudal relations of production as hierarchical and reciprocal. Hierarchical refers to the allegiance that peasants owed to their feudal lords, to whom they had to give their surplus produce; peasants farmed their own land, provided for themselves and gave the surplus they produced to their feudal masters. Reciprocal refers to the obligations of the lords to look after the peasants' interests by ensuring, for example, their physical security in 'exchange' for their allegiance.

A key development in the decline of feudalism was the enclosure of common land. This encouraged the development of commercial types of agriculture and the establishment of conditions where agriculture could produce a surplus. So early capitalists emerged from within the feudal system; commercial rather than subsistence agriculture led to people owning money rather than just land.

Marx argued that there were very clear differences between feudal and capitalist societies. In feudal societies, for instance, people were supposed to be paid on a fair, just basis rather than on economic calculations and they were bound to one another by mutual obligations. The feudal lifestyle was in sharp contrast to the emerging capitalist mode of production. The concern that Marx and Engels felt at the destruction of these feudal relationships and ties is illustrated by their comments in the first section of the *Communist Manifesto* (1848):

**The bourgeoisie, wherever it has got the upper hand, has put an end to all feudal, patriarchal, idyllic relations. It has pitilessly torn asunder the motley feudal ties that bound man to his 'natural superiors', and has left remaining no other nexus between man and man than naked self-interest, than callous 'cash payment'. It has drowned the most heavenly ecstasies of religious fervour, of chivalrous enthusiasm, of philistine sentimentalism, in the icy waters of egotistical calculation. It has resolved personal worth into exchange value. . . . In one word, for exploitation, veiled by religious and political illusions, it has substituted naked, shameless, direct, brutal exploitation.**

*(Marx and Engels 1952: 44–5)*

Marx emphasized the conflicts and contradictions in all societies, including feudal ones, and in contrasting feudal and capitalist economic systems, his portrayal of feudal relations as 'idyllic' is clearly somewhat idealized and exaggerated. The extract below is taken from a historical account of serfdom in medieval England.

**Hereditary servile status in medieval Europe was the lot, by and large, of the bulk of the peasantry. . . . The term normally employed by modern historians for unfree peasants is 'serfs'. . . . The end of the thirteenth century and beginning of the fourteenth was the time when the situation of the customary tenant was most affected by the servile legal status which had been elaborated in the courts to his disadvantage for over a century. . . . The villein (serf attached to a farm) could be made to pay for a licence fee before being allowed to sell any livestock; he would certainly have to pay for permission to marry off a daughter or even a son; his daughter would have to pay a fine if she became pregnant out of wedlock; his heir would have to hand over his best beast or chattel as *heriot* (as well as the second best beast as *mortuary* to the parson); he was not allowed to buy or sell land without permission; he was not allowed to leave the manor. These were the basic restrictions implicit in villeinage, and there might be more or less depending on the local custom. . . .**

**In a peasant society the fundamental freedom, obviously enough, was the right of the peasant, if not to the full product of his labour, at any rate to enough to sustain a traditional standard of living. But any medieval peasant knew, of course, that his surplus product was going to be taken away bit by bit by landowner, by lord, by Church and by State.** *(Hilton 1969: 9–30)*

To what extent does this account (a) support Marx's idealized picture of the feudal society (b) refute it?

### The capitalist mode of production: pursuit of profit

Marx stressed the importance of the system of production – of the economic base or substructure. In a capitalist society this system is based on the pursuit of profit. In this pursuit the capitalist, the owner of the means of production, must necessarily exploit the worker. For Marx, the essential element in the relationship between capitalist and worker is surplus value – basically the source of profit. Under capitalism the worker is paid a wage designed to enable him or her to survive, yet through the worker's labour power a product which has value over and above the cost of these wages is produced. As well as covering other costs that the capitalist might have – such as the buying of raw materials and renting premises – the surplus value also constitutes the capitalist's profit. For example, a person who works a forty-hour week may, in the first twenty hours of the week, produce all the value that will be received in wages; of the value produced in the remaining twenty hours, that person will receive nothing – it is stolen by the employers. Thus, the value produced by workers far exceeds the value of their wages.

Once a wage is fixed it is in the interests of the capitalist to get as much productivity as possible from the worker. Marx looked at the major ways of increasing exploitation used by capitalists; in *Das Kapital* he looked at how different forms of exploitation appeared and were used in different periods of history. Absolute exploitation would involve squeezing more output from the worker, by increasing the length of the working week perhaps. However, this is a very crude method and would be less likely to be used now. Nowadays the more usual way of raising productivity and therefore profit is to improve the efficiency of work without a commensurate rise in the labourer's wages rather than increase the time worked by the labourer. Marx saw this method of increasing profit as the dominant form of exploitation in the modern capitalist system.

The surplus value generated in modern capitalist societies has not only benefited the capitalists. The position of wage-earners has improved in certain ways. However, the fact that the working population may get more – in terms of better living standards, ownership of consumer goods and so on – is seen by Marxist writers as necessary for the survival of the capitalist system. To explain this point briefly. As capitalism is a system based on profit it depends on continual growth and, therefore, it makes sense to give the mass of the population surplus wealth in order to enable them to buy goods: the more goods they buy the more the system can produce. Of course, the wealthy capitalists will also have plenty of money to spend on luxuries. However, one person can only spend so much and it is more efficient to distribute surplus value around 20 million families rather than 20,000, then they can all buy televisions, washing machines, cars and cosmetics and thereby generate more production and profit. Personal wealth and savings are still heavily concentrated in a few hands, but most wages are now above subsistence levels and enable the mass of the population to buy a range of consumer goods.

## The contradictions in capitalism

In their account of Marx's analysis of capitalism, Cuff *et al.* (1990) suggest that he saw capitalism as a system characterized by:

1 Exploitation of many people by a few.
2 Tensions, strains and contradictions between different social groups.
3 The certainty of drastic change via some form of social revolution.

Adopting this categorization we shall examine each of these statements in turn.

First, Marx argued that there are basic contradictions within capitalist societies due to the conflict of interests between the various groups involved in the economic process, in particular the conflict of interests between an exploiting and exploited group, between the owners of the means of production and the non-owners. Under capitalism the main link between people is an impersonal cash relationship. Most people have only one marketable asset – their labour. A small number of industrial capitalists own the means of production, such as factories, land and raw materials, and provide the main means of employment for the majority. It is unlikely that individual capitalists regard themselves as exploiters; they are in business to make profits. To do this they have to beat competitors by reducing prices and a major way of reducing prices is to cut costs. The biggest recurring cost for most employers is likely to be labour, so capitalists, in trying to be competitive, have little option but to keep labour costs down. Essentially the capitalist wants as much work as possible from as few workers for as little pay as possible: this exploitation is not due to the 'evil' nature of individual capitalists, but is a necessary requirement of the whole capitalist system according to Marx.

Second, the capitalist system produces the very conflicts and tension that will eventually tear it apart. In particular, conflicts and tension over pay and conditions between capitalists and employees, but also conflicts and tension between different groups of wage-earners and between capitalists themselves. Marx believed that the tensions inherent in capitalism would intensify, due to certain developments or trends that were inevitable in a capitalist system. These developments included polarization, homogenization and pauperization.

**Definition**

### Polarization

**In modern industrial societies traditional skills were becoming redundant and there was a tendency for the working population to polarize into two distinct and hostile groups – the capitalists and the labourers.**

### Homogenization

**Within these two groups, individuals were becoming increasing alike (or homogenous). Among the capitalists, for example, competition was eliminating the smaller businesses and the successful ones were expanding, with the typical capitalist enterprise becoming a large and complex concern. Furthermore, workers would become increasingly homogenous as a result of their dependence on work in these large factories and the decline of traditional skills.**

### Pauperization

**In pursuing profit, capitalists need to keep their wage bills down. They need to ensure that the workers' wages do not rise in relation to those of capitalists, so that, in relation to capitalists, wage-workers are turned into paupers – they are 'pauperized'.**

### Questions

**What contemporary evidence is there to support the argument that there is (a) a polarization of the working population; (b) homogenization among major groups of workers; (c) pauperization of workers in relation to capitalists?**

Third, Marx argued that the capitalist system was doomed: the contradictions would grow and a social revolution was inevitable. Capitalism would disintegrate as developments such as polarization, homogenization and pauperization intensified. This would open the way for the establishment of a new, alternative type of social system. However, for a new system to be created a new consciousness would have to develop among the exploited workers – a consciousness that would reflect the interests of the workers. Marx felt that this new consciousness could develop only if the exploited group actively opposed the capitalist system; only through struggle would the old, false consciousness be eradicated. The old consciousness is false because it reflects the interests of the privileged ruling groups, not the interests of the bulk of the people. True consciousness for the mass of the population would come about only when they developed an ideology (a set of ideas and values) which supported their interests.

When this new consciousness develops and matures, the proletariat would, according to Marx, overturn the capitalist system. They would take over the means of production and the state – as the capitalists had done before them. This would lead to a fundamental shift in the relations of production and a new abundant society would emerge where everyone could work and live freely and enjoy equality of status:

**It will be possible for me to do one thing today and another tomorrow, to hunt in the morning, fish in the afternoon, rear cattle in the evening, criticise after dinner, just as I have a mind to, without ever becoming a hunter, fisherman, shepherd or critic.** ***(Marx and Engels 1976 vol. 5: 47)***

Only in this sort of liberated, communist society could humans fulfil their potential for creativity; in societies where one class group dominates the rest it is not possible.

This section has focused on the contradictions in the capitalist system: contradictions based on the exploitative relationship between owners and non-owners, between capitalists and workers. It is important to emphasize that we have looked at capitalism in a very general, simplistic manner. Contemporary capitalism differs considerably from early capitalism and from the model of capitalism that Marx wrote about. In the 1990s, instead of actually owning factories and industrial production, ownership usually takes the form of capital investment – stocks and shares. Marxists argue, however, that this does not alter the essentially exploitative features of capitalist society; the bourgeoisie may not make the goods but they still gain the benefit from the surplus value produced by workers. Although exploitation may not be as obvious as feudal masters extracting 'tithes' from their peasants (or as the exploitation of slaves), the relationship between capitalist and wage-earner is essentially the same.

## Alienation

**Work is external to the worker, that is it is not part of his nature . . . consequently he does not fulfil himself in this work but denies himself, has a feeling of misery, not of well-being, does not develop freely a physical and mental energy, but is physically exhausted and mentally debased. . . . [Work] is not the satisfaction of a need but only a means for satisfying other needs. Its alien character is clearly shown by the fact that as soon as there is no physical or other compulsion it is avoided like the plague.**

***(Marx, Economic and Philosophical Manuscripts, 1844, in Bottomore 1963: 124–5)***

The antagonistic and unequal class structure characteristic of capitalist societies leads to what Marx termed alienation. Alienation refers to the separation, or estrangement, of individuals from themselves and from others. It is a complicated concept as it involves individuals' feelings. Alienation describes the sense of frustration, pointlessness and lack of involvement felt by many working people. Marx saw alienation as a central feature of capitalism and one that could take different forms. As the quote above illustrates, workers became alienated from their work because what they produced was controlled by others. As well as work itself being an alienating activity, workers are alienated from each other. Relations in a capitalist society are those of competition (the 'dog eat dog' philosophy) rather than cooperation, even among the workers.

**Q**

Give examples of 'alienating work' in modern society.

Describe the extent and sort of alienation that might be found in the following occupations: nurse; shop assistant; car mechanic; taxi driver; food packager; teacher.

In what areas of life other than work might alienation occur?

**Definition**

### Alienation: Marxist interpretations

The notion of alienation has been given different emphases by the different versions of Marxism that have developed from Marx's work. These differing emphases can be seen in the two major divergent strands of Marxist theorizing – humanistic Marxism and structural Marxism.

The more orthodox, structural Marxism is concerned mainly with the economic laws of capitalism and the nature of the capitalist state; this approach formed the basis for the discussion of historical materialism and the contradictions in capitalism provided above.

In contrast, humanistic Marxism has tended to play down the importance of the economic base/superstructure division. The focus has been on Marx's analysis of the dehumanizing effects of the rise of capitalism and, in particular, Marx's writings on alienation. This approach developed from the early 1920s in the work of, among others, George Lukács, Antonio Gramsci and the Frankfurt School (see pp. 91–4). Humanist Marxism suggests that people are essentially cooperative but that the development of capitalism leads to their alienation. This alienation occurs not only in the economic context but also in other contexts due to the general influence of large bureaucracies, the mass media and oppressive forms of government. Alienation can be overcome only by abolishing capitalism.

Rather than stressing alienation, structural Marxism, exemplified in the work of the French Marxist philosopher Louis Althusser (1918–93), focuses on exploitation. The processes and structures of capitalism are seen as exploiting workers. This exploitation can be measured objectively; it is not based on speculative ideas about the 'human spirit'. Thus structural Marxism focuses on the economic base where the exploitative mechanisms are located, 'the base/superstructure distinction is of paramount importance – it renders Marxism a scientifically valid method of analysis' (Lee and Newby 1983: 118).

## The role of ideology

**The ideas of the ruling class are, in every age, the ruling ideas.**

*(Marx and Engels 1976 vol. 5: 59)*

The emphasis given to class exploitation and conflict raises the issue of why disadvantaged and exploited people accept their situation. Now, even in the modern, 'civilized' world a great deal of exploitation is exerted by pure force, particularly in states run by military and authoritarian regimes. However, that does not provide a complete explanation for the apparent acceptance of exploitation. In Marxist theory, ideas, values and beliefs perform a central function in maintaining inequalities and oppression. They act as ideologies supporting the (capitalist) system.

**Q** For a basically exploitative system such as modern capitalism to exist, either the inequalities (the fact that some people own Rolls Royces and yachts while others can barely afford household bills, for example) and exploitation must fail to be recognized by disadvantaged people or they must be persuaded that such a situation is acceptable and justified.

Why do you think disadvantaged groups put up with their situation?

What 'ideas, values and beliefs' might persuade people to accept their disadvantaged and exploited condition?

The importance of ideology highlights the crucial role of the superstructure – of society's cultural aspects and institutions – in ensuring that the economic system is considered legitimate. It also illustrates the importance of the notions of class consciousness and false consciousness to Marxist theory. Marx's theory of historical materialism is a good deal more complex than presented here. For instance, the relationship between the economic base and superstructure is not as rigid as we have perhaps implied. Marx was well aware that there was not a complete 'economic determinism' and that the superstructure had some influence on the economic system and could, indeed, influence the way in which the economic system developed. The variations in the capitalist system from one society to another demonstrate this: the different histories and cultures of Japan, the UK and the USA, for example, have affected the kinds of capitalist economic systems that prevail in those countries.

## Marx and social class

According to Marx there is a built-in antagonism and conflict between class groups in all societies; as his famous comment at the start of the *Communist Manifesto* puts it:

**The history of all hitherto existing society is the history of class struggles.**

*(Marx and Engels 1952: 40)*

Perhaps Marx's major intellectual aim was to discover the principle of change in society. However, he did not want just to describe divisions in society but to explain which groups had strong interests in maintaining the existing system and which in trying to change it. These groups, with differing interests, Marx saw as social classes.

Classes exist in all non-communist societies. In the Ancient mode of production the two main classes were the slaves and the slave owners. In feudal society they were the servile peasantry and the landed nobility. Under capitalism, there are, similarly, two main classes – the *bourgeoisie* who own the means of production and the *proletariat* who have only their labour power to sell. In any class system, then, there are two main classes and, because one exploits the other, they are antagonistic to one another. This antagonism provides the driving force for social change (as we highlighted in discussing the contradiction in capitalism, pp. 54–6).

For Marx, class consciousness was of central importance in defining social class. Members of social classes could be distinguished by two criteria, both of which are necessary for a fully developed social class to exist:

1 *Objective criteria* the sharing of a particular attribute, for example, a similar type of occupation or the same relationship to the means of production (being an owner or non-owner)
2 *Subjective criteria* grouping people in terms of a shared attribute does no more than create a category (all red-headed people could be lumped together in this way, for example); a category is only a possible or potential class and can be transformed into an active social class only when people become conscious of their position.

Marx summed up this distinction by stating that it was not enough for a class to be a *class in itself*, it had also to be a *class for itself* (with a full class consciousness and feelings of solidarity with others of that class). This distinction is central to Marx's theory of class and social change and the notion of class consciousness is central to his theory of working-class revolution. Awareness and consciousness is necessary for the existence of an active social class; only when a class becomes a class for itself does it exist as a political force.

Marx believed that the working class were bound to develop this class consciousness once the appropriate conditions were present. He believed the bourgeoisie were incapable of developing a strong overall consciousness of their collective interests, due to the inevitable competition between individual capitalists chasing profit.

One of the major problems of the Marxist analysis is that the working classes in most capitalist countries have hardly ever come close to acquiring this class consciousness and becoming a class for itself. Most western working-class groups have been content to squeeze the occasional reforms out of the ruling class, rather than challenging the whole basis of class inequality. Linked with this failure to mobilize has been the growth of the middle classes. For Marx, all non-owners of the means of production are, objectively, members of the proletariat. However, what distinguishes the middle class is that they help administer and perpetuate the capitalist system for the ruling class. They are not part of the ruling class but are its functionaries; lawyers, teachers, civil servants and so on are seen by Marxists as 'lackeys of the ruling class'. They enjoy more privileges than the exploited working classes but their power is no greater; without property to rely on for income the real interests of the middle classes are bound up with the working classes and in so far as they do not realize this they are victims of 'false consciousness'.

**Q** How might groups of workers develop a sense of collective identity and class consciousness?

What factors work against this in modern society?

Where do you think the interests of 'professional' workers and manual workers coincide? Where do they diverge?

## Weber and meaning

Max Weber is considered to be one of the 'trinity of founding thinkers' of sociology, along with Durkheim and Marx. Weber and Durkheim adopted quite distinct methods and theories in their sociological work. While Durkheim devoted himself to trying to establish sociology as an academic subject (founding journals and teaching departments), Weber was more a pure scholar, grappling with ideas. Like Marx, Weber was not 'just' a sociologist: his work extended into philosophy, economics, religion and history, for example. This work, however, has not led to the establishment of a coherent doctrine; there is not a 'Weberism' in the same way as a 'Marxism'. The focus of this introduction to Weber's work and its influence will be to examine some of the ideas and themes that Weber developed. His four major studies are:

- *The Protestant Ethic and the Spirit of Capitalism*, 1902
- *The Sociology of Religion*, 1920
- *The Theory of Social and Economic Organization*, 1922
- *The Methodology of the Social Sciences*, 1949

**Case Study**

### Max Weber (1864–1920)

Weber was born in Germany and spent his academic career there. His first teaching job was in law at Berlin University. As his intellectual interests widened he was appointed to professorships in political economy and then economics at the universities of Freiberg and Heidelberg respectively. However, mental illness and depression meant that Weber was unable to hold down full-time teaching positions throughout his whole life. In 1897 at Heidelberg, shortly after the death of his father, he suffered a nervous breakdown that cut short his career as it was beginning to develop. After that his academic life was spent writing and researching, with sociology becoming his main academic field.

Weber's lifetime spanned a period of massive change in German history. The unification of Germany led to the emergence of the modern German state and was accompanied by a phenomenal growth of industry; indeed it was around this time that Germany challenged and overtook Britain as Europe's leading industrial power. The attempts to create a German empire culminated in the First World War and defeat towards the end of Weber's life.

Weber's work has been described as a debate with the 'ghost of Marx'. Weber was clearly influenced by Marx, but was critical of some of his views. He criticized Marx's overemphasis on materialist explanations of historical development and argued that social divisions reflected more than solely economic or class conflict.

### Weber's work

Weber wrote about the nature of sociology and how to go about studying society. He argued that people cannot be studied using the same procedures as those involved in investigating the physical world: people are thinking, reasoning beings who attach meanings to what they do and sociology has to acknowledge this. Weber felt that sociology should adopt a sort of midway position between the 'hard' natural sciences and cultural studies such as literature, history and art.

For Weber the basis of sociological analysis was the meaning that individuals give to the social world and their situation in it. This necessitated sociology following a different kind of method from that of the natural sciences. Sociology could not proceed in the same manner as the natural sciences because individuals had a degree of free will which led to some unpredictability in their actions. Sociology had to aim to understand human action and to do this it had to acknowledge the particular and unique, rather than always expect to be able to generalize.

In contrast to the other founding writers, Weber was interested in explaining individual social action and what motivates it. The basic unit of investigation should, therefore, be the individual, whereas Durkheim emphasized collectivity and Marx the social class groupings.

In particular sociology had to adopt what Weber called *verstehen* – a German word meaning, roughly, empathetic or interpretive understanding – in order to show how people's beliefs and motives led to particular types of behaviour and action. Understanding and empathizing with the belief of others does not necessarily mean being sympathetic to or supportive of those beliefs. However, in order to gain a real appreciation of how others feel, we should try and think of ourselves as being in their situation and see things through their eyes.

While it might seem difficult to empathize with people from different cultures and periods of history, Weber saw *verstehen* as a method that could be applied to the understanding of events from different contexts: 'One need not have been Caesar in order to understand Caesar' (sense can be made of Caesar's actions by seeing them as an understandable sequence).

**Q** How might *verstehen* help in the study of (a) religion; (b) poverty; (c) crime?
What difficulties might someone adopting such an approach face?

Thus sociology, according to Weber, is the study of social action, and it is by placing meaning on and interpreting the behaviour of others that we are able to understand that behaviour. Of course, the meaning of an action requires an interpretation and the problem for sociology, as Weber sees it, is how to discover the meanings which other individuals and groups place on their behaviour. In interpreting behaviour, sociologists will inevitably be left with nagging doubts about their observations and analyses: 'How can I be sure that I have understood the subjective feelings of others? How would I know if I had totally misunderstood and misinterpreted them?'

These kinds of doubts and problems raise the issue of whether there is some standard of social action against which different types of behaviour can be related to and measured. Weber suggested that there were four basic categories of action that could provide such a standard.

1 *Traditional action* The individual is driven by custom and habit with behaviour often an automatic reaction. A great deal of everyday activity comes under this heading – eating, washing and so on.
2 *Affective action* The individual is guided by emotions. Such behaviour contains some distinctive and unconscious elements: it may involve seeking revenge or providing immediate sensual gratification, for instance.

3 *Value-rational action* The individual follows strongly held values and morals. Overall objectives or ends are seen as important and behaviour is guided by ideals – doing the 'decent thing'.
4 *Technical-rational action* The individual chooses the objectives and means rationally, with a full account taken of the consequences. It is this sort of behaviour that is most open to sociological understanding and analysis.

Weber argued that technical-rational action was becoming more and more dominant in western society and was driving out the other forms of action. This notion of rationality and the spread of it is a key principle of Weber's work.

**Definition**

**Ideal types**

**The categories of social action suggested by Weber are 'ideal types', a notion that is an important element of Weber's work. Essentially, an ideal type is a way of classifying things; it is an abstraction that Weber employed in trying to get to grips with the complexities of the social world. Social phenomena cannot always be understood in their entirety and it is often easier to emphasize certain key features. Thus, our ideal type of capitalism, democracy or whatever will not necessarily represent the 'real thing'; it will be a rather exaggerated and idealized version (a little like a cartoon characterization). Weber saw the ideal type as a sort of yardstick for comparing and evaluating other cases. It is quite possible for different ideal types to be constructed for the same phenomenon; there might be different ideal types of capitalism, for example.**

Weber's work was wide ranging and encompassed many topics. Here we shall focus on just two of his main concerns: the relationship between religion and the development of capitalism and the spread of bureaucratic administration in the modern world. As well as being extremely interesting and influential in their own right, both these areas of Weber's work give a good insight into the analytical methods he employed.

### *The Protestant Ethic and the Spirit of Capitalism*

Weber's most famous study, *The Protestant Ethic and the Spirit of Capitalism* (1902), attempted to explain how a particular type of religious belief came to influence economic behaviour, thereby making it more rational; this is an application of his argument that technical-rational action was becoming the predominant form of social action in the modern, western world.

Weber studied a range of cultures and religions of the non-western world in order to show that the reason they had not developed a similar sort of rational capitalism to the west was due to religious and cultural factors. This approach can be contrasted with Marx's emphasis on the importance of economic, class factors in the rise of western capitalism. Weber's work was critical of the Marxist view that religious ideas were always and inevitably shaped by economic factors. Weber did not deny that in certain situations religion may be shaped by economic factors, but he argued that this was not always the case. However, his main interest was in the ways in which religious ideas might affect and determine social change.

So, the 'Protestant ethic thesis' aimed to explain the development of capitalism in terms of the emergence of a particular form of Protestant religion. Weber tried to explain why capitalism had fully developed only in the western world and had flourished in northern Europe. He argued that religion provided a clue. He suggested that the ideas and practices of Protestantism were particularly appropriate to capitalist development in a way that was not true of other religions, such as Islam, or of forms of Christianity, such as Catholicism.

### *The capitalist spirit*

Weber argued that there was a capitalist spirit which was based on a desire to be productive and accumulate. In western society, hard work, investment and steady accumulation were seen as the 'proper' and correct attitudes, with idleness and over-consumption seen as wrong; elsewhere production was more geared toward the production of goods for immediate use. The sort of western attitudes that Weber identified with capitalist societies were, he felt, by no means natural. Why, for instance, not just produce enough for one's needs and then stop working? Why not spend when one can, rather than save?

In looking at Weber's definition of capitalism, it is important to bear in mind that he was writing at the beginning of the twentieth century and the attitudes and style of capitalism have changed since then. Also, his description is an 'ideal type': each capitalist society has its own peculiarities. None the less, the essence of capitalism is seen as an 'enterprise whose aim is to make the maximum profit and whose means is the rational organisation of work and production'. This desire for profit in tandem with rational discipline constitutes the historically unique feature of western capitalism. In all societies there have been merchants eager to make money, but what is unique is that this desire for profit should satisfy itself not by conquest and plunder but by discipline and science. Perhaps the term 'profit' does not fully describe Weber's emphasis on the idea of unlimited accumulation. The capitalist, according to Weber, does not limit his appetite for gain in accordance with tradition or custom, but is driven by a desire to keep accumulating.

**Capitalism according to Weber**

**Weber's definition of capitalism as an enterprise working towards unlimited acquisition of goods and functioning in a rational and disciplined way resembles Marx's definition but also presents various differences.**

**Similarities with Marx – The essence of capitalism is the pursuit of profit through the market; capitalism has utilized increasingly powerful technical means to achieve its ends – of extra profit.**

**Differences from Marx – The major characteristic of capitalism is rationalization, which would continue no matter who owned the means of production. The need for rational organization would persist beyond any revolution that might result in the state ownership of production; it would still exist in socialist or communist societies.**

With regard to the relationship between western capitalism and religion, Weber suggested that a certain form of Protestantism provided conditions that were particularly favourable for the growth of the capitalist economic system. The key elements of his findings and argument can be summarized as:

1 In areas of mixed religions (such as his own society, Germany) particular groups of Protestants possessed a disproportionate amount of wealth and important positions.
2 This indicated a spiritual affinity – a link – between the Protestant religion and the spirit of capitalism.
3 The different styles of religion in different societies help to explain why western capitalism did not develop elsewhere. Weber studied the religions of a number of areas of the world including China, India and the Middle East. He argued that a particular attitude to work, determined by religious belief, was the crucial factor present in the west and absent elsewhere which helped establish western economic dominance.

### *The Protestant Ethic*

What was the particular feature of this 'form of Protestantism' that Weber felt was so influential. The Protestant Ethic was a sort of Puritanism that was based on Calvinism (John Calvin was one of the great religious reformers of the sixteenth century and the founder of the Presbyterian religion). The principal features of the Protestant Ethic were:

1 The existence of an absolute, transcendent God who created the world and ruled over it.
2 This all powerful God has predestined each person to salvation or damnation; this predestination cannot be altered.
3 God created the world for his glory and everyone is obliged to work for the glory of God – whether they are to be saved or not.
4 Worldly things belong to the order of sin: salvation occurs only through divine grace.

Although each of these features exist separately in other religions, their combination in Calvinist Protestantism was, Weber argued, unique.

Weber saw a coincidence between certain requirements of this Protestantism and capitalist logic. The Protestant Ethic asks the believer to beware of the things of this world and emphasizes the importance of self-denial. To work rationally in pursuit of profit which is not consumed but reinvested is the sort of conduct that was necessary to the development of capitalism. This demonstrates an aspect of what Weber called the spiritual affinity between the Protestant and capitalist attitudes. The Protestant Ethic, according to Weber, provided an economic motivation for the 'strange' capitalist behaviour of accumulation for the sake of it – a behaviour which has no obvious parallel in non-western societies.

### *Predestination*

A central aspect of the Protestant Ethic was the idea of predestination, which is a religious conviction based on the belief that God's decrees are ultimate, impenetrable and irrevocable. Grace is either bestowed on an individual or it is not, and there is little the individual can do to alter this. This belief helps to explain the rejection of the sacraments by Protestant religions. In certain religions people can find 'grace' through, for instance, confession and absolution from sins or from last rites. For Puritan Protestants these practices would make no difference to whether an individual was saved or not.

The belief in predestination leads to the elimination of many of the mystical elements of belief and, for Weber, highlighted the increasing rationalization of religion.

Believers in predestination are faced by crucial questions such as 'How does one know that one belongs to the elect?' and 'What is the sign that one is saved?' The early Protestants believed that the sign of election could be found in a personal life that followed religious teachings and in the social achievements of an individual. Social achievement would include success in the individual's professional activity – in their 'calling'. Effective and good work demonstrates the glory of God so that a successful work career demonstrated a blessing on those activities and could, therefore, be interpreted as 'proof of election'. Individuals acquire the certainty of salvation through the strength of their faith that would be reflected in success at work.

This notion of successful worldly achievement demonstrating spiritual salvation poses a dilemma. Growing business success will lead to greater affluence, which does not fit in with the rigour of a true Christian life, where worldly possessions would be seen as unimportant. However, Puritan Protestants believed that it was not the acquiring of wealth that was wrong but the enjoyment of the things that money can buy and the temptations that it can bring. It was felt that individuals should take from their assets only what was needed for a life of personal sobriety and obedience to God's law and must follow an ascetic lifestyle.

The emphasis on hard work and productivity coupled with the rejection of luxuries led to a lifestyle that encouraged and influenced the spirit of capitalism.

**Definition**

### The Protestant Ethic and asceticism

**A lifestyle of asceticism was one based on self-denial and abstinence. In the context of the early Protestants with their emphasis on the virtues of hard work, it was felt that wasting time was a sin: God's time should not be wasted by idle talk, by too much sleep or by sociability, for example. In addition, people should accept the position that God had assigned to them; whatever work one has to do it should be done to God's greater glory. A person without a vocation was felt to lack the character demanded by asceticism; although irregular work might be unavoidable at times it was not a good thing. If individuals did not try to be as productive as possible in their work then they were refusing to be a good steward of God's gifts and were not following a calling. Asceticism was hostile to leisure and cultural pursuits. The theatre was obnoxious to Puritans, as was ostentatious dress; thus the plain clothing worn by Puritans.**

**The link between this religious asceticism and capitalism was that industry was provided with sober and conscientious workers. Furthermore, it gave an assurance that inequality was part of God's plan and was not to be questioned. Asceticism, and particularly the notion that hard work was highly pleasing to God, was not a new**

*(box continued)*

*(box continued)*

**phenomenon, nor was it unique to early Protestantism. However, the emphasis on work as a calling, and a sign of personal salvation, added an extra dimension to the ascetic idea. From a different perspective, it could be argued that the stress on work as a calling also provided a justification for employers' exploitation of their workforce, in that employers' business activities were also seen as callings, with profit-making viewed positively.**

### Questions

**Which particular stories or parables from the Bible could be used to 'support' the Protestant Ethic's emphasis on asceticism?**

**How has the Protestant Ethic influenced the way that people think about contemporary issues such as (a) unemployment and poverty; (b) divorce and changes in family structure?**

#### *The Protestant Ethic thesis: discussion points*

The Protestant Ethic thesis is essentially a reaction to the Marxist assumption that all social events are reducible to a single factor – the economic context or substructure. Weber's argument is not the opposite of historical materialism; as he put it, 'It is not my aim to substitute for a one-sided materialistic an equally one-sided spiritualistic causal interpretation of history and culture' (Weber 1974: 183). What he demonstrated is that economic activity may be governed by systems of belief, just as at certain times systems of belief may be determined by the economic system. Thus Protestantism was not seen by Weber as the cause of capitalism, but rather as one of the factors that led to its emergence and development. Weber's work has encouraged the recognition that there is no necessary determination of beliefs by economic and social reality, or rather that it is not justifiable to assume a determination of this kind to be the only and ultimate one.

Given its scope, it is not surprising that many doubts have been raised about the validity of Weber's thesis. First, although the early Protestant capitalists advocated an ascetic lifestyle and did not spend a great deal on luxuries, they did have power and status in their communities as well as financial security – and perhaps these things are enjoyments in themselves? Second, many of the early rich capitalists were not Protestants: there were also rich Catholic and Jewish business people. Third, while there probably was a link between capitalism and Protestantism, rather than Protestantism leading to capitalism, the reverse occurred and Protestantism developed as a rationalization for capitalism. It justified the wealth of certain people by suggesting that this wealth would be viewed favourably by God. Fourth, some Calvinist communities did not develop along capitalist lines immediately. Scotland for instance, although strongly Calvinist, had a slower capitalist development than other less obviously Protestant countries. Finally, the accumulation of investment capital in Britain, the Netherlands, New England in the USA and other early capitalist societies was arguably due as much to profiteering through trade with less developed countries as to careful saving by God-fearing Protestant business people.

Of course Weber realized that capitalism was not solely the result of Protestantism: he was aware of the developments in trade and technology. He felt, however, that the age in which capitalism developed, which was also the age of the Reformation, was one where religion was a major force in society and social scientists should examine and explain the extent to which religious conduct could influence other activities. Weber did not believe he had exhausted the subject as his comment in the last paragraph of *The Protestant Ethic and the Spirit of Capitalism* illustrates:

**Modern man [sic] is in general unable to give religious ideas a significance for cultural and national character which they deserve.** *(Weber 1974: 183)*

## Weber and bureaucracy

In the sociological study of organizations, Weber's work is generally taken as the starting-point. Weber examined, in particular, bureaucracy, the form of organization that he saw as becoming predominant in modern industrial society. In Britain, the word 'bureaucracy' tends to have negative connotations and be seen as something of a 'problem'; indeed the term 'bureaucrat' often doubles as a form of mild abuse. Nevertheless, the bureaucratic type of organizational structure would seem to be a fixed, permanent and perhaps even necessary feature of modern society.

Weber saw that as industrial societies developed they were characterized by the growth and spread of large-scale organizations – the Civil Service, the armed forces, churches, educational institutions, manufacturing companies and so on. Large-scale organizations were clearly having an increasing influence on all areas of social life.

Weber was particularly concerned with the problem of efficiency in organizations. The 'ideal type' blueprint for bureaucracy that he defined (see p. 69) was, he felt, the best way of ensuring efficiency in the administering of organizations. This 'ideal type' of Weber's was based on his analysis of alternative forms of power and authority. This analysis provides the context for an understanding of Weber's theorizing on bureaucracy.

*Power* was seen by Weber as the ability to get things done or to compel others to comply with one's commands. *Authority* also involves the ability to get things done but in situations where the particular order is seen as legitimate by those following it. Authority is, in essence, legitimized power, where legitimacy involves the acceptance of the rights of others to make decisions. So, power and authority are closely related concepts for Weber, but the notion of legitimacy is an important distinguishing feature. Weber then defined and distinguished three types of authority based on different 'types' of legitimacy. The three types were traditional, charismatic and rational-legal, and these were found, he argued, in one degree or another, in all forms of society.

Definition

### Weber's three types of authority

#### Traditional authority

This is based on the unquestioning acceptance of the distribution of power. Legitimacy is believed because it has 'always been so'; the leader has authority by virtue of the traditional status that the office of leader has.

#### Charismatic authority

This is based on the commitment and loyalty to a leader who is generally felt to possess very exceptional qualities. Charisma is a unique force that overrides tradition and law. In a system based on charismatic authority the word of the leader is seen as all important; by its nature, this type of authority is very unstable. First, the particular leader has to keep the loyalty of the masses and, assuming this can be achieved, it is difficult to pass charismatic authority on after the leader's death. Second, the authority of charismatic leaders tends to become routinized over time; they will need to get a staff of assistants as the job of leader evolves. Weber argued that charismatic authority will eventually change its form and become routinized or bureaucratized; it will merge with the third and final type of authority he defined – the rational-legal.

#### Rational-legal authority

This is based on a legal framework which supports and maintains the distribution of power among individuals and groups in society. This form of authority is characterized by bureaucracy; the emphasis is on the rules rather than either the leader (charismatic authority) or the customs (traditional authority). The organization is supreme, with no one being 'above the law' (remember that Weber was talking in ideal terms!).

### Questions

Give an example of (a) traditional; (b) charismatic; (c) rational-legal authority.

Give examples of people who illustrate or have illustrated each of these forms of authority.

In broad historical terms, Weber believed that the traditional and charismatic forms of authority existed in earlier, pre-industrial societies. In modern society, the rationalization process (by this Weber means the application of scientific thought and the influence of science in behaviour) has meant that authority has become increasingly rational-legal, based on formal rules. And, as suggested above, bureaucracy is the most typical form of rational-legal authority.

#### *Weber's 'ideal type' bureaucracy*

Bureaucracy was, for Weber, the characteristic form of administration in modern society. It was not just confined to the political arena but common to all other forms of administration, including education, religion, the business world and so on. Essentially, Weber's explanation for the spread of bureaucracy was because of its efficiency in relation to other forms of organization.

It is important to note that Weber's belief in the efficiency of bureaucracy did not mean he saw bureaucracy as necessarily a 'good thing'. An overriding fear at the end of his life was that modern society would be subject to a deadening, dictatorial bureaucracy. This fear was tied in with Weber's work on rationalization; bureaucratic development was a logical consequence of increasing rationalization, which was undermining and removing spiritual influences from the world. Rationalization was, for Weber, a key feature of modern society and occurred in the fields of both religious belief and economic activity.

Weber's 'ideal type' model of bureaucracy contained six basic principles:

1 *Specialization* official tasks and positions are clearly divided; each covers a distinct and separate area of competence.
2 *Hierarchy* there is an ordered system of superordination and subordination; every position or office is accountable to and supervised by a higher office.
3 *Rules* there are clearly established, general rules which govern the management of the office.
4 *Impersonality* everyone within the organization is subject to formal equality of treatment.
5 *Officials* they are (a) selected and appointed on the basis of technical qualifications (on some clearly recognized criteria); (b) full-time appointments, in that the particular post is the sole or major occupation of the individual; (c) subject to a formal career structure with a system of promotion according to either seniority or merit (in other words, there are objective criteria for promotions).
6 *Public–private division* there is a clear separation between official activity and private life (the resources of the organization, for instance, are quite distinct from those of the officials as private individuals).

Essentially, then, Weber's 'ideal type' bureaucracy meant ordered administration by officials. Weber laid particular emphasis on the central importance of rules. Rules reduce tension between people; they allow people to feel that they are following a rule rather than a particular individual. Furthermore, rules apply to everyone (in the ideal situation, of course) and they legitimize punishments in that the rule and sanction for breaking it is known in advance. Weber felt that the impersonal quality of bureaucracy was also particularly important: it ensured that everyone received the same treatment and that one could calculate in advance what would happen in particular situations and circumstances.

The major reason for the development and spread of this form of administration has been its technical superiority over other forms of organization. Precision, discretion, continuity and speed are all achieved to a greater degree in a bureaucratic structure. For Weber bureaucratization was simply the most efficient way of administering; there is a regular chain of command, always a higher authority to refer to.

**Q** **What organizations are you a part of or have regular contact with? Take each of the six elements of Weber's model of bureaucracy and describe briefly the extent to which they apply to these organizations.**

**Following on from these descriptions, evaluate whether Weber's classification is a good basis for assessing the extent to which a particular organization is bureaucratized.**

### *Weber and bureaucracy: criticisms*

Weber's argument that bureaucracy is the most efficient form of organization has been criticized by a number of writers. Robert Merton, an American sociologist and a leading figure in functionalist sociology between the 1940s and 1970s, wrote a famous paper 'Bureaucratic Structure and Personality' (1952), which focused on the harmful consequences of bureaucracy. He highlighted a number of *dysfunctions* (things that hinder the workings of an institution or activity) of bureaucracy. He suggested that the 'virtues' of discipline and efficiency could become exaggerated in practice, to the extent that officials become obsessed with organizational rules. At the extreme officials may become so enmeshed in the rules and 'doing things by the book' that they are unable to help their clients speedily or efficiently. Merton's argument is that bureaucracies create a bureaucratic personality – a personality that stresses conformity and, consequently, initiative and innovative behaviour are stifled and replaced with inflexibility and timidity. Merton also pointed out that strict conformity to rules can work against the achievement of organizational goals, particularly in circumstances of rapid change when new ideas might be necessary. Thus the dysfunctions or problems of bureaucracy are seen by Merton as due to the stress on rules that become too rigid and cannot be altered to fit special circumstances.

Weber's description of the ideal type bureaucracy does not include concepts such as trust, cooperation and flexibility. Alvin Gouldner (1954), in a study of a gypsum mining plant in the USA, argued that while a bureaucratic structure might work well in stable, predictable situations, it was too rigid to cope with situations of rapid change, where trust, cooperation and flexibility are essential. In the context of industrial bureaucracies a rule might be rational for achieving the ends of one group – management for instance – but might work against the interests of another group – the employees perhaps.

The importance that Weber attached to following rules was seen by Peter Blau (1963) as, on occasion, working against the efficiency of the organization. Some organizations function more effectively when workers gather into informal groups and disregard or break official rules. To illustrate his argument, Blau studied a federal law enforcement agency in the USA. He found that officers who infringed rules regularly achieved a higher success rate in enforcing the law. Blau argues that bureaucratic structures can be too inflexible. No set of rules can anticipate all the potential problems and it is important to study the informal workings of organizations as well as the formal structure.

Beaucracy in practice is often quite distinct from the ideal type on paper. It must be emphasized that although Weber believed bureaucracies to be efficient, he was not an uncritical supporter of them. Indeed, Weber saw the growth of bureaucratic administration, which he felt was inevitable, as a grave threat to individual freedom (along with other aspects of the general process of rationalization in modern societies). He argued that bureaucracies have an inbuilt tendency to accumulate power and that once established they tend to take on a life of their own and become extremely hard to dismantle.

## Contemporary sociological theories

This section discusses some important developments in sociological theory since the 1920s. Social theory did not come to an end with the deaths of the founding writers; rather their work has acted as a stimulus for a wide range of theoretical argument in sociology. This general introduction can provide only a flavour of the various complex developments in modern social theory; to capture the excitement and intricacies of these theoretical debates you will need to look at the original sources summarized here.

### Interpretive sociology

The title 'interpretive sociology' includes a number of more specific sociological theories, the best known of which are probably *symbolic interactionism* and *ethnomethodology*. As with other sociological theories, these approaches attempt to explain human behaviour and do this by examining the social influences on behaviour. However, rather than emphasizing the influence of the social structure and how it constrains people, interpretive theories argue that the most important influence on individuals' behaviour is the behaviour of others towards them.

Interpretive sociology concentrates on the micro-level of social life. Societies are the end result of human interaction rather than the starting-point and by looking at how this interaction occurs it is possible to understand how social order is created and maintained. In focusing on everyday life this theoretical approach offers a clear contrast with those theories that examine 'grand' questions and issues, such as 'What is industrial society?', and provide a general explanation of society as a whole. Thus interpretive sociology offers a different approach and style of investigating society to the functionalist and conflict, macro-theories and the work of the founding theorists looked at earlier in this chapter.

#### Meanings

These theories focus on the individual and the process of social interaction. They examine how people are able to understand one another; how they interpret what is going on around them and then choose to behave in particular ways. They emphasize the meanings that people give to actions and to things.

Human behaviour is seen as the product of conscious decisions and, in most cases, individuals have some choice as to how they act. Furthermore, actions are usually purposive: they are directed toward some goal. The particular goal or purpose that is followed is dependent on the way in which individuals interpret the world around them. People choose what to do in the light of their 'definition of the situation'. For instance, you might wake up on a wet morning and decide to work on an assignment or essay; if the weather brightens up you may decide to make the most of it and abandon the college work and go into town; in town you may meet a friend and decide to forget about any shopping plans and go to a café.

Theories that emphasize the meanings which individuals give to action clearly owe a great debt to Max Weber. The importance Weber attached to explaining individual social action and to the notion of *verstehen* (empathetic or interpretive understanding, see p. 61), demonstrate his role as the founder of the interpretive approach in sociology. However, Weber applied the idea of *verstehen* to the analysis of large-scale social change and did not examine in detail the day-to-day interactions of individuals in specific situations. Interpretivist sociologists have adopted Weber's approach and applied it to small-scale and specific contexts.

**Q** How can a greater understanding of social interaction on a micro-level aid our understanding of macro-sociological questions?

## Symbolic interactionism

There are a number of related theoretical perspectives that fit under the broad heading of interpretive sociology. Symbolic interactionism is perhaps the most well established and will be the focus for this introductory discussion. It suggests that human behaviour is different from that of (other) animals because it uses symbols and attaches meanings to them. When people interact with one another they use symbols, especially in the form of language – hence the name 'symbolic interactionism'.

This theoretical perspective emerged from the writings of US sociologists and social psychologists in the 1920s and 1930s, in particular Charles Cooley, William Thomas and George Herbert Mead. Mead, who began his career as a philosopher, published little while he was alive and his lectures formed the basis for his key role as the founder of symbolic interactionism.

Mead's work emphasized the relationship between the individual and society. He called his approach 'social behaviourism' because it was closely linked with social psychology – the study of social groups. The basic idea behind Mead's approach was that the perceptions and the behaviour of individuals are influenced by the social groups of which they are members. The existence of social groups is essential for the development of what Mead termed the 'self'.

The self is perhaps the key concept of the symbolic interactionist perspective. It refers to how individuals see themselves. We all have a self-image, an identity and some conception of who we 'really' are – which we refer to as the self. This concept of the 'self' is only meaningful in relation to other 'selfs'. We carry on a whole series of different interactions with different people; we are one thing to one person and another thing to another.

It is the ability to become self-conscious, to be able to stand outside one's own situation and look at one's behaviour retrospectively and from outside that provides the key to Mead's analysis. Questions such as 'What made me do that?' Mead saw as examples of reflexive questioning – of the individual 'taking the role of others'. So Mead's theory of self and socialization rests upon the individual's ability to take the role of others and so of the wider community. This requires the organization of the individual's whole self in relation to the social groups and the community to which that individual belongs. The organized community or group which provides this unity of self for individuals was given the term the 'generalized other' by Mead. The attitude of the generalized other is the attitude of the whole community to which the individual belongs. It is through taking the attitude of the generalized other that individuals are able to see themselves as others do and to understand the attitudes of others towards the various aspects of social life.

## The development of the self

The self develops or evolves through understanding the attitude and role of others. This development occurs through stages. Initially a young child adopts the role of particular individuals, for example through playing at being mummy, teacher, doctor and so on, and then gradually adopts the attitude of the whole community or society. The move from adopting individual to adopting general attitudes involves a change from copying behaviour to understanding behaviour. This development is exemplified in the change in a young child's reaction from 'Mummy says no' to 'One does not do this', where the child is relating to the generalized other.

Mead's theory of the development of self lays great stress on the individual's ability to interpret the behaviour of others. During social interaction the individual learns which behaviour is appropriate to particular situations. With experience the individual is able to generalize from specific instances and decide which types of behaviour are appropriate. Part of the process of socialization involves becoming aware of which particular role is applicable to a particular situation. So Mead regards the self as being made up of a series of roles, each of which relate to the social group which the individual is a part of. For a fully developed self, self-consciousness is necessary and is the core of the process of self-development.

Q

List the different roles you play during the course of one day.

Do any of these roles conflict with each other?

If so, how is this conflict resolved?

## All the world's a stage: the dramaturgical approach of Erving Goffman

Our discussion of the development of self looked at the ways in which individuals understand and adopt the role of others. The notion that in everyday life individuals play roles, negotiate situations and to a certain extent are forced to be 'actors' is the basis of the dramaturgical approach developed by Erving Goffman.

**Case Study**

### Erving Goffman (1922–82)

The view of the 'world as a stage', with individuals performing and acting for their audiences in everyday life, has been particularly associated with the work of Goffman. Goffman wrote a number of widely read and influential books between 1956, the publication of *The Presentation of Self in Everyday Life*, and 1981, when *Forms of Talk*, his last book, was published. In this discussion we shall use Goffman's work, and particularly *The Presentation of Self in Everyday Life* and *Relations in Public* (1971), as a specific illustration of this interactionist approach. Goffman was primarily an observer of social interaction who 'possessed an extraordinary ability to appreciate the subtle importance of apparently insignificant aspects of everyday conduct' (Manning 1992). He argued that individual behaviour follows intricate patterns; in our everyday lives we follow a set of implicit instructions that influence and determine this behaviour.

### Goffman's work

Goffman saw social encounters and interaction in theatrical terms, with his earlier work concentrating on how people present themselves and their activities to others. Using the theatre analogy, he talked about individuals' behaviour being 'performances' put on for audiences with different parts or roles played on different occasions. As we mentioned earlier, all of us have many different roles, with different expectations attached to them. Each of you may have a role as a student, where you are expected to sit in classes, reasonably quietly, look interested and do the work set; but you will also have numerous different roles which will involve you acting in quite different ways – as brother/sister, friend or worker, for instance. Goffman's work provides many examples of how we play different roles and try to create different impressions for others. Bearing in mind that Goffman's research was undertaken in the late 1950s, the following example illustrates female students acting dumb to avoid creating the 'wrong' impression:

**American college girls did, and no doubt do, play down their intelligence, skill, and determinativeness when in the presence of datable boys. . . . These performers are reported to allow their boy friends to explain things to them tediously that they already know; they conceal proficiency in mathematics from their less able consorts; they lose ping-pong games just before the ending:**

> **'One of the nicest techniques is to spell long words incorrectly once in a while. My boyfriend seems to get a great kick out of it and writes back, "Honey you certainly don't know how to spell."'**

**Through all of this the natural superiority of the male is demonstrated and the weaker role of the female affirmed.** *(Goffman 1969: 48)*

As well as playing roles and creating impressions, Goffman highlighted other ways in which everyday behaviour can be compared to a theatrical performance. There is often a division into a back region, where a performance is prepared, and a front region, where it is presented. As the audience in a theatre does not see backstage, so access to certain aspects of everyday behaviour is controlled, to prevent outsiders seeing a performance that is not intended for them. Backstage is private and it can be embarrassing if outsiders gain access to it; in hotels and cafés, for example, the differences between the front regions and back regions can be dramatic and customers might be disappointed, or horrified, if they saw backstage. Also, the communication that occurs frontstage and backstage can be quite different: customers who may be treated very respectfully to their faces may be caricatured, ridiculed or cursed as soon as they've gone.

When interacting with others most people want those others to reach a particular interpretation of their actions. It is possible to use dress, language, gestures and so on to organize and influence how others interpret behaviour and to ensure that they arrive at the desired interpretation. Although the police officer, businessperson or skinhead might make no apparent attempt to communicate with people who pass them on the street, they are creating an impression that will influence how others think about them. As a rule individuals will try to control or guide the impressions that others form of them and there are common techniques that can be used to create and sustain these impressions. A fundamental point that underlies all social interaction is that when one individual interacts with others the person will want to discover as much about the situation as possible. To do that it is necessary to know as much as possible about others. Of course, such information is not usually available (we don't know the likes, dislikes, background and so on of everyone we interact with). So in the absence of this knowledge we have to make guesses or predictions about others.

The importance of giving a convincing impression to others, and the obligation to live up to that impression, often forces people to act a role. What people think of one another is dependent on the impression given (as a certain type of person) and this impression can be disrupted if others acquire information that they are not meant to have – as the regular revelations of scandals in the private lives of public figures demonstrate!

**Q**

**What factors influence the first impressions you have of others?**

**How can these first impressions be either supported or altered as you acquire more information?**

**It is quite easy to think of examples from our own lives of instances where the 'wrong' person has seen or heard something that we would rather have kept hidden from them. Give examples of aspects of your own behaviour that you try and keep 'backstage' from others. What might happen if such behaviour was exposed 'frontstage'?**

Goffman was aware of the limitations of the theatrical analogy. In his later work he acknowledged the differences between face-to-face interaction in social life and on the stage. When watching a play the audience generally likes to see a complete performance and to hear all the lines of the actors whereas in daily life this is often not the case, with interruptions a normal part of social interaction. However, while not offering a complete account of everyday life, the dramaturgical analogy does contribute to our understanding and analysis of aspects of everyday life. It is clear in our interaction with others we play roles and display great skill in creating and managing impressions.

### Normal appearances

Goffman applied the dramaturgical perspective on social interaction to how individuals behave in public, looking in particular at the expectations people hold of what is normal and acceptable behaviour. We have particular ideas about what is right and wrong. Goffman cites a story from the *New York Times* to illustrate this point.

**A hit-and-run driver fooled several witnesses who saw him hit another automobile. The driver got out of his car after an accident, went to the damaged car and left this note: 'I have just hit your car. People are watching me. They think I'm leaving my name. But I'm not.'**

**The note was signed, 'the wrecker'.** ***(Goffman 1971: 312)***

This example illustrates the point that when people sense things are normal they will act in a normal manner. Acting normally or naturally is seen by Goffman as a key element in successful impression management. Indeed it is relatively easy to 'con' people because of the expectations that are held as to what is normal behaviour. This is not to say that it is morally a good or decent thing to do, just that it is often much easier than we initially think to fabricate lies and to make them seem natural.

Perhaps the best examples of the use, or maybe misuse, of normal appearances and expectations occur in the context of criminal behaviour. Criminals have regularly used normal appearances to deceive.

---

**Tokyo – The bandit, about 22 years old, wearing the white helmet and black leather jacket of a traffic officer, rode a stolen motorbike up to a bank car carrying bonus money for employees of the Toshiba Electric Co., 20 miles west of Tokyo. He told the unarmed bank men, from the Nippon Trust and Banking Co., that he had information that dynamite had been planted in the car. When the four got out, the bandit got in and drove away with the car and three metal boxes full of unrecorded yen banknotes worth $816,667. 'He looked just like a policeman', said Eiji Nakad, the driver of the auto. 'He said he had instructions from Koganei Police Station.'**

*(Goffman 1971: 360)*

---

## Ethnomethodology and the rules of everyday life

The term ethnomethodology means 'people's methods' and was used by Harold Garfinkel (1967) to describe a theoretical branch of sociology that he developed. Garfinkel felt that conventional sociology took social order for granted and assumed that the everyday social world we inhabit was a structured one. Ethnomethodology focuses on how people construct their social world; it investigates the background knowledge and assumptions that people hold and how they help to create and recreate social order. As with other interpretive approaches, there is an emphasis on how people give meanings to and interpret behaviour. However, ethnomethodology is particularly concerned with the processes by which this occurs; and specifically with the methods used by people to communicate with one another.

The importance of the meanings that we give to our actions can be clearly illustrated if we suspend the 'rules' of everyday life. Most of the time we, as individuals, live in a world that is taken for granted, we don't question what goes on. We don't think about the rules underlying everyday actions until something happens to interrupt the routine. During a college or school day it is a reasonable safe bet that nothing will happen to astound us. There is the possibility of a surprise – the building may catch fire, we might develop a passionate hatred or love for someone we meet. However, we all accept that what is going on is a routine, called college or school education. If this routine were not the case we would not get much done, we would constantly be being surprised by astounding happenings. Furthermore, even if a definite attempt were made to try something different this might soon become routine too. If a teacher went into the classroom and stood on a desk to teach, this would soon become routine if done regularly: there would be a change from 'Look what she's doing' to 'There she goes again'.

**Case Study**

### Rule-governed behaviour: Garfinkel's experiments

Various experiments have been carried out by interpretivist sociologists to demonstrate how rule governed our everyday behaviour is. Garfinkel (1967) organized a number of experiments that involved the disruption of everyday life. In one case he asked a group of his students to take part in a new type of counselling. They were to ask questions to an 'expert counsellor' who was to help them and give advice, but on the understanding that he would answer their questions only with a 'yes' or 'no' and no more. The 'counsellor' was, in fact, told to answer the questions by reading from a random list of 'yeses' and 'no's' which he had in front of him, paying no attention to the particular questions asked. Although the questions the students asked were meaningful, the answers given by the 'counsellor' were arbitrary and unrelated to the questions. However, because the students believed the answers came from an expert, they imposed meanings and relevance on to them. Indeed when asked by Garfinkel, the majority of the students said they felt the advice had been helpful. Garfinkel argued that this demonstrated how individuals construct meaning from chaos because of a need to fit things into underlying and understood patterns.

#### Questions

What rules and routines do you follow in everyday activities such as (a) getting up; (b) eating; (c) travelling?

How do you feel when you are forced to change your regular routines?

## Feminist theories

Feminist theory and feminist sociological research has developed significantly since the 1960s in what has been described as a 'second wave' of feminism; the first wave is generally taken to refer to feminist struggles for the vote in the late nineteenth and early twentieth centuries. Feminism has a rich history: the breadth of ideas and theory can be only touched upon in this introductory section.

Feminist sociologists have produced an extensive critique of conventional sociological theory. They have argued that sociological theories have been written from a male perspective which has meant that women's experiences have been marginalized. Not only have feminist theorists criticized male-centred theory but also they have written new theories of society which place women's experiences centrally and attempt to explain divisions between men and women in society.

It is important to briefly outline feminist criticisms of the founders of sociology. A key problem with their work is that the founders either paid little or no attention to the issues of women's subordination or treated this as normal. Durkheim and Weber assumed that it was natural for women to be located in the private sphere of the home and men to be active in the public sphere of paid work. Both associated women with nature, biology and emotion and men with reason, culture and rationality. They treated the sexual division of labour and women's subordinate position within it as natural and inevitable (Sydie 1987). Weber and Durkheim's analyses of social relations between men and women were shaped by assumptions that there were fundamental biological differences between women and men which suited the two sexes to distinctively different social roles. Sydie argues that for Durkheim and Weber

> **This belief in the significance of biological difference means that the hierarchies of power in society, which relegates women collectively to a subordinate status to men, are taken as givens that do not require sociological analysis.**
>
> *(Sydie 1987)*

This sort of biological approach to gender relations has been identified as problematic by many feminists.

Although Marx acknowledged inequalities between men and women he failed to treat gender as a crucial factor that shapes social experiences. His work focused on economic class relations and the exploitation of the working class, very much marginalizing gender relations and questions concerning the oppression of women. His theories were gender blind: the working class were treated as an undifferentiated mass, yet much of his work was concerned with male members of the proletariat. This failure to treat gender as a crucial determining factor of our social experiences has been a fundamental weakness of much sociological theory according to feminist theorists (Maynard 1990). Many feminists have formulated theories which place the question of women's subordination and gender relations much more centrally.

**Q** **Durkheim, Marx and Weber are sometimes referred to as the 'founding fathers' of sociology. What does this suggest about the origins and development of the subject?**

**Why are there no 'founding mothers' of sociology?**

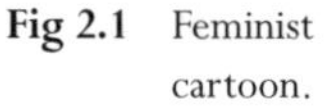

**Fig 2.1** Feminist cartoon.

When we examine feminism it becomes clear that there are many different tendencies within feminism and there is no one all encompassing definition of feminism. Indeed it is more appropriate to talk about feminisms than feminism (Humm 1992). Contrary to many common-sense interpretations of feminism, feminists do not always agree on ways in which we can explain gender differences and women's subordination. There are debates within feminism about the origins and causes of women's subordination and the strategies needed for change.

Q

**What characteristics do you associate with feminists and feminism?**

**Do you consider them positive or negative characteristics?**

**Consider where you have got these views about feminism from.**

**(After reading this section come back to these questions and consider whether any of your assumptions have changed.)**

We shall outline here four of the different strands of feminism: liberal feminism, radical feminism, Marxist/socialist feminism, and black feminism. Although any attempt at classification is likely to be incomplete and somewhat arbitrary, this approach provides a useful way of introducing feminist theorizing. However, it is important to note that some feminists cannot be assigned conveniently to a particular category, not all feminism is encompassed, nor do these strands represent entirely distinct feminisms. So, the four types of feminism introduced here represent key tendencies, but there are many other feminist perspectives – ecofeminism and post-modern feminism are just two examples. Feminism is a diverse, constantly evolving body of thought.

## Liberal feminism

Liberal feminism has its roots in the liberal tradition of the Enlightenment which stressed the principles of justice, rationality, citizenship, human rights, equality and democracy. The treatment of women in society violates many of these values. From the days of Mary Wollstonecraft and the publication of her seminal book in 1792 *A Vindication of the Rights of Woman*, liberal feminists have stressed that as rational beings women should be entitled to full personhood and hence have the same legal, political, social and economic rights and opportunities as men. They recognize that women are on occasion unfairly discriminated against on the basis of their sex. Much of this discrimination is informal and based on custom, the product of sexist assumptions and prejudice which still endure in our culture and are the product of gender role conditioning. Liberal feminists advocate political action and reform, favouring educational strategies and formal and legislative changes, in order to provide women with opportunities and challenge stereotypes and prejudices. Yet many have recognized that formal equality is not enough and have supported legislation which outlaws sex discrimination against women and men.

Some contemporary liberal feminists believe that if the state is to enforce equal rights and ensure equal opportunities it must make it economically possible for women to exercise these rights, hence the state should fund such things as childcare facilities and refuges for women who have experienced violence from their partners. Liberal feminists have historically put an emphasis on incorporating women into the mainstream, giving women the right to equal opportunities in the public sphere of education and employment. Some have suggested that having women in positions of power and influence will in itself have a knock-on effect with such women in high-status positions acting as role models for others and taking account of women's interests in the formulation of policy.

Betty Friedan's influential liberal feminist text *The Feminine Mystique* was published in 1963. Friedan argued that North American women had been offered fulfilment through motherhood and wifehood only to find dissatisfaction: this was the feminine mystique. She criticized this notion that women should only be home based carers and encouraged women to engage in paid work outside the home to provide more economic power and personal fulfilment. However, she has been criticized for not addressing how difficult it would be for women to combine motherhood and a career without challenging the notion of women as primary carers and considering the need for men to change. Black feminists pointed out that her theory was ethnocentric, i.e. based on the experiences of a particular ethnic group, in this case white middle-class women. Black women have historically had to work in the labour market and this has not bought them liberation.

Liberal feminists have been criticized for a range of reasons, many linked to what other feminists see as strategies that merely operate within the existing system rather than fundamentally changing social relations. While liberal feminism may bring opportunities and rewards for a few token women it brings little fundamental change in the lives of the large majority of women; despite some reform men still hold the majority of positions of power (Bryson 1992). Others argue that liberal feminism brings opportunities for women on men's terms, that women working within the status quo merely endorse the hierarchical and competitive structures of capitalism and patriarchy and indeed theoretically does not acknowledge these social relations.

Some feminists argue liberal feminism encourages women to be male clones, i.e. successful women adopt 'male' strategies and values. It has been suggested, for example, that Margaret Thatcher became very successful because she conducted her politics in the traditional masculine style and also that she did little to improve the position of women in British society during her years as prime minister. These concerns reflect a debate within feminism concerning whether women should be struggling for equality with men, which suggests they are the same as men, or recognize the differences between women and men (whether innate or socially constructed), and attempt to shape societies based on 'feminine' values and strategies which some feminists argue would create a more egalitarian, less competitive and a less destructive world order. The liberal feminist emphasis on the public sphere is seen as reinforcing the notion of two separate spheres, the public and the private, and devaluing the private (Jaggar 1983; Pateman 1987).

**Q** **How easy is it to think of women who have been successful in traditionally male dominated areas such as business or politics?**

**Would you describe the successful women you can think of as having adopted 'male' strategies and values?**

## Radical feminism

Contemporary radical feminism is associated with the women's liberation movement of the 1960s, yet although many of the ideas expressed by radical feminists were not new, in this period they began to be 'developed systematically as a self-conscious theory' (Bryson 1992). Some women within the movement argued that women's oppression was deeply rooted and that inequality between men and women was a primary source of oppression. This they felt was not being acknowledged in many existing social and political analyses and organizations which they identified as androcentric (male centred). As a result the struggle for women's liberation was being marginalized and a new approach which prioritized women's oppression was needed. Radical feminists argued that gender inequalities are a central and primary form of social inequality and constructed theories which acknowledged this. Radical feminists explain gender inequalities and women's subordination as the outcome of an autonomous system of *patriarchy*.

**Definition**

### Patriarchy

**Patriarchy is basically used to describe a structural system of male domination. It encapsulates the mechanisms, ideologies and social structures which have enabled men historically to gain and maintain their dominance and control over women. Stacey (1993) points out that radical feminists have found patriarchy to be useful theoretically as 'it has given some conceptual form to the nature of male domination in society' and has enabled radical feminists to describe 'how and why women are oppressed'.**

**Mies (1986) notes that it has provided a concept which captures the totality of women's oppression. Men dominate women in every sphere of life, all relationships between men and women are institutionalized relationships of power; this includes 'private', personal relationships, hence the feminists' slogan 'the personal is political'. Patriarchy is trans-historical, cross-cultural and universal; no area of society is free from male domination. Thus radical feminists are concerned to reveal how male power is exercised in all spheres of life and how patriarchy emerged historically.**

Kate Millett's *Sexual Politics* (1970) has been identified as an important radical feminist text because it introduced the concept of patriarchy and contains many typical radical feminist concerns. Millett described all societies as patriarchal, men dominate and women are subordinate, hence all relations between men and women are political relations of power. Patriarchy is maintained via a process of sex role socialization which takes place in the male-headed family. The family is a patriarchal unit which reflects the rule of men in other areas of society. She documents how education, religion and literature reinforce the notion of female subordination and male superiority. She also argued that a whole range of strategies were utilized to control women if they did not conform; these included physical and sexual violence. Similar concerns are evident in the work of other radical feminists.

Radical feminism now constitutes a large and diverse body of thought, with radical feminists taking different positions on a range of issues. Abbott and Wallace

(1990) identify three key issues of disagreement within radical feminism: the extent to which gender differences are the product of actual biological differences or are socially constructed; the relationship between feminist politics and personal sexual conduct; and the sort of political strategies that should be adopted to bring about change. An examination of the ideas of specific radical feminist theorists highlights these differences.

Unlike Millett, who stated that the differences between men and women are the product of socialization, the work of some radical feminists has been identified as proposing a biological basis for some differences between women and men. Rich (1977) argues that women's mothering capacity is at the core of men's oppression of women. Men are fearful of women's power to create life and men's sense that women's reproductive powers are somehow mysterious and uncontrollable. Rich and others have contended that as a result men have attempted to control women and even to control reproduction and birth itself. Feminists taking such a position are wary of developments in reproductive technology which are seen as a means of enabling further male control of reproduction (O'Brien 1981). Rich (1977) stresses that motherhood itself is not inherently oppressive for women but has become oppressive under patriarchy. She celebrates female biology and the potential for motherhood and argues this is an important source of power that women should reclaim. She goes on to suggest that woman-centred cultures and societies in which children are raised in line with feminist values of care and nurture can provide the basis for an alternative non-patriarchal society. For other radical feminists this biological approach to gender differences is unacceptable and reinforces traditional divisions and roles.

**Q** **Some people who have fought for sexual equality or whose beliefs overlap with feminism have refused to be labelled as feminists. What might be their reasons for doing so?**

Many feminists accept that women have had less power in sexual relationships than men but some radical feminists such as Catherine MacKinnon identify sexuality as central to patriarchy. Sexual relations are seen not simply as reflection of broader inequalities but as a source of power which men can exert over women. As MacKinnon (1982) puts it, 'Sexuality is the primary source of male power'.

For MacKinnon sexuality is male defined: in sexual relationships with men women are powerless and are merely objects to be used for male sexual pleasure. Heterosexual sex is based on relations of dominance and submission. Some radical lesbian feminists such as Jeffreys also place sexuality at the heart of women's oppression, specifically heterosexuality. According to Jeffreys (1994) the construction of heterosexuality as normal and natural and all other sexualities as deviant is the organizing principle of social relations of male supremacy; women are pressurized into heterosexuality and this serves the interests of patriarchy:

> **Without heterosexuality it would be difficult for individual men to extract unpaid sexual, reproductive, economic, domestic and emotional servicing from women.**
>
> *(Jeffreys 1994: 23)*

In heterosexual relations with men, women invest their physical, emotional and sexual energies and leave themselves open to exploitation. The term heteropatriarchy has been used by some lesbian feminists to describe a patriarchal system which is not only male dominated but also centred around heterosexuality (Penelope 1986; Wilton 1993). Within radical feminism some feminists have suggested that as heterosexuality was central to oppression to reclaim their selves it was necessary for women to reject heterosexuality and live a lesbian experience. This is sometimes referred to as political lesbianism.

Bunch (1981) argued that a lesbian existence in which women transferred their identity from men and put women first was an act of resistance in a world structured around the male. Part of the demand for a lesbian existence requires separatism, a strategy where women organize in a women-only context in order to create a space for women to develop an identification with other women and to regenerate women's energies and selves. This not only challenges patriarchy by withdrawing women's servicing of men but also provides a basis to develop alternative women-centred societies. Controversially some radical lesbian feminists such as the Leeds Revolutionary Feminists Group (1981) accused heterosexual women of sleeping with the enemy. By contrast, other feminists have argued that the rejection of heterosexuality is unrealistic for those women who identify themselves as heterosexual. Segal (1994) also contends that radical feminists' analyses of heterosexuality have dismissed the pleasure found by some women in heterosexual sex and have focused on heterosexual women merely as victims of male exploitation. This has ignored the possibility of women being active agents of heterosexual desire; being able to make choices, take some control and experience pleasure in heterosexual relationships. Wilton (1993) has pointed out a dilemma for lesbian feminists: on the whole it has been left to lesbian feminists to produce a critique of what she calls the 'heterosexual imperative', yet in producing this they are criticized for being divisive.

A whole range of radical feminists have identified violence, both physical and sexual, as a key source of male control over women. The identification of violence against women as a political issue and social problem has been seen as an important achievement of feminism and has been associated particularly with radical feminism; Brownmiller (1976) argued that the act of rape lies at the origins of men's oppression of women. Although not all radical feminists would identify violence as the original source of women's subordination, many have seen it as an important mechanism for maintaining the subordination of women (Kelly 1988). This violence is an expression of power and hatred which controls, humiliates, objectifies and disempowers women.

This brief discussion shows that radical feminists' ideas have generated much debate and criticism from feminists and non-feminists alike. Some non-feminists have identified radical feminism as a misguided political ideology which by identifying men as oppressors and women as exploited has actually fuelled conflict between the sexes (Lyndon 1992). The concept of patriarchy has been identified as a static and rigid category that doesn't allow for changing and varied gender relations across cultures and across history (Rowbotham 1982). A key criticism of radical feminism is that it has tended to lump women together as a universal group; this is problematic because it masks women's 'varied and complex social reality' (hooks 1984). It ignores and denies the different experiences between women, differences based on such factors as class, race, nationality, age and sexual identity. The emphasis on women as a group with shared experiences and common interests has been identified as particularly problematic by Black feminists who have pointed out that this ignores the way that racism has impacted on the lives of Black women creating different experiences for Black and white women. They also stress that women exploit and oppress other women and that white women have often been in positions of dominance in relation to Black women.

Black feminists have stressed that radical feminists have tended to treat all men as equally powerful, yet in systems such as slavery and imperialism Black men have been denied positions in the white male hierarchy; patriarchy is racially demarcated (Murphy and Livingston 1985). Hence it is difficult to claim that Black male dominance over women always exists in the same forms as white male dominance. Black feminists have pointed out that Black women have many common interests with Black men: the strategy of separatism and the need to organize separately from men, proposed by some radical feminists, have been unacceptable because of the common struggle against racism that they share with Black men. The identification within radical feminism of gender as the key source of inequality in society has been rejected by many. Marxist feminists, for instance, argue that gender inequalities are related to economic class relations.

## Marxist/socialist feminism

Marxist feminists have attempted to develop Marxist concepts to understand the subordination of women in capitalist societies. They have argued that it is essential to recognize that the oppression of women is inextricably linked with the capitalist order and that although Marxist analyses of society may have marginalized women, they provide insights into the structure of capitalist society and the position of women within it.

Case Study

### Marxist feminism

Many Marxist feminists have focused on how the economic class relations of capitalism produce women's continued subordination. They have argued that under capitalism a key cause of women's oppression is the sexual division of labour which shapes gender relations in a way that reinforces the capitalist relations of production. In this sexual division of labour men are defined as breadwinners and women have been defined as primarily domestic labourers and excluded from wage labour. They have been allocated an exploitative and restrictive role in the household reproducing the relations of production. The traditional nuclear family and the role of women's domestic labour has been a central focus of the Marxist feminist position. Women's domestic and reproductive labour has been identified as a very cheap way of reproducing and maintaining the working class and reproducing the next generation of workers. The value that this labour has to capitalism was the subject of the domestic labour debate in the late 1970s. The family was seen as a useful means of social control, disciplining male workers who must support their dependants, initiating children into restrictive gender roles and also acting as a useful unit of consumption. In terms of gaining liberation, Marxist feminists stressed the need to struggle for a communist society in which the social relations of the labour market and the family would be revolutionized, child care and domestic labour would be socialized and the responsibility of the state. They also emphasized the need for women to enter productive labour and struggle alongside male workers. Marxist feminists have been very active in examining the exploitation of women in paid work.

Marxist feminism has been criticized by feminists within the socialist tradition and outside. In historical terms Marxist feminism has been faulted for failing to account for the oppression of women prior to capitalism. It has also been pointed out that in revolutionary class struggles and supposedly socialist societies women have often found themselves occupying a secondary position with relations between men and women fundamentally unchanged. Many individual socialist women have found a contradiction between socialist values of equality, solidarity and anti-exploitation and the treatment they receive from socialist men (Phillips 1987). Some socialist women have therefore questioned the adequacy of Marxism for explaining women's subordination, as it failed to acknowledge men's role in women's subordination and emphasizes economic class relations at the expense of gender relations. Yet these feminists have also rejected radical feminism as it does not place centrally economic relations of capitalism.

Some feminists working in the socialist tradition began to place greater emphasis on patriarchal gender relations in their theoretical analysis. These have been referred to as socialist feminists to indicate a shift away from orthodox Marxism. Michelle Barrett's *Women's Oppression Today* (1980) paid attention to not only the economic but also the ideological conditions of women's oppression. She argued that women's oppression is the product of not only the economic needs of capitalism but also patriarchal gender ideology which existed prior to capitalism. The family household system is crucial to women's oppression. This system controls women's access to paid labour by handicapping women as the reproducers of children and sexual object for male pleasure. First, the family household structure consists of a *social structure*, the household, which consists of a number of usually biologically related people who depend on the wages of adult members, primarily a husband or father and also the unpaid labour of a wife and mother. Second, it consists of the *ideology* of the family which defines family life as naturally organized in the above way with a male breadwinner and financially dependent wife and children. So it defines the nuclear family and sexual division of labour as natural. Within this ideology are notions about 'natural' masculinity and femininity, while sexuality is defined as naturally heterosexual. With Mary McIntosh in *The Anti-Social Family* (1982), Barrett again emphasized the ideological significance of the family rather than the economic role. Barrett and McIntosh stressed that the ideological construct of the family as a haven not only masked the exploitation of women but also attracted attention away from social problems. They argued that the ideology of the family embodied principles that shore up the economic system – such as selfishness, looking after one's own or pursuing private property as opposed to altruism and community.

Some feminists went further, arguing that women's subordination is the outcome of two systems, patriarchy and capitalism. Exactly what effect these two systems have and how they work together has been the subject of much complex debate. These theorists have been referred to as dual systems feminists. Walby (1986; 1990) argued that capitalism and patriarchy are separate systems that at times interact. Although there can be a conflict of interests between capitalism and patriarchy, for example over women's labour, these conflicts are generally resolved and some compromise is made between the interest of capital and the interests of patriarchy.

In *Patriarchy at Work* (1986), Walby outlined a range of struggles between male workers and capitalists to illustrate these patterns of conflict and compromise. In contemporary society women are excluded from certain areas of the labour market which ensures men maintain economic and social privileges in the labour market and the household. Yet at the same time capitalism can utilize female labour in certain sectors of the labour market and pay lower wages by utilizing ideological notions of the male breadwinner, the secondary role of the female worker and women's suitability for certain types of work. Walby developed these ideas in *Theorizing Patriarchy* (1990) where she attempts to develop a theory of patriarchy which not only acknowledges how it interacts with capitalism but also acknowledges that gender and patriarchal relations can change. She also argues that in western history in the nineteenth and twentieth centuries there have been two major forms of patriarchy. *Private patriarchy* is based on household production in which a patriarch controls women individually in the household; this control is maintained through the exclusion of women from many aspects of the 'public' world. This reached its peak in the mid-nineteenth century when violence against women was formally condoned, divorce was difficult to obtain and women were formally excluded from many areas of education and paid work. *Public patriarchy* involves less emphasis on control in the household; patriarchy is maintained through other structures, women can enter the public arenas but are subordinated within them. The exploitation of women is performed more collectively: 'Women are no longer restricted to the domestic hearth, but have the whole society in which to roam and be exploited' (Walby 1990).

Most women enter paid work but have lower-paid lower-status jobs; women have citizenship right but form only a small percentage of elected representatives; divorce can be obtained but women remain responsible for children; cultural institutions such as the arts and media allow women's participation but usually in an inferior way. In contemporary British society the public form of patriarchy predominates.

Although dual systems approaches have tried to overcome some of the criticisms levelled at radical and Marxist feminism, they have been criticized by Black feminists for failing to incorporate race into their theories (Anthias and Yuval-Davis 1993). Black feminists have argued that socialist feminism is ethnocentric, for example its approach to the family does not consider women's varying experiences. Socialist feminists have tended to take the nuclear family as the only family, neglected other family forms and have approached the family as simply a site of oppression. Yet Carby (1982a) points out that at certain points in history the family has provided a 'site of political and cultural resistance to racism'.

## Black feminism

Black feminists have produced criticisms of each of the varying strands of feminism, and indeed have now developed an influential critique of what has been identified as white feminism. The key concerns about much of the theory and research produced by white feminists are that it has been ethnocentric and that it has failed to acknowledge differences between women and specifically the effects of race and racism on women's experiences.

Black feminists have not only criticized white feminists but also proposed new directions for feminist theory. Some Black feminists have pointed out that placing Black women's experiences centrally, looking at the world from a Black woman's standpoint, brings new insights into social relations (Hill-Collins 1990). hooks (1984) has noted that the experiences of Black women shows that oppression can be resisted, as Black women have in very adverse circumstances struggled to survive and resist oppression. Feminists need to focus these strategies and resistances to counter the tendency to talk about women as victims and to develop alternative forms of empowerment. Another thing that is learned about oppression from the experience of Black women is that it is complex. Many Black feminists have stressed that race cannot be simply added on to existing feminist approaches: this would be mere tokenism (Bhavnani 1993). They have rejected what have been called additive approaches which simply describe Black women as being exposed to a triple oppression of race, class and gender. This approach suggests that you can add together these three factors to end up with the sum of Black women's oppression: i.e. race + class + gender = Black women's oppression. Yet Black feminists argue that these factors interact not necessarily to produce a worse experience for Black women, but a qualitatively different experience. We can take women's experiences of contraception and abortion to illustrate this argument. In the 1970s and 1980s a key concern of white feminists around these issues was that white women's access to contraception and abortion had been restricted; struggles were focused on retaining legal access to abortion and increasing access to contraception and abortion. Yet Black feminists pointed out that Black women in Britain did not find it harder to get contraception and abortion, but that they experienced concerted attempts to get their fertility restricted. They were more likely than white women to be encouraged to have abortions and also more likely to be offered forms of contraception with possible damaging side-effects, such as the injectable contraceptive Depo-Provera. This Black feminist critique has led to the development of a broader reproductive rights movement which emphasizes the rights of women to have or not have children which has relevance to all women.

Black feminists have stressed that any theoretical model that deals adequately with the experience of all women must recognize and explore the *interlocking* nature of class, race and gender:

> **the realities of our daily lives make it imperative for us to consider the simultaneous nature of our oppression and exploitation. Only a synthesis of class, race, gender and sexuality can lead us forward, as these form the matrix of black women's oppression.** *(Amos and Parmar 1984)*

In the same vein some Black feminists have pointed out that it is impossible to list a universal hierarchy of oppressions or to list which set of social relations is the most important and most oppressive. bell hooks (1984) makes reference to her own experience to make this point:

> **I am often asked whether being black is more important than being a woman . . . all such questions are rooted in competitive either/or thinking, the belief that the self is formed in opposition to an other. Most people are socialized to think in terms of opposition rather than compatibility.** *(hooks 1984: 29)*

So she warns against theories that prioritize one form of oppression. Black feminists have proposed theories that begin to explore the *interconnectedness* of all forms of oppression i.e. examine multiple systems of oppression.

Similarly Hill-Collins (1990) proposes a theoretical model which she refers to as a matrix of oppression, which incorporates all relations of domination and subordination. Within this matrix race, class and gender must be viewed as axes that form part of a complex matrix which has other dimensions such as age, religion and sexual orientation. Feminism needs to explore the connections and interactions between women's oppression and other forms of oppression. In this model women's oppression is part of a more general system of domination; the liberation of women can be achieved only by part of a broader strategy which challenges all relations of domination and subordination. Similar issues have been raised by non-western feminists who have pointed out that the dominant voices of feminism have been white western women, hence the experiences and voices of Third World women have been marginalized within feminism. They have stressed that western feminism needs to incorporate the international relations of inequality if it is to be relevant to the lives of women in non-western countries and again stress the need to explore the interaction of gender relations with other social relations such as relations of colonialism (Mohanty *et al.* 1991).

Q What sort of analysis might each of the four strands of feminism provide for (a) government policy on single parents; (b) prostitution?

Would the different strands of feminism see an increase in the number of women in senior positions and top jobs as a positive step for women?

In 1995 women in the British army (unlike the US military, for example) do not actually fight in war situations although they may be present in other roles on the front line. Do you think women should be entitled to a combatant role? What arguments can you propose for and against women entering combatant positions?

## The pornography debate

Theoretical and strategic differences among feminists have manifested themselves in the ongoing debate about pornography. There are two general positions within feminism: the 'anti-pornography' approach and what has been called the 'anti-censorship' feminism. A key anti-porn feminist is North American radical feminist Andrea Dworkin, who has identified pornography as central to patriarchy, describing it as the 'nerve centre of patriarchy' and hence one of the main institutions of male supremacy.

**At the heart of the female condition is pornography: it is the ideology that is the source of all the rest.** ***(Dworkin 1983: 34)***

Many anti-porn feminists share Dworkin's concerns about the effects of pornography. They feel that pornography objectifies women; it constructs an ideology of women as sexual objects to be used by men, hence women are dehumanized within pornography. Some anti-porn feminists argue that pornography is actual male sexual violence against women. They argue that women used in the making of porn often suffer actual physical harm and draw on the testimonies of women coerced, harmed or abused in making of porn and women whose lives have been damaged by their partners' use of pornography. They have argued that pornography encourages sexual violence against women. They have drawn on various social and psychological research which indicates the use by sexual offenders of pornography prior to their assaults, that pornography desensitizes men to rape and makes men more sexually violent. Porn plays a role in shaping male sexuality and beliefs about female sexuality.

Itzin (1994) contends that it is always difficult to prove causation using scientific evidence but that it is possible to show correlation between two things. She argues that research on pornography shows that it contributes to a sexually violent culture which legitimizes violence against women. So pornography is a violation of women's civil rights that incites sexual hatred. It censors women by presenting them as one-dimensional sexual objects existing only to meet the sexual needs of men. Such representation plays an important role in reproducing sex discrimination and oppression. Anti-porn feminists have campaigned for anti-porn legislation which bans or censors pornography or enables women to seek compensation for porn-related harm. This anti-porn stance instigated by radical feminists was the dominant position within feminism and still has strong support but another position has begun to gain ascendancy.

Anti-censorship feminists Elizabeth Wilson and Gillian Rodgerson (1991) contend that porn merely reflects sexism in wider society; it did not create it. Rubin (1993) suggests that pornography is a modern phenomenon which women's subordination long predates; there are a whole range of social relations that are oppressive to women and focusing on pornography as Dworkin does marginalizes

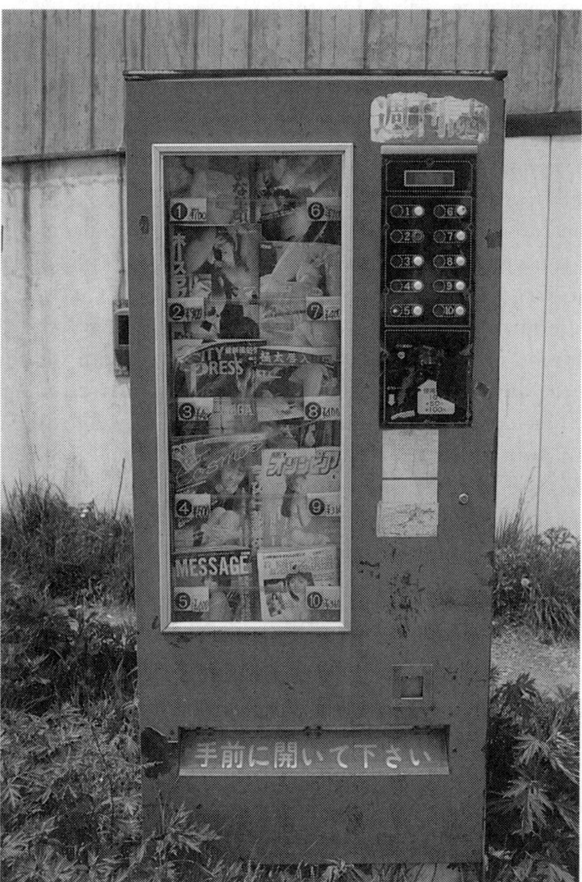


**Fig 2.2** Machine sex: a pornography vending machine, Hokkaido, Japan. (Photograph © Tom Ang, courtesy of Robert Harding Picture Library Ltd.)

these. Wilson and Rodgerson argue that feminism needs a broader cultural politics rather than a simple campaign against pornography. They say that pornography is not actual sexual violence; it is merely representational and a distinction must be made. Rubin (1993) claims that anti-porn feminists exaggerate the extent of violence depicted in porn and argues there is a considerable amount of porn in which women are portrayed as active participants who have their sexual needs met.

Anti-censorship feminists assert that despite the coercion of some women in the production of pornography, many women who work in the sex industry are not victims but chose to work in the sex industry. Feminists would be better struggling to improve working conditions for sex workers. Furthermore they contend that the links between pornography and sexual violence are not proven. Many of the studies of the effects of pornography on men are inconclusive; some even show that many men do not express more hostile attitudes to women after viewing porn (King 1993). They point out that in countries where pornography is widely available sex crimes are no higher than in countries where it is less available.

Anti-porn feminists argue that censorship in any form curtails choice and freedom and is anti-democratic. Campaigning for censorship will only support the moral right who oppose sexual freedom and women's liberation. They point out that censorship would and has been applied first and most strongly against lesbian and gay material rather than the material that feminists campaigners against pornography themselves identify to be most harmful.

This debate to a certain extent is linked to two different analyses of female sexuality. Radical feminists tend to see sexuality as male centred and male defined; pornography is a reflection of this male-centred model of sexuality which shores up patriarchy and controls and dis-empowers women. Lynne Segal (1994) argues that some feminists have not moved beyond understanding female sexuality in terms of something that is male defined and connected to sexual violation. In this analysis all women are defined as victims and this has been reflected in the anti-porn position. Anti-censorship feminists argue that radical feminism and the radical feminist analysis of pornography focuses on women only as sexual victims: women have gained some control over their sexuality and should have the right to the freedom of expression of their sexuality. Segal and Wilson, both socialist feminists, believe that women can be active agents of desire and can actively and willingly participate in a wide range of sexual practices and that some may enjoy the consumption of pornography. Anti-censorship feminists accept that much mainstream porn is sexist and misrepresents female sexuality yet they do not see censorship as the strategy to adopt: 'We believe feminism is about choice about taking control of our lives and our bodies and this must include our sexual choices' (Wilson and Rodgerson 1991: 71).

## A proliferation of voices

Clearly feminism is a diverse body of thought. In recent years because of the arguments of many feminists, particularly Black, non-western and lesbian feminists, there has been an acknowledgement of the diverse experiences that women face. The influence of post-structuralism has also led some feminists to suggest that although the concept and experience of being a 'woman' is important in feminist theory and politics it is misguided to search for one theory, one truth about women. Indeed the diversity within feminism can be interpreted as a strength:

**No one method, form of writing, speaking position, mode of argument can act as a representative model or ideal for feminist theory. Instead of attempting to establish a new theoretical norm, feminist theory seeks a new discursive space, a space where women can write, read and think as women. This space will encourage a proliferation of voices, instead of a hierarchical structuring of them, a plurality of perspectives and interests instead of the monopoly of the one. . . . No one form would be privileged as the truth . . . rather knowledges, methods, interpretations can be judged and used according to their appropriateness to a given context, a specific strategy and particular effects.**

*(Gross 1992: 368)*

## The Frankfurt School and critical theory

In the 1920s Georg Lukács and Antonio Gramsci criticized the mechanistic Marxist model of society that had become the dominant interpretation of Marxism after the Soviet Revolution of 1917. The mechanistic model, sometimes referred to as structural Marxism (see p. 57), stressed the determining effect of the economic infrastructure: human action was determined by the inevitable laws of economic history. In contrast, this new interpretation, sometimes known as humanist Marxism, emphasized the concepts of alienation and ideology and highlighted the value of human struggle against impersonal systems. Lukács and Gramsci attempted to place the individual back at the centre of the stage and stressed the importance of winning the hearts and minds of people in the political struggle for socialism.

These ideas are closely linked to those of the Frankfurt School, which was established in 1923 to 'criticise and subvert domination in all its forms' (Bottomore 1983: 182) and which developed a critical approach to both capitalism and Soviet communism. Faced with the failure of working-class revolution after the First World War and the rise of fascism in Europe at the end of the 1920s, the Frankfurt School developed a very pessimistic view of society and culture which held out little hope of revolutionary change in a world increasingly dominated by bureaucracy, mass culture and authoritarianism. The leading members of the school, including Max Horkheimer, Theodor Adorno and Herbert Marcuse, were forced into exile in the USA by the triumph of Hitler in the 1930s.

In an attempt to explain the failure of working-class revolution in the west, the critical theorists emphasized the power of culture and the declining importance of the individual. Instead of destroying capitalism the working class had become integrated into it by absorbing its culture and accepting its values and goals. The three most important features of this process were instrumental reason; mass culture; and the establishment of the authoritarian personality.

### Instrumental reason

Instrumental reason refers to the way in which rational thought had ceased to be a critical faculty and had become instead yet another instrument through which the powerful could exercise control and domination. During the Enlightenment and French Revolution of the eighteenth century reason had been celebrated as the source of liberation from tradition, superstition and religious bigotry. Under capitalism it had become 'domesticated' (Cuff *et al.* 1990: 119); according to Horkheimer, reason and science had become the tools of capitalism and bureaucracy. Instrumental reason is essentially the means by which we achieve the ends laid down by the system; it is the use of 'technocratic thinking' to achieve limited and practical ends or to solve immediate problems. This use of rational thought may produce short-term aims and personal success but it ignores long-term effects and moral questions about the ends themselves. Instrumental reason may tell us that certain qualifications will lead to more lucrative careers than others, but does not consider 'ends' such as personal fulfilment. Similarly, cost-benefit analysis demonstrates the efficiency gained by introducing new technology into the workplace but it takes no account of the resulting levels of unemployment. The laws of supply and demand reveal the economic necessity of committing more and more natural resources to the enterprise of industrial production even though this may lead to global destruction and pollution.

### Mass culture

Mass culture attracted the critical attention of the Frankfurt School because of the emphasis they gave to the power of ideas in explaining human action. In their view genuine art was seen as rising above the mundane and routine world of instrumental reason; indeed the Frankfurt School would seem to share Picasso's belief in the critical power of art as 'the lie which tells the truth'. This subversive element of 'true' culture has been undermined and superseded by a new popular culture which is not spontaneous, genuine or critical. Popular culture is a false culture devised and packaged by capitalism to keep the masses content.

**The culture industry concerns itself with the predominance of the effect. It aims primarily at the creation of diversion and distractions, providing a temporary escape from the responsibilities and drudgery of everyday life. However the culture industry offers no genuine escape. For the relaxation it provides – free of demands and efforts – only serves to distract people from the basic pressures of their lives and to reproduce their will to work.**

***(Bottomore 1983: 186)***

In *One Dimensional Man*, Marcuse (1964) argued that although modern culture created the illusion of freedom of expression and choice in reality we were becoming homogenous and less independent. Instead of engaging us in creative activity, modern culture simply encouraged the passive consumption of superficial products. In the short term this achieved escape and contentment but the long-term effect was to produce an uncritical and one-dimensional society in which the working classes were incapable of revolt and only a handful of intellectuals presented any challenge to the system.

### The authoritarian personality

The authoritarian personality is largely associated with the work of Marcuse and Adorno and their emphasis on the one-dimensional nature of the modern character. Using the psychoanalysis of Freud along with his own research, Adorno argued that the forces of instrumental reason and mass culture required the members of technocratic societies to possess conformist personalities suited to the hierarchical structure of society and the routines of modern living:

**Domination is not simply built into the culture industry, it requires a particular character structure, one that is not only receptive to domination but actually seeks it.**

*(Craib 1992: 219)*

Whereas early capitalism relied upon the repression of individualism and sexuality through strict upbringing and the development of strong personality, the modern age of mass culture and consumerism encouraged the abandonment of self-discipline and the expression of individualism through consumption. With a decline in parental control and the increasing influence of the culture industry, society was becoming inhabited by 'standardized' individuals who looked to the social system for approval. Instead of developing an independent personality based upon a strong father figure, the child turns away from the family towards the role models and icons provided by the worlds of politics and popular culture. The weak and anxiety-ridden modern personality is seen as uncritical and incapable of independent judgement. It craves domination and strong leadership to allay the doubts and fears which beset it in an increasingly complex and ambiguous world.

The authoritarian personality relies upon stereotypical and rigid thinking: racial prejudice and intolerance are characteristic symptoms; nationalism and fascism the potential outcomes.

**Rootless, lonely, directionless, 'mass man' thus constituted ready made fodder for totalitarian parties. . . . [they] offered him a means by which he might overcome his puniness and isolation, the psychic pain of responsibility, by merging his will with that of a mass movement.**

*(Hannah Arendt, in Bennett 1982: 36)*

The ideas of the Frankfurt School attracted a good deal of academic consideration and interest after the Second World War. They championed the cause of the individual in a world increasingly dominated by bureaucracy, strong state government and international capitalism. The critical approach to ideological control and mass culture seemed to focus on the concerns of the post-war period and the student movement of the 1960s expressed many of its ideas. However, the Frankfurt School became the victim of its own pessimism. It had rejected traditional Marxism and its optimistic faith in the working class and had nowhere to go. As these critical theories lost their influence, Marxist thought turned again to a consideration of its basic themes:

**the analysis of modes of production, structural contradictions and historical transformations, class structure and conflict, political power and the role of the state.**

*(Bottomore 1983: 76)*

Attempts have been made to rehabilitate the ideas of the Frankfurt School. Jurgen Habermas (1971), one-time research assistant to Adorno, developed a more optimistic approach which attempted to bring together the ideas of neo-Marxism and critical theory in order to expose the 'legitimation crisis' of modern capitalism.

Using a 'critical' approach, he expressed the hope that it would be possible to reveal the inadequacies of instrumental reason and undermine the attempts by the political, economic and cultural subsystems to maintain the legitimacy of the capitalist enterprise. He believed that this would seriously challenge the value consensus and result in either a genuine transformation of society or political repression. Either way the irrational and repressive nature of capitalism would have been exposed and the prospects for a free and rational society raised.

## Structuralism

Structuralist theories originated in the work of Durkheim and Marx and have since taken many forms both within and beyond sociology. Structuralism represents an attack on the importance of the individual 'subject' and advocates explanations of human consciousness and behaviour which refer to fixed and objective forces beyond our awareness and control. It implies that explanations for our thoughts, our actions and our culture are not to be found at the level of direct experience and personal awareness (surface structure) but rather in the hidden forces which construct our world and give it meaning (deep structure). In other words 'being human involves living in a world which has already been determined' (Trigg 1985, cited in Jones 1993: 104)

These ideas have had a particular influence in three areas of the human sciences: linguistics, anthropology and sociology.

### Linguistics

As with advocates of theories such as Marxism and functionalism, structuralists and post-structuralists believe that to explain social life it is necessary to look at structural influences beyond the individual. However, rather than focusing on institutional structures, they emphasize how systems of language provide us with our knowledge of the world: language defines our social reality. Linguistics is, then, clearly associated with the ideas of structuralism. In this context, the work of Ferdinand de Saussure (1857–1913) has particular importance. He made a crucial distinction between the everyday use of speech by individuals in their conscious communication with one another (parole) and the underlying system of collective language which is governed by rules of conduct and meaning (langue). Words take their meaning from this language system and it is the system we unconsciously learn and use to impose sense and order upon the world. We do this by learning to apply correct words to relevant concepts.

The importance of the rules governing grammar, sentence structure and sounds can be seen when we attempt to learn a new language. Nigel Barley (1986) reveals the importance of tone in changing the meaning of a word in the Dowayo language (from Cameroon, Africa):

**My rather wobbly control of the language was also a grave danger. Obscenity is never very far away in Dowayo. One day I was summoned to the Chief's hut to be introduced to a rainmaker. This was a most valuable contact that I had nagged the Chief about for weeks. We chatted politely, very much sounding each other out . . .**

**[and] agreed I would visit him. I rose and shook hands politely, 'Excuse me,' I said, 'I am cooking some meat.' At least that was what I had intended to say; owing to a tonal error I declared to an astonished audience, 'Excuse me, I am copulating with the blacksmith.'** *(Barley 1986: 57)*

As this body of rules already exists and has to be learned, it is correct to say that language is not a reflection of reality but the definition and creation of it; it can be seen as the underlying structure which gives meaning to our experiences and enables us to share them with others. When a 2-year-old child announces that she wishes to go to McDonald's even though she has never set foot in a fast-food restaurant she indicates the power of language to create conceptual categories that are independent of and prior to direct experience. The price we pay for this gift of communication is our enslavement by language through its power to constrain the way we think. As Doyle and Harris (1986) point out:

**You must learn from others the language you employ to describe even your most intimate and private feelings; thus even the way you describe yourself to yourself can only happen by using words publicly available, and learnt, by you.** *(Jones 1993: 103)*

The idea that words are only one form of communication has been applied by the science of signs known as semiotics. The work of Roland Barthes, for instance, has attempted to unearth the hidden message of popular culture. Barthes (1973) has tried to illustrate how all forms of cultural phenomena can be analysed as systems of signs that help us understand our society. According to this approach a sign is made up of two elements – the actual object ('signifier') and that which it represents ('signified').

In other words we inhabit a world of signs which exist on two levels. On the surface or 'connotive' level things have a purely empirical status as objects; but they also function at a deeper or 'denotive' level where they act as symbols for something else – they convey meaning. The task of semiotics is to decode the signs of everyday life (body language, adverts, fashion and so on) in order to establish what they denote. A simple example of this, borrowed from Sherlock Holmes by Asa Berger, is shown below.

**Case Study**

### Signifiers and signifieds

Many of us have followed the adventure of a detective who was (like all the classical detectives) a first class semiologist. I am talking about Sherlock Holmes. Inevitably there is some situation that arises that puzzles everyone, which Holmes then 'solves'. He does this by reading signs which others ignore as trivial and inconsequential. In one story, 'The Blue Carbuncle', Watson finds Holmes examining a hat that had been brought to him by a policeman. Watson describes the hat: it was old, its lining was discoloured, it was cracked, very dusty and spotted in places. Holmes asks Watson what he can deduce from the hat about its wearer. Watson examines the hat and says he can deduce nothing. Holmes then proceeds to describe, in remarkable detail, what

*(box continued)*

*(box continued)*

the man who owned the hat is like. He is, Holmes says: highly intellectual, has had a decline in fortune, his wife no longer loves him, he is sedentary, and probably doesn't have gas in his house. Watson exclaims, 'You are certainly joking, Holmes.' Holmes then shows Watson how he reached his conclusions. He examined the hat, noticed certain things about it (signifiers) and proceeded from there (described the implied signifieds).

| **Signifiers** | **Signifieds** |
|---|---|
| Cubic capacity of hat (large brain) | Man is intellectual |
| Good quality of hat but three years old | Man hasn't a new hat, suggesting a decline in fortune |
| Hat hasn't been brushed in weeks | Man's wife no longer loves him |
| Dust on hat is brown housedust | Man seldom goes out |
| Wax stains from candles on hat | No gas in house |

Holmes explains Watson's mistake. 'You fail . . . to reason from what you see. You are too timid in drawing your inferences.' Watson had failed to recognize the signifiers he examined for what they were. . . . The meaning in signs, and texts (collections of signs) is not always (or even often) evident; it has to be elicited. And too many people are like Watson, I would suggest – not bold enough in drawing their inferences.

(Adapted from A A Berger 1991: 9–10)

### Questions

**Take three current adverts and describe the messages that they are conveying. (Choose adverts for different types of products – perhaps American jeans; cleaning material; a car; soft drinks.)**

## Anthropology

In 1968 Vladimir Propp published his attempt to apply the ideas of structuralism to the fairy tale. Despite the range and variety of fairy tales around the world, he argued that all such stories are simply myths created to communicate deeper meanings about ourselves. They display universal similarities in form irrespective of the differences in content. These shared characteristics can be reduced to a basic menu of thirty-one functions from which all myths and stories are created. Asa Berger (1991) applied Propp's ideas to various texts to show that the underlying themes can be applied as easily to Frankenstein and Sam Spade as they can to Little Red Riding Hood. He demonstrates that the basic elements in fairy tales recur in various genres:

| *Genre* | *Elements from fairy tales* |
|---|---|
| Science fiction | Magical agents, magical powers, etc.; hero leaves home |
| Detective | Finding kidnapped heroines |
| Soap operas | Relations between members of families |
| Spy stories | Finding false heroes; hero (unrecognized) arrives in a foreign country |
| Situation comedies | Reversal of problem stories about royal families; stories about tricksters |
| Western | Hero and villain fight, a chase (reversed, with villian pursued) |

Claude Lévi-Strauss developed these ideas in the field of anthropology. He focused on the form rather than the content of particular cultures and attempted to explain all social phenomena as communication systems. He argued that myths and stories that might seem unintelligible to us made sense and could be shown to have a clear structure and order when studied as systems of signs and symbols. Lévi-Strauss adopted a similar approach in his examination of other aspects of human societies. His study of kinship structures, for example, revealed universal taboos of incest which he argued were simply a means of ensuring that marriage took place outside the family. As a result women became gifts between groups of men; gifts that expressed the value and respect which men had for one another. As with other forms of structuralism, what individuals themselves think or say they are doing is subjective and irrelevant. Ritzer points out that 'to engage in a science, the focus must shift from people to some sort of objective structure' (1992: 502). For Lévi-Strauss social phenomena are the products of the mind and should be interpreted as reflections of 'the permanent and logical structures of the mind'. Whereas anthropology usually highlights examples of cross-cultural diversity in human behaviour the structuralist model clearly suggests unconscious and universal similarities which unite human behaviour at a deeper level.

### Sociology

We have already acknowledged that the origins of structuralism can be found in the sociology of Marx and Durkheim and the emphasis they placed upon the importance of social and economic structures for a deeper understanding of the causes of personal behaviour. In modern sociology these ideas have been developed by functionalists, such as Robert Merton, and the Marxism of Louis Althusser.

In common with other modern structuralists, Althusser (1965) attacked the idea of voluntaristic action and the notion of 'the subject' which he argued was simply an ideological condition whereby we are deluded into giving individualistic and personal accounts of social behaviour. However, he rejected the analyses of linguistic structuralists such as Saussure and Barthes and their attempt to explain social phenomena in terms of language and the structures of the human mind. He saw this as a form of 'psychological reductionism'. In Marxism the emphasis is on external structures which exist independently of the human mind and shape our ideas and which change over time (historical materialism).

For Althusser, the humanist Marxism of Lukács and Gramsci was unacceptable because it returned 'the subject' to the centre of the stage. However, he also rejected mechanistic Marxism for placing too much emphasis on the base/superstructure model and the overriding importance of the economy. Althusser agreed that in modern societies the economy might 'in the last instance' determine all other social phenomena, but he also stressed the importance of other structures which could enjoy 'relative autonomy' from the economic base. These included the political and ideological structures of society which act to motivate and constrain the behaviour of individuals. He referred to these as 'structures in dominance' and classified them into two broad types: *repressive state apparatus* (including the armed forces, police and mental hospitals) and *ideological state apparatus* (including religion, education and the media).

This model permits a certain amount of flexibility and allows societies the room to develop in different ways. You do not have to be a professor of history to see that across cultures and through time societies experience different types of domination by different structures, even though they may share the same economic modes of production. In some capitalist societies the dominant structure may be an ideological one such as religion, whereas others may be dominated by the political structure. Despite the relative flexibility of this model, its critics would point to the dehumanizing tendency of explaining action in terms of social structures. Craib has used the puppet theatre as a metaphor for this tendency in structural Marxism:

> **Here we have the puppet theatre in full view: the strings originate at the economic level, the mode of production; they pass through the state and the ideological state apparatus, a second level of machinery that services the mode of production, keeping it in operation. And they finally work the puppets through an imaginary sense of being free, of choosing, of acting.**
>
> ***(Craib 1992: 171)***

## Post-structuralism

The importance of language and systems of communication continue as themes in the work of post-structuralists. Michel Foucault (1977), for example, stresses the importance of languages as ways of thinking and talking and uses the term 'discourses' to refer to them. However, the underlying assumption in structuralist theories of a universal and unifying principle is rejected. Rather the language and perspectives (discourses) that people learn to use to make sense of the world and to communicate with one another represent a form of power and control over them. Instead of looking for the origins of social organizations in the hidden and fixed workings of the human mind, post-structuralists look to the changing historical and social forces which created the discourses in the first place. This relationship between knowledge and power led Foucault to look at the ways in which knowledge can be used as a form of domination. Instead of being progressive or civilizing forces the discourses of medicine, science and technology were forms of mental domination and social control.

Foucault believed that the study of history should analyse how and why different discourses came to be established. Indeed Foucault's historical accounts of madness, sexuality and punishment aim to show how and why different discourses were established and accepted as defining such phenomena. With regard to madness, he argued that the origins of mental hospitals (initially called 'madhouses') could not be separated from the emergence of the power of reason (the opposite of madness), the medicalization of insanity and the vested interest of psychiatrists. The major explanation for this was institutional and almost accidental: the eradication of leprosy in post-Renaissance Europe had emptied the 'lazar houses' (which segregated lepers until the decline of leprosy in Europe) and provided the opportunity to segregate and incarcerate the mad.

Foucault rejected the idea that the provision of asylums for insane people was inspired by a genuine desire to provide the 'sick' with medical care; rather this represented a new age of incarceration in an increasingly rational world which sought to persecute the irrational and reinforce social control. In the new medical discourse, reason was the source of a healthy civilization, while madness was a sickness to be healed. Our resulting fear of madness ensures conformity and guarantees social control. Whether he was talking about medicine, punishment or sex, Foucault's unconventional ideas represent an attack on rational forms of knowledge as extensions of institutional control. They are not superior, they are simply dominant. This relativist approach to knowledge is shared by many post-modernist thinkers who also reject the notion that history is determined by the civilizing forces of science and reason.

Q Foucault and others have suggested that certain discourses represent a form of social control. How might this be applied to the way in which certain types of behaviour are defined as rational or insane?

Give examples of behaviour which is generally seen as rational or insane: why might society want to encourage the rational and control the insane behaviour?

## Post-modernism

Since the Enlightenment the search for the truth has dominated philosophy, social theory and scientific research. This search for 'the truth' has resulted in all encompassing theories of society and history known as *meta-narratives*. Meta-narratives claim to provide ever improving and logical accounts of historical progress and destiny (and are an essential part of what Crook *et al.* (1992) have called the 'continuous qualitative progression of modernity'). Such accounts have dominated sociological thinking since its infancy, in the optimistic predictions of Marx and the pessimistic warnings of Weber. In the twentieth century 'meta-narratives' surface in the theories of development put forward by Parsons (1966) and Rostow (1960) and in the post-capitalist theories of Dahrendorf (1959) and Bell (1973). An exponent of the 'project of modernity' is Francis Fukuyama (1989), who has argued that history has been the evolution and final triumph of liberal democracy and global capitalism:

**What we may be witnessing is not just the end of the Cold War or the passing of a particular period of post-war history but the end of history as such; that is the end point of mankind's ideological evolution and the universalisation of western liberal democracy as the final form of human government.**

***(Fukuyama 1989: 4)***

This triumph of western values may, however, produce 'soulless consumerism' and a world in which cultural and political differences disappear. This more critical view of modernity was summed up by Malcolm Muggeridge in *Things Past* (1978):

**What they all want . . . is what the Americans have got – six lanes of large motor cars streaming powerfully into and out of gleaming cities; neon lights flashing, and juke boxes sounding and skyscrapers rising, storey upon storey into the sky. Driving at night into the town of Athens, Ohio (pop. 3,450), four bright coloured signs stood out in the darkness – 'Gas', 'Drugs', 'Beauty', 'Food'. These signs could have shone forth as clearly in Athens, Greece as in Athens, Ohio. They belonged as aptly to**

**Turkestan, or Sind or Kamchatka. . . . There are, properly speaking, no Communists, no capitalists, no Catholics, no Protestants, no black men. No Asians, no Europeans, no Right, no Left and no Center. . . . There is only a vast and omnipresent longing for Gas, for Beauty, for Drugs and for Food.**

***(Muggeridge 1978: 125, quoted in Dizard 1982: 18)***

Whether we applaud the triumph of modernity or resent it, post-modernism resists the conclusion that we have reached the end of history. Instead the world described by Fukuyama and Muggeridge is simply a matter of perspective and represents the beginning of a new age – the post-modern.

In the work of writers like Lyotard (1985) and Baudrillard (1990) the end of modernism is celebrated and a post-modern world of disintegration, confusion and cultural choice opens up. The 'rational and rigid' guidelines of the meta-narratives of modernism have been swept away and replaced by the 'irrational and flexible' elements of a far more relativist position which says that 'anything goes'. This can be most clearly seen using examples from architecture where the terms 'modernism' and 'post-modernism' are widely used. For example, housing officials in London decided to 'post-modernize' their high-rise flats with architectural features from earlier epochs and styles such as classical roof shapes, decorative façades and ornate balconies (Strinati 1992).

In sociological theory the shape and impact of post-modernism is less easy to describe, in part because it is not a unified theory but a collection of different positions and ideas. However, there are several identifying features of post-modernist thought which provide some kind of identity, if only because they tell us what post-modernism is not.

Case Study

## Post-modernism and sociology: no special claim to the truth

First, the idea that social history is the rational and evolutionary progress of society towards some kind of end is rejected by post-modernists. The meta-narratives of Marx and Durkheim with their exclusive claims to truth have been replaced with a relativist perspective that treats their work as 'texts' rather than gospels. Post-modernism sees all points of view as valid with none able to claim superiority; they are simply different ways of looking at things. From this relativist position, all sociological accounts have equal validity. In a post-modern world, grand theoretical accounts such as Marxism and functionalism are obsolete. And sociology itself has no special claim to truth.

Second, post-modernists disdain the artificial classification of knowledge into separate disciplines; they emphasize the pluralistic character of knowledge. The boundaries between sociology, psychology, history, philosophy and so on are merely attempts to preserve one set of grand theories in opposition to all others. By dissolving such distinctions it is possible to become more eclectic in our approach – to 'pick and mix' from a range of disciplines and perspectives in order to create a more exciting blend of ideas. This can be seen in modern politics where the old organizing principles of class and party are being replaced by issues such as famine, civil rights and the protection of the environment.

*(box continued)*

*(box continued)*

Third, in post-modernist writing the importance of popular culture is often stressed especially in relation to the power of the media to create 'realities' – through advertising, popular music and television soap operas for instance. These new versions of historical reality have no respect for matters of fact or taste; they simply take what they need from the variety of characters, narratives and styles available and create new cultural forms – video games, adverts, comics. In Las Vegas there is a billion-dollar casino based on the Egyptian pyramids but it mixes together historical themes as diverse as Camelot, Henry VIII and characters from Charles Dickens. In this new pluralist culture, art is not the preserve of the elite but is available to all; there is no good or bad, there is simply choice.

The confusion of time and space and the fragmentation of cultural traditions is the characteristic of post-modern consumer society in which we experience the erosion of 'collective and personal identities'. On the one hand, Strinati (1992) argues, we have lost the traditional sources of social identity once found in factors such as social class, religion, community and family life. On the other hand, popular culture has failed to create anything worth while enough to provide an alternative source of security. Television is the supreme example of this 'candy floss' culture which 'speaks to everyone and no one in particular':

**TV is a constant flow which switches back and forth between different surface messages; it is not a genuine source of identity and belief. But . . . since there is nothing else, nowhere else, but the TV screen, people have no alternative (except perhaps to go to the shops) but to succumb to the TV image, to lose themselves in the blankness of the screen and the hollowness of its icons.** *(Strinati 1992: 7)*

Q

Every morning in Britain millions of viewers watch *The Big Breakfast Show*. The presenters have developed the ultimate post-modernist formula in which nothing is taken seriously. If you were the programme controller would you interrupt the show to announce any of the following news items? If so, how would you 'present' them?

- outbreak of war in central Europe
- the election result
- break-up of a royal marriage
- TV personality involved in sex scandal
- the birth of kittens to your pet cat
- dramatic twist in a popular soap.

In contrast to the modernist and post-modernist perspectives, there is also the argument that the world does have a clear destiny but it is one that is doomed to failure and collapse. In his pessimistic view of the future, Paul Kennedy (1993) argues the case for a world divided by crisis, domination and ecological decline. In the nineteenth century the predictions of Thomas Malthus that British society would be destroyed by the ravages of overpopulation and poverty were avoided through the opportunities offered by colonialism and emigration. In the twenty-first century the world will have no chance for escape. According to this view, the world is destined to face a crisis between the First World, based on a wealth explosion, and the Third World, which cannot avoid a massive explosion in population. In this unequal equation the values of the free market and liberal democracy will evaporate in the face of world domination by multinational companies and global oligarchies.

The end result will be disaster because the long-term problems of ecological decline cannot be grasped by short-term western political culture, which is incapable of confronting the crises of wealth creation. This view of the future is an indictment of modernist writers and their naive belief in the inevitable progress of science and reason. It is also a reminder of the limitations of post-modernist thinking and its obsession with western culture. Instead of engineering a new period of history we may simply be witnessing the disintegration of the old one.

## Summary

- In reviewing different theoretical approaches it is important to stress that sociology is more than the sum of different theories. The sociological perspective is not tied to one theoretical point of view and sociologists should be able to use a range of different theories.
- Durkheim helped to establish sociology as a distinctive academic subject. He outlined the scientific basis and methods that sociology should adopt. Durkheim's work emphasized the moral basis of social cohesion or solidarity, an approach that has developed in the functionalist perspective.
- Marx's analysis of society saw the economic base of society as affecting and determining all other aspects of social life. Marx argued that in all societies there are basic contradictions within this economic base, due to the conflict of interests between different social groups involved in the economic process – in particular conflict between dominant and subordinate classes. Since Marx's death a number of strands of Marxism have emerged. In sociological theory, two major forms of Marxism can be identified: (a) structural Marxism focusing on the importance of the economic base and class exploitation; (b) humanist Marxism stressing the alienation of the human spirit as a result of the rise of capitalism.
- Weber moved away from the structural theories of Durkheim and Marx and based his social analysis on the meanings that individuals give to the social world. He focused on social action and the motivations behind it. Weber developed this approach to suggest that structural Marxism, in particular, underplayed the role that non-economic factors might have in determining the development of society.
- There have been a number of important developments in sociological theory since the work of Durkheim, Marx and Weber.
- Interpretive sociology developed from the work of Weber and the importance attached to social action and includes a number of related theoretical perspectives. Symbolic interactionism focuses on the individual and the processes of social interaction. Ethnomethodology examines how people construct their social world. While emphasizing the importance of individuals' behaviour and of human interaction, interpretivists are aware that this cannot be divorced from the social situation in which behaviour and interaction occurs.
- Feminist sociologists argued that sociological theory has been written from a male perspective. They have attempted to redress this state of affairs by placing women's experiences as central to the development of social theory and by trying to explain

the divisions between women and men in society. There are various strands of feminist theory including liberal feminism, radical feminism, Marxist feminism and Black feminism.

- Critical theory, building on the work of Marx and Weber in particular, has emphasized the power of culture and the declining importance of the individual.
- Structuralism argues that the explanation for human behaviour cannot be found in the experience of the individual and that objective forces beyond our control have to be uncovered and examined. These forces can be found in systems of language and in the ideological and political structures of society. Post-structuralists look at how systems of language and ideological structures act as forms of power and control over people.
- Post-modernism suggests that the search for an ultimate explanation of and for human society is an enterprise doomed to failure. This perspective argues that all theoretical approaches are valid: none can claim to tell us the 'truth'.

## Further reading

This chapter has introduced and reviewed a wide range of sociological theories and theoretical writing and it really goes without saying that to gain a fuller appreciation of this work you would need to read the original sources referred to. Indeed it is often rewarding to read the 'real thing' and many of these sources are far more accessible and interesting than might be initially thought. Here, though, we highlight some more general texts that focus on sociological theorizing.

Bryson, V (1992) *Feminist Political Theory: An Introduction*, London: Macmillan.

Humm, M (ed.) (1992) *Feminisms: A Reader*, London: Harvester Wheatsheaf.

These are two detailed expositions of the various strands of feminist theory.

Craib, I (1992) *Modern Social Theory*, London: Harvester Wheatsheaf.

Layder, D (1994) *Understanding Social Theory*, London: Sage.

Ritzer, G (1992) *Sociological Theory*, 3rd edn, New York: McGraw-Hill.

These three studies provide thorough discussions of contemporary theories.

Cuff, E C, Sharrock, W W and Francis, D W (1990) *Perspectives in Sociology*, 3rd edn, London: Unwin Hyman.

Jones, P (1993) *Studying Society: Sociological Theories and Research Practices*, London: Collins Educational.

These are two clear general introductions to the different theoretical positions in sociology.

Lemert, C (ed.) (1993) *Social Theory: The Multicultural and Classic Readings*, Oxford: Westview.

There are numerous readers on sociological theory and edited collections of theoretical writing. We particularly recommend this collection, which covers a range of 'classic' and contemporary writing.

## Activities

### Activity 1 Sociological explanations of Christmas

How would the following sociological approaches interpret the rituals of Christmas?

(a) Functionalism (consider the functions and dysfunctions of Christmas rituals).

(b) Feminism (consider what women and men/girls and boys do at Christmas).

(c) Interpretive sociology (consider the 'games' people play at Christmas and the impressions people create at family gatherings).

(d) Marxism (consider who profits at Christmas and what ideological messages are conveyed by Christmas rituals).

(e) Post-modernism (consider the role of popular culture at Christmas: the fragmentation of cultural traditions/confusion of time and space).

### Activity 2 Why study sociological theory?

In the extract, Craib (1992) suggests that the problems which lead people to theoretical thinking are the problems that we all face in our everyday lives. It also provides an encouragement to those who 'don't like theory' because it shows that sociological theory can be applied to everyday events and can affect us as individuals.

I think the truth is that we all think theoretically but in a way which we are not often aware. What we are not used to is thinking theoretically in a systematic manner, with all the various constraints and rigours that involve. . . .

What, then, are the problems in response to which we all think theoretically without realising it? Most of us are affected in some way by events over which we have no control and the causes of which are not immediately obvious. . . . A member of the family might be made unemployed, for example, or fail to gain an expected place at university or college; some product or service might suddenly become unavailable because of a strike, or because of government or local authority economies. . . . We can do things to alleviate the effects of all of these, but they happen whether we as individuals like it or not, and it is by no means clear why they happen. There are similar, more intimate events in our personal lives: The slow change in the relationship between parents and children or between lovers, which no one wills but which nonetheless happen. I might suddenly find a friend has turned hostile for no obvious reason. . . .

In all these situations, wc try to find some explanation. Often it takes the form of blaming somebody or thing, frequently unfairly – I lose my job because of all the blacks coming over here. . . . Sometimes the blame is closer to the mark: I lose my job because of an economic situation largely created by government policy; . . . Sometimes the explanations are more sophisticated, but my point is that as soon as we start thinking about and trying to explain something which happens to us, over which we have no control, we are beginning to think theoretically. . . . Theory is an attempt to explain our everyday experience of the world, our 'closest' experience, in terms of something which is not so close – whether it be other people's actions, our past experience, our repressed emotions or whatever. . . . every social theory makes some propositions which are counter to our immediate experiences and beliefs, and this is in fact the way in which we learn from theory. The punk might believe that she is in full rebellion against the culture of her parents and authority, yet for the functionalist theorist, she is setting in motion a series of adjustments by means of which that culture and society continue to survive in a smoother-running way than before. The worker might believe she is getting a fair day's wage for a fair day's work but for the Marxist she is being systematically exploited. When I fail a student's exam paper, I might believe that I am applying a rule and upholding academic standards. . . . The symbolic interactionist would say that I am creating a failure. (Craib 1992: 5–10)

### Questions

List some of the 'problems' that you have had to or will have to deal with.

How might different sociological theories help you to (a) understand and (b) respond to each of these problems?

Chapter 3

# Sociological research: issues in the collection and organization of data

**Chapter outline:** Introduction • The scientific method and sociology • Different methods of research • Quantitative research • Qualitative research • Other methods of research • Feminist research • Triangulation • Summary • Further reading • Activities

## Learning objectives

When you have studied this chapter you should be able to address these key questions:

- What is sociological research?
- What different research methods are available to sociologists?
- What are the philosophies that underlie the collection and analysis of data?
- Why and in what ways have feminists criticized conventional sociological research?

## Introduction

> The sociologist [must] put himself [*sic*] in the same state of mind as the physicist, chemist or physiologist when he probes into a still unexplored region of the scientific domain. When he penetrates the social world, he must be aware that he is penetrating the unknown; he must feel himself in the presence of facts whose laws are as unsuspected as were those of life before the era of biology; he must be prepared for discoveries which will surprise and disturb him. (Durkheim 1964: xlv)

*The Rules of Sociological Method* was first published in 1895 and as Durkheim's comment illustrates, sociology had not then achieved the status of other academic disciplines (it also indicates the sexist language used by the early sociologists). The extent to which sociological research is accorded the same status as research in other disciplines is an issue that is still of concern to sociologists. Sociological research can provide explanations for issues that affect us both as individuals and as members of larger groups. It can help us understand how our social background can affect our educational attainment and why people in some countries are dying from diseases that have long since been eradicated in other parts of the world.

People hold a vast range of views on social issues, such as why certain people become criminals, why women are massively under-represented in positions of power in the political and business world, or why fewer people attend religious services. While the findings of sociological research might not help you to win arguments, they might lessen the misconceptions and prejudices that often accompany them.

Academic subjects require a 'methodology' to reach their conclusions; they must establish ways of obtaining relevant data and of analysing those data. In this chapter we shall consider which research methods are most appropriate for sociology and discuss the strengths and problems associated with different methods. As with other areas of sociological inquiry, there is no general agreement as to what is the most effective method of sociological research.

**Definition**

### Method, methodology and epistemology

**Method** refers to a technique for gathering information, such as a questionnaire or interview.

**Methodology** refers to the theory of and analysis of how research should proceed. It suggests a commitment to a particular way of practising research. Feminists, for example, have been active in specifying the ethics of feminist practice and the principles that should underpin research.

**Epistemology** refers to a theory of knowledge. It sets the rules for the validation of knowledge. It answers questions about who can be the 'knowers', who can say what truth is and what kinds of things constitute knowledge. Feminists argue that traditional epistemologies have excluded women as knowers and have seen men as the only authorized people able to decide what knowledge is.

A key question for sociology is whether it should adopt similar methods to those used in the natural sciences. At the risk of oversimplification, the basic issue is how far the study of human behaviour and social life is fundamentally different from the study of the natural world. There are two broad approaches in sociological research. The first advocates the application of scientific methods to sociological research – an approach that usually involves *quantitative* research. Second, the adoption of a more humanistic approach to research involves the use of *qualitative* methods.

Q

Think back to lessons you have had in chemistry, physics or other sciences. How were you taught to find out about things?

How might the methods you were taught in those subjects be used to find out about social issues, such as (a) why some groups get better educational qualifications than others; (b) why men commit more crime than women?

It is important to highlight the dangers of dividing all research into either quantitative or qualitative. There are various subdivisions within the two broad approaches, overlaps between quantitative and qualitative research, and many examples of sociological research that have adopted aspects of both approaches. None the less, this broad division provides a structure for examining the various research methods used by sociologists.

Definition

### Quantitative and qualitative research

**Quantitative research** involves the collection and presentation of numerical data that can be codified and subjected to detailed statistical testing. It follows the scientific method in so far as it attempts to discover and measure facts about society and social behaviour. Information is collected and analysed in order to test a specific hypothesis (see pp. 111–12). Methods of research include gathering social data through social surveys, questionnaires and structured interviews. These techniques usually involve studying large numbers of subjects so that the findings can be used as a basis for presenting general conclusions about social behaviour.

**Qualitative research** focuses on smaller units of society and on the understanding of social situations and the meanings that individuals attach to behaviour. It is a more subjective approach whereby the researcher aims to understand and interpret the experiences of the individuals involved, by viewing the world through the eyes of the individuals being studied. Methods of research include various forms of observation and unstructured interviews.

Although it is not possible to establish hard and fast connections between styles of research and particular theoretical positions, quantitative methods are likely to be used by those who favour a 'macrosociological' perspective and qualitative methods by those favouring 'microsociology'. Many of the early, 'grand' social theorists adopted a macro or large-scale approach in their writings. Karl Marx, for instance, set out to describe and explain the origins and development of modern industrial capitalist society. He examined different types of societies – tribal, feudal, capitalist and communist – and explored how one type of system evolved from another. He was not concerned with why some people might join a particular religious group or become involved in football hooliganism. Marx and other classic sociologists who are regarded as the founders of the discipline, including Durkheim and Weber, based their analyses of society on evidence from second-hand, general and historical sources rather than on original, first-hand research. At a similar period to the writing of these early sociologists, around the turn of the century, social reformers such as Charles Booth and Seebohm Rowntree were engaged in quantitative research in the form of large-scale surveys.

The concern of qualitative research tends to be with the small scale; a close-up view of society is taken. Such sociological research might focus on one aspect of social behaviour, perhaps a religious group or a juvenile gang. While this form of research might consider broad issues, the emphasis is different; there is less concern with generalizing about whole societies from particular instances. The importance attached to interpreting behaviour is indicated by the use of the general term 'interpretativsm'. Two other terms that are used in relation to the basic differences in approach to sociological research are positivism and phenomenology.

Definition

### Positivism and phenomenology

**Positivism** and positivist research is based on the logic and method of science and scientific inquiry. Positivism sees empirical science (science based on experiments that are testable) as the only valid form of human knowledge. Auguste Comte coined the term when arguing that the application of the methods of the natural sciences to sociology would produce a 'positive science of society'. In contrast, the phenomenological perspective maintains that there is a fundamental difference between the subject matter of the natural and the social sciences.

**Phenomenology** can be defined as the study of various forms of consciousness and the ways in which people understand and interpret the world in which they live. This perspective derives from the work of Max Weber. Although adopting a 'grand theoretical' approach, he argued that people cannot be studied in the same manner as the physical world. People attach meanings to what they do and sociology has to acknowledge this and attempt to interpret those meanings.

Many of the early sociological theorists adopted a positivist approach but this does not indicate that quantitative research came first and has been superseded by qualitative research. McNeill (1990) emphasizes the cyclical nature of trends in sociological research. After the Second World War the importance of objective data and statistical proof was stressed, particularly in the sociological work pursued in the USA and UK. During the 1960s a reaction against this kind of sociological research developed, and qualitative methods and participant observation in particular became the vogue. The 'debate' between those sociologists who advocated the scientific approach and those who argued that sociological researchers need to get involved in the lives of those they were studying has been described as a 'sociological war'. Using the same militaristic language, McNeill suggests that there has been an outbreak of peace in this methodological war and that it is now perfectly acceptable for sociologists to use a range of research techniques in their work (this development is discussed in the section on triangulation, pp. 142–3).

We shall consider the question of whether sociology is or should aim to be scientific prior to examining some of the specific methods of research favoured by sociologists.

## The scientific method and sociology

Science is usually taken to refer to the natural sciences and (in the educational context) to subjects such as chemistry, physics and biology, which aim to explain the natural world in a logical manner by using specific techniques – the 'scientific method'. Science aims to produce knowledge that can be trusted because it is known to be true in all circumstances and at all times. It produces knowledge that has been empirically discovered and tested, rather than knowledge based on belief or faith.

Whether the scientific method can be applied to sociological research is a question that has excited considerable debate and divided opinion in sociology. Positivism supports the scientific method of research. Positivist research in sociology tries to discover 'scientific laws', which could explain the causes, functions and consequences of social phenomena, such as rates of crime or suicide. The term 'laws' reflects a fairly hardline position; many positivists would aim to discover 'tendencies' rather than laws.

*Karl Popper* (b.1902) has been one of the foremost supporters of the positivist approach. In his view, scientific knowledge is the only valid form of knowledge. The development of knowledge is dependent on mutual criticism in that we learn about the world only by testing ideas against reality. In a society without the freedom to criticize, knowledge would not be able to grow. The emphasis on criticism comes from Popper's concern with the 'problem of induction', whereby science proceeds through the gathering of facts based on observations of events. Popper suggested that if we observe swans and note that they are all white then we can deduce that all swans are white. However, as soon as one black swan is observed the generalization becomes invalid. Thus a generalization can never be proved just by observation, although a generalization can be shown to be false on the basis of one counter-example. Science proceeds by the disproving of generalizations, by refutation, according to Popper. Science should make generalizations that are open to testing.

Popper's idea of science as a process of refuting hypotheses has been criticized, most notably by *Thomas Kuhn* (b.1922). Kuhn emphasizes the importance of social interests in shaping the things that are believed about the world. Scientific discovery does not just occur through open-minded inquiry; scientists are locked into particular theoretical positions that do not just depend on evidence but are influenced by the beliefs and interests of the scientific community. Kuhn suggests that 'social science' is almost a contradiction in terms.

Nevertheless Popper's view has been widely accepted as an accurate account of what scientists do and has been instrumental in establishing the 'hypothetico-deductive' method: scientific knowledge and theory develop from the deducing and testing of hypotheses. The procedure is essentially a set of steps that describe how a particular piece of research is carried out. These steps are illustrated using the example of football hooliganism:

1 Identification of a specific social issue or phenomenon that it is to be investigated: football hooliganism.
2 Formulation of a hypothesis: football hooliganism is caused by young people in 'dead-end' jobs that have little future and allow no scope for creativity and self-expression.
3 Selection or design of a particular research method by which the hypothesis might be tested: checking of police records of people arrested at football matches, followed up by asking those arrested what they feel about their employment situation.
4 Collection of information: examine police records and interview or give questionnaires to known football hooligans.
5 Interpretation and analysis of the information gained: relating the data gathered to the hypothesis being investigated, how many football hooligans were in 'dead-end' jobs?
6 Formulation of a theory based on the tested hypothesis and the interpretation of the data collected: there is (or is not) a causal link between employment situation and football hooliganism.
7 Reporting the findings and conclusions, which must be open to discussion and retesting by others who may be interested. In some cases, the findings might be used in the formulation of policy, perhaps in deciding whether to introduce identity cards as a requirement for entry to football grounds or whether to segregate and fence groups of football supporters into self-contained areas of the grounds.

The steps need not be followed in the exact order indicated above. For instance, a scientist may observe something happening and examine it without having any clear hypothesis in mind as to why it occurred; the hypothesis may emerge later in the investigation, perhaps after some information has been collected. In reality, research is rarely as clear cut as a textbook suggests.

**Q** Select another issue or phenomenon that sociologists might investigate and consider how steps 2 to 7 of the scientific method detailed above could be applied to it. Consider how this scientific method could be applied to an examination of (a) the extent to which the television portrayal of women influences children's attitudes towards the role of women; (b) the decline in attendance at religious services since the nineteenth century.

Consideration of the scientific method and its applicability to sociology highlights the relationship between sociological theory and method and the difficulty of looking at research methods in isolation. The formulation of a hypothesis and the type and style of questions asked will depend on the theoretical perspective favoured by the researcher. This theoretical perspective is also likely to guide the researcher toward certain 'facts'.

Hypotheses do not appear from nowhere: they might derive from beliefs and theories that are already held. In our example of football hooliganism, the hypothesis emphasizing the employment situation could derive from a criticism of government economic policy as having caused an increase in the sense of frustration felt by certain groups of people or from a wider theory about the alienating nature of work under capitalism.

The link between the researcher's theoretical stance and the research methods adopted raises the issue of whether sociology can be *value-free*. The positivist argument that sociology should attempt to be as scientific as possible is based on the belief that only science can provide the 'truth'. Scientists discover this truth by being completely objective, by dealing with facts. In their research, sociologists must be objective and neutral, must not take sides and should adopt an approach based on a position of value-freedom. Weber, a famous advocate of this approach, argued that sociology was not simply the subjective interpretation of action and that sociologists had to avoid making personal value judgements on the social phenomena they investigated.

This idea of value-freedom in sociological research – or indeed in scientific research in general – has not been universally accepted by sociologists. The facts collected in research depend on the questions asked and it has been argued that sociological research is inevitably directed by values – which are cultural products. From this perspective, knowledge is a cultural product. What a society defines as knowledge reflects the values of that society; another society and culture will accord other things the status of 'knowledge'.

Howard Becker is an advocate of the view that sociological research need not, and often cannot, be value-free. In his classic study of deviance, *Outsiders* (1963), he argues that it is difficult to objectively study both 'sides' involved in deviance – the rule-breakers and rule-enforcers – and that whichever group is chosen to study there will inevitably be some bias. Becker suggests that there is a strong case for sociologists representing the views and attitudes of the deviants as it is their views that will be least known about and therefore most open to misrepresentation. C Wright Mills in his renowned introduction to sociology, *The Sociological Imagination* (1970), also makes the point that social scientists cannot avoid choices of values influencing their work. Political and moral concerns are central to sociology and value-freedom is, therefore, impossible. In a similar vein to Becker and Wright Mills, Erving Goffman, in reflecting on his study of mental patients, *Asylums* (1968), argued that it was unrealistic to aim: to be value-neutral:

**To describe the patient's situation faithfully is necessarily to present a partisan view. For this bias I partly excuse myself by arguing that the imbalance is at least on the right side of the scale, since almost all professional literature on mental patients is written from the point of view of the psychiatrist.**

*(Goffman 1968: 8)*

These arguments contrast with the positivist view that scientists must aim to produce value-neutral knowledge and that sociology should aim to be value-free. In her study of the Moonies, Eileen Barker's (1984) approach to her research was guided by her view that sociologists should simply seek facts and not pass opinions or make value-judgements:

**I do believe that passing value-judgements should be an enterprise that is separate from social science. . . . There is little use in a research report that tells more about the researcher's personal values than the phenomenon studied.** *(E Barker 1984: 36)*

The merits of these different positions can be considered when we look at the different methods of research.

Case Study

## Value-freedom in sociology?

**This extract is taken from Alvin Gouldner's (1973) attack on the model of objectivity promoted by positivist sociology.**

Does the belief in a value-free sociology mean that sociology is a discipline actually free of values and that it successfully excludes all non-scientific assumptions in selecting, studying and reporting on a problem? Or does it mean that sociology *should* do so? Clearly, the first is untrue and I know of no one who even holds it possible for sociologists to exclude completely their non-scientific beliefs from their scientific work; and if this is so, on what grounds can this impossible task be held to be morally incumbent on sociologists?

. . . Does the belief in a value-free sociology mean that sociologists are or should be indifferent to the moral implications of their work? Does it mean that sociologists can and should make value judgements so long as they are careful to point out that these are different from 'merely' factual statements? Does it mean that sociologists do not or should not have or express feelings for or against some of the things they study? . . . Does it mean that sociologists should never take the initiative in asserting that some beliefs which laymen hold, such as the belief in the inherent inferiority of certain races, are false even when known to be contradicted by the facts of their discipline? Does it mean that sociologists should never speak out, or speak out only when invited, about the probable outcomes of a public course of action concerning which they are professionally knowledgeable? Does it mean that social scientists should never express values in their roles as teachers or in their roles as researchers, or in both? Does the belief in a value-free sociology mean that sociologists, either as teachers or researchers, have a right to covertly and unwittingly express their values but have no right to do so overtly and deliberately?

I fear that there are many sociologists today who, in conceiving social science to be value-free, mean widely different things, that many hold these beliefs dogmatically without having examined seriously the grounds upon which they are credible. Weber's own views on the relation between values and social science, and some current today are scarcely identical. If Weber insisted on the need to maintain scientific objectivity, he also warned that this was altogether different from moral indifference.

(Adapted from Gouldner 1973: 5–6)

### Questions

**In what ways might the values of a researcher influence the following stages of research: (a) the choice of research issue; (b) the formulation of a hypothesis; (c) the choice of research method; (d) the choice of questions asked (if any); (e) the interpretation of results; (f) the presentation of findings?**

## Different methods of research

When investigating a particular issue or phenomenon, the sociologist is not limited to any one method; indeed using more than one method could provide a fuller and so more valid account. Thus it is important to be aware of the characteristics, strengths and weaknesses of the various methods of research commonly used by sociologists. Our review relates to steps 3 and 4 of the procedure followed by the scientific method detailed earlier (p. 112): the selection of the research method and the carrying out of the research.

All sociology textbooks contain descriptions of different methods of research and cover the same basic areas. The specific methods of research tend to be either quantitative or qualitative, but it is important to emphasize that they only 'tend' to; there are inevitably pitfalls in trying to pigeonhole and categorize and the more sophisticated one's understanding of sociology the more one comes to recognize the overlap between different methods of research. Much sociological research uses aspects of both quantitative and qualitative research. None the less, these broad headings provide a structure for reviewing a range of methods.

We referred earlier to the dispute or 'war' between the advocates of different approaches to sociological research. While various methodological approaches tend to be popular at different times, the extent of the division into an 'either one or the other' approach should not be overstated. Pawson (1989) suggests that the supposed war between positivists and interpretativists has led to certain methodological myths being propagated, in particular, that the two traditions or approaches are mutually incompatible and in a state of permanent dispute. Pawson's position is that quantitative sociology can be based on non-positivist lines. Sociologists should not be afraid to admit that observation is influenced by theory: the fact that sociologists pick and choose the evidence they will examine according to their theoretical interests should not be seen as a failure of positivism. For example, in the sociological study of religion, one researcher might focus on the high proportions of people who believe in God and the growing numbers who express an interest in superstition and new forms of religious expression as evidence to demonstrate the continuing importance of religion in modern society. Another might emphasize declining attendance at mainstream churches as the key evidence on the importance of religion in society.

Pawson also points out that even in 'respected' sciences such as physics the data collected are influenced by theory; even the instruments used by physicists, such as thermometers, have been developed and constructed on the basis of complex theories.

Similarly, it is mythical to see qualitative research as a coherent and superior alternative that can get to grips with the special character of human meaning. Contemporary sociological research, according to Pawson, is essentially pluralistic: in many cases it is necessary to gather information by whatever means is practical and so to use both approaches. The combination of methods to gain a fuller picture of the area being investigated is now generally taken to be a sensible research strategy.

Definition

### Reliability and validity

Examination of the different methods of sociological research should consider the concepts of reliability and validity. The degree of reliability and validity acts as a sort of quality control indicator in the assessment of any particular research method.
**Reliability** occurs when repeated applications of the same technique of collecting or analysing information produce the same results. The extent to which a technique is seen as unreliable will tend to depend on the general perspective of the researcher(s). From a positivist approach interviews should be highly structured so that any interviewer would collect the same types of data from the same respondent. Interviewer unreliability would be a human error that could be eliminated. A non-positivist approach, in contrast, would emphasize the importance of the social context of the interview and would see interviewer 'unreliability' as an inevitable aspect of attempting to understand the social world.
**Validity** refers to the extent to which a technique measures what the researcher intends it to measure. This is an obvious requirement for good research, however the notion of validity applies differently to different approaches to research – to positivist and non-positivist approaches, for example. In general terms, it means the degree to which the findings of research can be relied on and it involves an evaluation of all the methodological objections that can be made about the particular research.

## Quantitative research

### Surveys

The survey is usually a large-scale method of research that involves collecting information from large numbers of people. While this information is typically gathered from questionnaires or interviews, a survey is not limited to any one technique of collecting information. In contrast to qualitative research, which provides a more in-depth study of social life, surveys tend to produce information that is less detailed but which can form the basis for making statistical generalizations over broad areas.

There are many well-known examples of large-scale surveys that have been used in sociological research, including the studies of poverty in the early years of the twentieth century undertaken by Charles Booth and Seebohm Rowntree, the Oxford Mobility Studies of the 1970s and the British Crime Surveys of the 1980s. The British Crime Survey was set up in 1982 to investigate crime through a sample survey of 11,000 households that asked people about their experiences of crime. It was established to address the limitations of official crime statistics, particularly the fact that those statistics include only crimes that are known to the police. The British Crime Survey asked this large sample of people whether they had been victims of crime and whether they had themselves committed any crimes over the previous year. The British Crime Surveys of 1983, 1985 and 1989 have shown that there is a great deal of crime, including serious crime, that does not appear in the official statistics.

Q

What kinds of questions could be asked to find out whether people have been victims of crime?

What do you think might be the problems with and limitations of surveys that ask about people's experiences of crime?

Surveys can be distinguished from other research methods by the forms of data collection and data analysis. Surveys produce structured or systematic sets of data, providing information on a number of variables or characteristics, such as age, sex or political affiliation. As questionnaires are the easiest way of getting such structured data they are the most common technique used in survey research. The analysis of data produced from a survey will provide standardized information on all the subjects being studied, for example, how much television a week people watch or how people intend to vote. Surveys can also provide detail on the causes of phenomena, such as variations in age, and suggest the extent to which this influences television watching or voting behaviour.

Surveys are one method of collecting and analysing data that usually involve large numbers of subjects. They are seen as highly reliable in that the data collected can be easily coded and analysed and should not vary according to the person(s) collecting it. In conducting a large-scale survey it is clearly impossible to investigate every single case or person, which raises the issue of sampling, and whether a smaller number can be used to represent a larger population. However, the fact that the data gained from surveys are necessarily restricted can be seen as a strength, in that it enables the analysis of these data to focus on standardized questions.

Case Study

### Can surveys measure social change?

Surveys involving the collection of information at one point of time are referred to as *cross-sectional surveys*; they provide a snapshot picture. The data gathered provide information such as who would vote for a particular political party or who belongs to a particular occupational grouping. Cross-sectional surveys that are repeated at different times, such as the British Crime Survey or the General Household Survey, allow some analysis of change over time.

*Longitudinal surveys* provide data that enable the analysis of change at the individual or micro-level. One of the best known longitudinal surveys in the UK is the cohort studies of the National Child Development Study in which a sample of children born in April 1958 have been followed from birth and interviewed at various stages of their lives. More recently the British Household Panel Survey has been established at the University of Essex. This is made up of 10,000 people who are to be interviewed annually throughout the 1990s. Such longitudinal surveys are concerned with the behaviour of people over time and are therefore well suited to the analysis of change.

(Adapted from Rose and Gershuny 1995: 11–12)

*Surveys and sampling*

Public opinion polls are an example of sampling for surveys that are particularly prevalent at election times. The key problem with taking a sample is making it representative; sampling is essentially the process of selecting people or information to represent a wider population. Different methods of sampling are available to the sociologist, including probability and non-probability sampling.

**Definition**

**Sampling methods**

**Random sampling** or probability sampling is where all the members of a population have a chance of selection – for instance, all schoolchildren of a particular age in a particular area – and perhaps one in every hundred is selected. Random sampling and quota sampling are the most commonly used methods of sampling.

**Quota or stratified sampling** is the major form of non-probability sampling. Here the technique is to deliberately make the sample non-random by splitting it up beforehand, usually into categories such as sex, age or class, and then selecting a certain number for investigation from each category. For example, if we wanted to find out whether most people in a school or college would prefer to have a longer winter break rather than a longer summer one, then a quota sample might be the most appropriate to use. Rather than just asking the first hundred people what they felt, the total population of the institution could be broken down into quotas, for example 10 per cent administrators, 10 per cent teachers, 10 per cent canteen/cleaning staff and 70 per cent students. A quota sample of one hundred would then include ten administrators, ten teachers, ten canteen/cleaning staff and seventy students.

**Snowball or opportunity sampling** is where one person selected and questioned recommends another person and so on.

**Questions**

What advantages and disadvantages can you think of for using a random sample, a quota sample and a snowball sample if you were conducting a survey of (a) religious attitudes of pupils in a comprehensive school; (b) leisure activities of retired men.

*Criticisms of surveys*

According to de Vaus (1986) the major criticisms of surveys can be classified as philosophical, technique based and political. Philosophical criticisms suggest that surveys cannot uncover the meanings of social action: they neglect the role of human consciousness, goals and values as important sources of action. To some extent these kinds of criticisms are linked with more general criticisms of quantitative sociology as being too rigidly scientific, too focused on hypothesis-testing and the collection of facts and statistics and as neglecting imaginative and creative thinking. Some surveys do, however, try to discover what people (say they) think: the British Crime Surveys ask respondents about their attitudes to crime.

Technique-based criticisms emphasize the restrictiveness of surveys due to their reliance on highly structured ways of collecting data. The statistical emphasis is seen as reducing interesting issues to sterile and incomprehensible numbers.

Political criticisms of surveys see them as being manipulative: the aura of science surrounding them gives power to those who commission and use the data. Survey data can be used to justify and further particular political interests. However, it is important to remember that surveys can provide unreliable information and are sometimes wrong. The surveys carried out before the 1992 general election in Britain predicted a very close-run election; however, the Conservatives were elected for a fourth term of office with an overall majority. The pre-election opinion poll surveys overestimated the Labour vote by 4 per cent and underestimated the Conservative vote by 4.5 per cent. Much of this difference was attributed by the Market Research Society to 'fundamental problems' in the way opinion polls are conducted. With regard to voting intentions there would seem to be a persistent and growing exaggeration of the Labour vote, which suggests that the sampling procedures used are missing a significant proportion of Conservative voters, or that some Conservatives lie about their voting intentions. Concern about the accuracy of survey polls has led to them being outlawed during election campaigns in some countries: in France, for example, they are banned for a period just prior to elections.

## Collecting quantitative data: questionnaires and interviews

Although a number of techniques of collecting information are available to sociologists who conduct surveys, information is usually gathered from questionnaires and/or interviews. While there are clearly differences between questionnaires and interviews – in terms of the way they are administered and the issues and problems they raise – we shall focus here on some of the common elements. Respondents (the subjects from whom information is sought) can be asked questions which are either written down in a questionnaire or presented verbally in an interview

### *Degree of structure*

The questions used in survey research can be asked in a more or less structured form. Both questionnaires and interviews can be very standardized and structured – providing only a limited number of possible responses such as Yes, No and Don't Know or ticking one of a list of statements – or they can be more open-ended and less structured.

The degree of structure affects the extent to which data can be coded and analysed. Using the example of the question on voting given overleaf, it would be straightforward to code Conservative, Labour, Liberal Democrat and Other as 1, 2, 3, 4: such coding would make the statistical analysis of the data easier.

### *Reliability and validity*

As they provide data that are both reliable and quantitative, the use of questionnaires and structured interviews is generally advocated by positivist research in an attempt to provide a scientific basis for sociology. However, these methods do raise some awkward questions concerning the reliability and validity of sociological

Definition

### Question styles

In a questionnaire that aimed to provide information on voting, a *closed-ended* question might be:

How did you vote in the 1992 general election? (please tick)

Conservative
Labour
Liberal Democrat
Other

An *open-ended* question might ask:

Why did you vote the way you did in the 1992 election?

with space left for a lengthy response.

In an interview the structure of the questions can similarly vary: in *structured* interviews the order and wording of the questions is predetermined and each respondent is asked the same questions. In *semi-structured* (sometimes called focused) interviews the questions focus on certain predetermined topics but the interviewers have scope to choose words, to alter the order of questions and to develop points as the interview proceeds. Such interviews are essentially conversations between the interviewer and respondent; the interviewer can follow up points of interest and allow the respondent to talk freely. This style of interview is favoured in the more in-depth qualitative approach and particularly valued by ethnographic researchers. The more structured and formal style, for both questionnaires and interviews, fits in with the quantitative approach to research.

research. How can we be sure that the people we want to interview or question will agree? If they do, can we be sure that they are giving honest answers?

Not only will the researcher have little control over these problems – it is not feasible to force people to be interviewed – but also there is the difficulty of ensuring that the way in which the question is asked does not influence the way that it is answered. It is important to be aware of the danger of leading questions and loaded words in the design of questionnaires and interviews.

#### *Order effect*

Another factor that can influence people's responses to questionnaires and structured interviews is the way in which questions are ordered. In research into *order effect* in survey questionnaires, Schuman and colleagues (1985) noted a marked difference in the responses to the same question. They asked first: 'Do you think the United States should let Communist newspaper reporters from other countries in here and send back to their papers the news as they see it?' and followed this with 'Do you think a Communist country should let American newspaper reporters come in and send back to their papers the news as they see it?' In that order, 44 per cent of Americans asked said yes to the first question. Using a split sample technique, where half the sample were asked the second question first, the numbers agreeing that communist reporters should be allowed to come to the United States

Definition

### Leading questions

**Leading questions are worded so that they are not neutral: they either suggest an answer or indicate the questioner's point of view.**

### Loaded words

**Loaded words excite emotions in the respondent that will be likely to suggest automatic feelings of approval or disapproval: the respondent reacts to the particular word or phrase rather than the question itself.**

**A classic and widely reported example of respondents reacting to a word concerns the different responses to the terms 'working class' and 'lower class'. A Gallup poll survey in the USA in 1933 found that 88 per cent of a sample of the population described themselves as middle class, while only 1 per cent said they were lower class. Members of the sample had been offered a choice of three alternatives – upper, middle or lower class. A similar survey was repeated shortly afterwards with the term 'lower class' replaced by 'working class'; this time, 51 per cent of the sample described themselves as working class.**

rose markedly, to 70 per cent. It would seem that an initial antagonism to foreign, communist reporters was significantly modified once people considered how they would feel about limitations on access to other countries for their 'own' reporters.

### *Bias*

Survey research, with the use of structured methods of collecting data, is seen as the most effective way to provide an objective science of society. As well as the doubts raised concerning the influence of the wording and ordering of questions on the objectivity of such research, the extent to which bias is eliminated from these methods has been challenged. The way in which people respond to questions may be influenced by *prestige bias*, in that answers which might be felt to undermine or threaten prestige may be avoided. People tend to claim that they read more than they do, for instance, or that they engage in more 'cultural' activities than they do. Answers to certain questions can reflect unfavourably on an individual's lifestyle: negative answers to questions such as 'Are you satisfied with your job?' could be seen as being too self-critical, admitting one's life to be a bit of a failure.

Finally, there is also the danger of *interviewer bias*. Even with tightly structured questionnaires and interviews, the respondent might still react to the interviewer – to their age, background or race, for example – and provide answers that it is felt the interviewer is looking for. In his research into the failure of Black children in the US educational system, Labor (1969) found that Black children responded differently to white and Black interviewers; with the white interviewer there seemed to be a sense of hostility that limited the responses from the children. Of course, race is not the only factor that influences interview responses. As Lawson (1986) puts it, 'the interviewee may be antagonistic towards interviewers for no other reason than a dislike of the clothes they are wearing'.

You want to find out about attitudes to (a) unemployment and (b) juvenile delinquency. Give examples of 'loaded words' that you should avoid in framing your questions.

Write down an example of a leading question for both areas of investigation.

Write down a 'neutral' version of those questions.

How might prestige bias and interviewer bias affect the findings from surveys?

In addition to the points listed above, what other factors should sociologists take account of in designing surveys?

This discussion of survey research has not covered the range of research methods that could be put under the heading of 'quantitative' and we shall look at some of the other methods used by sociologists later in the chapter. In essence, quantitative research attempts to follow the scientific method of positivism. The research should be reliable and replicable: the data should be collected systematically and be standardized so that, regardless of who collects the data, the same findings will always emerge. These findings should be generalizable, allowing laws to be established on the basis of them.

In the next section, qualitative research is examined. Here the interest is in the smaller-scale research; the focus is on 'meanings' and 'experiences'. An attempt is made to understand the lives of those being studied, as well as the less structured, informal interviews such research has emphasized the importance of observation. At the risk of being overly repetitive, it should be stressed again that sociological research is not simply an either/or choice and that the trend in recent research has been to use a number of different methods, both quantitative and qualitative.

## Qualitative research

This style of research is closely related to *ethnography*, an approach that has become increasingly popular since the 1960s. Hammersley (1992) highlights a basic disagreement over the definition of ethnography: some see it as a specific method of research and others as a more general approach to research. Here we adopt the latter usage advocated by Hammersley, ethnography being the in-depth study of a specific group or culture over a lengthy period. The emphasis of such study is usually on forms of social interaction (in, for example, a school, factory or juvenile gang) and the meanings that lie behind them.

### Observation

Observation can be either participant or not; however, in sociological research *participant observation* or *fieldwork* (the terms can be used interchangeably in introducing these methods) has been a widely and successfully used approach. Participant observation has its roots in anthropology and the studies of non-western societies by anthropologists such as Bronislaw Malinowski, Edward Evans-Pritchard and Margaret Mead in the first half of the twentieth century. These researchers lived with the peoples they studied, learned their languages and cultures and provided fascinating accounts of such societies. More recently, this approach to sociological research has been used to study groups and cultures within western societies. The work of sociologists at the University of Chicago in the 1930s (led by Robert Park)

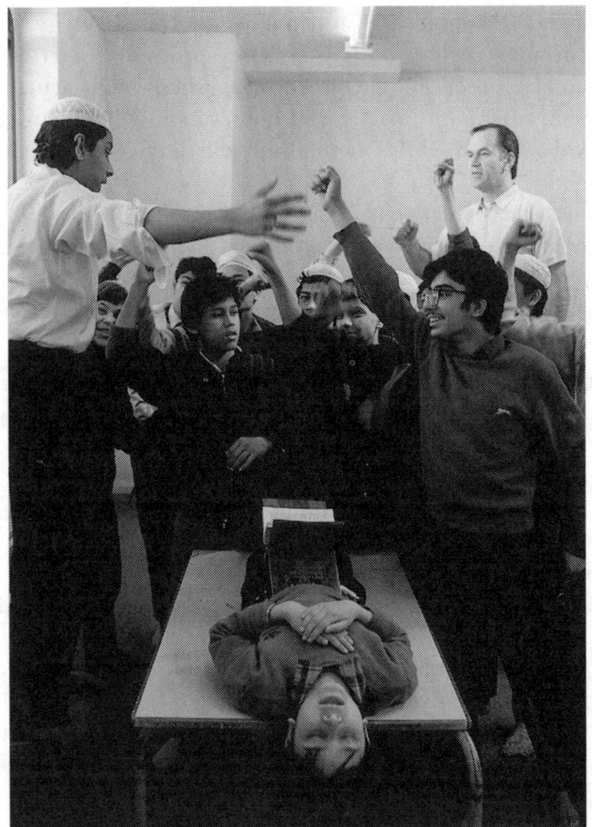

**Fig 3.1** By doing their research in 'real life' settings such as schools, ethnographers seek to understand the different cultural perspectives which influence the way that people act: rehearsal of *Julius Caesar*, East London Mosque school. (Photograph by Adam Woolfitt, courtesy of Robert Harding Picture Library Ltd.)

**Definition**

### Ethnography

Hammersley summarized the key assumptions that ethnography makes about the social world and how it should be studied:

1. An understanding of human behaviour has to be achieved by first-hand contact with it; thus ethnographers adopt a naturalistic focus and do their research in 'real life' settings.
2. Human actions do not consist of fixed or learned responses; to explain such actions it is necessary to understand the cultural perspectives on which they are based.
3. Research should aim to explore the nature of social phenomena rather than be limited to the testing of hypotheses; the emphasis should be on getting at the meanings and motivations that underlie behaviour.

These assumptions indicate why ethnography is linked with qualitative research and explain why ethnography uses methods of research that are less structured and do not follow the traditional scientific model discussed in the previous section.

applied anthropological techniques to the lifestyles they found in the city of Chicago (Park *et al.* 1923). They promoted participant observation, with researchers observing the life of social groups while actually participating in them. Our introduction to participant observation will look at examples of sociological work that have used this method and will discuss some of the issues raised by it.

Q

**Participant observation has been used particularly in the study of unusual and deviant behaviour. One reason for this is the fact that such behaviour is by its very nature liable to be secretive and/or illegal and thus often difficult to study by more conventional means. Why might participant observation be particularly useful for the study of crime and deviance?**

**Participant observation has also tended to be used when researching the less powerful groups in society. Why might this be?**

While other research methods such as questionnaires and interviews can be, and are, used to gain a wider and more general picture of society, participant observation enables the researcher to gain insight into behaviour through direct experience. This does not mean that it is an easy method to use; the observer has to remain neutral while at the same time being closely involved with those being studied. Howard Becker (1963), in his studies of the sociology of deviance, attempted to understand such behaviour through observation and close contact with the people he was studying. He described the role of the participant observer as someone who 'watches the people he is studying to see what situations they ordinarily meet and how they behave in them. He enters into conversations with some or all of the participants in these situations and discovers their interpretations of the events he has observed' (Becker 1982: 247).

### *Gaining access*

Participant observation involves the researcher becoming a part of a group or community in order to study it; initially, then, there is a need to gain access. Although this applies to all social research, it is particularly pertinent in qualitative, ethnographic study. For many researchers the issue of access is not usually problematic: the distribution of questionnaires, for example, does not usually raise this issue. However, getting permission to carry out research in a particular setting and with a particular group is not always straightforward. When Erving Goffman wanted to study a mental institution he took a job as a hospital orderly and in that role observed the day-to-day life of the hospital (which he recorded in his famous study, *Asylums*, 1968).

In reflecting on his research into child abuse, Steve Taylor (1992) highlighted the practical problems of gaining access to study a very sensitive topic. His research proposals were subject to close scrutiny by a number of people including the director of social services for the area where he was intending to conduct his research. As a result, he had to modify some of these proposals and guarantee absolute confidentiality. Once he had got access, Taylor still faced problems in making and keeping relationships with his subjects. He found that the social workers tended to feel scapegoated by the media – perhaps justifiably so as their position in the 'front line' makes them particularly vulnerable to complaints. He argues that researchers need to be sensitive to these kinds of feelings, and not look for and focus on cases that 'went wrong'. As well as the problems of being allowed access to investigate child abuse, Taylor also points out how he encountered examples of dreadful cruelty against children who were brought into care, and how amazed he was when these children were so openly and clearly affectionate to their abusing parents when they visited and tried to get them back.

Research into alternative religious movements similarly raises problems of access. Roy Wallis's (1976) research into the Church of Scientology illustrates this. Scientology was founded by L Ron Hubbard, a science fiction writer, who developed a religious doctrine based on the idea that humans can regain the spiritual powers they have lost through a process of training which would unlock the doors to these powers. The movement has attracted considerable controversy and following since the 1960s. Wallis's interest in studying Scientology was hampered by its reluctance to be investigated. As result he joined and followed an introductory course put on by scientologists and became a participant observer. As a secret or covert participant observer Wallis had difficulty in showing his support for and commitment to the beliefs of Scientology and did not complete the course. Although he later requested, and was allowed, to speak to Scientology leaders, the participant observation gave Wallis additional material and information on Scientology from the perspective of a potential recruit.

**Q** What problems of access would be faced by research into (a) inmate culture in prisons; (b) the divisons of household tasks between partners; (c) sexism and/or racism in the school playground; (d) the decision-making processes of business and companies?

### *The influence of the participant observer*

Once access has been gained, the extent to which the participant observer might influence the group or activity being studied has to be considered. People are likely to behave differently when they are being observed, though this will depend to some extent on whether the subjects are aware of the fact that they are being observed. This raises the important distinction between open (overt) and secret (covert) observation. If the observation is going to be done overtly, the researcher will need to inform the subjects of the research of his or her identity. If it is to be done covertly, the researcher will need to observe under some sort of guise. Even if the researcher does not tell the subjects and they do not know that they are being investigated, the presence of another person may still, unwittingly, affect their behaviour. Covert participation observation, in particular, highlights ethical issues about observing people without informing them (although, incidentally, this is habitually done by journalists reporting on celebrities).

The points raised above about the influence of the participant observer and the ethics of such observation can be illustrated by looking at examples of sociological research.

Eileen Barker's (1984) study of Revd Moon's Unification Church adopted several research methods, including participant observation. Barker considered the argument that in researching religion more information would be gained if the researcher pretends to believe in the religion being studied – if observation is done covertly. This raised for her the ethical question as to whether it was morally permissible to get information through false pretences. In rejecting the covert style of observation, Barker pointed to the psychological difficulties of pretending to hold beliefs and performing actions that go against one's conscience.

Although this sort of dilemma is not confined only to the sociology of religion, it does arise particularly in the examination of secretive religious movements unwilling to be studied. Barker argues that it is possible to carry out overt research even into fairly closed groups such as the Moonies. Although suspicious of outsiders and of publicity, the Unification Church gave her access to a great deal of information and supported her research. Their media image was so bad that the Moonies could not believe that someone who really tried to understand them and listen to them would come up with a worse account than that provided by the media. Barker also pointed out that covert observation can hamper the research by making it impossible to ask certain questions or to appear too curious. In contrast, the recognized, overt observer is expected to ask questions and exhibit curiosity; indeed, they might find themselves being sought out and told things that the believers want to share with a 'stranger' who is not part of the particular organization. Both overt and convert observers have to be careful of the extent to which they influence the behaviour they are meant to be observing.

Two studies of deviant groups that used the method of participant observation and which illustrate the issues and problems that are attendant on this style of research are described in the following case studies.

**Case Study**

### When Prophecy Fails

*When Prophecy Fails* (Festinger *et al.* 1956) is a classic covert participant observation study of a small deviant religious movement that predicted the imminent end of the world. In Christian-based movements this has usually referred to the second coming of Jesus Christ and the establishment of a new heaven and earth, accompanied by the destruction of all sinners. Movements such as the Millerites in the 1840s and the Jehovah's Witnesses have prophesied that the world would end at a certain time (although the Jehovah's Witnesses have now abandoned these specific date-centred predictions).

Festinger and colleagues were fortunate to find a small group who appeared to believe in a prediction of catastrophe due to occur in the near future. The group was located as a result of a story in a provincial paper, the *Lake City Herald.* This story detailed the prophecy of a Mrs Marian Keetch that Lake City would be destroyed by a flood before dawn on 21 December; Mrs Keetch had received messages sent to her by superior beings from the planet 'Clarion' who had visited earth and observed fault lines in its crust. The authors called on Mrs Keetch to discover whether there was a group of believers based around her. Their initial contact with her made it clear that any research could not be conducted openly. Given this, they described their basic research problem as 'obtaining entry for a sufficient number of observers to provide the needed coverage of members' activities, and keeping at a minimum any influence which these observers might have on the beliefs and actions of the members of the group' (Festinger *et al.* 1956: 234).

*(box continued)*

*(box continued)*

The bulk of the study describes how the group prepared for the end of the world and then how the followers came to terms with dis-confirmation of their beliefs. Fascinating though the whole study is, our interest is in the methodology of the research. On the whole, the authors and the additional hired observers they used were welcomed into the group as new converts. It was clear, however, that the involvement of a number of new observers-cum-believers was having a definite influence on the group itself, as the following extract illustrates:

> One of the most obvious kinds of pressure on observers was to get them to take various kinds of responsibilities for recommending or taking action in the group. Most blatant was the situation that one of the authors encountered on November 23 when Marian Keetch asked him, in fact commanded him, to lead the meeting that night. His solution was to suggest that the group meditate silently and wait for inspiration. The agonising silence that followed was broken by Bertha's first plunge into medianship . . . an act that was undoubtedly made possible by the silence and by the author's failure to act himself. (Festinger *et al.* 1956: 241)

As well as issues concerning access, influence and ethics, participant observation raises practical problems. Because of the difficulties involved in gaining access and trust, it is a time-consuming and therefore expensive method. Furthermore, it may well have significant effects on the lives of the researchers as well as the observed, as our second case study demonstrates.

**Case Study**

## Hell's Angels

Hunter Thompson's (1967) study of the notorious San Francisco Hell's Angels motorcycle gangs highlights the potential dangers of covert participant observation.

> My dealings with the Angels lasted about a year, and never really ended. I came to know some of them well and most of them well enough to relax with. . . .
>
> By the middle of summer (1965) I became so involved in the outlaw scene that I was no longer sure whether I was doing research on the Hell's Angels or being slowly absorbed by them. I found myself spending two or three days each week in Angel bars, in their homes, and on runs and parties. In the beginning I kept them out of my own world, but after several months my friends grew accustomed to finding Hell's Angels in my apartment at any hour of the day or night. Their arrivals and departures caused periodic alarm in the neighbourhood and sometimes drew crowds. . . . One morning I had Terry the Tramp answer the doorbell to fend off a rent collection, but this act was cut short by the arrival of a patrol car summoned by the woman next door. She was very polite while the Angels moved their bikes off her driveway, but the next day she asked me whether 'those boys' were my friends. I said yes and four days later received an eviction notice. (Thompson 1967: 52–6)

As well as losing his accommodation, Thompson's research proved physically painful.

*(box continued)*

*(box continued)*

On Labour Day 1966 I pushed my luck a bit too far and got badly stomped by four or five Angels who seemed to feel I was taking advantage of them. A minor disagreement suddenly became very serious. . . .

The first blow was launched without warning and I thought for a moment it was just one of those accidents that a man has to live with in this league. But within seconds I was clubbed from behind by the Angel I'd been talking to just a moment earlier. Then I was swamped in a general flail. As I went down I caught a glimpse of Tiny, standing on the rim of the action. His was the only familiar face I could see . . . and if there is any one person a non-Angel does not want to see among his attackers it is Tiny. I yelled to him for help but more out of desperation than hope. (Thompson 1967: 283)

## Questions

**How did being a participant observer influence Thompson's attitude toward the Hell's Angels and his relationships with people outside the group?**

**What other research methods could provide insights into the Hell's Angels? Give reasons for your answer.**

These case studies illustrate that research by observation is by no means straightforward. Observers, particularly when working in a covert context, have to be detectives – listening, probing and ensuring that their 'cover' is not blown. Some of the practical and ethical considerations that need to be taken into account when pursuing sociological research are examined further in Activity 1 at the end of the chapter.

### *Theoretical problems in participant observation*

In concluding this review of research by participant observation we shall refer to Howard Becker's (1982) reflections on the theoretical problems faced by those who adopt this method. Observational research typically produces vast quantities of descriptive material which the researcher has to analyse. This analysis, Becker suggests, needs to be carried out sequentially, while additional data are still being collected – and these additional data will take their direction from the provisional analysis. Becker distinguishes four stages involved in the analysis of data gathered from observational research:

1 The selection and definition stage. The observer looks for problems and issues that will help provide an understanding of the topic or organization being studied. The researcher will be using available data and material to speculate about possibilities. The credibility of the informants will also have to be considered: do they have reason to lie about or conceal information? In assessing the reliability of evidence, the observer's role in the situation has to be examined: was observation overt or covert?
2 The frequency and distribution of the data have to be checked. Are the events typical? Does every member of the group respond in the same way?

3 The data have to be incorporated into a model which will help to explain it.
4 The presentation of the evidence and 'proof' of the results. Quantitative, statistical data are relatively easy to present in tables and charts. However, the qualitative data gained from observation are much more difficult to present adequately. Such data are less easy to count and categorize; the data are also generally too detailed to present in full, which raises the issue of selectivity of presentation.

## Other methods of research

Our discussion of different methods of research has focused on those most often adopted in sociological investigations: questionnaires, interviews and observation. Other methods of sociological research include the use of experiments and official statistics, most favoured by those who suggest that sociology should aim to be as 'scientific' as possible. Case studies and life histories are used most by sociologists adopting an interpretive approach. Some methods involve sociologists analysing information that already exists and that has been gathered by other people and bodies: the use of official statistics and content analysis are examples of this sort of secondary analysis. By contrast, case studies and experiments are examples of methods that involve sociologists gathering fresh information and evidence in order to investigate social issues.

### Official statistics

Statistics collected by or for the government are referred to as 'official statistics'; they come from surveys conducted or commissioned by the government. These include the census (a survey of the whole population of the United Kingdom every ten years) and smaller surveys based on samples of the population such as the General Household Survey. Official statistics are available to the public through a range of HMSO (Her Majesty's Stationery Office) publications, including the *Annual Abstract of Statistics* and *Social Trends* which provide summaries of statistical information under specific headings, such as Education, Employment or Crime.

Official statistics are a useful source of material for sociologists: they are already available and provide very full information that can be compared from one year to another. However, official statistics are collected by persons other than sociologists for purposes other than social scientific research. Official Crime Statistics, for example, are collected and published by the Home Office and are based on police records of crime; these statistics, then, omit many activities that break the criminal law but remain unknown to the police. There is a 'dark figure of unrecorded crime'. It is impossible to say what this figure may be but common sense would suggest that for each crime the police know about there are likely to be many more that they are not aware of and so unable to record (problems with crime statistics are discussed in more detail in Chapter 13, pp. 523–4).

In addition to the amount of crime not recorded, the official statistics are also influenced by the way that the police enforce the law. Whether the police decide to arrest and recommend the prosecution of individuals or to 'warn' them will affect crime figures, as will the amount of police resources, including police officers. All the way through the process of dealing with crime, decisions are made about whether individuals are cautioned, arrested, charged and convicted, all of which affect the Official Crime Statistics.

**What kinds of problems might the sociologist face in using official statistics on (a) unemployment; (b) religious beliefs; (c) child abuse; (d) homelessness?**

## Content analysis

Content analysis concerns how people communicate and the messages conveyed when people talk or write. Content analysis is widely used to investigate how the mass media transmit ideas and images. If examining the position of women in society, for example, a content analysis of school textbooks would probably find that the majority of characters are males and that women are portrayed in a more limited number of roles than men. A content analysis of television programmes would determine the percentage of leading characters that are male and female. Thus the content of books, television programmes and films can reveal aspects of the society and culture in which they are situated and so can be an important source of information for sociologists.

## Experiments

While experimentation is the standard method used in the natural sciences, and is regularly adopted in psychology, it has not been widely used in sociology. People are liable to act differently ('unnaturally') in an experimental situation compared to how they would in 'real life'; it is difficult to study people in a laboratory and expect them to act normally. This lack of realism might be resolved by not informing people that they are being experimented on, which is an ethical issue itself. However, there are some important and well-known examples of the use of experiments in research into areas of social life.

In the social sciences, controlled experiments allow the researcher to manipulate an independent variable so as to observe and measure changes in a dependent variable. *Variables* can be any measurable characteristic of individuals, groups or societies – income, educational attainment or rate of unemployment, for example. Experiments have been used, for example, to study the effects of violence in the mass media on children's behaviour. Some children were exposed to violent programmes and others to non-violent programmes, followed by comparisons of how each group behaved when provided with opportunities to act violently. The *independent variable* was the amount and type of programme viewed and the *dependent variable* the age or gender of the children. One experiment involved children watching different television sequences – some violent, others not – and then being told that they could hurt or help a child playing in another room by pressing either the 'hurt' or 'help' button (Liebert and Baron 1972). The results of this and many other studies have shown that viewing violence produces increased aggression in the young. However, such experiments are difficult to generalize from; it has been argued that violence on television can make people more tolerant and less likely to engage in real life violence.

The issue of the ethics of experimenting on people was highlighted in the now (in)famous experiments conducted by Milgram (1974). Milgram's hypothesis was that cruelty is not committed by cruel individuals but rather by ordinary women and men who are quite capable of behaving in a cruel manner when they feel it is required of them. Individuals will perform acts they would normally condemn if they are carrying out orders given by an authority they accept.

The volunteers in Milgram's experiments were asked to play the role of either 'teacher' or 'learner'; the teachers were then told to deliver electric shocks to the learners as punishments when they made errors. Although the 'teacher' volunteers did not know the experiment was set up so that no electric shock was transmitted, the majority of them were prepared to deliver what they felt to be severe shocks. When these teacher volunteers were told to force the victim's hands on to the plate through which the shock was supposedly delivered, 30 per cent continued to fulfil the command until the end of the experiment. When the victims were hidden and their 'screams' were not audible, the figure jumped to 65 per cent. Milgram argued that it is quite easy to be cruel towards a person we neither see nor hear.

Milgram's conclusion – that cruelty is social in its origin, rather than just being a personal characteristic – is supported by another 'sociological experiment' undertaken by Zimbardo (1972). This experiment involved volunteers playing the roles of prisoners and prison guards. The experiment was conducted in as realistic a manner as possible, the 'prisoners' and 'guards' dressed appropriately, neither group was allowed to call the other by name and the guards were expected to enforce a range of petty and humiliating regulations. The volunteers were supposed to play their roles for two weeks; however, they became so involved in them that the experiment was stopped after one week for fear that the volunteers might suffer irreparable damage if it ran for the planned length of time. The guards' superiority and the prisoners' submissiveness encouraged the guards to indulge in shows of power: they forced the prisoners to chant filthy songs and to clean toilets with bare hands, for example. It appeared that the apparently normal volunteers had changed into cruel and sadistic monsters. The extent of this cruelty took Zimbardo and his colleagues by surprise. However, it was clear that this stemmed from the social situation of prisoners and guards not from any particular viciousness in the volunteers themselves. The experimenters concluded that many ordinary, generally law-abiding people will easily act in a cruel and even vicious way if such behaviour is required by a superior authority. They also found that a small number of the volunteers stood up to those in power and gave priority to their consciences.

**Q** **List the difficulties with the use of experiments in sociological research.**

**What advantages might experiments have over other methods of research? What particular insight might they provide into social behaviour?**

Due to the artificiality of laboratory-based experiments, researchers often conduct field experiments outside the laboratory. In a widely cited study examining the importance of teachers' attitudes on pupils' performance, Rosenthal and Jacobson (1968) tested how teachers responded to pupils of differing abilities. They randomly selected a number of pupils and told their teachers that they would improve significantly in the future. Although chosen randomly, Rosenthal and Jacobson found when they returned to the school the following year that these particular children had improved noticeably over their classmates.

### Case studies and life histories

Other qualitative approaches to sociological research include case studies and life histories. A case study investigates one or a few particular cases in some depth. Although case studies are only illustrative ('one offs'), they can be used as guides for further research. McNeill (1990) makes the point that, to a certain extent, any piece of qualitative research could be described as a case study given that all such research focuses on a relatively small group or on one particular institution.

A life history consists of biographical material that has usually been gathered from a particular individual, perhaps from an interview or conversation. As well as relying on people's memories, other sources of information are used to build as detailed a picture as possible of the experiences, beliefs and attitudes of that individual; these sources might include letters or newspaper articles. As with qualitative research in general, the emphasis is on the individual's interpretation of behaviour and events. Like case studies, life histories are unreliable as a basis for generalizing about social behaviour, but they can be valuable sources of insight for the sociologist.

## Feminist research

Feminists have been concerned with the techniques used in carrying out research, the way research is practised and more fundamentally with the processes via which sociological knowledge is formulated. They have been concerned with methods, methodology and epistemology. Feminists have produced a scathing critique of orthodox sociological research methodology (Abbott and Wallace 1990).

As research generates the raw material of sociological theory and knowledge, feminists have in turn challenged how sociological knowledge is produced (Spender 1981). They have recognized that knowledge is socially constructed, the product of social and cultural relations. All human beings may generate explanations of the world; not all of them become legitimized and accepted explanations. Women have been excluded as producers of knowledge and as subjects of sociological knowledge. Sociological knowledge has been primarily androcentric, i.e. male centred: 'The theories and methods of sociology, it seems, derive from the visions of the social world afforded to men' (Acker *et al.* 1983).

Feminists have aimed to produce research based on women's experiences which addresses women's oppression in society. They have moved beyond criticism and suggested principles that should underlie feminist research. Just as feminist theory is not a unified body of thought, similarly there is no one feminist methodology (Reinharz 1993).

**Q** Name as many sociology books or studies as you can that have been written by (a) women; (b) men; (c) both.

What topics were covered by the books and studies in your lists a, b and c?

Is there a pattern in the topics researched and written about by female and male sociologists?

## The feminist critique of conventional sociological research

Feminists have examined the sociological research community itself. This includes academic institutions, departments, funding bodies and publishing houses. Collectively these constitute what Liz Stanley (1990) has called the academic mode of production. She argues that the structure of this has contributed to the production of partial or limited knowledge. Certain individuals and groups have greater control over who can carry out research. Those individuals and groups with greater control include heads of department, professors, referees and editors; women are under-represented in these senior positions (Abbott 1991).

Abbott and Wallace (1990) have described orthodox sociological research as 'male stream'; they have described several levels on which sociological research has been male centred.

### *Exclusion of women from research samples*

Research has been androcentric because it has been based on male experiences. Women have often been absent from research samples. Conventional sociological research was carried out by male researchers and on male samples (Abbott and Wallace 1990). The majority of studies during the 1960s and 1970s in the sociology of work were of male paid labour. Findings and theories from these samples were often generalized to the whole population including women. Goldthorpe and Lockwood's famous Affluent Worker Study (Goldthorpe *et al.* 1968) suggested that manual workers were becoming increasingly affluent and were increasingly adopting the values and lifestyles of the middle class. Yet they were describing only the experiences of male workers; women have a different relationship to the labour market (see Chapter 7, pp. 293–308).

### *Deviant males*

Although some researchers acknowledged the presence of the female sex, there was a tendency for researchers to present or interpret their behaviour in a distorted and sexist way (Abbott and Wallace 1990). Women were often compared to a normative masculine standard. Until the work of Angela McRobbie (1991), sociological studies of youth culture tended to be studies of male youth cultures. Gender relations were scarcely mentioned and the subordination of girls to boys was taken for granted rather than analysed. Girls were portrayed as marginal or as playing out stereotypical roles.

Do girl 'punks' play out a stereotypical role? Do you think they are subordinate to the boys?

Think of some other youth cultures. What are the gender relations within those cultures?

### *Areas and issues of concern to women*

Men have set the research agenda and as a result areas and issues relevant to women have been neglected or marginalized. Topics such as sexual violence, domestic labour, childbirth and contraception received very little attention until the feminist

**Fig 3.2** Punks, London. (SS, courtesy of Robert Harding Picture Library Ltd.)

impact on sociology. Feminists believe that there must be feminist research which addresses issues and social problems that affect women. A key aim of feminist research is to make women visible, to observe, listen and record the experiences of women, and to write women back into sociological research.

Feminism has had an impact more broadly on sociology. Mary Maynard (1990) argues that feminism has begun to reshape sociology as many non-feminist sociologists are beginning to consider women and gender in their research and analysis. Feminists have stressed that men are influenced by gender relations, hence gender should be examined not only in research on women, but also in all research.

### Feminist principles

Stanley and Wise (among others) have argued that no one research method or set of methods should be seen as distinctively feminist: 'Feminists should use any and every means available for investigating the condition of women in sexist society' (Stanley and Wise 1983). Feminists have considered how the logistics of particular methods engage with feminist aims, yet it is the principles that underlie selected

Case Study

### Critique of positivism: male reason versus female emotion

Stanley and Wise (1983, 1993) have argued that positivism is problematic for feminists for several reasons. First, it is based on a series of dichotomies, science versus nature, objectivity versus subjectivity, reason versus emotion and male versus female. The problem is that positivism elevates science, objectivity, rationality and the masculine, hence denigrating nature, subjectivity, emotion and the feminine. Feminists have argued that in western scientific thought and culture the masculine is associated with reason, science and objectivity, the feminine with nature, emotion and subjectivity.

Second, Stanley and Wise argue that the positivist emphasis on objectivity divorces sociological knowledge from the social conditions in which that knowledge is produced. Positivistic methodology produces 'hygienic' research in which the researcher is absent (Stanley 1990). Feminists do not see research as orderly, they are suspicious of 'hygienic' research; 'hygienic research in which no problems occur, no emotions are involved, is "research as it is described" and not "research as it is experienced"' (Stanley and Wise 1983). Feminists argue that researchers are always part of the social relations which produce particular findings. Their beliefs and values will shape the research. The private and public spheres, the emotional and the rational, subjectivity and objectivity cannot be separated. Feminists have argued that personal subjective experience is political and important and should be recognized as such in research.

Third, feminists argue that the scientific approach produces a division and an imbalance of power between social science researchers and those people whose lives they research. Social scientists are seen to have special knowledge and skills, they control the research process, they come along and do their research on people. Feminists have been keen to involve women in the research process itself in an attempt to reduce the imbalance of power and hierarchical relations.

In challenging the concept of objectivity, feminists have challenged the view that research should be value-free and apolitical. Indeed they stress that feminist research not only must be of intellectual interest but also should further the political interests of women. Feminists argue that research should raise consciousness, empower women and bring about change (Harding 1987).

methods which distinguish a range of emerging feminist praxis (Stanley 1990). Feminist research involves a commitment to a particular way of practising research and this may shape how the specific techniques are utilized. Liz Kelly (1988) has suggested that feminist 'practice' would be a more appropriate term than feminist methodology to avoid the assumption that particular methods are feminist.

Not all feminists share a common view of research methodology: there is debate about what is and what should constitute a feminist methodology (Harding 1987). However, there does emerge a set of recurring themes and principles, four of which have been selected here, that are of particular importance to feminist, 'practice' (Kelly 1988):

- centrality of women's experience
- research for women
- rejection of hierarchy and empowerment
- critical reflexivity.

### *Centrality of women's experience*

Feminists in their research draw on new empirical resources, the most significant being women's experiences. Feminism moves away from the androcentric position which sees male experiences as central and places women's experiences as the foundation of social knowledge. The task of feminist research is to explore how women see themselves and the social world. McRobbie (1991) argues that the most important achievement of the growing body of feminist research is the revealing of women's hidden experiences both past and present. Underlying all feminist research is the goal of correcting both the invisibility and distortion of women's experiences by providing a vehicle for women to speak through. Women's experience must provide the raw material for theory construction.

Stanley (1990) argues that feminists should be committed to a belief that research and theorizing are not the result of the thinking of a group of experts different from those of 'mere people'. Stanley and Wise (1983) warn of the danger of the emergence of an academic elite of feminist researchers who distance their activities from the mass of women. They stress the need to ground theory in research and stress the two way relationship between experience and theory. Indeed many feminists reject any divide between theory and research.

### *Research for women*

Ramazanoglu (1991a) notes that there has been a distinct shift in feminist methodology from an earlier position which defined feminist research as research of and by women to research that has a political commitment to be for women. Duelli-Klein (1983) differentiates between research on women which merely records aspects of women's lives and research for women which 'tries to take women's needs, interests and experiences into account and aims at being instrumental in improving women's lives in one way or another' (Duelli-Klein 1983).

Feminist research is committed to improving women's position in society. Several feminists have stressed consciousness-raising as a key role for feminist research in the emancipation process. Pollert (1981) in her participation observation of women factory workers did not take a neutral stance but challenged both male managers and female workers about sexist assumptions that they made. She treated the situation as a consciousness-raising process for herself and the women in the factory.

### *Rejection of hierarchy and empowerment*

A basic principle of feminist methodology has been not only to challenge relationships typical of traditional research based on hierarchy and power but also to aim to democratize the research process. Feminists have attempted to restore their subjects as active participants in the research process and to ensure that knowledge and skill are shared equally between researcher and subject. There has been a range of feminist research aimed at empowering and actively involving the women involved (Lather 1988). The aim to change as well as to understand the world means that some feminists build conscious empowerment into the research design.

Kelly (1988) wanted to ensure that all the women she spoke to had some involvement other than releasing information in the research process. She carried out follow-up interviews in which she discussed the themes and analysis that she was developing, asking for and noting the women's opinions. This enabled 'joint interpretation of meaning', allowing the women to have an input into the findings.

The main objectives of the research by Hanmer and Saunders (1984) on violence against women were to feed back their findings into the community, to raise the profile of violence against women and to encourage women's groups in the community to undertake their own research into violence to women. They carried out community-based interviewing, using limited resources, in the Leeds area. This was at a time when Peter Sutcliffe (the so-called Yorkshire Ripper) was at large and they were interested in how this had affected women's lives. They visited organizations in the area whose work in some way concerned violence against women and consulted with neighbourhood groups. They fed the information gained back into the community in order to develop self-help among women. Research involvement led to a local support group for women being established.

Abbott and Wallace (1990) note that the logic of the feminist position on research seems to demand non-individual cooperative research, where the researcher helps the women involved to undertake their own research. The researcher acts as an enabler. Subject and researcher decide together how the findings are to be used, although in practice this is difficult to achieve.

**Q** Suggest how Abbott and Wallace's notion of cooperative research could be applied in the following areas: (a) male and female roles in the catering industry; (b) sexual harassment of girls at school; (c) homelessness; (d) the role of women in the police force

What are the arguments for and arguments against personal involvement in research?

Lather (1988) coordinated a group called the 'Women's Economic Development Project' in South Carolina. Low-income women were trained to research their own economic circumstances, in order to understand and change them. This participatory research design involved eleven low-income women working as community researchers on a one-year study of the economic circumstances of 3,000 low-income women. Information was gathered in order to bring action as a catalyst for change, to raise the consciousness of women regarding the sources of their economic circumstances, to promote community-based leadership, and to set up an active network of rural low-income women in the state to support new legislation concerning women's work and educational opportunities.

### *Critical reflexivity*

Perhaps one of the most challenging developments in feminist practice has been the demand that the researcher must be located in the same critical plane as the researched; if it is accepted that researchers cannot be detached from the process but are part of it then their beliefs, motives and social position must be scrutinized. Researchers should create self-reflexive designs, scrutinizing their own role.

Harding (1987) argues that the most desirable feminist analysis not only researches women's experiences but also locates the researcher directly within the whole process:

> **The best feminist analysis . . . insist that the inquirer her/himself be placed in the same critical plane as the overt subject matter, thereby recovering the entire research process for scrutiny in the results of research. That is, the class, race, culture, and gender assumptions, beliefs and behaviours of the researcher her/himself must be placed within the frame of the picture that s/he attempts to paint.**
>
> *(Harding 1987: 9)*

This is part of the attempt to restore subjectivity. It necessitates the researcher becoming visible and not the objective, detached, pretended object of orthodox research. This is a response to the recognition that the experiences, cultural beliefs and behaviours of feminist researchers shape the results of their analysis no less than do those of male researchers. Feminists must recognize that their role will always be central to the research product and be honest and explicit about this. The presence of the researcher as a human being cannot be avoided therefore; researchers must use this rather than pretend it doesn't exist.

Much of feminist research now shares this process of 'conscious reflexivity' (Kelly 1988). Feminists doing research examine their own role and also use their own experiences to help make sense of the women they are researching. Kelly interviewed women about their experiences of sexual violence. She openly acknowledges that her research was the end product of both the responses from the women she spoke to and her own interpretation of the experiences she was examining. It was a two-way process. In documenting her own involvement with the research, Kelly explains how while she had been involved in the women's refuge movement she became aware of the extent of violence against women, which led her to select violence against women as an area of research. She discusses how doing the research impacted on her life, how she became sensitized to instances of sexual violence in everyday life and herself recalled incidents of sexual violence while carrying out the research. This helped her to understand various aspects of her research, in this case how common it is to suppress painful experiences. She identified with women who did not have the words to tell or even understand what happened; this directly shaped her theorizing, leading her to explore in detail how sexual violence is defined by women.

Kelly stresses that the interaction of her experience with the women's experiences was crucial for understanding it and defends the feminist case for subjectivity:

> **Moving between the interviews and my own experiences and reactions was an integral part of the research methodology. Had I 'turned out' these responses I would probably not have noticed or fully understood the importance of the aspects of women's experience of sexual violence.** *(Kelly 1988: 19)*

Mirza (1991), in her research on the experiences of young black women in a comprehensive school, also builds in reflexivity. She identifies herself as a Black feminist who recognizes racism and sexism. She documents how she had experienced racism in school as a young woman. She argues that these experiences did not make her 'biased' but gave her a deeper understanding of the young women's experiences.

A research product is always filtered through the consciousness of the researcher, so it is argued that researchers must openly examine their beliefs, values and emotions. Feminists point out that researchers should not degrade or attempt to remove these but value and utilize them in their research.

## Feminism and method

While researching certain experiences of women, feminist researchers have found existing techniques, or the conventional ways of using these techniques, inappropriate. In her research on the transition to motherhood Oakley (1981) has exposed the limitations of conventional sociological criteria for interviewing. After six months as an observer on a maternity ward in London, Oakley met with and interviewed sixty-six women on four occasions during their pregnancy. In this context she found that as a feminist she had to reassess how she had been trained as a sociologist to carry out interviewing. She argues that in many textbooks the interview is presented as distanced from normal social interaction. Interviewing is often presented as a clinical research tool: in order to maximize data collection the subject must be put at ease, yet at the same time the interviewer must remain detached to avoid 'interviewer bias'. In order to gain cooperation, interviewers must strike up 'rapport' but avoid involvement. Interviewing is presented as a one-way process in which the interviewer gathers information and does not emit any information. The relationship between interviewer and interviewee is hierarchical and it is the body of knowledge possessed by the interviewer that allows the interview to proceed successfully. Oakley is critical of this model which, she argues, is a product of the desire for scientific status.

Feminist researchers argue that bias is introduced when an interview is taken out of ordinary everyday relations and becomes a constructed and artificial relationship. Stanley and Wise (1983, 1993) also argue that the traditional (scientific/orthodox) model is 'unnatural': people in social interaction do not act as automatons, it creates an artificial interaction, likely to produce unauthentic responses. The orthodox model is highly problematic for feminists whose aim is to validate the subjective experiences of women. Oakley (1981) points out that so-called correct interviewing is associated with a set of values that in our patriarchal culture are more readily associated with the masculine such as objectivity, detachment, science and hierarchy.

Oakley argues that interviewing, which relies on subjectivity and equality, is devalued as it does not meet the'masculine' standards of social science, rationality and scientific objectivity and that it has been seen as potentially undermining the status of sociology as a science. In the social science model of interviewing, feeling, emotion and involvement are conventionally denigrated.

The traditional model of research derives from a set of attitudes that regards people as objects to be manipulated; this contradicts feminist principles (Ehrlich 1976). The hierarchical model of interviewing is not conducive with feminist principles which challenge all relations of dominance and submission. Oakley suggests that when a feminist interviews women, it would be morally and ethically wrong to use prescribed interviewing practice.

In her research Oakley (1981) discussed with women personal and intimate issues in repeated interviews, which inevitably meant that a personal relationship evolved. Oakley built up relationships and became close friends with some of these women; she answered all personal questions and questions about the research. As she herself was a mother the women would ask about her opinion and experience of young babies and she would share her experience with them. Oakley argues that she could have taken no other direction than to treat the whole research relationship as a two-way process: the relationship cannot be left in the interview room but exists beyond the interview.

When interviewing women about their experiences of sexual violence, Kelly (1988) adopted an interviewing methodology similar to Oakley. She rejected objective aloofness and a refusal to enter into dialogue. She stressed how artificial, unnatural and impossible the orthodox approach would have been considering that she was speaking to many of the women about very intimate and for some traumatic experiences: 'It is difficult for me to envisage being detached when I remember how shaken many women were during or after my interviews' (Kelly 1988: 11).

Feminist methodology therefore rejects any paradigm that does not place the subjective centrally, that denigrates personal experience and involvement rather than recognizing its value: 'personal involvement is more than dangerous bias – it is the condition under which people come to know each other and to admit others into their lives' (Oakley 1981: 58).

Oakley and Kelly argue that their approach meant that women provided much more detailed and rich information than the traditional model ever could. Interviewing does not have to be exploitative but if practised in a more democratic way it can provide a vehicle for women to document their own lives.

**Q** Both Oakley and Kelly emphasize the importance of developing close personal relationships with the women they were researching.

What difficulties might they have in doing this?

How might this influence the information they gathered?

Do you think this matters?

---

## Quantitative or qualitative methods?

It is often assumed that feminist research involves only qualitative methods. Some feminist sociologists have been critical of quantitative methods. They have argued that questionnaires and structured interviews pre-code experience producing a false body of data which distorts the actors' meaning. Graham (1984b) claimed that survey methods and structured interviews 'fracture women experiences'. Surveys are seen to mask or misrepresent the position of women in male-dominated societies and fragment women's experiences.

Barbara Smith (1987) argues that there are aspects of women's lives which cannot be pre-known or predefined in such a way. Some feminists have stressed that the female subject gets lost in social science survey research. Oppression is such that it cannot be 'neatly encapsulated in the categories of survey research' (Graham 1984b). On many of these points feminist arguments overlap with ethnographic researchers.

**Q** On the whole feminists have favoured qualitative methods, claiming that they fit more comfortably with feminist principles as well as being more appropriate and sensitive to women's experiences of oppression. Why do you think feminist research has 'favoured qualitative methods'?

Although feminist research has tended to be defined in terms of qualitative research, a growing body of feminists have attempted to break down the distinction between quantitative and qualitative research. They have stressed that there is nothing inherently sexist with quantitative research methods and techniques such as surveys (Epstein Jayaratne 1993; Kelly *et al.* 1992; Pugh 1990). If used sensitively they can be utilized to compliment broader feminist research aims.

Case Study

**Women's Leisure, What Leisure?**

**Green, Hebron and Woodward (1990) used a social survey in combination with unstructured interviews and discussion groups in what is the most comprehensive study of women's leisure to date in Britain. They wanted to collect both general information about the types and levels of women's leisure participation as well as more detailed knowledge about women's perceptions and attitudes to leisure. They argue that as feminists are concerned both to understand patriarchal structures that oppress women and seek to change them they must utilize the strengths of quantitative evidence. They argued that using a survey enabled them to generalize from their results to the larger female population and to exert greater political influence. They wanted to provide a statistical body of research that could actually form the basis for more informed policy decisions. They pointed out that policy-making bodies were more impressed with statistical data and it was crucial that such bodies examine and take note of their findings. They were fully aware of the limitations of survey method in the context of women's lives and hence used qualitative research to compliment the quantitative data. Hence the shift towards triangulation (see pp. 142–3) is also reflected in feminist research. Feminists will use any method appropriate to expose and oppose women's oppression.**

Many feminists have also proposed that the use of qualitative methods does not necessarily overcome some of the problems identified with quantitative methods. Stacey (1988) has pointed out that although ethnographic methods seem ideally suited to research in that they involve empathy and allow for an egalitarian reciprocal relationship, they may expose the research subjects 'to greater risk of exploitation, betrayal and abandonment by the researcher than does much positivistic research' (Stacey 1988: 21).

## Feminist research: an overview

Feminist research has involved discussion and criticism, primarily from feminists themselves, which reflects the diversity of feminism (see pp. 79–88) and the feminist concern to constantly challenge the status quo. Stanley and Wise (1983) argue that research inevitably involves power relations and the question of exploitation has been raised by many feminists engaged in research: 'The researcher's goal is always to gather information, thus the danger always exists of manipulating friendships to that end' (Acker *et al.* 1983).

McRobbie (1991) argues that feminists must recognize that whatever methodology is used there is an unequal distribution of privilege. Feminist researchers often represent powerful educational establishments. They must acknowledge that this may be one reason why women are willing to participate in research. For example she criticizes Oakley (whose work was considered earlier) who she claims fails to consider the imbalance of power between herself as a researcher and the young mothers:

> **She does not concern herself with the fact that pregnant, in hospital . . . the women were delighted to find a friendly articulate knowledgeable woman to talk to their experiences about . . . their extreme involvement in the research could also be interpreted as yet another index of their powerlessness.**
>
> *(McRobbie 1991: 79)*

There is always the danger that some women will use experiences of women's oppression to further their careers, with women's suffering becoming a commodity. Angela McRobbie honestly speaks about the fact that doing research feels sometimes like 'holidaying on other people's misery'. She describes an interview with a 19-year-old women who had been brought up in care:

> **I was almost enjoying the interview, pleased it was going well and that Carol was relaxed and talkative. Yet there was Carol with her eyes filling up with tears as she recounted her life and how her mother had died.** *(McRobbie 1991: 77)*

McRobbie also challenges the assumption that the feminist researcher will necessarily understand the women because of their 'shared' oppression. Women have a multiplicity of experiences. Feminists may have valuable personal experience but they cannot assume this will be the same as those they are researching. While feminism attempts to foster sisterhood, it cannot naively assume that women are bound together purely on the grounds of gender.

Although the principles enshrined in feminist research cannot eliminate the possibility of exploitation they can serve as a check against it. As part of the conscious reflexivity feminists attempt to be explicit and open about power relations as they operate in the research process.,

There is a great deal of debate about what a feminist methodology should contain. It is important to remember that there is not one easily identifiable feminist research methodology (Reinharz 1993). Yet there is some consensus about principles that feminists should consider when carrying out research. Kelly notes this ambivalent position:

> **There is not, as yet, a distinctive 'feminist methodology'. Many of the methods used by feminist researchers are not original. What is new are the questions we have asked, the way we locate ourselves within our questions and the purposes of our work.** *(Kelly 1988: 5–6)*

## Triangulation

In this chapter we have introduced and discussed a range of methods by which sociologists gather new evidence and apply already existing information in order to address social issues and problems. We have tried to present these methods as complementary rather than mutually exclusive ways of pursuing research. The complementary nature of different research methods is shown when two or more methods are combined in one research project. The term given to the combining of research methods is triangulation. In these situations, the researcher does not have to rely on one method, so that the pitfalls of one particular methodological approach can be avoided or lessened by the use of another approach as well. Although sometimes described as a recent development, research that combines more than one technique for collecting information is by no means new. Most textbooks refer to examples of sociological research that have used triangulation and we shall look briefly at a couple of examples here.

Roy Wallis's (1976) study of the Scientology movement was mentioned earlier in the context of participant observation. Wallis not only followed an introductory course run by the movement as a participant observer, but also interviewed and sent questionnaires to Scientologists and ex-Scientologists to provide him with a broader picture of the movement.

Eileen Barker (1984) used a number of different research techniques in her work on the Unification Church of Revd Moon – the 'Moonies'. Barker adopted three main approaches – interviews, participant observation and questionnaires. About thirty in-depth interviews were carried out with a random sample of Moonies. These interviews extended over several hours and were fairly unstructured explorations of the attitudes and feelings of individual followers. Participant observation enabled Barker to examine the interaction and interrelationships between Moonies on a day-to-day basis. Finally, around 450 questionnaires were given to Moonies, along with another 100 to non-Moonies as a comparison, to provide statistical evidence of patterns and relationships within the movement and with the wider society. In reflecting on her research, Barker points out that each technique is interdependent. The questionnaire would not have been so thorough if she had not previously done a number of extended interviews with Moonies and actually lived with them and observed the so-called 'brainwashing' process at first hand; indeed the participant observation familiarized Barker with the appropriate language to use in the questionnaire. As well as these three approaches to collecting first-hand information on the Moonies, Barker's research involved discovering and reviewing what others had written about the Unification Church and other new religious movements. The reviewing of secondary literature – library work – is an important first step in all sociological research.

## Summary

- Sociological research involves the gathering of relevant material and data and interpreting and analysing them.
- In undertaking research the sociologist can use a variety of techniques. The method chosen will be influenced by the nature of the issue being examined and by the theoretical approach favoured by the researcher.
- One issue that has been central to the style of research adopted has been the extent to which sociological research should follow the methodological approach of the natural sciences. A by-product of this issue has been the debate over whether sociology can and should be value-free and the extent to which the data gathered by sociologists are reliable and valid.
- Quantitative research is most closely associated with the conventional scientific methodology. Surveys involve collecting data from large numbers of people, usually from questionnaires or interviews that ask people about their behaviour and attitudes. Surveys are typically based on a sample of respondents drawn from a specific

population. The use of official statistics and content analysis are other examples of quantitative research.

- Qualitative research gathers more detailed information from a smaller number of respondents. The focus is on the experiences of people and the meaning given to such experiences. Observation, in-depth interviews and case studies are qualitative methods.
- Feminist research has criticized orthodox sociological research methodology for being 'male stream', i.e. centred on men. Although feminist research is not a unified body of research, a major focus has been on women's experiences and how an understanding of them can help to explain and improve women's position in society.
- Throughout the chapter it has been stressed that sociological research is not confined to one or other specific method; indeed, a combination of methods is often the best strategy for the researcher to adopt.

## Further reading

Durkheim, E (1964) *The Rules of Sociological Method*, New York: Free Press.
With so many secondary sources available, there is a tendency not to consider reading the originals. However, Durkheim's key work on the studying of social phenomena is no more 'difficult' to read than some of the commentaries on it. It is a short study that sets out the requirements that rigorous sociological research needs to follow.

Gilbert, N (ed.) (1993) *Researching Social Life*, London: Sage.
This is a collection of papers that outlines the main ways in which sociologists gather data and describes a range of ways of analysing such data. The connections between quantitative and qualitative research methods and their theoretical bases are emphasized throughout. The papers are written by experienced social researchers who reflect on their own research experiences.

McNeill, P (1990) *Research Methods*, 2nd edn, London: Routledge.
Morison, M (1986) *Methods in Sociology*, London: Longman.
These are two short, introductory books that summarize and review the strengths and weaknesses of different research methods available to the sociologist.

Maynard, M and Purvis, J (eds) (1994) *Researching Women's Lives*, London: Taylor & Francis.
A series of papers written by key practitioners that detail the current debates within feminist research.

Pawson, R (1989) 'Methodology', in M Haralambos (ed.) *Developments in Sociology*, vol. 5, Ormskirk: Causeway Press.
This paper provides a strong critique of the tendency to divide sociological research into either positivism characterized by quantitative methods or phenomenology characterized by qualitative methods.

Stanley, L and Wise, S (1993) *Breaking Out Again: Feminist Ontology and Epistemology*, London: Routledge.
This updates and reviews the main arguments in feminist thinking and research since the original *Breaking Out* – an important feminist text, first published in 1983, that challenged conventional positivist practices in sociological research.

Becker, H S (1963) *Outsiders: Studies in the Sociology of Deviance*, New York: Free Press.

As well as 'methodology' texts, it is good practice to look at the methodological sections of specific sociological studies. Such sections may be found in the introductions to studies or as appendices. Chapter 9 in Becker's classic study of deviants, *Outsiders*, for instance, discusses some of the key issues attendant on studying deviant behaviour.

## Activities

### ■ Activity 1 Problems in researching a deviant religious movement

**This extract illustrates some of the difficulties of research into deviant religious movements. It is taken from the methodological appendix to *When Prophecy Fails* (Festinger *et al.* 1956), the classic study of a small group who believed that the world was about to be destroyed that we referred to earlier in the chapter (pp. 126–7).**

In our investigation of the group which gathered about Dr Armstrong and Marian Keetch, our observers posed as ordinary members who believed as the others did. In short, our investigation was conducted without either the knowledge or the consent of the group members. This situation presented a number of problems that merit detailed discussion. . . .

Both of our 'local' observers were under pressure at various times in mid-December to quit their jobs and spend all their time with the group. . . . Their evasion of these requests and their failure to quit their jobs at once were not only embarrassing to them and threatening to their rapport with the group, but also may have had the effect of making the members who had quit their jobs less sure that they had done the right thing. In short, as members, the observers could not be neutral – any action had consequence. . . .

Observing, in this study, was exhausting work. In addition to the strain created by having to play an accepting, passive role vis-à-vis an ideology that aroused constant incredulity, which had to be concealed, observers frequently had to stay in the group for long hours without having an opportunity to record what they had learned. . . .

The circumstances of observation made it impossible to make notes openly except on a single occasion, the meeting of November 23, when the Creator ordered that notes be taken. Apart from this, it was difficult to make notes privately or secretly, for the observers were rarely left alone inside the house and it was necessary to be ingenious enough to find excuses for leaving the group temporarily. One device used occasionally was to make notes in the bathroom. This was not entirely satisfactory, however, since too frequent trips there would probably arouse curiosity if not suspicion. . . .

Our observers had their daily lives to care for as well as the job, and were subject to occasional bouts of illness or fatigue from lack of sleep. The job was frequently irritating because of the irrelevancies (from the point of view of our main interest) that occupied vast quantities of time during the all-night meetings.

(Festinger *et al.* 1956: 234–46)

## Questions

You are a sociologist just starting a research project seeking information on ritualistic abuse. A friend tells you they know of a satanic cult meeting regularly in the area. Most of their activities are harmless but there is a rumour that an animal is to be sacrificed at Halloween. Your friend tells you they know of a member looking for new recruits. You feel this is a rare opportunity of getting access to the group which may not come up again.

How would you continue with your research? (Consider the advantages and disadvantages of alternative methods of research that might be used.)

Suggest the practical and ethical consequences of the methods of research that you propose to follow.

## ■ Activity 2 Problems in researching female factory workers

This extract is taken from a study of female workers in an electronics factory in Malaysia. It focuses on the problems faced by these workers, who were termed 'Minah Karan' (meaning, roughly, 'loose women'). Daud's (1985) research was carried out in a number of stages and involved several research methods: participant observation, in-depth interviews, official documents and surveys (based on questionnaires and including a follow-up survey five years after the initial research).

I started my fieldwork as a participant observer, by becoming a factory worker. It began in October 1976 and continued until June 1977. During the first five months I worked in the Variable Resistance Section (V.R.) and the Electrolytic Capacitor Section, working two-and-a-half months in each section. Then I carried out my in-depth interviews with 100 workers over a period of one month. At the end of the last two months of fieldwork I conducted a survey of 111 respondents to see the changes that had occurred between 1977 to 1982. . . .

Although work in the factory numbed the mind and tired the body, my research was strengthened by real knowledge of the long hours and tough working conditions. I discovered many advantages in becoming a worker in order to understand the real problems and situations of factory life. I could feel for myself the tiredness, depression, tension and other physical hazards; I discovered a lot of truth about the nature of a worker's life. For instance, cohabitation and illegitimate pregnancies were usually subjects for gossip. However, the workers talked about this only within their own groups. I believe that if I had not undertaken participant observation by becoming a factory worker, such private and personal matters would be very difficult to uncover. . . .

During the first few days of my work I had asked them whether it was true, as people claimed, that factory workers cohabit. They replied that it was nonsense. But when they had accepted me as one of them, they told the truth. . . .

There were drawbacks in becoming a worker and doing this 'undercover' work. Some of them are discussed below: The chief methodological problem was to keep my notes up to date while working normally with others. Each workers sat near another in the 'line' and I found there was a general interest in what I did and how I behaved since I was a newcomer. Only when there was a break could I write my notes in any detail. By becoming a worker I had to follow work regulations. Workers were not allowed to talk during work. . . .

A few seniors especially the 'line leaders' became suspicious and were unhappy with me. They feared that I might be appointed to the supervision post after my 'training'. They viewed this as unfair since they were senior to me. They resented me and refused to be friendly. It is undeniable that becoming a factory worker was a very good method of carrying out my fieldwork. In not disclosing my real identity, I always had to be careful and be on the alert for rumours and suspicion among the workers. . . .

The major advantage of using structured questionnaires is that it produces systematic data on information obtained during observation and in-depth interviews. But, there are also a few disavantages in using this method, namely: I noticed great differences in the quality of information obtained through the methods of participation and descriptive survey. . . .

For example, when I asked about their attitudes towards the management, during my period of anonymity, almost all the workers condemned the management and said they hated it. But when questioned during the descriptive survey, half the sample said the management was 'good'. I think this is because they were trying to be careful when answering the questionnaires administered by someone who was no longer their fellow-worker.

(Adapted from Daud 1985: 134–41)

## Questions

**What sort of information on factory work would each of the methods adopted by Daud be likely to provide?**

**To what extent can these different methods be seen as (a) valid sources of information; (b) reliable sources of information?**

Chapter 4

# Work

**Chapter outline:** Introduction • Marx and the labour process within capitalism • Braverman and *Labour and Monopoly Capital* • The organization of work • Industrialism and de-industrialization • *The Coming of Post-Industrial Society*? • Fordism and mass production • Post-Fordism and flexibility • The labour market • Unemployment • Trade unions • The globalization of economic life • Summary • Further reading • Activities

**Learning objectives**

When you have studied this chapter you should be able to address these key questions:

- What are the difficulties involved in defining 'work'?
- How has wage labour changed with the development of capitalist societies?
- Why have certain areas of employment expanded and others declined?
- What impact have these changes had on the structure of the labour market and on the role of trade unions?
- What effects has employment had on different groups in society?
- To what extent has capitalism become a global phenomenon?

## Introduction

People who speak grandiosely of the 'meaning of work' should spend a year or two in a factory.
(quoted in Fraser 1968: 12)

'So, what is it that you *do*'? This is a familiar question, one you will no doubt have been asked on numerous occasions. Although it is a question that seems obvious and commonplace it is worth some reflection as it makes huge assumptions about the way we live and how we categorize ourselves, our world and the knowledge we have of that world. The answer to this question, as we all instantly recognize, is to do with work. But what kind of work? Housework? The work we carry out as part of our hobbies or leisure activities? The work of caring for relatives or children? No, generally not. Almost always we tell people about our employment, the work that we are paid a regular income for, and those without such work might reply that they are currently without work or that they are 'not doing anything at the moment'.

Paid employment is, of course, by no means *all* that we do and people who are unemployed do not suddenly cease to exist – even if they may feel, and get treated, as though they do. Delineating between work and non-work is an extremely difficult thing to do. Imagine you come across someone sawing a piece of wood. They could be doing this as part of a hobby or doing it for a friend for a 'payment' of some kind. Perhaps the person involved is a joiner or maybe they are being forced to do it at gunpoint! The point is that simply observing a task will not serve as an accurate guide as to whether it will count as work or not. What is crucial is the context within which the activity takes place.

**Fig 4.1** Teaching a child to read may be seen as work when done by a teacher and non-work when done by a parent. (SS, courtesy of Robert Harding Picture Library Ltd.)

Q Identify two activities that are conventionally seen as (a) work; (b) non-work.

What are the characteristics that distinguish them?

What activities are seen as both work and non-work within different contexts (consider, for example, Fig 4.1)

In a society such as ours paid labour is most often equated with work – in the above example only the person sawing the wood as a joiner would be seen to be 'at work'.

The contemporary centrality of wage-labour in many societies cannot be assumed and is in no sense a 'natural' or fixed state of affairs. That it often appears to us in this way is the outcome of a complex mix of social and economic changes, upheavals and struggles played out over a long period of time (Marx 1970). But in an 'advanced' capitalist society like the UK it is paid employment that has come to form a cornerstone of many people's lives, their sense of self and well-being, and the nucleus around which the bulk of wider social relationships gravitate. Given this it is justifiable to begin with the classic analysis of wage-labour within capitalism, that of Karl Marx.

## Marx and the labour process within capitalism

For Karl Marx (1818–83) *labour* was the quintessential human activity (see pp. 51–4). Not in the narrow way in which we have come to understand labour today but labour in the broadest sense – a purposeful and sensuous interaction between people and nature. How people organized themselves in the act of production was the starting-point for Marx's materialist method: 'Thus the first fact to be established is the physical organisation of these individuals and their consequent relation to the rest of nature' (Marx 1967: 42). Individuals, for Marx, 'begin to distinguish themselves from animals as soon as they begin to produce their means of subsistence' (Marx 1967: 42). The manner in which people 'produce their means of subsistence' forms the basis of Marx's basic unit of historical categorization, the *mode of production*.

**Definition**

### The mode of production

This has two key components:

- **a labour process** the manner in which purposeful human activity fashions objects and the tools (often referred to as the means of production) with which this is done
- **the social relations of production** the relationships that form within and around the labour process.

It is only within the *capitalist mode of production* (CMP) that *wage-labour* comes to predominate. Essentially, within capitalism *labour power*, the mental and physical ability to labour, becomes all that a property-less working class has to sell to those who own the means of production – the ruling or capitalist class. Within the CMP, labour itself becomes a commodity. For an agreed period of time a worker relinquishes control of his or her labour power to the capitalist, who will then put it to use in an attempt to create surplus value and realize a profit in the marketplace. The CMP is thus an inherently exploitative, antagonistic and class-ridden socio-economic formation and it is within CMP that *alienation* becomes endemic to wage labour and a perennial condition and experience for workers (see pp. 53–7 for an elaboration of these concepts). As Marx states, 'The whole system of capitalist production is based on the fact that the workman sells his [*sic*] labour power as a commodity' (Marx 1967: 571).

## Braverman and *Labour and Monopoly Capital*

Harry Braverman (1974) attempted an extensive application of the Marxist analysis of the labour process for the twentieth century in *Labour and Monopoly Capital* (LMC). He argued that work within the twentieth century was undergoing a process of debasement and *deskilling* – hence the subtitle of the book, 'The Degradation of Work within the Twentieth Century'. In the era of 'monopoly capital' there was an intensification of the *division of labour* – the tendency towards a specialization of tasks – and the systematic, rational and 'scientific' application of managerial methods to work.

### Taylorism

The most important catalyst and representative statement for such a management approach, according to Braverman, was to be found in F W Taylor's (1967) book *The Principles of Scientific Management* (first published 1911). For Taylor, management's problem was essentially exerting total, or 'direct' (Friedman 1979), control over the workforce. Taylor reasoned that a workforce could not be trusted to maximize its output and efficiency on its own. 'Skill' represented something of an unknown to management and offered the workforce numerous opportunities to limit its output and subvert and deflect managerial authority. The following comment from Taylor is indicative of his perspective:

> **hardly a competent workman can be found in a large establishment, whether he works by the day or on piece work, contract work or under any of the ordinary systems of compensating labour, who does not devote a considerable part of his time to studying just how slowly he can work and still convince his employer that he is going at a good pace.** ***(quoted in Braverman 1974: 98)***

Thus, Taylor believed that skilled tasks had to be broken down into simple and more 'manageable' operations and subjected to detailed and intensive timing – via time-and-motion-study – and monitoring. An essential part of this was to ensure that 'All possible brain work should be removed from the shop and centred in the planning department' (Braverman 1974: 113). This was a process that Braverman laid great stress upon and described as the 'separation of conception from execution'. Braverman thought that this systematic 'deskilling' was inevitable within twentieth-century capitalism and would extend to all types of occupations throughout the economy. Thus the future for 'skilled' work and workers themselves within capitalism looked bleak.

Case Study

## Factory time

I work in a factory. For eight hours a day, five days a week, I'm the exception to the rule that life can't exist in a vacuum. Work to me is a void, and I begrudge every precious minute of my time that it takes. When writing about work I become bitter, bloody-minded and self-pitying, and I find difficulty in being objective. I can't tell you much about my job because I think it would be misleading to try to make something out of nothing; but as I write I am acutely aware of the effect that my working environment has upon may attitude towards work and leisure and life in general....

After clocking-in one starts work. Starts work, that is, if the lavatories are full. In an hourly paid job it pays to attend to the calls of nature in the firm's time. After the visit to the lavatory there is the tea-break to look forward to; after the tea-break the dinner-break; after the dinner-break the 'knocking-off' time. Work is done between the breaks, but it is done from habit and is given hardly a passing thought. Nothing is gained from the work itself – it has nothing to offer. The criterion is not to do a job well, but to get it over with quickly. Trouble is, one never does get it over with. Either one job is followed by another which is equally boring, or the same job goes on and on for ever: particles of production that stretch into an age of inconsequence. There is never a sense of fulfilment.

Time, rather than content, is the measure of factory life.

Time is what the factory worker sells: not labour, not skill, but time, dreary time. Desolate factory time that passes so slowly compared with the fleeting seconds of the weekend. Monday morning starts with a sigh, and the rest of the working-week is spent longing for Friday night. Everybody seems to be wishing his life away. And away it goes – sold to the man in the bowler hat.

People who speak grandiosely of the 'meaning of work' should spend a year or two in a factory. (Fraser 1968: 11–12)

### Questions

Can we draw any parallels between this type of factory work and other forms of work?

What do you think are the social/personal/economic consequences of the types of feelings described in the passage?

## Braverman and the labour process debate

Braverman's book proved to be extremely influential and was the catalyst for what was to become known as the *labour process debate* (R Brown 1992; Thompson 1983; Wood 1982). As a result of this debate LMC has been subjected to an intense and prolonged critique. However, the subsequent elaboration and further discussion of LMC's omissions and shortcomings have greatly enhanced our understanding of work and employment. It is therefore worthwhile spending some time reviewing some of the more pertinent criticisms of LMC.

### Braverman and skill

Given that Braverman's work has often been given the shorthand label of the 'deskilling thesis' and that the notion of skill obviously figures centrally within his investigations, it is somewhat surprising to find that nowhere in LMC does he systematically define, or even take to task, what 'skill' actually is or how it can be recognized. Braverman talks of 'skill' as though it were an axiomatic and unproblematic category which we all understand in a similar way. We should in no way dispense with the category of skill or portray it as being in some way false or illusory. However, it is important to bear in mind that the notion of skill is a socially and historically specific category which requires close sociological and empirical investigation.

Q What do you think constitutes 'skill'?

Why do you think the work that women do is often not seen to be skilled?

The creation of skill operates within relations of power and influence. Think of the ways that trade unions and professional bodies struggle to get their work defined as being 'skilful' in some way. We should reflect on why it is that the work women do (very often work that is extremely similar to that of men) is often not defined as being 'skilled', has less status and is consequently not so well rewarded financially. Much work away from the 'formal' sector of paid employment, especially domestic labour, is not regarded as being skilled or even 'proper' work. However, consider how much knowledge, physical effort and manual dexterity is involved in preparing, cooking and serving a meal for a group of people day after day. (If you doubt that there is any great skill involved in such a task then try it sometime!) That most of the work done which is regarded as skilled and/or has a high status is generally carried out by white men, often from a middle/upper-class background, is not a mere coincidence and requires some explanation.

The implicit datum from which Braverman judges work within the twentieth century is a romanticized 'Golden Age' of skilled craft workers, a masculine world of artisans using a creative combination of hand and brain to fashion intricate goods and artifacts. This is an accusation Braverman refutes without any real conviction: 'I hope that no one draws . . . the conclusion that my views are shaped by nostalgia for an age that cannot be recaptured' (Braverman 1974: 6–7). This is not to say that such workers never existed, or do not exist now, and that we should not lament their 'deskilling' but Braverman offers little proof that this was ever the work experience for the vast majority. Braverman does not operate with the norm or average from the past given that in the history of human toil it is probably fair to say that most people have been employed to pick things up and put them down again! Braverman also ignores the way that new 'skills' are created and have emerged throughout the twentieth century – for example, think of those people who work in the new telecommunications industries, with information technologies, computer programs and in the new service industries, to name but a few. Throughout the CMP the creation and recomposition of skills has always provided something of a counterbalance to the destruction of skills – however we define skill!

## Braverman and the influence of Taylorism

Braverman's assumption about the widespread influence of 'Taylorism' has also been cast in doubt (Burawoy 1985; Littler 1982; Wood 1982). It is by no means clear that Taylor and his writings had the profound impact on management practice that Braverman assumed to be the case. There was much resistance to Taylorist forms of management at all levels within many organizations. Leaving aside the huge amount of effort that a Taylorist 'direct control' strategy requires on the part of management there is no reason why the same principles of 'scientific management' could not be turned on management themselves – especially middle management. Braverman's rigid and dogged use of 'Taylorism' as a coherent and dominant set of practices also greatly underestimates the variety and range of managerial methods employed within workplaces to best ensure efficient production and maintain 'acceptable' and 'realistic' levels of control over the workforce. As Grint says, 'Taylorism, at least in its total form, as a unique and discrete managerial strategy, rather than just one more form of an increasingly rationalized approach to management, had a very limited application anywhere' (Grint 1991: 188). In many ways Taylorism can best be understood as a metaphor for the widespread intensification of the division of labour and the minute detailing of tasks within many workplaces in the twentieth century, part of Max Weber's all pervasive rationalization of many areas of social and economic life within capitalist societies (Gerth and Mills 1991).

## Braverman and workers' resistance

Another rather glaring omission from LMC revolves around Braverman's 'heroic' admission that 'no attempt will be made to deal with the modern working class on the level of its consciousness, organization or other activities' (Braverman 1974: 27). Braverman admits that this is a 'self-imposed limitation to the objective content of class and the omission of the subjective' (Braverman 1974: 27). Not to include an appreciation and discussion of workers' 'subjectivity' and 'agency' in his discussion of the development of the labour process greatly undermines the authenticity and power of Braverman's analysis. It is also something of a surprise, to say the least, for someone who was such a committed Marxist. The history of wage-labour within capitalism is fundamentally a history of struggle, resistance, subversion and sheer bloody-mindedness as well as being about domination, complicity and subordination. If we accept the Marxist understanding of the labour process outlined above it could hardly be otherwise.

Resistance from the workforce can materialize in a variety of ways. Strikes, walk-outs, go-slows and work-to-rule are only the most visible, and organized, instances of workers' resistance. Less obvious but at least as significant, when taken in aggregate, are the countless occasions when workers deliberately, and often literally, 'put a spanner in the works' and subvert, renegotiate and reorder managerial authority through their own 'subcultures' (Roy 1954). Willis put it well when he wrote that people 'thread through the dead experience of work a living culture which isn't simply a reflex of defeat' (in J Clarke *et al.*1979: 188). Workers can sabotage machinery, limit their output, deceive the person from 'time-and-motion', hide in the toilets, go 'on-the-sick', jam the photocopier, break the drill, destroy the accounts, stop for a 'ciggy'. . . . All of these actions, and a million others, have to be coped with in some way by management. Therefore it is crucial that we take into account the subjectivity of the workforce to properly understand the development of the labour process within capitalism (Littler 1982; Burawoy 1985). Resistance is not only derivative but also determinative of the labour process (Burawoy 1985).

**Case Study**

**Resistance**

The women protested and resisted the target and grading system, individually and collectively, on a day-to-day basis. The work-study analysts were often marked out as the main enemy and were constantly discussed – at times, more vehemently than higher levels of management. These women were seen as the perpetrators of a system which presented to the shopfloor targets which could not be reached, let alone surpassed to allow for a bonus to be earned. It is the encounter between the work-study analyst and the shopfloor worker which encapulates the collision between labour and capital, as this is the point at which the contract for the sale of labour power is realised and where labour power is turned into labour time and, thus profits for the company. . . .

[One] timed a woman and didn't ask if she could bring the clock out. It's against the rules. The girls are only timed if they agree to the clock coming out and it has to be visible to the girl. Well, this time it wasn't. She did it on the sly and when the girls found out they walked off the job. The nearest thing we've had to a strike here. We had to get John to sort it out. They have no idea what they are doing with their clocks and their minutes.

Outside the coffee bar, a row was developing which looked as though it might erupt into a walk-off. Gillian's unit had just been given minutes for making a baby garment – a tee-shirt which was edged, and had pants to match. Gillian was looking distraught and said: 'I hate this minutes thing; it's the worst part of my job. I feel sick, I've got a headache. Every time the minutes are given there is a row, every time.' Lisa, the assistant supervisor, was also looking very worried as the fury from the women grew. Some sat defiantly with arms folded while others talked together in small groups. The unit had disintegrated. (Westwood 1983: 49–51)

## The organization of work

We have seen that maintaining control over a workforce is no easy task. Such a recognition has been the catalyst for a huge effort on the part of managers and a whole host of analysts, consultants and academics to devise ever more efficient methods to organize, control and increase the productivity of a workforce. Evidence of this can be seen in the seemingly never-ending stream of 'new' managerial methods and techniques, the impressive edifices of management and business schools seen in many large cities and the appearance on bestseller lists of 'management books' (Peters and Waterman 1982; Peters and Austin 1985). A former chairman of ICI, John Harvey-Jones, even fronted a popular TV series in the guise of a managerial 'troubleshooter'. In the space available we can only outline some of the more influential discussions, managerial strategies and techniques of work redesign.

### Bureaucratic control

R Edwards (1979), in an influential study, offers a framework for understanding the development of managerial strategies within the twentieth century. This involves three stages (see box).

Definition

**Managerial strategies**

- **Simple control** management control via open displays of power and the personalized imposition of control and order
- **Technical control** an intensive division of labour and the pacing of work via machinery (classically, the assembly line)
- **Bureaucratic control** managerial authority becomes increasingly depersonalized and diffused through a hierarchical system of impersonal rules and procedures. Companies use internal career ladders and labour markets to reward workers' commitment to the ideals and aims of the company. Control here is embedded in the social and organizational structure of the firm.

Although R Edwards (1979) provides a useful shorthand account of attempts to exert control over the labour process he has been taken to task as to how prevalent such a system of bureaucratic control was (Grint 1991) and how successful it was in overcoming resistance and 'incorporating' the workforce. Rules and procedures, no matter how detailed, rarely cover every potentiality; control can never be that absolute. Further, rules can be subverted or they can be kept to rigidly – the basis of the long-established tactic of 'work-to-rule' – in such a way that the 'system breaks down'. The inflexible nature of bureaucratic and rigid systems can often be their Achilles' heel and when workers stop giving of themselves, organizations can often shudder to a halt (Gorz 1979).

### Giving the workers some 'responsible autonomy'

Friedman (1979) points out the limitations, some of which were discussed above, of *direct control* (DC) methods (exemplified by Taylorism). He suggests that managerial strategies have emerged to overcome these limitations and increasingly involve giving the workforce a measure of what he terms *'responsible autonomy'* (RA); we can also understand these changes as being part of a move from 'low trust' to 'high trust' systems (Fox 1974). RA methods seek to empower workers by giving them some degree of control and decision-making in the process of production and attempt to incorporate the 'subjectivity' of the workers through aligning them more closely with the goals and aims of the company. This has been part of a long-standing interest in the *'humanization'* of work.

## Work humanization and redesign

Two main techniques of work redesign are job rotation and job enlargement. *Job rotation* does nothing to change particular work tasks but entails moving workers around a number of jobs at regular intervals in order to reduce boredom and stimulate some interest through variety. *Job enlargement* involves merging a number of work tasks together to form a more complex and extended single operation. Obviously these methods carry with them dangers of having the opposite effect of that intended as both could lead to an intensification of tasks and a deterioration of working conditions.

*Job enrichment* revolves around an attempt to empower workers by giving them, in a way antithetical to the doctrines of Taylorism, not only a variety of work tasks but also an element of control and planning. Many repetitive and simplified production jobs could possibly be enriched, 'by the inclusion of tasks such as machine maintenance, elements of inspection and quality control, or machine setting' (Fincham and Rhodes 1994: 207). Again, such methods have met with mixed success. As one worker memorably put it

> **You move from one boring, dirty monotonous job to another dirty, boring monotonous job and somehow you're supposed to come out of it all 'enriched'. But I never feel 'enriched' – I just feel knackered.** *(Beynon and Nichols 1977: 16)*

Variants of *team working* have been tried within a wide range of organizations. *Quality circles* are the best known method of team or group working and are most closely associated with work experiments in Japan.

**Definition**

### Quality circles

An aspect of the Japanese model that receives attention is *ringi seido* or bottom-up management, which is operationalized through the use of quality circles. Quality circles involve small groups of between five and ten employees who work together and volunteer to meet regularly to solve job-related problems. Usually meetings take place during company time, but the frequency varies; some are weekly while others are monthly. Normally though not always led by supervisors, circles aim to improve quality, reduce production costs, raise productivity and improve safety.

Specific characteristics distinguish quality circles from other managerial techniques such as project groups, joint problem solving and job laboratories. Firstly, quality circles have a permanent existence and meet regularly, and are not *ad hoc* creations to solve specific problems. Secondly, participants decide their own agenda of problems and priorities. Finally, all circle members are trained to use specialized tools of quality management which include elementary statistics.

Three important assumptions underlie quality circles: one, all employees, and not just managers or technical experts, are capable of improving quality and efficiency; two, among employees there exists a reservoir of relevant knowledge about work processes, which, under conventional work practices, is difficult to tap; three, quality is an integral part of the entire production process. It is not an adjunct but the responsibility of every employee. (H Clarke *et al.* 1994: 364)

In the mid-1980s quality circles were found in at least 400 UK companies (H Clarke *et al.* 1994: 366). Organizing workers into collaborative work groups obviously represents a major break from the assumptions about workers' behaviour implicit within Taylorist or DC methods. Workers themselves can decide how to overcome production problems and reach production targets instead of all such responsibility being delegated to management; in some cases workers even have the power to stop the production line. At a company level there has been a move away from the classic bureaucratic and hierarchical firm, characterized above by Edwards, towards much 'flatter' and less stratified organizations with fewer layers of middle management between the workforce and top-level management. US computer giants IBM and Compaq are examples of 'flat' organizations that also utilize team working.

**Q** Consider the following occupations: shop assistant, waiter, teacher and cleaner.

How might 'job enrichment' be applied to these jobs?

What problems might arise from this?

---

### Japanization

Debates about the potential for the *Japanization* of production methods and work organization created a great deal of interest in the western industrial world in the 1970s and early 1980s (Sayer and Walker 1992; Thompson 1990). At that time many envious corporate eyes were casting anxious glances to the 'East', to the spectacular growth of the Japanese economy and the success of companies such as Toyota and Nissan. Such was the impact of a 'fact-finding' visit to Japan in 1980 on the head of Ford Europe (Bill Hayden) that it led to the company establishing a new calendar, replacing AD with AJ – 'After Japan'.

Japanization is a word that defies precise definition, being a catch-all term to describe a range of methods and production techniques – none of which, when taken in isolation, is particularly original – which essentially involves a combination of the 'holy trinity' of flexibility, quality and teamwork. These elements are central to the work organization most closely associated with Japanization; the *just-in-time system* (JIT). Put simply JIT 'is a system for delivering the exact quantity and defect-free quality of parts just in time for each stage of production' (Fincham and Rhodes 1994: 50). Such a system relies upon *total quality management* (TQM) whereby components must have 'zero defects' to ensure that production is not interrupted while faulty parts are being replaced. A system of *kanban*, where components are instantly replenished when required, and of *zero stocks*, not holding 'buffer stocks' of components or partially completed assemblies, is also crucial to the smooth running of the JIT system. Work innovations such as quality circles are used to help to ensure that production is closely monitored by workers and total quality can be maintained. Flexibility of labour is also a crucial requirement and JIT is a system that often entails the reworking of 'traditional' union practices (McIlroy 1995; Thompson 1990).

It is important not to exaggerate the importance of Japanization within western economies – in the UK in the mid-1980s Japanese companies employed about 15,000 workers compared to the 450,000 employed in US companies. Also the take-up of Japanese methods by western companies has been patchy and not enthusiastically embraced (Thompson 1990). Implementing QCs and JIT systems operate best within workplaces that are characterized by cultures of 'high trust' as opposed to the cultures of 'low trust' (essentially the culture of 'us-and-them') that are typical of many UK working environments. In many ways Japanization operates most powerfully as a motivating force for western management and workers, as companies strive to meet the challenge from the east, and as a term that serves as a summation of 'best practice' and a datum from which we should measure ourselves by.

## Industrialism and de-industrialization

### The march of industrialism halted?

For long period, particularly after the Second World War, capitalism and 'industrialism' were increasingly seen as panaceas for the ills of all societies. *Convergence theory* explained how many previously diverse societies, particularly those from the eastern bloc and the western industrial societies, were travelling along a basically similar trajectory of social and economic development (Kumar 1978). The USA, in particular, was seen to be at the end of this long evolutionary path (Burns 1969; Kerr *et al.* 1962; Rostow 1960). The development of industrial societies in the post-war period was linked up with powerful notions of 'progress' and 'modernity' and it seemed that most of the major social and economic problems in the industrialized world either had been solved or were about to be. Such extravagant claims were not solely down to the apologists for the capitalist system as the advanced industrialized nations had indeed experienced some remarkable social changes. Unemployment had to a large extent been contained (especially when compared to the misery of mass unemployment in the 1920s and 1930s), economic growth had increased consistently, and wage levels and 'spending power' had reached unprecedented levels for many millions of people across the western world. For the first time travel abroad became a realistic possibility for many, as did the purchase of, among many other things, cars, washing machines, television sets and record players.

To all intents and purposes capitalist industrialism, and the huge surpluses created by the manufacturing sector in particular, were seen to have solved most of the pressing social and economic problems encountered in the 'Great Depression' of the 1920s. However, as the 1970s wore on, the industrial world appeared to be undergoing a series of far-reaching changes. Prime among them was the onset of *de-industrialization* – the reduction, in terms of employment and output, of the manufacturing and extractive industries. Such was the importance attached to successive developments that some thought that we were on the threshold of another 'Great Transformation' (Kumar 1978).

### De-industrialization

Most advanced capitalist societies have apparently been undergoing some form and degree of de-industrialization. Although we have to be extremely careful how we measure de-industrialization (Allen and Massey 1988), for example employment can decline while output can actually increase in many industries, it seems to be the case that the composition of the workforce has changed dramatically in the post-war period. Certainly the statistics make for dramatic reading. In the UK in 1946 the manufacturing, construction and mining industries employed about 45 per cent of the labour force. By 1990 this had dwindled to around 20 per cent. The teaching profession now employs more people than mining, the steel industry and shipbuilding combined. To take the example of Scotland, one of the first industrialized nations, employment levels in a variety of occupational categories seem to show a marked shift away from the 'industrial sector'. In 1911 183,000 people were employed in the metals, minerals and chemicals industries; by 1993 this had declined to 36,000.

During the same period employment in banking, finance, insurance and business services rose from 23,000 to an astonishing 204,000 (Lee 1995). A similar statistical profile can be shown for the UK as whole and for other advanced industrial societies. The question arises, given the collapse of manufacturing employment and the general shrinking of industry (whatever definition we care to use), as to what extent we can continue to call a society like the UK 'industrial' in any meaningful sense? This is a question of great importance given that many of the occupations that are now disappearing were often the ones that were considered to be 'real' or 'proper' jobs. The trades, skills and work that made up these jobs – for example in mining, shipbuilding and engineering – were of course male dominated and classic sites of masculine occupational cultures (J Clarke *et al*. 1979; Morgan 1991). The iconography, meanings and powerful imagery of such occupations in many ways became synonymous, within industrial societies, with work generally and were often used erroneously as templates for all work. Something, incidentally, which much 'sociology of work' – not long ago subsumed under the general heading of 'industrial [*sic*] sociology' – has done relatively little to counter. This is why 'de-industrialization' is about more than simply the demise of particular jobs but involves, among other things, the dismantling of social and cultural relations and a renegotiation of the meaning of work itself – particularly as a vehicle for masculinity.

At a broader level de-industrialization, given the spatial division of labour (Massey 1994), varies across geographical areas. This means that the social fabric and economies of certain regions can be particularly badly affected. This is evidenced, in the UK, in the huge pools of unemployed labour and industrial collapse of areas such as the north east of England, Clydeside and South Wales as they deal with, often painfully felt, social and economic restructuring (Massey and Allen 1988; Allen and Massey 1988).

## *The Coming of Post-Industrial Society?*

Some observed the changes that were taking place within many advanced industrial societies differently and in an altogether more positive and optimistic light. The collapse of employment in industry, or the manufacturing and the extractive industries to be more accurate, has been seen as symptomatic of the emergence of a new order. In particular the growth of employment in the *service sector* is seen to be a development of great significance. Some commentators argued that we are witnessing, and living through, the emergence of a new social formation – a break with previous societies that was as clear and revolutionary as the break between agricultural and industrial society.

The best known and most influential statement of this *post-industrial* thesis or vision was put forward by Daniel Bell (1973) in *The Coming of Post-Industrial Society.*

For Bell the type of employment which is most common becomes a central and defining feature of society. Within pre-industrial societies, agricultural employment predominates, factory work is the norm within industrial society and, Bell argues, employment in the service sector becomes the largest occupational category of post-industrial society.

Within industrial society the rational pursuit of economic growth was the 'axial principal' around which large swathes of social and economic life were organized. People were now, according to Bell, less involved in the 'fabrication' of things and more involved in the manipulation, storing and processing of information and knowledge. For Bell post-industrial society was also the 'information society'; information processing and knowledge generation have become the 'axial principle' of post-industrial society.

The huge advances in information technologies and global communications networks had provided the catalyst, and offered the opportunities, for a revolution in the workplace. The new types of work that people do will involve less capitalist rationalization and control and will be less alienating than the jobs associated with 'industrial society'. 'White collar' (as opposed to 'blue collar') and professional jobs would become the norm. Knowledge and 'professional elites' will hold power and influence in society and will replace the marginalized and anachronistic industrial ruling classes. Indeed, given that the old industrial working class would wither away, so too would class lose its importance as a major social divide and source of collective identity. Centres of information, knowledge, innovation and dynamism, such as universities and centres of research-and-development, will become the nerve centres of post-industrial society, not the factory or the industrial complexes of old. The new knowledge elites could utilize the new technologies available to plan and forecast the future more effectively, thus freeing society from the fluctuations and cyclical uncertainties of the old industry-based economy. Generally, post-industrial society would be a more stable and harmonious society within which there would be more time for creative and leisure pursuits and the drudgery of most people's work would be alleviated through the sensitive and systematic application of new technologies.

All versions of post-industrial theory (Touraine 1971) have been subjected to a sustained and thorough critique (Kumar 1978, 1995; Webster 1995) but they continue to display a remarkable longevity and resilience. Perhaps this is because they tap into widely held notions and fears about the pace of change of social and economic life and the ambiguous role of the bewildering range of new technologies. Post-industrial visions paint a generally positive and possibly comforting picture which many people find appealing and are wont to cling to. However, the shortcomings of 'post-industrial' theory are many and far reaching.

## The difficulty of defining services

The move to a service economy and the growth of people working in service occupations are central to discussions about post-industrial society and are used as incontrovertible evidence that we are undergoing a change of great significance. However, the definition of a service occupation or the service sector is notoriously difficult to achieve (Massey and Allen 1988). 'Services' are sometimes described as being 'anything that can not be dropped on your foot', the absence of a physical product being crucial. However, we immediately run into problems given that a wide variety of tasks which are generally included within most classifications of the service sector such as catering, laundering and many financial services very often do deal with a tangible product or 'thing'.

Definition

**Services**

There are four different uses of the term 'services'.

- **Service industries** these make up the service sector.
- **Service occupations** these are present in all sectors of the economy and alert us to the fact that clerks, accountants, cleaners, catering staff, among others, are common and integral to many different industries and organizations, whether they be engineering plants or advertising agencies.
- **Service products** these refer to the fact that even manufacturing firms produce these in terms of 'follow-up services', service contracts, information services, etc.
- **Service functions** this category draws attention to the ways that many manufactured goods provide a 'service' to some degree, e.g. TVs and videos provide a 'home entertainment' service and washing machines and irons service people's laundry needs.

(Gershunny and Miles 1983)

The problem of operating with a 'service sector' and 'manufacturing sector' distinction is that it blinds us to the interdependent and hugely complex nature of modern economies and the division of labour – something which Durkheim brought to our attention a long time ago. The use of labels such as 'services' and 'the service sector' tends to homogenize a heterogenous group of activities. This is sociologically and empirically problematic as it glosses over a myriad of different labour process, work environments and experiences. The term 'services' is a highly unsatisfactory social construction. However, it is probably unrealistic to expect people to dispense with the term completely but we have to treat it with great caution. The 'service sector' is a 'rag-bag of industries as different as real-estate and massage parlours, transport and computer bureaux, public administration and public entertainment' (Jones, quoted in Webster 1995: 42). It is difficult to see how such a definite and crucial change as the move from industrial to post-industrial society could be based on such a flimsy and fractured foundation.

## Post-industrialism: a radical change?

The extent of the change brought about by the developments discussed above is a matter of some controversy. Commentators such as Toffler (1970, 1980) maintain that we are witnessing nothing short of a revolution. However, as Kumar (1978, 1995) notes, service jobs have long been critical to any capitalist society; in fact Scotland's 'service sector' was the major employer as long ago as 1900. No capitalist nation in fact has ever had the majority of its workforce employed in the manufacturing sector – with the exception, for a brief time, of the UK (Webster

1995). Also post-industrial theorists give no compelling reasons as to why the decline in manufacturing jobs is such a cataclysmic change any way. Why not, for instance, highlight the collapse of employment in agriculture and forestry? We have given some statistics which highlighted the decline of manufacturing in Scotland (p. 161). Over the same period employment in agriculture and forestry plummeted from 238,000 in 1911 to only 27,000 in 1993 (Lee 1995). As Kumar suggests, if there *has* been a startling change in the structure of capitalist societies then it has been of one from agricultural employment to service employment (Kumar 1978). However, we rarely hear of discussions about a 'post-agricultural society'.

Wage-labour (for Marx, the basis of the whole system of capitalist production) is still of course the predominant employment relationship. Many types of work often included within the service sector, such as work in the tourist industry, catering and cleaning, are poorly paid, casualized, characterized by insecurity and subject to the same kinds of rationalization and control that were supposed to be the preserve of industrial work.

Certainly 'fast-food' restaurants, to take one example from a growing sector of employment, often display a level of control and systematization that Ford and Taylor would have been proud to have achieved. At McDonald's we are told that a 'quarter pounder is cooked for exactly 107 seconds. Our fries are never more than 7 minutes old when sold . . . [we] aim to serve any order within 60 seconds' (quoted in Abercrombie and Warde 1992: 180).

**Case Study**

## McDonald's

The sheer number of fast-food restaurants has grown astronomically. For example, McDonald's, which first began franchising in 1955, opened its 12,000th outlet on March 22, 1991. By the end of 1991, McDonald's had 12,418 restaurants. The leading 100 restaurant chains operate more than 110,000 outlets in the United States alone. There is, therefore, 1 chain restaurant for every 2,250 Americans.

The McDonald's model has not only been adopted by other hamburger franchises but also by a wide array of other fast-food businesses, including those selling fried chicken and various ethnic foods (for example, Pizza Hut, Sbarro's, Taco Bell, Popeye's, and Charley Chan's). . . .

This American institution is making increasing inroads around the world as evidenced by the opening of American fast-food restaurants throughout Europe. (Not too many years ago scholars wrote about European resistance to fast-food restaurants.) Fast food has become a global phenomenon; consider the booming business at the brand-new McDonald's in Moscow where, as I write, almost 30,000 hamburgers a day are being sold by a staff of 1,200 young people working two to a cash register. There are plans to open 20 more McDonald's in the remnants of the Soviet Union in the next few years, and a vast new territory in Eastern Europe is now laid bare to an invasion of fast-food restaurants.

Already possessing a huge Kentucky Fried Chicken outlet, Beijing, China, witnessed the opening of the world's largest McDonalds', with 700 seats, 29 cash registers and nearly

*(box continued)*

*(box continued)*

1,000 employees, in April 1992. On its first day of business, it set a new one-day record for McDonald's by serving about 40,000 customers. In 1991, for the first time, McDonald's opened more restaurants abroad (427) than in the United States (188). The top 10 McDonald's outlets in terms of sales and profits are already overseas. By 1994, it is expected that more than 50 percent of McDonald's profits will come from its overseas operations. It has been announced that starting in 1992, McDonald's will start serving food on the Swiss railroad system. One presumes that the menu will include Big Macs and not cheese fondue. (Ritzer 1993: 2–3)

**Questions**

**How far do you think a society like the UK shows evidence of 'McDonaldization'? Give examples.**

**What spheres of work and employment do you think would be impossible to 'McDonaldize'?**

As Beynon suggests,

> **If we take industrialisation to mean the production of commodities through the use of machinery aided with rational systems of organisation, the post war period can be seen as one in which areas of life hitherto unaffected by the march of capital were subjected to this process. . . . Add to this the mechanisation of banking, transportation and the home and we have the bones of an on going industrialisation thesis and the *extended* rather than the *post*-industrial society.**
>
> *(quoted in Abercrombie and Warde 1992: 180)*

Certainly Beynon's prognosis can be further supported if we look at the growth of industrialism as an international rather than a national phenomenon. Countries such as Taiwan, South Korea, Indonesia and Brazil are all experiencing rapid economic growth which is based on an unbridled capitalist industrialism. So the case for post-industrialism becomes even more difficult to sustain if we look at the global picture (Webster 1995).

## Fordism and mass production

More than anything else the image of people working on an assembly line (immortalized in Chaplin's film *Modern Times*) epitomizes the way that many of us think about work in the twentieth century Henry Ford's creation – the Model T – has become the emblem of *mass production*. Ford pioneered the organization of mass production (within which the assembly line was only *one* element) for the production of complex commodities such as the Model T.

**Definition**

**Fordist mass production**

Sabel describes this as 'the efficient production of one thing' (1982: 210); it operates along the following principles:

- long runs of standardized commodities, the Model T being the classic example
- the use of fixed or dedicated machinery which is tooled up to produce many thousands of identical components
- the widespread use of unskilled labour within the production process
- an intensive and extensive division of labour.

With the systematic application of these fairly simple principles the Ford Company was able to achieve incredible levels of relatively low cost production and Ford's plant in Detroit was quickly churning out vast quantities of cars; by 1913 Ford were producing around 180,000 vehicles a year, more than three times the output of all British companies (McIntosh 1991).

Of course the production of vast quantities of identical, or similar, commodities is pointless if they do not meet a demand in the marketplace. One answer was to increase the purchasing power of the workforce. This was done at Ford in 1914 through the introduction, in a qualified and partial way, of the (in)famous 'five dollar day' (Meyer 1981). It is unclear as to whether the introduction of the five dollar day really was a deliberate attempt to increase the spending power of the Ford workforce or, as seems more likely, was done in order to 'buy off' any organized resistance to the intense pace of work within the Detroit plant and reduce the number of employees leaving the company. Ford plants had exceptionally high levels of labour turnover: in 1913 Ford required around 13,000 workers to operate his plants and in that year alone around 50,000 workers quit (Beynon 1975: 19).

However, the growth of purchasing power for a large section of the working class during the Fordist era came to be seen as part of the Fordist 'bargain' – 'high' wages and spending power and 'continuous' employment in return for putting up with 'alienating' and repetitive work conditions.

Mass production thus required a corresponding *mass consumption*. Mass marketing and the mass media were used to 'create' demands for a bewildering array of products and commodities. Mass unionism, a state-regulated industrial relations framework and, in the realms of politics, general cross-party support over several key objectives – a commitment to 'full employment' being central – provided the essential regulatory mechanisms (often referred to in the UK as the 'post-war consensus') to keep the economy in dynamic equilibrium. Such a series of social and economic arrangements were thought to be particularly prevalent during the classic era of Fordism – roughly the post-war period up to the early 1970s.

'Fordism' has come to refer to more than the mass production of particular commodities and is used as a shorthand way to characterize the organization of a whole social system and a particular historical time period or epoch – the 'Fordist Era' (Gramsci 1971; Harvey 1989). Many areas of social life and a host of activities are said to have been Fordized. Symbols of Fordism are not only automated factories, typing pools or people working 'on the line', but also large housing estates like Drumchapel in Glasgow or Hulme in Manchester, holiday camps, tower blocks and, more grimly, Nazi concentration camps which were organized to mass produce death (Bauman 1989).

### The limits of Taylorism and Fordism: Fordism in crisis?

However, in the late 1960s and early 1970s it appeared that Fordism was showing signs of stress and breakdown. There were a series of shocks to the Fordist system culminating in the 1973 'oil crises'. Many western economies were showing signs of a slowdown of economic growth and a falling away of levels of labour productivity and profits. The long and stable post-war boom was apparently coming to an end. Why? An important reason was to do with the apparent inability of the Fordist labour process to secure further increases of productivity within the manufacturing sector and the inapplicability of Fordist methods to other sectors of the economy, especially the 'service sector'. The technical limits of Fordism had been reached. Waves of strikes across the western world and apparently chronic and endemic problems with workforce resistance and unrest seemed to suggest that workers had also reached their limits within Fordized workplaces. The very inflexibility of the Fordist labour process was showing itself to be a unforeseen Achilles' heel. Consumers were increasingly making demands for individualized goods. Newly emerging social developments such as 'youth' and 'pop' cultures and styles, and shifting patterns of taste and demand exposed the rigidity of Fordism. The stability of the Fordist global system, underwritten and maintained by the huge economic, financial and military might of the USA, was being challenged by the rise of other economies, especially West Germany and Japan.

## Post-Fordism and flexibility

Given the break-up of mass production, mass markets and mass consumption, some commentators have argued that we are witnessing a widespread move towards *post-Fordism* (Hall and Jacques 1989). The key term here is *flexibility*. As within the post-industrial discussion there is an important role for new technologies such as computer-integrated manufacturing systems and new social innovations at work, such as less hierarchical organizations, team working, flexi-time and a range of more flexible work practices – some of which were discussed above, particularly in relation to Japanization.

**Definition**

**Post-Fordist production**

The following are the key elements of a post-Fordist labour process:

- flexible production systems
- a move from economies of scale to economies of scope
- flexible work organization – for example team working and JIT – and a concomitant restructuring of union practices and collective bargaining
- a decentralization of production into more spatially diverse and smaller units
- niche versus mass marketing

Some commentators see these tendencies coming together in the form of the *flexible firm*. The best known and most influential discussion of the flexible firm is that of Atkinson (1984).

Within the flexible firm, management are able to 'flex' production up and down to meet changes of demand in the marketplace. This is achieved through a reorganization of working practices, increased subcontracting and use of agency workers and employing workers on a range of different contracts of employment. This leads Atkinson to make a distinction between a group of '*core*' workers who are multi-skilled and therefore have 'functional flexibility', and a '*peripheral*' group who are employed variously on a part-time, seasonal or casual basis and can be hired-and-fired when required. This group Atkinson describes as having 'numerical flexibility'. Certainly at least one report has given some empirical support to this polarization, stating that the number of people in full-time permanent jobs has fallen dramatically since the late 1970s, from being 55.5 per cent of the workforce in 1979 to 35.9 per cent in 1993 (reported in *Guardian* 3 April 1995).

Flexibility has become a buzzword for managers in a range of different workplaces and environments. Many areas of local government, for example, are seen to

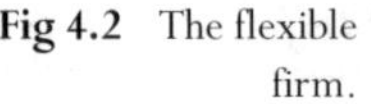

**Fig 4.2** The flexible firm.

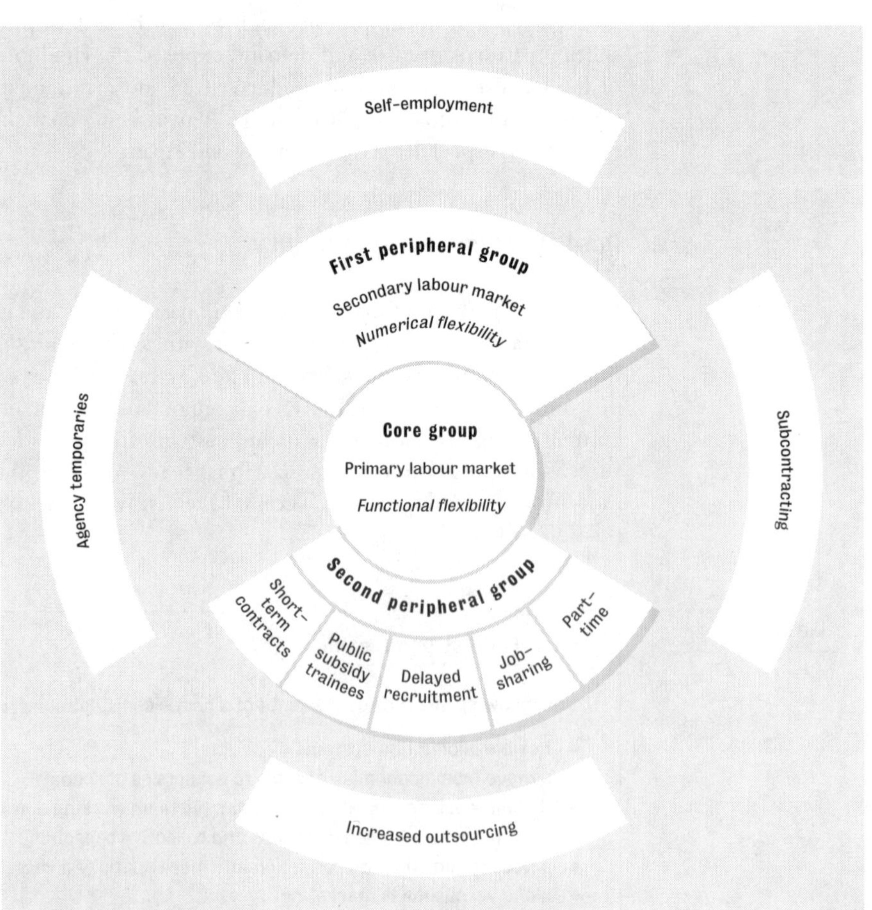



*Source:* Atkinson 1984

be reorganizing along more flexible and post-Fordist lines (Stewart and Stoker 1989; Burrows and Loader 1994). As a supervisor in a council cleansing department indicates, the 'new' world of flexible working practices can take its toll on workers and managers alike:

**We have had to become more 'business like' if you know what I mean, we have to price jobs up and be more careful in what we do. . . . we have to respond more quickly and we have to be flexible and be able to respond immediately. Before you could leave things to the next day. Labour has to be far more flexible, work has to be done on the same day so it's important that they go out and do it and don't come back until it's finished.** *(McIntosh and Broderick 1996)*

**Q** How might 'flexible' work practices benefit or disadvantage:
(a) management; (b) workers; (c) society as a whole?

The whole notion of 'flexible' working practices as a desirable, new and widespread phenomenon has come under much scrutiny (Pollert 1988a, 1988b). The bandying around of the terms 'flexibility' and 'flexible specialization' (Piore and Sabel 1984) often serves to give a gloss of sophistication to many changes that are taking place in UK workplaces. Basically 'flexibility' often amounts to the very unsophisticated and long-established practices of shedding labour, increasing workloads and employing workers on a variety of seasonal and temporary contracts.

Similarly, the notion that post-Fordism represents a radical break from Fordism has been questioned (Kumar 1995; Sayer and Walker 1992; Webster 1995). To begin with we have to question whether Fordism as it is often portrayed is a valid construction in the first place. Companies such as Ford have long been able to change production to meet changes in demand and have always hired and fired workers to maintain some flexibility in working arrangements. As one man who worked at Ford's Manchester plant in the 1920s says: 'If they got a bit slack they fired people and if they got a bit busy they took them on' (McIntosh 1995: 75).

Talk of Fordism's demise is also seen to be wide of the mark. K Williams *et al.* (1987) point out that techniques of mass production are still very much in evidence. A whole range of 'new' commodities, such as compact disc players, dishwashers, flat-pack furniture, TVs and camcorders are still mass produced and 'consumed' in their millions.

As with discussion of industrial and post-industrial society, debates around the move from Fordism to post-Fordism operate with sharply drawn 'binary-histories' (Sayer and Walker 1992). Such a perspective can lead us easily to construct erroneous dichotomies into which we force 'relevant' bits of evidence. Underlying continuities get lost in the attempt to perceive dramatic change. The 'reality' is that Fordism and a range of flexible working practices can operate quite happily side-by-side – Japanese methods are a good example of this – and capitalism has long displayed an ability to adapt to changing socio-economic environments and pressures.

## The labour market

When people look for employment they become involved in the *labour market*. It is through the labour market that people secure employment. We cannot understand this as a single market located at a particular place at a certain time. We have to think of the labour market in the abstract, a label attached to a hugely complex set of relationships.

**Definition**

### Labour market

Fevre (1992) has identified five 'functions' served by labour market:

- **informing employers** about the availability of workers for employment
- **informing workers** what jobs are available, through Job Centres, word of mouth, newspapers and other means
- **screening workers** what skills and attributes workers have and how much or little they are prepared to work for
- **screening employers** what the job pays and involves and how secure it is
- **making an offer of employment** which may or may not be bound up with a contract of employment.

An understanding of the workings of the labour market can have crucial implications for the way you come to view the world of work and paid labour. For some, generally on the right of the political spectrum, the labour market is seen to operate like any other: there will be a price (the wage) at which demand and supply will eventually meet. What is important for such people is that market forces should be left as far as possible to work themselves through in an unfettered manner. From this point of view there should be little or no 'interference' in the workings of the labour market from governments, trade unions and welfare systems. People should 'price themselves into a job' even if this means the driving down of wage levels. Essentially it is understood as a largely homogenous single entity.

However, most would agree that this is a rather simplistic view of the world, although it may well have a powerful political influence. If you have looked for some paid employment you will quickly realize that the world is not so clear cut. The labour market is not a single entity but is fractured and divided and best understood as a whole series of labour markets which can operate at local, regional, national or international levels at different times and places and is always undergoing change and variation.

People enter the labour market (or a particular labour market to be more accurate) on different terms. They bring with them different resources and attributes, skills and abilities. The labour market does not operate in a vacuum but is inextricably implicated within the society within which it operates. Thus if within society at large we see people divided and discriminated against along lines of class, gender, ethnicity or religion then it should come as no surprise to see such prejudices at work or emerging within the labour market. Sexism and racism limit the entry of women and Black workers into the labour market and proscribe the kind of employment they can attain. Similarly with people with disabilities. This is of course evidenced in terms of the jobs that people do and the rewards they can get. For example women on average earn about 75 per cent of the wages that men get, even if they do similar types of work. The sexual division of work is extremely pronounced in the UK: women and men are segregated into occupations that are seen to be 'appropriate' for the genders, for example the vast majority of clerical workers, nurses and canteen assistants are women (see pp. 293–308 for a fuller discussion of the gendered division of labour).

To take such factors into account, and to acknowledge people's differential access to the labour market, notions of the *dual* or *segmented labour market* have been put forward (Massey and Allen 1988). This corresponds closely to prior discussions of 'core' and 'peripheral' groups of workers and has similar consequences in that relatively powerless groups of workers find themselves trapped in disadvantaged 'segments' of the labour market characterized by low pay, insecurity and periods of unemployment.

## Unemployment

Given previous discussion about what we actually count as being 'proper' work it follows that what 'unemployment' means is not as straightforward as we might first assume (Whiteside 1991; Gallie 1989; Gallie *et al.* 1993). Unemployment is generally understood as referring to those out of paid employment which as we know is a limited understanding of the notion of 'work'. Many people who are not directly involved in the formal economy often 'work' extremely hard – people (mainly women) who carry out the huge numbers of domestic tasks in the home, caring for children, elderly or sick relatives, people who might 'work' constantly on hobbies or who put in thousands of hours of voluntary work. Most of this work is generally ignored within discussions of unemployment.

However, not being part of the world of the formal economy and paid employment is most often for people a miserable state. Given the aforementioned centrality of work and the way that it can be a central source for one's identity and sense of self, it should come as no surprise that to lose a job can be a devastating experience for many people (Fineman 1987; Gallie *et al.* 1993). Employment helps provide a temporal structure without which many people become lost and stupefied. As one man says:

> **I spend the odd hour or two walking up and down the stairs, counting each step. I still manage to read but my concentration is almost shot. In fact, half the time I am unable even to think. . . . I am six stones overweight and pulling my brain and fat together isn't easy.** ***(Independent 9 February 1994)***

The loss of social contacts and being forced into a kind of semi-isolation is also a major problem for people who lose their jobs. Unemployment also, of course, often results in financial hardship, crippling debt and a state of grinding poverty.

Official classifications of 'unemployment' have shown a great deal of flexibility since 1979. For example at least fourteen changes were made to official definitions of unemployment between 1982 and 1986 which had the effect of removing about

400,000 people from the total (Whiteside 1991; Gallie 1989). Thus there is general agreement that the official unemployment figures (just under 2.5 million people were claiming benefit in December 1994, around 8.6 per cent of the workforce) greatly underestimate the 'real' rate of unemployment which would see at least another million people added to the figures (Unemployment Unit 1995).

Unemployment levels of course display great regional disparities. This should come as no surprise given the variable nature of economic restructuring and processes of its de-industrialization discussed above. Scotland had 9.4 per cent (235,000 people) of its labour force claiming benefits in the summer of 1994. The figure for East Anglia was 6.6 per cent (72,500), 11.1 per cent (158,000) for the North of England and 12.8 per cent (434,200) for Greater London (Unemployment Unit 1995). Of course these figures, which are still for large areas and large populations, tend to average out the effect that unemployment has on particular places in the UK where almost no one works in full-time employment.

Unemployment also impacts differentially upon different 'groups' within society. The Unemployment Unit (1995) lists unemployment rates 'by ethnicity'. Whereas the rate for whites in 1994 was 9.1 per cent, for 'Black Caribbeans' it was 22.2 per cent, for 'Black Africans' it was 33.8 per cent, for Pakistanis 23.9 per cent and for Bangladeshis 33.1 per cent. Again this draws our attention to the way that discrimination is structured into the workings of the labour market and employers' strategies. Young people have been particularly affected by unemployment and there are now almost 1 million people under the age of 25 who are without a job. Predictably young Black people are suffering the most, with about two out of three Black men in London between the ages of 16 and 24 out of work. We now face the very real prospect that, for the first time in the post-war period, a large number of people will *never* be in full-time and permanent employment. Thus whereas in the not so distant past 'full employment' was seen to be a key objective of all British governments, now the very notion seems to have a rather utopian ring to it. Unemployment is seen by many to be an unfortunate but unavoidable problem within modern societies. This, however, ignores the way that employment and unemployment are social and political categories, they are not timeless or immutable, and 'work' itself can be reorganized economically and reinterpreted socially and culturally in such a way that 'full employment' need not be such an unattainable goal.

**Q** How might employment be reorganized in order to reduce levels of unemployment?

What would be the likely obstacles which would prevent such a reorganization taking place?

## Trade unions

Millions of workers around the world are members of trade unions. Although the structure, size and power of unions show considerable variation, all unions attempt to provide workers with a degree of collective strength and to defend the interests of their members in relation to management and capital. In the UK, which has the world's oldest unions, they are a familiar part of the social, economic and political landscape. Unions and their activities are a constant source of copy for newspapers and the centre of endless discussions about their appropriate position and place within public life. Unions themselves often appear not to have a clearly defined role: are they defensive and sectional organizations concerned only to look after their members' pay and conditions or can they have a more 'progressive' role in terms of being vehicles implementing partial, even revolutionary, social change? This is something of an ongoing dilemma for many unions that has never been satisfactorily resolved.

### Unions and social and economic change

As McIlroy says, 'Trade unions are inseparable from the society in which they are created and recreated' (1995: 1–2). Unions have of course been affected by, and have had to adapt to, contemporary changes to employment, such as those outlined above. Membership of trade unions in UK grew steadily through the post-war period and union density (the proportion of employed workforce in unions) peaked in 1979 at 55 per cent – a total of just over 13 million people. In the mid-1990s around 9 million people are members of unions and union density has dropped to around 35 per cent. Such a figure means that the UK is still one of the most highly unionized countries in the world, although a long way behind Scandinavian countries such as Sweden, which has a union density of 80 per cent. Much of the fall in union membership can be accounted for by the impact of de-industrialization and the collapse of the manufacturing sector. Some of the UK's once largest and most powerful unions have fallen away drastically. The most dramatic example is that of the miners' union, the NUM, whose quarter of a million membership in 1979 crumbled in 1994 to a mere 8,000 – a figure dwarfed by membership of the actors' union Equity, which is estimated at around 42,000.

Generally the industries that have contracted – such as mining, engineering and shipbuilding – were ones that had high union densities. A number of unions have maintained their membership levels at consistent levels – the National Association of Local Government Officers (NALGO, now UNISON) increased its membership

**Fig 4.3** Sir Harold Wilson, Labour Prime Minister 1964–70 and 1974–76, addresses the Miners' Gala, Durham; since 1979 membership of the NUM has fallen from a quarter of a million to 8,000. (Courtesy of Robert Harding Picture Library Ltd.)

from 753,000 in 1979 to a marginally greater figure of 759,000 in 1992. However, the restructuring of the economy and occupational changes have to a large extent altered the face of British trade unionism. It is worth noting that women's presence in unions is growing, even if not at the top level, and they now make up about 40 per cent of union membership (*Socialist Review* September 1994). The growing numbers of women joining unions seriously challenges long-held notions that women are not 'interested' in union matters (Cockburn 1983).

Unions themselves are having to adopt to the new labour market environment, given that the classic location for union organization was within the masculine work environments of the manufacturing industries. The post-war stability of the 'traditional' industries allowed for the development of powerful occupational cultures that provided the necessary social organization and networks and cultural resources that are crucial for the development of grassroots unionism. This form of unionism became the template for union organization in the UK and unions are now being faced with the difficult task of reorganizing and rethinking their practices to meet the demands of a post-industrial society, a fragmented workforce, the decline of full-time male employment, disparate working environments and the dispersal of plants away from the traditional urban base of British trade unionism. Lane (in Allen and Massey 1988) notes that a typical large company now has around a hundred plants dispersed around a number of 'greenfield' sites, the largest plant could employ up to a thousand workers and the smallest around fifteen. Many 'service' sector jobs (retailing, catering, tourism), all of which having been growing in employment terms, have proved difficult to unionize. Such 'industries' are characterized by high labour turnover, part-time work and short-term contracts and a lack of a 'union culture'. The Union of Shop, Distributive and Allied Workers (USDAW) has a membership of which 40 per cent are part-time and around 30 per cent leave the union each year.

Trade union power and ability to organize has also been severely curtailed through the efforts of a Conservative government fundamentally hostile to unions. Unions in the UK have no direct or 'legitimate' role to play at a national level in terms of exerting an influence on government thinking or economic policy. Throughout the 1980s and 1990s, a range of sweeping legislation – for example the Employment Acts of 1980, 1982 and 1988 and the Trade Union Act 1984 to mention a few – has been passed with the aim of limiting the effectiveness of unions in defending their members' interests. What constitutes a 'proper' and 'lawful' trade union dispute has been limited, time off from work for union representatives has been reduced, all secondary action is now unlawful, seven days' notice is now required for industrial action, and a host of other attacks (McIlroy 1995) on union power has severely limited their range of operation.

Unions have also had to face the might of giant 'transnational corporations' which can move production around the globe and set up plants in a number of different countries. Multinational companies can thus undermine national agreements and put immense pressure on unions to meet their demands for accepting no-strike deals, single union agreements and flexible work practices. If unions do not accept such conditions, these giant enterprises can simply build their plant somewhere else. Ford did exactly this when it laid down a variety of conditions to unions before commencing building a factory in Dundee in 1987; when the unions involved failed to reach an agreement Ford built the proposed Dundee plant in Portugal.

Unions, then, face difficult times but their resolve and importance – at least as defensive organizations – should not be underestimated. There has been very little decline in union organization in workplaces where collective bargaining was already well established and workplaces with over 200 employees largely continue to keep union recognition and organization (*Socialist Review* March 1995). According to numerous opinion polls and surveys, unions are regarded in an overwhelmingly positive manner. Eight out of ten people see unions as being essential for defending workers' rights and only a minority of people think they have 'too much power' (McIlroy 1995). Thus despite the formidable challenges to unions it is clear that they will continue to played crucial role in millions of people's working lives.

Q What do you think are the benefits of a union organization for a workforce?

How might the developments mentioned above provide major obstacles to effective unionization?

## The globalization of economic life

The world, it is often said, is getting smaller, or as Harvey (1989) would have it, we are witnessing 'time–space compression'. This certainly seems to be the case in respect of the movement of capital around the world. Capitalism has long operated at an international level. However, capitalist economies since the late 1960s have become increasingly integrated, encouraging talk of a 'global capitalist system' or a 'world economy' (Frobel *et al.* 1980). Production, trade and finance, with the aid of new information technologies, satellite and telecommunication systems, can now be organized at a global level rather than at a national or even international level. The most obvious protagonists of this capitalist world system are the multinational or *transnational corporations* (TNCs). TNCs are the linchpins of what Frobel *et al.* (1980) call the 'new international division of labour'. Car firms such as Ford in the early 1970s began the production of their 'World Car', the Fiesta, and reorganized production around the globe. Carburettors and distributors were built in Belfast, axels were built in Bordeaux and various bits of assembly were put together in plants in the UK, Spain and Germany. The world market allows TNCs such as Ford to distribute and sell products to all corners of the globe. Although it is important to note that most of the investment by TNCs is *within* the 'industrialized' nations, production can also be relocated in order to tap into cheap, and generally non-unionized, pools of labour in many 'developing' countries. The breakdown of production processes means that each operation can be done with minimal levels of skill, so labour need have few industrial skills.

Such a relocation and restructuring of capital has huge implications for work and employment in the 'old' centres of production and industry such as the UK. Increased competition from around the world and the movement of sites of production can accelerate the process of de-industrialization and decimate regional economies; one has only to think of the catastrophic impact that global competition in the shipbuilding industry had on regions in the UK such as Tyneside and Clydeside.

It is also increasingly difficult to think of these vast organizations as actually 'belonging' to a particular country in any meaningful way. One of the flagships of UK multinational capital, ICI, employs more people in its plants outside of the UK than it does within the UK. Thus to what extent we can still apply a 'British' tag to a company like ICI, or BP for that matter, has to be cast in some doubt; indeed firms such as ICI and BP *prefer* to be known as 'international companies'.

However, some sectors of the UK economy, and thousands of jobs, are completely dependent and integrated into the global system. This is most obviously the case with the vast array of financial institutions in the 'City' of London. London is one of the big three financial nerve centres of the global economy; New York and Tokyo are the others. These cities are also home to a disproportionate number of TNC head offices from which companies can orchestrate their global operations. In 1984 London had 37, New York 59 and Tokyo 34. In the mid-1980s foreign TNCs owned 402 of the UK's biggest 1,000 companies (McIlroy 1995: 78). Thus hundreds of thousands of jobs in the UK are dependent on the global economy – and perhaps even more in the UK are directly threatened by it.

TNCs are huge. In financial terms, relatively few countries are bigger than the largest TNCs. In 1983 the sales of BP (almost $50 million) were equivalent to the gross national products of Iraq and Ecuador (Giddens 1993a). IBM in 1992 had a revenue of $65 billion and General Motors was worth $133 billion in the same year. Multinational companies account for about 25 per cent of all the world's production. Their immense economic power means that they set the tone in terms of pricing, market innovation and leadership and control of subsidiaries. It is estimated that they employ 44 million people around the world (Webster 1995). Given the gargantuan size, huge resources and economic, political and financial power of TNCs, it is debatable as to what extent we can still meaningfully talk about 'national economies'. The management of TNCs are not noted for paying too much attention to the dictates of 'national economic policy': if nations do not want them to locate production on their territory (very unlikely given that most national governments actively compete with each other to offer the most attractive packages for TNCs to locate production within their borders) they can fairly easily move to another, more amenable, part of the globe. Other supranational organizations such as the World Bank, the EC and the International Monetary Fund have all had the effect of eroding the sovereignty of nation-states and limit their ability to withstand world-wide competitive pressures and offer protection to national industries and jobs. The capitalist global economy looks set to gather pace and wield its immense power over us for some time to come.

**Summary**

- Defining precisely what constitutes 'work' is problematic. 'Wage-labour', or 'paid employment', is often equated with work generally but much unpaid and largely unacknowledged work gets done within contemporary societies.
- The classic and most influential discussion of wage labour within capitalism is that of Karl Marx.
- Braverman (1974) utilized and extended Marx's analysis of the labour process and applied it to work within the twentieth century. Braverman thought that work had undergone a process of 'deskilling' and the main catalyst for this was attempts by management to exert total control over the workforce. Taylorism exemplified this managerial strategy.
- Braverman has been strongly criticized on a number of points. The widespread influence of Taylorism has been questioned. Braverman's understanding of 'skill' was seen to be lacking and he failed to take adequate account of workers' resistance.

- A wide range of managerial strategies has been developed to control and maximize the productivity of a workforce. This has included giving the workforce some 'responsible autonomy', 'humanizing' work tasks and the reorganization of work through team working and 'Japanese' methods.
- Industrialization was seen by many to be an inevitable tendency for most countries of the world; however, this was cast in doubt with the emergence of 'de-industrialization' and the decline of employment in a number of sectors of industry.
- Writers such as Bell (1973) foresaw the emergence of a 'post-industrial' society based on an economy where employment in the 'service sector' was dominant. Such ideas have been criticized as being overly optimistic, inaccurate and based on an erroneous interpretation of changes taking place within many capitalist societies.
- Fordism was a term used to describe a socio-economic system based on mass production and mass consumption which was seen to be dominant during the post-war period. It is argued that Fordism reached its limits in the early 1970s and was increasingly replaced with more flexible methods of production and work organization. The term post-Fordism is often used to describe these changes. The distinction between Fordism and post-Fordism has been criticized for being too polarized and based on an empirically weak foundation.
- Labour markets are where employers and prospective employees can 'meet' and/or gather information about each other. Labour markets can often display similar patterns of racism and sexism that are present within wider society to the extent that we can talk of dual or segmented labour markets.
- Unemployment is a feature of many modern societies and is generally experienced as a profoundly depressing and miserable state for most individuals. Rates of unemployment vary for different regions and for different 'groups' of people.
- Trade unions are a crucial part of our society. Unions have had to adapt to a changing socio-economic environment brought about by de-industrialization, falling membership, hostile legislation and transnational corporations but they still provide an important function for millions of workers.
- Capitalism has to be understood as a world phenomenon. Production, trade and finance, with the aid of new information technologies, satellite and telecommunication systems, can now be organized at a global level and massive transnational corporations wield enormous power and influence around the world.

## Further reading

Braverman, H (1974) *Labour and Monopoly Capital: The Degradation of Work within the Twentieth Century*, New York: Monthly Review Press.
Regarded as a classic, if flawed, Marxist analysis of work in the twentieth century.

Brown, P and Scase, R (eds) (1991) *Poor Work: Disadvantage and the Division of Labour*, Buckingham: Open University Press.
Emerging alternatives to permanent employment and the experience of unemployment.

Gallie, D, Marsh, C and Vogler, V (1993) *Social Change and the Experience of Unemployment*, Oxford: Oxford University Press.
A detailed look at changes in local labour markets in Britain, unemployment and people's work and family histories.

Grint, K (1991) *The Sociology of Work*, Oxford: Blackwell.
Concise introduction to the major issues within the sociology of work.

Kumar, K (1995) *From Post-Industrial to Post-Modern Society* Oxford: Blackwell.
Balanced discussion of post-Fordism, the 'information society' and post-modernity.

McIlroy, J (1995) *Trade Unions in Britain Today*, 2nd edn, Manchester: Manchester University Press.
A comprehensive introduction to trade unionism in Britain.

Thompson, P (1990) *Work Organizations: A Critical Introduction*, London: Macmillan.
A guide to the major changes taking place in work organizations.

Webster, F (1995) *Theories of the Information Society*, London: Routledge.
Contains critical discussions of post-industrialism and post-Fordism.

Webster, J (1996) *Shaping Women's Work: Gender, Employment and Information Technology*, London: Longman.
Shows how gender relations in the workplace and sexual division of labour affect the direction and pace of technological change. An innovative look at a major service sector which combines theory with empirical research.

Wood, S (ed.) (1982) *The Degradation of Work?*, London: Hutchinson.
Covers most criticisms of Braverman and major issues of the 'labour process debate'.

## Activities

### Activity 1 Full-time workers fall by 35 per cent

The proportion of the working population in full-time tenured employment has fallen by about 35 per cent over the last 20 years, says a new economic report released today, and 15 per cent of British homes now have no member in work.

Paul Gregg and Jonathan Wadsworth of the Centre for Economic Performance at the London School of Economics and the National Institute for Economic and Social Research say **only 35.9 per cent of the working population held full-time tenured jobs in 1993, down from 55.5 per cent in 1975.**

In a survey of the British labour market in the current edition of the Oxford Review of Economic Policy they report that jobs have become much more unstable with the typical duration of any individual's job falling by 20 per cent over the last 20 years.

However, while the average man's job now lasts 6.4 years compared to 7.9 years in 1975, women's employment patterns have become stabler – with the median job for a woman lasting 4.3 years in 1993 compared to 3.9 years in 1975, still lower than men's.

Labour turnover is rising especially for older workers and for unskilled men, they say. More and more older men are leaving the labour market altogether, and this has been driving the decline in full-time tentured jobs.

The jobs market is becoming two-tiered with a secondary sector 'characterised by higher labour turnover among the least skilled, young, and old and those in atypical employment'. A new insecurity has been concentrated on a minority for whom a job for life will be the 'stuff of legends'. But they dismiss government claims that this flexible labour market is necessary for employment.

They argue that 'current patterns of job creation are becoming less and less helpful in reducing the unemployment count.' The consequence will be 'long-run poverty among families systematically disenfranchised' from earning a living.

(Will Hutton, *Guardian* 3 April 1995)

## Questions

The *Guardian* report indicates that a series of dramatic changes may be taking place to the labour market and the nature of employment within the UK.

What are these changes?

How might these developments be explained by someone adopting (a) a 'post-Fordist'; (b) a 'post-industrial'; (c) a Marxist perspective?

What impact do you think the tendencies noted in the report will have for trade union organization in UK workplaces?

## ■ Activity 2 Working in a nursing home

**This article is drawn from ethnographic doctoral research undertaken in two homes for older people in the South West of England.**

### The bedroom job

The bedroom was the main site of work for the auxiliaries and most of the patients' time in the home was spent there. Morning work was virtually all bedroom work and was officially begun by the auxiliaries entering patients' rooms on the tea round. This was a point of the day at which cups of tea were served and bottoms were washed. It was customary to present the patients to the new shift intact, clean and quiet in their rooms for 8am. Presenting well ordered bodies seemed to symbolise the job properly done. The next shift spent all the morning in the bedrooms, washing and dressing patients. The workers spent most of the morning getting patients ready, then taking them down to the lounge. By lunch time they were all down, but straight after lunch it was time to put them back to bed for a nap and later get them up again.

In the evenings work again revolved around the bedrooms as staff got patients ready for bed. By the time the night shift came on all patients were in bed. In this way the auxiliaries' work could be said to revolve around the bedroom. And it was in this private world that they were able to decide the rules and had total hidden control.

Making jokes at the patient's expense was seen as 'having some fun with the patients' (Vera) and workers argued it involved patients in some way with the work. For example, patients who could not walk properly were told to 'race' down the corridor, and jokes would be made about Nigel Mansell etc. Patients who were crying in pain would be told to buck up and smile. Mimicry was also common, with staff copying the words of confused residents. Most patients either could not hear, see or understand jokes that the workers made at their expense, while others became distressed at them. But 'joking' appeared to help auxiliaries get through the work; it broke up the stress and gave them some sort of control.

### The hard culture

Auxiliary work in nursing homes is hard work: low paid, low status, dirty, physically backbreaking and tiring. However, far from complaining about the conditions of their work the nursing auxiliaries appeared to have elevated the notion of personal hardship with their subculture. Personal hardship and hard behaviour towards patients seemed central to auxiliaries' understanding of what they were supposed to do. They spoke about others, such as residential home workers, and trained staff, as too 'soft'. A strong emphasis was placed upon coping and getting on with the the work, even avoiding the use of hoists and aides, despite a frequency of serious back problems.

Auxiliaries were not only trying to make sense of their work, given the poor working conditions, but also to make it easier and give themselves a clear role and place in relation to trained nursing workers. In response to this the auxiliaries at Cedar Court became the 'hardest' workers. (Lee-Treweek 1994)

## Questions

The jobs discussed in the above extract are ones that are generally considered to be part of the 'service sector'. Do you think that they fit well into Bell's vision for 'service employment' within a 'post-industrial' society?

Can we draw any parallels between the work discussed by Lee-Treweek and work that takes place within other environments such as industry? You should have another look at the extract 'Factory Time' on p. 153.

Chapter 5

# Politics

**Chapter outline:** Introduction • International political structures • The political structure in Britain • Parties and political theories • Political participation • 'Old' and 'new' politics • Summary • Further reading • Activities

## Learning objectives

When you have studied this chapter you should be able to address these key questions:

- How widely should 'politics' be defined?
- How do political structures operate at an international and a national level?
- What are the main factors that influence the extent and form of political participation?
- In what ways has there been a movement from an 'old' to a 'new' style of politics?

## Introduction

Radicals today recognise that freedom is interconnected and indivisible – how can I be truly free if you are not ? A century of growing and widespread activism for equal treatment and half a century of United Nations accord on human rights have had a marked effect on attitudes and policies in many parts of the world. Yet in large parts of the globe the basic human freedoms are far from being respected, and our growing awareness and understanding of oppression and disempowerment only serve to show what elusive goals freedom and self-determination are. (Button 1995: 21)

In this chapter the emphasis is on how politics influences and is influenced by relationships between people, rather than on the finer details of how political systems are organized. Brief descriptions will be provided of some aspects of political systems, but these are intended to give a grounding to our principal analysis of people and politics. This analysis includes the various issues identified by Button (1995) as fundamental, including attitudes and activity, human rights and freedoms, claims of oppression and disempowerment. Button refers to the elusive nature of political progress on all of these issues; indeed, it is possible to take either an optimistic or a pessimistic stance. We could emphasize political achievements in holding disparate societies together or we could emphasize failures in creating genuinely cohesive and caring societies.

Q Before reading further, compose your own definitions of 'politics', 'democracy' and 'citizen'. Discuss these with other students. Can you agree on how these terms should be defined?

Even definitions of the term 'politics' are problematic. At a basic level the term could be reduced to the Greek word *polis*, which refers to a 'city', the central focus for public debate in ancient Greece. Narrow definitions of 'politics' tend to offer the most positive connotations because they are primarily concerned with descriptions of how formal institutions and systems function, evolve and adapt (as, for example, in the United Nations: see pp. 183–4). Wider definitions tend to be less positive because they include social critiques of unequal power relationships and the inadequacies of political outcomes (see feminist criticisms, pp. 204–5). The boundaries of politics as an academic discipline are also difficult to identify because politics consists of many subdisciplines (including sociology, history, philosophy, economics and psychology); this chapter focuses on political sociology, with its emphasis on contemporary group behaviour.

The concept of 'democracy' provides a focus for many themes encountered in political sociology, and again there are disagreements about how the term should be defined. Even the simple definition of 'rule by the people' (from the Greek words *demos*, meaning 'people', and *kratia*, meaning 'rule') tells us very little. In ancient Greece all 'citizens' were entitled to influence government – but women and slaves were excluded from citizenship! A simple definition of 'democracy' as 'rule by the people' therefore ignores power relationships and fundamental assumptions about human rights. Wider definitions would include some sort of recognition of those who are excluded from influence. According to Riley (1988: 15–16) democracy is 'a variable concept, meaning popular control of those in power. It stresses certain basic rights: to assemble,to criticise, to vote unhindered by the authorities, to hold minority opinions and free elections'. This suggests that debates about human rights should play an important part in our study of political sociology.

We can see that during the twentieth century some states have continued to exclude large proportions of their populations from political influence and that warfare has been experienced on a massive and international scale. (See, for example, the extract about Iraq in Activity 2, p.218.) It is clear that 'politics' therefore encompasses political systems and power relationships, not only within individual states but also at an international level. In this chapter we start with a narrow definition of politics by looking at formal political structures at an international level moving on to formal political structures in Britain at national and then local level. We move progressively towards applying wider definitions of politics, developing the theme of changes from 'old' to 'new' politics along the way.

## International political structures

It would be difficult today to find any state that is truly isolated from the complex web of international political, economic and cultural systems, communications networks, multinational companies and so on. A brief description of the activities of the United Nations and European Union not only highlights the interdependence of national and international political structures and processes but also demonstrates the long-term impact of two world wars and the ongoing fear of atomic war.

The League of Nations was created after the First World War in an effort to keep peace between the nations of the world and maintain a sense of collective security. In the 1930s Japan, Germany and Italy withdrew from the League and by the start of the Second World War the League had been totally undermined. The Second World War resulted in more debates about human rights at an international level and to the creation of the United Nations.

### United Nations

Fifty countries signed the founding charter of the United Nations in 1945; its stated aims were to

**save succeeding generations from the scourge of war, which twice in our lifetime has brought untold sorrow to mankind, and to reaffirm faith in fundamental human rights, in the dignity of the human person, in the equal rights of men and women and of nations large and small.**

Definition

## Institutions of the United Nations

### International Court of Justice

Countries can refer their disputes to the International Court of Justice and abide by its decision in an effort to avoid the resolution of conflict by force or war.

### General Assembly

Each member state has one vote in the Assembly and important resolutions must be passed with a two-thirds majority. However, these are only recommendations and cannot be enforced by law.

### Security Council

The Council consists of fifteen members. Ten of these are elected for two years by the General Assembly. Five (China, France, the USA, Russia and Great Britain) are permanent. Each of the five permanent members can cancel a decision made by other members. The Security Council can respond to conflict by providing its own teams of negotiators, asking member countries to supply troops to form a peacekeeping force, sending unarmed observers to monitor a permanent ceasefire, instructing its members to impose trading sanctions on one or more warring parties, intervening directly in extreme cases (UN resolutions could be enforced by multinational forces).

### Humanitarian agencies

UN agencies include the World Health Organization (WHO), International Monetary Fund (IMF), United Nations Children's Fund (UNICEF), United Nations Educational Scientific and Cultural Organization (UNESCO), and United Nations High Commissioner for Refugees (UNHCR).

## Question

In view of the aims stated in the founding charter why do you think the UN did not intervene more forcefully to abolish apartheid in South Africa?

## European Union

As in the case of the United Nations, the foundations of the European Union were laid after the Second World War. During the war the British Prime Minister, Winston Churchill, proposed that a European council should be created, which would include at least ten states and would have its own army and law courts. He called this 'a kind of United States of Europe'. However, during negotiations with France, Italy and Belgium in 1949 he refused to allow such a joint European body to take decisions over the head of the British government. He said that Britain was 'linked but not compromised' with Europe.

Churchill's reservations set the tone of political debate in Britain: politicians have often expressed mixed feelings about the relationship between Britain and the rest of Europe. Many have wanted to see closer economic links but have been anxious to maintain national sovereignty (sovereignty means the right to own and control an area of the world, thereby maintaining the supremacy of British law over European law).

Some sort of economic cooperation has nevertheless been seen as a way of rebuilding the economic structures that had been damaged by the war and of enhancing long-term peace. Economic cooperation started on a relatively small scale with an emphasis on coal and steel in the 'Benelux' agreement of 1951 between Belgium, the Netherlands and Luxembourg. This economic cooperation was expanded in 1957 when the six original members of the European Economic Community (Belgium, France, Germany, Italy, Luxembourg and the Netherlands) signed the Treaty of Rome. This was primarily a customs union in which members agreed not to put tariffs on goods imported from other member states. By 1995 what had become the European Union had fifteen member states, the additions being Austria, Denmark, Finland, Greece, Ireland, Portugal Spain, Sweden and the United Kingdom. (The UK and Ireland became members in 1973.)

Since 1957 the pressure for closer economic and monetary union has increased. Plans were drawn up in the Maastricht Treaty of 1991 to abolish all of the individual currencies within the union and create just one currency and interest rate. The 'ecu' is proposed as a common currency with a common central bank implementing a common monetary policy. However, there have been differences of opinion about a single common currency throughout the European Union. British Conservative governments have been in favour of a 'hard ecu' (without the constraint of a central bank or common monetary policy) and retained the right to keep the pound even if the other member countries should form their own common currency.

The differing policies of the British Labour and Conservative parties are particularly noticeable when social issues are considered. The European Union's 'Social Chapter' attempted to codify European practice on many social issues. These included the extension of basic citizens' rights and entitlements in the workplace: for example part-time workers' rights, minimum wages, maximum working hours and pension rights. British Conservative governments have refused to sign the Chapter, thereby preventing its implementation in Britain. However, as the Social Chapter complements the Labour Party's policies on workers' rights, a Labour government would sign and implement the Chapter. This is just one example of the difficulties involved in creating effective links between states with different political institutions, party policies and perhaps even different political cultures.

**Definition**

### Institutions of the European Union

**The European Union functions through four main institutions.**

#### European Commission

**This institution is based in Brussels and has twenty-one members. Each country has at least one member and the larger countries (Germany, Italy, the United Kingdom, France and Spain) have two. The Commission proposes new laws for the Council of Ministers to consider. It is also responsible for the implementation of decisions once they have been finalized.**

*(box continued)*

*(box continued)*

**Council of Ministers**

This is the main decision-making body of the European Union. The Council discusses proposals from the Commission and aims to reach agreement. Each country has one seat on the Council, although the occupants of those seats vary, as different specialists attend according to what is being discussed On some issues all countries have to agree and the veto of one country can block a new law.

**European Parliament**

The European Parliament acts as a forum for discussion, scrutinizing proposals from the Commission and Council of Ministers and suggesting amendments. In 1995 there were 639 Members of the European Parliament (MEPs). Those states with the largest populations have the most MEPs (for example, the United Kingdom has a population of approximately 58.3 million and 87 MEPs) and those states with the smallest populations have fewest MEPS ( for example, Luxembourg has a population of approximately 0.4 million and 6 MEPs).

**European Court of Justice**

This institution considers any infringement of European Union law and any queries about the interpretation of the law.

Q He's not a man of great weight. After all, to have been prime minister of Luxembourg is a bit like having been chairman of Basingstoke District Council.

(Lord Tebbit on Jacques Santer, new president of the European Commission, July 1994, quoted in McKie with Bindman 1994)

What does this quote reveal about the attitude of certain sections of the Conservative Party to Europe?

The European Commission has often been lampooned in the British press for allegedly spending much of its time legislating on the exact curve of a banana or the contents of Cornish pasties. What problems might you face if you had to draw up laws for the whole of the European Union?

## The political structure in Britain

One fundamental difference between political systems emerges from their attitudes to the doctrine of the 'separation of powers'. According to this doctrine the powers of the legislature (parliament or assembly), executive (government and civil service) and judiciary (legal system) should be kept separate in order to avoid the concentration, and possible abuse, of power. This doctrine is strongly adhered to in France and the USA but is barely acknowledged in Britain, where, for example, the monarch and Prime Minister both have powers that relate to the legislature, executive and judiciary.

## Monarchy

The Queen is the official head of state and we now have a 'constitutional monarchy': the role of the monarch is largely symbolic and most power has been transferred to politicians. The Queen retains some powers in the form of a 'royal prerogative'; which entitles her to open and dissolve parliaments, head the Church of England and the armed forces, appoint prime ministers and judges, confer peerages and other titles. However, she exercises these powers on the 'advice' of her ministers; this is seen by critics as a source of supplementary government power.

The Queen's powers are regarded as significant only at times of uncertainty, for example, if there is no parliamentary majority. In such circumstances, she could – in theory – take over the role of Prime Minister and could declare a state of emergency. She is immune from prosecution, as all criminal prosecutions are made in the name of the Crown. As head of the Commonwealth she is the head of state in many other Commonwealth countries. However, her status is constantly challenged by republican movements within some of these states; for example Paul Keating, the Australian Prime Minister, announced in 1992 that new citizens would swear allegiance to Australia and not to the Queen. He also refused to bow to her when she visited the country.

Where other European states (such as Sweden, Norway and the Netherlands) retain monarchies, they have none of the status, remaining powers or wealth of the British monarchy. Most states in the world have no monarchy and the role of a national figurehead is taken by an elected or nominated head of state, most commonly the president of a republic. There has also been a long history of republicanism in Britain, dating back through the centuries to include the English Civil War (1642–51) between royalists and roundheads and, in 1791, the publication of Thomas Paine's book, *The Rights of Man*.

## Parliament

The legislature of any state consists of its consultative chamber(s) or assembly(ies) for political debate and the scrutiny and passing of legislation. As in the USA and many other European countries Britain has a bicameral parliament, which means that there are two chambers – the House of Commons and the House of Lords – although the word is often used to refer to only the House of Commons (the 'lower house') and its 650 Members (in 1995) of Parliament.

## Prime Minister

The Prime Minister's role in various European states has evolved in different ways: For example, in France the Prime Minister is subordinate to the President, who is head of state and has the greater control of government policy. In Britain the electoral system means that the Prime Minister must be leader of the party with a majority in the House of Commons. This provides extra power for the Prime Minister, who is the unofficial head of state ('advising' the monarch), head of the executive (Cabinet and civil service), effective head of legislature, and not entirely separate from the judiciary (the government's Home Secretary heads the police and prison service). During the 1990s British prime ministers have experienced growing criticism of their, apparently, growing powers; for example, to designate non-elected, yet powerful, quangos (quasi-autonomous non-governmental organizations) and nominate their members.

## Cabinet government

The British Cabinet consists of ministers responsible for the main executive functions of the government. There are so many junior ministers that the Cabinet would no longer be a small forum for debate if all were included; it therefore comprises senior ministers, but can call other ministers to attend. All junior and senior ministers are appointed by the Prime Minister and are members of the party with a majority in the House of Commons, although they can come from either House.

Throughout the twentieth century Cabinets have been criticized for not including a representative social mix. Conservative Cabinets, in particular, have been criticized for being mostly (sometimes entirely) male, middle-class or upper-class, privately educated, graduates and businessmen.

The salaries of government ministers are high in relation to average wages, but considered relatively low compared to those of heads of industry or to their counterparts in other states. This means that their salaries are often cited as one of the reasons why former ministers engage in financial activities when out of office and have been accused of exploiting their position when in power.

Q

**What would be the benefits of a greater social mix among Cabinet members?**

**Would more women in the Cabinet make a difference?**

**How could these be achieved?**

Before the 1970s there were two commonly recognized conventions affecting Cabinet members but, since then, these conventions have fallen into disuse. The convention of collective responsibility asserted that, once a decision was taken in Cabinet, members would not refer in public to disagreements between government ministers. The convention of ministerial responsibility asserted that ministers would accept ultimate responsibility for any major problems in their department and would therefore resign.

Since the 1960s the convention of collective responsibility has fallen by the way and politicians have become increasingly prone to reveal their disagreements. For example, during the Labour governments of 1964–70 there were many open disagreements. In the 1980s Margaret Thatcher took many decisions herself, or with a small clique of trusted advisers. For example, before the poll tax was introduced Mrs Thatcher created an internal departmental committee, working in secret, under the leadership of Kenneth Baker and William Waldegrave. This sort of reaction can at least partly be seen as a response to the number of leaks from the Cabinet. Some of these could be seen as unintentional, as (generally male) ministers have shared Cabinet matters with their wives or girlfriends, while some could be seen as intentional, as information has often been manipulated to create a good image via the press.

Similarly the convention of ministerial responsibility has occasionally been disregarded. For example, Nigel Lawson remained in place as Chancellor despite apparent evidence of extensive economic incompetence within the Exchequer. In 1995 the Home Secretary Michael Howard was issued with a writ by the head of the prison service alleging excessive and damaging intervention in prison administration. Howard challenged the writ, thus indicating a move away from the convention, while the issuing of the writ presented an image of a not so submissive civil servant.

### Civil service

As government employees, civil servants must sign the Official Secrets Act 1989, which is intended to prevent them from disclosing any information (no matter how trivial) about their work. The claim that secret information has been disclosed in the public interest is no longer (since the 1989 Act) accepted as a defence. This tightening up of the law can be seen as a response to some revelations by civil servants during the 1980s. Some civil servants were forced to resign or were prosecuted by the government (for example, Clive Ponting and Sarah Tisdall in the mid-1980s: see p. 579).

There is more generalizable evidence of tensions between civil servants and the government. Before the 1980s civil servants were commonly regarded as politically neutral, discreet servants of any government, irrespective of its party affiliation. However, since then the relationship between government and civil service has become more confrontational, as morale seems to have disintegrated. Cuts in public spending led to cuts in the civil service and the abolition of the Civil Service Department, which had been seen as an avenue for promoting the interests of government personnel. In 1981 major industrial action was taken by the civil service; this action included personnel at the Government Communications Headquarters (GCHQ) in Cheltenham, from which various intelligence operations are run. The government saw the civil service unions as growing increasingly militant and was concerned that employees at GCHQ, who were handling sensitive communications, would experience divided loyalties. Without any prior consultation, in 1985 the government announced that trade union membership at GCHQ would be prohibited. The unions sought an injunction to restrain the Prime Minister from altering the terms of their employment, and were initially successful, but on appeal the decision was overturned in favour of the Prime Minister.

In 1984 the civil service unions participated in a campaign for more freedom of information and the reform of the existing Official Secrets Act, but when the Act was reformed in 1989, the regulations regarding secrets became even more constricting. In general, civil servants were concerned that they were being informed rather than consulted. This concern has been compounded as fewer civil servants in the lower ranks come from elitist backgrounds and resentment escalated concerning the promotion of mandarins who were sympathetic to government objectives. For example, in 1987 Peter Levene, who was formerly involved in the arms industry, was made head of the Ministry of Defence Arms Procurement Agency. This was an illegal appointment according to Orders in Council of 1982.

### Local government

Until 1995 there were two types of local authorities, those sited in predominantly urban conurbations (metropolitan), and those in less urban (county) areas. In metropolitan areas district council administered the most localized services and joint boards administered joint services for the whole metropolitan area. Joint boards had replaced the metropolitan councils (for example, the Greater London Council) that previously had Labour majorities. The joint boards were widely criticized for being largely unelected quangos.

In rural areas district councils were responsible for the most localized services and county councils for joint services relating to all districts. Regular elections were held for district and county councils and the absence of joint boards made the government of non-metropolitan areas less controversial.

In 1994 a Report by the Local Government Commission recommended that most of Britain should have unitary (single-tier) authorities. This would replace a system in which there were already unitary authorities for twenty-four counties, but a two-tier system for fifteen counties. In the local elections of May 1995 unitary authorities were elected throughout Wales and in some other areas.

Relationships between central and local government have become increasingly difficult throughout a lengthy period of Conservative government because there have been Labour majorities in many local authorities. The central government has encountered problems in the local implementation of some of its policies (in particular in education and housing) and local authorities have found the government-initiated cuts in spending difficult to implement. Even Conservative councils have faced problems in satisfying central government, as they too face cuts in their spending and occasional scandals (for example the homes for votes scandal in the Westminster council, reported in the *Guardian* 5 November 1994).

## Parties and political theories

Our earliest experiences of political theories are often at the level of party politics and involve quite simplistic distinctions between left and right, socialist and conservative. This is partly because politicians and the media tend to talk in terms of extremes (after all, it makes better copy) and partly because of the inherently adversarial nature of British politics. The virtual domination of the British political scene since the Second World War by the two largest parties, the Labour Party and the Conservative Party, has meant that political debates often appear to the public to be less about the issues involved and more about political point scoring. In the past it was relatively easy to distinguish what was right or left wing and to characterize the traditional Conservative or Labour voter or politician. Now, however, an increasingly complex political scene reflects the complexities of the modern world. Traditional loyalties may be put to the test by issues such as new road building, Sunday trading or the export of live animals which arouse fierce opposition from all parts of the political spectrum. Looking beyond Britain, the dramatic changes in world politics mean that the same terms can mean very different things in different countries and political environments. For example someone who held essentially right-wing views might be called a conservative in Britain, but in one of the former

**Fig 5.1** Sunday trading is an issue which puts traditional party loyalties to the test. (Photograph © Adam Woolfitt, courtesy of Robert Harding Picture Library Ltd.)

eastern bloc countries such as Russia or Poland a conservative would be a supporter of the old communist regime.

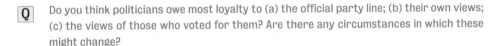

**Q** Do you think politicians owe most loyalty to (a) the official party line; (b) their own views; (c) the views of those who voted for them? Are there any circumstances in which these might change?

It is important to develop a good, critical understanding of various political terms and perspectives before pursuing political sociology any further. The following terms are frequently used in political studies. General political ideologies are described first and then political perspectives and parties in Britain.

## Political ideologies

### *Totalitarianism*

In a totalitarian state opposition to the dominant political group and its associated policies is not allowed. A totalitarian state can be extremely left wing or extremely right wing or have some other (often military) political identity. We can therefore see a similarity between the extremes of communism and fascism. Although based on radically different philosophies (which are considered on pp.192–3) neither leaves room for alternative theories and each has been associated with an element of force. This could be seen if we compared the atrocities of Hitler's concentration camps with the horrors of Stalin's Gulags. In such circumstances there is apparently no room for opposition, yet we have seen a process of gradual change from fascism to 'pluralism' in Spain and from communism to 'pluralism' in the former eastern bloc.

### *Pluralism*

When trying to explain the meaning of pluralism Woolf (1969) used the image of a weather vane (central and local government) responding to the wind (of public opinions). Government responses are portrayed as compromises between a plurality and fragmentation of influences. Efforts are made to avoid the alienation of any particular section of interests. Power is spread across a wide range of social locations, and organizations representing various interests and democracy exist because no one interest group is allowed to dominate. According to this view individuals (by themselves as voters, in pressure groups, political parties, etc.) can genuinely influence those who hold power. As sociologists we can see how this relates to Durkheim's argument that social solidarity is based on an acceptance of diversity (see pp. 43–5).

At least two types of pluralism have been identified by political scientists. First, conventional pluralism represents the government as neutral umpire, balancing inputs (of influence) with outputs (policy) in such a way that influence is balanced among a plurality of groups. A second type, neo-pluralism, observes the state negotiating with some groups (particularly influential pressure groups) and individuals (experts) more than others. This is similar to the image of corporatism that we consider later (p.194).

### *The extreme right: fascism*

Fascist movements have historically arisen in situations of great economic and social turmoil. The most obvious example would be the rise of the Nazis in a Germany which had been devastated by the First World War. In such situations fascist leaders exploit the desire for strong leadership by offering the promise of order, security and prosperity. Common fears and hatreds, nationalistic alliegancies and, usually, racism, could be exploited in order to generate unquestioning support. For these reasons fascist states, are inevitably totalitarian and authoritarian.

It would, however, be wrong simply to describe fascists as extremely right wing. In some ways fascists have been as suspicious of free market capitalism as communists: the economy of Franco's Spain was heavily regulated. Fascist leaders try to achieve a popularist image, which may include appeal to working-class and left-wing supporters. For example, Oswald Mosley (1896–1980), the leader of the British Union of Fascists before the start of the Second World War, was formerly a junior minister in the Labour Party. Hitler's fascist party was the National Socialist German Workers' Party (NSDAP). Even during the mid-1990s, the warring factions within the former Yugoslavia could be distinguished primarily by their national and cultural identities, rather than by their positions on a left- to right-wing polarity of perspectives. Fascism therefore tends to draw on common fears, and/or the appeal of superiority and domination over others.

### *The extreme left: Marxism and communism*

Marx was particularly inspired by Hegel's philosophy of history (see Hegel and Knox 1952), that humanity advances and progresses only because of the struggles of the oppressed against their oppressors. As Hegel said that progress is not created by peace and harmony, real advancement could be only through conflicts, wars and revolutions.

Marx was also influenced by Feuerbach's (1957) denial of the 'sacred' origin of royal authority. He saw power as concentrated in the hands of the dominant economic group, and therefore social class, in society. Political structures were perceived to be serving the needs of the dominant class. Schattschnieder wrote (1969: 31) that 'the flaw in the pluralist heaven is that the heavenly choir sings with a strongly upper-class accent'.

Since Marx, Marxists have refined or adapted his theories. One notable adaptation is Habermas' (1971, 1976) theory of legitimation crisis. According to this theory, capitalism is inherently unstable, the state regularly intervenes in the economy to try to maintain stability. Voters see social problems as political rather than economic, and therefore question the legitimacy of the state. Ultimately the state is overburdened by responsibilities in its efforts to ameliorate the effects of capitalism.

**Q** What are the similarities between extreme right-wing and extreme left-wing political movements in terms of the situations they flourish in and the way they operate?

Think of two contemporary examples which illustrate your argument.

### *Elitism*

**the elite case is that most societies act in a manner which *systematically* excludes the majority from anything like an even break over the whole range of societally significant institutions.** *(Dowse and Hughes 1986: 160)*

According to this perspective, elitist states systematically exclude the majority from political influence, and rely on the deference of the masses, created by their socialization into an acceptance of elite domination. Power is held by an elite group of political experts, and not just by an economically dominant group (as suggested by Marxist theories). Although an elitist government works in the elite's interests this could be seen as enabling the system to run efficiently. The elite may claim that a limited democracy exists, and full democracy is worth sacrificing in favour of rule by experts. Elite influence is cumulative and transferable between institutions, and the elite determines access to elite positions (an example being the role of elite public schools in providing personnel).

Dahl's elite model (1958) stresses the following conditions that must be met in order to identify elite rule:

1 The ruling elite is a well-defined group.
2 There are several instances of cases involving key political decisions to which the preferences of the ruling elite group run counter to those of any other likely group that might be suggested.
3 In the cases described in (2) the preferences of the elite group regularly prevail.

Most elite theorists do not see elite dominance as a matter of deliberate manipulation, but of subscribing to an ideology in which elite domination is seen as natural. This ultimately means that some writers (such as Mosca 1939; Pareto 1935; Schumpeter 1976) take a very low view of the capabilities of the masses for self-government, or of their desire for it.

### *Oligarchy*

Oligarchy describes a political structure in which an individual (oligarch) or small group (oligarchy) control the decision-making processes. Michels (1959) studied trade unions, which were apparently examples of egalitarianism, and concluded (his Iron Law of Oligarchy) that, once elected or accepted, officials and leaders will systematically exclude others from the decision-making process.

### *Corporatism*

In a corporatist state some large interest groups have become more powerful than others in the political and economic arena. Decision-making is generally by compromise between representatives of labour (unions), capital (employers) and the state. They come together to coordinate the economy and provide a balance between private enterprise and state control.

Is Britain now, or has it ever been, a corporatist state?

Japan and Sweden are often cited as examples of a corporatist state. Look at the political structure of either, or both, of these states. Do they in any way fit the above description of corporatism?

### *Hegemony*

The concept of hegemony illustrates Marxist and elitist theories about the control of the masses. It helps to explain how the powerful can exert their domination over the masses without much resistance. Socialization processes result in the dominant ideology and associated status quo being internalized and accepted without challenge. Rousseau explained this succinctly in the third chapter of *The Social Contract* (1762)

**The strongest man is never strong enough to be always master unless he transforms his power into right and obedience into duty.**

## Political perspectives

### *The New Right*

There are many political perspectives within the Conservative Party, two of which we will look at. Both the New Right and one nation conservatism emphasize economic freedom, sovereignty and individualism, but the New Right emphasizes all of these with more vigour and with less inclination to compromise (hence the image of Margaret Thatcher as the 'iron lady'). An early reflection on attitudes within the Conservative Party points the way to the popularization of New Right views.

**It is part of the conservative intuition that economic freedom is the most precious temporal freedom, for the reason that it alone gives each of us, in our comings and goings in our complex society, sovereignty - and over that part of existence in which by far the most choices have in fact to be made, and in which it is possible to**

**make choices, involving oneself, without damage to other people. And for further reason that without economic freedom, political and other freedoms are likely to be taken from us.** *(Buckley 1959: 166)*

First, the New Right is particularly critical of Keynesian economics, according to which government spending (on welfare, housing, etc.) is productive because it minimizes unemployment, results in greater affluence for all and increases purchasing power. In contrast, the New Right sees government spending as counter-productive because it increases the amount of money in circulation, causes inflation and reduces consumers' purchasing power. They argue that the government should spend less (on welfare services, etc.), reduce taxation and allow unemployment to find a natural level. The emphasis is therefore on letting market forces operate naturally, without government interference. This is by no means a new idea, as it can be traced back to Adam Smith (1776, *The Wealth of Nations*). He too claimed that free market forces would operate more efficiently than government planning.

Second, and in particular since the 1960s, Conservative governments have argued that a search for consensus within a diverse population is a waste of time. All of the people cannot be pleased for even part of the time. Margaret Thatcher compounded this claim by stating: 'There is no such thing as society. There are only individuals and their families.' Returning to wider sociological theories we can see that, although functionalism has often been seen as 'conservative', Durkheim's brand of functionalism, with its emphasis on the organic community, was the antithesis of this view (see pp. 44–5).

A third argument is that state bureaucracies are not to be trusted as they can act in their own interests and become too expansive. They and their activities should therefore be kept to a minimum.

Finally, the New Right has particularly emphasized the theory of state overload (Brittan 1983; Friedman 1962). According to this theory the state and its bureaucracies have become overburdened as a result of their efforts to satisfy the ever-increasing demands of various interests (as can be seen in the increasing pressures on the National Health Service).

### *One nation conservatives*

Benjamin Disraeli, Conservative Prime Minister during Queen Victoria's reign, regretted the

**two nations; between whome there is no intercourse and no sympathy; who are as ignorant of each other's habits, thoughts, and feelings, as if they were dwellers in different zones, or inhabitants of different planets; who are formed by different breeding, are fed by a different food, are ordered by different manners, and are not governed by the same laws. . . . *THE RICH AND THE POOR.*** *(Disraeli 1835: 22–5)*

Disraeli therefore advocated social reform, which would generate a more equal, but not totally egalitarian society.

Tory 'wets' have criticized the New Right for disregarding the needs of those unable to thrive in an enterprise culture and thus recreating two nations of rich and poor. Although these more moderate Conservatives still see society as a hierarchy, they have a benevolent, paternalistic attitude and a sense of *noblesse oblige*, combined with a fear of unrest. They see their own wealth as held in trust for the common good, and this helps to explain why many Conservatives supported the development of a welfare state after 1945.

Nevertheless they still have in common with other Conservatives a rejection of egalitarianism, the image of a chain of command, deference to authority, respect for the law, allegiance and patriotism. The common zeal about social control and law and order issues is based on concern about the inherent depravation of the individual (associated with a fallen and sinful human nature) and its destructive potential.

### *Liberal Democrats*

The former Liberal Party and its successor the Liberal Democratic Party have often been perceived as forming the moderate centre ground between the Conservative and Labour parties. Indeed some voters may support them because of this public perception. Most Liberal Democrats would, nevertheless, argue that this is not the case, as their policies are radical and seek major social changes. They aim to defend and enhance civil rights, freedom of belief and speech, the protection of minorities, tolerance, and equal opportunities. Rather than being seen as a centrist party, they seek recognition that some of their radical policies have been 'stolen' by other parties.

Liberals first espoused the idea of a welfare state and (after 1909) Lloyd George's Liberal government started to introduce various welfare schemes. In 1942, the Liberal, William Beveridge produced his *Report on Social Insurance and Allied Services*, which laid the foundations of a welfare state. However, the Labour Party won the 1945 general election and received most of the credit for implementing the report's recommendations.

The origins of the complex relationship between eighteenth-century liberalism, twentieth-century Liberalism, Conservatism and the Labour Party are too intricate to consider here. We can see traces of it in the Labour Party's commitment to equal opportunities, the Conservative Party's focus on individual human effort and economic freedom and the Liberal Democrats' continuing emphasis on personal liberty and civil rights. Both Conservatives and Liberals have been influenced by Adam Smith's (1776) emphasis on *laissez-faire*, although during the twentieth century the Liberal Party strongly allied itself to the economic theories of the Liberal, J M Keynes (1936), while the Conservative Party changed from its previous acceptance of Keynesianism to embrace some of the theories of another Liberal, F A Hayek (1967).

Liberal Democrats have also aimed for radical political change via the decentralization of power. and the reform of an electoral system that has regularly produced a disproportionately small proportion of Liberal Democrat MPs when compared with their actual votes. During the 1990s the Labour Party developed a greater acceptance of both of these aims, and it is reasonable to ask how much difference there is between the Liberal Democratic Party, New Labour and the 'new' politics we will be addressing later (p. 214).

### *Socialism and New Labour*

'The reason we have been out of power for 15 years is simple – society changed and we refused to change with it' (Tony Blair, July 1994). It may have been appropriate to describe socialism and New Labour separately. However, it is very difficult to describe one without referring to the other and in the mid-1990s New Labour, unlike the New Right, is still in a relatively early stage in its development. 'New Labour' is the name which Tony Blair used increasingly in 1994–5 to signal the changes that had taken place in the Labour Party under his leadership. Although his predecessors Neil Kinnock and John Smith had made moves to make Labour less dependent upon its traditional industrial working-class base, Tony Blair took the Labour Party into new territory with the high profile abandonment of Clause 4 of Labour's Constitution which, in theory, had bound the party to a policy of nationalization of industry. Tony Blair's 'New Labour' by contrast embraces the concepts of enterprise, individual responsibility and the market economy, and seeks to address the concerns of what political commentators have labelled 'Middle England'. Whereas the New Right has been criticized for being a strong version of conservatism, New Labour has been criticized for being a weak version of socialism. Marquand, a former Labour MP who had joined the Social Democratic Party until he rejoined Tony Blair's New Labour, suggested that New Labour has consigned aspects of socialism 'to a pauper's grave'.

**Case Study**

### The life after death of socialism

Before consigning socialism to a pauper's grave, it would be as well to re-examine the corpse. Exactly what has died, and how? Has anything survived? The first thing to notice is that the corpse is a more complicated creature than the conventional wisdom allows. Socialism had at least five dimensions.

It was, in the first place, an ethic. It was a difficult ethic to put into words, and socialists disagreed among themselves about how best to do so. Central to almost all their gropings, however, were words like co-operation, commonwealth and fellowship. In non-sexist language, we might call it 'community'.

Secondly, socialism was an economic theory. Socialists of all kinds, Fabians as well as Marxists, gradualists as well as revolutionaries, took it for granted that social ownership would be more efficient than private, and a planned economy more than the free market. The mighty productive powers of modern industry were held back by the chaos of private competition. In a socially-owned economy . . . these powers would be liberated. The result would be a Promethean upsurge of wealth creation, freeing mankind at last from the tyranny of want.

Not only was socialism an economic theory, it was also a science of society. Society, they assumed, followed a determinate path towards a knowable goal. That goal was socialism. It was coming, not only or even mainly because it was right but because it was inevitable. Socialism thus had two faces. Socialists were, of course, committed partisans, embattled advocates of human emancipation. But, in their own eyes at least, they were also dispassionate inquirers, teasing out the laws of social development as physicists and biologists teased out the laws of nature.

Fourthly, socialism was the vehicle of a social interest – the instrument, inspiration and mentor of the labour movement. Socialist doctrine, again whether revolutionary or gradualist, allotted a unique, redemptive role to the proletariat. It was a school for citizenship, a source of self-discipline and self-respect. It threw a glow of principle over the everyday struggles of the factory floor, and gave dignity and meaning to lives which market economics treated as commodities.

*(box continued)*

*(box continued)*

Finally, socialism was a secular religion. It had a heaven and a hell; saints and sinners; martyrs and persecutors; heretics and heresy-hunters; saved and damned; clergy and laity. Above all it had eschatology – a science of last things. One day, the expropriators would be expropriated, the humble would be exalted and a new society, free of exploitation and injustice, would arise from the ruins of the old.

(David Marquand, 'The life after death of socialism', *Guardian* 5 June 1991)

**Marquand goes on to argue that the only dimension to remain intact in New Labour is the first, the socialist ethic.**

### Questions

**Consider the five dimensions described by Marquand.**

**Do they fit your own definition of 'socialism'?**

**How many dimensions remain in the current Labour Party?**

**What evidence is there to support Tony Blair's claim that in the 1980s the Labour Party failed to reflect changes in society?**

## Political participation

Political participation is not the same as political activity. 'Participation' suggests involvement in political decision-making but an individual may be politically active without exerting influence. We have already started to adopt a wider definition of 'politics' because even trying to limit ourselves to descriptions of political structures proved difficult. By discussing structures and outlining some political theories we have started to confront power relationships and the balance of political influence. The next step is to consider the processes by which public opinion is monitored and possibly contributes to political decision-making.

### Elections

Franchise and suffrage both mean the right to vote. The word 'franchise' goes back nearly two thousand years to the kingdom of Frankish Gaul where only the Franks had full rights. Gradually the word has come to apply to the 'privilege' of voting, as there has been pressure throughout history from those who want to be granted the privilege of voting.

In Britain general elections take place at the instigation of the governing party, at intervals of a maximum of five years. By-elections occur when an individual MP has died or resigned from a seat. Local authority elections take place every year, but only one-third of councillors are subject to re-election each year.

### *First-past-the-post system*

This voting system has been used in Great Britain for the election of local councillors, MPs and MEPs; the single transferable vote (STV) system has been used in Northern Ireland for some elections since 1977. In 1995 there were 650 seats in the House of Commons, each representing a single constituency. Voters put a cross next to only one candidate on their voting slip. The candidate with the most votes would therefore win the seat by a simple majority. This means that a candidate has often been elected with a very small proportion of votes. For example, if there are three candidates one may be elected despite 60 per cent of the votes in that constituency going to other candidates.

Every British government since 1945 has been elected with less than half of the total vote. In 1951 Labour obtained 48.8 per cent of the votes, and the Conservatives 48 per cent but the Conservatives had the majority of MPs. In February 1974 Labour received fewer votes than the Conservatives, but Labour had the majority of MPs. In 1987 Conservatives received only 42.3 per cent of the votes but had 102 more seats than the rest of the parties put together.

### *Proportional representation*

Britain is the only member of the European Union that does not use a system of proportional representation (PR); the European Parliament has agreed that all member states should use some form of PR. There are several versions of PR, but all aim to make the proportion of seats held by each party reflect the proportion of the electorate voting for that party. In Britain PR is favoured by the Liberal Democrats and Green Party. There are mixed views within the Conservative and Labour parties, although the Labour Party takes this issue more seriously and has suggested some sort of PR for the election of its proposed Scottish parliament.

An independent campaign group, the Electoral Reform Society, favours the single transferable vote system, which is used in Northern Ireland for local and European Assembly elections in order to give the minority Catholic population some representation. It is also used in the Republic of Ireland, Australia (for the Upper House), Malta and Tasmania.

An STV system involves the creation of large constituencies represented by between two and six MPs. On the ballot form voters rank the candidates in order of preference. The quota of votes needed by any candidate in order to be elected is calculated: for example, if three MPs are to be elected to represent the constituency a candidate will need at least a quarter of the votes. A candidate is elected by gaining more than the necessary quota. The second preferences listed by this candidate's supporters are then weighted and added to the votes for other candidates. After second preferences are allocated, the candidate with the lowest number of votes is eliminated and the second preferences of this candidate's supporters are allocated. When this is done the next candidate with the lowest vote is eliminated and the process continues until all seats are filled. In Greece, the Netherlands, Sweden, Turkey, Israel and Guyana a list system is used. In this system there are no local constituencies and the vote is for a party rather than an individual. Winning candidates are then drawn from the top names on a party's list.

The British Green Party favours the additional members system (AMS) used in Germany, which involves two votes on the ballot paper, one for a local MP and one for a party. Half of the MPs in the German Bundestag are elected by a single majority vote and the other half are elected according to the proportion of votes cast regionally for their party.

**Q** What do you think would be the positive and negative consequences if Britain changed to a system of proportional representation?

### *Presentation of social groups in the political system*

The methods used by political sociologists are often regarded as more statistical than those used by other social scientists. It is easy to see why: political sociologists often aim to monitor grouping in the social structure (especially gender, race and social class) and how these are represented in politics. The results of their work often lead to statistics laid out in tabular form. We will start by considering the representation of some groups among MPs and then appraise the monitoring of public opinion in general, theories about voting, and the relationships between gender, race and social class and voting behaviour.

### *Social backgrounds of Members of Parliament.*

MPs have traditionally been more middle class, highly educated and affluent than the general public, and these features are usually monitored in election studies (psephology). However, if we concentrate on those features in particular, we obscure the finer distinctions between political parties regarding social class and occupation. Table 5.1 shows Curtice's (1994) findings about changes over time.

Labour has consistently had more working-class MPs than the Conservatives, but the percentage declined between 1951 and 1992. Labour has also consistently had fewer MPs from the business community. In the Conservative Party many of the MPs classified as 'Professional' are from the legal profession, while in the Labour Party, teachers and lecturers are strongly represented in this category.

Between 1945 and 1983 the number of women MPs was fairly stable but very low indeed. There was a dramatic rise in the number of women MPs in 1987 and 1992, but still very few women MPs overall – just 9.2 per cent of all MPs after the 1992 general election. Twelve out of the hundred Members of the European Parliament elected in the United Kingdom in 1992 were women; of all MEPs, 19 per cent were female. In general, more women act as representatives of other member states.

**Table 5.1** Occupational background of Conservative and Labour MPs (%).

| | Conservative | | Labour | |
|---|---|---|---|---|
| | 1951 | 1992 | 1951 | 1992 |
| Professional | 41 | 39 | 35 | 42 |
| Business | 37 | 38 | 9 | 8 |
| Miscellaneous | 22 | 22 | 19 | 28 |
| Workers | – | 1 | 37 | 22 |

*Source*: adapted from Curtice 1994: Tables 3.2 and 3.3

**Table 5.2** Women MPs after general elections (numbers).

| General election | Number of women MPs | General election | Number of women MPs |
|---|---|---|---|
| 1918 | 1 | 1955 | 24 |
| 1922 | 2 | 1959 | 25 |
| 1923 | 8 | 1964 | 29 |
| 1924 | 4 | 1966 | 26 |
| 1929 | 14 | 1970 | 26 |
| 1931 | 15 | 1974 | 23 |
| 1935 | 9 | 1974 | 27 |
| 1945 | 24 | 1979 | 19 |
| 1950 | 21 | 1983 | 23 |
| 1951 | 17 | 1987 | 41 |
| | | 1992 | 60 |

*Source*: updated from *Labour Research* January 1991

Although Margaret Thatcher successfully led the Conservative Party through three general elections, the very low number of women Conservative MPs and Cabinet ministers is often obscured. The Labour Party and other political parties tend to have proportionally more women MPs. Since 1992 the Speaker of the House of Commons has been Betty Boothroyd (originally a Labour MP) and most of the women MPs in Table 5.2 have been in the Labour Party. The deputy leader of Labour in the early 1990s was also a woman (Margaret Beckett). Labour has been trying to have more women on the shortlists of candidates in winnable seats. Conservatives want more candidates but, unlike Labour, have refused to use positive discrimination in the selection of shortlists.

The Labour Party includes a pressure group called 'Emily's List' which aims to have more women elected as Labour MPs. During the 1990s, there have been fervent debates about the morality of positive discrimination. Members of the all-party 300 Group aim to encourage and enable more women to stand for Parliament and increase the number of women MPs to about 300. Yet divisions between feminists have been particularly noticeable, as some feminists claim that just increasing the number of women MPs simply addresses electoral issues and does not deal with more fundamental issues regarding the role of women in politics.

Similar concern has been expressed about the racial mix of MPs. 'Black' candidates have been more successful in local authority elections than in parliamentary elections. The first Black MP was in office as long ago as 1922–9: Shapurji Saklatvala was the Communist and Labour MP representing North Battersea. However, for many years since then, all MPs could have been described as white. In the 1979 general election there were five Black candidates and none was elected; in the 1983 general election, there were eighteen Black candidates and again, none was elected. This can at least partly be explained by the 'unwinnable' seats in which Black candidates stood (Saggar 1992: 165–8) and the kinds of seats in which they tended to be most successful (generally inner city areas). In the 1987 general election there were thirty-two Black candidates and four were elected; by the 1992 general election, there were even more Black candidates but only six were elected. To assess fully the representation of various social groups among MPs, electoral processes would, therefore, have to be studied in considerable detail.

## Public opinion

Political sociology is perhaps best known for its interest in monitoring public opinion (usually shown in general attitude surveys opinion). It would not be possible for us to analyse various survey findings in detail, but some general comments must be made about political research methods, theories about voting behaviour, and the relationships between gender, race, social class and voting behaviour.

### *Problems with opinion polls*

At the 1992 general election the error in forecasting the gap between the Conservative Party and Labour was greater than ever before (an average of 8.9 per cent error in the final polls by the leading organizations, compared to 4.0 per cent in 1987, 3.6 per cent in 1983 and 2.4 per cent in 1979). Denis Kavanagh (1992) suggested some explanations for the inaccuracy of the polls:

Case Study

#### Problems of prediction

1 *Sampling methods* It is possible that the use of quota sampling resulted in an unrepresentative sample and that the more expensive, random sampling would have been more accurate. We could add that the polls did not include overseas voters (who were most likely to vote Conservative) and, as their voting rights had been extended, there were substantially more of them in 1992.
2 *Non-registration* It is possible that significant numbers of people (mainly Labour supporters) tried to avoid payment of the poll tax by failing to register to vote.
3 *Time of polling* Most opinion polls were carried out during the week. It has been argued that more Conservative voters are available at weekends.
4 *A late swing* A dramatic last-minute swing of voters towards the Conservative Party could explain the apparent discrepancy in the opinion poll findings. It is not clear that this happened in 1992, although it seems that there was a larger than usual number of late deciders. Gallup polls found that 14 per cent decided in the last two or three days before the election, compared to 8 per cent in 1987.
5 *Differential turnout* It is possible that some of the people who told pollsters that they would vote Labour did not actually vote. Further research has suggested that up to half the polls' errors could be accounted for by last-minute changes or to non-registration.
6 *Tactical voting* It is possible that the forecast of a hung Parliament with a small Labour majority induced a late Conservative swing.
7 *Conservative refusals* After the election ICM found that 'undecided' and 'don't knows' voted disproportionately Conservative. This could invalidate polls in general.
8 *Contradictions* It is possible that there was a difference between stated attitudes to pollsters about taxation and public spending (many said that they favoured high taxation in order to fund public spending) and attitudes towards these issues when voting (some favouring a party associated with low taxation).

Crewe (1992) argued that 'Had the campaign polls consistently shown the Conservatives to be ahead - as they probably were - the government might not have mobilised the anti-Labour vote so effectively and hence may not have survived in office.'

*(box continued)*

*(box continued)*

**Questions**

**Do opinion polls still play an important role in British politics?**

**What are the arguments for and against the banning of opinion polls in the last week of an election campaign'?**

## Theories about voting behaviour

During the 1960s Butler and Stokes developed what is often defined as the party identification (or expressive) model. This includes an emphasis on family influence on voting behaviour. They also describe the four 'ages of political man' to explain the process of political socialization and how awareness and attitudes develop and change over time. Furthermore, they identify three criteria by which an issue can be judged in terms of its impact on voting behaviour: the issue must be associated differently with the political parties in the voters' minds, there should be considerable strength of feeling about the issue, and opinion on the issue must be skewed (i.e. it must strongly favour one side of the argument).

Crewe (1992) developed a rational choice (or consumer) model, which argues that political issues and self-interest are particularly influential. According to this model, party identification is conditional and parties must persuade voters that their policies are valid.

David Denver has developed a model (1989: 76, Figure 4.1) which addresses the relationship between social location (party identification model), policy preferences (rational choice model) and party choice. He presents three possible relationships between the three potential influences. Unbroken lines indicate causal paths, and broken lines indicate an indirect relationship.

### *Denver's models of influences on voting behaviour*

In one possible relationship social location determines both party choice and policy preferences, resulting in an indirect relationship between party choice and policy preference (Fig 5.2a).

**Fig 5.2a** An indirect relationship between party choice and policy preference.

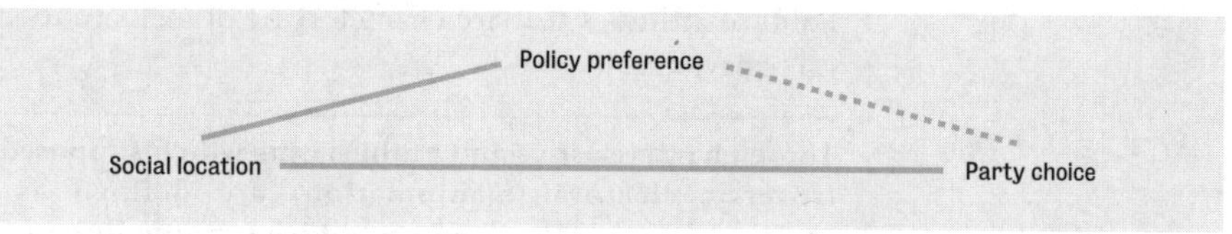


*Source*: Denver 1989: 76

In a second relationship social location determines policy preferences, which determines party choice. This results in an indirect relationship between social location and party choice (Fig 5.2b).

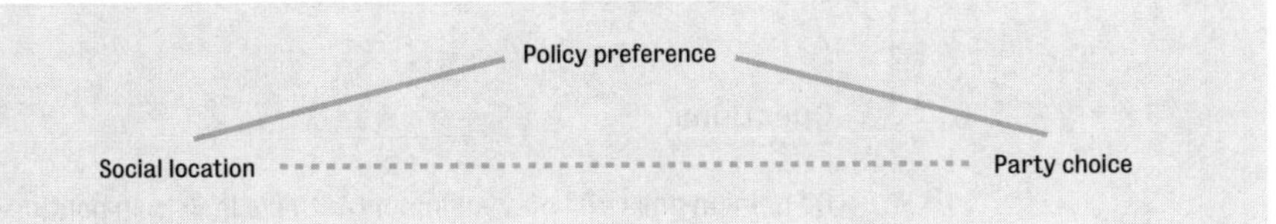


**Fig 5.2b** An indirect relationship between social location and party choice.

*Source*: Denver 1989: 76

In a third relationship social location determines vote, and policy preferences are adjusted to accommodate party choice. This results in an indirect relationship between social location and policy preferences (Fig 5.2c).

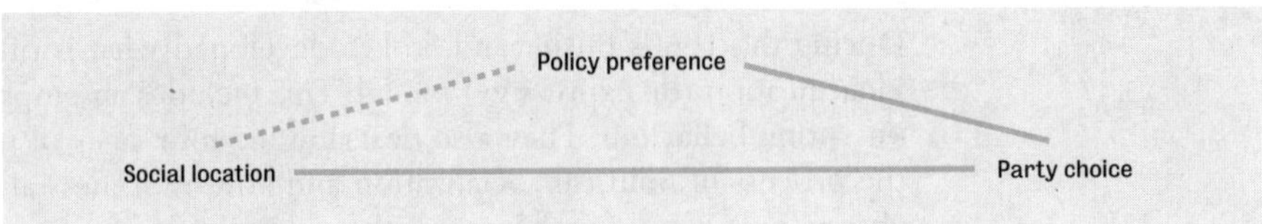


**Fig 5.2c** An indirect relationship between social location and policy preferences.

*Source*: Denver 1989: 76

**Q**

Compare Butler and Stokes' theories with other findings and theories in order to discuss the extent to which family background influences voting behaviour.

Assess the usefulness of Butler and Stokes' three criteria for judging the impact of an issue.

Assess the usefulness of Denver's model as an explanation for voting behaviour.

## Gender and voting behaviour

When sociologists consider gender and voting behaviour they are interested not only in gender differences in voting behaviour, but also in gender differences in levels of political participation and feminist critiques of political scientists. Before proceeding to analyse gender differences in political behaviour it is therefore important to bear in mind the following feminist criticisms of social scientists:

1 They sometimes 'fudge the footnotes', which includes producing misleading statements or statements that are unsupported by references.
2 They may assume that men influence women's political attitudes, but not vice versa.
3 Political attitudes that are characteristic of men are used to define mature political behaviour.

> **Those characteristics and enthusiasms which supposedly sway men (wars, controversy, electoral manipulation) are defined as political, while those characteristics and enthusiasms which supposedly sway women (human need for food, clothing, shelter, adherence to consistent moral principles, a rejection of war as rational) are simply not considered political**
>
> ***(Bourque and Grossholtz 1984: 118)***

4 The political contribution of women is equated with their role as mothers.

5 Feminists often claim that there has been a tendency among political scientists to separate the public world of politics and employment from the private world of the family and interpersonal relations. This idea is embodied in the notion of the private woman and the public man. For example, Siltanen and Stanworth (1984) argued that politics must intervene in private situations in order 'to protest against abuses of freedom and dignity. Intimacy and privacy are neither licences for, nor protection against, inhuman conduct' (1984: 207). They were concerned that the idealized image of the family 'offers no solace to battered women and children who suffer from the neglect of our political institutions in the name of personal freedom (1984: 207).

You should consider these potential criticisms when analysing Table 5.3.

Crewe (1992) noted that the swing to Labour in 1992 was greater among men (3.5 per cent) than women (1.5 per cent) and claims that this can be partially explained by John Major's replacement of Margaret Thatcher as party leader. He argues that Mrs Thatcher's 'macho' image appealed to men but repelled women.

**Table 5.3** Vote by sex in the general election compared with the 1987 and 1979 elections.

| | Con | Lab | Lib Dem | Con lead over Lab | Swing to Labour |
|---|---|---|---|---|---|
| **Men** | | | | | |
| Vote in 1992 | 41 | 40 | 19 | +1 | +3.5 |
| Change from 1987 | -1 | +6 | -5 | -7 | |
| Change from 1979 | -4 | -1 | +5 | -3 | +1.5 |
| **Women** | | | | | |
| Vote in 1992 | 45 | 36 | 19 | +9 | +1.5 |
| Change from 1987 | +1 | +4 | -5 | -3 | |
| Change from 1979 | -2 | -1 | +3 | -1 | +0.5 |
| **First-time voters** | | | | | |
| Vote in 1992 | 35 | 40 | 25 | -5 | +9.5 |
| Change from 1987 | −10 | +9 | +2 | −19 | |
| Change from 1979 | −11 | +3 | +8 | −14 | +7.0 |
| **People aged 22–29** | | | | | |
| Vote in 1992 | 43 | 41 | 16 | +2 | -1.5 |
| Change from 1987 | +7 | +4 | -11 | +3 | |
| Change from 1979 | +7 | -4 | -3 | +11 | -5.5 |
| **People aged 30–44** | | | | | |
| Vote in 1992 | 39 | 39 | 21 | 0 | +5.0 |
| Change from 1987 | -3 | +7 | -6 | -10 | |
| Change from 1979 | -9 | +3 | +5 | -12 | +6.0 |
| **People aged 45–64** | | | | | |
| Vote in 1992 | 44 | 35 | 21 | +9 | +2.0 |
| Change from 1987 | -1 | -3 | -2 | -4 | |
| Change from 1979 | -3 | -6 | +8 | +3 | -1.5 |
| **People aged 65 and over** | | | | | |
| Vote in 1992 | 48 | 37 | 14 | +11 | +2.5 |
| Change from 1987 | 0 | +5 | -6 | -5 | |
| Change from 1979 | +2 | 0 | -3 | +2 | -1.0 |

*Notes*: figures show the three parties' share of the three–party vote; 'swing' means the 'Butler swing'; because of rounding rows do not always add up to 100%; the table slightly over-estimates the actual 1987–92 swing to Labour because the 1992 Harris/ITN exit poll figures were Con 4.1%: Lab 36% when the actual result was Con 43%: Lab 35%

*Source*: Harris/ITN exit polls, 3 May 1979, 11 June 1987, 9 April 1992, adapted from Crewe 1992:4, Table 2

Cynthia Cockburn (1987) presents a view that reflects the third item on our list of feminist criticisms. She argues that the interests of women are not included within definitions of 'politics' (see the reference to democracy and citizenship in ancient Greece, p. 182). Furthermore she suggests that behaviour that may be labelled 'naive' is actually a rejection of the terms of political debate (Cockburn 1987; see also Lovenduski and Randall 1993: 157–60).

### Race and voting behaviour

You can read elsewhere in this book about the problems researchers have in categorizing 'race' (pp. 318–23). As Britain's Black and mixed race voters are heterogeneous, and include other significant social groupings (such as social classes, genders, religions, age groups and geographical areas) it is possible that researchers could find no race-related voting patterns. However, Zig Layton Henry (1989) identified differences in the voting behaviour of 'Asian' and 'Afro-Caribbean' voters. Afro-Caribbean adults have been less likely to be registered to vote in a general election (a Harris poll found that the actual turnout in the general election of 1987 was 75.3%, 72% of all adults said they would vote, but 74% of 'Asians', and only 51% of 'Afro-Caribbeans'). There also seems to be more Black support for Labour, especially from voting Afro-Caribbeans. A Harris poll of 1983 found that this support was consistent across Blacks in all social classes, but they were attracted by Labour's traditional support for the working-class population, rather than the interests of the Black population. This seems strange in view of the Liberal Party, Social Democratic Party, and now Liberal Democratic Party's strong and long-standing support for minority rights, anti-racism and opposition to severe immigration controls.

### Social class and voting behaviour

Many political sociologists associate changes in the relationship between social class and voting behaviour with post-modernism. We will be referring to the work of John Curtice (1994: 33–42) throughout this section because he acknowledges diversity within social classes (a feature of post-modernism) but argues that the effects of this on the British political system seem to have been exaggerated by many analysts.

Curtice acknowledges the changing sizes and characteristics of social classes; with more white-collar workers now than blue-collar workers, more home ownership, more voters with a higher education, and a reduction in religious adherence. Yet, he argues that our main interest is in the proportion of Conservative and Labour votes that come from different classes. If the proportions for each of these parties have become similar to each other we can claim that there has been a decline in relative class voting.

In order to judge this we will consider the two important theories of class dealignment and partisan dealignment.

### *Theories of class dealignment*

Many researchers have observed that, since the 1970s, there has been a fundamental decline in the relationship between social class and loyalty to one political party. In addition to the changing characteristics listed above we should consider the difficulties today in defining social class. The former 'working class' now includes workers who have shares in their companies, and do not therefore conform to the proletariat of Marx's lifetime.

Divisions in the middle class can also be perceived, including the different political allegiances of many public and private employees. It is argued (Dunleavy 1980) that production and consumption sectoral cleavages may be better indicators of voting behaviour than simple definitions of social class, such as the Registrar General's Scale (which, in the late 1990s, is being revised and updated). In Leadbetter's analysis of the divided workforce (Riley 1988: 313) we can also see additional differences between workers based on their level of job security.

If class dealignment has occurred the implication is that the 'working class' has been weakened as a political force. The long term of government by the Conservative Party, from 1979, also led to fears that Britain was moving out of multi-party politics into hegemonic rule by one party.

At this point you should reflect on Table 5.1 (p. 200) and the section above it, which describe the occupational backgrounds of Conservative and Labour MPs. Curtice notes that there have been some changes in the social composition of these MPs, but there are still some clear and long-standing differences, for example in the 'Workers' and 'Business' categories.

With regard to class dealignment Curtice states that, although changes in the size and identity of social groups have been a net disadvantage to Labour, the impact on Labour's support has been small compared with the scale of its relative decline in the polls. Other factors must also be considered. In addition, the occupational backgrounds of MPs in the two main parties still follow traditional patterns which make it difficult for voters to perceive any fundamental change in their differing social backgrounds.

**Table 5.4** The divided working class: the parties' share of the vote among different groups of manual workers (%).

| | The new working class | | | | The traditional working class | | | |
|---|---|---|---|---|---|---|---|---|
| | Lives in South | Owner occupier | Non-union member | Works in private sector | Lives in Scotland or North | Council tenant | Union member | Works in public sector |
| Conservative | 40 | 40 | 37 | 32 | 26 | 22 | 29 | 36 |
| Labour | 38 | 41 | 46 | 50 | 59 | 64 | 55 | 48 |
| Liberal Democrat | 23 | 19 | 17 | 18 | 15 | 13 | 16 | 16 |
| Con or Lab majority in 1992 | Con +2 | Lab +1 | Lab +9 | Lab +18 | Lab +33 | Lab +42 | Lab +26 | Lab +12 |
| Con or Lab majority in 1987 | Con +18 | Con +12 | Con +2 | Lab +1 | Lab +28 | Lab +32 | Lab +18 | Lab +17 |
| Swing to Labour 1987–92 | +8.0 | +6.5 | +5.5 | +8.5 | +2.5 | +5.0 | +4.0 | -2.5 (to Con) |

*Source*: Gallup/BBC survey, 10–11 June 1987; Gallup post-election survey, 10–11 April 1992, in Crewe 1992:5 Table 4

### *Theories of partisan dealignment*

Since the 1970s there has been a dilution of loyalty to the two major political parties' philosophies and policies. Voters are less likely to have a lifetime commitment to one political party. Their vote may change over time and according to the context of the election (for example voting differently at general elections and local authority elections). 'Floating voters' may be open to persuasion at election time and may, for example, be politically apathetic or primarily influenced by the issues of the day (see our earlier résumé of some 'Theories about voting behaviour').

Curtice argued that there was no real evidence of a pattern of partisan dealignment. First, he argued that the effects of social change and electoral volatility had been exaggerated, and that these theories underestimate the resistance of political systems to social change. An important part of this resistance is the first-past-the-post electoral system (see p. 199) as it would not accurately reflect partisan dealignment.

Even if social change had been responsible for a collapse in the strength of the two-party system at the popular level, we would have had to conclude that its impact on the way that Britain is governed had so far been muted. For the impact of social change upon politics is mediated by the political – and that includes the constitutional – rules as well as the actions of politicians (Curtice 1994: 42).

Above all, social class remains an important cleavage at both elite and mass level. Rather than the helpless plaything of sociological forces, post-war British politics has been vitally shaped by political choices and developments (Curtice 1994: 41). Curtice argued that, rather than a straightforward pattern in the relationship between class and vote, the period between 1964 and 1992 indicated a 'trendless fluctuation' which could be explained by the particular circumstances of each election. He found, for example, that class alignment was weakest at the end of periods of Labour government, which may reflect a disillusion with Labour's performance while in office.

## Who are the activists?

We have already considered political participation with regard to elections and voting behaviour. Here we will ask how politically active people are and what is the nature of their activity? Before looking at some research findings, we will ask you to assess your own political activity.

**Case Study**

**How politically active are you?**

- Individually, and honestly, decide whether you fit any of the following categories 1–7. If you do not fit any, how do you define yourself?
- In a group, list the categories on a board, together with the numbers in the group who fit each category (or do not fit any).
- What problems have arisen?
- How would you describe your group's level of political activity?
- Are you, as students of political sociology, representative of the wider population?

*(box continued)*

(box continued)

1 Inactive: do not vote regularly or have any other involvement
2 A voting specialist: only vote
3 A group specialist: involvement only in a group context
4 A party campaign specialist: have campaigned for a political party
5 A contacting specialist: have contacted politicians (by letter, by telephone, at the politician's surgery or in other ways)
6 A protesting specialist: participating in marches, demonstrations, protest letters
7 A complete activist: active across the board from 2 to 6.

The Political Participation Study, carried out by Parry *et al.* (1989) comprised a national sample (1,578) survey of the population of England, Wales and Scotland (carried out in 1984/5) together with a survey of citizens and leaders in local communities.

The researchers observed that an issue must be identified as susceptible to individual influence, and they list four main reasons why people take action.

1 *Instrumentally* to defend or promote their own interests.
2 *Communitarian* for the good of the community at large.
3 *Educative and developmental* increasing understanding of society or politics.
4 *Expressive* stating your position on a matter that may or may not affect you and on which one might not expect immediate return in terms of changed policy.

Parry *et al.* (1989) note that an individual may take action for more than one of the above reasons. Very little action was taken on issues that were considered to be beyond their respondents' sphere of influence. More action was taken on relatively local issues (such as housing, the environment, education and transport) that were perceived as both affecting the household directly and most amenable to influence.

Perhaps the most substantial findings about political activity relate to the social location of the particularly active or inactive. The British Political Participation Study found that professionals were 'massively over-represented', among complete activists, by about five times their relative size in the population. Some other non-manual grades were also over-represented.

**one can see very clearly that being part of the participatory elite corresponds very closely to being from the non-manual, and especially managerial, strata of society. Most members of the middle class are not political activists. . . . Conversely, those from manual occupations, and particularly those from households outside the economically active sector, are under represented. In the latter case, we may be observing some age-related effects. Whatever the case, however, in social terms, both they and the proletariat are conspicuous by their relative absence. The 'chorus' of complete activists clearly sings with an upper-class accent.** ***(Parry et al. 1989: 29)***

Although the majority of 'complete activists' are middle class, it was not found that the majority of middle class were activists. It has already been noted that over 75 per cent respondents in the British Political Participation Study did nothing more than vote in elections. Even among the relatively active middle class, 'complete activists' were in the minority.

Q Parry *et al.* (1989) categorized respondents according to level of political activity as follows (compare these findings with your group findings):

25.8 per cent were inactive did not vote regularly or have any other involvement
51.0 per cent were voting specialists only voted
8.7 per cent were group specialists involvement only in a group context
2.2 per cent were party campaign specialists
7.7 per cent were contacting specialists contacted politicians, etc.
3.1 per cent were protesting specialists marches, demonstrations, letters
1.5 per cent were complete activists active across the board.

These findings are supported by more findings about action and assertiveness from various British Social Attitude (BSA) surveys (for example, Jowell *et al.* 1992). Levels of local and national assertiveness were measured and an apparent increase (between the BSA 1983/4 and 1985 findings) in national assertiveness was found. Comparisons in local assertiveness were made over time, using the 1960 study (Almond and Verba 1965) and a survey carried out for the Redcliffe Maud Committee (1969) on local government during the early months of 1965. These are rather dated but useful for assessing changes in attitudes over time.

Almond and Verba (1965), Redcliffe Maud (1969) and various BSA surveys all provide evidence of the greater willingness of individuals to act on their own account when roused by some proposed local action. The most highly educated and most affluent people are more likely to act.

It long been claimed that more men than women take action. However, there are criticisms of how action is defined and of sexism in political studies (see pp. 204–6). It would be useful to consider these criticisms, together with the implications of the following:

1 More full-time employees and trade unionists are active.
2 Women may be more tied to the home.
3 The most highly educated people tend to express feelings of political efficacy. Even at a time when girls seem to be achieving more than boys in school-leaving examinations, more men than women in the older population have had a higher education.
4 Bourque and Grossholtz (1984) argue that women might simply be more realistic:

**One might offer the alternative hypothesis, that given the very limited number of issues that citizens can effect, the lower sense of political efficacy expressed by women is a perceptive assessment of the process. Men, on the other hand, express irrationally high rates of efficacy because of the limitations of their sex role which teaches them that they are masterful and capable of affecting the political process. In fact, few of us have any political influence in any case.**

***(Bourque and Grossholtz 1984: 107)***

## Participation theories

Few people are politically active beyond just voting in an election; one possible explanation arises from Maslow's (1970) theory of a hierarchy of human motivations. According to this theory, an individual's material needs and psychological safety need to be satisfied before more expressive needs can be satisfied. Expressive needs include such emotions as affection, esteem and self-actualization and although there is some overlapping of the hierarchy (affection can, for example, be felt in the most dire circumstances), expressive needs are considered less important than physical and spiritual survival. Political activity could be assigned to Maslow's fifth (and lowest) tier of needs ('self-actualization').

---

**Disempowerment through inertia is exactly what so-called civilised, democratic governments like best, especially those most intent on maintaining the status quo. It allows them to assert, in the absence of a large-scale and vocal opposition, that they are acting on behalf of the 'ordinary person in the street'. The 'ordinary person in the street' would never resort to nasty demonstrations or shout at public meetings. Or would they?** ***(Button 1995: 11)***

---

There is more about changes in political activity in the next section, which draws on the theories of Claus Offe (1985) and Richard Inglehart (1977).

**Q**

Would you be more likely to act on a local issue than a national issue?

Suppose a regulation were being considered by your local council that you considered very unjust.

What do you think you would do?

What action, if any, would you take if Parliament was considering a law which you regarded as unjust or harmful?

List and discuss possible reasons for lack of political activity.

## 'Old' and 'new' politics

Changes in the social composition of left- and right-wing parties and the changing characteristics of trade union activities have been cited as illustrations of a 'new' style of politics in western democracies. Political analysts claim that an 'old' style of political participation (involving social class alignment, partisan alignment, and formal pressure group activity) has been replaced, or is in transition towards, a 'new' style of political participation (involving class dealignment, partisan dealignment, and loosely linked campaigns for social and political change with greater emphasis on wider moral concerns).

We have already considered class and partisan alignment and dealignment but have not yet explained what we mean by pressure groups. Definitions generally include most of the following: that they are highly organized and hierarchical groups, defending their members' self-interest, exerting pressure within the political system, but not seeking elective office for themselves, nor presenting a programme covering a wide range of policies.

This means that the trade union movement is often described as a pressure group, or as an 'old' social movement to be compared with 'new' social movements (such as the women's liberation movement, the peace movement, the environmental/green movement). Yet, when you consider changes within trade unions and claims that some groups can be called 'pressure movements', you will see that labels are not easily attached. The Black civil rights movement in the USA and the anti-poll tax movement are similarly difficult to categorize.

## 'Old' politics

The 'old' style of politics is often associated with modernist themes, such as industrialization, mass production, an emphasis on class conflict, Marxist critiques, the trade union movement, and pressure group activity working within formal political systems. However, it is important not to accept too easily what may be a rather simple image of the past. For example, Button (1995) suggests that there are some remaining elements of 'old' politics.

First, Button claims that the gap between the haves and the have-nots has been widened by economic policies favouring a market economy. Second, he argues that those policies have promoted money as the only valid measure of value. In the second half of the twentieth century, commercial and relatively covert political tactics have helped to disempower the silent majority and have increasingly replaced overt social and military power tactics. His third suggestion is that the power establishment have retained some oppressive, elitist views. Finally, Button observes that political activity by pressure groups remains, although many groups have adjusted to a new political environment.

## Institutional influences on political change in Britain

To identify important aspects of political change in Britain we will reconsider political participation, relate it to developments in the political structure, and ask how democratic and pluralist the British political system is. This helps to explain 'new' politics' concern with moral issues, civil rights and personal freedoms.

We have seen that opportunities for voters to influence policy are minimized by the British (first-past-the-post) electoral system. It is possible, not only for a British government to be elected by a minority of all votes, but also for it to have less electoral support than any other government in power in a European democracy. Furthermore, Britain has no entrenched constitution to limit what the party with a parliamentary majority (but a minority of the vote) may do. During the Conservative governments of the late twentieth century most of their electoral support has been in the south of the country, leaving many voters feeling alienated from power.

A large proportion of voters and politicians still favour the first-past-the-post system because it provides a relatively straightforward result and (usually) a clear parliamentary majority. The most common criticism of proportional representation is that it leads to coalition governments, and uncertainty, as competing factions disagree. However, PR is also praised for limiting the power of a Prime Minister or President and forcing compromise between parties, thus ensuring that policies are acceptable to a wider span of voters. You were asked earlier if Britain had a pluralist or corporatist system. If you found that it had elements of one, or both, of these you may feel that pressure groups have provided avenues of participation to compensate for possible problems with the voting system.

Concern remains that a single-party government with voting discipline in Parliament gives the British Prime Minister a power base that few leaders have elsewhere in Europe. A lengthy period of government by one political party has also provided it with the time to implement radical changes. Conservative governments have been able to increase their powers because of four terms of continuous office (e.g. via the centralization of education policy, the reduced influence of local govern-

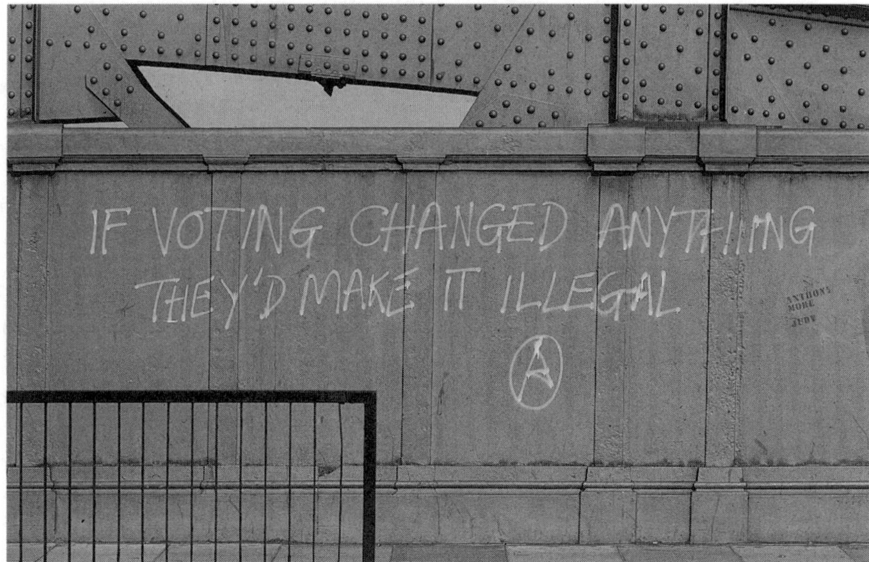


**Fig 5.3** Political graffiti at Royal Oak Station, London. (Courtesy of Robert Harding Picture Library Ltd.)

ment, increased controls over trade unions, the Criminal Justice Act, etc.). They have been accused of having a combination of ideological certainty and authoritarian instincts (Riley 1988) and, in the early 1990s the 'sleaze' factor (of various government scandals) became a topic of national debate. Whether this factor is a uniquely modern phenomenon is debatable. In 1887, for instance, Lord Acton made his celebrated claim: 'Power tends to corrupt, and absolute power corrupts absolutely. Great men are almost always bad men.' This claim can be disputed, but growing concern about government power could be associated with changes from an 'old' to a 'new' political style in Britain and in other countries.

Perhaps the most important problem relating to political change in Britain is the lack of political activity (beyond voting) by most of the population (see Parry *et al.* 1989; see also pp. 208–11). This helps to explain the rise of a 'new' pattern of political activity.

---

**Today's decision-makers grew up in a postcolonial, post-global war world, where women and foreigners and racial minorities and homosexuals and the sick and the disabled and children and old people are known to have rights, even when those rights are deliberately thwarted. The big difference is that until our parents' generation people could be blinkered and still semi-legitimately excuse themselves for being blinkered. 'We didn't know. There wasn't anything we could do. They deserved it.' Having reached the end of a century of extremes we now live in an age where there is no excuse not to know and no excuse not to take a stand.**

***(Button 1995: 44)***

---

**Q** Do you agree with Button's contention that 'we now live in an age where there is no excuse not to know and no excuse not to take a stand'? What kind of stand (a) should we take; (b) can we take?

## 'New' politics

Button also claims that when he refers to 'radicalism' it can most closely be associated with empowerment and that 'a new fearlessness has emerged – a realization that oppressive centralised power must be resisted and balanced by "people power"' (Button 1995: 12).

This 'new' style of politics is also associated with post-modernist themes: such as the diversification of production, and loss of social class and other identities, class dealignment and partisan dealignment. It is important not to accept too easily what may be a rather simple image of changes that are associated with the second half of the twentieth century, and still in a process of development. It is, nevertheless, possible to identify a growing concern (in 'new' politics and 'new' social movements) that has less to do with social class and more to do with wider examples of inequalities (e.g. women's liberation; racial issues; children's rights; gay liberation; elderly, poor and disabled people; animal liberation), wider moral issues, rights and oppression.

This clearly involves a particular interest in civil liberties and citizenship; much has been written about civil liberties in the past (Marshall 1947), and more recently (McKie with Bindman 1994). In keeping with some aspects of 'new' politics are new academic debates about communitarianism (in the USA, e.g., Etzioni 1993) which emphasize a balance between the rights of individuals and their responsibilities to the community. It aims to remove severe impediments to community relationships; for example, providing education for parenthood, helping parents to help themselves, and devolving considerable government power to a local level.

Another important difference between 'old' and 'new' politics and social movements is in the change from a politics that focuses on material issues to a politics that seeks cultural change. For example, the women's liberation movement aims to change, not only material and social inequalities between women and men, but particularly the attitudes that lie behind them. This involves enlightening men and women and empowering women in their social and personal lives. Similarly, the gay liberation movement seeks to change social inequalities and the attitudes that support them. For some movements this involves providing a strong cultural backing to support their supporters (for example, in the gay liberation movement, this involves the movement's own newspapers and magazines, pop music, nightclubs and other local and national groupings). Here can be seen an emphasis on both political change and improvements in the quality of life. It can also be seen that there is likely to be an overlap as some individuals support a number of movements.

These attitudinal and cultural changes have been addressed by many writers (see e.g. Dalton and Kuechler, 1990). An additional dimension can be added by looking at Inglehart's materialist/post-materialist hypothesis. Inglehart (1977) claims that, once their basic material needs have been satisfied, people are free to develop post-materialist interests. Materialist interests are associated with 'old' politics, post-materialist interests with 'new' politics.

## Pressure movements

It is difficult to label some movements as either 'old ' or 'new' social movements; a third form of political grouping may be seen as including some of the features of each style of movement. Tonge (1994) found that the anti-poll tax movement included features of both the 'old' and the 'new', and that 'pressure movement' might be the best label to attach to it. He identified five characteristics of a pressure movement:

1 It is concerned with political aims.
2 Its aims are limited to single-issue campaigns.
3 It may possess a class base, but not a class force.
4 It is likely to adopt a highly centralized form.
5 It is likely to bypass political parties as agents of change.

He concludes that, although he can define the anti-poll tax movement as a pressure movement, it would be difficult to find others.

**Q** Consider the trade union movement, women's liberation movement and black civil rights movement in the USA.

How would you label each of them: for example, a pressure group, 'old' social movement, 'new' social movement, pressure movement, or something else?

Why did you choose that particular label?

Another feature of 'new' politics and movements is seen in the increasing use of less formal (compared to 'old' politics) channels of political participation. Protest movements of the 1960s left a legacy of sometimes large-scale protest, and unorthodox methods. For example, in their protests against the storing of nuclear missiles at Greenham Common, activists' tactics included knitting the gates shut and having a teddybear's picnic on the missile silos (Barker 1992). Most of this action is peaceful, as violent behaviour would challenge the very aims of 'new' social movements. However, this chapter will end by contrasting peaceful activity with extreme and sometimes violent action.

## Extreme and/or violent political action

Within any political organization (for example, a political party or pressure group) or movement, there are likely to be several flanks, representing differences of opinion about policies and/or action. Extremists who create a radical flank can either discredit the image of the whole movement or indirectly support the moderates' case by suggesting that political decision-makers have little to fear from moderate elements. Malcolm X provided a figurehead for the extremist Nation of Islam, but explained how he felt that his group of radicals could help the whole black civil rights movement in the USA.

**I want Dr. King to know that I didn't come to Selma to make his job difficult. I really did come thinking that I could make it easier. If white people realize what the alternative is, perhaps they'll be more willing to hear Dr. King.**

*(Malcolm X 1965, quoted in Haines 1988: 1)*

Martin Luther King was not easily impressed and predicted

**The more there are riots, the more repression will take place, and the more we face the danger of a right-wing take-over, and eventually a fascist society.**

*(Martin Luther King, quoted in Haines 1988: 1)*

It is easy to see how radical flanks can become terrorist organizations. Some radicals may feel that their peaceful methods have been unsuccessful and that the only alternative is to use violence. In his deprivation theory. Gurr (1970: 24) proposed that 'the potential for collective violence varies strongly with the intensity and scope of relative depravation among members of a collectivity'.

There is also the possibility that radical flanks can attract individuals who join because they are more interested in violence than in the movement's aims. Terrorism aims to inspire terror, by using violence, or the threat of violence, intimidation and a rejection of compromise. This, of course, means that some political systems answer that description (as we saw near the start of this chapter) and the old problem of distinguishing between freedom-fighters and terrorists remains. It is likely that relationships between political systems, social movements and political violence will vary considerably.

Q

Which of the following political groups are least likely to spawn violence: (a) pressure groups; (b) 'old' social movements; (c) 'new' social movements; (d) pressure movements?

Would you describe the African National Congress (before the end of apartheid) as (a) a terrorist organization; (b) a group of freedom fighters; (c) some sort of social movement?

How would you label South African governments during the time of apartheid?

Devise your own model(s) of relationships between states, violence and social movements.

## Revolutions

We started this chapter by considering the struggle for human rights and freedoms, forced exclusion of some social groups from citizenship and the problems associated with achieving a democracy. Although this included references to warfare, it excluded revolutionary change because it is difficult to define 'revolution', and activity that can be considered 'revolutionary' (Kimmel 1990, cited in Giddens 1992: 323). The word 'revolution' could be taken literally and represented by a state, social or economic arrangement revolving until it is upside-down. This can be seen, to some extent, in the French Revolution (starting 1789) and Russian Revolution (starting 1917. However, when other 'revolutions' (such as the industrial revolution and the revolutions in eastern Europe of 1989 and onwards) are analysed the picture is even less clear.

Q

To what extent are all revolutions violent?

To what extent are individual social movements revolutionary?

In the first box of this chapter you were asked to define 'politics'. Define it again to consider any similarities and differences between the two.

Have you personally been aware of a change from 'old' to 'new' politics? Explain your answer.

## Summary

- A narrow definition of politics emphasizes formal political structures, including international bodies such as the UN and EU and British institutions such as the monarchy, Parliament and civil service. A wider definition would encompass political theories and processes, including voting and other forms of political participation.
- Basic classifications of political parties and governments divide them into right wing or left wing. However, this categorization is far from straightforward; totalitarian states can be either extremely right wing or left wing and fascist movements and leaders have appealed to those who would see themselves as basically left wing.
- Political participation suggests an involvement in political decision-making. In modern mass societies, studies of political participation have focused on patterns of voting. Models of voting behaviour include the party identification model that emphasizes the influence of background on voting; the rational choice model highlighting the voter's self-interest and more complex models of relationships between social background, policy preferences and choice of political party.
- Political decision-makers are usually more middle class, highly educated and wealthy than the general population, and much more likely to be male and white.
- The continued success of the Conservative Party in British general elections between 1979 and 1992 encouraged research into class background and political support. The decline in the relationship between social class and loyalty to a particular party is known as class dealignment and the decline in loyalty to particular political philosophies and policies is termed partisan dealignment.
- Changes in the nature of political parties and the movement away from strong political loyalty and commitment to one political position have been seen as evidence of a 'new' style of politics. The old style of politics was characterized by class loyalty to one party, trade union support and political pressure groups; the new style is associated with a decline in the relationship between social class and party loyalty and with a growing interest in civil liberties and citizenship.

## Further reading

*Dod's Parliamentary Companion* (annually) London: Dod's Parliamentary Companion Ltd.

*Keesing's UK Record* (bimonthly) and *Keesing's Record of World Events* (monthly) St Andrews: Cartermill International.

These detailed reference books include information on politicians, legislation, constituencies, the EU and recent political events in the UK and abroad.

Stirk, PMR and Weigall, D (1995) *An Introduction to Political Ideas*, London: Cassell. An exellent source of information about political theories.

## Activities

### Activity 1 A case study

Present a case study of one pressure group, social movement, pressure movement, or terrorist organization.

Your central question will be: What has been the role of [name of movement or group] in a changing political environment?

You can consider how this particular movement has influenced, and been influenced by, the continually changing political scene. How has it responded to its circumstance? This provides an opportunity to consider features of the movement/group, while drawing together appropriate aspects of the whole chapter (and additional reading) to provide the necessary depth. The features could include: how it fits (or does not fit) definitions of (and theories about) movements and other groups; its origins, aims, organization and tactics. Be selective in your references to the rest of the chapter (or book), thinking carefully about the relevance of various theories to the central question.

Your emphasis should be on discussion, rather than description, and you should avoid 'padding' with irrelevant detail.

### Activity 2 'Vulnerable society ripe for cracking': political participation in Iraq

The Ba'ath Party seized power through a military coup in July 1968, taking advantage of a weak state, 'Ba'athising' the army and forming several competing security forces equipped with up-to-date instruments of surveillance and coercion. Individuals inside and outside the party who disagreed with the leadership around the first president, Ahmad al-Bakr, and Saddam Hussein were removed or killed.

The leaders used the state and its institutions to assert their own power, the maintenance of which lay at the core of most of their policies. Although party membership increased rapidly, the Ba'ath became less important as the regime entrenched itself, although the organisation remained useful as an instrument of co-option, manipulation and artificial mass mobilisation. . . .

In a society where the state is omnipotent and its actions arbitrary, where the rule of law barely exists and the individual is powerless alone, meaningful participation in politics has become impossible. Political involvement in Iraq is either opportunistic (if in the service of the state) or almost insanely dangerous (if in opposition to it).

This political alienation and the related unreliability of state institutions has strengthened family, village and communal ties. In this way, Iraq's regime has restrained, rather than promoted, national integration.

Such regimes also try to galvanise their populations by presenting them with threats to their existence, real or imaginary, whose defeat requires their unswerving loyalty.

(M Farouk-Sluglett and P Sluglett *Guardian* 18 January 1991)

#### Questions

What is a 'military coup'?

Looking at the definitions of terms at the beginning of this chapter, and at the political theories we define later, do any of them help to explain the political system in Iraq? Can you find any other terms that help to explain the system?

Why did political alienation strengthen family, village and local ties?

Assess the success, or otherwise, of using external threats to galvanize populations into 'unswerving loyalty'.

Chapter 6

# Social stratification and class

**Chapter outline:** Introduction • Systems of stratification • Explanations of stratification • Theoretical concepts of class • Operationalizing the concept of class • The class structure in modern society • 'Class is dead; long live class' • Summary • Further reading • Activities

## Learning objectives

When you have studied this chapter you should be able to address these key questions:

- What are the major forms of stratification?
- What explanations have social scientists offered for the advantages and disadvantages that follow from membership of particular social classes?
- Is class analysis still useful in understanding social structure and social opportunities?

## Introduction

I conceive that there are two kinds of inequality among the human species; one, which I call *natural or physical*, because it is established by nature, and consists in a difference of age, health, bodily strength and the qualities of the mind and the soul; and another, which may be called *moral or political inequality*, because it depends on a kind of convention and is established, or at least authorised, by the consent of men. This latter consists of the different privileges, which some men enjoy to the prejudice of others; such as that of being more rich, more honoured, more powerful, or even in a position of exact obedience.

(J-J Rousseau, quoted in Bottomore 1965: 15)

In a class society everyone lives as a member of a particular class, and every kind of thinking, without exception, is stamped with the brand of a class.

(Mao Tse-Tung 1966: 2)

Q

What kinds of inequalities can you identify which are natural or physical?

Which ones would you regard as moral or political?

Do you feel that you are a member of a particular social class?

If so, which class and what influence does it exert on your life?

If not, do you feel that you are a member of any other sort of social grouping that affects your everyday life?

While more and more people own more and more consumer goods than ever before, we do not have to look very far to find evidence of gross inequalities. Some people can afford to live in large houses with two or more expensive cars to drive around in while others live in overcrowded and run-down accommodation or sleep rough and will never own a car.

The examination of inequalities has been a major (if not the major) area of sociological inquiry; issues of inequality are central to many social theories and are the key to understanding the different social opportunities available to different social groups and individuals. Sociologists suggest that the origins of inequality can be found in the cultures and social structures of societies themselves. This is not to deny that there are innate and natural differences between people and that such differences contribute to inequality; however, the sociological approach emphasizes how cultures and social structures can create and maintain individual inequalities.

In this chapter we focus on how inequality in societies leads to systems of social stratification, particularly stratification by social class. Chapters 7 and 8 look at stratification by gender and race.

Definition

### Inequality and stratification

Although not synonymous these terms are often used interchangeably. *Inequality* refers to differences between people in terms of their abilities and rewards. We notice these differences from an early age. Why am I stronger than my brother? Why is my sister smarter than me? We become aware of their social implications as we grow up. Why do some people (particularly some men) get better jobs? Why are some jobs paid more highly than others?

Inequality leads to *social stratification* when people are ranked hierarchically according to their possession of attributes such as income, wealth, power, age, gender and status. This sort of ranking leads to groups of people being classified into layer or strata – like geological rock formations – hence the term stratification. Stratification can be thought of as referring to structured inequalities that persist over time.

Inequality and stratification profoundly affect the quality of people's lives and can make the difference between, say, working in a well-paid job or being unemployed, eating well or going hungry, keeping warm or freezing during cold winters, living to an old age or dying young.

## Systems of stratification

While our focus is on stratification in contemporary society, the origins of social inequality can be traced back to ancient times. Historically four systems of social stratification can be identified: slavery, caste, estates and social class.

### Slavery

The oldest and most extreme form of stratification involved the enslavement or ownership of others as a result of conquest, trade, kidnapping, hereditary status or the repayment of a debt. The early civilizations of Babylon, Egypt and Persia relied heavily on slave labour, as did the Greek and Roman empires. Between the fifteenth and nineteenth centuries the industrial and financial might of modern European powers was directly related to the trade in African slaves. This slave labour was crucial to the economic development of the New World and the establishment of black populations in the Americas and the Caribbean.

Although in earlier civilizations slavery was sometimes only temporary, with individual slaves occasionally enjoying high status and the opportunity to earn their freedom, usually it was a permanent state whereby an individual was the property of someone else for whom he or she worked with no prospect of reward, freedom or legal protection. Despite being abolished in the British Empire in 1833, slavery has by no means disappeared. In 1984 the United Nations investigated claims that the West African former colony of Mauritania still allowed 100,000 people to be kept in slavery. Anti-Slavery International has continued to monitor the use of forced labour as well as child prostitution on a global scale.

Case Study

## Anti-Slavery International and the fight against slavery

**Why does the world still need Anti-Slavery International, its oldest human rights organization?**

Because the most basic of human rights are still being flouted. In spite of international condemnation of slavery, the number of slaves world wide continues to run into hundreds of millions. Anti-Slavery International believes it is not enough to seek changes in law alone; it takes constant pressure to persuade governments to take real action to solve the problems.

**How are people enslaved today?**

Although traditional slavery still exists, modern slavery can take many other forms. The United Nations identifies other categories of slavery, including:

- **Debt bondage** Where people pledge their labour against debts, that they are unlikely ever to be able to repay. This bondage can then be inherited by subsequent generations.
- **Child labour** In the poorest families children are some times forced to leave home to work. This makes them particularly vulnerable to exploitation and abuse.
- **Servile forms of marriage** Where women are given in marriage without the right to refuse.
- **Forced labour** Where governments forcibly recruit labour for a variety of purposes.

(Information from Anti-Slavery International, Stableyard, Bromgrove Road, London SW9 9TL)

## Caste

The caste system is mainly associated with Indian society and the Hindu religion. It involves a complex and strictly defined division of labour in which occupations are assigned to one of four closed status groups (Varna). Rank order is not necessarily related to power or money but rather to traditional values which place the Brahmin priests at the top and those responsible for 'unclean' tasks, known as 'untouchables', as outcasts below the four main castes. There is no possibility of social mobility as these positions are determined by birth. Indeed a person's position is believed to be based on what was achieved in a previous incarnation. As a result of these beliefs, it is held that the structure of society is divinely ordained and individuals are obliged to accept it and to carry out their duties within it 'without ambition to change' (Dharma).

These beliefs are further reinforced by social taboos governing social interaction, pollution and marriage. Despite being officially abolished in 1947 this system still survives, especially in rural areas, as do the religious beliefs that have underpinned it for the past 3,000 years. The term 'caste' has also been used to describe societies based upon racial segregation such as South Africa under apartheid and the southern states of the USA prior to the civil rights movement.

### Estates

In the feudal system of medieval Europe a ranking of status groups known as estates became the dominant system. The three major estates were the aristocracy (headed by the divine monarch), the priesthood, and the commoners (peasants, servants, artisans, etc.). This system was closely related to property and political power with landownership as the key. In a relationship of rights and obligations known as *noblesse oblige* the commoners were allowed use of land in return for providing service and rents to their landlord, who in turn promised protection and support. Just as the tenant was a vassal (dependant) of the lord, so the lord was in debt to the monarch. This interlocking system of rights and obligations was seen as divinely ordained. However, the estate system was not as strictly tied to religious belief as the caste system and some historians have argued that feudalism allowed for a degree of social mobility, especially in the towns.

### Social class

In the previous systems of stratification the social position of an individual was fixed by law, custom or inherited status. These positions were reinforced by a set of norms which clearly governed the relationship between members of the different groups; group membership was often ascribed at birth. Such systems are characterized by very little social mobility and are sometimes referred to as 'closed' societies because individuals' life prospects are predetermined. Under the process of industrialization the traditional aspects of these stratification systems gave way to a more open system which was characterized by competition and a higher degree of social mobility. Customary divisions and traditional distinctions were replaced by 'class' distinctions based upon property and authority. Class position is therefore largely determined by an individual's place within the economic system and is to some extent achieved. Ideally such a society should become a *meritocracy* (a hierarchy based on achievement and ability) in which class origins are irrelevant to where an individual is 'placed' in the economic system. However, despite this conception of society as a hierarchy of positions based solely on merit, most sociologists still regard modern industrial societies as being stratified on the basis of social class. Indeed the idea that contemporary societies can be and are divided into classes is one which is not only popular with sociologists, but also shared by members of society at large. A large part of this chapter will be taken up with a fuller discussion of the meaning of class and of its continuing importance in modern society.

## Explanations of stratification

Inequalities between people and the stratification of entire societies have always required some form of explanation. Such explanations often tend towards either justification or condemnation and as such can be regarded as ideologies rather than theories. From ancient times these explanations have emphasized divine, natural or social intervention, while more recently (post-Enlightenment) the moral assumption that we are all born equal (in an increasingly divided world) has only increased the speculative interest in this debate.

### Divine explanations

Peter Berger has claimed that religion has a special authority when it acts as an ideology of justification, 'because it relates the precarious reality constructions of empirical societies with ultimate reality' (quoted in Daly 1991: 132). This notion of 'ultimate reality' can be applied to various forms of inequality. The Indian caste system is supported by the Hindu belief in reincarnation and the identification of social rank as a sign of spiritual purity. The twin concepts of Karma and Dharma are central to this moral justification of a closed social system:

**Karma teaches a Hindu that he or she is born into a particular caste or sub-caste because he or she deserves to be there as a consequence of actions in a previous life. Dharma, which means 'existing according to that which is moral' teaches that living one's present life according to the rules (dharma) will result in rebirth into a higher caste and thus ultimate progression through the caste system. Both existing inequalities of caste, therefore, as well as any possibility of change in the future, are related to universal religious truths and are thus beyond the reaches of systematic sociological examination.** *(Crompton 1993: 2)*

Similar justifications were provided for the estates system by the Catholic Church, which sanctified the feudal hierarchy with the argument that it reflected the celestial order of things and blessed the king with a divine right to rule.

**One of the greatest achievements of the Middle Ages was the development of this idea of a universal human society as an integral part of a divinely ordered universe in time and in eternity, in nature and supernature, in practical politics and in the world of spiritual essences.** *(Southern 1988: 22)*

This universal human society laid great stress on duty and order and allowed for little social mobility. 'Everyman had his station in society, and few men were allowed to sink very much lower or to rise very much higher than the station into which they were born' (Southern 1988: 43). To seek for personal improvement through the pursuit of wealth was condemned as a sin (of avarice) while poverty was cherished as a humble virtue. Such ideas may have originated in the Middle Ages but they persisted into the industrial revolution and the age of the rise of capitalism.

**In 'primitive' societies religious explanations were used to come to terms with phenomena which were beyond understanding, but gradually these beliefs and explanations became justifications and legitimations for keeping society as it was. Thus, for example, in the sixteenth and seventeenth centuries, the idea of a 'great chain of being' existed in which the social hierarchy of Gods, kings and bishops, lords, freemen and serfs was argued to be natural and God given. Similarly, in the eighteenth and nineteenth centuries many people thought it was largely senseless to try to do anything about poverty since it was God who had created the rich and the poor, and it was therefore immoral and ungodly to try to change things.**

*(Thompson 1986: 36)*

Religious explanations have been used to justify both racial and sexual inequality. The relationship between religion and race has always been troublesome. In those societies that depended upon African slaves for their economic power, theological debates raged over the 'humanity' of black Africans. The Dutch Reformed Church in South Africa persistently sanctioned apartheid from the pulpit. In its 'Statement on Race Relation, no 1' (November 1960) the Dutch Reformed Church stated that it 'could not associate itself unreservedly with the general cry for equality and unity in the world today'. Its statement after the Sharpeville riots of the same year made clear its approval of separate development (apartheid):

**The Nederduitse Gereformeerde Kerk has made it clear by its policy and by synod statements that it can approve of independent, distinctive development, provided that it is carried out in a just and honourable way, without impairing or offending 'human dignity'.** *(Unesco 1972: 178)*

The universal subordination of women throughout history has also been explained and approved of by almost all religions. Whether it is through creation myth, spiritual teachings or ritualized practice, the subjugation of women by men has often been given the status of holy law. O'Faolain and Martinez (1979) have shown that holy teachings and practices have provided powerful ideological support for the oppression of women.

Case Study

### God the Father

**Mary Daly (1991) has argued that world religions (and Christianity in particular) are part of a conspiracy to retain the status of women as 'sexual caste' through their own consent via the process of 'sex role socialization', which hides the truth of their caste status. Daly suggests that 'the entire conceptual systems of theology and ethics . . . have been the products of males and tend to serve the interests of sexist society' (Daly 1991: 4).**

The biblical and popular image of God as a great patriarch in heaven, rewarding and punishing according to his mysterious and seemingly arbitrary will, has dominated the imagination of millions over thousands of years. The symbol of the Father God, spawned in the human imagination and sustained as plausible by patriarchy, has in turn rendered service to this type of society by making its mechanisms for the oppression of women appear right and fitting. If God in 'his' heaven is a father ruling 'his' people, then it is in the 'nature' of things and according to divine plan and the order of the universe that society be male-dominated.

Within this context a mystification of roles takes place: the husband dominating his wife represents God 'himself'. The images and values of a given society have been projected into the realm of dogmas and 'Articles of Faith', and these in turn justify the social structures which have given rise to them and which sustain their plausibility . . . however, change can occur in society, and ideologies can die, though they die hard.

As the women's movement begins to have its effect upon the fabric of society, transforming it from patriarchy into something that never existed before – into a diarchal situation that is radically new – it can become the greatest single challenge to the major

*(box continued)*

*(box continued)*

religions of the world, Western and Eastern. Beliefs and values that have held sway for thousands of years will be questioned as never before. (Adapted from Daly 1991: 14)

**Questions**

In what ways is traditional religion patriarchal? Can you think of any religious beliefs or practices which illustrate this ? What does the controversy over women priests in the Church of England tell us about the extent to which the women's movement has successfully challenged patriarchal religious beliefs? How would you feel about being married by a woman priest?

## Naturalistic explanations

From ancient times to the present day the explanations of differences between individuals and groups in terms of natural differences have been popular. It appeals to 'common sense' to suppose that the differences and similarities which appear at an early age between members of the same family are caused by nature. Whether a child is regarded as 'a chip off the old block' or 'the black sheep of the family', the cause can be easily accommodated within a model that explains physical, psychological and intellectual characteristics in terms of genetic inheritance. It is a short step to assume that all inequalities within society are part of the same natural condition; 'boys will be boys' is used to explain why brothers are treated differently from their sisters; the idea that the aristocracy have 'blue blood' in their veins is taken to mean that they were 'born to rule'. There are important differences between different types of natural explanations; biological and psychological explanations, for instance, are not interchangeable.

As with divine explanations, appeals to the laws of nature can operate as very powerful conservative ideologies. While Aristotle was insistent that the domination of both slaves and women by freemen was a condition ordained 'by nature', so Plato argued that the clear differences between the three basic classes of human stock (gold, silver and bronze) in an ideal society should be maintained by a form of state-regulated eugenics.

**Definition**

**Eugenics and the Eugenics Movement**

Eugenics refers to the improvement of the human race through genetic policies that would discourage certain people and social groups who were felt to be 'inferior' from breeding and encourage others, who were thought to be more intelligent or superior in some way, to breed.

By the late nineteenth century, scientific interest in the new fields of genetics and evolution led to a Eugenics Movement which had a powerful influence on many areas of social investigation and policy, particularly in the USA.

The importance of selective breeding for the maintenance of a stable class structure (especially in the face of a population explosion among poor people) was stressed in the work of Francis Galton and his admirer Cyril Burt. Both believed that individual talent (and its absence) was essentially inherited and that the unequal rewards found in society were no more than a reflection of this natural distribution of ability throughout the population. If social classes existed, that was merely a reflection of groupings in nature. The Eugenics Movement was also concerned with the issue of racial purity and campaigned for the sterilization and incarceration of disabled and mentally ill people as well as the introduction of strong immigration controls. In the nineteenth and early twentieth centuries the threat to the Anglo-Saxon stock (in Britain) was identified as Celtic and Jewish. Later this fear was extended to African and Asian people. Early on in Britain's imperial history scientists were ready to explain the differential treatment of other racial groups in terms of natural differences between the races. This led to the development of what Peter Fryer (1984) has called 'pseudo-scientific racism' which is clearly linked to attempts to demonstrate that differences in intelligence, aggression and personality have a racial origin. During the twentieth century the work of some psychologists has been used to suggest that the social failure of some racial groups is the result of inferior IQ.

In 1916 Lewis Terman introduced the Stanford-Binet Test by highlighting its capacity to distinguish between the abilities of different racial groups in the USA and expose the 'feeble mindedness' of some groups in particular:

> **Their dullness seems to be racial, or at least inherent in the family stocks from which they come. The fact that one meets this type with extraordinary frequency among Indians, Mexicans and negroes suggests quite forcibly that the whole question of racial difference in mental traits will have to be taken up anew. . . . Children of this group should be segregated into special classes. . . . They cannot master abstractions, but they can often be made efficient workers. . . . There is no possibility at present of convincing society that they should not be allowed to reproduce . . . they constitute a grave problem because of their unusually prolific breeding.**
>
> *(quoted by Kamin 1977: 374–7)*

This debate grabbed the headlines again in the early 1970s when psychologists like AR Jensen (1973) began to repeat the claim that Black Americans were intellectually inferior to whites. In the early 1990s Charles Murray and Richard Herrnstein initiated a return to the arguments with their claim that Black people in the USA scored on average 15 points below whites in IQ tests. In their book, *The Bell Curve: Intelligence and the Class Structure* (Herrnstein and Murray 1994), they argue that a three-part class structure has emerged based upon inherited intelligence. Society is dominated by a 'cognitive elite' (IQ 125+) and serviced by a middle class of average IQ, beneath whom a largely black underclass with IQs of 75 or less survive and multiply (*Observer* 23 October 1994).

The historical subordination of women and the domination by men of all positions of economic and political power have been given similar treatment by biologists and psychologists who sought to show that gender differences can be traced back to the natural differences between men and women. (According to this view, women achieve very little outside of their caring role within the family because they are physically weaker, emotionally unstable and intellectually inferior.)

Nineteenth-century phrenologists argued that in terms of head shape the areas responsible for love, approbation and secretiveness were larger in the female, but less well developed than those for aggression, self-sufficiency, firmness and ingenuity. Later attempts to locate the source of the differences targeted the brain, hormonal balance and genetically transmitted differences in intellect and personality.

By 1914 the German psychologist, Hugo Munsterberg, concluded that the female mind is 'capricious, over-suggestible, often inclined to exaggeration, is disinclined to abstract thought, unfit for mathematical reasoning, impulsive [and] over-emotional' (Fairbrother 1983). As Hugh Fairbrother has pointed out, such conclusions have a strong whiff of male prejudice about them and very little to do with scientific rigour:

**What we need to do is remind ourselves constantly that our behaviour is not only, or even mostly, at the whim of our physique and physiology. As social beings we share responsibility for each other's behaviour. We create the sexist society which in turn spawns sexist science. . . . The crude stereotypes of 'male' and 'female' that the scientists set out to validate have changed and continue to change.**

*(Fairbrother 1983: 8–9)*

In the modern age the advances in technology have meant that the 'harmless' speculations on genetic engineering of Aristotle and Plato have become distinct and disturbing possibilities; not only in the prophetic pages of Aldous Huxley's *Brave New World* (1932), but in the real world of genetic engineering and social policy. Hitler's *Lebensborn* policy of eugenic breeding to create a 'super race' was the flip side of the 'final solution' coin.

**All the good blood in the world, all the Germanic blood that is not on the German side, may one day be our ruin. Hence every male of the best Germanic blood whom we bring to Germany and turn into a Teutonic-minded man means one more combatant on our side and one less on the other. I really intend to take German blood from wherever it is to be found in the world, to rob and steal it wherever I can.**

*(Heinrich Himmler, speech to officers of the Deutschland Division, 8 November 1938, quoted in Henry and Hiltel 1977: 143)*

In California scientists are rumoured to be trying to engineer 'super kids' using sperm banks and artificial insemination, but the prospect of cloning identical families is still very far away. 'Problem populations' may be dealt with through birth control and immigration legislation. Rather than being old-fashioned philosophies these ideas are now more powerful and potentially dangerous than they ever have been.

### Social explanations

Within sociology various explanations have been offered for the persistence of social inequalities. Much emphasis is placed on the role of personal experience, culture and deprivation in explaining why some individuals succeed and others fail, while the openness of the opportunity structure is also a crucial part of the debate. For the moment however we shall concentrate on the purposes and consequences of inequality for society from three perspectives: the market forces model, the functionalist model and the conflict model.

### *The market forces model*

The market forces model, which is closely associated with individualistic and naturalistic explanations, emphasizes the importance of an open and free market for talents and abilities so that those with the most marketable skills are rewarded for their ability and motivated to work hard and compete with others for the highest rewards. Neo-liberal economists (sometimes known as 'the New Right') have argued that unequal reward encourages self-interest and competition which in turn sponsor personal initiative and technological innovation. Capitalism is seen as a dynamic system which gets the best out of individuals by rewarding talent and hard work and penalizing feckless and idle people. As a result we all benefit from the inspiration of creative individuals and harnessing the power of their ideas and effort. Whether we approve of them or not we inhabit a world which has been greatly influenced by individuals such as Henry Ford, Richard Branson and Rupert Murdoch. Without an unequal reward structure we would never have heard of any of them or enjoyed the benefits of mass-produced motor cars, the Virgin Megastore and satellite TV. According to writers like Friedrich Hayek (1976) and Milton Friedman (1962), any attempt to tamper with the 'spontaneous order' generated by the capitalist reward structure serves only to reduce the 'social energy' produced by inequality.

### *The functionalist model*

With more emphasis upon the social importance of inequality and its relationship to a complex division of labour and a set of rational values, the functionalist model tends to share the view of the Economic Right that social stratification reflects the 'spontaneous order' created by inequality and furthermore enjoys the approval of the majority because it is seen as providing just reward for those jobs which are of high social value. According to Talcott Parsons the 'spontaneous order' is not simply a product of market forces but also the result of social consensus ('normative order') over the most important skills (such skills might be bravery, hunting or intelligence) and the extent to which they should be differentially rewarded. Davis and Moore (1967) argue that stratification is both inevitable and functional in any society which requires its most important tasks to be carried out efficiently:

> **Social inequality is an unconsciously evolved device by which societies insure that the most important positions are conscientiously filled by the most qualified persons.** *(Davis and Moore 1967: 48)*

By compensating those who train to become qualified for the most important positions, this system ensures that the most able individuals are allocated to the key roles in society and motivated to work hard while they are employed in them. As a result social efficiency is maintained while the high value placed on certain skills is reinforced. At the centre of this model is the assumption that competition for the key places is open to all and that roles are allocated according to individual merit. This is clearly summarized in Turner's (1961) model of 'contest mobility'.

> **Applied to mobility the contest norm means that victory by a person of moderate intelligence accomplished through the use of common sense, craft, enterprise, daring and successful risk taking is more appreciated than victory of the most intelligent or the best educated. . . . The contest is judged to be fair only if all the players compete on an equal footing. Victory must be won solely by one's own efforts.**
>
> *(Turner 1961: 183)*

Saunders (1987) has argued for a return to this model, maintaining that as long as people are guaranteed political and legal equality, the best system must be one in which everyone has an equal opportunity to be unequal.

### *The conflict model*

Melvin Tumin's (1967) attack on the 'principles of stratification' outlined by Davis and Moore (1967) is well documented elsewhere; essentially his argument challenges the assumption that some positions are inherently more important than others, and that stratification provides an efficient mechanism for attracting the most talented individuals in society to these positions. Instead of promoting functional efficiency and fairness, such systems can be socially divisive and dysfunctional, promoting resentment, demotivation and conflict, while the skills and talents that are encouraged by unequal rewards have little to do with intelligence or social worth:

> **Wealth and power tend to accrue to those who are ruthless, cunning, avaricious, self-seeking, lacking in sympathy and compassion, subservient to authority [and] willing to abandon principle for material gain.**
>
> *(Chomsky 1972, quoted in Anderson 1974: 82)*

As a result, systems of stratification encourage self-perpetuating elites who pass on their privileges through inherited wealth, private education and inter-marriage. As Bottomore (1965) pointed out, social stratification operates to resist the dynamics of openness and social change:

> **Indeed, it would be a more accurate description of the social class system to say that it operates, largely through the inheritance of property, to ensure that each individual maintains a certain social position, determined by his birth and irrespective of his particular abilities.** *(Bottomore 1965: 16)*

The arguments of Tumin (1967), Bottomore (1965) and Chomsky (1972) clearly indicate a lack of agreement with the fundamental idea of modern, stratified societies as meritocracies. Instead they would see Turner's (1961) model of 'sponsored mobility' in which status is ascribed rather than achieved as being more appropriate:

> **Sponsored mobility . . . rejects the pattern of the contest and substitutes a controlled selection process. In this process the elite or their agents who are best qualified to judge merit, call those individuals who have the appropriate qualities to elite status. Individuals do not win or seize elite status, but mobility is rather a process of sponsored induction into the elite following selection.**
>
> *(Turner 1961: 183–4)*

Q Briefly suggest how the different social 'models' – market, functionalist and conflict – might explain the position of (a) a rich entrepreneur; (b) an unemployed 18 year old; (c) a social worker.

## Theoretical concepts of class

**The discourse of class has become one of the key concepts through which we can begin to understand [the modern world]. Class, therefore, is a major organising concept in the exploration of contemporary stratification systems.**

*(Crompton 1993: 4)*

**I think we need a classless society, and I think we need to have what I refer to as social mobility. And what I mean by social mobility is the capacity of everybody to have the help necessary to achieve the maximum for their ability.**

*(John Major 1990, quoted in Edgell 1993: 121)*

These two quotes highlight quite contradictory stances on the importance of class in contemporary societies. In the first, class is seen as an essential aspect of such societies whereas John Major's comment suggests that class is becoming less important, with an individual's position increasingly based on that person's own ability. As we mentioned when looking at systems of stratification (pp. 221–3), sociologists would tend to support Crompton's comment and emphasize the continuing importance of social class in modern societies. The 'discourse of class' continues to have a wide and general usage. In thousands of different ways we generate and interpret clues about ourselves and others which indicate class position. How we dress, speak and eat are all indicators of social class. The concept of social class is part of our culture; embedded in this culture are judgements about how we earn our money and what we purchase with it, how we educate our children and where we spend our leisure time.

**Case Study**

### The Duke of Westminster's housing estate

In 1937 the Duke of Westminster made a present of the Page Street housing estate to the Westminster Council on the condition that it should be used exclusively as 'dwellings for the working class . . . and for no other purpose'. Almost fifty years later the 1985 Housing Act gave sitting tenants the 'right to buy' council rented property. Westminster Council attempted to implement this policy, but ended up in the High Court when they insisted that the phrase 'working class' no longer had any meaning. The current Duke of Westminster successfully defended his ancestor's wishes when Mr Justice Harman ruled that parliament 'does not determine the meaning of those words in ordinary English speech'. He concluded that the term was 'as valid today as when it was made'. (*Guardian* 27 November 1990)

#### Questions

What does the term 'working class' mean to you?

Would you want to live in a classless society?

Could a classless society exist?

## Marx and social class

Marx died with his aim of providing a precise definition of social class an unfinished project. Nevertheless, the concept remains at the centre of his work. Unlike Durkheim, who rarely used the term, or Weber, who gave it specific and limited meaning, Marx saw class not only as a descriptive device but also as a way of understanding how society and history interact, the maintenance of social order and the dynamics of social change. Sometimes he talks of 'Society . . . splitting up into *two* great hostile camps'; on other occasions he says that 'wage labourers, capitalists and landlords, form the *three* great classes of modern society'. In more empirical mood Marx allows for six different groups (in Germany) and seven (in Britain) where the working class can be subdivided into productive (factory workers) and non-productive (servants). In his mention of 'intermediate' classes Marx seems to anticipate some of the arguments developed later in Wright's discussion of 'contradictory class positions' (see p. 236). To understand the different ways in which Marx used the term we can distinguish between *objective* and *subjective* class position (see p. 59).

**Definition**

### Objective class position

For Marx, a person's class can exist independently of their awareness of it and affect them in ways they are not conscious of. In this sense class operates as a social force which influences opportunities, governs relationships (between groups) and transforms conflict into change.

As Lee and Newby (1983) have pointed out, Marx used this objective notion of class position both theoretically and empirically. First, it was used to explain the inevitable antagonism that would develop between the bourgeoisie and the proletariat as a result of their diametrically opposed interests and the gradual proletarianization of society, work and politics. The eventual outcome of this class conflict would be a revolutionary transformation of society and the victory of socialism.

Second, objective class position was used in a more static and descriptive way to provide a snapshot of the various social classes actually in existence at any particular time without making much comment on the relational aspects of these groupings. This explains why Marx can describe the existence of several classes alongside his more theoretical attempts to explain the importance of the two dominant ones.

### Subjective class position

Although Marxism is often accused of being structuralist and deterministic in its emphasis upon the objective nature of social class, Marx himself clearly realized that antagonistic interests did not automatically guarantee social conflict and revolutionary change. People had to be conscious of their interests and committed to achieving them; only when this *class consciousness* developed could a class be transformed from a 'class *in* itself' to a 'class *for* itself'. This development of a class consciousness involved people in an ideological struggle in which 'false consciousness' is replaced by class awareness and a revolutionary consciousness. In the *Communist Manifesto* Marx makes it clear that workers will achieve nothing until they share a common consciousness.

## Weber and social class

Like Marx, Weber did not finish his analysis of the concept of class, but he did give a more complete picture of what it meant to him by distinguishing the 'multidimensional' aspects of stratification. According to this view, society cannot be stratified by economic factors alone; status and party coincide and overlap with class as alternative bases for stratification. John Hughes (1984) has argued that rather than reducing inequality to economic factors, Weber regarded *power* as the primary relationship between unequal groups in society with class representing only one form:

> **Power, according to Weber, is the ability of an individual or group to get what they want even against the opposition of others. . . . Power can be divided into three spheres of activity: the economic, the social and the political. Within each of these, individuals can be grouped according to the amount of power they are able to command.**
> *(Hughes 1984: 7)*

These three spheres of activities are more commonly referred to as class, status and party and we need to examine each one to understand the extent to which Weber differed from Marx on the issues of class and stratification.

### *Class*

It is not surprising that Weber did not share Marx's beliefs about social class. Weber had a commitment to the possibility of value-free sociology and cautiously welcomed the growth of capitalism and bureaucracy as the inevitable progress of rationality. He was also a Christian with some faith in the possibility of social reform. However, his writings on social class show that he was in close agreement with Marx on the importance of economic classes and the shape that these classes took at the end of the nineteenth century. Weber defined class in clear economic terms and accepted that it often provided the basis for shared social position, life chances and political action. He defined 'class situation' as:

> **The typical chance for a supply of goods, external living conditions, and personal life experiences, in so far as this chance is determined by the amount and kinds of power, or lack of such, to dispose of goods or skills for the sake of income in a given economic order.**
> *(Weber, quoted in Edgell 1993: 12)*

Like Marx, he accepted that 'class situation is by far the predominant factor' in determining social position with ownership (or lack) of property being the 'basic categories of all class situations'. As a result Weber acknowledges the existence of positively and negatively privileged classes, separated by a growing middle class. His description of the prevailing class structure resembles that put forward by Marx:

> **[Weber] identified as 'social classes' (a) the working class as a whole; (b) the petty bourgeoisie; (c) technicians, specialists and lower-level management, and (d) 'the classes privileged through property and education' – that is, those at the top of the hierarchy of occupation and ownership. In short, *at the descriptive level*, Weber's account of the 'class structure' of capitalist society is not too different from that of Marx.**
> *(Crompton 1993: 30)*

In four other respects, however, Weber's views on social class formation and class action are very different from those espoused by Marx: first, class situation is not simply determined by property relationships, but by the shared life chances that people enjoy (or are denied) as a result of the value of their skills and possessions in the marketplace. This means that possession of particular skills or qualifications may be just as important as the possession of property in determining class situation. It also implies that a person's class position will change with fluctuations in the market.

Second, class position is associated with potential for consumption (income) rather than the relationship to the mode of production.

---

**For Marx, class relationships are grounded in exploitation and domination within *production* relations, whereas for Weber, class situations reflect differing 'life chances' in the *market*.** *(Crompton 1993: 30)*

---

This emphasis upon consumption and lifestyle is central to Weber's idea of status.

Third, despite his apparent agreement with Marx over the four essential classes of capitalist society, Weber's definition allows for 'multiple classes' because he recognized 'important differences in the market situation of all groups, especially with respect to the various skills and services offered by different occupations' (Hughes 1984: 7). This means that on top of the differences between his four main classes he also emphasizes possible differences *within* these classes. Instead of society becoming polarized into two simple homogenous classes, Weber's view was that the number of different classes would multiply with the expansion of society. Thus, Weber's conception of the social stratification structure in general, and the class structure in particular, is extremely complex and pluralistic.

Fourth, Weber rejected Marx's *dynamic* view of social class. He did not see class conflict as inevitable nor did he accept it as the engine of historical change. Weber believed that people are essentially individuals and their class situation is only one of many possible sources of consciousness and political activity. Classes were seen as (merely) representing possible and frequent bases for communal action.

While Marx saw something inevitable in the connection between class position, class consciousness and political revolution, Weber was quite cynical about the political potential of the working classes and very pessimistic about the direction of world history. Working-class people could just as easily be motivated by patriotism and religious fervour as they were by class interest. He believed that rationally organized capitalism was more likely to dominate the future than revolutionary socialism.

### *Status*

For many writers, Weber's greatest contribution to the stratification debate is his view that social differences can be as important as economic ones in the identification of social position even if the two seem very closely related:

---

**'Classes' are stratified according to their relations to the production and acquisition of goods; whereas 'status groups' are stratified according to the principles of their consumption of goods as represented by special 'styles of life'!**

*(Weber, quoted in Hughes 1984: 8)*

---

Although you may feel that 'lifestyle' is determined by class position, Weber says this is not necessarily the case:

**Money and an entrepreneurial position are not in themselves status qualifications, although they may lead to them; and the lack of property is not in itself a status disqualification, although this may be a reason for it.** *(Weber, quoted in Ritzer 1992: 128)*

Status position is derived from the prestige or 'social honour' which the community attaches to a particular individual or role as well as the expected 'lifestyle' that attaches to it. A community will judge someone's social status according to cultural standards like education, occupation, speech and dress, as well as the more obvious trappings of a privileged lifestyle.

Weber's concept of 'status group' has allowed modern sociologists to recognize that factors like age, gender and race are related to 'life chances' in much the same way as class differences are and, for the individuals concerned, may even be more important.

Q How would you assess the following people in terms of class and status position? Queen Elizabeth II, Gazza (Paul Gascoigne, football player), Mother Theresa, Harry Enfield as 'Loadsamoney', Wayne and Waynetta Slob, Richard Branson.

### *Party*

Just as the social order is given autonomy from economic forces, so Weber argues that the political sphere cannot be reduced to economic interests either. In this third arena of Weber's stratification system, people exercise control over others and inequalities of power become another way in which differentiation manifests itself. Sometimes people will organize themselves into political parties which represent their economic interests (e.g. the Parliamentary Labour Party), but this is not the only basis for political organization. When political power results from such organization it can be used for the benefit of party members at the expense of other groups in society. In the former Soviet Union, for example, party membership was closely related to social status and economic privileges.

Corruption scandals in western democracies emphasize this point; political power may be used as a device to increase economic privilege and social differentiation. In developing societies, too, political power may be a source of economic privilege. On the other hand political policy may be directed towards social reform and the eradication of economic inequality. In both cases, political power is not simply the reflection of economic relations, but appears to have a life of its own which sometimes runs in the opposite direction.

## Modern concepts of class

The debate over the concept of class has continued. The main contemporary contributors derive their inspiration from both Marx and Weber with some clearly representing a neo-Marxist position and others proclaiming a neo-Weberian stance. In the middle there are those who attempt to use Weber's insights to 'round out' Marx.

### *Nicos Poulantzas*

In the face of changes in modern society, the apparent failure of communism and the emergence of humanistic Marxism, structuralist writers like Louis Althusser (1969) and Poulantzas (1979) argued for a return to 'scientific Marxism' (see p.57). This was largely an attack upon individualism and subjectivism within Marxism and sociology, but it was also an attempt to re-emphasize the importance of class position as determined by the mode of production. For Poulantzas classes are defined not by shared life chances or market situation, but by their *role* in the production of *surplus value*. Consequently, those groups who appear to be 'working class' because of similarities in pay and working conditions with other workers cannot be included unless they are directly involved in the production of surplus value. On the political and ideological levels these classes may support one another and pursue the same interests, but they may not be classified together at the economic level. Instead, Poulantzas distinguished between productive and unproductive labour, with only those directly involved in production being allowed the classification 'proletariat'.

### *Erik Olin Wright*

Wright is another neo-Marxist whose ideas developed not only in response to the work of Poulantzas (1979), but also as an attempt to provide an operational concept of class for use in empirical study. He followed the example set by fellow American Marxist, Harry Braverman (1974), when he developed a more flexible 'class map' than Poulantzas' (1979) rigid 'production model'. In Wright's view the structure of class relations in modern capitalism is defined not primarily by economic production, but also by power relations, i.e. control of the workplace and work processes. By including this factor of control into his analysis, Wright allows a much more complex model to develop which is based upon Marxist notions of exploitation and control, but also allows for the ambiguous nature of class relationships that develop between different groups in a complex society.

---

**According to Wright, the two major classes have unambiguous locations with respect to all three dimensions [control]. The capitalist controls investment, organises labour power and decides upon the nature of the productive process. The proletariat, on the other hand, is excluded from all forms of control. Other classes, however, have contradictory locations, the new middle class most of all.**

**(*Hughes* 1984: 13)**

---

The concept of 'contradictory class locations' was used to accommodate managers, small employers and self-employed workers into his 'class maps'. In his later works Wright attempts to recognise that over and above the exploitative power of the owners, the middle classes also found themselves in positions where they could exploit others. (Edgell 1993: 17-27).

### *Anthony Giddens*

Giddens (1973) puts forward a model of the class system which is very close to Weber's. In this model the power that people enjoy in the bargaining process derives essentially from their 'market capacities' (i.e. the value attached to their possessions and skills). He suggests that modern societies tend towards a three class model in which class position is determined by market capacity:

| *Class* | *Market capacity* |
|---|---|
| Upper class | Capital ownership |
| Middle class | Educational credentials |
| Working class | Labour power |

Giddens is aware of cultural variations on this model and acknowledges the internal fragmentation that can occur within each group (e.g. the distinction between professional, technical, managerial and clerical workers within the middle class), but he still prefers to simplify the class system into its three major components, based upon 'the possession of property, qualifications and physical labour power' (Edgell 1993: 53).

### *W G Runciman*

Following Weber, Runciman (1990) has taken the three major stratifying elements in society to be 'ownership' (of property), 'control' (of power/authority) and 'marketability' (of skills), but instead of associating each source of privilege with a particular class he has argued that these criteria for differentiation cut across simple class boundaries, producing a much more fragmented model of the class structure in which the differences within broad classifications are celebrated rather than disguised. The result is a seven class model in which a small 'upper class' share a dominant position with regard to all three criteria. At the other end a significant 'underclass' are identified who possess no property, exercise no control over events and have few marketable skills. The two extremes are separated by two broad classes ('middle' and 'working') internally differentiated by variations in access to property, authority and skill.

### *Frank Parkin*

Probably the best known exponent of the neo-Weberian perspective, Parkin (1972) has made clear his opposition to Marxist concepts of class. Embracing Weber's idea of status he has argued that ownership of property is only one means of social dif-

**Table 6.1** The Runciman classes.

| Class | Size in 1990 |
|---|---|
| Upper class | <1% |
| Upper middle class | <10% |
| Middle middle class | 15% |
| Lower middle class | 20% |
| Skilled working class | 20% |
| Unskilled working class | 30% |
| Underclass | 5% |

*Source:* Runciman 1990: 389

ferentiation and identified occupational status as the most significant criterion for distinguishing between groups in society.

**The backbone of the class structure, and indeed the entire reward system of modern western society, is the occupational order. Other sources of economic and symbolic advantage do coexist alongside the occupational order, but for the vast majority of the population these tend, at best, to be secondary.** *(Parkin 1972: 18)*

In Parkin's model the major distinction appears to be that made between manual and non-manual jobs with higher professionals at the top of the hierarchy of occupations and unskilled workers at the bottom. Instead of society being driven by class conflict, struggles between status groups are more important. Through a variety of techniques of social closure, status groups ensure that they maintain their positions of prestige in society by exclusion of less desirable groups. As a result class boundaries are not created by some objective relationship to the means of production or market situation, but by the conflict between the strategies and techniques adopted by particular status groups.

**Q** Exactly what strategies do you think status groups adopt on a day-to-day basis to maintain their own prestige and exclude others?

## Operationalizing the concept of class

Apart from the theoretical problems posed by the concept of class in sociology there is also much disagreement over its categorization for the purposes of empirical study. This is an important issue because if sociologists cannot agree on the best way of operationalizing social class (i.e. turning the concept into a measurable variable), they will use different methods for classification and measurement and end up with data which are not comparable. If this is the case, apparent changes in social life like voting behaviour or social mobility patterns may be nothing more than distortions created by changes in our definition and measurement of social class.

### Official definitions of 'social class'

The earliest attempts to classify economically active groups in society did not involve class analysis at all. The first Census in 1801 simply adopted general and vague categories of general employment:

- agriculture
- manufacture, trade and handicraft
- others.

Such a scheme may have been useful for assessing proportional shifts in the working population, but it made no attempt to classify people according to their position within the economic and social hierarchy. The revised Census of 1851 simply increased the range of categories of employment and only added to the confusion. It was not until 1911 that the classifications were revised again 'to represent as far as possible different social grades'. The five grades that were introduced formed the basis of what we now know as the Registrar-General's Scale and is 'the nearest thing we have to an official definition of "social class"' (Nichols 1979: 158).

Definition

**Registrar-General's Scale of social classes**

1 Professional occupations
2 Intermediate occupations
3 Skilled occupations
4 Partly skilled occupations
5 Unskilled occupations

The General Household Survey is a seven point scale which identifies people by socio-economic groups and is used for some official investigations, while the advertising industry uses a six point guide to social position which emphasizes consumer potential.

A Upper middle class
B Middle class
C Lower middle class
D Skilled working class
E Semi-skilled working class
F Low level of subsistence.

In sociology the occupational scale has become adopted as the most convenient means of converting the problematic concept of social class into a variable which we can easily use. In Goldthorpe's work this neo-Weberian approach is clear to see. He identified 'market situation' and 'work situation' as the important determinants of class consciousness and used an occupational scale for his important empirical studies of class consciousness (Goldthorpe *et al.* 1968, 1969) and social mobility (Goldthorpe *et al.* 1980). His revised version shows how 'social classes' reflect gradations in the workplace and the labour market (Goldthorpe *et al.* 1980).

Definition

**Goldthorpe's class scheme (revised version)**

1 Classes I and II All professionals, administrators and managers (including large proprietors), higher-grade technicians and supervisors of non-manual workers
2 Class III Routine non-manual employees in administration and commerce, sales personnel, other rank-and-file service workers
3 Class IVab Small proprietors, self-employed artisans and other 'own-account' workers with and without employees (other than in primary production)
4 Class IVc Farmers and smallholders and other self-employed workers in primary production
5 Classes V and VI Lower-grade technicians; supervisors of manual workers and skilled manual workers
6 Class VIIa Semi-skilled and unskilled manual workers (other than in primary production)
7 Class VIIb Agricultural and other workers in primary production

### Advantages of using occupational scales

The occupational scale incorporates the idea of social status and recognizes the growing importance of the 'middle classes' against the decline of the ruling and working classes.

In modern societies occupation has become 'the primary status fixing device'. In modern mass societies characterized by large impersonal bureaucracies and a complex division of labour, occupational position becomes a shorthand method for recognizing others. It is often the first question that we ask someone we are meeting for the first time.

In order to measure the possible influence of social class upon life chances it is necessary to have some generally agreed means of categorizing people. Much valuable research has been conducted using occupational scales and the data produced have been used to inform debate and influence policy making.

### Criticisms of occupational scales

Occupational scales confuse 'class' and 'status'. In this merging of two distinct terms, the emphasis shifts away from 'property relations' and 'the process of production' in favour of 'prestige' as the main measure of social position.

Occupational scale is a *descriptive* device which is good at providing static snapshots of the occupational hierarchy, but it does not *explain* the relations between classes. This criticism comes from Marxist writers who believe that class division, class conflict and the dynamics of class struggle are obscured by scales which simply rank the working population by prestige.

Although they appear to offer a neat solution to the difficulty of operationalizing the concept of class, occupational scales are extremely problematic for four reasons.

First, people may be classed together by occupational group despite large differences in reward and prestige *within* each occupation, e.g. junior hospital doctors and consultants in private practice.

Second, different occupations may be placed in the same social grade despite differences *between* those occupational groups, e.g. Goldthorpe has been criticized for including managers, high grade technicians and professional workers in Class 1 along with 'large proprietors' (Edgell 1993: 32).

Third, accounts based upon occupational scale target the working population and, by definition, overlook those who have retired or do not have a job. It is also difficult, in such schemes, to classify the 'idle rich' who may live by an invested income, but not have a recognized occupation. Nichols (1979: 165) has referred to the absurdity of 'a sort of bald class structure' which has a 'working class' and a 'middle class' but 'nothing on top'.

Fourth, feminists have attacked scales such as Goldthorpe's for classifying women according to the occupation of the male head of household and producing 'gender blind' accounts of social structure and social change so that women are seen as 'peripheral to the class system'. Writers like Oakley and Oakley (1981), Stanworth (1984) and Crompton (1989) have argued for a more 'gendered' approach to the class structure by replacing the 'head of household' classification with one which recognizes the increasing contribution of women in the workplace (see pp. 293–302).

**Q** What kinds of assumptions do you make about people based on their occupation?

What assumptions would you make about individuals in these occupations: (a) professional footballer; (b) doctor; (c) sociology lecturer; (d) secretary? (Consider political views, leisure activities, tastes.)

## The class structure in modern society

Whether it is still useful to talk of a class structure is a matter of continuing sociological debate; this debate is informed by the theoretical positions outlined in the previous section and by empirical research based upon the attempts to operationalize the concept of class.

### The demise of class

In the latter half of the twentieth century, the traditional notions about the significance of social class have been questioned. Such questioning has been inspired not only by Weberian-influenced criticisms of Marxism – by writers such as Parkin (1972), Dahrendorf (1959) and Pahl and Wallace (1988) – but also by those such as Saunders (1987) who reject Weber's conception of class along with Marx's on the basis that 'they continue to employ essentially nineteenth century ideas to analyse late twentieth century conditions' (Saunders 1987: 319). According to this general viewpoint it is claimed that changes in the structure of society, the nature of work and the formulation of consciousness have reduced the value of class analysis so that, according to Pahl, 'class as a concept is ceasing to do any useful work for sociology' (quoted in Crompton 1993: 99).

This position is based on the following factors:

1 changes in the quality of life
2 social reform and the idea of 'citizenship'
3 changes in the organization and nature of work
4 social mobility and the fragmentation of class structure
5 the end of ideology and the embourgeoisement thesis.

#### *Changes in the quality of life*

According to Marx, the 'pauperization' of the working class was an essential condition for the survival of capitalism and its eventual downfall. However, since the 1950s the living standards of many working people have improved due to wage rises and the increasing cheapness of basic goods and mass-produced consumer items. For skilled workers who have retained their jobs and especially for those 'work rich' households which have more than one income, material lifestyle has clearly improved. The relative affluence of these groups has promoted an optimistic notion of workers becoming incorporated into a diamond shaped 'middle mass' society. Pahl and Wallace (1988) argue that patterns of consumption have replaced productive activity as the means of fixing social identity and position:

> **If the symbol of the nineteenth century city was the factory chimney, the equivalent symbol at the end of the twentieth century in Europe and North America is the shopping mall.** *(Pahl and Wallace 1988, quoted in Crompton 1993: 103)*

The fact that many working people can now afford the 'luxuries' previously associated with well-off people as well as buying their own houses and shares in public utilities is taken as further evidence of the existence of the 'affluent worker' and the limitations of the 'pauperization' thesis.

### *Social reform and the idea of 'citizenship'*

In 1963 T H Marshall published the text of his now famous lectures on citizenship and social democracy. He argued that the social and political reforms of the nineteenth and twentieth centuries, the establishment of a welfare state and the belief in 'Keynesian' economic policies meant that a liberal democratic state had emerged which reflected and guaranteed the interests and rights of all people in society. No matter what class people belonged to they enjoyed the same rights of citizenship. Within liberal democracies, people had civil and political rights that guaranteed their freedoms before the law as well as the opportunity to participate in the political process, but what was special for the citizens of such democracies was their right to a decent standard of living established through the welfare state. The battle for 'social citizenship' was seen as an essential part of the war against capitalism; its aim was to assist 'the modern drive towards social equality' and reduce class antagonism. According to Marshall, social citizenship would establish

> **a general enrichment of the concrete substance of civilized life, a general reduction of risk and insecurity, an equalisation between the more and less fortunate at all levels – between the healthy and the sick, the employed and the unemployed, the old and the active, the bachelor and the father of a large family. Equalisation is not so much between classes as between individuals within a population which is now treated for this purpose as though it were one class. Equality of status is more important than equality of income.** *(Marshall 1963, quoted in Jordon 1984: 110)*

As well as providing a 'universal right to a real income', Marshall's social citizenship had at its centre the right to a decent education which in turn would widen opportunities and increase rates of social mobility. Under such circumstances it was envisaged that the sharp divisions of capitalism would be reduced and the resulting class antagonisms blunted.

### *Changes in the organization and nature of work*

In the traditional model of the class structure, people were clearly stratified according to their position within the system of production. The decisions about planning, investment and development would be made by those who owned and therefore controlled the means of production (factories, mines, railways, for example). This class of manufacturing entrepreneurs employed large groups of workers whose labour power was essential for the production of mass-produced goods. Entire communities emerged which were solely dependent upon traditional industries and skills. Within these communities work was often regarded as central to a person's status and the identities of male workers were inextricably bound up with the work they did.

At the end of the twentieth century many traditional industries have declined to the point of extinction. In Britain the steel industry, coal-mining, shipbuilding and deep sea fishing have all but disappeared. The service industries which have replaced them (in areas such as banking, leisure and retail) require different types of skills and different attitudes towards work. People are now told not to follow 'a trade' but to pick up as many 'transferable skills' as they can in order to take advantage of the new pick'n'mix job opportunities thrown up by an ever changing economic environment. No one can expect a job for life and everyone needs to be able to adapt. There are many consequences of these changes for the modern class structure but two in particular stand out.

First, the emergence of a new middle class which has, at the top end, taken over some of the administrative functions of the entrepreneurial class of owners and at other levels has expanded through the development of the professions and the rapid increase of the non-manual sector. This has given rise to the idea that apart from a very few rich people at the top and an increasingly marginalized underclass at the bottom, society is now characterized by a large and contented middle class. Despite there being little sociological evidence for this 'middle-class classless' society the idea has been extremely popular with social commentators and politicians (Edgell 1993: 119); it is certainly true that the majority of working people are now to be found in what may be loosely termed middle-class occupations.

Second, within this growth of non-manual, service sector jobs another pattern has emerged – the replacement of men by women. Whereas women in the first half of

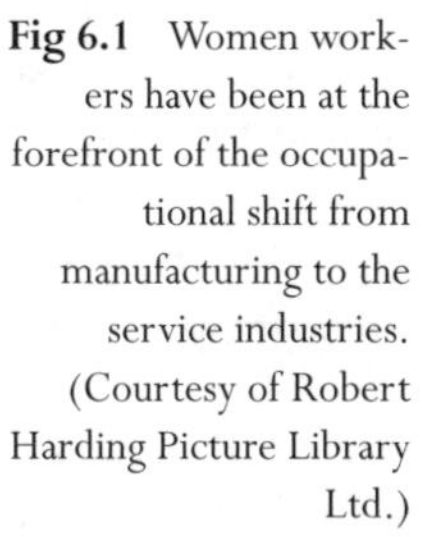

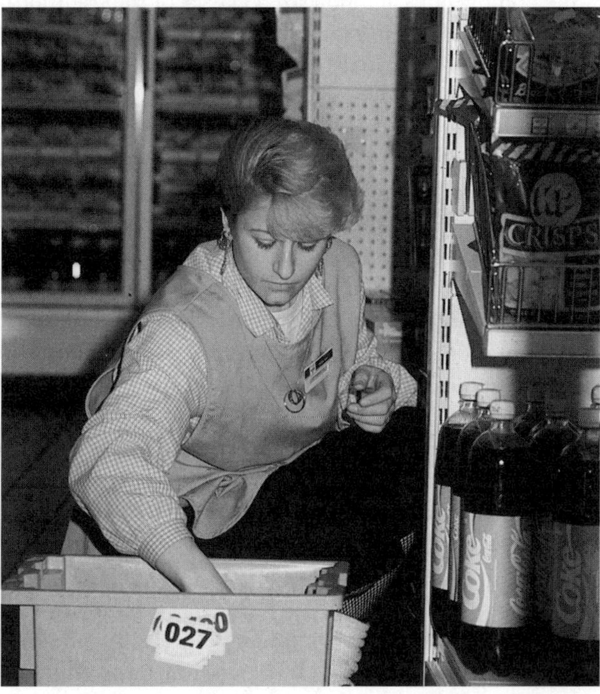


**Fig 6.1** Women workers have been at the forefront of the occupational shift from manufacturing to the service industries. (Courtesy of Robert Harding Picture Library Ltd.)

the twentieth century were largely excluded from the economic structure by their roles as wives and mothers and the 'ideology of domestication' that accompanied these roles, the penetration of women into the labour market and their increased importance as family breadwinners has been remarkable. The Labour Force Survey published in September 1993 found that most new jobs being created are part time and filled by women (in the latter part of 1992, 80 per cent of the new jobs on offer in Britain were part time and 80 per cent of these jobs were filled by women).

This 'feminization' of service work has several implications for the debate about the class structure. Women workers have been in the forefront of the occupational shift from manufacturing to service industries so that as men in traditional industries are made redundant they are replaced in the occupational structure by women in a range of 'non-manual' occupations. Despite the evidence that many of these women are being recruited into low-paid and part-time routine jobs, the non-manual nature of the work creates the impression that the class structure is becoming more middle class. Although many women may go to work simply to make ends meet, where their income combines with other household incomes, sociologists such as Pahl and Wallace (1988) have argued that 'work rich', dual income families, who enjoy relatively high living standards, emerge. Again the impression of a new middle-class family being created by changing patterns of work and income has established itself; this reinforces the impression that modern society is increasingly dominated by middle-class households able to afford a middle-class lifestyle.

### *Social mobility and the fragmentation of class structure*

The growth of a new middle class and the increasing opportunities for social mobility for people from both middle-class and working-class origins has led to the idea that the homogenous and polarized classes of the traditional model have become so fragmented by differences in skill, pay and consciousness that it no longer makes sense to talk of a class structure. According to writers like Dahrendorf (1959), the traditional upper class has undergone a process of decomposition largely as a result of increasing share ownership and a *managerial revolution* which has effectively seen ownership and control of the means of production slip from their grasp (see also Burnham 1945; Galbraith 1967).

At the same time the working class has become fractured by differences in employment opportunities and pay. Not only are there divisions between skilled, semi-skilled and unskilled workers but also an underclass of 'work poor' families has emerged characterized by unemployment and poverty (Smith 1992). This idea of fragmentation clearly undermines the Marxist notions of class formation and class consciousness and has been used to support the argument for the growth of a new middle class. However, it has been argued that even the middle mass of society is becoming increasingly fragmented by differences in skill and pay and that this has created a hierarchy of differentially rewarded status groups who see the social structure in very different ways (Roberts *et al.* 1977).

### *The end of ideology and the embourgeoisement thesis*

Despite predictions of a proletarian revolution made by Marx, the failure of the working class to develop a 'class consciousness' which has translated into 'class action' has led many sociologists to challenge the basic assumption that class position, consciousness and political action are automatically linked (Rose 1988). Instead of becoming committed to a radical value-system, most working people have rejected rebellion in favour of a more individualistic set of attitudes towards social change. In attempting to explain why workers do not necessarily adopt radical attitudes, Gordon Marshall and colleagues (1988) have distinguished between theories of working-class ambivalence and theories of working-class instrumentalism, which we shall summarize in the last part of this section.

*Theories of working-class ambivalence*

The political passivity of workers is explained in relation to the fragmentation and middle mass arguments mentioned above. On the one hand it is suggested that a fragmented working class becomes heterogenous and divided and as such cannot achieve its role as a revolutionary class. On the other hand, it is argued that sections of the working class become incorporated into the dominant value-system and subordinate to it. This view was clearly expressed in the *embourgeoisement* thesis put forward to explain the decline in working-class support for the Labour Party in the 1960s. According to this thesis the increasing affluence of working-class family life undermined the attraction of radical or social democratic policies for change. Being able to afford the trappings of a middle-class lifestyle had encouraged working-class people to become more conservative. This thesis was partially revived in the 1980s to explain the dramatic success of consecutive Conservative governments in appealing to the 'collective acquisitiveness' of some sections of the working class.

*Theories of working-class instrumentalism*

In their famous study of affluent workers in Luton, Goldthorpe and colleagues (1968) set out to test the embourgeoisement thesis and effectively demonstrated its limitations as a general economic explanation for the political behaviour of a whole class. Essentially they noted that despite economic improvements, the workers in their study had not become 'middle class' nor had they become Conservative. They did conclude, however, that a 'new working class' had been created in the post-war environment of full employment, citizenship and consumerism; their goals were increasingly 'privatized' (home-centred) and their political strategies were still collective but clearly instrumental. In other words affluent workers were prepared to support their trade unions and vote Labour as long as this guaranteed their affluent lifestyle. It has been the defection of this group of skilled manual workers to the Conservatives since 1979 after promises of tax cuts, 'right to buy' schemes for council tenants and the privatization of public utilities which has kept the Labour Party out of power ever since.

In their attack on the Marxist model of class and class consciousness, Pahl and Wallace (1988) refute the deterministic approach as 'simple minded' and romantic. They argue that the decomposition of the working class along with the dealignment of politics caused by Thatcherism has shown that there are other determinants of political outlook. Drawing on the research of sociologists and political scientists at the University of Essex (Marshall *et al.* 1988) as well as their own study of family life and class in the Isle of Sheppey, Pahl and Wallace argue that the class alignment of working people has been 'fractured' by changes in occupational structure and lifestyle. Four factors in particular provide alternative sources of social identity:

1 An increasing number of people are 'non working' class and depend increasingly upon state benefits for their income. It is their experience of unemployment that crucially affects their consciousness.
2 The increasing numbers of women in the workplace means that traditional (male head of household) notions of work, identity and class consciousness have to be re-examined.
3 Differential access to private and public services means that differing patterns of consumption appear which may be seen as a more important source of consciousness than occupation. Home ownership, private education, private health care and the ownership of shares may all become points of departure from a traditional class alignment.
4 In the world of work itself further divisions have occurred which are related to the form that work takes rather than the nature of the job. A self-employed maintenance worker may have very different views from one who works for somebody else. Whether that person was employed in the private sector or the public domain may also affect political attitudes.

As a result it is argued that the 'cultural privatization' of home-centred working-class lifestyle can result in the demise of class identification and class politics. This view is developed further by Pahl and Wallace, who suggest that social identity and consciousness is too complex to be reduced to social class. The social world is experienced through the everyday life of families and it is people's own experiences of their domestic life cycle which forms their consciousness of the real world: 'Social images, we suggest, may be constructed less in terms of class and more in terms of family and personal biography' (Pahl and Wallace 1988: 136).

The Isle of Sheppey study found little evidence of any radical consciousness ('rebels in red') nor did they discover the widespread deference often associated with privatized workers ('angels in marble') but the collective identity they did come across took rather surprising forms. First, steel plant workers on the island had combined against pickets from other plants to defend their jobs rather than join in a broader struggle. (The defection of the Nottinghamshire miners during the national strike in 1983–4 is perhaps a better known example of a similar phenomenon.) Second, trade union membership and organization were purely instrumental and were not linked in any traditional way to the Labour Party. Indeed, trade unionists were as likely to be actively involved in the Conservative Party – although the popularity of the Conservative Club seemed to rest upon the price of beer as much as anything else! Third, the general collective identity had deep historical roots which went beyond class and touched on the themes of nationalism and patriotism. The victory celebration at the end of the Falklands War in 1983 was seen as an example of 'relatively spontaneous collective action'.

Alongside this rather conservative form of collective identity Pahl and Wallace (1988) also claim to discover 'a strong element of working class individualism', a resentment of 'less respectable' families and a deep-rooted commitment to the values of domesticity. It was within this broader social consciousness that the politics of 'dynamic conservatism' made its mark at the end of the 1970s with the rise of 'Thatcherism':

**She presented herself to the working class as the champion of the taxpayer against the Treasury, the worker against the trade union, the council tenant against the landlord and the citizen against the state.** *(Jenkins 1987: 53)*

Q Summarize the problems that may arise in trying to 'measure' the following indicators of the importance of social class: (a) changes in quality of life; (b) the importance of social reform; (c) changes in the nature of work; (d) the extent of social mobility; (e) the extent of working-class instrumentalism.

## The persistence of class

Many sociologists, particularly those adopting a Marxist perspective, would reject the conclusion that class analysis is no longer useful, although few would argue that the class structure has been unaffected by social and economic change. From this point of view the major divisions in society are ones of class. These divisions still affect life chances and have a major effect on the way that people see themselves and the structure of society.

**The view that class is dead derives from a very narrow and misleading understanding of class. Properly understood, class points to fundamental social divisions that cross-cut Britain and all other modern societies. Taken along with the closely interlinked themes of gender, race and ethnicity and age, class defines the nature of social stratification, which remains the sociological key to understanding the structure of society.** *(Scott 1994: 19)*

Despite the differences already mentioned sociologists who have been influenced by Marx and Weber still talk of three major classes and emphasize the underlying conflict in the relationship between these classes. In examining the extent to which social class is still important we shall look at some of the evidence and arguments that suggest that the upper, middle and working classes continue to be important and distinct groups in modern society.

## The upper class

Traditionally the upper class are associated with ownership of property and in particular the ownership of land. The landed aristocracy began to be replaced in the nineteenth century by those whose economic power derived from manufacturing industry, retail and banking, although a certain amount of overlap occurred between these investments. More recently it has been argued that a 'managerial revolution' has stripped this class of its power to control events and that a new managerial elite of administrators has taken over.

Occupational scales tend to obscure the existence of the 'super rich'. Research is thin on the ground with rich people tending to keep details of their wealth secret, so it is easy to be persuaded by the idea that this group have all but disappeared. However, there is clear evidence that as a class they have adapted in order to survive and even become more powerful through a diversification of interests.

Definition

### The 'super rich'

On a global scale the super rich represent a tiny group of dollar-billionaires, the top 101 of whom now control wealth valued at approximately $452 billion. According to *Fortune* magazine (28 June 1993), these top individuals and their families could be found in the following categories:

| Source of wealth | Number of billionaires | Total wealth ($billion) |
|---|---|---|
| Property/construction | 11 | 50.8 |
| Manufacturing | 18 | 79.9 |
| Media/publishing | 16 | 68.9 |
| Monarchs and nobles | 9 | 80.2 |
| Finance/trading | 31 | 93.5 |
| Retailing | 16 | 75.5 |

Some of these people are famous but the interesting thing about the 'top ten, super-elite' listed below is that with one or two exceptions they are not household names:

| | | Source of wealth | $billion |
|---|---|---|---|
| 1 | Sultan of Brunei (Brunei) | Head of state/oil | 37.0 |
| 2 | Walton Family (USA) | Retailing | 23.0 |
| 3 | Forrest Mass Family (USA) | Confectionery | 14.0 |
| 4 | Minoru and Akira Mori (Japan) | Property | 13.0 |
| 5 | Si and Donald Newhouse (USA) | Publishing | 10.0 |
| 6 | King Fahd (Saudi Arabia) | Head of state /oil | 10.0 |
| 7 | John Kluge (USA) | Media | 8.8 |
| 8 | Gad and Hans Rausing (UK) | Packaging | 8.5 |
| 9 | Queen Elizabeth II (UK) | Head of state/property | 7.8 |
| 10 | Toichi Takenaka (Japan) | Construction | 7.1 |

(Adapted from *New Internationalist* September 1994: 17–20)

On a national level, writers including Miliband (1969), Scott (1991) and Westergaard and Resler (1976) in Britain and Barron and Sweezy (1968) and Zeitlen (1989) in the USA have argued that the managerial revolution is more imagined than real. The idea that the managerial elite are a group of essentially neutral technocrats operating in the public interest is roundly rejected. The modifications of the class structure in recent times have not altered its essential nature:

**Property, profit and market – the key institutions of a capitalist society – retain their central place in social arrangements, and remain the prime determinants of inequality.** *(Westergaard and Resler 1976: 17)*

At the apex of these key institutions remains a dominant class of between 5 and 10 per cent of the population who derive their position from property ownership and the control that they exercise over resources and other people's lives:

**The core assumptions of our society (property, profit and market) are firmly in line with the interests of one small group. That group comprises top business people and large property owners. It also includes those who derive substantial privilege from their association with this central cluster: the highly prosperous and well established professions, the senior ranks of officials in public service. . . . Capital with its associates is still the effective ruling interest. It is not just one elite among several.**

*(Westergaard and Resler 1976: 252)*

This homogenous view of a capitalist class has been modified more recently by models which suggest a variety of interests constituting a powerful group at the top whose ownership of property confers power. Giddens (1986: 159) has identified three categories of rich people in Britain.

1 *Jet set rich* this includes writers, sports professionals and rock stars who amass large fortunes very quickly as a result of well-marketed publicity. This group represents a very small section of the wealthy and would not normally be regarded as part of the capitalist class. An example is Paul McCartney.
2 *Landowners* people whose fortunes have been largely inherited, their estates having been passed down over generations. The concentration of landownership means that a small group of landed families are still prominent. Because of the responsibilities and costs involved in maintaining such estates, as well as the legal restrictions covering such property, this group are not as wealthy as they may appear and do not control the kind of liquid assets which make other rich people very powerful. The Duke of Westminster is an aristocrat who inherited both land and title.
3 *Entrepreneurial rich* a group who derive their position from the ownership of stocks and shares. The concentration of ownership of these resources puts the control of manufacture, banking, insurance and the retail trades in the hands of a very few people. Although they may not be as wealthy on paper as some aristocrats, these people control assets that give them substantial power. Richard Branson and the Guinness, Cowdray and Forte families are examples.

John Scott (1991) has researched the exclusive 'business class' at the centre of the major enterprises which dominate British economic activity. In his view the landed aristocracy and the highly paid are not necessarily members of the business class simply because of their affluence. The important consideration for Scott is the involvement of wealthy and influential individuals who hold key positions ('economic locations') at the centre of capitalist activity.

**Capitalist economic locations are positions within a structure of ownership and control over property, and there are two bases for location within the capitalist class: direct participation in control through personal property holdings and administrative participation, as directors and executives, in the impersonal patterns of control through which business enterprises are ruled.** *(Scott 1991: 8)*

Behind the rise of joint-stock companies and institutional share ownership there still exists a core of capitalists who represent a business class. Scott suggests that this group may be classified in the following manner:

1 *Entrepreneurial capitalists* through their personal property holdings they enjoy direct control over corporate policy in one organization where they have a major or complete stake. The Moores family's domination of the Littlewoods empire is a good example.
2 *Rentier capitalists* they have less day-to-day involvement with company policy, and their personal investment is spread over a range of different companies, return on investment rather than control is the major consideration – they 'speculate to accumulate'. They have multiple shareholdings and make their money out of share dealing. By their nature, such individuals tend to work behind the scenes and so are not very well known.
3 *Executive capitalists* they have official full-time positions (e.g. Chair) within organizations but do not necessarily hold a large or controlling stake in the business. The senior executives of large concerns such as ICI, British Airways and British Telecom would fit this category.
4 *Finance capitalists* they enjoy multiple non-executive directorships across a range of separate companies. These people are not simply passive shareholders, but might represent the interests of big financial institutions on the boards of large companies and as a result may be regarded as a sort of 'inner circle' of the British business class. An example is the Conservative MP, Sir John Henderson.

Although Scott has indicated a more differentiated model of the upper class than that offered by Westergaard and Resler (1976), for instance, he is clear that they still represent a privileged group in society:

> **Occupants of all these capitalist locations are able to secure advantaged opportunities and life chances for themselves and for their families and they are able to live a life of privilege.** *(Scott 1991: 10)*

Case Study

## The business elite in Britain

### Directors' pay rises

Research into directors' pay by the *Guardian* reveals that the highest paid in the UK's biggest companies received pay increases of just under 9 per cent last year. Although less than the rises gained in previous years, such a rise is well above both the rate of inflation and the rise in average earnings in the UK. And this overall pay rise figure hides a much larger average increase for the executives of certain companies, in particular the big privatized public utilities such as British Gas and the regional water boards. In addition, the pay rise figures do not reflect the increases in the pension contributions that are made to top executives nor do they take account of windfall profits gained from the sale of share options by directors. Thus it is difficult if not impossible to calculate the entire remuneration packages provided for Britain's 'top executives'.

*(box continued)*

*(box continued)*

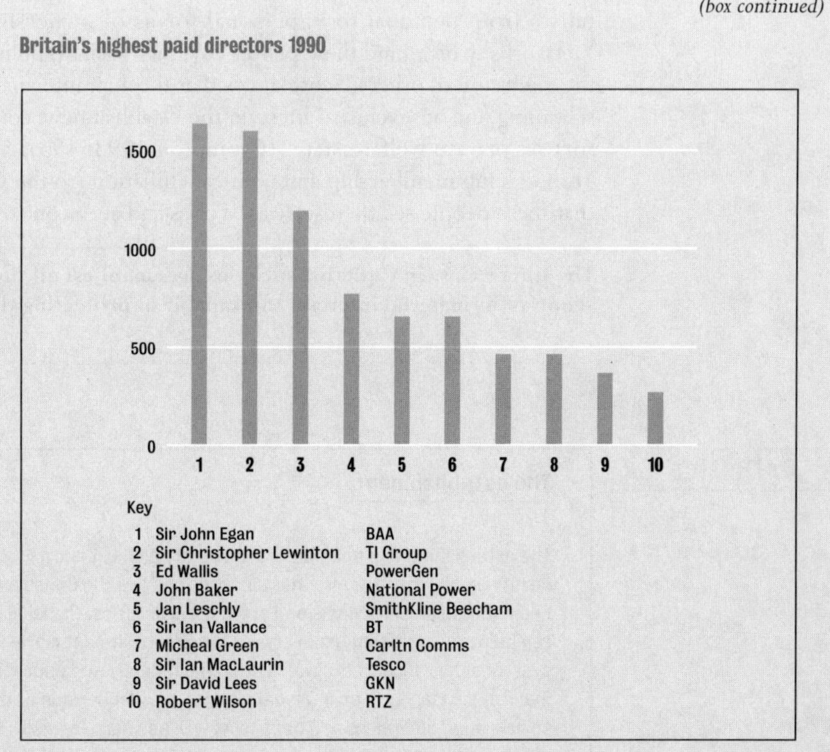


**Fig 6.2** Windfalls – share option profits, £000s.

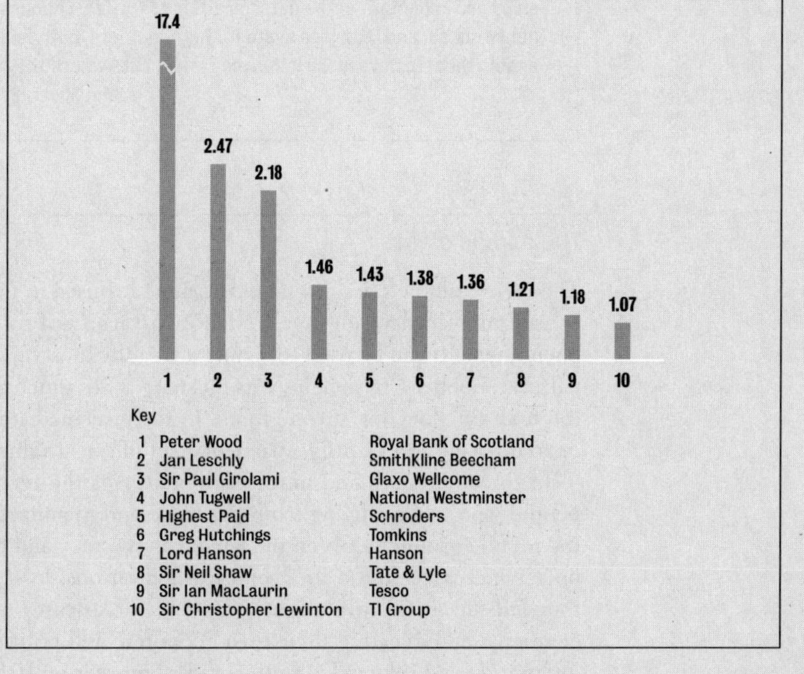


**Fig 6.3** Big earners – FTSE's top ten pay packages, £m.

(Adapted from L Buckingham, 'How Boardrooms Scale the Perks', *Guardian* 1 July 1995: 38)

According to Scott, this group survives *as a class*, despite the transformation of capitalism from personal to impersonal forms of ownership, because of a series of 'networks' which bind these people together socially, politically and economically to the exclusion of others. Scott shows that through intermarriage and kinship, private schooling and an exclusive lifestyle the establishment continues to assert itself as a sort of 'private welfare state' (Crompton 1993: 193). Similarities of social background, club membership and political affiliation (to the Conservative Party) means that these people see themselves as a class and act as one. As Crompton concludes:

**The upper class in capitalist societies *does* manifest all the signs of being both conscious of its material interests and capable of protecting them.**

*(Crompton 1993: 198)*

Definition

**The establishment**

The establishment is not simply a group of people; it is a group of people allied around certain social institutions. These institutions are the Conservative Party, the Church of England, the public schools and ancient universities, the legal profession and the Guards regiments. . . . In its informal aspect the Establishment is the 'old boy network', the system of social contacts which stem from family and education. Such contacts 'are maintained largely in an informal manner by membership of the London clubs, by the social round of dinners and parties as well as, more formally, in business meetings and at official events'. The contacts which constitute this informal network of social relationships are important in the determination of the life-chances of those who go through the public school and Oxbridge system. Their contacts 'both facilitate their careers and enable them to have more influence in the posts where they eventually land'.

(John Scott 1992, quoted in Giddens 1992: 88)

## The middle class

The term 'middle class' is one of the most misused in the sociological dictionary. It is used in everyday language to denote a variety of social, economic and cultural phenomena. It can be used to signify a wealthy lifestyle, a managerial occupation or cultural snobbery. In sociology its meaning is not much clearer; it has been used as a catch-all category for anyone found in the intermediate strata of industrial society or to describe and identify a particular set of social values.

In the eighteenth and nineteenth centuries the term tended to refer to those people who made a living from the trade and manufacture of goods and inhabited the middle ground between the landed aristocracy and the poor. As their economic power increased so did their political aspirations. In some countries (e.g. France) they led successful revolutions against the aristocracy, establishing republican governments and exerting their own economic and political domination. In Britain, integration and reform led to the gradual merger with the aristocracy to form what is loosely referred to as the 'upper class'. In both situations the class that had been in the middle was now at the top, which made the continued use of the term even more confusing. According to Marx the industrial bourgeoisie had become the new ruling class in opposition to the other major industrial class (the proletariat). In between he also recognized a class of small traders, self-employed artisans and landlords whom he referred to as the petty-bourgeoisie. However, as economic competition and the growth of monopolies forced them out of business, Marx expected that this group would eventually sink into the proletariat as society divided more clearly into 'two hostile camps'. As we have noted (pp. 233–5) Weber disagreed fundamentally with Marx here and predicted an increase in the growth of the middle class. In the twentieth century the number of people in 'non-manual' occupations has undoubtedly grown at the expense of traditional manual occupations. The percentage of the working population in manual occupations is now lower than 50 per cent in many industrialized countries with the non-manual sector representing anything between 50 and 60 per cent. This shift has been accompanied by a growth in female employment in the service sector and increasing levels of education and social mobility:

**With the general rise in living standards, the spread of higher education and the transformation of Britain from an industrial to a service economy the middle classes, however defined, have made up an increasingly large proportion of the population.** *(Williams 1986: 112)*

Over time, then, the term middle class has ceased to be used to define a class (of manufacturers and traders) and been applied instead to a status group who are distinguished by the non-manual nature of their work and whose attitudes and values differ from the traditional industrial working class. In 1948 Herbert Morrison generalized the middle class as 'that varied section of the community that works with its brain rather than its hands'. They were also seen to be better paid and to have earned a salary (paid into a bank account) rather than a weekly wage (placed in their hand). Along with this they were more likely to have a mortgage and to pay income tax. Some of these distinctions between manual and non-manual workers may have diminished in significance but the middle class is still defined in economic and social terms. Sociologists and advertisers refer to the middle class as those who inhabit grades A, B and C on an A–E scale where the distinction is still drawn between skilled manual (C2) and skilled non-manual (C1) occupations.

As this non-manual status group is so broad it is unhelpful to talk about all non-manual employees as if they belong to one homogenous and conscious class, sharing similar economic, social and political interests. As a result most writers seem to accept that the differences within this group are as important as the similarities that may exist:

**It is, indeed, much more accurate to talk about the *middle classes* rather than about one single middle class. There is an enormous difference in income, status and lifestyle between the stockbroker at the upper end of the upper middles and the shorthand typist hovering uncomfortably between the ranks of the lower middle classes and the skilled manual workers.** *(Williams 1986: 112)*

Since the 1950s a distinction has been made between the 'old' middle class whose position derived from property and the 'new' middle classes which include a range of 'white-collar' occupations. There is some dispute about the future of the old middle class, but it is clear that some small-scale entrepreneurs have survived. Optimists believe that this class may reassert itself as a result of government support for small businesses and enterprise initiatives. However, the high failure rate of such initiatives and the collapse of small businesses as a consequence of the recession and a jittery banking sector may lead us to question the long-term revival of a petty-bourgeois class.

The 'new' middle classes, on the other hand, have been dramatically successful in expanding their size and influence. There is little dispute that the service sector has grown, and that professionals, managers and administrators have become a significant part of the occupational structure. This growth has created a demand for new groups of specialists whose function is to service the emotional and cultural needs of the new middle classes. Media pundits, psychotherapists, fashion designers and health gurus are part of this 'new petty bourgeoisie' which has blossomed in response to an ever growing appetite for difference in the post-modern age of mass consumption (Crompton 1993: 179–80).

### *The service class*

This section of the 'new' middle classes is that which is closest to the capitalist or upper class by virtue of the control and servicing functions that it carries out on behalf of the upper class and because of clear differences in income, education and lifestyle which mark it out from other non-manual groups, but similar to the dominant group in society. As a result this group clearly has 'a stake in the status quo' although there is continuing debate about whether they are so privileged that they have become part of the dominant class.

An attempt to make sense of the factors that confuse our analysis of the middle classes at this level can be found in the work of Mike Savage *et al.* (1992). According to their view it is possible to understand the lifestyle and structuring of the upper middle and service classes in terms of the different assets that they possess. These are property, cultural and organizational assets, which are the key to their success and the life chances they and their families enjoy. These assets also correspond to the formation of different groups within the middle class and may explain the differences in cultural outlook at this level.

#### *Property assets*

Property is the most important form of asset. It is easy to store and quick to utilize; it represents the most obvious way in which members of this class can establish themselves and get things done. Although property assets are most obviously connected with the formation of the entrepreneurial classes, they can also be important in establishing and maintaining the class position of members of the service class – some of whom enjoy six figure annual incomes and lucrative share options. The overnight fortunes made in the City after the Big Bang in 1986 also provided the basis for the formation of a young and upwardly mobile sub-class. The 'yuppie' phenomenon may have been short lived but it demonstrates the enduring power of property assets to affect class formation. Because, in Savage's model, this group is almost indistinguishable from what we have already called the upper class, it is safe to assume that they exist within (or on the fringes of) the network which

Scott identified as the establishment. Private education, intermarriage, membership of exclusive clubs and the Conservative Party are all badges of 'social exclusion'. Savage, however, has identified a post-modernist trend among the yuppies of the 1980s whereby cultural taste is less determined by traditional patterns of consumption and is more hedonistic and eclectic in nature. The old divisions between high cultural forms and mass culture disappear in the free market of commodity choice as new patterns of consumption and taste emerge (see Chapter 2, pp. 99–102 on post-modernism).

*Cultural assets*

Along with property, and sometimes instead of it, the 'cultural capital' achieved through exclusive and high levels of education can become the key to membership of the professional wing of the service class. This professional middle class clearly takes advantage of the education system to secure the cultural advantages that can lead to social success. These assets may not be as fluid or as effective as property, but a 'good education' is an investment in the future which can withstand inflation and the vagaries of the marketplace.

As a result cultural assets have enabled a powerful professional middle class to emerge 'alongside but subordinate to [the] propertied class' (Scott 1994: 2). As this group is high on cultural capital but low on economic assets, it is not surprising that in terms of consciousness and lifestyle they can be seen as different from the propertied middle class. This is especially true of those professionals who work in the public sector who may have different tastes as well as unexpected political allegiances. Their lifestyle has been described as healthy, intellectual and culturally radical; Wynne (1990) called this group 'sporters' because of their ascetic and athletic lifestyle. In political terms they are also less likely to support the Conservative Party. Whereas top professionals have been described as a 'conservative force' this does not apply to all members of the professional middle class. Research has shown

**Fig 6.4** 'Yuppies out', graffiti against development, London Docklands. (Photograph © Adam Woolfitt, courtesy of Robert Harding Picture Library Ltd.)

that while top professionals in the private sector who are employed within an entrepreneurial model tend to be conservative, those who work in public service areas like health and education may support and become actively involved in the Labour Party (Callinicos and Harman 1987: 40–5; Crompton 1993: 204–5).

*Organizational assets*

The least valuable form of asset are those skills that relate only to the organization being served. Although administrative skills have made managers, as a class, indispensable to large organizations (see p. 244), they provide only a short-term and inflexible basis for membership of the service class. Managers may become redundant as a result of restructuring or new technologies and discover that their skills are no longer required anywhere else. This makes organizational assets alone a very unstable guarantee of middle-class position and lifestyle, especially in Britain where the managerial middle class have historically been recruited separately from those with cultural assets. This may explain why the children of managers are likely to be well educated and are encouraged to 'trade' their organizational assets for cultural ones. As a result the children of managers are more likely to become professionals than to follow their parents into management (Savage *et al*. 1992: 148).

### *The lower middle class*

The other element of the 'new' middle classes is a lower or intermediate class which is comprised of lower-paid non-manual workers engaged in routine white-collar work. While some writers seem happy to lump this group together with other members of a general middle class characterized by their ownership of educational and technical qualifications (Giddens: see p. 237), there is widespread disagreement among sociologists about the class position of routine non-manual workers. Some would argue that the pay, status and working conditions of these workers make them a distinct 'intermediate' class occupying the social territory between the service class and the working class; others, however, would prefer to see them as part of a broader working class which makes no distinction between mental and physical labour. In essence this debate concerns the process of proletarianization which Marx predicted as the fate of industrial capitalism. Colin Ward (1972) provides a clerical worker's view of office routine:

**One occupational hazard facing a clerk is always the sense of futility he [*sic*] struggles against, and is more often just overwhelmed by. Unlike even the humblest worker on a production line, he doesn't produce *anything*. He battles with phantoms, abstracts; runs a paper chase that goes on year after year and seems utterly pointless. How can there be anything else other than boredom in it for him?**

*(Ward 1972: 22)*

**We argue that, once a person's place in the relations of production is taken as the key to his or her class position, then three groups of white-collar workers must be distinguished: 1. a small minority who are salaried members of the capitalist class, participating in the decisions on which the process of capital accumulation depends; 2. a much larger group, the 'new middle class', of highly-paid white-collar workers, most of whom occupy managerial and supervisory positions intermediate between labour and capital; 3. the majority, routine white-collar workers having as little control over their work as manual workers, and often less well-paid. The cru-**

**cial conclusion we draw from this analysis is that the growth of this third group represents the expansion, not the decline, of the working class.**

***(Callinicos and Harman 1987: 9)***

Westergaard and Resler (1976) maintain that the apparent growth of this 'middle class' is really no more than an expansion of opportunities for low-paid drudgery with little prospect of promotion. This is especially true for women who have 'moved from domestic service jobs and skilled manual work into semi-skilled jobs in offices and factories' (1976: 294). Crompton and Jones (1984) have emphasized the continuation of deskilling in the workplace and the proletarianization of the social and economic position of white-collar workers. Crucial to this process is the 'feminization' of clerical work and the restricted opportunities for women in these organizations relative to men (see pp. 243–4).

The proletarianization thesis has been attacked by sociologists influenced by the Weberian perspective. In their view those in white-collar occupations form a distinct 'intermediate class' who can be clearly distinguished from the service class above them and a manual working class below (Goldthorpe *et al.* 1980). In his early *Blackcoated Worker* study, David Lockwood (1958) argued that despite a deterioration in relative pay and status, clerical workers enjoyed better job security, pension provision and promotion prospects when compared with manual workers. In his revised edition, Lockwood (1989) concluded that changes in the workplace may have benefited white-collar employees.

**Regardless of the extent to which clerical work may be said to have been proletarianised, there are no grounds for thinking that the majority of clerical workers have experienced proletarianisation. The promotion opportunities of male clerks and the fairly rapid turnover of female clerks more or less guarantee that this is not the case. Secondly, the view that clerical work itself has undergone widespread 'degradation', as a result of rationalisation and mechanisation, is not one that has found much support. Indeed, the most detailed recent surveys and case-studies of the effects of the new technology lead to just the opposite conclusion: namely, that reskilling, even job enrichment appear to be the most general consequences.**

***(Lockwood 1989: 250)***

Support for this view has been provided by the research of Stewart *et al.* (1980) whose study of male white-collar workers showed that for over 50 per cent of their sample, clerical work was a route to promotion and social mobility. By the age of 30 less than 20 per cent were still in clerical work, which led them to conclude that in the experience of most clerical workers proletarianization did not characterize their work. This view has been endorsed by Marshall *et al.* (1988) whose research shows very little evidence of deskilling and proletarianzation among clerical workers but indicates a fragmentation within the lower middle class between this group and personal service workers (e.g. shop assistants) for whom the process of proletarianization is more significant.

There are clearly problems in using a term like 'middle class' to accommodate all of those people who neither own property nor work with their hands. Although the term is used widely in everyday language, its use within class analysis is fraught with difficulties which stem from the fragmentary and contradictory nature of the group who make it up. Abercrombie *et al.* (1994) provide a clear summary of these difficulties:

**We conclude that the occupational category usually referred to as the middle class is divided into two unequal sections, with some intermediate strata in between. The larger part has a market and work situation generally superior to that of the working class but with proletarianisation occurring in certain categories. The smaller part has much more advantageous situation. In between these two sections is a further set of occupations largely composed of lower management, parts of the lower professions, and technicians, who may have better market and work conditions than clerks or shop assistants, but who have neither the control over their work nor the rewards of higher managers and professionals. These groups are particularly vulnerable to . . . rationalising and deskilling processes.**

***(Abercrombie et al. 1994: 188)***

### The working class

We have already noted that the idea of an homogenous manual working class with its roots in traditional forms of manual work, community culture and political allegiance has come under attack as a result of technological and economic change. These criticisms also brought into question the relationship between class position, class consciousness and class action. As a result the revolutionary role of the working class has been rejected in favour of models which stressed working-class, ambivalence and instrumentalism. However, the idea that the decline in the number of people working in some areas of industrial production means saying 'farewell to the working class' (Gorz 1982) has been challenged by many sociologists and Marxist writers who have argued that the working class has simply been transformed by changes in the structure of the labour market. The nature of work, reward and lifestyle of these workers still distinguishes them from others, while the political consequences of these changes may have been exaggerated. While acknowledging the disagreement over the nature of the working class in modern society, we shall attempt to categorize the different broad groups who may be said to constitute the working class: a traditional working class; an expanded working class; and an underclass.

#### *The traditional working class*

This group is made up of people (usually men) who work in the traditional areas of industrial production. In the past these industries have included textiles, steel production and coal-mining; more recently light engineering and the car industry have formed part of this changing area of the economy. Classical sociological studies of family life, work and the community have painted an homogenous and possibly romantic stereotype of a working-class culture dominated by the male pursuits of sport, drink and trade union politics, but characterized also by a strong matriarchal family (Dennis *et al.* 1956; Tunstall 1962; Young and Willmott 1957).

By the early part of the nineteenth century it has been argued that in Britain a strong working class with its own distinctive culture had emerged. Working-class people were conscious of their membership of this culture and their separate interests as a class (E P Thompson 1968). According to Callinicos and Harman (1987) these interests developed into a fully fledged class consciousness based upon collective values and action as a result of 'three waves of industrial struggle' between

1850 and the 1930s. This old manual working class established the basis for collective action through a variety of organizations such as family, community, trade unions and the Labour Party.

Since the 1950s the homogeneity and strength of purpose of the traditional working class has been under attack from the processes of 'embourgeoisement' and 'privatization'. Goldthorpe *et al.*'s (1968, 1969) classic study of 'affluent' workers in Luton repudiated the idea that the working class had adopted middle-class norms and values as a result of a more affluent lifestyle (see p. 245). However, their conclusion that a 'new working class' had emerged who were more interested in a privatized lifestyle and an instrumental attitude to work (and politics) has also been criticized. At the time John Westergaard (1970) disputed the idea that increasing materialism made workers less interested in class action (in fact he suggested the reverse). In the early 1990s Fiona Devine returned to Luton in order to test the 'new workers' hypothesis in the aftermath of a protracted recession and a decade of Conservative government. Her conclusions suggest that Goldthorpe *et al.* (1968–9) had 'exaggerated the extent of change in working class lifestyles . . . [and] incorrectly gave primacy to changing working class norms and values' (Devine 1994: 7). Workers moved to Luton in search of jobs and affordable housing (not to become socially mobile) and, once there, retained ties of kinship and friendship with communities as far afield as Northern Ireland, Scotland and the South East of England. These workers identified with the concerns and aspirations of other workers (especially the threats of redundancy and unemployment) and felt that trade unions and the Labour Party were a 'collective means of securing working class interests'. What had appeared as a 'new' working class in the 1960s had all but vanished in twenty years.

Although the number of people employed as manual workers in the traditional industries has clearly fallen, this does not eradicate their significance as a class. Manual workers still play an important role within the economy and continue to account for a large proportion of the workforce. Depending on how we define manual workers, this group still constitutes around 50 per cent. In some parts of the world the proportion is even lower (approximately 40 per cent in the USA) but in areas of recent industrialization the manual working class will constitute the majority class into the twenty-first century.

The pay and life chances of manual workers have remained a significant part of working-class experience. Despite the fact that some white-collar workers take home less pay than some manual workers it is still clear that *on average* the comparison favours those in non-manual occupations.

**Case Study**

### Pay differentials

**In the year to April 1994 average gross weekly earnings of full-time employees rose by £8.70 (or 2.8 per cent) to £325.70. Retail prices increased by 2.6 per cent in the year to April, so that average real pay went up by just under 0.2 per cent.**

**The gap between manual and non-manual workers, which has been widening, since the 1970s widened again but mainly for women. Average weekly earnings of full-time employees at April 1994 were as follows:**

*(box continued)*

*(box continued)*

**Table 6.2** Average weekly earnings of full-time employees (April 1994).

| | Manual | Non-manual | All |
|---|---|---|---|
| Men | 280.7 | 428.2 | 362.1 |
| Women | 181.9 | 278.4 | 261.5 |
| Men and women | 262.7 | 359.5 | 325.7 |

**These figures are taken from the *New Earnings Survey* – a sample survey of the earnings of employees in Britain carried out in April each year by the Department of Education and Employment and covering all industries and occupations.**

The *New Earnings Survey* showed that manual workers depended far more than other groups on overtime payments for their total earnings and that they worked longer hours. It is also still the case that manual workers enjoy fewer privileges at work (time off, sick pay, holidays) and have lower levels of job security. They have fewer opportunities for promotion and they are less likely to belong to pension schemes. As a consequence, manual workers are also less likely to enjoy the life chances available to other groups in society. In the areas of health, housing, education, social mobility and leisure, major differences still occur which reveal the significance of being 'working class'. As Ivan Reid's (1989) work demonstrates, individual life chances are still tied to class background with very little likelihood of improvement for those at the lower end:

> **It is difficult to see that political activity and social change in the 1980's has done much other than to sustain, or even increase, existing class differences. Indeed the large body of unemployed, especially the long-term, may be seen as a new class whose deprivations are many and severe. There is, in short, no evidence to suggest that class differences are anything but alive and well at present and that they will feature prominently . . . into the 1990's and beyond.** ***(Reid 1989: 397)***

### *An expanded working class*

As noted earlier the 'proletarianization' debate raised the issue of the class position of the lower middle classes. It has been argued that as the nature of work has changed to increase the demand for routine clerical and service workers, the conventional distinction between manual and non-manual work has been rendered useless. Instead the view of neo-Marxist writers like Callinicos and Harman (1987) is that the routine nature of this work and its relatively low levels of pay and status make this form of employment virtually indistinguishable from manual labour.

In the 'hierarchically structured' world of white-collar work they estimate that a prestigious group of administrators and managers have emerged who represent between 10 and 15 per cent of the workforce and operate as part of the 'service class' (they use the term 'new middle class'). Below the minority are an 'intermediate grade' of administrative and clerical staff (approximately 15 per cent of the workforce) who aspire to membership of the 'new middle class' but in reality exist just above those on 'routine manual grades' and as a result must be regarded as simply another group of 'exploited workers'. Alongside this group has emerged a strata of lower professionals such as classroom teachers and lower-paid nurses who also exert little control over their work and only have their labour power to rely upon. In conclusion they argue that 'the restructuring of industry has produced a restructuring of the working class, *not* the growth of a new class alongside and comparable in size to the working class' (Callinicos and Harman 1987: 86). If the surviving blue-collar workers and the lower grades of white-collar and routine non-manual workers are combined together they represent an 'expanded working class' which accounts for 70 per cent of the working population

### *The underclass*

In the debate over the persistence of the working class, the idea of a growing underclass has emerged which relates to a variety of sociological and political issues. In this discussion we shall have to overlook many of these important issues and focus on the relevance of the underclass to class analysis. In particular we are concerned with the way in which the underclass is defined and with its relationship to the wider class structure.

The idea of an underclass is not new. Marx used the term *lumpenproletariat* in the nineteenth century to refer in disparaging terms to a 'surplus population' living in the most destitute conditions. The writings of Mayhew (1949) and Booth (1889) also painted lurid and frightening portraits of life among the dangerous classes in Victorian London (Chesney 1991). In the twentieth century the term underclass was coined in order to make sense of the experiences of those living in the black ghettos of the USA or the townships of South Africa. This racial dimension has always made its application to British society problematic, but since the 1960s the term has been widely used to refer not only to inner city deprivation among ethnic minority groups (Rex and Tomlinson 1979) but also to those suffering from the urban decay found on many of the (predominantly white) post-war housing estates on the fringes of major cities.

Writers like Giddens (1973) have used the term broadly to describe those people in modern capitalist society who survive in a twilight world between unemployment and the secondary labour market. But Runciman (1990) and Field (1989) prefer to highlight welfare benefits as the key to defining the underclass. As Field puts it:

**I accept that Britain does now have a group of poor people who are so distinguished from others on low income that it is appropriate to use the term 'underclass' to describe their position in the social hierarchy.**

***(Field 1989, quoted in Murray 1990: 37)***

He goes on to suggest that the underclass includes three main groups: 'the very frail, elderly pensioner; the single parent with no chance of escaping welfare under the existing rules . . . and the long-term unemployed' (Field, quoted in Murray 1990: 39).

Smith (1992) makes a case for defining the underclass in structural terms which are specifically related to legitimate opportunities for regular work:

**The underclass are those who fall outside [the] class schema, because they belong to family units having no stable relationship at all with the 'mode of production' – with legitimate gainful employment.** ***(Smith 1992:4)***

According to this view structural changes which are a direct result of economic recession have led to long-term unemployment becoming a way of life for many people. Changes in benefit rules and cuts in welfare expenditure have increased the likelihood that this way of life will be characterized by poverty, while the gap between 'work rich' and 'work poor' households increases. Studies have indicated that a growing number of people in Britain are living on or below the poverty line. The Joseph Rowntree Foundation report, *Income and Wealth* (1995), concluded that inequalities of income and opportunity were widening: the 'top' 10 per cent were becoming better off and the 'bottom' 10 per cent worse off. These findings are supported by the Department of Social Security report, *Households Below Average Income* (1994), which showed that the poorest tenth of the population suffered a 17 per cent fall in real income between 1979 and 1992 while the richest tenth enjoyed an increase of 62 per cent. It also highlighted an increase in the number of people living in poverty. Overall 13.9 million children and adults (25 per cent of the population) were living below the official poverty line of half the average income after allowing for housing costs in 1992, compared with 5 million (9 per cent of the population) in 1979.

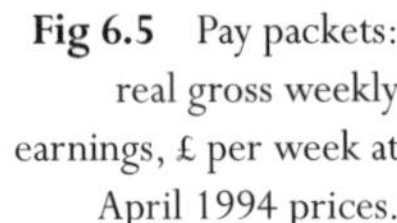

## Case Study

### The gap between rich and poor

**Data from the 1995 edition of *Social Trends* highlights the widening gap between the rich and poor. The gap between the richest and poorest tenths of male workers grew from £203 per week in 1971 to almost £402 per week in 1994. For women workers, the equivalent gap grew from £118 to £279. The share of total household income received by the poorest 20 per cent of the population fell from 10 per cent in 1979 to 6 per cent in 1992, while the proportion received by the richest 20 per cent rose from 35 per cent to 43 per cent.**

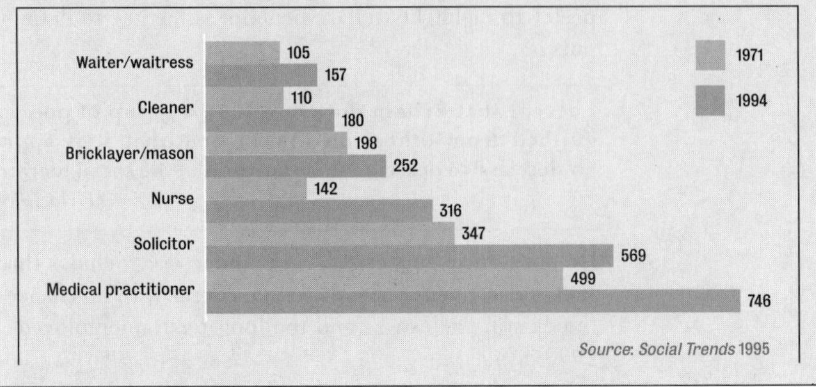


**Fig 6.5** Pay packets: real gross weekly earnings, £ per week at April 1994 prices.

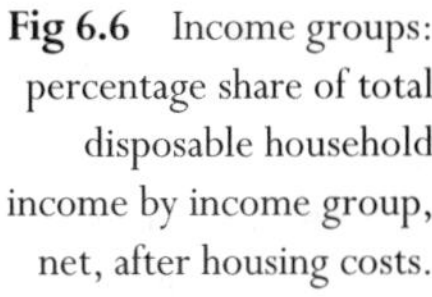

**Fig 6.6** Income groups: percentage share of total disposable household income by income group, net, after housing costs.

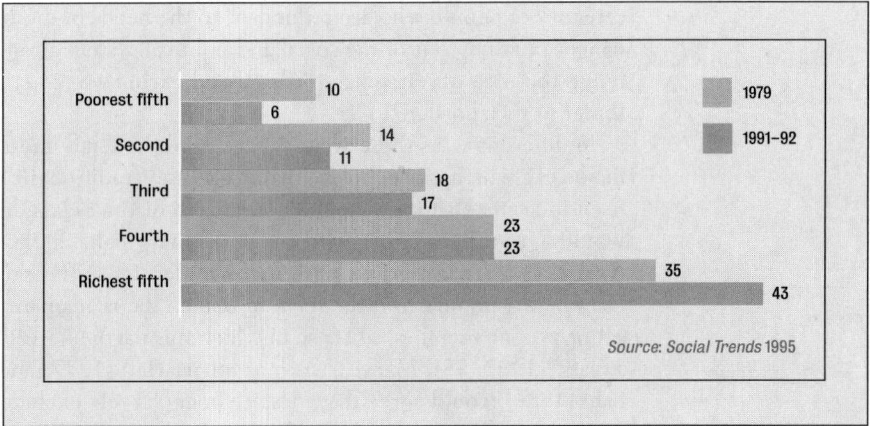


In contrast to this structural perspective a more controversial point of view has developed which stresses the *cultural* aspects of the underclass. This view can be seen as making a distinction between the 'respectable' and the 'rough' (or 'undeserving') working class. These ideas emerged in Oscar Lewis's (1960) work on the 'culture of poverty' in the 1950s and were apparent in Sir Keith Joseph's policy initiatives in the 1970s which targeted the 'cycle of deprivation' (see A Walker 1990: 51). In the 1980s the work of Charles Murray became part of a New Right perspective on poverty which identified the emergence of an anti-social ghetto culture:

**During the last half of the 1960s and throughout the 1970s something strange and frightening was happening among the poor people in the United States. Poor communities that had consisted mostly of hardworking folks began deteriorating, sometimes falling apart altogether. Drugs, crime, illegitimacy, homelessness, drop-out from the job market, drop out from school, casual violence – all the measures that were available to the social scientists showed large increases focused in poor communities. As the 1980s began, the growing population of 'the other kind of poor people' could no longer be ignored, and a label for them came into use. In the US we began to call them the underclass.** ***(Murray 1990: 2–3)***

When asked to apply his ideas to Britain, Murray found no difficulty in discovering a similar group defined by their 'deplorable behaviour' rather than their structural position. This subculture not only marks them off from the respectable working class, but also serves to transmit underclass membership from one generation to the next:

**I am not talking here about an unemployment problem that can be solved by more jobs, nor about a poverty problem that can be solved by higher benefits. Britain has a growing population of work-aged, healthy people who live in a different world from other Britons, who are raising their children to live in it, and those values are now contaminating the life of entire communities.**

***(Murray, quoted in Sunday Times 26 November 1989)***

A slightly more sympathetic view, which still adopts a culturalist perspective, is that of Ralph Dahrendorf (1992) who argues that, partly through choice but also due to changes in long-term unemployment and family structure, there is now a distinct category of people who are redundant to the needs of modern capitalism and are in danger of falling out of the social and political system altogether. As such they challenge the idea of 'citizenship' discussed earlier (p. 242) and indeed represent a threat to social order.

In different ways these writers have used the term underclass to denote a group in society which exists below or beyond the traditional class structure. The term itself indicates that they should be seen as a distinct class; however, few sociologists would agree that people who are poor, marginalized and out of work should be treated as a separate class with its own identity, interests and lifestyle. Although Dahrendorf popularized the term in Britain, he is adamant that 'there is no technical or proper sociological sense in which this particular category can ever be called a class' (1992: 55). Marxists such as Stuart Hall (1977) and Weberians such as Ray Pahl (1984) would agree that, despite being largely excluded from the opportunity structure of society, it is misleading to represent the underclass as a permanent and stable class, conscious of its own interests. Rather it has tended to be seen as constituting a fraction of the working class, despite the fact that it may have a distinctive social character in terms of ethnicity, gender, age and cultural attitude.

Although it has excited a good deal of theoretical interest, the underclass has not been subjected to much empirical scrutiny. However, Anthony Heath (1992) used information from the 1987 British Election Survey and the 1989 British Social Attitudes Survey to study the attitudes of members of the underclass, investigating orientation to work and political attitudes of two samples (which he termed the long-term and the short-term) of the underclass. He concluded that it was difficult to identify the underclass as a distinct community with negative attitudes towards family values, work and other mainstream institutions.

## 'Class is dead; long live class'

In this chapter we have examined the concept of social stratification and, in particular, the relevance of social class. Discounted by many writers as an outdated notion more suited to the 'two nations' of nineteenth-century Britain, it retains for many sociologists a significance at the end of the twentieth century that has hardly been diminished by social, economic or political change. As Scott puts it, 'class remains the sociological key to understanding the structure of society' (1994: 19).

For Scase (1992) the relevance of class for ordinary people may be somewhat vague, but for sociologists 'it remains a concept that is vital for understanding the structure of present-day capitalist society'. As a Marxist, he argues that it is not possible to contemplate society without reference to the role played by social classes in the formation and maintenance of capitalism:

**The analysis of class is inherent to the study of capitalist society. Western industrial societies are capitalist and, hence, their economic development is determined by the interplay of class forces of one kind or another. The fact that the prime objective of capitalist corporations is to make profits means that they are characterised by relations of exploitation and control and, hence, consist of class relations. . . . It is for this reason that social class will continue to remain central to sociological analysis.**

*(Scase 1992: 81)*

To some extent this view is matched by Edgell (1993), who emphasizes the importance of social class as the major source of structural social inequality. The significance of social class as the basis of social identity and political action may have been diluted over time but this is largely due to the power of capital and the relative weakness of the 'propertyless classes'. Instead of raising the question of the extent of class consciousness in contemporary society we should be questioning the assumption that society has become a classless meritocracy:

**The main obstacle to the establishment of a multi-class or non-egalitarian classless democratic society is the persistence of class inequalities. . . . Hence, what needs to be explained is not the presumed demise of class, but the tenacity of class-based patterns of inequality and politics, and much else besides. In the meantime, class rules and classlessness remains a dream rather than a reality.** *(Edgell 1993: 122)*

The relevance of class analysis, particularly in areas such as health, housing and education remains clear. However, as indicated in our discussion of Weber, social class is not the only means by which social inequality is transmitted. Since the early 1970s sociologists have become more aware of the relative importance of gender and race as the bases of structured inequality and discrimination. These two areas are examined in Chapters 7 and 8.

Summary

- Historically most societies develop some form of stratification system.
- Most sociologists regard modern industrial societies as being stratified on the basis of social class.
- Sociologists have provided various theoretical 'class maps' and class categories based on Marxist, Weberian and functionalist models.
- The significance of social class in the latter half of the twentieth century is a matter of continuing sociological debate.
- On the other hand, it has been argued that changes in the structure of society have reduced the importance of class as a tool for sociological analysis.
- On the other hand, while acknowledging that the class structure has been affected by social and economic changes, there is evidence that social class continues to affect lifestyle, opportunities, consciousness and behaviour; the upper, middle and working classes continue to be important divisions in modern society.

## Further reading

Crompton, R (1993) *Class and Stratification*, Cambridge: Polity.
A detailed examination of the complexities of class and status, especially recommended for pursuing this area of study beyond foundation undergraduate level.

Edgell, S (1993) *Class*, London: Routledge.
A clear introduction to many of the ideas introduced in this chapter, it tackles some complex theoretical issues in an accessible manner.

Lee, D and Turner, B S (1996) *Conflicts about Class: Debating Inequality in Late Industrialism*, London: Longman.
An important assessment of the relevance of class in late-twentieth-century Britain.

Reid, I (1989) *Social Class Differences in Britain*, 3rd edn, London: Fontana.
An excellent review of the correlations between class position and life chances that covers areas such as wealth, pay, health, education and housing.

Scott, J (1991) *Who Rules Britain?*, Cambridge, Polity.

Scott, J (1994) *Poverty and Wealth: Citizenship, Deprivation and Privilege*, London: Longman.

One of the few sociologists to undertake a comprehensive analysis of the rich and powerful, these are up-to-date summaries of the patterns of wealth and poverty distribution at home and abroad.

Smith, D (1992) *Understanding the Underclass*, London: Policy Studies Institute.
A collection of readings from the key contributors to the underclass debate, such as Dahrendorf, Murray and Field.

Regular sources of updated empirical material are in the journal *Labour Research*, publications of the Child Poverty Action Group and *Social Trends*.

## Activities

### ■ Activity 1 Value, status and (in)dispensability

#### Occupational scales

Attempts to reconcile the differences over class and status in evaluation of an individual's position in society have generally involved classifying people according to their job based on the assumption that some jobs are more prestigious/important than others. Rate the following jobs in order of importance from I (most important) to 6 (least important): coal-miner; electrician; refuse collector; director of advertising agency; nurse; high court judge.

#### Are you a worker?

What is a worker? That's the question . . . provoked by our criticism of the Greenham Common protesters as predominantly middle class.

Ann Roderick, for example, naturally enough feels insulted when she is put – as a school teacher – in the same category as 'vicars' wives'.

The issues raised here are very important. A majority of the workforce in Britain, along with other advanced industrial countries, does white-collar work. Does that mean, as ruling class propagandists (and even some socialists) claim, that the working class is disappearing?

##### Class

The answer depends, obviously, on what you mean by class. Academic sociologists attach great deal of importance to status – to how the job is seen by those doing it, and by others. Historically, there has certainly been a difference of status between manual and white-collar jobs. This is reflected in the fact that even today most white-collar workers work shorter hours and enjoy better pension rights than their manual counterparts.

Does this mean that they belong to different classes? Not according to Marx. For him, a person's class position is determined by his or her relation to the means of production. And this relationship is crucial because control over the means of production gives you the power to exploit the labour of others.

Equally, lack of such control makes you liable to be exploited. So, anyone who is compelled by their economic position to sell their labour-power is, according to Marx, a worker. A worker is someone who has the choice between working and starving because they do not control the means of production.

Control

From this standpoint a shorthand typist or word-processor operator is as much a worker as a miner or engineer. Both . . . must sell their labour-power to live.

So what has happened in the past 40 years is that the structure of the working class has changed. There are fewer manual workers in industries such as mining and manufacturing, but more typists and other clerical workers.

The size of the working class has increased overall, not shrunk . . . Most white-collar workers are not middle-class.

But this isn't the end of the story. All white-collar workers aren't middle class, but some of them are. Those that form what is sometimes called the 'new middle class'.

(Alex Callinicos, *Socialist Worker* undated)

## Questions

What criteria did you use in 'rating' the six occupations? Which of these criteria were objective and which subjective?

Does the order coincide with classifications based on the conventional division between manual and non-manual occupations?

The article by Alex Callinicos looks at problems with the division between manual/working-class and non-manual/middle-class occupations. What difficulties do you think there are with this method of categorizing occupations?

## ■ Activity 2 The underclass

The underclass spawns illegitimate children without a care for tomorrow and feeds on a crime rate which rivals the United States in property offences. Its able-bodied youths see no point in working and feel no compulsion either. They reject society while feeding off it: they are becoming a lost generation giving the cycle of deprivation a new spin. . . . No amount of income redistribution or social engineering can solve their problem. Their sub-life styles are beyond welfare benefit rises and job creation schemes. They exist as active social outcasts, wedded to an anti-social system.

(Charles Murray, *Sunday Times* 26 November 1989)

## Questions

What evidence can you find to support Murray's view?

What 'solutions' do you feel Murray would offer to deal with the problem of an underclass? What criticisms can be made of this approach?

There have been various publicity stunts by Conservative politicians who have claimed that they and their families have managed to live quite adequately for a week on income support. Find out how much you would get on income support and work out how you would spend your weekly payments. What kind of changes would you have to make to your current lifestyle? What are the strengths and weaknesses of approaching a social problem in this way?

Chapter 7

# Gender

**Chapter outline:** Introduction • Gender and transvestism • Explaining gender differences • Social construction of gender • Representing gender: media and popular culture • Gendered labour • Sexuality • Summary • Further reading • Activities

**Learning objectives**

When you have studied this chapter you should be able to address these key questions:

- What is meant by gender?
- What are the major theoretical approaches to gender differences and inequalities?
- How are femininities and masculinities constructed in different areas of social life?
- What are the major gender divisions in contemporary British society and how do they reinforce the subordinate position of women in society?
- How does gender interact with other social factors such as race and class?

## Introduction

Kate: We are told that there are only two genders in the world, and I'm saying that just doesn't make sense. There is nothing else in nature that is two and only two, everything else has all these limitless possibilities but for some reason we figure there are only two genders and I'm saying there are more. . . .

Interviewer: Are you really saying any more than that old classical idea that there is a bit of male and a bit of female in all of us?

Kate: I would say what I'm saying incorporates that idea, that yes we have a man and woman in us but I'm saying that there is so much more than that, I'm saying that outside the realm of men and women there are other identities and why limit ourselves? Why not be able to explore more identities? What is a man? What is a woman? Why do we have to be one or the other? Those are questions that aren't asked in this culture. . . . Whenever you have something of two, a binary, there's going to be an imbalance and in this culture and in most cultures in this world women have come up short, men have oppressed women.

(From an interview with Kate Borstein, *Woman's Hour* BBC Radio 4 September 1994)

Borstein is the author of *Gender Outlaw: On Men, Women and the Rest of Us* (1994), and she describes herself as a transgender person and male to female transsexual.

To avoid being treated as a 'man' or 'woman' is clearly a struggle. Gender is a key factor which shapes social behaviour and social institutions. Yet gender differences are something that we often take so much for granted, which seem so 'normal' that they often remain invisible to us.

**Q** Think about walking down the main street of any western city or town. What gender distinctions are there between shops and between departments in shops? What gender distinctions are there among the staff in shops? Are most shoppers women or men? Are most car drivers women or men? Are most van and delivery drivers women or men?

What other gender distinctions between women and men might you see on the street?

Connell (1987) describes the street as a 'gender regime', which he defines as

**The state of play in gender relations in a given institution is its gender regime.**
*(Connell 1987: 120)*

The gender regime consists of the social relations based on distinctions between women and men. The street is a place where meanings about gender are communicated and rules and patterns concerning gender are reinforced. But what goes on in the street cannot be understood in isolation; social settings and institutions are interconnected. Connell points out that all social settings including formal organizations and more informal ones have gender regimes:

**Compact formal organizations like schools perhaps have particularly clear gender regimes, but others have them too. Diffuse institutions like markets, large and sprawling ones like the state, and informal milieu like street corner peer-group life, also are structured in terms of gender and can be characterized by their gender regimes.**
*(Connell 1987: 120)*

He stresses that it is impossible to identify a select group of social institutions that are concerned with gender because 'gender relations are present in all types of institutions' (Connell 1987: 120). So wherever we look we cannot escape gender relations. It would be impossible in one chapter to explore the wide range of gender regimes that make up the social world we inhabit. Here we can focus on only some of these gender regimes, to illustrate some key issues and approaches in the developing field of the sociology of gender.

Traditionally sociology has neglected gender as a factor that shapes our social experiences. Feminism in its struggle to understand women's oppression has placed gender on the broader sociological agenda. Increasingly it is recognized that gender is a crucial factor in shaping individual experience and identity, as well as social institutions, and must be taken into account by sociologists for a full understanding of all social processes. Indeed it has been argued that the study of gender is now reshaping sociology (Maynard 1990). The sociological study of gender continues to show that gender shapes the experiences of women and men differently in many areas of social life and remains a source of inequality in society.

## Gender and transvestism

Cultural rules and expectations surrounding gender and sexual identity often become visible only when they are transgressed, when people break the rules. If a man walked into a women's clothes shop and began to examine the clothes and try them against himself he would probably be perceived as strange or unusual. Woodhouse (1989) argued that societal responses to transvestisms make visible taken-for-granted assumptions and 'rules' about gender-appropriate behaviour. She uses the term *transvestite* to refer to a man who does not alter his biological sex, and identifies himself as a man but enjoys altering one cultural variable of the gender role, dress; he dresses up creating the appearance of a woman. *Cross-dressing* is also a term used to refer to women or men who dress in clothes to create a look associated with the opposite sex. This is different from a *transsexual* person, who has a gender identity which does not correspond to his or her biological sex and may chose to have surgery to alter their physical sexual characteristics. Borstein (1994) refers to transgendered individuals as people who refuse to accept the label and identity of female or male.

**Definition**

### Sex and gender

In the 1970s sociologists began to make a distinction between sex and gender. **Sex** has been defined as

The biological aspects of a person involving characteristics which differentiate females and males by chromosomal, anatomical, reproductive, hormonal and other physiological characteristics. (Lindsey 1990)

Sex is taken to mean some sort of anatomical differences between men and women.

**Gender** has been defined not as a fixed biological category but a socially created construct, which

Involves the social or cultural and psychological aspects linked to males and females through particular social contexts. What a given society defines as masculine or feminine is a component of gender. (Lindsey 1990)

This distinction between sex and gender implies two concepts that can be separated unambiguously; it also implies that while gender is shaped by social factors, biological sex is not and is based on an assumption that there are two distinct biological sexes. Some sociologists and natural scientists question these rigid distinctions.

Woodhouse (1989) argues that in our culture it is generally assumed that sex and gender and gender appearance fit together, that a 'feminine' appearance denotes the female sex and a 'masculine' appearance the male sex. This assumption is so deeply ingrained in our everyday lives that we rarely question the sex of most people we meet but make a judgement based on their physical appearance. Woodhouse describes an incident at the transvestite/transsexual group she was attending as part of her research into transvestism:

**While chatting with a transvestite I had met previously, I noticed someone standing at the counter. She looked different from the other persons present, dressed in a quiet manner with light make-up and glasses. Her own hair was done in an ordinary, unelaborate style. . . . Not having met her before, I wanted to introduce myself and, hopefully, find out more about her. But I found myself unable to approach her until I knew 'what' she was. In other words, I realised that my social manner towards her would be determined by my knowledge of her sexual status. The everyday, taken-for-granted assumption that gender appearance indicates biological sex broke down in this setting and thus the fragility of that commonplace expectation was thrown into sharp relief. She could have been transvestite, or indeed, she could have been a real woman. I was unable to tell. The very fact that I had to ascertain her biological status from someone else before approaching her underlined the ways in which social interaction is firmly based on the unconscious expectations we use to identify people and place them in stereotyped categories.** *(Woodhouse 1989: 29–30)*

This illustrates the way social interaction is firmly based on unconscious assumptions we make in order to identify people's gender and place them in the appropriate category of female or male.

When you meet people how do you make judgements about their sex from their physical appearance?

Once you have decided that person is female or male in what ways does that categorization affect how you interact with them?

What is your reaction to transvestism? How do you feel about seeing a man dressed in 'women's' clothing?

Can you think of any other groups who deviate from expected gender norms? Are they stigmatized ?

Woodhouse (1989) proposes that we assume that sex, gender and gender appearance should fit together in a particular fixed pattern. Men in our culture who enjoy wearing women's clothes are perceived generally as strange, ridiculous or even perverted. Such behaviour is incongruous to us; it transgresses the cultural component of the sex–gender link, the appropriate gender appearance assigned to the male. She does not see the distinctions between women and men, feminine and masculine as arbitrary but as part of a social system based on hierarchical gender relations, which she calls the sex/gender system:

**Clearly the assignation of gender, as opposed to sex, in terms of appropriate behaviour, activities, clothing language and gestures is neither accident nor a cultural anomaly. It establishes a hierarchy whereby a sexual division of labour ensures an imbalance of power and control weighted in the favour of male supremacy.**

*(Woodhouse 1989: 5)*

Woodhouse locates transvestism in a culture not only of gender *difference* but also of gender *inequality* and hierarchy. Social reaction to transgression such as transvestism can be harsh and censorious because the transgression challenges the status quo. Transvestites are stigmatized and rejected in order for the gender system to remain intact. Although there may be some room for non-conformity the division of masculine and feminine is rigid and carries punitive sanctions for those who go against the grain.

Woodhouse points out that deviation in terms of appearance is more likely to be tolerated in women, for example it is more widely accepted for women to wear trousers than for a man to wear a skirt. Women can appear in masculine-style clothes without immediately losing status provided they remain identifiably feminine. To explain this she argues that the gender divide is not one of equal balance; the scales of power and control tip decisively to the side of the masculine, which is given primary status. Thus to deviate from this status is to take a step down and to adopt the trappings of the second sex. To protect the primacy of the masculine, this cannot be allowed to happen; it questions the primacy of the masculine and the split between masculine and feminine.

However, the wearing of trousers by women in certain social settings is still not acceptable. In 1995 some secondary school girls staged a protest against school rules that prohibited them from wearing trousers. The girls argued that these rules violated equal opportunities laws. Imagine the outcry at many schools if boys wore skirts!

In 1993 Lisa Cresswell was awarded compensation by an industrial tribunal after she was dismissed from her job for wearing trousers. Her male employers described her appearance in trousers as 'horrendous' (*Independent* 3 October 1993). This notion that trousers are unfeminine has only recently been challenged. Historically trousers have been defined in British culture as masculine; the phrase 'You can tell who wears the trousers in that house' is used to describe a household where the man is supposedly not 'in charge' and the woman is taking on a controlling masculine role. Clothes have been analysed by feminists as a means not only of marking out gender but also for reinforcing inequalities. Feminists in the 1880s and 1890s pointed out that the skirt (then long) was encumbering and restrictive and proposed the bloomer, shocking at the time, as a liberating alternative. Contemporary feminists have also argued that clothing restricts women's mobility and physical freedom and signifies their oppression.

Although dress is a means by which gender distinctions between the female and the male are marked out it can also provide a means of challenging distinctions and expectations (E Wilson 1986). Women have resisted and worn 'masculine clothes'. Some male celebrities in Britain have publicly worn skirts. In the 1990s it is increasingly common to see men with long hair. Indeed at various periods throughout history it was acceptable for men to wear their hair long, for example during the reign of Charles II and in the 1960s. Also in many cultures it is acceptable for men to wear skirt-type clothing, which demonstrates the historical and cultural variability of gender norms.

Taking appearance and specifically clothing as an example we have seen that there are social norms about appropriate behaviour for men and women; cultural artefacts and practices communicate messages and construct meanings about gender distinguishing between the feminine and the masculine, and these distinctions can be interpreted as part of a system based on a hierarchy. Although sanctions exist to encourage conformity, transgressions occur and can challenge or subvert dominant expectations and meanings about gender.

## Explaining gender differences

Definition

### Difference and inequality

Two key themes reoccur in sociology theory and research on gender: difference and inequality.

**Difference** concerns how distinctions are made between women and men. Various theoretical approaches have been proposed to explain these differences. Sociologists have been concerned with examining how different social relationships, institutions and processes distinguish between women and men and create meanings about femininity and masculinity.

**Inequality** concerns how gender distinctions are linked to inequalities, hierarchy and power relations. Sociologists have examined whether social distinctions between women and men create or reinforce inequalities between them, and the unequal distribution of resources and/or access to opportunity.

Feminist sociologists have developed and established the sociological study of gender. They have argued that distinctions between women and men have placed women at a disadvantage and have been central to the subordination of women. Gender differences are part of a social structure which ascribes more power and status to the male gender. There is a whole range of sociological research and theory which highlights that although gender relations are dynamic and changing, gender inequalities persist in various areas of social life, including the labour market and the household.

### Biological beasts or social subjects?

Sociologists have concerned themselves with the biological category of sex because sex differences have often been proposed as explanations for the differences in social roles performed by women and men. Sociologists have engaged in the 'nature–nurture' debate (see pp. 9–10) on whether differences in personality, behaviour and social roles between men and women are the product of biological or socio-cultural factors. Are women and men naturally different or are they made so by the society they live in? This debate has been of particular importance for feminist writers, who have argued that certain interpretations of women's biology have been used not simply to mark out their difference from men but to justify their subordinate and secondary status and to exclude women from certain areas of society. Gender inequality refers to this inequitable allocation of social status, opportunity and resources (economic, political and social) on the basis of gender.

There has also been a concern that the male sex has been taken as the norm and women have been defined as deviant, lacking, second rate or, as Simone de Beauvoir (1974) argued, 'other'. In the 1980s and 1990s, some sociologists have been concerned that on the basis of gender men have also experienced restriction, for example being defined primarily as breadwinners has meant they have been deprived of involvement with child-rearing and nurturing activities.

### *Born to be a man/woman*

Essentialist or biological arguments attribute the different social roles performed by women and men to underlying biological structures particularly, reproductive differences or hormonal difference. The 'natural' differences between women and men are seen to contribute to an organization of social relations in which women nurture and men go out to work. Biologically deterministic explanations of sexual difference have a long history in scientific and pre-scientific thinking though the form of the biological arguments has changed over the years as scientific techniques and knowledge develops. Essentialism and biological determinism are umbrella terms for a range of approaches which emphasize biological factors. In the 1950s the functionalist sociologist Parsons argued that there are natural differences between women and men which mean they are suited for particular roles in society (Parsons and Bales 1955). Women have an instinct to nurture which suits them for an 'expressive' role in the nuclear family. Male biology which leads men to be more aggressive and competitive means that men are suited to an 'instrumental' role in the family, providing economic support and links with the outside world. Biological differences constitute a practical and 'natural' basis for the sexual division of labour. Biological theories also often present heterosexuality as the 'normal' and 'natural' expression of human sexuality, and identify women and men as having different sexual needs and desires. Biological explanations are now marginalized within sociology but they still abound in our culture and new biological theories are often proposed. For example Moir and Jessel (1989) in their book *Brain Sex* bring together what they argue is evidence to support pre-natal hormone theory.

Moir and Jessel (1989) argue that at around 6 weeks, when the male foetus begins to produce hormones different from the female, key differences are laid down. As the brain is developing in the male foetus, male hormones, chiefly testosterone, are released; these shape the body and brain in a particular way which in turn determines thought processes and emotions. At adolescence during puberty another rise in male hormones exaggerates and confirms these differences. They argue that these changes in the brain have a real effect on personality and capabilities. To simplify, these hormonal differences mean that in effect the wiring of the brain is different in women and men. In women language and social skills are controlled by both sides of the brain whereas in men these are controlled by the left side. This has profound effects on personality and abilities. Men are more single minded, they are able to ignore anything but factual information hence enabling them to focus and make decisions more quickly than women. These differences impact on the contemporary social structure and this theory can be used to explain a range of contemporary gender differences. For example women are not in top jobs because they do not have the same drive to be on top; men are more aggressive and competitive:

**the pursuit of power is overwhelmingly and universally a male trait . . . to rise in the hierarchy, men are much more prepared than women to make sacrifices of their own time, pleasure, relaxation, health safety and emotions.** ***(Moir and Jessel 1989)***

Yet Moir and Jessel are keen to stress that they are not presenting a theory of female inferiority; women should be seen as different but not inferior and they stress that women's verbal and people skills should be increasingly valued in the labour market.

For many years socio-biologists have provided a whole range of theories for gender differences, connected to Darwin's theory of evolution. Desmond Morris (1977), a popular socio-biologist, connects much of social behaviour to evolutionary drives and proposes a model of human development that is linked to his belief in 'man the hunter'. In this model in pre-history women remained at the base camp with the children while the men went off to hunt as a result of men's higher levels of testosterone, which lead to greater aggressiveness and physical strength. As a result of evolutionary selection males with more aggressive qualities have left more copies of themselves and females with more maternal genes have been selected.

A key criticism of these essentialist approaches is that they are biologically deterministic and neglect social influences on behaviour (Bem 1993; Oakley 1972). They also neglect how biological features themselves interact with the environment in which it is situated: socio-biology 'massively underestimates the contribution of cultures and histories to that interaction' (Bem 1993).

Biological approaches also assume rigid distinctions between women and men and rely on the assumption that the categories women and men are universal groups sharing a universal biology and personality. Hence these theories do not account for diversity. They do not account for biological women who display masculine behaviour and take on masculine roles and biological men who display feminine traits, except to define them as biological deviants. There is a great deal of autobiographical evidence from individuals who feel that their gender identity does not correspond to their biological sex or who feel restricted by a culture that allows gender identity to be expressed only in terms of the female–male dualism.

Sociologists point to the variation across cultures of what it means to be a woman or man. There is a great deal of anthropological and sociological research evidence which shows cultural variation in gender roles. Margaret Mead's (1935) famous study in New Guinea of three different groups of tribal peoples – the Arapesh, Mundugumor and Tchambuli – provides an example of variation. Among the Arapesh both female and male were gentle, passive and sharing. There was not a rigid definition between the responsibilities and personalities of women and men, and there was a more egalitarian community. Among the Mundugmor there was more defined sexual division: men were aggressive, hostile and dominant and women were responsible for child care and subordinate. Among the Tchambuli peoples Mead found what could be interpreted as a reversal of conventional western gender behaviour: men had a greater responsibility for domestic labour and care of the young and adorned themselves whereas the women had a greater involvement in leadership and food hunting and were more aggressive.

Within many contemporary societies women are effectively performing conventional male roles in, for example, the military (Fig 7.1); similarly men can be found involved in child care and non-traditional masculine work. Some sociologists have

**Fig 7.1** A woman soldier trains other soldiers to use Uzi submachine guns in Israel. (Courtesy of Robert Harding Picture Library Ltd.)

argued that we have become blinkered by gender distinctions. In our culture we make a rigid distinction between female and male and then judge everyone in relation to this dichotomy and attempt to place them within one of two categories. We impose social meanings on to our human biology. In the 1970s Oakley (1972; 1974b) argued that it was misleading to think in terms of two distinct sexes and more useful to think in terms of the female and the male being placed at the ends of a continuum with overlap. Many sociologists now challenge the notion of two distinct sexes and propose that the male–female dichotomy itself is a social construct. Post-structuralist thinking has influenced gender studies challenging rigid categories. Butler (1990) argues that the body makes sense to us through cultural discourses; the categories 'woman' and 'man' are created through these discourses rather than having a biological basis.

**Case Study**

### Refusing to be a Man

**John Stolenberg (1990) parodies the social distinctions between men and women that are made in our culture and the importance that is assigned to biological differences.**

I'd like to take you, in an imaginary way, to look at a different world, somewhere else in the universe, a place inhabited by a life form that very much resembles us. But these creatures grow up with a peculiar knowledge. They know that they have been born in an infinite variety. They know, for instance, that in their genetic material they are born with hundreds of different chromosome formations at the point in each cell that we would say determines their 'sex'. These creatures don't just come in XX or XY; they also come in XXY and XYY plus a long list of 'mosaic' variations in which some cells in a creature's body have one combination and other cells have another. . . . The creatures

*(box continued)*

*(box continued)*

in this world enjoy their individuality; they delight in the fact that they are not born divisible into distinct categories. . . .

These creatures are not oblivious to reproduction; but nor do they spend their lives constructing a self-definition around their variable reproductive capacities. They don't have to, because what is truly unique about these creatures is that they are capable of having a sense of personal identity without struggling to fit into a group identity based on how they were born. These creatures are quite happy actually. They don't worry about sorting other creatures into categories, so they don't have to worry about whether they are measuring up to some category they themselves are supposed to belong to . . . perhaps you have guessed the point of this science fiction: Anatomically, each creature in the imaginary world I have been describing could be an identical twin of every human being on earth. These creatures in fact, are us – in every way except socially and politically. The way they are born is the way we are born. And we are not born belonging to one or other of the two sexes. We are born into a physiological continuum on which there is no discrete and definite point that you can call 'male' and no discrete and definite point that you can call 'female'. . . .

What does all this mean? It means, first of all, a logical dilemma: Either human 'male' and human 'female' actually exist in nature as fixed and discrete entities and you can credibly base an entire social and political system on those absolute natural categories or else the variety of human sexedness is infinite.

(Stolenberg 1990: 33–6)

## Questions

**Do you believe that male and female are fixed, separate identities in relation to (a) sex; (b) gender? If not, what are the implications for our daily social interactions?**

Stolenberg (1990) suggests that humans have imposed one of many interpretations on a set of biological characteristics and that difference rather than sameness has been emphasized. Birke (1992) explores the idea of sex differences arguing that there are differences between women and men, but these are massively exaggerated. She also stresses that scientific work on differences usually takes an average but within the population as a whole there are individuals who deviate from these averages, for example female bodybuilders who have a much greater muscle mass than many men.

Birke (1992) has pointed out that it is difficult to make a firm separation between fixed biological sex and culturally shaped gender, and encourages us to think how the biological and social interact. She identifies two key problems with the concept of biological causes of difference: it treats biology as a fixed concept and excludes other factors. Biological factors are themselves socially constructed. Physical characteristics can be shaped by the social, for example people's physical strength can be shaped by dietary and exercise programmes. With the example of pre-natal hormone theory (p. 275) testosterone leads to aggression but the process is two way because aggressive behaviour leads to the production of testosterone. Birke (1992) argues that gender identity is a continual process of construction and reconstruction. Rather than biological factors and cultural factors being treated separately they should be viewed as 'interacting' factors. What is important is how humans culturally interpret biology and how the biological is shaped by the social.

Many sociologists have doubted the reliability of 'objective' scientific results which claim to connect behaviour to biology or nature. Bem (1993) notes how science has historically provided unreliable evidence of differences between men and women, specifically evidence of women's inferiority. Feminist writers among others have pointed out that scientific knowledge itself is not value free but can be shaped by cultural, political and ideological values.

The theory of *vitalism*, popular in the late nineteenth century, is an example of this type of now discredited scientific work. This theory proposed that humans have a vital electrical force and the amount of energy within us is constant. Nineteenth-century scientists argued that women's reproductive function drew vital energy from the brain, limiting intellectual capacity. This was used by writers such as Edward Clark (1873) in *Sex in Education* to argue that higher education was not suitable for women: education would divert energy from the development of women's reproductive organs, which would be damaging to women's health.

The argument that science can be a vehicle for ideological beliefs and can be utilized to justify various forms of inequality has formed an important part of feminist criticisms of many biological theories. Even if there are biological differences between women and men this does not explain why the male gender has higher status; to understand this we have to look to social and political factors. Feminists and other sociologists argue that these distinctions serve as a form of social control, giving greater value, status and power to men and the masculine while subordinating women and the feminine. 'A discourse of gender difference serves as an ideology to neutralize, rationalize and cover disparities of power. . . . Difference is the velvet glove on the iron fist of domination'(MacKinnon 1989).

## Social construction of gender

The predominant view in sociology has been that many of the differences between women and men are the product of social and cultural process. Sociologists have focused on gender as a learned set of behaviours and have explored the social processes through which we all learn to be either feminine or masculine. A whole range of social processes have been identified as sites where gendered categories of femininity and masculinity are constructed. Sociologists have explored the diverse meanings attached to femininity and masculinity, so much so that there has been a shift towards talking about femininities and masculinities (we shall examine this shift in more detail on pp. 285–6).

### Learning gender

According to social learning theory we learn what is considered gender-appropriate behaviour via socialization, which begins at birth. Girls and boys experience gender socializiation in different ways, learning appropriate behaviours, personalities, gender roles and developing their own gender identities (own feelings and consciousness).

Sociological and psychological research has paid attention to various components and stages of gender development. In the 1970s and early 1980s particularly there was a mass of research which examined the differential learning processes of boys and girls. This included studies of such things as post-natal care, books and magazines, clothing and toys. Many researchers have reported that there are different practices or expectations in relation to girls and boys which encouraged or reinforced 'feminine' behaviour in girls and 'masculine' behaviour in boys.

Information technology is becoming an increasingly important part of our culture and everyday lives, yet it seems that females and males have a different relationship to it. For example computer games contain within them different roles for women and men. The main active characters are usually male; female characters are under-represented and when present they tended to be glamorous sex symbols or more passive characters waiting to be rescued by male characters. The male characters fight and destroy various enemy or alien characters; they are brave, physically tough and take action. Also the technology itself is presented as something masculine; advertisements for Sega and Nintendo games target boys, for example one system popular in the 1990s is the *Game Boy*®.

Social learning theory assumes that in our culture there are certain roles, behaviours and characteristics that are stereotyped as either 'feminine' or 'masculine'. Examine the list of characteristics below and decide for each one whether they are considered desirable for a woman or man in British society generally.

Affectionate
Flatterable
Analytical
Cheerful
Self-reliant
Forceful
Soft-spoken
Independent
Tender
Gentle
Leadership abilities
Makes decisions easily
Sympathetic
Sensitive to others' needs
Strong personality
Ambitious
Childlike
Athletic
Warm
Yielding
Individualistic
Does not use harsh language
Dominant
Loves children

Was it easy to allocate characteristics to categories?

If you were asked to allocate them in line with your own opinions of women and men's personalities and capabilities rather than what is considered more desirable and appropriate in British society generally, would there be differences in how you allocated them?

Did you feel that some could not be allocated to a discrete category?

Tick those traits that you would use to describe yourself. Have you ticked mainly 'masculine', mainly 'feminine' or a mix of both traits?

These characteristics are taken from the Bem Sex Role Inventory (BSRI). Bem (1993) stresses that the traits that were included on her inventory were not selected on the basis on how females and males describe themselves but 'on the basis of what was culturally defined as gender appropriate in the United States in the early 1970s'. She determined this by asking a sample of US citizens who she saw as her 'cultural informants' to identify for each of the traits whether they were seen as more desirable for a woman or a man 'in American society generally'. Bem went on to develop the BSRI using these traits; the inventory involves individuals assessing their own personalities. From the results of her work Bem has argued that humans are androgynous, expressing a range of 'feminine' and 'masculine' traits. She also argued that those people who were androgynous were more psychologically healthy than people who expressed more rigid feminine or male traits. Bem favours a social approach to understanding gender differences; her work suggested that women and men express a range of 'feminine' and 'masculine' traits yet also acknowledged that there are socio-cultural factors which encourage feminine behaviour for women and masculine behaviour for men; this rigid socialization is restrictive, making it difficult for individuals to express whatever aspects of their personalities they feel, be these deemed 'feminine' or 'masculine' in our cultures.

### *Good girls*

Examining how girls learn to be women has been very important for feminist theorists who have argued that feminine gender roles and dominant ideologies of femininity have been restrictive for women channelling them into social roles to which lower social status is attached. Dominant notions of femininity have emphasized passivity, dependence, emotion and nurturing characteristics which have often disempowered women. Many feminists have pointed out that these characteristics are not inherently negative but have been denigrated and unvalued. Socialization into roles that stress romance, marriage and motherhood have been seen as particularly restrictive and as providing an effective way of obtaining female subordination, by consent. Hence it has been crucial for feminists to explore how femininity is constructed and to challenge these processes. Sharpe (1976) in *Just Like a Girl* mapped out the process of gender socialization for girls. She found that children's activities performed in the home which distinguished between girls and boys and parental expectations rehearse girls and boys for future roles. Girls were encouraged to be girlfriends, wives and mothers with primary responsibility for domestic labour. Although they expected to engage in paid work this was seen as temporary or secondary and the jobs they aspired to were conventional low-paid female jobs; girls were being encouraged to have limited aspirations and hence restricted choices. Sue Sharpe went back to speak to young girls and boys in 1991 and repeated the research she had carried out originally in 1972. She found that in terms of teenage girls' views and expectations:

> **While their range of job expectations showed surprisingly little change, there were striking differences in attitudes to education, marriage and family life. Change was also evident in girls' personal opinions. They now placed a greater stress on equality with men, and on their own needs. I was greatly impressed by their comparative assertiveness and confidence, and their strong belief in women's ability to stand on their own two feet and not have to depend on, nor be dominated, by men.**
>
> ***(Sharpe 1994b: 15)***

Case Study

### There's a Good Girl

Marianne Grabrucker (1988) recounted her experience of attempting to bring up her daughter free from gender stereotyping. In writing a diary she became aware of the subtle ways in which she treated her daughter in a specific way simply because she was a girl and also the other social forces that conspired to teach her child gender consciousness. Despite her own efforts not to relate to her daughter in a sex-typed way she found that there were many influences outside her control in the social environment that communicated messages about gender difference. The child responded to advertisements and gender hierarchies she saw in her everyday environment, for example she saw men mainly on motor bikes and hence associated these with men. Children's literature which challenges gender sterotypes has been produced, Babette Cole's (1988) book *Princess Smartypants* is the story of a princess who scares off all her suitors and sets them unachievable tasks so she can spend her life on her own doing her own thing. However, cultural images that provide alternative messages tend to be the exception in children's books, games, films and television programmes.

### *The beauty myth*

A recurring theme in the work on the representation of women in the media is that women's physical bodies are represented in a particularly limited way. In films and magazines women's bodies are likely to be 'glamorous', 'beautiful', 'sexy' and 'thin'. Some theorists argue that the media play a key role not only in constructing notions of feminine ideals of beauty to which women are encouraged to aspire but also in feminine socialization

The beauty industry has been identified as a set of practices and ideas which restrict women's lives. Feminist work on fashion, beauty and adornment has tended to interpret women's concerns with these practices as a product of ideologies of femininity designed to control women's lives, undermine women's autonomy and the development of unities between women by establishing competition between women (Chapkis 1986; Wolf 1991). The feminine ideal is impossible to achieve because the images and icons of the beauty industry are themselves fabricated and also because the ideal is constantly being redefined with a waif-like thin body in one year and a buxom look the next. Beauty and fashion culture have been seen as closely intertwined with capitalist relations:

> **Feminists in the second wave originally explained the fashion culture in terms of patriarchy in league with capitalism. Femininity in this analysis is false consciousness.** *(Gaines 1990: 4)*

The 'fashion, beauty, diet' industry is identified as big business within capitalism and also serves to reinforce differences between women and men and undermine, control and restrict women. Feminists such as Naomi Wolf (1991) feel that the beauty myth has taken over other ideologies in undermining women's confidence. The beauty myth involves ideal standards of feminine beauty and body shape to which all women must aspire. For Chapkis (1986) this ideal is white, youthful and able bodied. Hill-Collins (1990) points out that not only are eternally defined standards of beauty 'white', which can create anxieties for Black women who cannot live up to the white-skinned, blue-eyed, straight-haired ideal, but also this white ideal exists only in opposition to the Black 'other'. This illustrates how women's experiences vary depending on their racial identity, and how gender ideologies interact with a wide range of factors including race. It also illustrates the reality that women are a diverse group with differential access to social power and prestige.

---

**Judging white women by their physical appearance and attractiveness to men objectifies them. But their white skin and straight hair privilege them in a system in which part of the basic definition of whiteness is superior to blackness.**

***(Hill-Collins 1990: 79)***

---

Wolf (1991) argues that the beauty myth is the most insidious ideology yet undermining girls and women individually and collectively. At work and at leisure women can never fully be themselves and focus their energies as they must always be concerned about how they present themselves, anxious about whether they match up to the 'beauty myth'. For Wolf the 'beauty myth' plays a key role in controlling and undermining women. The pressures to aspire to the 'beauty myth' reduces women's confidence and saps their energies. Young girls may no longer prioritize getting married but they want to look like and perhaps become supermodels. So the diet industry and cosmetic surgery thrive on exploiting women's anxieties and insecurities. Hill-Collins stresses the importance of self-definition and the creation of a new aesthetic for beauty based on individual uniqueness.

### *Bad boys: men's studies and dominant masculinity*

Gender studies have tended to concentrate on girls and women. Yet not only are women's lives shaped by gender but also men are gendered beings affected by ideologies of gender. Men may have been the key subjects of sociological research but they had not been approached as gendered beings (Morgan 1981). As well as feminist writers examining the social construction of masculinity, increasingly masculinity is receiving more attention from male sociologists. Some men listened to feminism and have responded with new ways of understanding men's behaviour. Masculinity is taken to be socially constructed; being a man is considered something that men become rather than an innate property of the male sex.

Feminists had pointed out that traditional masculinity often disempowered women and led to their subordination. Masculinity was therefore approached as problematic and certain aspects of male behaviour particularly so – men's violence and aggression, their sexual activity and their domination of women. Hearn (1987) identifies men as the gender of oppression and points out that they oppress other men as well as women. The study of men and masculinity has attempted to explore the processes that lead to this domination and to recognize the emotional costs to men of their dominance as well as to women (Seidler 1989).

It has been recognized that although feminism has challenged men's domination no fundamental changes in gender relations can take place without changes in men. Seidler (1989) has considered the consequences for men of what he identifies as the dominant western form of masculinity, which is taken to be natural to men. He argued that far from being natural this is a relatively recent historical development.

In this model of masculinity, the male mind has come to be seen as separate and superior to the body, masculinity is identified with reason, objectivity and superior mental power. Masculine identity is tied closely to the 'public' realms of work and political life. The consequences of this identity for many men is that they are restricted in developing a more personal sense of self and this makes it hard for men to recognize their own or other people's needs. Dominant masculinity stresses aggression, assertion, competition and reason rather than emotion. Within this model of masculinity for men to acknowledge their emotional needs is seen as weakness. Men are then locked into a competitive struggle to prove their masculinity. This has implications for male sexuality. Seidler argues that as part of this competitive struggle men approach sex as something closely connected to individual achievement and something which signifies their position in the pecking order of masculinity. Male sexuality is part of the development of a masculine identity in which sexuality is seen in terms of power and conquest. Sex becomes a way of proving manhood (see pp. 312–13).

Phillips (1993) in *The Trouble with Boys* described what she saw as the cruel transition to manhood that boys undergo. She argues that in our society we are still raising boys to find and express themselves by standing alone, appearing strong, being independent and proving themselves through competition. In contrast girls are encouraged to develop relationships and gain affiliative skills. It is at the level of emotional relating where the most profound effects of gender can be seen; girls spend hours practising emotional skills, whereas boys' energies are directed towards mastering physical skills. Although boys do have feelings they are rarely taught to identify and understand them. The feelings they do practise are feelings of competition and aggression. These may serve boys well in the world of competition but fail them in other settings. They find it hard to recognize vulnerability; signs of tenderness and need make them uneasy; they deal with this by competing and appearing not to need. From this viewpoint men are seen as emotionally crippled.

### *Men in crisis?*

As men have been placed under the microscope some people have talked about a crisis in masculinity, as conventional masculinity is challenged. Feminism not only demanded changes for women but also identified a need for men to change. To what extent men have changed is much debated. In the early 1990s the media began to talk about the 'new man'. This construct is typified by a man who plays an active role in parenting and domestic labour, takes his partner's sexual needs into consideration and is generally in touch with his emotions (Collier 1992).

Sharp (1994b), while arguing that the expectations and views of girls in the 1990s have changed distinctively since the 1970s, believes that boys have not moved as far: 'Unfortunately boys growing up today have less egalitarian expectations. Although they are being made aware of the issue of gender equality inside and outside the schools, boys are unlikely to make it a priority in their own lives' (Sharpe 1994b: 15).

## Femininities and masculinities: discourses of gender

Much of the sociological work on femininity and masculinity has adopted a socialization perspective, in which the main concern has been how people learned gender stereotypes and internalized them. Although many sociologists accept that gender is learned and that socialization plays a key role, an increasing number have pointed to the problems with taking a straightforward learning approach. Social learning theory acknowledges that gender roles and identities are not fixed and may change over history and across cultures. Walby (1990) argues that this approach still operates with a static and unitary conception of gender differences: femininity is one set of characteristics that girls and women learn and masculinity another set that boys and men learn. She argues that this takes insufficient account of the different forms that femininity and masculinity can take and hence it does not account for diversity among women and men. This approach implies that each person is equally conforming to gender ideology and does not explore how masculinity and femininity vary according to a whole range of social factors such as class, age, race and ethnicity. It treats people as relatively passive in their acquisition of gender identity. The emphasis on the passive learning of dominant ideology does not adequately recognize that people may resist, reject or subvert dominant meanings about gender.

This has led to an exploration of the varied content of femininities and masculinities and a shift in emphasis from examining simple sex stereotyping to exploring the *processes* by which a range of femininities and masculinities are constructed. This shift is the product of a recognition that there are different messages about female and male behaviour, communicated for example via the media and education and not simply one ideology. Sociologists examine how social structures act as vehicles for transmitting these different ideologies or discourses of gender (Walby 1990). This does not mean that all ideologies have the same power and influence; indeed some theorists acknowledge that some ideologies are more dominant and powerful than others. We can find advertisements that are not quite so gender stereotyped, and do not simply portray women as wives, mothers or sex objects. These advertisements can be understood as providing alternative messages about femininity. Yet we can still find many conventional notions of femininity communicated in advertising, women talking about their experience with washing powder products and endless examples of 'beautiful' women sexualized to sell a whole range of products. Approaches to the construction of gender which try to identify the varied messages/ideologies about gender Walby refers to as *discourse theory*.

Femininity has been identified in the past very much as a set of characteristics and behaviours that women learn and which then constrain women's lives. Yet some researchers have explored how femininity and feminine identification can be part of social identification from which women can gain positive identity and meaning. Similarly, although masculinity has been approached as a fixed set of characteristics which disempowers women and restricts men, it has been acknowledged that men may feel uncomfortable with some constructs of masculinity and that there are alternative masculinities. Questions have been raised about the extent to which all men conform to the traditional model of masculinity and whether all men are uncaring and insensitive to the needs of others.

Morgan (1992) emphasizes that there are a range of 'masculinities'. For example he points out that middle-class masculinity places emphasis on success at work whereas working-class masculinity, although incorporating the role of breadwinner places great emphasis on physical strength and prowess.

**Q** What characteristics do Prince Charles, Arnold Schwarzenegger and Julian Clary share?

In what ways are they different?

Do you think it is accurate to describe them as sharing similar 'masculine' traits?

## Representing gender: media and popular culture

Sociologists have examined how gender differences are represented in the media and how the media have shaped meanings about gender and gender identity. Winship (1986) argues that women's and men's lives are culturally defined in markedly different ways; what we read or watch and how it is presented to us reflect and are part of that difference. Media representation is political because different groups have more power to produce representations and definitions which may serve the interests of those particular group. Feminists have pointed out that women have had less control over cultural representation.

Some sociologists have approached the media as a site where stereotypes about gender, dominant gender ideology and gender inequalities are reinforced. Women are represented in a restrictive and stereotypical range of ways, as sex objects or in a peripheral or supporting way. The representation of women is determined by the 'male gaze', that is women are represented in ways that suit men's interest and pleasures. Feminists are concerned that the cultural representations of women as weaker and less capable than men not only create barriers for women in many spheres of society, but also justify and contribute to inequality. There have been demands for a wider range of representations of women of varying age, race and class, and for women to have a greater role in the production of media of all forms.

In the late 1980s and 1990s the construction of masculinity in the media has received attention. Although men may have a greater presence in the media, some theorists have been critical of the narrow definition of masculinity in popular cultural forms and have considered how representations of women shape men's views and treatment of women. As well as being produced through social practices and relations, masculinity 'is produced through cultural and ideological struggles over meaning'(Jackson 1990: 223). Some theorists have pointed out that while it is crucial to examine the restrictive ideologies of gender constructed by the media, it is important to recognize that men and women are not simply brainwashed by the media but may resist, criticize and subvert information and messages conveyed in the media.

There has also been a shift towards acknowledging that people will read and make sense of media texts in varying ways. Gamman and Marshment (1988) have argued that the media are not simply vehicles for patriarchal ideologies: there is space in the media for the 'female gaze', for women to express their viewpoints and experiences and hence present alternative images. Popular culture does not simply serve capitalism and patriachy, 'peddling false conciousness to the duped masses'(1988: 1), and the media can be seen as a site of struggle where many meanings are contested and where dominant ideologies can be disturbed. It can provide a site for alternative meanings; representations can be produced that are challenging and subversive. The media are seen as a vehicle for ongoing struggle over meaning:

**Between the market and the ideologues, the financiers and producers, the directors and the actors, the publishers and writers, women and men, heterosexual and homosexual, black and white, between what things mean and how they mean is a perpetual struggle for control.** *(Gamman and Marshment 1988: 1-2)*

So even in the mainstream of the media it is possible to present alternative images and challenge dominant meanings about gender. They identify television programmes such as the US police series *Cagney and Lacey*, which followed the 'public' and 'private' lives of two female police officers, as a media form that provides identification for female viewers, validates women's abilities and challenges stereotypical and sexist beliefs about women.

Q Can you think of television programmes or particular characters which provide identification for women and challenge sexism and gender stereotypes?

How does the character of Patsy Stone in *Absolutely Fabulous* challenge or confirm sexual/gender stereotypes?

## Magazines

### *Women's magazines*

Walk into any newsagent and you will be confronted by a massive array of magazines clearly targeted at specific audiences in terms of gender and age. The vast range of titles for women includes weekly magazines such as *Woman* and *Woman's Own* and monthlies such as *Cosmopolitan, Options* and *Marie Claire*. This proliferation of titles has led to fierce competition among magazines; the circulation of both *Woman* and *Woman's Own*, for example, dropped from over 1 million in 1987 to just over 700,000 in 1992 with these 'lost sales' going to newer publications such as *Marie Claire*, whose circulation rose by 39 per cent in 1992 alone (Peak 1994). Although there are now several men's general interest magazines such as *GQ*, magazines aimed at men tend to be special interest magazines focusing on cars or sport, for example.

Q List magazines aimed at the following social groups: (a) young girls/young boys; (b) teenage girls/teenage boys; (c) young women/young men; (d) middle-aged women/middle-aged men.

What is it about the magazine that identifies it as being aimed at a particular group?

Although often read at a glance for leisure purposes, feminist writers have argued that women's magazines should not be trivialized but approached as a cultural form which informs us about the social world and as such is part of relations of gender, femininity and inequality. Women's magazines and the role they play in constructing femininity have been interpreted in a range of ways.

McRobbie (1982) argued that girls' and women's magazines define and shape women's lives and expectations at every stage of their lives from childhood. Her research into girls' youth culture led her to examine the magazines that young girls consumed, specifically *Jackie*. *Jackie* is no longer produced but there are a whole range of similar magazines aimed at adolescent girls, such as *Just Seventeen*. Beauty, fashion, boys and popstars formed the main staples of *Jackie*. Indeed this almost exclusive focus on personal romance problems, fashion and pop led McRobbie to claim that these magazines communicated the message that all else was of secondary importance to girls. The stories contained in *Jackie* focused on romance and emotions, with themes like a girl must fight to keep her man, you cannot trust another woman and, despite this, being a girl and romance itself are fun. McRobbie describes an ideology of adolescent femininity, the most pervasive element of which was the focus on going out with and finding a boyfriend. She refers to this ideology as 'romantic individualism' and sees it as a powerful influence on young girls; the message in *Jackie* is that girls, although they may seek advice from their friends, are on their own in the search for boys and once they find a boy they can move away from the world of girls. She claimed boys are not exposed to this type of pressure in the same way and felt that 'This whole ideological discourse, as it takes shape through the pages of *Jackie*, is immensely powerful' (McRobbie 1982: 282).

Some analysts have pointed to the similarity of images, representations and ideologies of femininity contained in women's magazines. Focusing on women's magazines Ferguson (1985) argued that the construction of femininity contained in them was restrictive for women. Women's magazines perpetuated the 'cult of femininity'; indeed she described them as the high priestesses of this cult, which defines what it is to be a good and real woman. The magazines lay out the rituals, rites, sacrifices and obligations which women must maintain. Rituals attached to beautification, child-rearing, housework and cooking are all part of this cult. Ferguson examined women's magazines from the 1940s to the 1980s and claimed that although the rituals change slightly, the cult of femininity remains fundamentally unchanged. Until the late 1970s the dominant themes were 'getting and keeping your man', 'the happy family', 'self-help', 'be more beautiful' and the 'working wife is a bad wife'. Ideal femininity was represented in the self-reliant, resourceful, domesticated wife and mother who kept herself looking good for her man. In the late 1970s and 1980s many of these themes endured but there was one new theme for the emerging 'new woman': this was 'the working wife is a good wife', economic activity was now compatible with femininity. Key themes were still self-help, individual resourcefulness and energy to achieve perfection and overcome misfortune. There is, she accepted, some differentiation, yet overall the messages about femininity still fit within the same parameters. On the surface the range of messages and the roles and expectations have widened beyond the earlier emphasis on romance and marriage. Now we find representations and articles about the independent woman who has a career, but to be complete and satisfied she is still expected to get a man and be a successful wife and mother. The magazines contain two conflicting messages: show the world you are someone yet at the same time ensure you are a good wife and mother. These conflicting messages are the product of socio-economic changes, such as women's increasing role in the labour market and changing attitudes to sex and marriage. Women's magazines do not just reinforce and teach women traditional and emergent beliefs about the place of women in society; the covert message of the cult is that there is a feminine way of being that all women share and that women are fundamentally different from men (Ferguson 1985).

Case Study

## From cookery to sexual liberation

Whereas Ferguson (1985) approached women's magazines as cultural forms which are highly oppressive to women, Winship (1986) places more emphasis on the differences between magazines and changing ideals of femininity. She looked at the pleasure women derived from them and argued there were qualitative differences between magazines and the way they represent femininity, and, as an example, compared *Woman's Own* and *Cosmopolitan*. The results of this analysis are summarized below:

| | Woman's Own | Cosmopolitan |
|---|---|---|
| Audience | Housewife and mother, predominately white perspective | Career woman, young, middle-class, successful |
| Regular features | Domestic matters, family and fashion, cookery | Beauty, fashion, personal health and fitness |
| Social issues | Not politically engaged | Tackles broad range of issues in some detail offering wide range of view points |
| Sex and relationships | Marriage normal and inevitable but not ignoring problems such as affairs and divorce | Sexually explicit, champion of female orgasm, sex should be fun for those in and out of partnerships but constructed as heterosexual |
| Tone | Caring, reassuring | Fun, sexy, 'tough, tender and in touch' |

Winship (1986) agrees that magazines such as *Cosmopolitan* in the 1980s expand the bounds and possibilities of femininity but put new pressures on women by requiring personal qualities such as self-confidence, assertiveness, determination and practical know-how: the image of the new woman is very similar to that of the successful man in a competitive, materialistic society.

However, Winship also claims that because women tend to be more isolated from each other their pleasure and sense of identity are often marginalized in a predominately masculine culture. Women' s magazines play a valuable role in validating women's traditional skills and interests. They create a sense of a woman's world which may not actually exist but gives women a reassuring sense of community and pride in their own identity.

### Questions

How much influence do you think women's magazines have on the way women see themselves?

Do they pressurize or liberate?

Consumption dominates women's magazines which are packed with advertisements and articles on beauty goods, food ingredients and so on. The emphasis on consumption can be understood on two different levels. Winship (1986) proposes that in the 1950s women's magazines educated women about their role as consumers, a work which reflected not only their femininity but also their class status and the kinds of individuals they were. Women's magazines still provide this advice and take this role seriously, but at same time they are concerned with making money and with creating a culture of individuality. Advertisements tap into dreams and fantasies, and magazines make these obtainable via the purchase of a product; pleasure is increasingly something we buy. Winship suggests that magazines provide a whole range of pleasures to women, the quality and look of the magazine, identification with heroines, exciting creativity, peeping in on the lives of the rich or the troubles of everyday people.

Several theorists have acknowledged women's pleasures in consuming certain forms of popular culture and indulging in feminine behaviour. Ballaster *et al.*(1991) were aware that women's magazines can act as both vehicles for dominant ideology and bearers of pleasures. Many women's magazines are popular because they do contain contradictory messages and these resonate with the contradictions of women's lives. A magazine may contain a radical article on sexual harassment at work but this will be set against articles which reinforce ideologies of domesticity and romance. Ballaster *et al.* stress that women's magazines must be understood as a cultural form in which definitions and understandings of gender difference have been negotiated or contested rather than taken for granted and imposed; in them femininity is something which is not simply fixed but something which is struggled over and contested.

*Magazine readers*

Dutch sociologist Joke Hermes (1995) felt that many studies of women's magazines had not really let women speak for themselves; indeed some had denigrated women readers, presenting them as a brainwashed group in need of feminist enlightenment. She focused on the views of readers, exploring the meaning of the magazines in the context of readers' daily lives. She identifies herself as influenced by post-modernism and sees readers themselves producing meaning rather than just absorbing it passively from the texts: each individual brings with them different views and a range of identities. Hermes carried out ethnographic research and interviewed eighty Dutch and British women about their experiences of reading a range of women's magazines; she analysed the different ways women interpreted and talked about magazines, identifying recurrent themes or repertoires. She felt that women's magazines are less oppressive than some feminists claimed, but they still mainly represent women as heterosexual and white. She describes the different reasons identified by the women in her research which made magazines meaningful to them. A key theme was that magazines were 'putdownable', that is they could be read quickly without much attention, they were not demanding and filled empty spaces, and were relaxing. Underlying these themes were the 'repertoire of practical knowledge' and the 'repertoire of emotional learning and connected knowing'. Practical knowledge encompassed women getting 'tips' and 'picking things up', for example recipes, shopping and medical advice, interior designs and film reviews, so magazines provide value for money in the information provided. The repertoire of emotional learning and connected knowing focuses on emotions and how to deal with them. The magazines enable women to explore their wide range of 'selves'. The magazines are used to 'learn about other people's emotions and problems, in other cases readers are more interested about their own feelings, anxieties and wishes' (Hermes 1995: 41) so women empathize with others and recognize themselves in stories and articles. Both repertoires 'help women to gain a sense of identity and confidence, of being in control or feeling at peace with life, that lasts while they are reading but dissipates quickly when the magazine is put aside' (Hermes 1995: 48). Although there are many different reasons why women read magazines, it is important not to overestimate their cultural significance. Unlike some femininists, Hermes argues they are not central to shaping gender identity. The most important aspect of the magazine for readers was that it blended in with other obligations, duties and activities.

### *Men and the media*

Sociologists have commented on the role of the media in constructing masculinity. Easthope (1986) stresses that 'the masculine myth' saturates media and popular culture: 'there is a natural and universal masculine identity based on strength, competitiveness, aggression and violence'. He argues that men internalize these features and a key source of of the conscious and unconscious process of learning masculinity is in popular culture. Within films, advertising, comics and popular music lyrics, men are presented as masterful, in control of both nature and women, physically strong and heterosexual. The action heroes of the 1980s and 1990s seem to live out this myth, for example Arnold Schwarzenegger, Jean-Claude Van Damme and Bruce Willis. Although Easthope acknowledges that men do not swallow the image wholesale, he suggests it is difficult for them to escape some influence on their gender identity;

**Clearly men do not passively live out the masculine myth imposed by the stories and images of the dominant culture. But neither can they live completely outside the myth since it pervades the culture. Its coercive power is everywhere – not just on screens, hoardings and paper but inside our own heads.** *(Easthope 1986: 167)*

*Beano* comic has been popular with boys and to a lesser extent girls for many years. Easthope considers how two contrasting characters who generally appear in the same story, Dennis the Menace and Walter, communicate messages about desirable male behaviour. Walter is presented as very weak, soft, pathetic and 'girly' whereas Dennis is physically strong, tough and daring:

**Dennis and his mates keep getting into trouble; Walter and his softies play nursery rhyme games. . . . The pairing of Walter and Dennis gives the dominant codes for masculine and feminine across a wider range of boys' behaviour.** *(Easthope 1986: 31)*

Case Study

## Unmasking Masculinity

David Jackson (1990) considered the comics he read as a boy in terms of their role in constructing his masculine identity. In the late 1940s he avidly read *Rover, Hotspur* and *Wizard* and felt that they played a 'small but significant part in the ideological construction of my masculinity' (Jackson 1990: 223). Reading comics was his key leisure interest after playing football; indeed many of the stories focused on sporting successes or adventure. Characters such as the Cannonball Kid presented a win-at-all-costs rounded superhero. The comics contained lots of actions but few words; events took place in the public arena rather than in a more personal sphere. These comics appealed to young boys' fantasies about achieving 'a fully formed masculinity through physical strength and competitive performance' (Jackson 1990: 127). At the time he was reading these comics he was insecure about his masculine identity, disappointed at the frailty of his body and experienced bullying from other boys. Part of his strategy to deal with this was through the fantasy of the stories in his comics. What grew out of this was the striving to appear more manly that shaped his notion of what it was to be a man:

> Boys' comics prepared the way for a 'natural' acceptance of a striving, individualist energy and a single determination to win at all costs. (Jackson 1990: 240)

Gender analyses of men's magazines, apart from pornography, are less developed than women's magazines; indeed it is only in the late 1980s that a modern group of general interest, glossy 'men's magazines' have emerged. Titles such as *GQ*, *For Him* and *Loaded* contain articles on health, sport, fashion and personal care, women, sex and employment. Collier (1992) points out that the depiction of masculinity in these magazines has received little attention. He scrutinized them to see if their presentation of men and masculinity depicted the 'new man', the caring, child-centred, sensitive man, so talked about in the media; he found there were different and contradictory messages about masculinity:

> **the masculism of the new men's magazines involves two simultaneous and contradictory developments. On the one hand the rewriting of an old and familiar and traditional masculinity; and alongside this notably with regard to work, sexuality and fatherhood the development of a masculinity which in some respects rejects out and out sexism and seeks instead progressive, non-oppressive relations with women, children and other men.** *(Collier 1992: 35)*

He found that paid work, material success and economic power remain fundamental to the 'dominant form of masculinity on offer by the magazines'. He compared the ethos of the magazine to that of the corporate business world. Issues of sexuality were up-front, explicit and humorous; in the same way that women's magazines construct conflicting notions about female sexuality, men's magazines express a 'deep ambiguity about male sexuality'. Men are presented as both sexually and emotionally vulnerable yet sexually powerful, in control and dominant. Many images of women in the magazines draw on the soft porn genre and presented women as sex objects. The magazines celebrate a heterosexual masculinity. He found similar confusion and contradiction regarding fatherhood: the 'ideology of new fatherhood' present in some magazines addressed issues of shared parenting and represented men as active fathers. Yet at the same time masculinity is presented in terms of material and economic success which he suggests relies on and endorses the privilege, hierarchy and material benefits which accrue to men. For Collier there is a tension in the new men's magazines' depiction of masculinity. They have been informed to a certain extent by feminism and the anti-sexist men's movement but in the end,

> **the failure to address the need for structural change and their own reliance on higher earning advertisement revenue which produces a consumerist defined masculinity results in a little more than updated version of the old man.**
>
> *(Collier 1992: 38)*

In fact some new men's magazines are not even attempting to redefine masculinity. *Loaded*, launched in 1994, is aimed at and presents the image of the 'new lad' and has one of the largest circulations for a men's magazine. It contains features on partying, including lots of beer drinking, sport (particularly football), features and interviews with famous 'beautiful women' and male heroes. Women are presented as sex objects and there are many soft porn images of women's bodies. Real men get 'loaded', 'shag' women and watch football. This magazine stakes out the bounds of a particular type of masculinity.

## Gendered labour

The 'public' world of paid work has often been referred to as separate from the 'private' sphere of the family, yet feminist theorists have questioned this notion of two separate spheres, arguing that gender relations in the labour market are interrelated to gender relations in the family and household. For example Garmarnikov *et al.* (1983) claim that domestic labour performed to a greater extent by women is crucial in enabling men to devote all their energies to a competitive labour market.

Although challenging the notion of separate public and private spheres, feminists have pointed out that the public–private dichotomy has had a very powerful ideological role in constructing gender relations. The public–private split reflected a sexual division of labour within which men were defined as active in the public world and paid work, and women were defined primarily as domestic labourers located in the private sphere of the home. Feminist theorists and male sociologists in the field of men's studies have argued that this division has had a central role defining femininities and masculinities. For feminists it has meant that women have been excluded from and placed at a disadvantage in paid employment; for some theorists of masculinity it has meant a restrictive definition of masculinity. Historically western masculinity is defined by men's breadwinning role and men's relationship to the public sector. Morgan (1991) argues that employment provides a key site for understanding men; it has been a key source of masculine status and prestige.

## Unpaid labour

Before we turn our attention to paid employment it is important to examine unpaid labour. Gender relations in the household interact with and shape paid employment. Throughout the world both women and men perform unpaid labour; a large proportion of this is domestic labour. Feminists have stressed that this labour is real work and can be taxing in ways that paid work is not. Oakley (1974b) carried out in-depth interviews with forty London housewives. She found that women spent an average of seventy-seven hours per week on housework. She applied the criteria used by industrial sociologists such as Goldthorpe and Lockwood (Goldthorpe *et al.* 1968, 1969) to the work performed by housewives and found high levels of dissatisfaction, monotony, loneliness and feelings of low status. Numerous studies have shown that despite some shift towards equality, women still perform an unequal share of domestic labour in the home and child care. Despite the claim by sociologists Young and Willmott (1973) that as a result of more women going out to work the division of labour between women and men in domestic spheres was changing with the family taking on a symmetrical form, much research reveals persistent inequality. Fawcett and Pichaud (1984) detailed the cost of child care to individuals in terms of time and found that the time cost was overwhelmingly borne by mothers. The Family Policy Studies Centre report *Inside the Family* (Henwood *et al.* 1987) found that women were still primarily responsible for domestic and caring tasks: although 50 per cent of couples claimed to share child care, women were mainly or solely responsible for almost three-quarters of all housework. Jowell and Witherspoon (1985) similarly found that women performed more domestic labour but they also found what other researchers have noted – a gendering of tasks.

Weelock (1990) examined in what ways the divisions of domestic work between wives and husbands changed when men became unemployed. The thirty working-class couples with children she interviewed in Sunderland, Wearside, were representative of social and economic trends in the area where opportunities for manual workers had declined but low-paid women's work remained relatively buoyant. She examined the relationship between economic restructuring and the internal dynamics of the household. She hypothesized that under such family circumstance, gender roles would change as men out of work would have more time to undertake domestic work while women, being in the labour market, would have less. She found substantial change with men taking on a considerable proportion of domestic labour in 20 per cent of households, some change in 47 per cent of the cases, no change in 13 per cent and regressive change in 10 per cent. She concluded that on the whole unemployment leads to a positive change in the distribution of domestic work as men demonstrated a degree of flexibility and responded pragmatically to the overall changing family/work situation. She noted that there remained a gendering of domestic jobs: some tasks were gender segregated and others gender neutral. Washing up, tidying up, using the vacuum cleaner and making beds tended to be gender neutral; cooking the main meal and thorough cleaning were almost exclusively female, and washing clothes and ironing were done predominantly by women. Tasks with a managerial element like shopping and handling the household budget were done predominantly by women. Predominantly male tasks included gardening, mowing the lawn, household repairs and taking the rubbish out. Wajcman (1983) in a study of women who worked full time also found this: husbands perform certain domestic duties, but they are different from those that women do in that they are neither routine nor continuous but involve a few tasks, at intervals and often outdoors; female task are regarded as less skilled.

Case Study

## Food for thought

Despite the flamboyant male chefs who feature in many television cookery programmes, the *British Social Attitudes Survey* (Jowell *et al.* 1992) found that in 70 per cent households women mainly made the evening meal, in 9 per cent of households men mainly do it, and in 20 per cent of households it was a shared task. Interestingly 54 per cent thought that the task should be shared equally. Mennell (1992) suggests that men can cook but have more choice as to whether they do or not, and may do an occasional special meal, whereas many women have no option, having greater responsibility for the day-to-day family cooking. Cooking in our culture remains part of the ideology of wifeliness or motherhood. Women are expected to cook food which their partners or children like and hence adapt their food choices to suite these tastes. Research throughout the world has found that when food is scarce, women will often reduce their own portions first. In underdeveloped countries in which food is limited, women are more likely to suffer malnutrition (Wells 1993).

There is limited research on the gendering of food choice available at present; however, one contemporary issue that has received some comment is the consumption and non-consumption of meat (Timperley 1994). Among the 3 million vegetarians in the UK, there are more women than men (5.8 per cent of women as opposed to 3.2 per cent of men) and young women constitute the largest growing proportion of vegetarians (16 per cent of teenage girls). Some theorists have linked this to inequality, masculinity and male dominance.

### Meat to Live

Even in the nursery, we are fed the image of the king in his counting house who consumes four and twenty blackbirds, while his queen dines daintily on bread and honey. So money, meat and masculinity are indelibly juxtaposed on impressionable minds . According to Carol J Adams in *The Sexual Politics of Meat* it is an insidious method of perpetuating patriarchy: 'People with power have always eaten meat'.... Meat is a symbol of male dominance. The implication is that by eating animal muscle, human beings increase their own muscle mass.... During the Second World War, when meat supplies for civilians were strictly rationed, the per capita consumption of meat within the armed forces was approximately double that of the civilian population. An army marches on its stomach and its military puissance depends on that stomach being fed meat. Fifty years on the link between carnivorism and clout is just as strong. The Meat and Livestock Commission's multi-million pound 'Meat to Live' advertising campaign features athletic bronzed beefcakes exuding vigour and vitality from hoardings and the pages of lifestyle magazines. The unsubtle message is that if a guy wants pecs and sex, he' d better stick to steak.

Much of this is rooted in the tradition of man as hunter. And it follows that if man is hunter, woman must be gatherer. In other words, he brings home the bacon but she picks the mushrooms that accompany it .... Women are as a rule more directly concerned with the purchase and preparation of food and with the health and well-being of their families. They have traditionally reserved the pick of the first class protein for

*(box continued)*

*(box continued)*

their menfolk, which often meant going without themselves . . . . Even the very metaphor of food reflects this masculine/feminine divide. Weighty topics are described as 'meaty' and are 'beefed up'; bravery is red blooded behaviour. In contrast vegetables are dull, unexciting and intellectually improving. Quite apart from the positive/negative implications, there is an active/passive subtext: men as aggressors and initiators, women as passive recipients. (Timperley 1994: 24)

## Questions

**In the extract on meat, which of the author's points do you agree with and which do you disagree with?**

**The preparation of food involves labour; does gender influence the preparation of food?**

**How is what we eat shaped by gender relations?**

**In the households that you have experienced, who has done the food preparation? How do you explain the arrangements in those households?**

Household and family responsibilities also involve broader caring obligations, particularly in relation to sick, elderly and disabled relatives. Women are the major providers of unpaid health care in the home (Graham 1984a); about 75 per cent of adults caring for elderly relatives are women. Finch and Groves (1983) argue that caring is central to women's lives. It is the medium through which they gain admittance into both the private world of the home and the public world of the labour market. It is through caring in an informal capacity (as mothers, wives, daughters, neighbours and friends) and through formal caring (as nurses, secretaries, cleaners, teachers and social workers) that women often occupy their place in society.

Other inequalities in the household have been identified in the areas of economics, decision-making and leisure. Pahl (1989) argued that the family is not simply a unit of consumption in which resources are shared equally; power relations exist which determine how those resources are allocated. Pahl found among the couples in her study that the most common model of decision-making involved women making day-to-day domestic decisions but men making the infrequent but important household decisions. Pahl points out that women may have control over household budgets but this by no means ensures them a position of power. Men's greater economic power was reflected in the greater share of family resources they received. Green *et al.* (1990) found in their research on women's leisure that men were still able to claim as a right a high proportion of the family income for their personal leisure use, such as drinking in the pub, while women's leisure was restricted because they still had greater domestic and caring responsibilities and tended to have access to less money. Another constraint on women's leisure were ideologies of femininity which defined only certain leisure pursuits as suitable for women.

On a global scale women's unpaid labour not only includes child care, cleaning and cooking but also involves a whole range of tasks which have economic value, such as gathering cow dung for fuel in Ladakh, India, or trading goods in Lagos. The UN *Fifth Annual Human Development Report* (quoted in *Guardian* 8 August 1995) on women's economic status in more than eighty countries found that two-thirds of women's work and a quarter of men's work are unpaid and constitute 70 per cent of the world's annual global output of $23,000 billion. This research revealed that women work on average 13 per cent more than men, yet there are marked differences between countries. In Italy women work 28 per cent more compared to 2 per cent less in Denmark; in rural Kenya women work 35 per cent more and in Nepal 5 per cent more. Women's labour in all its forms seems to be undervalued.

## Paid labour

The sexual division of labour has changed dramatically since the Second World War; references to male breadwinners and housewives are misleading and conceal a diverse and complex range of social relations (Allen and Walkowitz 1987; Pascall 1995; Walby 1990). Pascall (1995) argues that since the mid-1970s women's position in the UK labour market has changed distinctively. Women have increasingly entered paid employment since the Second World War and in the mid-1990s form 46 per cent of the workforce (Pascall 1995). This is not only through shifts towards gender equality but also because of economic restructuring: manufacturing jobs have declined whereas employment in the service industries has increased. Men have traditionally dominated many sectors of manufacturing, whereas women have been concentrated in the service industries, hence many of the new jobs created have been taken by women. This pattern is found in many countries throughout the world; women now represent 41 per cent of all workers in developed countries and 34 per cent world-wide, yet their wages are 30–40 per cent less than those of men for comparable work (*New Internationalist* 270 August 1995).

These changes have led some commentators to argue that a 'genderquake' is taking place, that women are gaining equality at last and even that an emerging shift in power from men to women is taking place. Yet feminist researchers have argued that despite significant changes in the patterns of female and male employment women are still disadvantaged in paid employment compared to their male counterparts. These persistent inequalities are linked to the different types of work that women and men perform: 'Men and women are largely segregated into different occupations and into different layers of the same occupations' (Pascall 1995: 2).

### *The segregated labour market*

*Horizontal segregation* describes the tendency for women and men to be concentrated in different occupations (Hakim 1979). Martin and Roberts (1984) found that 63 per cent of women were in jobs done only by women and 81 per cent of men were in jobs performed solely by men. Women are concentrated in a narrow range of occupations and sectors of the economy.

**Q** List six occupations you would describe as female dominated and six as male dominated. Why do you think these jobs are 'gendered'?

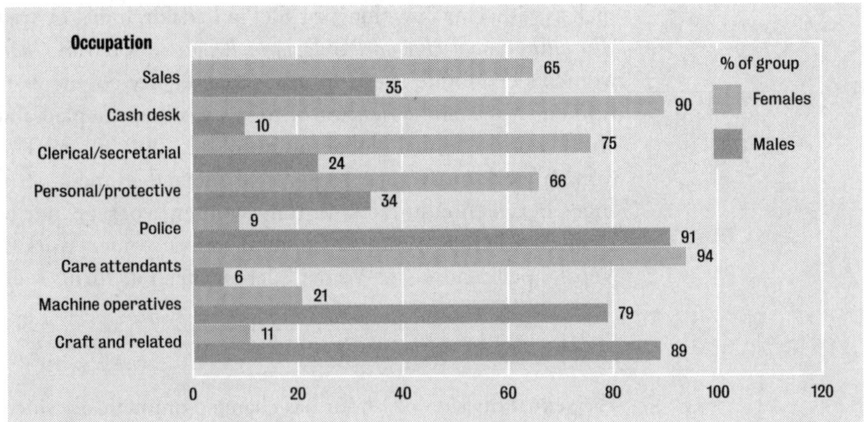


**Fig 7.2** Employment by occupation, 1993.

*Source: Labour Force Survey* 1994

Figure 7.2 shows the gendered nature of selected employment groupings. The *New Earnings Survey* (EOC 1995) showed that over 70 per cent of full-time female workers are concentrated in three occupational sectors, first, clerical work, second, professional and similar occupations in education, welfare and health, and third the personal services such as hairdressing and cleaning. The fourth major employer for women is retailing. Feminists have argued that the sectors in which women are concentrated are associated with low status, low pay and poor working conditions.

*Vertical segregation* describes how the division of labour between occupations is paralleled with that within them (Hakim 1979). When women and men work together in the same sector or organization, men are higher up the job hierarchy in better paid high-status conditions. In the 1990s researchers still find this vertical segregation: although women have broken into many male-dominated areas of employment they are still under-represented and virtually absent from high-status positions. The *'glass-ceiling'* describes the phenomenon whereby women are progressing into high-status professions, but are not making it to the top jobs even though they are as talented and able as the men who hold those positions.

A whole range of disadvantages face women in organizations. Recruitment and promotion practices tend to operate against women. Even though it now violates equal opportunities legislation, employers may ask female interviewees if they plan to have children or marry or make decisions based on the assumption that they will and that this will affect their job performance. In an Institute of Management Survey, *The Key to the Men's Club*, Coe (1992) found that women in management make more sacrifices than men and that many women managers have opted out of having children: Coe (1992) found that the image of the woman boss is still a stereotypical one of a harridan in tweeds or a vamp power-dresser in suit and stilettos. One-fifth of men said they would find it difficult to work for a woman and gave reasons ranging from women simply do not make good managers to women crack under pressure. Workplace organizations are mostly still structured in a way that lacks the flexibility required by women workers who have children. They often have to find child care to cover them for long hours; work-based crèches are quite rare.

Career breaks, job shares and flexible hours, all which improve women's chances, challenge the way professionals have worked and are also seen as expensive to initiate and require commitment from individual companies.

In many professions the membership of old boys' networks has been identified as an important way of learning about opportunities and actually being considered for particular positions. As well as not being part of male networks that get people jobs, women may be excluded or feel alienated from male work-based cultures which are a crucial part of making contacts and gaining promotion in some organizations, professions and industries. Kanter (1977) revealed how male friendship and sponsorship networks act to exclude women from the knowledge and contacts necessary for corporate success.

Liberal feminists have stressed the importance of getting women into senior positions; they argue that these women could act as role models for other women, challenge assumptions that a particular job can be performed only by a man, and suggest that women may be more likely to incorporate women's needs into their decision-making and policy formulation and to bring new skills and approaches. Many initiatives have been established in many professions to increase the number of women in senior positions, for example 'Opportunity 2000' launched by the Conservative government in 1991. Companies voluntarily join the scheme and set their own ten-year targets to improve women's position; although welcomed, the initiative has been criticized for relying on the goodwill of employers and lacking any legislative backing.

**Q** Is there any evidence to support the idea that if more women are in senior positions they (a) act as role models; (b) actively help other women in their careers; (c) bring new skills and approaches to their work?

### *Women's work, child care, pay and equal opportunities*

In 1992 45 per cent of women workers were part time compared to 6 per cent of men. Walby (1990) argues that the division between part-time and full-time work is the most important new form of labour market segmentation in Britain since the 1940s. Part-time work has lower rates of pay than full-time work and part-timers have less secure contracts and fewer employment rights. Part-time women workers earned 56 per cent of men's hourly rates in 1986; full-time women earned 74 per cent of men's hourly rates. Part-time workers who are employed for fewer than eight hours per week do not qualify for certain employment rates such as the right to claim unfair dismissal, maternity benefits, holiday pay and redundancy pay. Those who work between eight and sixteen hours qualify for these rights when they have been with the employer for five years. Thus part-time workers provide a cheap and flexible source of labour.

Part-time jobs are particularly attractive to women who have child-care responsibilities. While some theorists argue that women opt for part-time work out of choice, others stress that this choice must be understood within the context of social and economic constraints. In a society where state child-care provision is limited and private child-care expensive, part-time work is the only option for some women. Child care shapes women's labour market opportunities and is a clear example of domestic responsibilities shaping choices in the labour market.

As Ramazanoglu (1991b) notes, women are faced with the personal and private problem of resolving a structural problem which requires major socio-economic transformation.

Rapid labour market changes with increasing numbers of women going out to work have taken place against a background which encourages families to care for their own children. The lack of state nursery provision has placed costs and responsibilities on parents for day care of pre-school children. As a result most women stop work to have children and women's economic status is related to child-rearing. Professions such as medicine which require intense career building in the early stages present a special barrier to women. Yet a shift towards a more continuous 'Swedish' pattern of work has begun in the UK. Brannen and Moss (1991) studied women who kept their employment after child-birth. They argue that this pattern improves the terms on which women combine parenthood and paid employment, yet they concluded that

**Dominant ideologies about motherhood emphasise women's primary responsibility for children and remain highly ambivalent about women with very young children having full time jobs. Fathers did not equally share childcare or other domestic tasks nor did they accept equal responsibility for these areas. Support from social networks was important in some ways for some women but generally inadequate. Many women who returned to work experienced hostile attitudes from relatives, friends and work colleagues . . . women were forced to rely largely on personal solutions to the demands and tensions of managing the dual earner lifestyle which fell largely upon them.** ***(Brannen and Moss 1991: 251–2)***

### *Pay*

In a capitalist society the pay that people receive is a measure of the value of their labour. Compared to their male counterparts, women workers get less for their labour than male workers: in 1993 women's wages constituted 72 per cent of men's wages (*New Earnings Survey,* EOC 1995). These differences in pay persist despite the existence of the Equal Pay Act 1975, which in its original form had little impact. There was evidence that employers deliberately introduced segregation by gender in jobs where there had been none before to avoid giving female workers equal pay. In 1984 the Act was amended to refer to jobs of equal value; it was hoped that comparisons could be made across jobs and many women performing jobs in which traditionally few men have been employed would come within the scope of the Act. While some individual successful cases have been won, problems with the legislation remain. Many women are unaware of the existence of legislation or reluctant to make claims because of fear of victimization by colleagues and employees. More fundamentally, differential pay is related to the structure of the labour market and the Equal Pay Act has little impact on this structure. The Equal Opportunities Commission (Humphries and Rubery 1995) recommend that the work that women predominantly perform must be revalued as no major impact would be made through individual cases. Yet in the early 1990s there were no signs of a shift towards the revaluing of women's low-paid work.

Case Study

## Hairdressing

**The abolition of wages councils in 1993 is an example of how policy changes have further undervalued women's low-paid work. Although the scope of wages councils had been reduced since 1979, they had set minimum rates for pay for 2.4 million workers, 80 per cent of them women including many from ethnic minorities. About 95 per cent of workers covered by the wages councils were in hotel and catering, retailing, clothing and hairdressing, where the basic rates had been set between £2.66 and £3.30 per hour. Two-thirds of the workers are employed part time. The *Guardian* reported the case of a hairdresser:**

> One young hairdresser in the midlands, who wants to remain anonymous for fear of dismissal, asked her employer recently to pay her the minimum rate of £2.88 an hour when she qualified as a 21 year old on 4th September. In the mid-Eighties the government removed wage protection from workers under that age. Her employer informed her that from the 30th August there was no such entitlement and that she would be continued to be paid £2 an hour – £80 for a 40-hour week. (*Guardian* October 1993)

**This legislation has implications for all low-paid workers but it clearly has a gendered effect, hitting female workers to a greater extent. Women's position in the labour market and the pay levels they can command have serious implications for their power and choice in other areas of society. Women's low pay is a key cause of female poverty and reinforces women's dependency on men or the state.**

### *Employment, race and gender*

Paid employment is one area that demonstrates the interaction of gender with a whole range of other factors. Black feminists have pointed out that Black women have had a different relationship to the labour market than white women; this differential positioning is the product of historical, economic and ideological factors. Whereas white women have found themselves excluded from paid labour and defined as domestic workers, Afro-Caribbean women, since slavery, have been seen as the 'mules of the world', capable of heavy work. Different ideologies of femininity have shaped the experiences of Black and white women. Afro-Caribbean women have always worked, which is still reflected in their higher rates of economic activity. Yet evidence suggests that they face discrimination in the labour market: professional Black women are in jobs with lower pay and status than equally qualified other workers.

The exploitation of domestic migrant workers, which attracted some media attention in the 1990s, illustrates how gender, race and nationality interact. Migrant domestic workers, predominantly women from the Third World, come to Britain with families who act as their employers. They find themselves in a highly vulnerable position as the conditions under which they reside in the UK, laid out in current immigration law, class them as visitors and not residents. Tied exclusively to the employer with whom they came to the country, they have no independent right to work, which often traps them in exploitative working conditions.

*Britain's Secret Slaves*, a report commissioned by Anti-Slavery International (1993) and Kalayaan, who campaign for the rights of domestic workers, found that they worked long hours for low pay and often experienced a range of abuses. In their study 89 per cent of workers were subject to psychological abuse and 33 per cent suffered physical abuse. If workers leave the family or the family discontinues their employment, they are classified as illegal immigrants and face deportation. With no right to work legally, illegal low-paid work is the only option. The experiences of these workers highlight the claim by bell hooks (1989) that to understand women's oppression we have to acknowledge the differences between women in order to explore the complex interaction of gender, class, race and the international relations of subordination and domination.

## Explanations for gender segregation in the labour market

A range of explanations has been put forward to explain gender segregation in the labour market and specifically why women generally undertake jobs which are relatively low paid and which are perceived as having low levels of skill:

- economic theories
- Marxist and feminist approaches
- capitalism and patriarchy: the dastardly duo
- sexuality on the job.

### *Economic theories*

Sinclair (1991) identifies 'orthodox economic theories' as being influential because of the important role they play in 'determining the ideology and policies according to which the economy is run' (Sinclair 1991: 3). These theories focus on the supply and demand for female labour within the economy to understand women's position in the labour market. One example is human capital theory.

Women have less human capital than men; they get paid less because they have less skill and labour market experience as a consequence of freely chosen decisions to allocate more of their time to other domestic responsibilities. Women's work as carers of children prevents their acquisition of qualifications and labour market experience. Human capital theory attempts to explain occupational segregation as well as low pay: women choose those occupations for which their lesser skills will give the best reward and in which they will be least penalized for their intermittent work patterns. This theory assumes that women believe that they will spend fewer years in the labour market than men. The occupations in which women are concentrated require fewer skills and fewer penalties for interrupted work patterns which women choose to pursue. This is the type of approach to the labour market taken by the Institute of Economic Affairs, whose report *Equal Opportunities: A Feminist Fallacy* (IEA 1992) proposed that the Equal Pay Act and anti-discrimination legislation weaken the freedom of contract between employer and employee and undermine equality before the law.

This theoretical approach fails to account for women who have equal experience and training (equal human capital) but are not appointed to certain positions or fail to get promotions when placed against lesser or equally qualified men, that is they ignore the evidence of sexual discrimination in the labour market. It also assumes that skill is an objective category, that there is consensus about what is skilled work and that all skills are recognized as such. Human capital theory completely neglects the structural factors within the labour market and outside, which place women at a disadvantage in the labour market. It is to these structural factors and social relations that other theorists have turned.

Phillips and Taylor (1980) argue that skill definitions are saturated by sex bias. The work of women is often deemed inferior simply because it is women who do it. They argue that we need to rethink the meaning of skill itself and that it is the sex of those who perform the work rather than its content which leads to its identification as skilled or unskilled. Skill is not an objective category, rather it is 'an ideological category imposed on certain types of work by virtue of the sex and power of the workers who perform it' (Phillips and Taylor 1980: 80).

Several feminists have noted that women's work does not get labelled as skilled because such jobs generally involve quite short periods of training, or use skills which it is assumed women learn informally within the home (e.g. cooking). Feminists have stressed that much of the work that women perform is an extension of the nurturing and caring work that women are culturally expected to perform in the home. These sorts of skills are seen as natural feminine skills, rather than developed through experience. However, some work that entails long periods of training such as hairdressing does not get labelled as skilled. Phillips and Taylor (1980) argue that what has been labelled skilled is the outcome of a continuous battle between male craft workers and capital over the control of production. They argue that in these struggles craft has been increasingly associated with masculinity.

### *Marxist and feminist approaches*

Various Marxist theorists acknowledge that women's labour is exploited and some suggest that this can be understood by considering how the labour market is itself split into two key sectors which provide very different experiences and opportunities. Barron and Norris (1976) identified two segments in the labour market:

*Primary sector*: skilled secure work, good pay and working conditions, promotion prospects

*Secondary sector*: unskilled, poor working conditions, insecure pay, few prospects.

Employers segment the labour market as part of a divide-and-rule strategy to control the workforce. They utilize pre-existing social divisions based for example on gender or ethnicity. Women are concentrated predominantly in the secondary sector, easily fitting into this sector because they will work for less money as they are not so committed to paid work because of their domestic roles. Women frequently leave work of their own accord and are less likely to join trade unions, making them easier to dispense with; the social distinction between the sexes means women are demarcated from men and becomes a useful way of dividing the labour force (Barron and Norris 1976).

This approach pays little attention to the role of men in excluding women from work and the role of trade unions in maintaining the segmented labour market. Dex (1985) argues it is inaccurate as some women are employed in the so-called 'male' primary sector and also there are distinctions between women workers themselves. Some models have been developed which are more complex and propose a high degree of segregation rather than a twofold division, with many different labour markets arising as employers seek to divide and rule the labour force. However, feminists have been unhappy with this type of approach as it fails to take into account the fundamental effect that gender has on the labour market.

Marxist feminists also explain the experience of women in the labour market as the outcome of the capitalist economic system yet they identify the exploitation of women's labour as central to the functioning of capitalism and hence to the subordination of women. In much Marxist feminism the sexual division of labour in the family and family ideology have been seen as crucial in placing women at a disadvantage when they enter the labour market. There is a range of explanations proposed by Marxist feminism.

Marx had noted that capital accumulation required a *reserve of labour* to prevent workers from being able to bargain up their wages and conditions in times of increased demand for labour. Beechey (1978) applied this theory to women, arguing that they constitute a flexible reserve of labour which can be bought into the labour market when boom conditions increase the need for labour and let go to return to the home in times of recession. This type of approach has been applied to women's employment during the two world wars, when due to the shortage of male labour, women were required and encouraged to enter the labour market, particularly in munitions factories, and to engage in trades which had been a male preserve. Images such as 'Rosie the Riveter' were part of the wartime strategy to encourage women to enter the labour market. Women were let go at the end of the war to make way for the returning men and governments were able to utilize ideologies about domesticity and motherhood, women's suitability as wives and mothers and the need for mothers to rear their children and also about men's right to work.

**Case Study**

## Women's employment in Russia

After decades of paying lip service to the principle of sexual inequality, Russia has reverted to unashamed male chauvinism. Now the small but growing band of Russian feminists are having to stand up for their rights as western women did 20 years ago. Thirty-nine million Russian women, about half the female population, have jobs, but so dire are the economic prospects in the newly democratic Russia that the position of women in the workplace is being challenged. Sex discrimination comes close to being official policy. Last month the labour minister, Gennady Melikyan, asked, 'Why should we employ women when men are unemployed? It's better that men work and women take care of children and do housework, I don't want women to be offended, but I don't think women should work while men are doing nothing'.

Small wonder that women account for 70 per cent of the 600,000 people so far registered as out of work, and that employers can get away with placing job ads that specifically discourage women applicants. Yelena Yershova, chairwoman of the independent Gaia Women's Centre, is furious with Mr Melikyan. 'If any minister in the west had spoken as he did, it would have been political death for him', she said. 'But we will fight, because 10 million women in Russia are bringing up children on their own and have absolutely no choice but to work.' . . .

One of the public organisations which has the right to see and comment on draft legislation [is the Gaia Centre]. Ms Yershova, 59, founded it in 1990, when she retired from her job as an academic at the Institute of USA and Canada. . . .

*(box continued)*

*(box continued)*

I was impressed at how much American women have managed to achieve for themselves compared to women in the Soviet Union, where the laws on paper at least, were good. Now that is changing. Even the right we had we are losing'. Ms Yershova is particularly concerned about a draft law, which . . . would make the family, rather than the individual, the most important unit of Russian society. 'This may sound innocent,' she said 'but all totalitarian societies focus on the family, at the expense of the individual.'

Ms Yershova said she believes that Russia, with its increasingly influential Orthodox Church, could be heading down the conservative path taken by Catholic Poland. When it comes to sexism, Russian women are their own worst enemies, she admitted. Throughout the Soviet era they bore a heavy double burden, doing most of the house work while going out to work as well. Now in these times of acute economic crisis, they are under heavy pressure simply to survive. So it is tempting for them to surrender to men's suggestions that they stay at home.

Gone are the women railway workers and tractor drivers of Soviet propaganda, she says. Beauty contests, clubs teaching etiquette to wives of wealthy business men, prostitution, pornography are features of post-communist Russia.

(Helen Womack, 'Why employ women when there are men out of work? It's better that women do housework', *Independent* 21 March 1993)

**Questions**

**How could you apply the reserve army of labour theory to these changes in Russia?**

**Why do you think some women have achieved greater success in the USA?**

Marxist feminists generally have been criticized for focusing simply on the needs of capitalism and for paying insufficient attention to patriarchal relations and how these impact on the labour market. Hence the role of male workers and trade unions in constructing a gendered labour market has been ignored.

Cythia Cockburn raises this issue:

**We can see that men and their unions do share responsibility with employers . . . Though they have sometimes paid lip-service to the idea of equal pay for females (as indeed most do today), they have never made it part of their industrial strategy.**

*C Cockburn 1983: 200)*

### *Capitalism and patriarchy: the dastardly duo*

Some feminists have tried to understand women's position in the labour market as a product of both the economic relations of capitalism and patriarchal gender relations; this reflects a broad change of direction in socialist feminism. Hartmann (1981) argued that segregation by sex and women's low pay can be explained only be exploring the way patriarchy and capitalism work together to form a system which she referred to as *patriarchal capitalism*. The basis of male power in this social system is men's control over female labour, in both the family and the labour market. Segregation by sex in the labour market has secured male dominance and men's demand for a family wage ensures that men have higher wages and economic power in the household. She argues that men have organized via trade unions to exclude women from certain areas of work. Capitalist employers have benefited from this arrangement chiefly by obtaining women's labour cheaply in many areas of the labour market.

Walby (1986) has also taken a dual systems approach but she stressed that patriarchy and capitalism are two separate systems which interact together in a variety of ways, and not always harmoniously as Hartmann proposed. Walby suggested that these two systems have conflicting interests over women's labour. Men dominate in the labour market but this is in tension with capitalist relations as employers are keen to exploit all forms of labour and particularly women's. Women's access to paid work on an equal basis to men would give women greater power and hence undermine patriarchy and male privilege. Walby identifies a pattern of struggles and compromises between employers and male workers and examines a range of historical and contemporary events to illustrate her theory. For example she considered the Factory Acts passed in the late nineteenth century. Women were entering factory employment in large numbers and capitalists were happy to use their labour. Yet this threatened the patriarchal family. In excluding women, male workers and trade unions did not simply have the health and safety of women workers at heart but the dominance of male workers. Eventually a compromise was reached: women were excluded from certain sectors of the labour market. Although groups of women opposed this exclusion their voice was not heeded.

Cockburn (1985) has considered how trade unions have organized to exclude women from certain areas of the labour market. Her study of the printing trade found that historically the print trade unions have organized to resist women's entry into the trade and also how male workers via trade union struggle have shaped work processes themselves in a way that constructs that job as masculine. The workers felt that the presence of a woman doing a job devalued that job and she argued that the entrance of women into male jobs for the male workers disturbed the world as it should be, demarcated by gender.

### *Sexuality on the job*

Adkins (1995) has argued that explanations of the differential experiences of women and men in the labour market fail to acknowledge the centrality of sexuality in the labour market. Her work based on research in the tourism industry has led her to explore how relations of sexuality are central in constructing women and men as different types of workers. She argues that feminists have concentrated on how women's labour is controlled through women's exclusion from jobs and wages or via segregation within jobs. All gender divisions in the labour market are seen to stem from this control: capitalism structures jobs into a hierarchy and then patriarchal control of women's labour restricts women's access to these jobs. Adkins argues that the hierarchy itself 'is intrinsically structured by patriarchal relations' and that the labour market is more gendered than dual systems approaches suggest.

The labour market is not only a site of inequality but also a site where meanings about gender and sexuality are constructed. Adkins noted that jobs in hotels were gender segregated with positions such as receptionists and housekeepers being performed by women and porters and kitchen hands by men. Yet she also points out that the job specifications for posts at the hotel provided by personnel not only demonstrated this segregation but laid out certain qualities which were expected for 'female' and 'male' posts. Occupations in which women were concentrated required similar specifications; one specification that was not requested for male posts was 'attractiveness'.

Q What are the key differences in qualities required for 'female' and 'male' jobs? Why are these different?

Adkins argues that the control of women's labour in tourism involves sexuality and the compulsion for women to be what she refers to as 'sexual workers'. Women and men may do the same job, but they are different kinds of workers, as women's work involves 'sexual servicing':

> **Men and women were constituted as different kinds of workers within these workplaces even when they were located in the same job. To be workers women had to be 'attractive workers' and carry out forms of sexualized work, whereas men did not have to do this. Thus . . . women not only took orders, served food and drinks and cleared tables, they (and only they) also provided sexual servicing for men, both customers and co-workers. Women were thus not only 'economically productive' but also sexually productive workers. The fact that it was only women who were required to carry out sexual servicing as a condition of their employment shows that men and women participated in the two workplaces with substantially different relations of production.** *(Adkins 1995: 147)*

Adkins describes the gender relations at 'Funland' to illustrate her notion of sexual servicing work. The majority of female staff were employed as catering staff or retail assistants, as waitresses, checkout workers, or bar staff. Male workers were employed to run the rides as operatives; this role was defined as a male job because of its associations with strength and technology although all rides were mechanized and repairs were carried out by a specialized repair team. The only women operatives were on the children's rides; these were young women who had been perceived as more 'butch'. Catering staff were predominantly female and were expected to present themselves in a particular way; there was an explicit feminine look with 'feminine' make-up which the female workers were expected to adopt. Some male catering staff had been sacked for reasons of hygiene but none had lost his job for simply not appearing the right way as had happened to female staff. Adkins argues that this is part of the service women workers provide. Female bar staff found themselves allocated a uniform which they had to wear, including a short skirt, and the bar manager told the women they had to wear their blouses off their shoulders. Hence they were required to present themselves in a sexualized manner in a way that male bar staff did not have to. Adkins provides just one study of an organization which exposes how gender and sexuality are constructed in the labour market and shape the choices and opportunities of workers.

Increasingly theorists are treating the labour market as a site where meanings about femininity, masculinity and sexuality are constructed. Some researchers have turned their attention to the ways in which female and male behaviour is constructed. Several researchers have considered how aspects of women's work require certain 'feminine' qualities including the sexual attractivness of women workers. Broadbridge (1991) examined female sales assistants' perceptions of their work, experience of pay and working conditions and prevalent assumptions about skill and expected behaviour in a number of department stores in central London. She argues that the customers expect good quality personal service, which may include product knowledge, submissiveness, friendliness and an attractive appearance. Shop assistants are expected to possess these characteristics, to dress in a business-like manner and to wear their make-up in a particular way, with more stringent expectations for women selling cosmetics. Broadbridge argues that these characteristics are fundamental in the construction of the female shop assistant as an essential ingredient of the consumer package. She argues that a sexual element also characterizes the relationship between shop assistants and customers. Sexual harassment of female assistants by male customers was frequently reported but the women believed that they had to grin and bear it. Expectations and responses to assistants vary according to gender, with customers tending to behave more respectfully to male assistants.

Case Study

### Masculinity and the military

David Morgan (1994b) points out that meanings about femininity and masculinity in the labour market are not uniform. Focusing on masculinity he argues that there are a range of meanings within organizations and in different occupations. The military is an example where masculinity is most directly 'constructed, reproduced and deployed'. The warrior/soldier is a key symbol of masculinity and is associated with 'aggression, courage, a capacity for violence, and, sometimes, a willingness for sacrifice. The uniform absorbs individualities into a generalized and timeless masculinity while also connoting a control of emotion and a subordination to a larger rationality' (Morgan 1994b: 166). The organization is designed to produce a particular notion of masculinity; training entails the actual disciplining of the body, control, subject to danger and physical deprivation and military culture contains entrenched sexism, racism and homophobia. Yet Morgan points out that even in this organization there is a complex range of masculinities. The military is a hierarchical organization: at different levels group solidarities develop, perhaps around race and class, and there may be resistance to official models of masculinity and conflicts between masculinities. The increasing entrance of women into the military upsets the association of only the masculine with armies and the soldier. He stresses that battle and war themselves also provide 'the opportunity for the display of other characteristics more conventionally associated with the feminine than the masculine'. There is a whole body of literature which demonstrates care for others, fear and grief experienced by soldiers involved in war.

**Q** Consider the different kinds of work in a restaurant, a shop, an office and a school. What jobs are performed mainly by women and mainly by men? If they are performing a similar or the same job do they perform them in different ways? What are the expectations for female and male workers in these areas of work?

## Sexuality

Sex is everywhere you look, on television, in magazines, and on advertising billboards selling everything from cars to ice cream. This cultural obsession with sex has been reflected in a considerable and diverse sociology of sexuality; we can only touch on some key debates here. Feminists and lesbian and gay theorists have argued that sex is a political phenomenon tied up with power relations. Feminists have been keen to analyse sexual relations and their implications for women and women's oppression.

### Surveying sex

Considering the public interest, there is limited large-scale social research on sexual activity. Until the publication of *Sexual Behaviour in Britain* (Wellings *et al.* 1994) anyone who wanted information about human sexual behaviour based on large-scale research had to look to the work of Kinsey *et al.* (1948, 1953) or Masters and Johnson (1966, 1970). The 1994 study was more extensive and more characteristic of the general population than the Kinsey study. The sample of 18,876 people interviewed was representative of the British population in terms of social class, education, ethnic background, age and region. The survey produced a vast amount of descriptive information about reported sexual behaviour. It also raised a whole range of methodological issues concerning the study of sexual behaviour. For example the survey found that six in every hundred men said they had had some homosexual experience in their lives. Some gay activists have stressed that these numbers may be an underestimation because respondents questioned about 'partners' may have counted only long-term relationships. They also said that the home interviews used by the researchers would have lead to an under estimation, as 'Closeted Gays are unlikely to admit their homosexuality to a total stranger who turns up on their door and asks them personal questions about the intimate details of their private life' (Peter Tatchell, quoted in I Katz, 'Rights Group scorn one in 90 gay survey', *Guardian* 22 January 1994).

Despite media which often seem saturated with sexual imagery, sex as a serious topic of conversation is still taboo in many contexts. This is exacerbated by powerful discourses which construct only certain expressions of sexual desire and behaviour as normal and acceptable. Hence some gay, lesbian and bisexual individuals may not feel able to come out in a homophobic society. This creates difficulties for social researchers as many people may not want to talk about their sexual experiences or may not feel able to talk openly or honestly about them.

**Q** Why do you think there has been limited research on sexual behaviour? If you were asked to research patterns of sexual behaviour among the British public what methods would you use?

**Fig 7.3** Coming out: a gay and lesbian demonstration, London. (Courtesy of Robert Harding Picture Library Ltd.)

## Normal sex?

Sexuality is often defined as a natural instinct or drive which is part of the biological make-up of each individual and demands fulfilment through sexual activity. This view of sexuality as a natural biological entity is referred to as *essentialism*. Much essential thinking links sex as a natural instinct to reproductive activity. Weeks (1986) points out that in this approach there is a clear link between biological sex/gender and sexuality:

**Modern culture has assumed an intimate connection between the fact of being biologically male or female (that is having appropriate sex organs and reproductive potentialities) and the correct form of erotic behaviour (usually genital intercourse between men and women).** ***(Weeks 1986: 13)***

This view leads to a distinction between the sexual needs and desires of men and women; men are defined as having a stronger sex drive than women and a natural tendency to promiscuity. According to this discourse human sexuality is rooted in biology, and a normal sex drive is a heterosexual drive intended for procreation. Any deviation is considered to be pathological. Thus lesbian, gay and bisexual women and men have been defined as deviant, unnatural, perverse and not real women or men.

**We learn very early on from many sources that 'natural' sex is what takes place with members of the 'opposite sex. 'Sex' between people of the same 'sex' is therefore, by definition, 'unnatural'.** ***(Weeks 1986: 13)***

Heterosexuality is the norm in this model for both women and men, and sex is properly expressed in stable, monogamous, ideally marital relationships.

A key critic of essentialism has been Jeffrey Weeks, who rejects any approach that does not consider the social and historical forces that shape sexuality and which does not acknowledge the diversity of sexual identity and desire. He rejects the idea that there is a true essence of sex, an 'uninformed pattern' which is 'ordained by nature itself' (Weeks 1986: 15). He argues that it is simplistic to reduce a complex pattern of sexual relations and identities to biological factors.

## Constructing sex

There are a whole body of theorists who agree that our sexual desires may seem to be natural yet our sexual responses and identities are actually socially constructed. We learn not only patterns of behaviour but also meanings attached to such behaviour. Our sexual feelings, activities, the ways in which we think about sexuality and our sexual identities are all the product of social and historical forces. Sexuality is shaped by the culture in which we live; religious teachings, laws, psychological theory, medical definitions, social policies and the media all inform us of its meaning. This does not mean that biology has no influence: limits are imposed by the body and we experience different things depending on whether we have a vagina or a penis. Yet the body and its anatomical structure and physiology does not directly determine what we do or the meaning this may have. The body gains certain meanings only in particular social contexts. Different parts of the body can be defined in different ways. For example in the 1960s a new cultural context emerged with liberal attitudes that supported sexual liberation for women: the 'G-spot' was discovered, books were published and classes held to help women explore their bodies and find the G-spot; the physical anatomy of women was the same as before but it had a different social significance. This particular part of the body was given sexual meaning and this constructs desire.

**All the constituent elements of sexuality have their source either in the body or the mind, and I am not attempting to deny the limits posed by biology or mental processes. But the capacities of the body are given meaning only in social relations.**

***(Weeks 1986: 15)***

### *Foucault and discourse theory*

Michel Foucault (1981) has been very influential on the social constructionalist position. He argued that there was no one truth about sex and that various discourses – law, religion, in particular medicine and psychiatry – have produced a particular view of the body and its pleasures, a set of bodily sensations, pleasures, feelings and actions which we call sexual desire. It is these discourses which shape our sexual values and beliefs and meanings attached to the body. Sex is not some biological entity governed by natural laws, but an idea specific to certain cultures and historical periods. Sex and how we make sense of it is created through definition and in particular the creation of categories such as heterosexual and homosexual, lesbian and so on.

Weeks, like Foucault, stresses that sexual identities are historically shaped. He has been concerned with the ways in which sexuality generally and homosexuality in particular has been shaped in a complex and ever changing history over the past 100 years. He cites his influences as feminists, lesbian and gay activists and Foucault. His hypothesis is that the sexual categories that we take for granted, that map the horizons of the possible and which seem so 'natural' and secure and inevitable are actually historical and social labels. He has stressed that it is important to study the history of sexuality in order to understand the range of possible identities, based on class, ethnicity, gender sexual preference. He argues it is reductionalist to reduce the complexities of reality to an essentialist biological truth. Sexual identity is not achieved just by an act of individual act or will or discovered in the recesses of the soul.

Both heterosexuality and homosexuality are, then, social constructions. Some writers have pointed out that there is no essential homosexual experience, that gay history is complex and the experience of being homosexual varies. Indeed the use of the term 'homosexual' to describe a certain type of person is a relatively recent phenomenon (Foucault 1977; Weeks 1990); in many historical periods a woman who had sex with another woman would not think of herself or be regarded as lesbian.

## Sexual desire and gender

The work of Foucault, although recognized as very important by feminists, has also been criticized for not paying enough attention to the way gender influences sexual desire and identity. Many researchers have argued that men and women have different attitudes to sex and relationships. Shire Hite (1981) has examined men and women's sexual behaviour and attitudes to sex. She claimed that although men were diverse in their feelings, attitudes and sexual experience, they were more likely than women to claim that their sense of self-identification was gained through sex.

### *Male sexuality: power and anxiety*

Brittan (1989) proposes that in masculine ideology real men are heterosexual, sexually active, initiators of sexual relations and have a powerful sex drive. Many theorists have argued that men's sexual identity is in some way shaped by masculine ideology. Sexuality has been defined as important to male gender identity because within this ideology genital sex has been a way of confirming masculinity. For Metcalf and Humpries (1985) this identity involves performance and conquest as sex becomes another area in which men feel that they have to prove themselves. Seidler (1989) suggests that if a man has not had sex with a woman there is a great deal of pressure on him to pretend that he has had sex to prove his masculinity; sex and masculinity are inextricably linked. Seidler (1991) has stressed that the way men approach sex is often shaped by a dominant notion of masculinity: men should deny their emotions and feeling within relationships. As sexual relations are often intimate, men fear losing control of their feelings, feel uneasy and this may make them withdraw after sexual contact as a strategy to prevent emotions and feelings coming to the fore. Some theorists have stressed that for men sex is related to maintaining control, power and conquest. The key to being a true man in masculine ideology is being in control and exerting power; this applies in sexual relations.

Case Study

## Dominant masculinity and rape

Since the mid-1970s feminists have drawn attention to the high levels of violence that women experience at the hands of men. Kelly (1988) found that most women have experienced some form of sexual violence; she identified a continuum of violence, from verbal harassment to rape and murder, which she argues acts to instil fear and control women.

To explain rape feminists have turned their attention to the broader context of unequal gender relations, the social construction of masculinity and a culture which condones violence against women. Some theorists have directly linked the construction of dominant masculinity and male sexuality to violence against women, including rape. The view that, for men, sexual expression is linked to conquest and maintaining power and control, has been utilized to understand the violence women experience on men. A recurring theme in the analysis of male sexuality is that as part of their socialization men learn to separate sex from emotion, that they must be dominant in sexual relations and that they learn to see women as sexual objects to please men.

Rape is understood as an act which exerts power over and controls and disempowers the victim. Rape acts to keep women in their place. A key point Brownmiller (1976) made was that rape is not purely a sexual act, where the rapist derives sexual pleasure, but an act of power designed to control and humiliate. In this type of approach rape is not a biological drive or a purely sexually motivated act, it is an act of aggression and hostility and it flourishes where cultures encourage it.

Feminists have also pointed out that in many cultures women are sexually objectified and this objectification has been crucial in the legitimization of the sexual abuse of women by men. The ability to distance oneself from the person involved in the sexual encounter, to objectify the other person, to ignore the needs of the other and meet one's own desires are key features of an abusive relationship. John Stolenberg identifies objectification as part of the process that leads to violence: 'The depersonalization that begins in sexual objectification is what makes violence possible for once made a person a thing, you can do anything to it you want' (Stolenberg 1990: 59). This focus on violence emphasizes male sexuality as a source of power. However, some researchers point out that male sexual identity is diverse and that sex can be an area of anxiety (Seidler 1991).

### *Female sexuality: pleasure and pain*

A key feminist demand has been the right for women to have freedom of sexual expression and choice; implicit in this is an assumption that female sexual expression has been more tightly controlled than men's and that women have had less power in sexual relations. Although research in the 1990s suggests that young women are taking more control in heterosexual relationships and making greater demands, it seems that women and men are still caught up in power relations.

Many have argued that there is an enduring sexual double standard whereby men are judged positively if they engage in sexual encounters, whereas women are judged negatively. Sue Lees (1986, 1993) in her interviews with young adolescent girls found evidence of this double standard in the 1980s and 1990s. Young girls who got a reputation for 'sleeping' with men would be labelled 'slags', whereas girls who got a reputation for not engaging in sexual relations were labelled 'tight', 'drags' or 'lessies'. Lees argues that this verbal abuse not only demonstrates the sexual double standard but also serves as one way of controlling female sexuality.

Many feminists agree that gendered power relations are found within heterosexual relationships and these needed to be challenged. Women have been exploited within sexual relationships and experienced a great deal of sexual abuse, they had less power and control in sexual relationships, sex has been centred around vaginal intercourse, male pleasure and specifically male orgasm. Some theorists stress that the way sexual relations have been institutionalized through heterosexuality has served to control and oppress not only lesbian, gay and bisexual men and women but all women. For some individuals, heterosexuality and the social relations that accompany it (such as marriage) have been crucial to the persistence of male dominance. Other theorists have explored the complexities of women's experiences of both the pleasures and dangers of sex. They have rejected theories which define all women as sexually passive and men as sexual aggressors.

## Summary

- The sociology of gender has been developed by feminist writers concerned with how gender differentiation has meant the subordination of one sex, women, who have been assigned certain gender characteristics and roles. Gender is socially constructed. Both men and women are gendered beings.
- The media have constructed meanings about femininity and masculinity and can shape people's gender identities. Some theorists identify magazines as a vehicle for promoting conventional and oppressive meanings about gender, others point to a more complex range of messages about femininity and masculinity. People read magazines in different ways and construct different meanings.
- Some progress towards equality for women, in the household and in the labour market, has been achieved but inequality persists. Gender ideologies still structure labour market choices and opportunities for women and men. The labour market is a site where meanings about femininity and masculinity are constructed and reinforced.
- Gender is a crucial social factor in producing adequate explanations of social behaviour and the organization of social institutions. Gender relations have been researched in all areas of social experience. This is reflected in the fact that many chapters in this book consider gender; and perhaps one day there won't be a separate chapter such as this one in sociology textbooks – if gender distinctions and divisions are eroded and gender studies becomes fully integrated into sociology.

## Further reading

Anthias, F and Yuval-Davis, N (1993) *Racialized Boundaries: Race, Nation, Gender, Colour, Class and the Anti-Racist Struggle*, London: Routledge.

This book considers how race interacts with gender among other factors to shape social experience. It summarizes Black feminist criticisms of much feminist theory and explores the relationship between gender, race, class and nation.

Bem, S (1993) *The Lenses of Gender*, New Haven, CT: Yale University Press.

Sandra Bem is a pioneering writer within gender studies; she addresses fundamental questions about the causes of gender differences, reviewing a whole range of approaches and proposing her own perspective which stresses the cultural construction and imposition of gender distinctions.

Brod, H and Kaufman, M (1994) *Theorizing Masculinity*, London: Sage.

This collection of papers, written by some key writers on masculinity, spans a range of diverse topics which include a variety of approaches to theorizing masculinity.

Edley, N and Wetherell, M (1994) *Men in Perspective*, London: Havester Wheatsheaf.

A very readable and accessible overview of research and theories on men and masculinities which provides a good introduction to the study of men and masculinities.

*Polity Reader in Gender Studies* (1994) Cambridge: Polity.

This collection of extracts from key texts on gender relations is structured into three sections relating to theory, work and identity, and sexuality and power. The book gives a taster of the work of some key writers and debates.

Richardson, D and Robinson, V (1993) *Introducing Women's Studies: Feminist Theory and Practice*, London: Macmillan.

A comprehensive introductory text with chapters on a wide range of areas of women's experience, including feminist theory, education, history, motherhood, health, work, family, representation and popular culture, sexuality and violence. Each chapter outlines and summarizes key research, debates and theories.

Sharpe, S (1994) *Just Like a Girl*, 2nd edn, Harmondsworth: Penguin.

An updated version of Sharpe's 1976 study of how girls learn to be women, this text provides an insight into the social construction of femininity and the changing experience of growing up female in Britain.

Walby, S (1990) *Theorizing Patriarchy*, Oxford: Blackwell.

As well as developing her own feminist analysis of gender relations and women's subordination, Walby reviews a range of approaches to gender relations and divisions in paid employment, household production, the state, culture, violence and sexuality.

Weeks, J (1986) *Sexuality*, London: Tavistock.

A useful introduction to various approaches to sexuality, sexual desire and identity written by one of the key British writers in the field of sexuality and gay and lesbian studies.

## Activities

### ■ Activity 1 Women's and men's magazines

Select three or more magazines – at least one that is seen as a woman's magazine and one as a man's (and you might include one magazine you read and one you have never looked at).

What does the title communicate? What about the cover?

Look at the checklist below – what topics does the magazine feature?

Beauty/make-up/personal grooming
Fashion
Fitness
DIY and home décor
Cookery/food
Politics and social issues
Feminism and women's rights
Personal relationships
Sex
Others (please list)
People (a) ordinary (b) celebrities
Paid work/careers
Parenting
Sport
Offers/competitions
Fiction
Holidays/travel
Consumer items
Sewing/craft work

What written style does the magazine adopt – chatty, racy, investigative or serious?

What type of reader do you think the magazine is addressed to? (Consider age, socio-economic status, etc.)

What would you say are the key interests and concerns of the people who read the selected magazines?

What messages about femininity and masculinity are communicated in this magazine? Is there one particular ideology that you can identify or are there varying discourses about femininity and masculinity?

Carry out an interview with a woman and a man who read one of the magazines. Why do they read it? Do they agree with all the features? Are they critical of any aspects of the magazine?

### ■ Activity 2 Personalizing gender

Write your own autobiography focusing on gender relations and how they have affected your life.

Among other areas and aspects of your life you might consider (a) relations with and between family members; (b) the importance of gender relations at significant stages of or events in your life – births, weddings, going to new schools, joining clubs, starting work and so on.

How did gender influence your schooling, the jobs you have done or are hoping to do, your leisure pursuits – what you do and what you would like to do?

Chapter 8

# Race

**Chapter outline:** Introduction • Modern Britain: a crisis of identity? • Theories of 'race' • Theories of racism • Immigration to Britain since 1945 • Racial inequality in Britain • Ethnicity • Nationalism • Summary • Further reading • Activities

**Learning objectives**

When you have studied this chapter you should be able to address these key questions:

- What are the main sociological theories of race and racism?
- How do the employment, housing and educational experiences of ethnic minorities differ from those of the white population in Britain? What explanations are there for such differences?
- How does policing of Black communities differ from policing of white communities?
- To what extent have Jewish migrants to Britain been 'racialized'?

## Introduction

The irony of 'race theories' is that they arise almost invariably from a desire to mould others' actions rather than to explain facts. (Barzun 1937: 284)

Imagine a world in which people are classified and graded according to eye colour. Those with brown eyes enjoy proportionately better housing, employment conditions, education and social status. Those with blue eyes are frequently, though not exclusively, marginalized in political life, absent from high-status occupations, and are portrayed in the media as problems that the brown-eyed population has to, at best, tolerate. Blue-eyed people protest about the treatment they receive from the brown-eyed population, but are disillusioned by the bias they see in the institutions and political laws of the land; even their protests are defined by politicians and newspapers in negative terms. The situation seems hopeless, though there are moves within the blue-eyed communities to resist and challenge this discrimination.

Such a situation seems absurd and fantastical; no society, surely, would organize itself according to something as trivial and unimportant as eye colour. Yet if we replace the word 'eye' with 'skin' and the adjectives blue/brown with black/white, the descriptions in the passage start to take on meaning and relevance. Even when physical difference would appear to have little relevance in defining the way that people are classified – for example, with the Jewish population and with the citizens of the former Yugoslavia – racial and ethnic prejudices shape how we see, and consequently treat, other people.

**It is a mark of the highly contested nature of the word 'race' that its status in social theory still remains the subject of controversy.**

***(Brah 1994: 806)***

The treatment of people according to perceived differences of class, sex, religion or age forms the basis of much sociological analysis and debate and the concept of 'race' has long been recognized as an important factor in social interaction but one which is extremely difficult to define. Yet whatever the problems of defining such terms as 'race', 'racism' and 'ethnicity' (which we shall address later) there can be no doubt that the issues connected with these ideas have a real and profound effect on people's lives on a daily basis. They experience racist violence and discrimination, they have to endure racist taunts and to cope with a society in which they are often portrayed as 'other', as inferior, different, threatening, 'not British'. There is also a more positive side to 'race', a sense of identity and pride which for example might be reflected for people of African descent in the emergence of Black Studies (see pp. 357–8). But it can be difficult to appreciate when people belonging to ethnic minorities often struggle to get a good education, a job or even adequate housing.

## Modern Britain: a crisis of identity

Much of the discrimination which members of ethnic minorities experience stems from the prejudice that they are not properly 'British' but as Cohen (1994) illustrates in his book *Frontiers of Identity: The British and the Others* the construction of the British identity has been a long and complex one:

**Multiple axes of identification have meant that Irish, Scots, Welsh and English people, those from the white, black or brown Commonwealth, Americans, English-speakers and even 'aliens' have had their lives intersect one with another in overlapping and complex circles of identity-construction and rejection. The shape and edges of the British identity are thus historically changing, often vague, and to a degree, malleable.** *(Cohen 1994: 35)*

Q

Imagine you have to describe yourself to someone who hasn't met you and doesn't know your name: (a) which words or phrases would you use? (b) in what order (most important first) would you put them?

Did you mention the colour of your skin?

One of the most widely believed myths which has contributed to a climate of prejudice and discrimination is that the Black presence in Britain dates no further back than the 1950s and post-war immigration from the Caribbean. In fact there have been Black people in England for hundreds of years and in the eighteenth century there were as many as 20,000 who came as seamen or as the children, slaves and servants of returning planters and colonial administrators. Far from all being dependent on their white masters, a significant proportion were successful and independent, enjoying their own social scene in London of balls, parties and concerts (Gerzina 1995). During the eighteenth and nineteenth centuries Black communities grew up in many of Britain's western seaports, especially those connected with the slave trade such as Bristol, Cardiff and Liverpool. Many Black people fought (and died) for Britain in both world wars, as did Asians and Jews.

Case Study

## The Wonderful Adventures of Mary Seacole

Mary Jane Seacole (née Grant) was born in Kingston, Jamaica, in 1805 of a Scottish father and a Jamaican mother. During her Jamaican upbringing she acquired the knowledge of traditional Creole medicine which had evolved from the herbal medicine that slaves had brought with them from Africa. In the boarding house which her mother ran Mary developed her medical skills which were much in demand from European naval and military personnel stationed in Jamaica. In 1840 she embarked by herself on travels which took her first to Central America where her medical reputation was further enhanced by her success in dealing with cholera and yellow fever epidemics. In 1854 she volunteered to assist the British army fighting in Crimea. Despite official rebuttals she set up on her own initiative a 'British Hotel' where she both nursed the sick and provided food for healthy soldiers. She won many admirers for her courage in going into the field of battle to attend the wounded. All her efforts were entirely self-financed and in the end the war bankrupted her. She was rescued from debt by a high profile campaign in her support in London. In 1857 her account of her travels in Central America and the Crimea, published under the title, *The Wonderful Adventures of Mary Seacole in Many Lands*, became a bestseller. She died in 1881 in west London.

### Question

Why do you think Mary Seacole is not as well known today as Florence Nightingale?

It is important to see Britain's current race relations problems in a historical context because as Fryer (1991) points out in his book on *Black People in the British Empire*:

> **There is no more significant pointer to the character of British society than the exclusion of Black people from our history books . . . Without knowing something about black history we can neither understand the world of today nor see the way forward to the world of tomorrow . . . By disguising or glorifying the true history of colonialism, and by writing black people out of British history, the official historians have marginalised and thus further oppressed those whose history they have distorted or concealed. Their distortions and omissions have had the clear purpose of maintaining the existing power structure.** *(Fryer 1991: 11–13)*

Though writing about Black people in this instance, Fryer's argument could just as easily be applied to Jews, Asians, Irish and many others who have all contributed to the multiracial and multicultural nature of Britain but have been equally marginalized and discriminated against. As Miles (1993) has reminded us, racism against Black people has long coexisted with racism against Irish and Jewish people.

**Case Study**

### Racism, nationalism and anti-semitism: the Jewish experience

Though there had been Jewish communities in Britain for many hundreds of years the nineteenth century saw a massive influx into Britain of Jews from eastern Europe and Russia – a wave of migration which was exceeded only by the numbers of immigrants from Ireland after the potato famine of the 1840s. Those Jews who arrived in Britain during the late nineteenth century were mainly agricultural workers who sought to escape a combination of economic deprivation and persecution, while those who came in the 1930s were mainly middle-class professionals escaping persecution under the Nazi regime – approximately 50,000 Jews came to Britain between 1933 and 1939 and a further 10,000 arrived during the Second World War (Holmes 1988: 119,163).

Towards the end of the nineteenth century the racialization of Jewish migration manifested itself with calls for limits on the number of immigrants allowed into the country and Jews were signified as a 'degenerate' race. 'Jewishness' was portrayed as a 'quality determined by blood' (Miles 1993: 135) and was thought to encourage criminal activity, venereal disease and sexual perversion (Gainer 1972: 46-5). This ideology which portrayed Jews as a 'degenerate' race treated the Jewish bourgeoisie (who were mainly British subjects) and the Jewish working class (who were mainly immigrants) as equal threats to 'civilized' society, with the Jewish bourgeoisie using their capital to buy control and the working classes threatening revolution.

In the 1920s, Karl Pearson, a professor of human biology prominent in the Eugenics Movement (see p. 226), claimed that the 'national stock' had been adulterated by the influx of an 'alien race', the Jews, who he claimed were both physically and mentally inferior to the indigenous population. Though there was no scientific evidence for his claims they were frequently cited by fascist organizations in Britain during the 1930s:

> Thus for the 1870s through to 1939, the idea of 'race' was central to the signification of Jews in Britain as a distinct and alien population... Moreover the final solution was legitimised by the theory of biological inferiority. ( Miles 1993: 139 )

Contemporary British racism is often explained as the legacy of a colonial history which could justify itself only by the assertion of the biological inferiority of Black people but, as Miles points out, the economic and social circumstances of Jews in the nineteenth and twentieth centuries cannot be understood in terms of colonialism or the reification of skin colour (Miles 1990). So we must ask ourselves what is racism and the ideas of race it is founded on.

## Theories of race

### Pseudo-scientific theories of race

The attempt to classify *Homo sapiens* into distinct biological types corresponding to racial groupings can be traced back at least as far as the nineteenth century and is in part a legacy of the Enlightenment – an intellectual movement of the eighteenth century which sought to apply rational and 'scientific' methods to all areas of human experience. The French anatomist George Cuvier and his associate Charles Hamilton Smith sought to link physical differences to distinct temperaments and the Comte de Gobineau in the 1850s attempted not only to describe the differences between groups of people but also to explain them by dividing all of humankind into three distinct groups – 'white', 'black' and 'yellow'. He believed that these three groups had specific racially determined, cultural characteristics so that whites had superior intellects, Blacks were mystical and the 'yellow races' were cunning and sly.

Michael Banton (1987) identified three main types of theories which classify human beings in terms of different biological or racial groups:

1 Race as lineage
The idea of race as lineage originated from Christianity and the belief that all human beings are descended from Adam and Eve. After the expulsion from Paradise and various other disasters such as the Flood, humans were scattered across the globe which resulted in distinctive lineages or races. These races developed physical characteristics which corresponded to their geographical environments. As Banton says, the message was 'each people was adapted to its own environment and therefore should stay where they were'.

2 Race as type
The theory of race as type was based on the belief that racial differences had occurred from earliest times and were either the result of a natural catastrophe or an act of God. These ideas were developed especially in North America resulting in Nott and Gliddon's *Types of Mankind* (published in Philadelphia in 1854) which asserted not only that there were also different types of human beings which behaved differently from one another but also that these groups were naturally antagonistic to one another.

3 Race as subspecies
This theory combining elements of the other two originated with the work of Charles Darwin and the publication of *On the Origin of Species* in 1859 in which he explained the differences between humans with the theory of evolution. According to this theory humankind is a species which through a process of natural

selection has developed from a common origin into a number of distinct subspecies or races which are constantly evolving to adapt most effectively to their environment – the survival of the fittest. 'Social Darwinism' also encompassed the idea that certain subspecies or races were less developed and therefore inferior to others according to a classification system elaborated by Herbert Spencer, an English sociologist of the nineteenth century (Andreski 1971).

**Case Study**

### Biology as destiny

Contemporary socio-biology is in many ways a modern reworking of some of the ideas of Social Darwinism. The work of writers such as Desmond Morris (1968, 1977), Konrad Lorenz (1965, 1973) and Richard Dawkins (1976, 1977) can be seen as representing a resurgence of theories which attempt to explain the world through reference to genetic variations which shape personality traits and social behaviour. Socio-biology sees a propensity to hostility and violence between humans who look 'different' from one another (as formerly in South Africa for example) as rooted in genetic structures which act as fixed determinants of behaviour. Richard Dawkins, a prominent socio-biologist, argues that:

> Conceivably, racial prejudice could be interpreted as an irrational generalisation of a kin-selected tendency to identify with individuals physically resembling oneself and to be nasty to individuals different in appearance. (Dawkins 1976: 108)

### Questions

Socio-biology could be seen as providing a 'scientific' or 'rational' explanation for the existence of racist beliefs, and, most importantly, for hostile and racist behaviour. What do you think are the dangers involved in explaining racist violence in this way?

## The limitations of race as biology

Such biological theories of race seek to link *genotype* – the underlying genetic differences between groups of people – with *phenotype* – physical characteristics such as skin or hair colour which are a result of the interaction between genotypes and the environment. Rapid advances in genetic science, however, make this increasingly problematic. According to Steve Jones (1991), a leading geneticist who has reappraised biological theories of race in the light of these advances, there is no genetic justification for distinguishing different races even though there are genetic differences between groups of human beings. We know that human beings are the product of as many as 50,000 genes (sometimes described as the building blocks of the human organism) but changes in fewer than ten genes determine skin colour and there is far greater genetic diversity (about 85 per cent of those variations which occur) between individuals from the same country than there is between countries within the same continent (about 10–15 per cent):

**The overall genetic differences between 'races' – Africans and Europeans, say – is no greater than that between different countries within Europe or within Africa. Individuals – not nations and not races – are the main repository of human variation.**
*(Jones 1991, quoted in Haralambos and Holborn 1995: 656)*

Jones goes on to say that there can be no scientific basis for genetic or biological theories of race and that 'much of the history of the genetics of race – a field promoted by some eminent scientists – turns out to have been prejudice dressed up as science'. This leads us inevitably to wonder why such ideas were so widespread and so popular for so long and it is difficult to escape the conclusion that not only did they bring with them a comforting sense of innate superiority but also they legitimized the process of colonial expansion of the nineteenth and early twentieth centuries, a process which often had disastrous consequences for the people being colonized.

## The social construction of race

As mentioned earlier there is considerable debate about the definition of the concept and indeed the use of the word 'race'. While most sociologists would reject the scientific validity of the concept of 'race' there is a recognition that the widespread belief in the idea of 'race' and its influence on the way people interact justifies its use as a social category:

**Social categories depend for their existence on the subjective definition given to them by social actors. Race is no exception. So long as it exists in the minds of men [*sic*] there will be race relations problems to study.** *(Rex 1970: 192)*

There have been a number of attempts to explain the continuing use of the concept of 'race' in a social context which draw on social psychological theories of group behaviour and personal stereotypes and prejudices. Of the more explicitly sociological theories it is worth examining the theory of race relations and Marxist and neo-Marxist theories of race and racism.

## Race relations

The race relations perspective attempts to explain the different treatment accorded to ethnic minorities in their relations with the rest of society. Analysis focuses on situations in which members of minorities are defined by their distinctive identities and social treatment (Rex 1970: 160) and this is generally at least in part defined by their status as immigrants. Thus society is seen at certain points in time as racially stratified and 'disfavouring' certain races in the allocation of housing, employment opportunities and education provision. As Miles (1989) points out, the problem with the race relations approach is that it leads to a situation in which the minority group is inevitably classified as 'racially disadvantaged' with social action directed towards helping the 'victim(s)' overcome the conditions associated with their racial status. The race relations model has frequently been applied in the field of social policy and in government legislation and has been adopted by the media when reporting incidents such as inner city riots involving Black youths. However, though it ostensibly recognizes the social factors which contribute to race conflict and discrimination, it can also be interpreted in such a way that it leads to a 'blame the victim' attitude:

> **Difficulty in race relations arises from the speed of the arrival of immigrants and their concentration in certain areas. This has led to social changes being imposed on the people already living in those areas, who perhaps find it hard to accept them.**
>
> ***(Reginald Maudling 1971, quoted in Miles and Phizacklea 1984: 73)***

### Neo-Marxist accounts of race and racial discrimination

While Marxism has, for theorists such as Cedric Robinson (1983) and Paul Gilroy (1987, 1993a), been equated with Eurocentric, economistic accounts of Black experiences, the accounts examined in this section do represent genuine attempts to explain patterns of inequality in society through reference to social and economic factors. In short, Marxist theories of racial discrimination move away from a concern with physical differences and innate personality traits, towards an investigation of the relations between racist beliefs and the capitalist social system.

In addressing Marxist theories of race and racism, we can see how many accounts in this tradition see racist practices and beliefs as both the product of the capitalist class system while having the function of reinforcing capitalist class relations (see e.g. Cox 1970; Wallerstein 1983). Such accounts take the concept of class as their starting-point with racial oppression defined as a tool of the 'capitalist' classes. In dividing the Black worker from the white, through racist beliefs and discriminatory practices, the working class is conceptualized as effectively split in two and a Black 'underclass' created.

Writers such as Cox (1970) and Wolpe (1980) address (through reference to the systems of slavery and apartheid, respectively) what they see as an intrinsically economic motive for the creation and application of racist beliefs. In the case of the former, the supply and exploitation of Black labour is understood as stemming not simply from racist attitudes, but from a combination of demographic and economic forces (Mintz 1974). That beliefs about the intrinsic inferiority of Blackness were mobilized to explain and legitimize the exploitation of African slaves is not denied but the priority of economic motives and practices retains a primary role.

How, then, might Marxist accounts of race explain the continued disadvantages faced by the Black population in Britain today? While race and racism are perceived to be important factors in explaining the specific type of discrimination encountered by Black and Asian people in the labour market, it is the nature of the capitalist accumulation process that is of primary importance. For Marxists, capitalism exploits the worker regardless of race or gender: it is only when supply of labour exceeds demand that exclusionary practices which draw on racism may occur (Miles 1989: 128; Fevre 1984).

Contemporary Marxist theories of race and racism are useful in addressing the relation between racist beliefs, practice, and the broader social structure. Where the contributions of Marxism are not so clear is in relation to the apparently autonomous and independent nature of racist beliefs. In defining racism as shaped by economic forces, the potential of racist practices themselves to shape economics is not considered in any depth. Furthermore, the continued expression of racist beliefs by employers and workers which are to the detriment of the capitalist system through encouraging rioting and conflict is difficult to explain (Sivanandan 1990).

### Neo-Marxism and the new racism

A number of sociologists based in the Centre for Contemporary Cultural Studies in Birmingham developed a neo-Marxist approach to race and racism in *The Empire Strikes Back* (1982). In it they argued that racism predated colonialism and was shaped by a variety of historical and political factors as well as economics. They believed that it was important to take into account the part played by ethnic minorities in resisting and challenging racism and that the nature of racism was not fixed but dynamic and constantly changing. They also identified a new form of racism which was not centred on the biological superiority and inferiority of different 'races' but saw the different cultures of Afro-Caribbean and Asian immigrants as a threat to the 'British' way of life. According to this view, being truly 'British' was a question not simply of citizenship but of embracing 'British' culture and values.

Paul Gilroy, who was one of this group, developed these ideas further in *There Ain't No Black in the Union Jack* (1987). Gilroy sought to examine 'race' and ethnicity in conjunction through his theory of race formation, a process by which groups continually redefine themselves and organize themselves around ideas of race.

## Theories of racism

Although there is much discussion in sociology textbooks of the difficulties involved in defining racism, there is no shortage of definitions available including the psychological theories of the Frankfurt School and Marxist theories of institutionalized racism. The concept of *racism* refers to beliefs and social practices which draw directly or indirectly upon the belief that there are racial groups which have distinct physical or cultural characteristics which are usually but not exclusively defined in negative terms. John Solomos defines it as

> **those ideologies and social processes which discriminate against others on the basis of their putatively different racial membership.** ***(quoted in Haralambos and Holborn 1995: 689)***

While Giddens describes a racist as

> **someone who believes that a biological explanation can be given for characteristics of superiority or inferiority supposedly possessed by people of a given physical stock.** ***(Giddens 1993a: 255)***

One distinction which it is helpful to make is that between racial prejudice – the holding of racist views and beliefs – and racial discrimination – the unfavourable treatment of a person or persons because of their real or imagined membership of a particular 'race'. Different theoretical perspectives have attempted to explain racial discrimination in, for example, the areas of housing, education and employment by focusing on specific aspects of racism such as beliefs and values or social practices and in the following sections we shall look at these areas of discrimination in greater detail. In considering the most extreme form of discrimination – racist violence – however, it is not possible to make this distinction between beliefs and action:

**A vast majority of racist incidents are perpetrated by people not affiliated to any racist organisation, and without clear, elaborated (political/ideological) racist frameworks of thought. These incidents are racist, however, because the victim(s) are attacked because of the colour of their skin, or because of their alleged nationality, religion or colour.** *(Witte 1996: 11)*

What role does racism play in understanding racial discrimination in employment in Marxist accounts?

How would Marxism explain the different employment positions of Black and white workers? Which is the most important factor, class or 'race'?

Why do writers such as Robert Miles place inverted commas around 'race' and not class?

### Racism and the state: institutional accounts of 'race' discrimination

Political or state-centred accounts of racism derive in part from the Marxist theorization of race yet choose to focus in more detail on the covert incorporation of racist beliefs and attitudes into social and political policy. The existence and perpetuation of racial difference in the social structure is explained through reference to the effects of state policies which result in the exclusion of subordinate groups in society.

Described and defined in the writings of theorists such as Blauner (1972), Sivanandan (1982) and Hall *et al.* (1978), the notion of institutionalized racism reflects an attempt to move away from the individual as the focus of attention in understanding how racism works. To quote from Blauner:

**The processes that maintain domination – control of whites over non-whites – are built into the major social institutions thus there is little need for prejudice as a motivating force. Because this is true, the distinction between racism as an objective phenomenon, located in the actual existence of domination and hierarchy, and racism's subjective concomitants of prejudice and other motivations and feelings is a basic one.** *(Blauner 1972: 10)*

Drawing on a combination of racist sentiments, notions of Britishness and the nation-state, xenophobia and political strategy, British political policy since the post-war migration experience is defined by writers in this tradition as inherently racist in nature. Rejecting a common-sense race relations perspective, Miles and Phizacklea (1984), for example, examine the ways in which racism in the sphere of political policy defines Black people as a 'problem' in need of legislation. Through building such beliefs into policy directives and party political debate, while claiming that they represent the sentiments of the people, racism is covertly reproduced at the level of the state and the individual.

To take one example, Hall *et al.* (1978) considered how social problems such as crime and violence have become racialized through state and media discourses. In creating a moral panic around the myth of the 'Black mugger' in the 1970s, they argued that themes of immigration and personal safety became fused into one. Miles and Phizacklea, too, examine the strategic location of the threat to the (white) British citizen in discourses of race and culture, and address the role of the media in the institutionalization of racist explanations for manufactured social problems. Indeed, media representations of the muggings – which in fact constituted only 0.9 per cent of total recorded serious crimes in London in 1981 – can be seen as contributing to a social definition of a perceived problem in racial terms. Witness the *Daily Mail* on the crime problem in Handsworth:

> **All the sentenced youths are either coloured or immigrants and live in one of Birmingham's major problem areas. Police and social workers have been battling for years to solve community problems in Handsworth, where juvenile crime steadily worsens and there are continuous complaints about the relationship between the police and the predominantly coloured public.** ***(Daily Mail 21 March 1973)***

Texts and discourses of the state – specifically government inquiries – are described by Gilroy (1987) as in part reflecting the strength of the state institution to both define and solve what, exactly, constitutes the race problem. In this way, Gilroy sees the state as playing a crucial role in the reproduction of racial discrimination. In the Scarman report on the relation between crime, the police, and the community, the link between racial categorization and policy formation is striking:

> **Many agencies are equally responsible for the communal good and find themselves locked in conflict with black adolescents. I am sure that the solutions lie in the sharing of perceptions not only with these agencies but, more vitally, with those who have managed to gain the trust of the black teenager.** ***(Scarman 1982)***

In relating patterns of racial discrimination to an understanding of the role of the state, and state institutions, such accounts ascribe the state system a central role in the following social practices:

- the defining and racialization of social problems
- the development of social and political policy which reproduces racism through its location of Black people as the 'problem' and which inhibits the promotion of a genuinely anti-racist political agenda
- the reproduction of an institutional and structural framework which is strategically geared towards the privileging of a white, colonial experience (in, for example, the racist teaching of the Black culture in schools.

## Immigration to Britain since 1945: a study in race relations

The history of immigration to Britain since 1945 and the legislation which has been introduced both to control it and to cope with its perceived effects on British society provide a fascinating opportunity to examine ideas of structural racism and to look at the ways in which a climate is produced in which the racialization of social problems occurs. Though we do not have the space here to go into this history in the detail it deserves (and this has been done very adequately elsewhere: see further reading) one thing is apparent from a very quick glance at the legislation listed: there is considerably more legislation which curbs immigration than that designed specifically to improve race relations or reduce discrimination.

**Q** Why do you think this is? What do you think might be the main problems involved in drawing up legislation which promotes good race relations?

Case Study

## Legislating race

Some key Acts concerning immigration and race relations since the Second World War:

**British Nationality Act 1948**
Made a distinction between British subjects who were (a) citizens of the United Kingdom and (b) colonies and Commonwealth citizens but both groups retained the right to enter, settle and work in Britain. Citizens of the Republic of Ireland retained the right to unrestricted entry and settlement.

**Commonwealth Immigrants Act 1962**
Withdrew right of entry of all Commonwealth immigrants unless they (a) were born in the UK, (b) held UK passports issued by the government or (c) were included on the passport of someone exempted from immigration control under (a) or (b) (Macdonald 1983: 10–12). Effectively it distinguished between British citizens in general and those from the Caribbean and Asia. A voucher system was instituted for those who did not qualify, classifying people according to whether they already had a job or particular skills which the UK needed.

**Race Relations Act 1965**
Banned discrimination on grounds of 'race, colour or ethnic or national origin' in places of 'public resort' such as hotels, restaurants and public transport. It also made it illegal to incite racial hatred through speech or written word. The Act was criticized for failing to cover discrimination in the crucial areas of housing and employment and for being 'toothless': between 1965 and 1969 only fifteen cases went to court and of those five involved members of the Black Power movement (Witte 1996). The Race Relations Board set up in February 1966 established local centres for reporting discrimination but most of the complaints received proved to be outside its jurisdiction.

**Commonwealth Immigrants Act 1968**
All citizens of the UK or colonies with a British passport became subject to immigration controls unless they had one parent or grandparent born, naturalized or resident in Britain.

**Race Relations Act 1968**
Extended the provisions of the Race Relations Act 1965 to cover employment, housing, commercial and other services but still did not cover the police (who dealt with complaints internally) and though the Race Relations Board was given the power to institute legal proceedings it had to provide substantive evidence that discrimination had taken place.

**Immigration Act 1971**
All aliens or Commonwealth citizens who did not qualify under the terms of the Commonwealth Immigrants Act 1968 could now enter Britain only with a work permit which usually had to be renewed after twelve months. Unlike the voucher system, these permits did not grant permanent residency or the right of dependants to settle. Immigrants had the right to apply for citizenship after four years but the Home Secretary also and the right to deport anyone who might be seen as a threat to the public good. In effect it put Commonwealth citizens on a par with any other aliens who wanted to come into the UK.

*(box continued)*

*(box continued)*

**Race Relations Act 1976**
Made indirect discrimination illegal. This meant that if for example employers advertised a job stating that all applicants had to be born in the UK they could be charged with indirectly discriminating against members of ethnic minorities unless they could provide a reasonable justification for so advertising.

The Commission for Racial Inequality was established to promote racial harmony. It was given greater powers than its predecessors and has had some success initiating new legislation and exposing discrimination in a wide range of institutions as well as raising awareness of racial issues.

**British Nationality Act 1981**
Established three categories of UK and colonies citizens: (a) British citizens; (b) citizens of British dependent territories; (c) British overseas citizens. By stating that British citizenship could pass to children born overseas only if their parents were born in the UK it effectively discriminated against first generation settlers from Asia and the Caribbean. The Act also stated that people married to British citizens had to be resident in the UK for three years before they could apply for citizenship.

**Immigration Act 1988**
Took away the right of dependants of men who had settled in the UK before 1973 to join them unless there was proof that they would not be dependent on state benefits.

**Asylum and Immigration Act 1993**
Designed to streamline procedures and to eliminate so-called 'economic refugees'. In late 1995 Home Secretary Michael Howard promoted a Bill designed to streamline procedures further by introducing a 'white list' of countries presumed to be safe so that any appeal for asylum from a country on the list would automatically be rejected.

On examining this legislation in chronological order it becomes clear that irrespective of which party was in power, British policy towards immigration since 1962 has progressively diminished the right of entry and settlement in the UK of Commonwealth citizens and has consistently discriminated against Black and Asian people. Despite the passing of a number of Race Relations Acts designed to improve community relations the underlying assumption which this legislation is based on (and the often openly stated belief of policy-makers and politicians) was, and still is, that these community relations had become a problem only because too many Black immigrants had been 'let in' and were threatening the British way of life. It is of course impossible to know to what extent popular, common-sense perceptions of Black immigration as a threat influenced policy and to what extent the legislation which was passed confirmed these fears. Certainly politicians and the press did little to assuage people's concern that the Black immigrants coming in brought an alien culture with them which would undermine British traditions and values and that they would prove a drain on the newly created welfare state.

Case Study

## For their own sakes: stop them now!

The media played a significant role in establishing a link between social and economic deprivation and threats to law and order on the one hand, and the presence of the Black migrant communities on the other. Often this causal connection was established implicitly in newspaper articles as in the Sunday newspaper *The People* on 25 May 1958 where an article was headed 'For their own sakes stop them now!' The article continued 'With the greatest possible urgency *The People* now asks the government to put a bar against the free admission of coloured immigrants in Britain. We are not yielding to colour prejudices. But the wave of immigrants rolling over our shores has now risen to threatening proportions' (quoted in Witte 1996).

I think it means that people are really rather afraid that this country might be swamped by people of different cultures. The British character has done so much for democracy, for law, done so much throughout the world that if there is any fear that it might be swamped, then people are going to be rather hostile to those coming in. (Margaret Thatcher 30 January 1978, quoted in Solomos 1989: 129; Fryer 1991: 397)

### Questions

The two extracts show that between 1958 and 1978 little had changed in terms of some people's perception of the threats posed by Black immigration. Do you think people still hold these views today? To what extent do you think Britain is a multiracial, multicultural society?

In the immediate aftermath of the Second World War the acute shortage of labour meant that for a short time companies such as London Transport actively recruited in the West Indies and labour immigrants of all kinds were welcomed. In fact though much publicity was given to the arrival of 417 Jamaicans aboard HMS *Empire Windrush* in May 1948, the most important source of migrant labour in this period was Europe and, in particular, Ireland: 'between 1945 and 1951 between 70,000 and 100,000 Irish people entered Britain'(Solomos 1989).

As soon as the number of Black and Asian Commonwealth immigrants began to increase in the 1950s, however, public attitudes began to change. As Solomos observes: 'throughout the 1950s the debate about immigration in parliament and the media began to focus on the need to control black immigration' (Solomos 1989).

The Notting Hill riots of 1958 are often seen as marking an important point in the racialization of social, economic and law and order issues; although there is evidence to suggest that this process was already underway, the riots certainly brought race and immigration issues to the top of the public and political agenda, and were used by those calling for stronger immigration controls to justify their arguments. These arguments were developed even further by Enoch Powell in his infamous 'Rivers of Blood' speech which he delivered in Birmingham in April 1968. In it he claimed, 'As I look ahead I am filled with foreboding. Like the Roman, I seem to see the River Tiber foaming with much blood' and he went on to warn that immigration was causing 'a total transformation to which there is no parallel in a thousand years of British history'. This transformation meant that white Britons 'found their wives unable to obtain hospital beds in childbirth, their children unable to obtain school places, their homes and neighbourhoods changed beyond recognition, their plans and prospects for the future defeated'. The speech cost Powell his place in the Shadow Cabinet but a poll carried out in May 1968 showed that 74 per cent of those polled agreed with him.

Views like these have played an important part in shaping the experience of Black and Asian people in Britain and in the next section we look at the consequences of this process of racialization.

## Racial inequality in Britain

### Employment

**Racism and racial discrimination account for most of the discrepancies in the employment statistics of black people. Generally, the over representation of blacks on the unemployment register and in low paid jobs still prevails, and now there is consistent research data to verify this in the private as well as public sectors. . . . there will no doubt be a steady growth in black business, but this is not going to resolve the economic crisis faced by the black community.**

***(Bhat et al. 1988, cited in Skellington 1992: 132)***

#### *Periphery to metropolis: migrant labour and inequality*

According to Cashmore and Troyna (1990) the system of domination, which characterized the historical experience of empire, produced a well-regulated supply of labour from the periphery (colonies) to the centre of the system – the metropolis. In the early period of the empire, labour transference from the periphery to the centre was achieved by force – through slavery. However, in more recent times migrants have moved voluntarily to the centre:

**On, and for some time after arrival, the migrants tend to be disadvantaged relative to the metropolitan population and are compelled to accept only the undesirable jobs. Thus, migrants are almost disproportionately represented in the lower grade employments.** ***(Cashmore and Troyna 1990: 74)***

Migrants tended to be utilized in the public service sector. Wage levels here trailed behind those in the private sector. Migrants were also channelled into industrial jobs characterized by low pay, long hours and 'unpleasant' working conditions (C Brown 1992: 47). Such conditions correspond with the conditions described in the 'secondary' labour market.

#### *The dual labour market theory*

This model, advocated by writers such as Piore (1973), suggests that the labour market is divided into primary and secondary sectors. The primary market, characterized by high pay, security, good prospects and good working conditions, attracts the 'stable' worker. Conversely, the secondary market, characterized by low pay, insecurity and poor working conditions, attracts 'unstable employees – women, ethnic minorities and other marginal and relatively docile groups' (Blackburn and Mann 1981: 77). In this scenario the 'stigmatized' minority groups find themselves caught up within a vicious circle. They can obtain jobs only in the secondary labour market and their over-representation within this market merely serves to reinforce their inferior social status (Richardson and Lambert 1995: 78).

Colin Brown (1992) suggests that for both employees and the indigenous workforce the invitation to immigrant workers was not an open one; rather it was a 'last resort'. This point was made clear by employers in the interviews during the first of the Political and Economic Planning Studies:

**The initial decision to employ them was almost invariably taken reluctantly, apprehensively and after a perhaps prolonged struggle with shortages of staff and unsuccessful attempts to recruit enough white employees. Inevitably the sectors in which circumstances had forced employers to accept coloured employees, through the shortage of white personnel, had been those of acute manpower shortage or those in which the type or location of the jobs were especially unattractive to white people.** *(Daniel 1968, quoted in C Brown 1992: 47)*

### *Immigrants: the new reserve army of labour*

According to Marxist writers Castles and Kosack (1973), immigrants form the new industrial reserve army of labour in the metropolitan centres. Capitalism creates a situation of underdevelopment in former colonies which in turn produce large reserve pools of cheap labour to be drawn on as required when metropolitan centres experience labour shortages. This, as we have seen, happened in the post-war period in Britain. The employment of immigrant workers has important socio-political functions for capitalism. Migrants do not simply enter a class society; they have an impact upon it. For Castles and Kosack (1972) a division is created between immigrant and indigenous workers along 'national' and 'racial' lines. Working-class cohesion is divided because

**Many indigenous workers do not perceive that they share a common class position and class interest with immigrant workers. The basic fact of having the same relationship to the means of production is obscured by the local workers' marginal advantage with regards to material conditions and status.** *(Castles and Kosack 1972)*

This marginal advantage enjoyed by indigenous white labour creates, for large sections of the working class, 'the consciousness of a labour aristocracy, which objectively participates in the exploitation of another group of workers' (Castles and Kosack 1972).

In Castles and Kosack's analysis, indigenous workers do not regard immigrant workers as comrades but as an alien presence which poses an economic and social threat. The fear is that they will take jobs from white workers and will be used by employers to force down wages and break strikes. Castles and Kosack (1972) point out that such racialism not only prevents working-class unity but also aids capitalism in its programme of 'divide and rule'.

### *Discrimination and employment in contemporary Britain*

In the mid-1990s, over half the Black population were born and educated in Britain. Consequently the position of Black people in the labour market in contemporary Britain cannot be explained in terms of low aspirations of immigrants. Evidence suggests that inequalities in the labour market are largely caused by racial discrimination.

### *Patterns of discrimination in employment*

**If you can't be looked at and be seen as white, then you're going to be disadvantaged in employment. It's as simple and easy as that.** *(Oppenheim 1993: 116)*

Elizabeth Burney (1988) stated that Black workers in Britain were no better off than they were before the second Race Relations Act became law in 1968. Her report concluded that in the absence of positive action members of ethnic minority groups would consistently fail to be part of mainstream economic life (Burney 1988, cited in Skellington 1992: 133). Colin Brown (1992) claims that there was no evidence produced during the 1980s to suggest a drop in the extent of discrimination in the labour market. Research carried out by Brown and Gay in 1985 in London, Birmingham and Manchester found that at least one-third of private employers discriminated against both Afro-Caribbean and Asian applicants (C Brown 1992: 60).

The 1988 BBC TV series *Black and White* used secret cameras to record 'real' attitudes of 'ordinary' people living in a 'typical' British city (Bristol). Two reporters, one Black (Geoff Small) and one white (Tim Marshall), spent two months monitoring discrimination in employment, housing and accommodation and leisure. The series highlighted the often invisible nature of direct, deliberate discrimination:

**The landlady of the Ashley Arms, for example, who was not just nice, but seemed to go out of her way to explain exactly how and when the bar jobs had gone, turned out to be giving me an elaborate brush-off; but I would never have suspected, had it not been for our concealed camera, and the follow up visit of Tim, who was promptly told that the job was still open.** *(Geoff Small, The Listener 14 April 1988)*

Studies suggest that young Blacks and Asians have been excluded from those government training schemes that are most likely to lead to permanent employment (C Brown 1992: 61). For example, the Youth Employment and Training Unit (YETRU) claimed in 1989 that racial discrimination was widespread on Youth Training Schemes (YTS) – most notably among 'prestigious' employers that had outlets in large cities where Black communities are concentrated (Skellington 1992: 137–8).

The Gifford Report (1989) examined 'race relations' in Liverpool. Among its area of focus were inequality and the struggle for jobs in the city. Examples of incidents often encountered by Job Centre staff highlighted the discriminatory practices of would-be employers. They included:

**The employer who said the vacancy was filled once he saw the applicant was black.**

**The employer who said the vacancy was filled once he heard the applicant speaking on the telephone with a non-English accent.**

**The employer based in the South Liverpool area who will not use the Toxteth job centre (South Liverpool) for filling vacancies.** *(Gifford 1989: 136)*

Q Why is discrimination in the workplace difficult to detect?

Why might it be detrimental to people to claim that they were discriminated against at work?

Why might people not realize they had been discriminated against in the workplace?

### *Black women and the labour market*

**In general black women are to be found in the lower echelons of all the institutions where they are employed, where the pay is lowest and the hours are longest and most anti-social. In accordance with gender divisions, black women tend to be employed in particular sectors of the Welfare State: catering and cleaning, nursing and hospital ancillary work.** *(Mama 1992: 83)*

Studies of post-war migration have often presumed that female migration to Britain was a 'passive following of menfolk' (Peach 1972). Conversely, Doyal *et al.* (1981) contend that while that this was partially true, a substantial number of Caribbean and African women migrated independently. Migrant female labour, following the patterns of migrant male labour, tended to occupy low-paid jobs vacated by the socially mobile indigenous workforce.

Doyal *et al.* (1981) contend that immigrants constituted a source of cheap labour in the NHS. In contemporary Britain, Black nurses are disproportionately represented in unpopular specialist areas such as mental health and genetics (Radical Statistics Health Group 1987). Mama points out that public expenditure cuts in the NHS since the early 1980s have disproportionately affected Black workers across the board. Additionally, 'persistent discrimination ensures racist recruitment patterns in those areas being expanded and developed' (Mama 1992: 84).

Mama contends that Black women's role as workers (most notably in the African and Caribbean communities) is particularly important because they are more likely to have unemployed partners and more dependants than white women (Mama 1992: 85).

### *Discrimination and the professions*

Thus far attention has been focused on inequality in the less prestigious areas of the labour market. However, it would be misleading to assume that all Black labour is located in low-status occupations. Research in the late 1980s and early 1990s has focused on discrimination in the professional sphere of the labour market. Areas of direct and indirect discrimination included accountancy (CRE 1987a), graduate employment (CRE 1987b) and journalism (Alibhai 1990).

Labour Force Survey (LFS) statistics for the years 1987, 1988 and 1989 show that 41 per cent of employed men of Indian origin were located in professional and managerial positions compared to 35 per cent for the white population.

A 1991 survey of 15,000 young (under 35) Black people found that 30 per cent of respondents were qualified to degree level and a quarter held professional or vocational qualifications. Despite this, two-thirds of the men and one-third of the women surveyed claimed they had experienced discrimination in work and in promotion (Skellington 1992: 142).

Case Study

## Racism, discrimination and the criminal justice system

### The Bar

In 1990, Kate Muir examined the situation relating to Black lawyers at the Bar. Although a Bill had become law in November 1990 outlawing race discrimination at the Bar, it was unlikely to make any difference to Black lawyers 'in the world of old boys committees and Oxbridge degrees which constitute the legal establishment'.

Muir focused on 'sets' (groups of barristers sharing 'chambers'). Describing the situation as 'legal apartheid', she argues that Black sets are treated as inferior, inefficient, 'poor relations' by the white sets. Ethnic minority sets tend to be less busy than their white counterparts and tend to specialize in less lucrative and prestigious areas such as family and criminal law and commercial law.

Muir pointed out that in 1988, 182 chambers had no Black members. In 1989, out of a total of 269 chambers which responded to a Bar Council survey, 16 contained 53 per cent of all non-white barristers. Muir maintained that a non-statistical way of describing the situation was 'ghetto'. (Adapted from Kate Muir, 'Legal apartheid', *Correspondent Magazine* 11 November 1990)

### The judiciary

Law Society figures produced in March 1991 revealed great disparities in relation to the number of men, women and members of ethnic minority groups both on the bench (the judiciary) and among the reserve of potential candidates from which the bench is selected.

**Table 8.1** The composition of the judiciary in England and Wales.

| Judges | Total | Women | % | Ethnic groups | % |
|---|---|---|---|---|---|
| House of Lords | 10 | 0 | 0 | 0 | 0 |
| Court of Appeal | 27 | 2 | 7.41 | 0 | 0 |
| High Court | 83 | 2 | 1.66 | 0 | 0 |
| Circuit judges | 429 | 19 | 4.4 | 1 | 0.2 |
| Recorders[a] | 744 | 42 | 5.7 | 3 | 0.4 |
| Assistant recorders[a] | 443 | 27 | 6.0 | 2 | 0.4 |
| **The candidates** | | | | | |
| Practising barristers | 5,994 | 1,246 | 21.0 | 376 | 6.0 |
| Practising solicitors | 54,734 | 12,683 | 23.2 | 709[b] | 1.3 |

*Notes:* [a]Part-time
[b]16,622 respondents to the Law Society survey declined to specify their ethnic group

*Source:* Adapted from Skellington (1992: 104), based on Lord Chancellor's Department 1991; Law Society 1989–90; Bar Council 1989–90

The table suggests the presence of an institutionalized manifestation of racism within the British criminal justice system. Moreover, there is a clear indication that discrimination and inequality cuts across 'class'. In the primary as well as the secondary labour markets there are still major disparities.

### Question

What measures might be taken to increase the numbers of people from ethnic minorities in the judiciary?

### *Unemployment*

Unemployment rates have been consistently higher for Black people and other ethnic minority groups than for white people. During the period 1989–91 the male unemployment figure for Black people and other ethnic minority groups stood at 13 per cent – almost double the rate for white people (7 per cent). The pattern in unemployment rates for women was similar: 12 per cent compared to 7 per cent (House of Commons, Hansard, 21 May 1992).

High rates of unemployment particularly affected people from Bangladesh and Pakistan. In 1989-91, the figures stood at 21 per cent for men and 24 per cent for women (House of Commons, Hansard, 21 May 1992). In 1989–91, 22 per cent of young men (aged 16–24) from Black and other ethnic minorities were unemployed, compared to 12 per cent of young white men. The figures for young women were 19 per cent and 9 per cent respectively (House of Commons, Hansard, 21 May 1992).

In 1989–91, the unemployment rate for ethnic minorities with high qualifications stood at 6 per cent compared to 3 per cent for white people with the same qualifications. The unemployment rate for ethnic minorities with 'other' qualifications stood at 13 per cent compared to 6 per cent for white people with similar qualifications ('Ethnic origins and the labour market', *Employment Gazette*, Department of Employment, February 1993). (This section is based on Oppenheim 1993: 116.)

**Fig 8.1** Unemployment rates by ethnic origin, Spring 1992 (Great Britain).

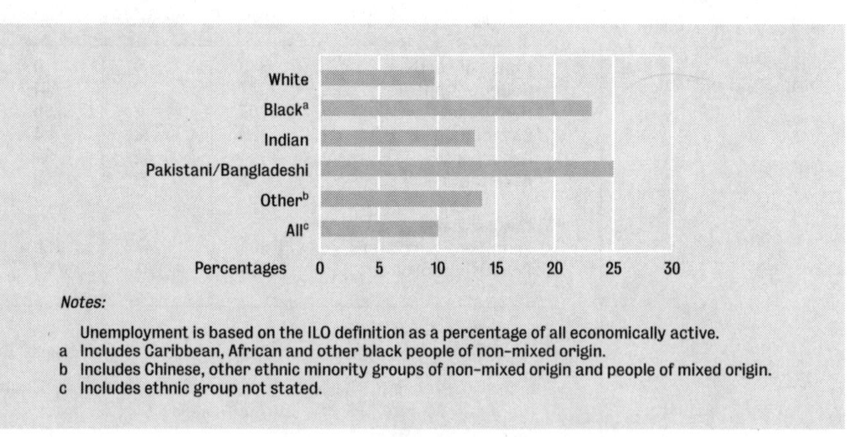


*Source*: *Labour Force Survey*, Employment Department 1992

---

## Housing

**Black people in Britain generally live in worse housing than white people, largely as a result of direct and indirect discrimination. Whether they are home owners, private tenants or council tenants, black families are more likely to live in accommodation which is older, more crowded and situated in areas regarded as less desirable.** ***(Gordon and Newham 1986: 20)***

---

Skellington (1992) points out that the general improvement in housing conditions in Britain since the 1950s has benefited ethnic minority groups along with the rest of the population. However, major disparities in housing outcomes still exist. From the late 1980s and into the 1990s a series of reports from the Commission for Racial Equality (CRE) have highlighted covert and overt discrimination in housing policies and practices, including institutional racism, which has created and perpetuated ethnic minority disadvantages in housing (Skellington 1992: 93).

At the risk of over-generalization, we can distinguish two basic types of housing in Britain: private housing, including home ownership or private renting, and public or local authority housing, conventionally termed council housing. We shall look briefly at these two housing sectors and consider factors that might lead to racial inequalities within them.

### *Prejudice and discrimination in the private sector*

Discrimination occurs in the private sector of housing through the actions and attitudes of what Skellington (1992: 109) terms 'key individuals'. These individuals include vendors, landlords and landladies, estate agents and building society officials. Their subjective racism may attempt to exclude Black people from specific neighbourhoods.

In their research in Liverpool and Birmingham, Karn *et al.* (1983) identified stereotypical views among mortgage lenders that West Indians and Asians will want to purchase property only in specific areas where their communities are located. Moreover, the white population will not want to buy or even remain living in such areas (cited in Ginsburg 1992: 119).

In Bedford, Sarre *et al.* (1989) identified a process whereby the institutionalized stereotyping of mortgage applicants by building society officials produced a 'status hierarchy'. Prospective Italian and Asian buyers were viewed positively whereas Afro-Caribbeans were defined in negative terms as 'unreliable and disorganised [and] having irresponsible attitudes to finance . . . they are judged to have failed to display the thrift and resourcefulness so highly valued by the building society movement' (Ginsburg 1992: 119).

Subjective racism may also be linked to institutional practices. Ginsburg (1992) points out that building society officials, solicitors, surveyors and estate agents operate within frameworks which often lend themselves to institutional racist practices. Moreover institutional racism in the owner-occupier sector can be defined as the product of a combination of common-sense subjective racism and structural forces:

> **The exclusion of certain areas, property or people with low or insecure incomes has a common sense financial and administrative legitimation, to the extent that a building society manager can claim that lending on such properties or to such people is too risky . . . black people on average have lower incomes than white people, a feature of structural racism.** ***(Ginsburg 1992: 119)***

Skellington (1992) contends that while signs stating 'No Blacks' or 'No Irish' may have disappeared in the wake of race relations legislation, evidence suggests that racial bias persists in the private rented sector. The CRE (1990) report *Sorry, It's Gone* showed that one in five accommodation agencies in thirteen different locations discriminated against ethnic minority group applicants. Moreover, one in twenty private landlords and landladies also discriminated against these groups.

Research in Bristol for the TV series *Black and White* (see p.333) illustrated the often invisible nature of subjective racism:

> **As the filming progressed it struck me more and more that there was no real way of knowing how to interpret people's behaviour. As we went after flats . . . some of the people who were nicest to my face, who went out of their way to be helpful, were the ones who were discriminating.** *(Geoff Small, The Listener 14 April 1988)*

**Q** What influence could (a) estate agents and (b) building society officials have on patterns of housing for white and Black people?

Why might they try to exclude Black people from specific neighbourhoods?

### *Prejudice and discrimination in local authority housing*

Administrative processes in local authority housing departments – as with building societies and estate agents – have resulted in the unfavourable treatment of Black people. These processes cannot be explained solely in terms of subjective racism among individual staff within such institutions. Rather they are legitimized by a combination of negative stereotyping of Black people and a failure to recognize their specific housing needs. Ginsburg (1992) suggests that racial inequalities in housing that are linked to the practices of local housing authorities can be defined in terms of institutional racism. He argues that institutional racism in the area of council housing manifests itself in three major forms. First, there is the desire to match specific tenants to specific properties. A report on the allocation of housing in Tower Hamlets, east London, highlighted a process of 'ghettoization' that was most notable among the Bengali community: 'The view that all social security and black tenants should be put together on certain estates was expressed to the researcher on several occasions by different [council] officers' (Philips 1986: 34).

In a similar vein, a Commission for Racial Equality study in Liverpool in the late 1970s revealed that Black people were allocated to the least desirable estates in the city. The study also highlighted the number of instances whereby Black applicants were subject to overt racism by council officers. A West Indian male stated: 'After seeing a vacant flat I went to the district office where I was told the flat was not "for your kind of people"' (CRE 1984: 80–1).

A follow-up study in the mid-1980s provided further evidence of direct discrimination with Black applicants nominated to housing association property being treated less favourably than white applicants in terms of the property they received (CRE 1989, cited in Ginsburg 1992: 112). This study found that white people were twice as likely to be offered new properties than Black people, were four times more likely to be offered purpose-built properties, and four times as likely to get an offer of a council house with a garden. Liverpool Council were subsequently taken to the High Court by the CRE in 1993 for failing to comply with CRE directives to end discrimination in housing allocation in the city.

Second, housing officers anticipate that there will be racial harassment directed against Black tenants by established white tenants on certain estates:

---

**Certain estates have been regarded as unsuitable for black tenants mainly it seems because of white tenants' objections to cooking smells. . . . Some council employees may have been prepared to let white tenants dictate the pattern of housing allocation.**
***(Philips 1986: 34 )***

---

Ginsburg suggests a 'head to head' merger of subjective and institutional racism. Discrimination against those who are perceived as a threat to the 'smooth running' of estates creates 'institutionalised acceptance of racial harassment or the threat of it' (Ginsburg 1992: 114).

Third, there are the value judgements of council officers who identify a 'deserving' and 'undeserving' status. A study in Nottingham in the mid-1970s revealed that on average Black families were larger in size than white families and therefore required larger properties. The council did not have many larger properties available and those it did have were in varying states of disrepair. As a consequence Black people waited longer for housing or rehousing from overcrowded accommodation. Furthermore, they tended to be offered the 'poorer' properties by housing officials (Simpson 1981: 257).

**Fig 8.2** Black mother standing in room at home, with young children. (Courtesy of Tony Stone Images.)

Ginsburg points out that this particular manifestation of institutional racism which ignores the particular housing needs of Black families is common to many housing authorities. Moreover large families have traditionally been viewed as 'less deserving'. The notions of deserving, less deserving or undeserving have adversely affected not only Black people but also Irish people, single mothers and unemployed people (Ginsburg 1992: 112–14).

**Case Study**

### Gentrification: perpetuating inequality

The process of 'gentrification' has been cited as perpetuating inequality in housing in contemporary Britain. 'Gentrification' refers to the middle classes moving into areas of towns and cities that have become run down. Private landlords are encouraged to sell their large run-down properties to property developers for high prices. The properties are then renovated and sold or rented out to better off, middle-class tenants from outside the area.

The run-down areas that become gentrified tend to be in inner-city areas and to have high concentrations of ethnic minority groups. Invariably these ethnic minority populations are forced to move to accommodation outside the gentrified area, which has now been priced beyond their means. On average, Black people have lower incomes than white people and therefore are effectively excluded from enjoying the benefits of living in gentrified areas. Jacobs ( 1988) comments that in Britain, as in the USA, the process of gentrification 'has had the effect of reinforcing the relative deprivation of ethnic minorities' (Jacobs 1988: 111).

### *Government housing policies and inequality*

Ginsburg has commented that government housing policies have played a structurally racist role in producing inequality in housing in Britain. Since the mid-1970s both Labour and Conservative policies have focused on home ownership and withdrawal of support from council housing and council tenants. Government support for home ownership has included housing improvement grants, capital gains tax exemption and mortgage tax relief – all of which have differentially benefited higher income groups, among whom Black people are poorly represented (Ginsburg 1992: 120).

The promotion of council house sales since the Housing Act 1980 has further amplified inequality. Over 1.25 million local authority dwellings have been sold since that Act was passed; those homes that have been sold tend to have been on 'better' estates with, for instance, their own gardens, again effectively excluding Black applicants:

> **These estates are populated mostly by white working class households who benefited from the racialised allocation policies of the previous decades. Thus local institutional racism of the past combined with contemporary central government policy produce a powerful inegalitarian effect.** ***(Ginsburg 1992: 121)***

Furthermore, cuts in public expenditure on the maintenance and construction of council housing represents another facet of structural racism which directly affects black people and thus perpetuates inequality. According to the Chancellor's Autumn Statement in 1988, public expenditure on housing was cut by 79 per cent between 1979 and 1988: ' The restraint in spending on council housing allied with council house sales has solidified and extended the racial inequalities already existing'.

### *Centre, twilight and periphery: housing classes*

In Chicago in the 1920s, Robert Park, Ernest Burgess and Roderick McKenzie (1923) identified clear, demarcated sections of the city that were occupied by specific groups. These sections were found to form roughly concentric zones spreading out from the city centre. Park and his colleagues categorized these zones. The central area was essentially a business zone. This was surrounded by a zone of transition – an area characterized by run-down, dilapidated property and a general air of social disadvantage, with poverty and crime prevalent. Beyond this zone they identified three others, one occupied by the working classes and the other two by the 'privileged' classes. In this model the more powerful and affluent sections of society obtained the more desirable property at the periphery of the city.

Park and Burgess' model was adapted by Rex and Moore (1967) for a study in the 1960s based on the Sparkbrook area of Birmingham. Rex and Moore identified specific types of residents that corresponded to specific spatial zones of the city. The upper-middle class, for instance, lived in large houses in peripheral areas away from industrial locations. By contrast, ethnic minority groups tended to be concentrated near the centre of the city, in twilight zones. These twilight zones were similar to the zones of transition identified in Chicago: they were run down, crime ridden and generally undesirable places to live. People living in such areas had limited access to the more desirable forms of accommodation in the outer spatial zones. In these cases, it is the city itself that generates inequalities which are separate from and additional to inequalities that occur in other areas such as work and education.

Moving away from the traditional Marxian approaches which identify two main classes in terms of their relationship to the means of production, Rex and Moore adopt a more flexible, Weberian approach which identifies a variety of classes according to their 'market situations' – and one such market is housing. Thus they introduce the notion of 'housing classes' (Richardson and Lambert 1995: 73).

In this scenario an individual might occupy a powerful position in the labour market but this does not necessarily reflect power and influence in the housing market. Therefore:

---

**A Pakistani worker might be relatively well qualified and have a position of seniority that pays well; but he [*sic*] may still be crushingly disadvantaged in his access to desirable housing. The opposite case may hold for a white labourer who has reasonable quality accommodation.** *(Cashmore and Troyna 1990: 108)*

---

### *Housing, racial harassment and inequality*

---

**Racial attacks, racial harassment and the threat of them at home are thus very significant in perpetuating racism and racial inequalities in housing in contemporary Britain** *(Ginsburg 1992: 124)*

**An Asian woman who reported a series of attacks to the police was stopped in a lift on a Merton estate by a man with a knife who threatened to kill her if she went to the police again.** *(Gordon and Newham 1986: 22)*

**A three year old boy suffered a broken leg after he was run over by a youth on a bicycle. The incident took place on a council estate in Wandsworth, South London. The boy's mother has suffered racial abuse for three years. She has had blood smeared on her front door, stones thrown and pellets fired at her. This was one of 24 cases reported to the Wandsworth and Merton Racial Harassment Unit over a two week period.** *(Gordon and Newham 1986: 22)*

---

Skellington (1992) argues that up until the mid-1980s the response of most councils to allegations of racial harassment or direct attacks on white estates was to treat them as private matters between neighbours. Ginsburg (1992) points out that the major policy issues for local housing authority departments in such cases are the removal (transfer) of victims and the removal (eviction) of perpetrators. The former is the easiest option while the latter response is only rarely adopted: 'Victim transfer is disastrous as a long-term solution, yet it is being widely implemented' (Ginsburg 1992: 125).

Skellington suggests that in such cases Black tenants are usually transferred back to overcrowded estates which contain large populations of minority ethnic group tenants. Action by housing departments against the perpetrators of racial harassment on housing estates is rare. Problems relating to legal interpretations and definitions of racial harassment have resulted in few councils taking such action.

In 1984 Newham became the first local authority to evict a white family for the persistent and violent harassment of their Asian neighbours. However, by the end of 1987 only six cases had been brought against white tenants and only three of these had succeeded in forcing the eviction of the perpetrators of racial violence and harassment.

Q

Why might local councils not wish to take action against tenants accused of racial violence/harassment?

Do you think racial harassment should lead to eviction? Explain your answer.

Case Study

### Homelessness

The risk of becoming homeless is higher for people living on low incomes, for people from ethnic minorities and for single parents. (Oppenheim 1993: 53)

**The growth of homelessness in Britain in the 1980s and 1990s has particularly affected Black people – both families and young single people – as the following findings demonstrate.**

In 1988 research in London found that minority ethnic group households were up to four times as likely to become homeless as white households.
(NACAB 1988, cited in Skellington 1992: 99)

A CRE study spanning the period 1984–85 in Tower Hamlets suggested that a process of overt institutional racism affected homeless Bangladeshis. In particular, it found that there were 'significant differences' in the period spent in temporary accommodation by Bangladeshis in comparison to white people. Evidence also suggested that Bangladeshis were offered inferior temporary accommodation often miles away from the area. (CRE, cited in Ginsburg 1992: 122–3)

Young people, and most notably young single people, are particularly susceptible to homelessness. A survey of 24 London boroughs in 1989 highlighted the problem. In Brent and Southwark, for example, a disproportionate number of the single homeless were young and black. There was also evidence to suggest that an increasing number of the single homeless were young Asian women.
(SHIL and LHU 1989, cited in Skellington 1992: 99)

*(box continued)*

*(box continued)*

A more recent study by Centrepoint, Soho in London (1992) that focused on young people who stayed at their night shelter during the period 1981–91 found that 36 per cent were from black and ethnic minority backgrounds. (Oppenheim 1993: 88)

The effect of homelessness on educational attainment was highlighted by an HMI survey in 1990. It found that 'homeless children tended not to be enrolled at school, were frequently absent, performed relatively poorly in class, and suffered from low self-esteem and expectations.' (cited in Skellington 1992: 99–100)

## Education

Commentators such as Cashmore and Troyna (1990) have pointed out that the benefits of the formal education system are premised on three main assumptions. First, it enables individuals to develop as 'aware, sensitive and contributing members of society'. Second, individuals can improve themselves both socially and economically by obtaining qualifications, which in turn can be directed towards occupational success. Third, knowledge of 'other' cultures can free individuals from the ignorance and 'prejudice' of previous generations. These assumptions are underpinned by the belief that each individual should be allowed the opportunity of full intellectual development through unhindered access to educational institutions and the qualifications they offer (Cashmore and Troyna 1990: 121).

In theory, therefore, factors such as children's social background should not interfere with educational opportunity and educational attainments would reflect ability. In practice, however the type of education received or the educational qualifications gained are closely linked to social background (see pp.455–70).

### *Multicultural and anti-racist approaches*

David Milner (1983) and Bernard Coard (1971) contend that the British education system has consistently failed to encourage positive self-images among Black pupils. Milner points out that Black children's self-concepts and educational achievements are impeded by the Eurocentric nature of the curriculum (Milner 1983: 189). Coard (1971) drew similar conclusions, arguing that blame for academic failure of Black children rests with the schools themselves:

> **The black child acquires two fundamental attitudes or beliefs as a result of his [*sic*] experiencing the British school system: a low self image and consequently low self expectations in life. These are obtained through streaming, banding, busing, ESN schools, racist news media and a white middle class curriculum: by totally ignoring the black child's language, history, culture and identity. Through the choice of teaching materials, the society emphasises who and what it thinks is important, infinitesimal, irrelevant. Through the belittling, ignoring or denial of a person's identity, one can destroy perhaps the most important aspect of a person's personality – his sense of identity, of who he is. Without this he will get nowhere.**
>
> *(Coard 1971: 31)*

**Q** Think back to when you were at school. What kind of history were you taught?

Did you learn about Black contributions to culture, art or science?

What perceptions did you gain of Africa and its people?

There can be little doubt that such negative perceptions can disadvantage Black pupils in the classroom situation. Should we conclude that such stereotypical labelling is racist? Jeffcoate (1979) has pointed out that it would be misleading to make such an assumption. He defines it as a manifestation of institutional racism; institutional racism and individual racism are mutually reinforcing:

> **the individual racism represented by demeaning stereotypes is both an expression of the institutional racism deeply embedded in the educational system and a guarantee of its survival.** *(Jeffcoate 1979: 98)*

Jeffcoate supports the development of multicultural educational policies – a pluralistic model which promotes a recognition of cultural differences and lifestyles rather than suppression of them. Supporters of multiculturalism contend that the multiracial school environment 'can become a place where pride in race is affirmed, and where interracial friendship and understanding are celebrated' (Jeffcoate 1979: 122).

### *Multicultural education: a critique*

Multicultural educational policies have attracted criticism. Carby argues that instead of alleviating disadvantage, multiculturalism merely perpetuates it. In focus-

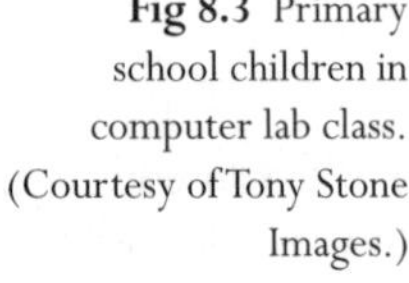

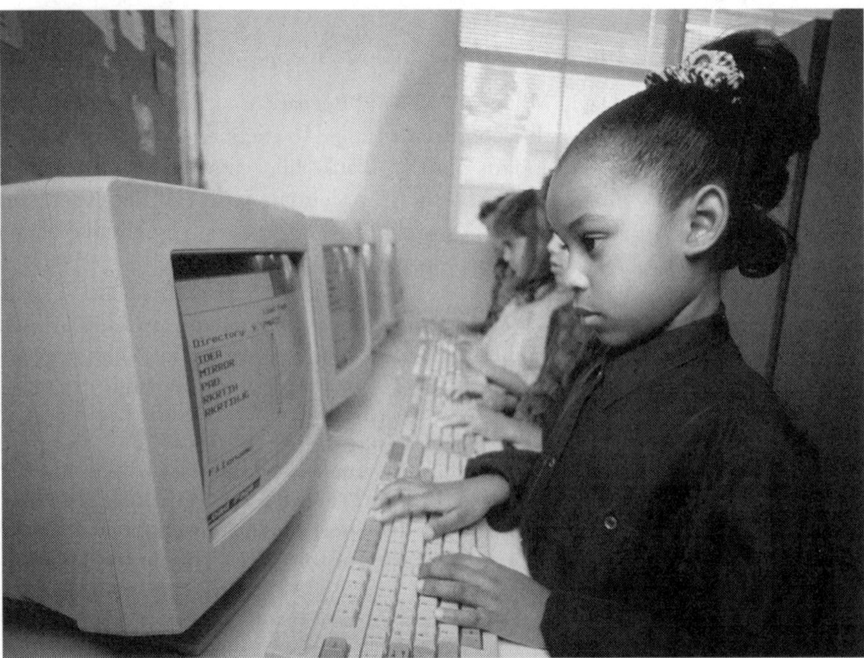

**Fig 8.3** Primary school children in computer lab class. (Courtesy of Tony Stone Images.)

ing on culture, the spotlight has been taken away from institutional racism (Carby 1982b: 194). Stone (1981) has pointed out that such policies are 'diversionary': Black pupils do not suffer from low self-concepts. Therefore, policies which focus on 'changing attitudes' rather than the 'mastery of skills' are likely to perpetuate disadvantages (Stone 1981, cited in Cashmore and Troyna 1990: 141). For Mullard (1982), multicultural policy is little more than a 'revised' version of the assimilation model of the 1960s and 1970s (cited in Burtonwood 1986: 150). Carby views multiculturalism as another form of social control over Black pupils:

> **The multicultural curriculum was from its inception, part of state strategies of social control. Black culture and history were what the schools said they were. The state recognised the danger of the demand for black studies and determined to exercise control over what black students were taught.** ***(Carby 1982b: 194)***

Multicultural education has also come under attack from the New Right. Antony Flew rejects the idea that all cultures may be equally valuable, arguing some are more 'instrumentally valuable' than others (Flew 1984, cited in Francis 1988: 101).

To conclude, Mullard (1982) argues that anti-racist rather than multicultural education is a more valid way of combating disadvantage because it is a Black rather than a white response to the problem focusing on structure rather than culture (Burtonwood 1986: 131).

## The policing of Black communities

### *A history of oppressive relations 1919–59*

The defining of Black people in Britain as a 'problem' is not a new phenomenon. In the period between the First and Second World Wars the expanding Black communities of maritime cities such as Liverpool and Cardiff were seen as 'an unwanted presence by the various levels of government, including the police' (Cashmore and McLoughlin 1991: 22).

Racial disturbances, traceable as early as 1919 in Cardiff, Newport, Glasgow, Tyneside and east London, resulted in calls for the repatriation of Black seamen. Studies carried out in the late 1920s suggested a relationship between Black men, crime, prostitution and disease. During this period the police not only actively involved themselves as 'key local spokesmen' in favour of repatriation (Rich 1986) but also actively engaged in the harassment of Black people through the enforcement of the 1925 Special Restriction Order on 'alien seamen' (Ramdin 1987). Cashmore and McLoughlin (1991: 23) conclude that the labelling of Black people as a source of social problems during this period laid the foundations for the subsequent relationship between the police and the Black communities in Britain.

The arrival in post-war Britain of non-white immigrants in large numbers from 'New Commonwealth' countries served to heighten the perception that Black people were a problem. John Solomos (1989) suggests that the police played a key role in the construction of this imagery. He points to a 'manifest racial prejudice within the police force dating back to the early stages of migration' (Solomos 1989: 101).

Police handling of the Notting Hill riots in 1958 was strongly criticized by some commentators of the period for its heavy-handed, abusive and openly prejudicial treatment of Black people. The long-term implications of such policing was summed up by Herbert Hill in 1959:

> **Repeatedly one is given a sense that these people feel completely deserted and that, if effective and reasonable forms of protest and redress are not provided, irrational forms of protest and explosions of anger are inevitable.**
>
> ***(Herbert Hill, New Statesman, 9 May 1959)***

In the period that followed these 1958 riots the policing of Black communities was described by Hunte (1965) as 'malicious and exceptionally hostile, in his report *Nigger Hunting in England?* so called after a spate of anti-Black operations which the Brixton police themselves called *Nigger hunting* (Witte 1996). Some writers have pointed out that this facet of law and order represented the 'hard' side of a policing designed to implement a ruling class's assimilation and integrationist ideology which was, in turn, based on a 'colonialist-paternalist' mentality (Cashmore and McLoughlin 1991: 24). In this scenario those sections of the Black communities which refused to respond to the 'hard sell' of assimilation were defined in terms of an ongoing threat to social order. Consequently new strategies were devised to counter this threat.

### *Mugging: the 'problem' redefined in the 1960s and 1970s*

Popular media images of Black youth in inner-city areas had, by the end of the 1960s, established a link between Black youth and crime. The link was redefined in the early 1970s as public concern was focused on the spectre of the 'predatory' Black mugger. Hall *et al.* (1978) explain that the mugging panic heralded a call for the re-establishment of law and order. This emphasis on law and order was not directed at Black youth alone but at the wider sources of political, social and economic unrest which 'threatened' the fabric of the post-war consensus. Such sources of conflict included politicized youth protest, women's movements, industrial unrest and an acceleration of violent protest in Northern Ireland. For Hall, the crisis of the Black mugger is directly linked to a broader crisis – a crisis within capitalism itself. From this period 'black youth became a metaphor for every fear and anxiety that existed in British society' (Cashmore and McLoughlin 1991: 27).

### *A confrontational approach in the 1970s and 1980s*

From the early 1970s onwards violent confrontations between Black youth and the police became regular occurrences in inner-city areas (Solomos 1989: 101). Paul Gilroy explains that the subsequent fear and anxiety generated by the mugging crisis enabled the police to justify a move towards a more authoritarian and aggressive approach to inner-city policing. The eventual outcome of such policing was seen by Cashmore and McLoughlin as 'the civil disturbances of the 1980s' (1991: 27).

**Q**

Why do you think Black seamen, in particular, were considered a problem in the early 1900s?

Why do you think that Black youth, in particular, were signified as a threat in the 1970s and 1980s?

## Urban violence in the 1980s

The 'riots' of the 1980s have exerted considerable influence on debates surrounding the politics of 'race' in contemporary Britain. They have played a key role in discussions which focus on reforms and policy changes designed to stop the reoccurrence of such events. We consider four broad explanations:

- the role of the police
- urban deprivation
- political exclusion and marginalization
- a 'cry for loot'.

### *The role of the police*

It is difficult to assess the extent to which the events of the 1980s were a consequence of the relationships between the police and local Black communities. Cashmore and McLoughlin (1991) suggest that the 'authoritarian' and 'racist' features of inner-city policing were ultimately responsible for producing the violent protests that characterized the 'civil disturbances' of the 1980s.

The Scarman Report (1982), which not only focused on the Brixton disorders of April 1981 but also considered the disorders that occurred elsewhere in the summer of that year, drew attention to the strained relationship between the police and local Black youths: 'Tension between the police and black youth was, and remains, a fact of life in Brixton' (Scarman 1982: 3:23). Furthermore, Scarman maintained that the disorders of 10 April 1981 which preceded the more serious rioting of the 11th were 'a spontaneous act of defiant aggression by young men who felt themselves hunted by a hostile police force' (Scarman 1982: 3:25).

Similarly, some accounts of the riots of 1985 drew attention to the potentially explosive relationship between the police and Black youth. In their examination of the causes of rioting in Toxteth, Liverpool, in 1985, (Solomos and Rackett highlighted the tense relationship between the police and Black youth: 'As in Brixton and Handsworth, police relations with youths, and especially young black people were a significant factor in the explosive mixture' (Solomos and Rackett 1991: 48).

However, although the Scarman Inquiry made reference to the 'tense' relationship between police and Black youth, it did point out that this was one face of a complex set of variables which created 'a predisposition towards violent protest' (Scarman 1982: 2:38)

### *Urban deprivation*

Unemployment and urban deprivation featured prominently as issues during the 1980 and 1981 disturbances in Bristol, London, Liverpool and Manchester and in the 1985 disturbances in Birmingham and north London. Media representations created images of 'urban decay', 'tinderbox cities' and 'ghetto streets'. In a parliamentary debate on the 'civil disturbances' of July 1981, Roy Hattersley, the Shadow Home Secretary, rejected the idea that the police were instrumental in 'sparking' the riots:

**I do not believe that the principal cause of last week's riots was the conduct of the police. It was the conditions of deprivation and despair in the decaying areas of our old cities – areas in which the Brixton and Toxteth riots took place.**
*(Hattersley 1981, cited in Solomos 1989: 111)*

*Political exclusion and marginalization*

The Scarman Report highlighted the feelings of powerlessness and political marginality endured by the Black community in general and Black youth in particular:

**In addition they do not feel politically secure. Their sense of rejection is not eased by the low level of black representation in our elective political institutions. . . . Rightly or wrongly, young black people do not feel politically secure, any more than they feel economically or socially secure.** *(Scarman 1982: 2:36)*

Analysis of urban unrest in the USA also emphasized political marginality as a factor which influenced involvement in violent protest (e.g. Skolnick 1969; Fogelson 1971).

However, it has been pointed out that this line of argument was kept off the public agenda by those in power because it defined the disorders and disturbances in terms of political responses to political exclusion rather than as irrational acts of criminal elements (Solomos and Rackett 1991: 53).

**The attempt to depict the riots as irrational was very important. It denied legimitimacy to the rioters, their actions and their views. It made them events without a cause.** *(Kettle and Hodges 1982, quoted in Solomos 1989: 114)*

*A 'cry for loot'*

The ideology which denied a legitimacy to arguments highlighting the political marginality of Black communities also denied a legitimacy to analyses suggesting that poverty, unemployment and deprivation were factors in precipitating the riots.

Enoch Powell rejected outright notions that social and economic deprivation were the key factors and major causes. Without actually using the term, he argued that 'race' was the main causal factor (Solomos 1989: 105). Right-wing discourse articulated by commentators such as Geoffrey Partington (1986) claimed that anti-racist education policies produced a 'new racism' which fostered 'hatred of British institutions, values and beliefs' (P Gordon 1988: 99). In an article in the *Journal of the Police Federation*, Partington (1982) claimed that the roots of the riots could be traced to classrooms which adopted anti-racist teaching: 'Long before violence erupted on the streets there was uproar in the playground, corridors and classrooms. Provocation of teachers preceded and paved the way for harassment of police' (quoted in P Gordon 1988: 99).

Geoffrey Dear, Chief Constable for the West Midlands, defined the 1985 riots in that area in criminal terms as a 'cry for loot' rather than uprising against harsh inner-city policing or unbearable social conditions (Solomos and Rackett 1991: 59).

Other right-wing arguments emphasized the supposed 'pathological nature' of the West Indian family, again defining the 'riots' as something which went beyond the government and the police.

**Q** What criticisms can you make of (a) the urban deprivation; (b) the political exclusion and marginalization; (c) the 'cry for loot' explanations for the urban violence of the 1980s?

**Case Study**

### Black people and the criminal justice system

Black people are still disproportionately represented in the criminal courts. One third of those appearing before magistrates on criminal charges are black even though less than 5 per cent of the population are defined as black. (CARF 3 June/Aug 1991)

Black people are more likely than their white counterparts to be stopped by the police. If stopped they are more likely to be arrested. If arrested more likely to be charged. If charged more likely to be remanded in custody and if convicted more likely to receive a sentence of imprisonment. (S Shaw, 'Black jail figures would shame South Africa', *Independent* 7 August 1989, quoted in Skellington 1992: 107)

Black people are more likely to be assaulted in police custody, wrongfully arrested and have evidence fabricated against them. (CARF 3 June/Aug 1991)

One in ten black youths will have been sentenced to custody before they reach twenty one and once in prison black people are systematically discriminated against. (CARF 3 June/Aug 1991)

In 1990 the Metropolitan Police paid out over £500,000 in damages for assaults, wrongful arrests and malicious prosecutions. Of this £1 30,000 was paid to the family of Winston Rose who choked on his own vomit and died after being assaulted by four police officers, handcuffed and thrown into the back of a police van. (CARF 3 June/Aug 1991)

95 per cent of all arrests for the possession of crack were of black people, in spite of the fact that over half of crack users in this area were estimated to be white and 79 per cent of all known drug users in the area were white. (CARF 3 June/Aug 1991)

**BBC Nine O'Clock News on 8 April 1991, ten years after the Brixton disturbances, reported that only 12 out of 300 police officers in the Brixton area were Black. A survey conducted by *Today* newspaper in 1990 showed that out of the 51 police forces in Britain only 1,308 officers (0.9 %) were drawn from ethnic minority groups.**

## Lessons for the future

Solomos (1989) argues that in the years since 1981, rather than addressing the causes of unrest, the government has become preoccupied with the building of defences. Consequently the police have been provided with increased resources, training and equipment with which to 'deal with' urban unrest and riots when they occur. And with right-wing political and ideological beliefs becoming firmly entrenched throughout the 1980s and into the 1990s the prospects of social disadvantage and institutional racism being addressed at national level have been further reduced (Solomos and Rackett 1991).

In the absence of 'radical' and imaginative reforms Solomos and Rackett point to the likelihood that 'during the 1990s there will be further outbreaks of violent unrest' (1991: 63). This prediction seems to have been well founded, as the rioting in Bradford in June 1995 illustrated.

**Table 8.2** Numbers of Black and Asian police officers in Britain.

| Force | Total strength | Minority ethnic group officers | Force | Total strength | Minority ethnic group officers |
|---|---|---|---|---|---|
| Metropolitan Police (including City of London) | 24,468 | 463 | Lancashire | 3,167 | 18 |
| Avon and Somerset | 3,080 | 20 | Leicestershire | 1,743 | 44 |
| Bedfordshire | 1,047 | 31 | Lincolnshire | 1,197 | 0 |
| Cambridgeshire | 1,187 | 20 | Lothian and Borders | 2,440 | 2 |
| Central Scotland | 638 | 1 | Merseyside | 4,810 | 43 |
| Dumfries and Galloway | 363 | 0 | Norfolk | 1,400 | 0 |
| Dyfed, Powys | 943 | 0 | Northampton | 1,141 | 18 |
| Cheshire | 1,865 | 4 | Northern Scotland | 624 | 0 |
| Cleveland | 1,497 | 9 | Northumbria | 3,593 | 12 |
| Cumbria | 1,144 | 2 | North Wales | 1,327 | 1 |
| Derbyshire | 1,793 | 23 | North Yorkshire | 1,379 | 2 |
| Devon and Cornwall | 2,846 | 2 | Nottinghamshire | 2,344 | 50 |
| Dorset | 1,281 | 3 | Royal Ulster Constabulary | 8,260 | 6 |
| Durham | 1,375 | 3 | South Yorkshire | 2,937 | 21 |
| Essex | 2,902 | 18 | Staffordshire | 2,202 | 17 |
| Gloucestershire | 1,164 | 11 | Strathclyde | 6,825 | 14 |
| Grampian | 1,158 | 1 | Suffolk | 1,204 | 6 |
| Greater Manchester | 7, 008 | 108 | Surrey | 1,659 | 9 |
| Gwent | 1,002 | 4 | Sussex | 2,960 | 9 |
| Hampshire | 3,173 | 9 | Tayside | 1,036 | 3 |
| Hertfordshire | 1,685 | 19 | Thames Valley | 3,685 | 47 |
| Humberside | 1,989 | 3 | Warwickshire | 1,007 | 9 |
| Kent | 2,991 | 20 | West Mercia | 2,023 | 19 |
| | | | West Midlands | 6,859 | 165 |
| | | | West Yorkshire | 5,279 | 82 |
| | | | Wiltshire | 1,098 | 9 |

*Source: Today* 2 October 1990

From this brief historical review it is apparent that 'outbreaks of violent unrest' involving, among others, Black people are part of a continuing tradition in Britain. Few lessons seem to have been learned from our recent history.

## Ethnicity

Ethnicity is used in ethnic relations literature to refer to a sense of cultural awareness and identity within groups that share a common history or heritage. In contrast to biological theories of race, the process of cultural identification or, more frequently, *non*-identification, has a determining role in explaining the different social experiences of Black and white people. Issues of common identity and cultural difference are mobilized to account for the fear and hostility of the host population towards the ethnic Other; in constructing boundaries between the Self and the Other, ethnicity is the key cultural variable.

**Ethnicity refers generally to the perception of group difference and so to social boundaries between sections of the population. In this sense *ethnic difference* is the recognition of a contrast between 'us' and 'them'.** ***(Wellman 1977: ix)***

Different experiences of Black and white people in areas, for example, of housing and employment are thus explained for writers in the ethnic relations framework through reference to exclusionary practices which derive from both Self-identification, and Other (mis)recognition, of cultural differences.

While the ethnic relations focus represents a significant shift away from the implied biological associations of the race relations approach in addressing the relation of cultural characteristics – of dress, customs, religion, food – to practices of social exclusion, there remain serious theoretical problems with this approach (see Miles 1982: 71). As with racial labelling, the notion of ethnicity and ethnic groups conveys a sense of closure, of a homogeneity that is unchanging and impenetrable; questions of class and gender differences *within* ethnic groupings are not considered in any detail. Moreover, there are grounds for concluding that the notion of ethnicity is little more than the outcome of a race plus culture formula: in short, the socio-biological claim that culture is itself ultimately determined by phenotypical or physical features.

## New cultural theories of 'ethnicity' and difference

The second tradition associated with the notion of ethnicity is to be found in the work of contemporary writers such as Stuart Hall (1992), Jonathan Rutherford (1990) and Homi K Bhabha (1990). Such approaches are less concerned with explaining *structural* inequalities experienced by the Black population than with the reproduction and maintenance of the race notion in society. Indeed, it can be suggested that it is only through understanding processes of labelling, identity and resistance, that the motives behind continued discriminatory practices can be understood and ultimately challenged.

We shall briefly examine the approach of Stuart Hall (1992) as representative of a shift towards the analysis of what he terms 'new ethnicities'. As with writers in the early 'ethnicity school' (e.g. Wellman 1977), Hall's definition of ethnicity locates culture and history as core elements in the formation of identity:

**The term ethnicity acknowledges the place of history, language and culture in the construction of subjectivity and identity, as well as the fact that all discourse is placed, positioned, situated, and all knowledge is contextual.** *(Hall 1992: 257)*

And yet the 'new cultural analysts' differ from those writing in the shadows of the race relations perspective through a focus *not* on ethnic boundaries and exclusion, but on the possibilities for the mobilization of cultural ethnicity as a liberating force. We are *all* ethnically located – Black and white – and in recognizing the diversity of all cultural experiences, can work towards breaking down the negative connotations of Blackness, Otherness and race in society.

**The new cultural politics is operating on new and quite distinct ground – specifically, contestation over what it means to be 'British'. The relation of this cultural politics to the past, to its different 'roots' is profound, but complex. It cannot be simple or unmediated. It is . . . completely mediated and transformed by memory, fantasy and desire.** *(Hall 1992: 258)*

New theories of cultural identity represent, positively, a break with theorizations of Black people as victims requiring care and understanding by the 'white community'. Moreover, writers in this tradition focus on the *political* nature of new ethnicities, a term which would appear to finally break away from the limiting associations of race and physical characteristics.

Their approaches, however, have been criticized by writers such as Callinicos (1993) as profoundly idealist and insensitive to the continued oppression suffered by those defined as different from the white majority. Celebration of cultural diversity and difference are of little comfort for those excluded from the labour market on the grounds of such perceived difference.

Q What is the relation between 'race' and ethnicity? Do white people constitute a distinct ethnic group? Do we need to use inverted commas around the word 'ethnic'?

How can new cultural theories of ethnicity help explain structural inequality between Black and white people in society?

## Nationalism

Racism can be defined as a socially constructed ideology which lays emphasis on biological differences. 'Racism is in the lining of nationalism' (Miles 1987, quoted in Cashmore and Troyna 1990: 6). Nationalism can also be defined in terms of a socially constructed ideology which lays emphasis on cultural determinism. That is, world populations are divided into 'nations' rather than 'races':

> **each nation is unique and exhibits a particular cultural profile, from which it follows that each people should inhabit a territory (its own country) within which it should ensure cultural homogeneity and govern itself.**
>
> ***(David Smith 1983, quoted in O'Donnell 1993: 134)***

Anthony D Smith (1995) points out that the revival of ethnic nationalism in the latter part of the twentieth-century Europe has manifested itself in various ways. For instance there are the brutal ethnic conflicts in the Basque regions, Ireland and the former Yugoslavia. There is a strand of nationalism which lends legitimacy and coherence to those 'dangerous and sinister tendencies such as violent xenophobia, neo-fascism, racism and anti-semitism' (A D Smith 1995: 13).

Smith points out that ethnic nationalisms have different origins and 'outlooks' from those of fascism. Historically, neo-fascism and neo-Nazism have manifested themselves in the wake of ethnic or civic nationalisms failing to achieve their stated goals: 'Identity and exclusion feed on each other' (A D Smith 1995: 18).

New Right discourse lays great emphasis on the idea of 'nation', 'race' and rootedness of British culture. According to commentators such as Powell (1981), the multicultural nature of contemporary society has had the effect of 'dislodging' the national identity:

> **We have no unique distinguishing characteristics: the formula is 'a multiracial, multicultural society'. A nation which thus deliberately denies its continuity with its past and its rootedness in its homeland is on the way to repudiate its existence.**
>
> ***(Powell 1981, quoted in Levitas 1986: 109–10)***

Case Study

## Incidents of anti-semitism

The Board of Deputies of British Jews monitored an 85 per cent increase in reported anti-semitic incidents between 1984 and 1992.

Attacks include the desecration of a Jewish cemetery in Southampton in 1993 with neo-Nazi and anti-semitic slogans, and the circulation of a letter accusing Jews of the ritual murder of children.

The Institute of Jewish Affairs' third annual report found incidents of anti-semitism in 1993 increasing by 18.5 per cent in Britain compared with 1992, when a 9 per cent increase was recorded over 1991.

Increasing tension between Jewish students and Muslim fundamentalists at universities in London and Manchester coincided with a rise in support for the far right.

The clandestine group Combat 18 listed among its aims 'to weed out all Jews in the government, the media, the arts, the professionals' and 'to execute all Jews who have actively helped to damage the white race and to put into camps the rest until we find a final solution for the eternal Jew'.

In Germany, the Netherlands, Austria and the USA extremist neo-Nazis are using computer networks to spread anti-semitic and other hate material. Guidance on how to make bombs and articles inciting violence have been found in Europe. Computer disks trivializing the Holocaust and denying the existence of the death camps were circulated in Vienna in 1993. A US fascist group has distributed a neo-Nazi magazine by computer. Thus far, computer networking in Britain has limited itself to tracts denying the Holocaust.

Britain has joined a list of countries with growing anti-semitism headed by Romania, Turkey and the Ukraine.

(Adapted from Louise Jury, *Guardian* 28 January 1994, 22 June 1994)

### Questions

What reasons can be given for the rise of right-wing extremism and anti-semitism in Europe?

Jewish people are well 'assimilated' in contemporary society: why have they been targeted by neo-fascist organizations?

## Summary

- Many theories have attempted to explain 'race', racism and patterns of racial discrimination. Biological theories developed in the nineteenth century stressed physical differences in human characteristics displayed in different groups of people. This theoretical position underwent a revival in the 1960s and 1970s under the guise of 'socio-biological' theories that emphasized the importance of genetic variation in shaping both individual personalities and social behaviour.
- There are a number of sociological theories. The 'race relations' approach focuses on the types of relations experienced by minority groups. Society is seen as racially divided in a way that works in favour of certain ethnic groups and against others. Marxist theories highlight the relationship between racist beliefs and practices and the capitalist economic system. Racial oppression is seen as a tool of capitalism – a mechanism for splitting the working class thereby lessening its potential as a force for

change. Political or state-centred theories examine how social and political policy excludes subordinate groups in society – through, for example, categorizing Black people as particularly prone to commit certain types of violent crime.

- Other theorizations of race have stressed the importance of cultural identity in explaining the different experiences of Black and white people, with the term 'ethnicity' used to refer to the cultural identity of particular minority groups. Culture and history are seen as the key elements in the formation of different cultural identities.
- There is plenty of evidence of continued racial inequality in Britain. With regard to employment, large numbers of Black people have worked in the British labour market since the 1950s, when migrants from the old colonies of the British empire were recruited for low-paid and low-status work. These ethnic minority groups have been seen as part of a secondary labour market or a reserve army of labour, with less security and fewer prospects than the indigenous white population. Today, although the majority of the Black population in Britain have been born and educated in Britain, marked inequalities remain. Racial discrimination in the labour market is indicated by research and reports from a variety of bodies including the CRE and the Gifford Report. Discrimination occurs in both manual and professional occupations.
- Although there has been a general improvement in housing conditions since the 1950s, there is still clear evidence of inequalities in housing between different ethnic groups and particularly between Black and white people. In the private housing sector Black people tend to be directed away from the 'better' areas and towards less prestigious and 'poorer' areas. Local authority housing policy tends to operate in favour of the family structure most common among the white population, i.e. small, one-generation families. These policies and strategies combine to ensure that Black people live in poorer quality housing in the less prestigious areas of Britain's towns and cities.
- The type of education received and qualifications gained are strongly influenced by social and ethnic background. Attainment levels of Afro-Caribbean children are well below those of the general population. Ethnic minority groups have been seen as suffering from the same disadvantages as the working classes.
- Black children are additionally disadvantaged by the Eurocentric nature of the curriculum, which helps to promote a poor self-image among Black children.
- There have been a number of 'racial disturbances' in British cities in the 1980s and 1990s; these are part of a tradition stretching back through the twentieth century. Explanations for urban violence have highlighted the poor relationship between Black communities and the police, the deprivation faced by Back people living in run-down inner-city areas and the political marginalization of Black people.
- Racism and racial inequalities are not felt exclusively by Black people. Other migrant groups to Britain, including Jews, have experienced racial discrimination and prejudice. The racism directed against Jews and other migrant groups can be related to the rise of ethnic nationalism in the twentieth century.

## Further reading

Braham, P (ed.) (1992) *Racism and Anti-Racism: Inequalities, Opportunities and Policies*, London: Sage.

A detailed critical text which examines the nature and the extent of racial discrimination in contemporary Britain.

Cashmore, E and Troyna, B (1990) *Introduction to Race Relations*, London: Falmer.

A clear introductory text to the field of race relations that looks at key areas such as immigration laws, work, housing, education, rioting, fascism and the media.

Centre for Contemporary Cultural Studies (1982) *The Empire Strikes Back: Race and Racism in 70s Britain*, London: Hutchinson.

A radical account of racist practices and beliefs in Britain of the 1970s, written from a 'Black' perspective.

Cohen, R (1994) *Frontiers of Identity: The British and the Others,* London: Longman.

An accessible and fascinating examination of the way the identity of the British people is constantly redefined through various ethnic and national identities both within and outside the UK.

Fryer, P (1984) *Staying Power: The History of Black People in Britain*, London: Pluto.

Provides a detailed history of Black people in Britain.

Levitas, R (ed.)(1986) *The Ideology of the New Right*, Oxford: Polity.

Critically examines a range of views put forward by New Right thinkers.

Miles, R (1989) *Racism*, London: Routledge.

Miles, R (1993) *Racism after 'Race Relations'*, London: Routledge.

*Racism* provides a concise yet comprehensive historical account of the concept of 'racism'. Miles (1993) focuses on the multiple definitions of the concept of racism and contests the view that racism is experienced only by Black people.

Rex, J and Mason, D (eds) (1986) *Theories of Race and Ethnic Relations*, Cambridge: Cambridge University Press.

A good introduction to the 'race relations' tradition of analysis.

Skellington, R (1992) *'Race' in Britain Today*, London: Sage.

This study focuses on various areas of contemporary debate and provides an insight into 'race' and discrimination in Britain today.

Witte, R (1996) *Racial Violence and the State: A comparative Analysis of Britain, France and the Netherlands*, London: Longman.

The first comparative study of racist violence in three major European countries covering the history, theory, policy and practice of state responses to racist violence.

## Activities

### Activity 1 'Race', housing and the 'twilight zone'

**Read the following extracts from Rex and Moore's study of Sparkbrook, Birmingham, in the 1960s (*Race, Community and Conflict*) and consider how their findings relate to areas you live in, have lived in or are familiar with. The questions at the end of the extracts ask you to apply Rex and Moore's model.**

#### Race relations in the city

The most important contribution of Park and his colleagues, from our point of view, was their differentiation of the various residential zones of the city. It does not seem to us to matter very much whether these are to be regarded as forming concentric zones or as being arranged in sectors. [Their work] indicates the existence within the city of several important sub-communities . . . that of the lodging-house zone, that of the zone of working men's homes, that of the middle-class areas, and that of the commuters' suburbs. . . .

We envisage a further stage of development characterised above all by the emergence of suburbia. This occurs when the lower middle classes . . . forsake the centre of the city for a way of life in which, with the aid of credit facilities, they may more closely approximate to the life of the upper middle classes. Their deserted homes then pass to a motley population consisting on the one hand of the city's social rejects and on the other of newcomers who lack the defensive communal institutions of the working class, but who defend themselves and seek security within some sort of colony structure. . . .

In studying a zone of the city . . . we must find out who lives there, what primary community ties they have, what their housing situation, economic position and status aspirations are, what associations they form, and how these associations interact and how far the various groups are incorporated into urban society as citizens. . . .

In many areas of his life, however, the immigrant finds himself not simply enjoying his social rights as a citizen, but having to satisfy his needs in the market. This is particularly true with regard to finding a job and a home. . . .

Competition for the scarce resource of housing leads to the formation of groups very often on an ethnic basis and one group will attempt to restrict the opportunities of another by using whatever sanctions it can. (Rex and Moore 1967: 8–16)

**The zone of transition**

We believe that in large measure what is happening in Birmingham is something which might happen in any West European or North American city. . . .

Before we can begin to understand what the problems of the zone of transition or the twilight zone are, it will be necessary . . . to distinguish the different types of access to housing which are possible in a modern city.

We distinguish the following types of housing situation:

(1) that of outright owner of a whole house;
(2) that of the owner of a mortgaged whole house;
(3) that of the council tenant a in a house with a long life;
b in a house awaiting demolition;
(4) that of the tenant of a whole house owned by a private landlord;
(5) that of the owner of a house . . . who is compelled to let rooms in order to meet his repayment obligations;
(6) that of the tenant of rooms in a lodging-house.

It is likely that these types of housing situation will have a definite territorial distribution in the city depending on the age and size of the buildings in different zones. . . . The six housing situations . . . take the order 1–6 in a scale of desirability according to the status values of British society. . . .

Situations (1), (2) and (3a) do not merely enjoy high prestige. They enjoy legitimation in terms of the value standards of the society as a whole. Situations (1) and (2) are legitimated in terms of the ideal of 'a property-owning democracy'; situation (3a) in terms of the values of 'the welfare state'. Situation (3b) is regarded as an unfortunate transitional necessity in terms of welfare state values. Situation (4) is of declining importance because of the gradual disappearance of the private landlord. Situations (5) and (6) are seen as highly undesirable in terms of welfare state standards, and especially in terms of public health standards. The number of those who can make the transition to situation (3a) is limited by the resources available and the standards which operate. . . .

Local councils are likely to reflect the interests of the long-established residents who form the majority of their electorate. Thus a basic distinction is drawn between local people and immigrants, and between those with normal family situations and isolates and deviants. These will live in the lodging-house. . . .

It will be the case, however, that for most people in the zone of transition, there is a sub community of some kind in which they feel culturally and socially at home. . . .

In a strict sense this does not produce a ghetto. A ghetto would appear to imply a segregated ethnic community, and as we have seen the zone of transition includes ethnic communities, transitional people awaiting rehousing and isolates and deviants of all sorts. . . .

Clearly this situation (in the zone of transition) is not a stable one. One possibility is that . . . the punitive policies of the host community and their elected representative might be checked by the active resistance of immigrants themselves. This later stage of development in the twilight zone may already have been reached in some American cities. (Rex and Moore 1967: 272–80)

### Questions

Consider the town or city you live in – or the nearest to where you live. Use an Ordnance Survey or street map and divide it into 'housing zones'.

How easy was this to do? What problems did you face?

Describe the populations of each of your zones.

Where do different minority groups live?

What explanations can you offer for the spread of population?

How might the work of Rex and Moore help you interpret the housing pattern – and particularly the position of minority groups – in your town? Can you recognize and locate the six types of housing situation distinguished by Rex and Moore?

How might the notion of a zone of transition or twilight zone help an understanding of the urban disturbances of the 1980s and 1990s (see pp. 346–8)?

## ■ Activity 2 What is Black Studies?

Black Studies emerged in North American universities in the 1960s and 1970s. Its growth was closely associated with the Civil Rights movement in the USA but it built upon a long-standing concern of the Afro-American community that their history and culture should not be marginalized by the dominant white educational establishment.

Where it has been taken up in Britain the purpose of Black Studies has not been to portray a cosy image of multiracialism (indeed many of the biographies uncovered chronicle a daily experience of racial insults and discrimination) but to challenge simplistic notions of nationhood based on an idealized past of racial purity before the era of 'mass immigration'.

Though Black Studies clearly helps redress the exclusion of the Black experience from the education syllabus it has no particular methodology of its own and inevitably raises the question of what is 'Black', a question which Paul Gilroy explores in a collection of essays on Black British culture, *Small Acts* (1993b).

> In England, as elsewhere, the effortless certainties that guided the creation and the use of dissident black cultures in earlier times have evaporated in stressful new historical conditions for which no precedents exist. The fundamental, time-worn assumption of homogeneous and unchanging black communities whose political and economic interests were readily knowable and easily transferred from everyday life into their expressive cultures has, for example, proved to be a fantasy.
>
> (Gilroy 1993b: 2)

He goes on to express his regret that there has emerged

> a new condition in which the old commitment to debate and discussion as a means to strengthen the culture is being replaced by a mood that reduces race politics to little more than a form of communal therapy and makes critical judgements on black culture impossible to articulate. In this climate to be critical or analytical is often perceived to be an act of betrayal. (Gilroy 1993b: 3)

## Questions

Do you think that Paul Gilroy's assessment of the current level of Black cultural debate is a fair one? What do you think he means by 'a form of communal therapy'?

Compare Black culture in the UK and the USA by researching a specific area of cultural life such as films, books, art or music and analysing the number of Black people (a) involved in the artistic production of the piece of work; (b) occupied in the technical production; (c) represented in the piece of work; (d) involved in its promotion.

(If for example you were to look at books you might look at how many Black authors were on the bestseller list, how many Black people worked in publishing and how many Black booksellers there were in the UK and the USA.)

Chapter 9

# Global inequality and development

**Chapter outline:** Introduction • Language and meaning • Sociological theories of development • Modernization theory • Underdevelopment theory • World system theory • Articulation of modes of production • Globalization • Rates of development • Third World debt • Aid • The demographic time-bomb • Summary • Further reading • Activities

**Learning objectives**

When you have studied this chapter you should be able to address these key questions:

- What are the strengths and weaknesses of sociological theories of development?
- What explanations do sociological theories offer for the continuing economic disadvantages experienced in many societies?
- What is the extent of global inequality?

## Introduction

There are only two families in the world, as a grandmother of mine used to say: the have's and the have not's. (Cervantes, *Don Quixote*, quoted in Simpson 1994)

What do we mean by development? Perhaps up to the 1970s few people would have problems answering this question. Ask anybody from your grandparents' generation about development in their lifetimes and you would probably hear about changes that have taken place within their homes – electricity, phones, television, hot and cold water, inside toilets, owning a car – all kinds of things which many people now take for granted but which seen in the context of the whole twentieth century represent huge changes in society. These changes relate to the astonishing record of economic growth and technological development since the end of the nineteenth century. However, the benefits of this development have never been shared equally. There are huge inequalities within societies and between societies of the advanced industrial world – Europe, North America and Japan – and the rest of the world. Even in societies which have benefited most from development there is now an increasing awareness that the material prosperity associated with development has been brought about at the expense not only of the poor people of the world but also of the environment itself.

In this chapter we shall look at the ways in which social scientists have explained development. We shall also challenge the assumptions we make that some societies are more 'developed' than others. We shall see that the very idea of 'development' with its implications of everybody travelling along the same predestined path of economic growth and technological advance is open to question.

Q What do the terms developed and underdeveloped mean to you? How would you measure development? Explain why you interpret these terms in this way.

Of the money spent on HIV/AIDS research and treatments, 90 per cent is spent in the 'developed' world, where only 8 per cent of the sufferers live. Why do you think this is? What do such statistics tell us about global inequalities?

Until the late 1960s and 1970s (a period of profound change following the oil crises), the sociology of development sought to describe a progression from one condition to another, from 'undeveloped' to 'developed', in simple terms of western values, thoughts, ideas and cultural practices, which were seen as superior to all others. The sociology of development had until the 1970s implied that other societies are becoming, or must become, like 'us'; for the most part the role of sociology was to measure the pace of such change and the obstacles to it. In this chapter we hope to demonstrate how such views may at last be changing.

In the 1990s we live in a world in which poverty, hunger and inequality are a normal part of the lives of billions of people. Contrasted with this image of global poverty and misery is the material wealth enjoyed in many western capitalist societies; high living standards, material abundance and developed systems of social welfare provision all illustrate a grossly unequal world. Although the notion of two polarities – affluence for the few and deprivation for the many – is oversimplistic, this picture of glaring opposites still retains a force in the minds of western politicians, United Nations officials and development agency directors and in the governments of the 'Third World'. It is this need to change, improve, grow, expand, but above all 'develop' which propels much of the efforts of the majority of the world's population. Many of the world's poor people have seen a vision of their own future and it looks at least in part 'westernized' and 'materialist'.

## Language and meaning

The language of development studies is based upon a specific vocabulary, developed over time and saturated with ideological baggage. Early terms and concepts used in development studies were mostly of a pejorative nature, reflecting an arrogance or superior self-image of the rich nations. Most were short-hand concepts which in a single word or term tried to encapsulate the totality of an economic, political and social system.

**Definition**

### The four worlds

The **First World** refers to affluent industrialized and developed societies. The USA, Britain, France, the Netherlands, Germany and others, such as Japan from the mid-1960s onwards, are examples of First World countries.

The term **Second World** was first applied to the communist or socialist societies of eastern Europe, and later included Cuba and countries of communist Asia. Second World societies might be industrialized, as demonstrated by the former Soviet Union, former East Germany or Hungary. However, these nations had failed to reach the rates of social and economic development reflected in high levels of consumption and general affluence within the First World.

The term **Third World** has considerable symbolic meaning. It was first used by French sociologists and demographers and meant, quite simply, the third level of the world – *'le tiers monde'*. In using such a term the classical sociological ideas of writers such as Spencer, Durkheim and even Marx, with their implication that there exists a natural gradient from poor to rich, undeveloped to developed, appears to be accepted. As an English language concept Third World was first popularized within British sociology by Peter Worsley (1964). Worsley rejected the seemingly negative connotations associated with the concept Third World adopted by the French in favour of a much more sympathetic emphasis, although even the idea of support and sympathy for the Third World could be construed as patronizing or insulting. For many French and British sociologists the world could indeed be divided into three. In the strict academic sense employed by sociologists and economists, the concept Third World means those societies that have yet to undergo industrial development, or those in the process of developing but still with some distance to go before they could be considered industrialized. Any nation outside the economic orbit or control of either the USA or, until the early 1990s, the former Soviet Union was seen to be a Third World nation, ranging from societies such as Brazil, which had large industrial sectors and pockets of affluence, to those nations that were utterly destitute with little if any economic growth.

*(box continued)*

*(box continued)*

Prior to the collapse of communism a new term was added – the **Fourth World.** This even more pejorative description makes a distinction between those Third World societies which have the potential to develop, such as many oil-rich societies, and those societies that appear destined to remain non-industrial and poverty stricken: societies such as Bangladesh, Afghanistan and Ethiopia were all once regarded as Fourth World societies, simply because of their dire poverty.

Since the late 1980s with the collapse of communism the term Third World is still used but it remains to be seen for how long.

The 'four world' terminology reflects a very ideologically loaded world-view that is based on hostility between two major economic systems, led on the one hand by the economic and military might of the USA, and on the other by Soviet-style socialism. In subscribing to such linguistic descriptions we are, either consciously or unconsciously, accepting the polarization of the world into two major economic and social systems, with the vast majority of the world's population locked out of economic growth, consumer affluence and wealth.

## The terminology of development studies

### *Undeveloped and developing*

*Undeveloped* has been frequently employed within sociology and development studies to describe a range of societies. This is clearly a loaded term, often used within modernization theory and functionalism during the 1950s and 1960s to describe those societies with little or no industry, commerce and low levels of growth; for the most part it implies backwardness. As a linguistic short-hand it was sometimes used by western politicians in the 1950s and 1960s. Even in the 1990s, despite the UN recommending in 1951 that it should not be used, some western politicians are prone to use it.

Other less deprecating terms such as *developing* have been employed within development studies. It is used to convey progression, implies gradual change, and has been regarded as inappropriate, because it still has at its centre the concept of developing towards an ideal condition, that ideal being western industrial society.

### *Underdeveloped and developed*

The terms *underdeveloped* and *developed* have been used extensively in the work of western Marxists and neo-Marxist writers within the field of development studies.

### *Globalization*

The origins of the term *globalization* can be found within classical Marxist sociology. Marx referred to capitalism as a global process, while Lenin in his study of imperialism saw the globalization of capitalism as dependent upon the expansion of imperialism by societies such as Britain and Germany. Giddens (1990) and others (e.g. Featherstone 1991a) have restored an interest in the process of globalization that takes it beyond the narrow domain of development studies and into mainstream sociology. Many books on the sociology of the media, political sociology, or medical sociology employ the term globalization; economists and politicians also use the concept in one way or another. The definition by Giddens (1990) is probably most appropriate for an understanding of globalization as a process: globalization simply reflects a growing interdependency of world society. The changes implied by this view of globalization are quite profound, suggesting the creation of a world society in which the image of nation-state and national identity may give way to world-wide social interaction. While most sociological analysis focuses on the negative aspects of globalization, such as economic shifts and decline in one place being matched by economic expansion and growth in another, Giddens' view contains within it an optimism hitherto lacking within development studies. For Giddens the process of globalization has equally the potential to empower and unite citizens as to divide them. So while the process of globalization of industry or the mass media might allow vast wealth or influence to accumulate into the hands of a small minority of 'global' entrepreneurs, the potential for human understanding of problems common to everyone, such as increasing population growth, pollution and threats to the environment, are the more positive side of globalization.

### *Tiger economies*

A new concept that has entered the vocabulary of development studies is *tiger economies*, which refers to those nations on the Pacific rim that are undergoing dramatic rises in economic growth rates. Social science appears to be divided as to how to explain such high levels of economic growth which combine high levels of social solidarity within largely authoritarian political regimes, yet existing within clearly capitalist economic structures. Tiger economy refers to the strength of these emerging nations and the uncertainty as to their underlying driving forces and hence their futures.

**Q** Many of the terms and concepts used to describe poor and less affluent countries have pejorative overtones; terms like Third World imply third rate societies. How do you think such language conditions our perceptions of non-western societies?

Think of the ways in which such societies are described by the media. Is any of this language unfair or untrue?

## Sociological theories of development

We shall discuss five theories:

- modernization theory
- underdevelopment theory
- world system theory
- articulation of modes of production
- globalization.

## Modernization theory

Walt Whitman Rostow (b. 1916), a US economist and historian, is the leading exponent of modernization theory, a theory of development which Rostow (1960) described as a non-communist manifesto. The key to modernization theory is the idea that all modern capitalist societies, such as the USA, have a system of cultural values that makes them advanced. The cultural values of capitalism are held to be those of openness, democracy, innovation, individualism and achievement. The cultural values of primitive and agrarian societies are held to be those of control, anti-individualism, anti-democracy and anti-achievement.

**Definition**

### Rostow's five stages of development

**1 The traditional society**

The most basic form of all societies, this does little more than economically survive, shrouded in mysticism, pre-scientific with rigid social hierarchies and a weak division of labour.

**2 The preconditions for take off**

In this form of society the division of labour increases as population increases, freeing up social organization, in turn allowing for the growth in knowledge, innovation and specialization. Very important to this stage are revolutionary developments taking place in agriculture that allow the growing urban population to be fed without the usual cycle of famine.

**3 The take off**

In this society manufacturing industry has started to emerge and a complex division of labour exists, dependent upon an increasingly complex system of economic organization and distribution.

**4 The drive to maturity**

For Rostow this is a crucial period in which the forces for modernization are allowed to develop, or else society would slip back into a state of economic decline and rigidity. In this period a society defines the economic direction it will take.

**5 The age of high mass consumption**

At this point in the economic evolution of a society, affluence has become widespread. The division of labour is now at a highly refined level in which the full potential of the population is utilized, providing both high economic rewards and levels of satisfaction for workers. Equally, it is a society in which the emphasis is now placed upon consumption of goods and services, including social welfare. (Adapted from Rostow 1960)

Rostow believed that while some communist countries had engaged in process of development, even modernization, their cultural values in essence prevented them reaching the final fifth stage; ultimately they would have to develop the cultural values of capitalism or slip back to an earlier and less developed stage. Moreover, Rostow believed that it was possible for Third World societies to develop and become capitalist in much the same way that the USA had. As the Third World societies became capitalist and advanced, the USA, Britain, France, Germany and other developed nations would derive benefits from this process of modernization. The expansion in industry in the Third World would produce new markets for the goods and services produced in the developed world. As the developed world moved to service-based industry, a new world economic division of labour would emerge, with industrializing and developing societies providing many of the simple manufactured goods it required.

For Rostow and other modernization theorists it was important that developing societies overcome the obstacles to modernization that exist within their own society. They must rid themselves of outdated structures, institutions and practices; they must accept the value systems employed in successful western capitalist societies. Modernization theorists such as McClelland (1961) have suggested that the process of change would come not only through diffusion of capitalist values to these societies, but also through trade, cultural exchange and commerce. Modernization theory argues that the more rational and clearly better practices and forms of organization employed in the west will gradually filter through into these societies.

Clearly modernization theory has within it a highly *ethnocentric* vision of the world: capitalism is seen as 'good' and socialism 'bad'. Such a view should not surprise us, for the ideological climate of the USA in the 1950s was one of fundamental opposition to all things communist; this was the decade of the 'McCarthy witch-hunts'. US society was effectively engaged in a struggle with the Soviet Union and communist bloc for economic, political and military world domination.

As with much sociological theorizing, modernization theory was a specific product of its place and time. It appeared to represent the ideological triumph of the advance of western economies, in particular the growing economic power of the USA. In the 1960s this domination both in the wider economic world and at the level of sociological analysis began to be challenged.

## Underdevelopment theory

In many ways underdevelopment theory offers a mirror image of modernization theory, only this time the Third World's struggle against capitalism is seen as a 'just struggle'. André Gunder Frank (b. 1929) writing from an ideological position sought to challenge the central orthodoxy of modernization theory (Frank 1967). For Frank, Rostow's theory of modernization simply provided academic smog behind which a process of domination and exploitation, as rigid and destructive as that which occurred in the nineteenth century under imperial and colonial expansion, was justified. Moreover, the idea that by adopting the necessary cultural values Third World societies may themselves become modern was anathema to Frank.

While he accepted that the rich west could be regarded as developed, and that most other societies must be seen as underdeveloped, these conditions did not exist in isolation from each other, but rather were fundamentally joined. The developed, and modern, condition of a small number of western societies was in effect dependent upon the deliberate underdevelopment of the majority of other societies. Quite simply, for there to be rich nations, poor nations had to be kept poor. For Frank this was a contemporary process as well as being a historical fact. Modern capitalist societies could have become so only through their exploitation of other societies in the past. Frank stated that historically capitalism created a chain of exploitation that reached from the centre, or what he terms the 'metropolis', the capitalist west, to the edge, or 'periphery'. The peasant farmer of the Third World and the capitalist manufacturer of the west existed under one mode of production, the capitalist mode of production.

According to Frank capitalism has polarized the world into what he terms the central metropolis and the peripheral satellite. Satellite societies channel what they produce to the centre, but even within these satellites there are centres which are fed into by the outlying satellites' areas. Thus there is a gigantic chain of capitalist exploitation reaching down to the individual at the centre. At each stage those above will exercise economic power and control over those below. As power increases closer to the centre, the centre is able to use the surplus it extracts from the periphery for its own ends.

**Definition**

## Frank's underdevelopment theory

### Capitalist world metropolis

**The cities of London or New York are examples of the very heart of the capitalist world system to which the maximum surplus or profit is drawn, supporting fabulous wealth and affluence for those at the very centre.**

**Fig 9.1** São Paulo, Brazil, where wealth and affluence exist alongside deprivation. (Photograph © David Lomax, courtesy of Robert Harding Picture Library Ltd.)

*(box continued)*

*(box continued)*

**National metropolis**

These are cities in the Third World from which products (often raw materials such as coffee, tea or copper) are exported. São Paulo in Brazil, Lagos in Nigeria or Chittagong in Bangladesh are examples, with pockets of vast wealth and affluence existing alongside deprivation and misery for the masses.

**Regional centres**

Here goods, mostly in the form of raw materials, are brought and traded. It is often in these centres that the multinational companies purchase goods and natural resources used in manufacturing.

**Large landowners/merchants**

These act as middlemen between the producer and the regional centres. Often large landowners will rent out their land to peasant producers at high prices, inducing crippling debt for the peasants that can be paid off only through even harder work, and sale of the items to the landowner/merchant.

**Small peasants/tenants**

Those who either own or rent the land on which they work producing goods that are sold to the merchants, but managing to retain only a very small fraction of the real values of what they produce

**Land-less labourers**

In some cases local landowners or even multinational corporation such as the North American giant United Fruit will employ workers to work their land. In this way the relationship of the worker is simply one of wage slave with no control whatsoever over what is produced.

Q

Take an everyday food item such as tea, coffee or sugar and trace the steps from the original agricultural production to the processing and manufacture of this item, to its distribution and sale, and ultimately to your table.

Where was the item originally grown/produced?

Who produced it?

What was its cost in its raw form?

Where was it exported from?

Which companies were involved in its processing and packaging?

What is the cost of the item to you the consumer?

Does this help us understand what Frank had in mind?

By tracing the steps from the periphery to the centre can you see any underlying weaknesses in Frank's model?

For Frank the obstacles to development by societies on the periphery are numerous, both external and internal. Externally, the centre will not allow the development of the periphery, because this will in turn reduce the level of exploitation and surplus that is extracted by the centre. So, for example, if mass consumer industries such as cars are produced at the periphery this will add competition to the same industries at the centre, competition which is unwelcome. It is only when the capitalist industrial centre switches its production to other goods and services that it will allow production of the old goods to take place at the periphery.

In Brazil and Mexico car manufacturing has, Frank accepts, been allowed to develop. However, these facilities mostly produce models that are outdated, for example VW Beetles in Mexico. The Beetle is a very popular car in Mexico, frequently used as taxi cabs, and VW have also found a small niche market in the USA by exporting them to enthusiasts. The same may be true, Frank argues, for commodities such as coffee, tea or sugar. If coffee was processed and packaged in the countries in which it was grown much of the profit from the 'value adding processes' of such processing and packaging would be lost to the company selling the coffee to the supermarkets of the capitalist world metropolis.

Processed goods are often re-exported back to the country where they originated in their raw form. Most of the instant coffee drunk in Brazil, for example, is provided by one of two large multinational companies, Nestlé, who produce Nescafé and are based in Switzerland, and United Foods, the US food producer of Maxwell House coffee. At the periphery it is often the agents or employees of these large multinationals (the export managers, shipping agents and government officials) who form the base of the consumer market for western goods, often living lifestyles very similar to those of their counterparts at the centre. The west employs structures and systematic policies that prevent development taking place in the periphery. The refusal to export technology, such as machine tools, computers and processing equipment, is an example of this. Such external formal barriers are not the only tools employed by the west; others include protective tariff barriers to prevent goods produced at the periphery undercutting those produced at the centre.

Many western companies will actively create at the periphery structures which have a vested interest in maintaining the chain of exploitation. Internally groups exist which depend upon their link with the centre – local landowners, politicians and the military, for example. According to Frank they will often form an alliance with the centre to prevent opposition developing. Indeed the unflattering term 'Banana Republic', meant to signify a backward and corrupt society, was originally coined to explain the control exercised by US fruit companies, such as United Fruit, over Latin American countries. Countries like El Salvador and Nicaragua were under the control of local oligarchies or families, who were paid employees of such US companies. So the term 'Banana Republic' is more an index of exploitation and control than a description of a corrupt and primitive country.

Underdevelopment theory believes that the only real way forward to economic growth and prosperity for the majority would involve breaking the chains that link the periphery to the centre. In the past some attempts have been made to do this; thus the nationalization of the Suez Canal by the radical Arab nationalist leader Gamal Abdel Nasser, President of Egypt, in 1956 led to an invasion by the combined forces of Britain, Israel and France. For Frank such independent action by small countries should be avoided in favour of a more cooperative and unified approach between exploited nations. This could be done through the formation of *cartels* such as the Organization of Petroleum Exporting Countries (OPEC). Indeed OPEC was an example of how societies previously exploited by the west can gradually gain a position in which they were able to use their natural resources against the developed world. In 1973 OPEC trebled the price of oil overnight, forcing countries like the USA, Britain and Japan into economic recession. The effects of the oil crisis are still with us in the 1990s, symbolized by the growth of nuclear power, the exploration and development of North Sea oil reserves and moves towards ever increasing levels of fuel efficiency in cars, in an attempt to move away from externally produced forms of energy to a position of near self-reliance.

During the 1970s OPEC was very successful both economically and politically: countries such as Saudi Arabia, Iran and even Nigeria provided an example of how change might be accomplished. However, it can be argued that OPEC was a victim of its own success; in forcing the west to acknowledge its dependence on oil, many western capitalist societies sought to reduce such dependence, which in turn lowered world demand for oil and weakened OPEC. Thus the strategy of cartel development does not appear to offer the success of economic independence envisaged by Frank. Additionally, while the west became less reliant upon oil as its major source of energy, efficiency measures and substitution (i.e. the development of North Sea oil and nuclear power in Britain), many Third World countries felt the full effect of the oil price rise. In this way the action of the OPEC in 1973 and 1980 hit the poorest nations harder than the richest.

Another, and perhaps far more direct strategy for development was through social revolution and a move towards independent development via *socialism*. Socialism, Frank assumed, would rid peripheral societies of the massive internal inequalities that existed. Cuba in the late 1950s and early 1960s is an example of the Frankian message in practice – social revolution leading to a new and more equal social structure. Cuba's revolutionary leader Fidel Castro pledged to Cuban citizens that it would no longer be a puppet of US imperialism and multinational corporation control. Yet in reality the revolution in Cuba depended to a large degree on the economic and military support provided by the Soviet Union. With the increasing economic strains faced by the Soviet Union in the mid-1980s, leading to its eventual collapse in 1990, the level of economic support and subsidies to peripheral socialist states vanished. Since the 1960s the USA has maintained an economic blockade against Cuba that has prevented Cuba from exploiting its own natural resources and full economic potential. Living standards in Cuba have continually dropped; discontent and counter-revolutions have been prevented only by an exodus of people to the USA. At first this exodus was gradual and orderly but during the summer of 1994 economic conditions in Cuba deteriorated so badly that an estimated 1,200 people per day were leaving. Many of these individuals took to the high seas on rafts made of little more than inner tubes and wood. The US Coast Guard estimated that of the 1,200 leaving per day, only 800 were picked up or made it to the USA: the human cost of the economic blockade has been very high. Despite the communists winning a long and bitter war of national independence, first against the French, then against the USA, Vietnam has suffered a similar economic blockade to that imposed on Cuba. For the most part, the USA says that it will lift its blockade only if the communist government in Vietnam accept policies of economic liberalization and moves towards 'democratization'. In Vietnam at least, economic collapse has been avoided only by policies of economic liberalization and the development of capitalist markets:

**As the Vietnamese government abandons socialism to make way for the free market, the services millions of Vietnamese have come to depend on under communist rule are crumbling. In government schools, students are being asked to pay for their books, and in some cases classes. Vietnam's health care system, once free and considered a model for the developing world, is giving way to a private system.**

***(Guardian 22 November 1994)***

A development in Vietnam, which is being followed in African countries such as Malawi and Zambia, is that of eco-tourism. In the early 1990s, under the communist government's policy of economic liberalization, large tracts of land are being given over to the formation of national parks. Most of the money to finance such schemes comes from the United Nations or the World Bank. However, many of these areas have had their indigenous peoples moved out for western-style tourist hotels to move in.

Q What do you understand by the term eco-tourism? What might be the dangers of implementing such a policy?

## World system theory

Writing a few years after Frank, Immanuel Wallerstein (1979) sought to enhance the idea implicit within Frank's work that a world system existed which was based upon the capitalist mode of production. Central to Wallerstein's model was the concept of the 'social system'. The history of the world, he argued, could in effect be seen not as the development of distinct nation-states that are exploited by other nation-states, as in Frank's model, but rather, as the evolution of quite distinct social systems. Essentially these social systems resemble Marx's modes of production, although in Wallerstein's model there are three modes of production, rather than the five of Marx.

Wallerstein argued that it may be possible for some peripheral societies to move to the semi-periphery while other semi-peripheral societies are forced to the periphery by changes in the world economic conditions and, importantly, by decisions made at the capitalist core. This world system came into existence at about the same time as the colonization of the new world and the European agricultural revolution. Over the following centuries this system became ever more refined and complex. As with Frank, for Wallerstein control of this system lies at the core, those nations that are economically and politically able to control the periphery. These nations are basically the technologically advanced west, including nations such as Japan, and they are able to use the powers they have to maintain their position of dominance and control over the periphery. In turn the periphery is economically reliant upon the centre. Under the world economic system the same basic economic principles, those of capitalism, apply everywhere; however, at the same time a significant degree of political heterogeneity is allowed among those nation-states encompassed within it. Under this system the political structure and freedom enjoyed within any society is limited by the economic control exercised by the global economic system. In this model clearly there appears to be a return to the Marxist orthodoxy of 'economic determinism' in which non-material factors play no part, the economy is the motor of social change.

It is possible to apply some of Wallerstein's ideas to Britain. It is often said by commentators on the political left that Britain is ultimately under the control of the world monetary system, most effectively through organizations such as the International Monetary Fund (IMF), and even through economic speculators, who can influence, if not dictate, social and economic policy for Britain. Thus the economic power of, say US or Japanese bankers can force the pace of social and political change in any society, including Britain. An example of a British government being forced to adopt economic policies not of its own choosing came on 16 September 1992 when currency speculators, and in particular one man, George Soros, 'broke the pound' (*Guardian* 4 December 1992) and forced a withdrawal of the British currency from the European Monetary System. This compelled the Conservative government to adopt economic and political policies which they had previously rejected. The period between 24 August 1992, when share values fell by £10 billion, and December 1992 illustrates the volatility of financial capitalism and global financial markets.

Wallerstein's model explains the significant level of exploitation that takes place in many Third World countries by reference to their place in the wider international division of labour. It also allows us to understand the way political structure and internal mechanisms of control may vary from nation to nation, but are ultimately subordinated to the global capitalist economies. In many ways Wallerstein's model is a highly pessimistic analysis of the global economic system, arguing that control is removed from democratically elected governments and placed in the hands of the impersonal forces of capitalism. Such a position (as we shall see) is not without its critics.

## Articulation of modes of production

One of the key elements stressed by both Frank and Wallerstein was that the world was now encompassed by the capitalist system. For Frank, even the poor peasant farmer living in Chile, growing coffee beans for sale to the developed world, was part of a system of capitalist exploitation. In effect, he argued, there was now only one mode of production, capitalism, a system that was rigid and unbending in applying the same economic logic throughout the globe. Wallerstein's world system theory introduced a degree of flexibility that went beyond Frank's original ideas; different political systems were allowed to operate, but one overarching and all-powerful economic system remained in control – capitalism. In Wallerstein's model, political and social policies may be adopted in one country as long as they do not impinge on the operation of the world capitalist system itself.

Writers such as Ernesto Laclau (1977), following on from the pioneering work of French anthropologists such as Rey (1976), felt this argument was both inaccurate and misleading. Laclau challenged the idea of a distinct capitalist core and periphery. He believed that while capitalism may exist in the centre, at the periphery different modes of production existed. For Laclau the simple test of whether capitalism existed at the periphery was to ask: what relations of production existed there? For Laclau it was impossible to regard the relationship of the peasant farmer, who decides what to produce and when to produce it, to the landowner as equivalent to the relationship that existed between a worker on a production line and the owner of that factory at the developed capitalist core. In each of these modes of production there are specific social and economic relations of production. Although these may result in both the production line worker and peasant being at the bottom of the economic ladder, to say they are both on the same ladder is, for Laclau, totally misleading. The relationship to the ownership of the means of production, be it the land or the factory, is quite different in each case. In essence Laclau challenges Frank's argument (and to a considerable degree Wallerstein's) in suggesting that the relations of production that exist at the periphery are not, and need not be, capitalist for the process of exploitation to take place. Laclau argued that capitalism would use different modes of production for its own ends; it did not need to expand its own direct economic control and its form of economic relationship directly to the periphery in the way that Frank assumed it must. Moreover, the way that capitalism used different modes of production at the periphery was very sophisticated and far more complex than allowed for in either the Frankian model or in Wallerstein's world system model.

**Definition**

**Laclau's notion of the process of 'articulation'**

This is a concept first developed by Laclau in his critique of dependency theory. In dependency theory Frank and Wallerstein both made the assumption that only one global model of production existed – capitalism. For Laclau it was possible to have several modes of production operating at the same time across the globe. A mode of production, in classical Marxist terms, is an integrated system that links together complex economic, productive and social forces. In capitalism the mode of production involves specific economic, social and productive relationships between worker and owner of the means of production which signifies that they are in opposition to each other. Under feudalism these relationships will vary. Thus it is possible for non-capitalist modes of production to exist apart from, but be used and *articulated* by capitalism, without becoming capitalist. In this way it is in the interests of capitalism to preserve the feudal mode of production if this serves capitalism or at least does not act in opposition to it. Thus Laclau's focus on Latin America allowed him to describe the mode of production that existed there as semi-feudal. Capitalism simply accentuates and consolidates such exploitation for its own ends.

Laclau accepts that there is a real division between the capitalist centre and the underdeveloped periphery, and that peripheral countries perform vital services and roles that allow the affluence of the developed world to be sustained and even expanded. In essence a key function performed by the periphery is the provision of an indirect wage for the developed world. In the developed world workers not only are paid a wage by their employer, but also receive certain indirect amounts of income in the form of welfare services such as education, hospitals and social security payments, the so-called indirect wage. This indirect wage is paid by the state to the workers and their dependants. For the most part these indirect wages fulfil a number of functions, ensuring that workers are educated to a high enough level to enable them to take their place in the process of production and ensuring that the workforce is fit and healthy. It can also function to buy off potential discontent by higher living standards. Thus the social security net that exists in many western capitalist societies, and which provides the indirect wage, to a certain degree prevents the immiseration of the workforce and the potential for working-class discontent and revolution. (The term *immiseration* was coined by Marx and is the process by which the poor become poorer.)

A good example of how the process of articulation works is provided by an examination of *labour migration* (LM), where workers are drawn into the centre, that is the heart of capitalism, to perform the menial unskilled and low-paid jobs that the capitalist system is built upon, and which, at least during times of economic boom, western workers are reluctant to take. They are paid a wage by their employer, but this is often very low by western standards. While they perform a vital function in the labour process of capitalist economies they are not provided with any substantive form of indirect wage. Examples of the type of employment that such migrant workers perform is work in the service sector – catering, cleaning, household domestic work, transportation and textiles. However, the capitalist economic cycle necessarily includes both booms and slumps; as demand fluctuates within capitalism the migrant workers are the first to be laid off (and often sent home, away from the centre) during periods of economic recession. As they have no citizenship rights, and may often be deprived of even basic civil rights in their host country, it is relatively easy to dispense with their services at short notice and with very little fuss. Forced to return to their own country, they are paid no social welfare benefits or wages by the capitalist centre and must either depend upon their savings, or eke out an income through the existing economic structure (for example, subsistence farmers hawking goods in large cities). When the capitalist centre or core returns to a phase of economic boom, these displaced workers are drawn back into the capitalist economy. In this way the real costs of the worker are not met by capitalist employer or the society at the centre, but rather from the precapitalist, or articulated mode of production.

**Case Study**

### Guest workers

The *guest worker system* used in many European countries, particularly Germany, France and Switzerland, illustrates articulation in operation. A more widespread and disagreeable form of LM is found in South Africa and many southern states of the USA. Under the *apartheid* regime in South Africa it was illegal for black workers to live in white areas, yet many employers would require their 'domestic servants' to be available 24 hours a day if required. Such workers were often provided with very basic accommodation, living away from their families, who they would be able to see only on their limited days off. In the USA many *'illegal aliens'* from Mexico and Central America are employed in fruit harvesting or as domestic servants, as low-paid workers undertaking very menial jobs. Their illegal status excludes them from any of the civil, political or social rights enjoyed by citizens. As with the guest worker system employed in Europe, it is very easy to dispense of such workers when required.

In Laclau's (1977) model of articulated modes of production, capitalist economies are given a level of flexibility which allows them to sustain high living standards at the cost of continuing poverty and deprivation in the Third World. Any attempt at development by Third World nations is prevented by the economic control of the capitalist centre, when developed societies operate policies of import substitution, or play one society off against another, restricting economic development. The only way that non-capitalist societies might develop would be by a radical change in the world system that actively encouraged far greater equality between nations. This would require sacrifices on the part of the rich societies that they appear to be unwilling to make.

While the articulation of modes of production model is a useful analytical tool that seems to explain a number of different situations, it does have its own inherent difficulties. It fails to recognize significant differences between peripheral countries. There is a tendency in Laclau's work to see the world as divided between the capitalist mode of production and the articulated non-capitalist mode of production. The former comprise a small number of western societies, while the latter are the majority of the world's nations. In reality, its critics argue, there is as wide a level of variation between peripheral societies as between core and peripheral societies. At the periphery there are societies quite different from each other in terms of economic, political and social structures.

There is evidence that non-capitalist or pre-capitalist societies can take their own path to capitalist development, for example Japan during the post-war period. With the help of US capital, Japan transformed itself from a semi-feudal and rigidly controlled society into a modern and vibrant capitalist economy. Indeed so strong is the Japanese economy and industry that both North America and Europe have called for some form of restrictions on Japanese exports, lest their own industry collapse under the weight of competition. Japan's example is in turn being followed by many of the so-called 'tiger economies' or NICs (newly industrialized countries) of South East Asia. The fact that some societies are able to transform themselves into modern, advanced capitalist economies suggests that the rigid division of the globe into capitalist and non-capitalist modes of production is both misleading and inaccurate.

## Globalization

The development of capitalism radically reshaped the economic, political and cultural systems in those societies in which it first emerged. Initially this new economic force was highly localized, confined to northern European societies such as Britain, the Netherlands and France. However, in the past five hundred years capitalism has expanded to become the dominant world socio-economic system. In the post-war period this position of global dominance has further strengthened. The fall of communism signalled by the collapse of the Berlin Wall in 1989 appeared to herald the final victory of capitalism over the only alternative economic system in place since the end of the Second World War. It led the Harvard historian Fukuyama (1989) to publish an article entitled 'The End of History?' (see p. 99). In this article, which was widely discussed in the corridors of power in Washington, Bonn, London and Tokyo, Fukuyama proposed that the economic and ideological struggle between communism and capitalism had now been won by capitalism.

Since the late 1960s the pace of global capitalist economic expansion has increased dramatically. However, the process of globalization is much more than the workings of capitalism on a world level. While the former Soviet Union, eastern

Europe and China had, until 1989, offered an alternative economic, political and ideological path to industrial and technological development, that path has appeared to reach a dead end. Meanwhile capitalism, with its associated system of liberal democracy and emphasis on materialism and consumer culture, has transformed societies across the globe.

However, the traditional dominance of the established capitalist societies, particularly in the USA, is now being challenged. At the global level the rise of Japan and China as both manufacturing and military powers has raised doubts about the continued leading role of the USA. Mass unemployment in many societies is believed to mark a shift in which the power of wealth and global economic control is moving towards the Pacific rim countries. Others see the process of globalization as not merely the shifting of power between nation-states, but rather involving a radical change to the very idea of the nation-state itself. Rosenau (1990) argues that the intense pace of change makes the idea that nation-states can independently exercise power very uncertain. He believes that as capitalism becomes truly global the very idea of the nation-state, with its fixed boundaries and fixed structure, must be challenged. For Rosenau the main imperative of globalization has been the process of technological development brought about by capitalism.

What distinguishes capitalism from other economic and social systems is its flexibility, versatility and, for Rosenau at least, its central use of technological innovation in pushing cultural, ideological and economic barriers back. Clearly then for some writers, such as Fukuyama, the process of the 'globalization' of the world economy is synonymous with the triumph of capitalism and it is assumed that western societies play a leading, if not key, role in this process. What marks this process of globalization off from the expansion of 'capitalism' in the past, is the way in which the previous division between 'developed' (north) and the 'underdeveloped' (south) is no longer applicable. For Sklair (1991) globalization acts at three levels – economic, political and cultural ideological. Transnational corporations (TNCs) such as Shell Oil or the North American telephone company AT&T operate at not only a global economic but also a global political level. Their desire to accumulate profits through the development of new oil fields or markets for telecommunications have had significant impacts on nations with oil within their territory, or without developed systems of communication. Companies such as Shell and AT&T are virtually able to dictate the terms under which they will exploit such oil reserves or install telecommunications systems and for the most part they are able to extract agreements that reinforce their position of global importance. The question of relations between TNCs and Third World governments was graphically illustrated by the controversy surrounding Shell's activities in Ogoniland in south east Nigeria, following the execution of Ken Saro-Wiwa and eight other environmental activists in November 1995.

In the modern global world, knowledge, finance, manufacturing and even crimes know no national boundaries. Just as capital or manufacturing can flow easily from one country to another, so too can global tides such as drugs and the associated criminality flow from one part of the world to the next. Moreover to fight such tides of world-wide criminality, global policing is now emerging. In July 1994 the United States Federal Bureau of Investigation (FBI) opened an office in Moscow with the aim of exchanging information with its Russian counterpart, and to gather intelligence information which might be useful to other organizations such as Interpol, but perhaps more importantly to attempt to stay one step ahead of organized crime operating at a transnational and even global level.

With the internationalization of capitalist production, social relations have become international, rather than simply national. As an example of this the British computer company ICL has subcontracted its software design to a company in Puna, India. Here qualified software designers are paid the equivalent of about £3,000 per year, ten times less than an equivalent worker in Britain would earn. UK customers of ICL software are put through to the Puna engineers when they make telephone enquiries in Britain.

Giddens (1990) suggests that local conditions have less and less importance than at any time in the past. For example during the early 1980s the fate of the British mining industry was sealed by the actions of the Conservative government following free market principles and allowing the fate of the British coal-mining industry to be determined by the world price of coal. If British miners could produce coal at world market prices, pits would stay open, if not they would close. Foreign coal, particularly coal from Poland, was cheaper and led many users of coal, including the electricity generating companies, to switch suppliers. This reduction in demand for British-produced coal led to the decimation of an industry that had once been a central part of British life and certainly was one of the key working-class industries. Coal-producing areas such as South Wales and the Midlands faced economic ruin, social upheaval and increasing deprivation. The community culture, tradition and political outlook developed over generations was simply wiped away. However, the negative effect of such processes felt by miners in South Wales contrast with the positive effects in Upper Silesia, Poland, as pits expanded and miners were employed.

But what are the causes of globalization – the desire of capitalists for ever greater accumulation, as assumed by Marx? The inexorable workings of capitalist rationality as the most efficient economic system, as postulated by Weber? Or the world-wide spread of capitalist values, as argued by modernization theory? For Giddens there is no logical flow or implicit direction to the process of globalization, rather contradictory and often conflicting tendencies operate which nevertheless work in a dialectical process. This is perhaps reflected in the ways in which capital will create within NICs the most advanced structures that are clearly part of the global network of production and consumption, alongside what might be regarded as the most basic social structures and forms of existence. For example, the shanty towns of Brazil are set beside the gleaming skyscrapers of São Paulo (see Fig. 9.1, p. 366), and the cardboard city of homeless people is just yards away from the London Stock Exchange. For Giddens globalization is an uneven process. Its effect of disembedding social relations from their local context, and re-embedding them across space and time, may lead to powerlessness at the local level.

One of the most important implications of the process of globalization is the potential weakening of national autonomy and the further strengthening of supranational bodies such as the EU, OECD, IMF, G7 and WTO (see pp. 377–8). However, evidence to support the shift in power to such supranational organizations is far from conclusive. Writers such as D Gordon (1988) argue that decisions made at the level of the nation-state still maintain an impact at the level of operation of international capital. This can perhaps be illustrated by the strategy of the British government during the 1980s and 1990s to attract inward investment into the UK in the face of attempts by other European Union countries to do the same.

The British government utilized a number of devices, including tax concessions, financial inducements and infrastructure projects to attract several Japanese car companies such as Honda (Swindon), Nissan (Sunderland) and Toyota (North Wales). The current precarious demand for cars in world markets means that without such inducements these multinational companies would find themselves in very difficult circumstances. There is just as much to gain by TNCs in adopting flexibility and compromise towards national governments as there is bullying them. D Gordon (1988) argues that a mutuality exists in which the power and role of the nation-state should not be underestimated.

A central aspect of globalization is the development of a new international division of labour, in which many former colonies of western capitalist countries are taking a leading role. Many NICs have developed their economic potential by utilizing productive capacities and technologies originally developed in the western capitalist economies. Much of the manufacturing capacity of societies such as Singapore, Hong Kong, South Korea, Taiwan and Malaysia is based on established western capitalist manufacturing companies setting up branch plant manufacturing and providing training for managers and workers. For the most part these branch plants utilize labour-intensive assembly-line methods of production. In the 1980s and 1990s both Korea and Malaysia have developed their own export oriented car industries that have successful penetrated European markets. Much of the plant, technology and components for these vehicles come from Japan. Thus, outdated production lines and older models are given a new lease of life in another country while Japan develops its products at the higher end of the global market.

**Definition**

## Global organizations

### IMF (International Monetary Fund)

Often regarded as the rich countries' central bank, this world financial organization was set up by the USA after the Second World War to provide economic support for industrial expansion primarily in the west, but during the 1960s onwards provided loans to countries in the developing world such as Brazil and Mexico. Usually loans provided by the IMF come with strings attached. There are strict rules on overdrafts and loans, but these are far harsher than high street banks would impose, for example, demanding economic, political and social change in societies receiving loans.

### World Bank

Effectively an arm of the IMF, the World Bank grants loans to Third World countries. As with the IMF and developed societies, rules on lending are strict. However, during the 1960s a general flexible expansion in credit took place as the world economy expanded. Many Third World and developing nations borrowed heavily at what were then favourable rates of interest. Following the oil price rises after 1973, interest rates climbed and the cost of servicing such loans became immense. More loans were taken out to pay back the interest on earlier loans. In the late 1970s and early 1980s some Third World countries threatened to default on their loans unless interest rates were reduced. As a result an international banking crisis ensued from which we are only now recovering.

*(box continued)*

*(box continued)*

**G7**

This group of leading industrial economies comprises the USA, Japan, Germany, France, the UK, Italy and Canada. The **G10** group also includes Belgium, the Netherlands and Sweden. Since the early 1990s, Russia has attempted to gain access to this 'club' in the hope of influencing global economic policies. To date it has been refused entry due to what are termed 'structural deficiencies in the Russian economy', most probably the lack of truly developed capitalist markets and 'liberal democratic freedoms'.

**OECD (Organization for Economic Cooperation and Development)**

Formed by a larger group than G7, the OECD includes countries such as Iceland, Finland, Denmark, Sweden, Switzerland and New Zealand. OECD reports on individual member economies are taken seriously, not only within the organization, but also by the country itself.

**GATT (General Agreement on Tariffs and Trade.)**

Under the Bretton Wood Agreement of 1948, post-war western governments decided that the only way to prevent a future war was by free trade between nations. This would allow a general rise in living standards for all western societies, thus preventing the rise of fascism as in the 1930s. Since the 1980s leading capitalist countries such as the USA have tried to further liberalize world trade and open up markets in the developing nations.

**Uruguay Round**

The most recent agreement within the GATT nations will allow an expansion in the level of world trade by the removal of import barriers between nations. For some developing nations there is a real fear that their emerging industries will be swamped by competition from the developed nations, in particular in the fields of new technology.

**WTO (World Trade Organization)**

This organization will take over responsibility for policing world trade from GATT; like so many global or supranational bodies it is based in Washington, DC. Its formal role is to monitor world trade and employ sanctions against those member nations who impede free trade.

**NAFTA (North American Free Trade Agreement)**

This is an agreement signed by the USA, Canada and Mexico to open up their countries to each other's goods and services. During 1993, while NAFTA was being negotiated, the US trade union movement launched a political campaign to derail it, arguing that NAFTA would lead to the export of US manufacturing jobs as companies relocated in Mexico to take advantage of low wage rates.

Central to the process of globalization has, as Rosenau (1990) points out, been the pace of technological change within capitalism. Trade and communication have been transformed since the 1960s. Changes in telecommunications, computing and information technologies have led to the emergence of what Marshall McLuhan (1962) termed the 'Global Village'. Greater global interconnection has had a profound influence in shaping all our lives. Every year, the processing power of computers has doubled during the 1990s, while the real cost of computer technology has fallen, mostly due to the low wages paid to workers in the NICs who assemble such products, but also and importantly due to rapid advances in semiconductor technology. More computing processing power has been squeezed into ever smaller and cheaper computer chips. As a result of this computers have become smaller, vastly more reliable, far cheaper and more readily available.

**Q** Look around your home or college and list any electronic consumer items. Do the product names sound either high tech or Japanese? How much do they cost? Has the cost of the item fallen since it was purchased? Has the specification of the equipment improved for the same price? Where were these goods made?

**Case Study**

### Financial services

In the financial service markets technology has been used to dramatic effect. Throughout the 1980s stock markets in London, New York, Hong Kong, Frankfurt and Tokyo utilized developments in computer technology to facilitate massive growths in trading capacity and overall efficiency. The move away from trading in paper shares or paper currency to electronic transactions has meant that many more dealings can take place. Linking in satellite communications with these very fast computer systems has had profound effects that shape our lives; stock market computers in several countries are in direct contact twenty-four hours a day.

In the 1990s the development of the first truly global financial system has enabled stocks and shares once traded only in London to be instantaneously available in Hong Kong and San Francisco.

Sklair (1991) has pointed out that these kinds of transactions are largely beyond the control of national governments. The growth of world-wide financial service industries has supported the development of the transnational capitalist class, who are reliant upon the global operation of capitalism.

International communication via computers and satellites have further facilitated the ability of capital to flow from one country to another. In the 1980s the free market policies of Ronald Reagan in the USA and Margaret Thatcher in Britain further removed remaining legal and political constraints on the free flow of capital between nations. Just as flows of capital have meant the relocation of manufacturing from one part of the globe to another, benefits have been drawn back into the west. In Britain, many of the pension funds hold stocks and shares in developing global markets. The fate of manufacturing industry in Taiwan or Korea may have an effect on the living standards of future pensioners.

Between 1965 and 1985 the number of televisions world-wide grew from 190 million to 710 million (Unesco report 1989). The developing world accounts for 20 per cent of all television sets world-wide, a figure that is increasing year by year. There is in constant geostationary orbit a belt of satellites – mostly controlled and developed by the USA, Japan and Germany – which facilitate telephone, radio and television contact with every part of the earth. These satellites monitor weather patterns, provide instantaneous communications between countries and assist trade and capital flows. Satellite communication allows other economic and cultural dimensions to be added to the process of globalization. Since the early 1990s, many satellites have been launched, in particular as China and European nations enter the space race, with the explicit intention of widening the market for capitalist goods and services. Featherstone (1991b) points out that this may result in the increased repression or submersion of national culture in favour of a highly commercialized materialist and capitalist culture.

Such developments inevitably further the reach of capitalist values and its attendant consumer-based culture. In the late 1980s the Hong Kong entrepreneur Sir Run Run Shaw launched a communications satellite on the back of a Chinese space rocket. This satellite, named 'STAR', has a 'footprint' that extends over China, South East Asia and as far as India, broadcasting to an audience and market in a total of thirty-eight countries. In 1992 Rupert Murdoch's News Corporation entered into partnership with the owners of STAR, providing Murdoch with another forum for broadcasting most of his readily available programming developed for BSkyB. Many people living in Indian cities such as Calcutta now regularly tune into STAR; it is quite common to see arrays of satellite dishes pointed skywards to receive western soap operas dubbed into Hindi.

Much of the complex technology and computer chips which support these satellites are produced in the developed world. The current technological lead held by the west has led some to believe that new forms of colonialism are developing. Electronic colonialism and consumer colonialism have no national boundaries, are not controlled by national governments and answer only to the owner of the satellite and the producer of the broadcast images. The satellite owners and broadcasting

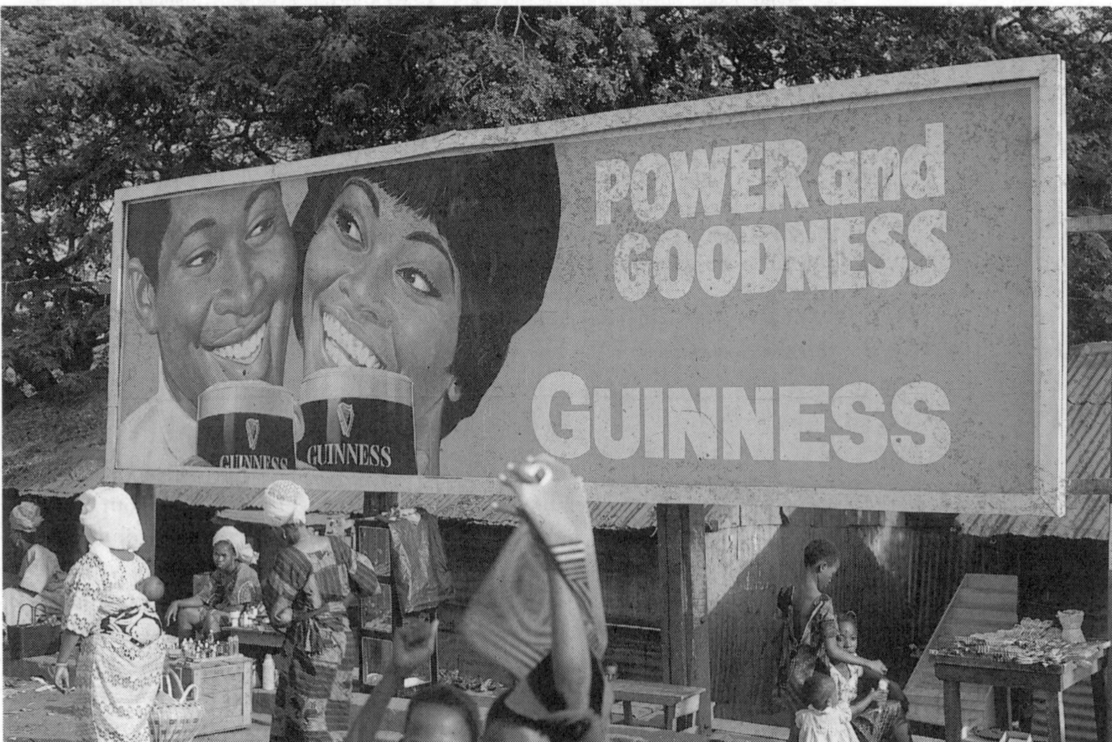


**Fig 9.2** Guinness advertisement, Nigeria; manufacturers have adapted their campaigns to suit particular societies. (Courtesy of Robert Harding Picture Library Ltd.)

companies have been quick to utilize the opportunities offered by globalization, but so too have manufacturers and advertisers. The US soft drinks company Coca-Cola was the first to break into truly global advertising of its products. Jingles such as 'I'd Like to Teach the World to Sing' (first broadcast in 1971) demonstrate how both product and culture are being packaged for a global audience. Advertising companies who promote Coca-Cola world-wide have done so through a process of 'glocalization', adapting their global campaigns so that they do not affront the local sensibilities of particular local societies. TV adverts in the Philippines or Korea less frequently show smiling American kids on skate boards drinking coke and more often Asian children in 'culturally specific settings' enjoying a coke. In fact these ads are mostly written and produced in the USA using suitable looking bilingual actors. Coca-Cola is now the most widely known (and used) consumer product in the world. Its advertising message is simple, its product immediately recognizable and its taste the same in every part of the world. Where Coca-Cola led others have followed. Products such as Kodak film, Levi jeans and McDonald's hamburgers have all become household names and household products across the globe.

Should we see such developments in a totally negative way, as unavoidable results of progress? Such pessimism ignores the essential diversity of human cultural practices that fight against such homogenizing influences. As Giddens (1990) acknowledges, while the process of globalization may indeed be driven by the accumulation needs of capitalism, its effects on people may be unintended and result in reactions not necessarily beneficial to capitalism. For Featherstone (1991b) the development of a global culture may offer the prospect of unity through diversity in which the increased level of cultural contacts can draw people together in realization of their common aspirations.

One of the most profound implications of the process of globalization is its effects on our way of thinking and acting. This is vitally important to sociology, which emerged as a discipline in direct response to the changing world of nineteenth-century Europe and North America. Since the 1970s the pace of change has accelerated, but it would appear our ability to comprehend such change in the way of grand theorists such as Marx, Weber or Durkheim has yet to. For the most part sociology confines itself to the local and immediate and while such concerns clearly have a validity, the very pace of globalization may make any 'answers' to local questions quickly redundant.

## Rates of development

Since the 1960s the gap between the rich countries and poor countries has grown wider. Simpson (1994) argues that Gross National Product (GNP) can be used as a measure of the wealth and degree of development of a society. In effect the GNP of a society is the total value of the goods and services produced within that society. Thus tables which give the GNP per person of various societies give a very good idea of the overall wealth of one society in comparison to another. However, as Simpson cautions, such figures do not indicate how that wealth is spread within a society; a society can be very rich, but with massive differences between the people at the top and the bottom.

**Fig 9.3** GNP per head (US dollars).

| Key | |
|---|---|
| GB | Great Britain |
| Bh | Bangladesh |
| Ba | Bolivia |
| Et | Egypt |
| Ea | Ethiopia |
| Fr | France |
| D | Germany |
| Hi | Haiti |
| Ia | India |
| Isa | Indonesia |
| S | Sweden |
| USA | United States of America |
| Ze | Zaire |

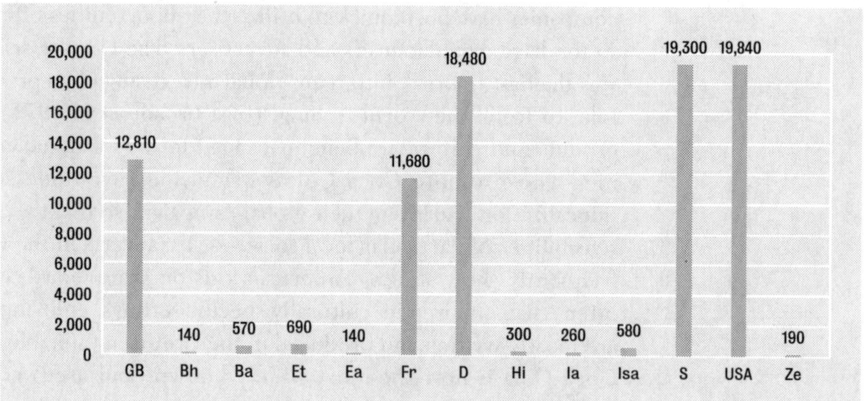


*Source*: Based on data supplied in *World Development Report*, (UN 1984)

**Fig 9.4** Daily calorie intake in relation to life expectancy.

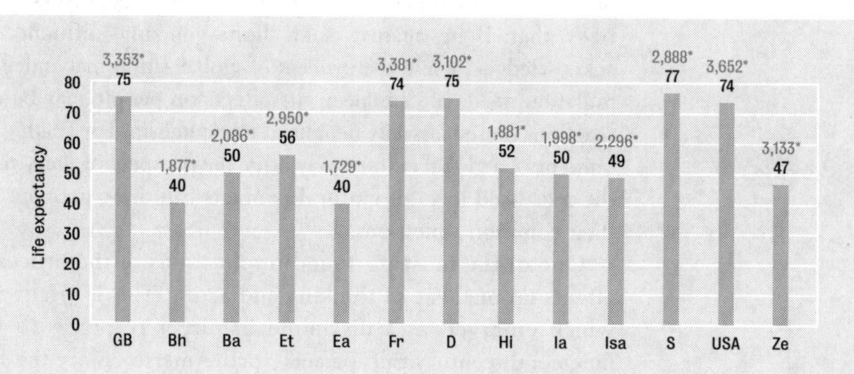


*Note*: *Daily calorie intake
*Source*: Based on data supplied in *World Development Report*, (UN 1984)

**Fig 9.5** Infant mortality per 1,000 live births.

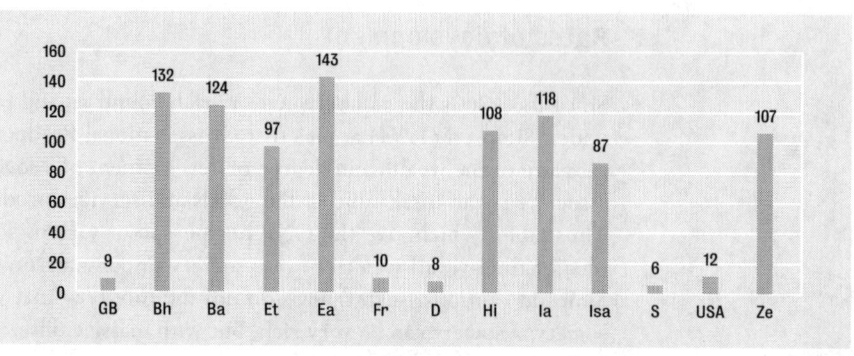


*Source*: Based on data supplied in World Development Report, (UN 1984)

The level of GNP of a society directly relates to the ability of that society to feed itself. The poorer a society, the less its ability to pay for the importation of food. The richer a society, the more it can spend on food. Countries such as Ethiopia, Afghanistan, Columbia and many others use their precious agricultural land in the production of agri-exports, attempting to earn foreign currency which will allow them to survive. The majority of their population live on basic, meagre diets while people in the developed world are mostly overfed on a wide variety of foodstuffs.

Average calorie intake per individual varies considerably between rich developed societies and poor developing nations. Food and calorie intake is related to life expectancy: the lower the amount that a society is able to spend on food, the lower the average life expectancy and the higher the rate of infant mortality rates in that society. The basics that any individual needs to survive are clean water, adequate diet and shelter. In many Third World societies these basics are becoming harder to obtain.

## Third World debt

During the 1960s and early 1970s many Third World countries borrowed massive amounts from the IMF, World Bank and even commercial western banks with the hope of boosting their own economic activity and thus forcing development to occur. However, the expected expansion in world trade never occurred. Indeed in 1973 the dramatic rise in oil prices led to a world debt crisis which affected both the developed and developing world. The tight fiscal policies adopted by many western nations had two effects on Third World nations; first, an increase in their own debt level forced them to abandon or significantly reduce their aid levels to the Third World, and second, they were much less willing to accept imported goods from other Third World countries.

In the early 1980s many western banks started to believe that these Third World countries would have difficulty paying off their loans. The cost of loans had risen dramatically in the years following 1973, with interest payments becoming an increasing burden on developing societies. In many cases countries had to take on new loans to help them pay off their earlier loans. The repayments on new loans can account for 10–15 per cent of export earnings. These problems were illustrated when Mexico defaulted on its international debt in 1982 leading to the so-called *Third World Debt Crisis*. Latin American countries were among those that faced the largest debts – Mexico $103 billion, Brazil $117 billion and Argentina $59 billion. The cost of this to individuals in these countries was disastrous. Individual income fell by 1.5 per cent per year during the 1980s, while in the west individual income was growing at the same rate. Linked to the international debt crisis were the fiscal crises of many Third World and developing societies. The attempt to sustain living standards while paying external debts forced inflation rates to climb dramatically in many countries, including Brazil, Argentina, Nigeria, Algeria and the Philippines (in 1990 Brazil had an inflation rate of 1,000 per cent, for example).

The cost of such debt in human terms is immense. In Ghana, an African economic success story, growth rates doubled between 1985 and 1995 – far faster than in many other African countries. However, to service its external debt, Ghana has to spend one-third of its export earnings, money that is not available for schools, health or food. The British aid agency, Oxfam, calculates that for every £1 spent on health by African countries in 1993, £3 was spent on servicing debt repayments.

## Aid

In 1992 the USA provided nearly $1 billion in foreign aid; in cash terms it is the largest aid donor to developing countries, although it provides less than 0.2 per cent of its GNP in aid.

Simpson (1994) points out that since the early 1970s most major donor nations have substantially reduced their aid budgets in real terms. While Britain provided 0.32 per cent of its GNP in 1994 in aid, this was a reduction from 0.47 per cent GNP in 1965. For most developed countries, aid is often linked to trade. Donations of aid give the impression that the rich nations are indeed helping their less fortunate friends. In reality aid is often a double-edged sword.

**Fig 9.6** Aid as a percentage of GNP 1991.

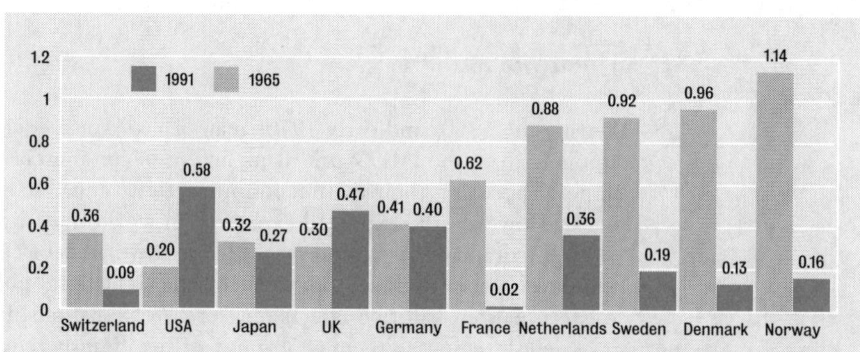


*Source*: Based on data supplied in *World Development Report*, (UN 1984)

**Case Study**

**Pérgau Dam Project**

The British government granted aid in excess of £234 million in 1991 to help the Malaysian government build a large dam, which, it was argued, would provide hydro-electric power to a rural part of Malaysia. The non-governmental and voluntary aid organization World Development uncovered the fact that this project was linked to the purchase of British weapons by the Malaysian government. In effect the dam was built by British taxpayers' money, but only in return for substantial purchases of military equipment by Malaysia. John Pilger (1994), the investigative journalist, brought to the world's attention that most aid is associated with trade, often trade of military equipment, much of it propping up corrupt military and undemocratic regimes in the Third World.

The ESAP programme adopted in Zimbabwe is one example of a move towards a free-market-led capitalist path to development. The move away from collectivized agriculture based upon the 'Soviet Model' gained momentum in the mid-1980s. Countries such as China, Vietnam, Cuba and parts of Africa have all moved away from socialist forms of economic management. In agriculture this has led these societies to focus on production for export. Thus it is possible to buy exotic fruits

Case Study

**Zimbabwe: the effects of western aid policies**

Western policies of aid to developing countries are now more cruelly wedded to trade than ever before. During the drought years of 1988–93 the Socialist government of Zimbabwe was forced to adopt stringent economic polices by the IMF and World Bank. In particular the Economic Structural Adjustment Policy (ESAP) placed far greater emphasis on agricultural production for export than agriculture for self-sufficiency. Subsidies to village communities have been cut, welfare policies abandoned and educational changes introduced for school children. Zimbabwe is now forced to spend hard-earned foreign currency importing maize, a staple of the Zimbabwean diet, and a product once exported to neighbouring countries. The emphasis placed upon the acceptance of western ideas, economic systems and cultural values has been to the detriment of many people of the Third World.

and vegetables from China, Ethiopia and Brazil, for example, year round at your local supermarket, yet the cost of such developments has been horrific in the Third World.

**As famines loom, Ethiopia is growing flowers. Not the kind of flowers you can eat, no – but roses, carnations and chrysanthemums. The country has joined Third World competition to supply fresh flowers to northern decor lovers. . . . Flower growing is the most polluting form of agriculture known to man. Nobody will buy a bloom that has been half eaten by bugs. So every hectare must be fed 10 tonnes of fertiliser and pesticides every year; the soil must be biologically dead. . . . The cruellest cut is that this takes money out of the Third World. The grower earns only 10% of the wholesale price of every flower: the other 90% is made by air freight and trucking firms in the north, wholesale dealers and the ever expanding flower auctions in Holland.** ***(N Maharas, 'Downside of Third World Boom', Guardian 7 November 1994)***

## The demographic time-bomb

The western world's population remains static or declines, while rates of population growth in the developing world have increased. In an effort to maximize their income many families in the Third World increased the number of children they had out of economic necessity. In 1950 the annual growth in world population was 28 million per year; by 1960 it was 72 million. By the year 2000, annual population growth is predicted to reach 94 million: the number of babies born each year will equal the current total population of Germany. UN statistics show that in 1991 there were 5.3 billion people in the world; by 2050 there will be 10 billion people. The US-based World Watch predicts that population levels could reach between 10 billion and 14 billion by 2050, with the biggest increase in population taking place in Asia and Africa.

The UN World Population Conference in Cairo in 1994 recognized that the biggest threat to world stability is not the proliferation of arms, but rather population growth. The developed nations offered advice to the developing nations on

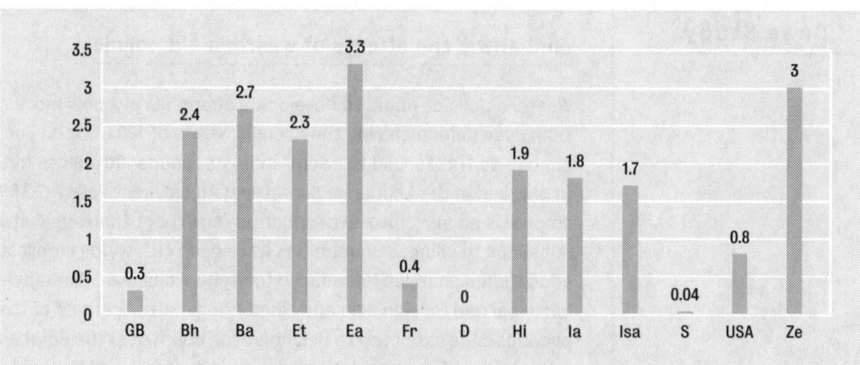


**Fig 9.7** Population growth rates for year 2000.

*Source*: Based on data supplied in *World Development Report*, (UN 1984)

ways of curbing population growth. As with aid, such advice appears to be more out of self-interest, rather than humanitarian concern.

Population growth rates are static or declining in the developed world, but in the developing world they are increasing by 2 per cent per year – a doubling of population every thirty-five years. It is clear that in those societies with expanding populations some form of action needs to be taken to reduce population growth. The developed world commands the majority of the world's income, but its population at 1.2 billion is only 29 per cent of the developing world.

**Case Study**

### Global inequality and the extent of poverty

**In the 1960s the richest 20 per cent of the world's population received 70 per cent of world income, and the poorest 20 per cent only 2.3 per cent. By 1990 the poorest 20 per cent of the world's population saw their share of world income drop to 1.4 per cent, while the richest 20 per cent saw their share increase to 83 per cent.**

**In 1995 the World Health Organization (WHO) showed that one-fifth of the world's population live in extreme poverty, almost one-third of the world's children are undernourished and half the global population lack regular access to essential drugs. It found that 12.2 million children under 5 die every year, 95 per cent from poverty-related illnesses. More than 1 million children die of measles every year when vaccines to save them would cost only 9p each.**

**(WHO reported by Chris Mihill, *Guardian* 2 May 1995)**

In many Latin American countries, poor half-starved children roam the streets, often searching rubbish bins for scraps of food, stealing to survive. Such has been the large number of these children and their 'perceived threat to public order' that right-wing death squads routinely shoot these children and dump their bodies in rivers and sewers, believing that they have done society a favour, by ridding it of vermin. In India it is estimated that despite child labour laws, 55 million children are forced to live as little more than slaves. Often these children work twelve hours per day, seven days a week producing carpets, pottery, leather-goods and other items for western markets.

Part of the solution to the demographic time-bomb is the greater empowerment of women in regard to their reproductive life. However, in many societies, both developed and less developed, cultural barriers, in particular lack of education, prevent women having access to and making decisions over contraceptives and abortion. At the 1994 Cairo conference both the Vatican and Islamic delegates joined forces in condemning any weakening of traditional family structures and encouragement of what they perceived as permissive behaviour.

However, the demographic outlook is not all bleak. As was demonstrated at Cairo, some countries have had remarkable success in introducing programmes to reduce population increase.

---

**In country after country, average fertility rates have been falling dramatically over the last 20 years. . . . Bangladesh is one of the most interesting examples of this so-called 'reproductive revolution'. It is one of the world's poorest nations, with high infant mortality and a large agrarian society, in which most families still depend on children for their labour and security in old age. But between 1970 and 1991, fertility rates declined from 7 to 5.5 children per woman (a 20% reduction). And key to that was the increase in the number of married women using contraceptives; up from 3% to 40% In short, contraception is the best contraceptive, not development.**

***(Guardian 2 September 1994)***

---

In the early nineteenth century Thomas Malthus argued that any attempt to increase the living standards of the poorest section of the population above subsistence level was bound to fail because it would lead to an increase in the general or total population that would be unsustainable. Since 1950, the growth in world trade, the impact of the so-called 'green revolution' in agriculture and the use of technology has prevented the type of global catastrophe predicted by Malthus from occurring. However, there is disagreement as to the effects of these demographic changes. Some bodies such as the UN Food and Agricultural Organization (FAO) believe that high yields and the further application of technology to agriculture will ensure that growth in population is matched by growth in food levels. Other organizations such as Green Peace and World Watch believe the technological quick-fix can no longer be applied. Indeed, they argue the further use of science and technology in the form of the genetic engineering of crops and the increased use of organ-ophosphate fertilizers will lead to a real deterioration in the 'carrying capacity' of the planet.

**Q** What do you think the implications of population growth are for (a) natural resources; (b) climatic and environmental effects; (c) food supplies; (d) levels of poverty?

As the wealthy nations retain and increase their share of global wealth, for individuals in Third World societies more members in the family may mean the difference between survival or death. Why do you think this is so?

**Summary**

- Early sociological theories of development aimed to explain the 'development' of societies; the sociology of development has reflected this notion of the superiority of the advanced, capitalist world, for example, the hierarchy of 'worlds' from 'First World' to 'Fourth World'.
- Modernization theory illustrated this ethnocentric thinking and was criticized by Marxist influenced writers such as Frank (underdevelopment theory) who 'blamed' the rich capitalist nations of the west for exploiting the rest. Other theories that have emerged as critiques of these positions (such as world system and articulation theories) have themselves emphasized the crucial role of the capitalist mode of production.
- Globalization is a concept illustrating the growing interdependence of world economies and therefore societies. The decline of communism following the fall of the Berlin Wall has been interpreted by writers such as Fukuyama as evidence that capitalism is the only economic system able to offer Third World countries a path to a developed status: liberal democracy and capitalism have passed the test of time. Globalization is reflected in the increasing domination of the world economy by transnational capitalist companies. This process has weakened the autonomy of nation-states.
- In spite of growing world interdependence, global inequality (specifically the gap between rich and poor nations) shows little sign of diminishing. This inequality is reflected in (among other things) the food eaten and the life expectancy rates in different countries. Expansion of the world economy and world trade has led many of the economically weaker nations to borrow from the richer ones. The cost of repaying these loans has had disastrous consequences for such nations.
- For the past five or more centuries there has been an implicit assumption that progress (most often material progress) is both desirable and sustainable. The west, more by good fortune in being the first to develop manufacturing technology, has been able to maintain a steady increase in living standards, material prosperity and economic growth. However, since the 1960s there has been a gradual shift in sociology away from grand theories, or meta-narratives, be they pro or anti-capitalist. Our new understanding of the process of globalization presents us on the one hand with a stark realization of the potential for planetary catastrophe while on the other hand allows some room for optimism. In attempting to understand the effects of western materialism and consumerism on the cultural practices and lifestyles of the Third World, sociology can also offer a critique of such practices and lifestyles in the capitalist world.

## Further reading

Harris, G (1988) *The Sociology of Development*, London: Longman.

This provides a short, clear introduction to theories of development.

Simpson, E S (1994) *The Developing World: An Introduction*, 2nd edn, London: Longman.

As well as providing a great deal of up-to-date data on rates of development, fertility, mortality, etc., Simpson introduces the basic issues of development in the Third World and examines how particular nations are attempting to secure sustainable economic development.

Hulme, D (1990) *Sociology and Development: Theories and Practice*, London: Harvester Wheatsheaf.

This is particularly good on the complexities of agricultural production in the developing world.

Lemert, C (ed.) (1993) *Social Theory: The Multicultural and Classic Readings*, Oxford: Westview.

Worsley, P (ed.) (1991) *The New Modern Sociology Readings*, Harmondsworth: Penguin.

Both these books include a range of useful readings which will provide you with an introduction to and flavour of the work of writers discussed in this chapter – both 'classic' and more recent development theorists.

Toye, J (1993) *Dilemmas of Development*, 2nd edn, Oxford: Blackwell.

This book provides a detailed examination of the effects of western economic policies (and particularly the policies promoted by Reagan in the USA and Thatcher in the UK) on the developing world.

## Activities

### ■ Activity 1 Third World images

The image of the Third World supported by modernization theory is one in which war, poverty, famine, disaster and drought are either natural disasters or self-inflicted wounds which visit these societies on occasion. These disasters or social upheavals are often explained in terms of the general inefficiency or even corruption common to such societies or because of their lack of rational values or scientific or professional processes of management.

Such views are not uncommon and often condition the way that we see and relate to the Third World. The Band Aid concert to raise money for the starving people of Ethiopia in 1984 or the Oxfam appeals in the 1990s for help in Somalia or Rwanda appear to deny the west and developed world any part in creating such situations. Charitable appeals ask us to respond in humanitarian ways, but while they are generally hugely successful in terms of raising money they do little to prevent those problems re-occurring. Our attention to such disasters is often brought about by media coverage, including media appeals by the rich and famous on behalf of charities. Such appeals are intended to prick our consciences and then ease them by credit card payments over the phone.

Search through a selection of recent newspapers for stories, features or adverts which relate to Third World countries.

#### Questions

What images are portrayed of the particular societies? Do you feel these images are accurate?

Are any explanations offered for the situations or conditions being described?

What sort of response is being invited from the reader?

What do you think are the advantages and disadvantages for Third World countries of accepting charitable aid from the west?

## Activity 2 Understanding dependency

This activity is intended to help develop an understanding of the concepts surrounding sociological theories of development. A useful way of helping to identify or empathize with the predicament of dependent nations is to consider the options that are open to individuals when they are financially dependent on others and the effects which the choice of particular options might cause. Does it make things better or worse? Do the long-term effects outweigh the immediate benefits?

Imagine that you are at the end of the first year of your course and now have a large overdraft at the bank. Next year you know that such an overdraft will entail bank charges.

### Questions

What strategies might you adopt to resolve this problem? What effects would such strategies have? List these strategies and effects in the two left-hand columns on the chart.

Are there equivalent strategies open to national governments. What effects would such strategies have for these governments? List the strategies and effects suggested for governments in the two right-hand columns on the chart.

| Individual | | National | |
|---|---|---|---|
| Strategy | Effects | Strategy | Effects |
| Example: Sell your possessions | Low price for goods. May have to replace later at inflated prices. Poorer lifestyle. | Example: Sell off national assets | National assets controlled by outside interests |
| | | | |
| | | | |
| | | | |

# Chapter 10

# The family

**Chapter outline:** Introduction • Changing family patterns • Marriage, divorce and cohabitation • Single parent families • Homosexual families • Elderly people • Theoretical perspectives on the family • Current issues in the sociology of the family • The ever-changing family • Summary • Further reading • Activities

## Learning objectives

When you have studied this chapter you should be able to address these key questions:

- What problems arise in trying to define concepts such as the family, marriage, childhood and old age?
- What is the relationship between family patterns and wider social and physical environments?
- Does the rise in rates of divorce and cohabitation mean that the family and marriage are no longer valued?
- How are specific groups affected by social expectations within the family and society at large, for example single parents, homosexual couples, elderly people, children?
- What are the major areas of debate within the sociology of the family?

## Introduction

My father was frightened of his mother; I was frightened of my father, and I am damned well going to see to it that my children are frightened of me.

(George V, quoted in Donaldson 1976: 10)

The stereotype of the family epitomised by the husband as the sole wage earner, wife as full time housekeeper and mother with dependent children living at home (that is, the family which is featured almost exclusively in the advertising world), in fact comprises only a minority of households at any given point in time.

(Henwood *et al.* 1987: 3–4)

The family is regarded as one of the most basic and important institutions in society. In fact, what the family is, and should be, is regarded by some as such unquestionable common sense that it became central to the British Prime Minister's call for a return to traditional values in 1993, a theme that was intended to run through all areas of government policy in the years to follow:

**It's time to get back to basics: to self-discipline and respect for the law, to consideration for others, to accepting responsibility for yourself and your family, and not shuffling it off on the state**

*John Major's address to the Conservative Party Conference, November 1993)*

However, the fact that some felt a moral crusade to strengthen family values was needed at all reveals that contemporary British society is experiencing considerable social change in relation to attitudes, values and structures concerning family life. (In fact the career of the 'back to basics' theme was rudely interrupted by the abject hypocrisy surrounding a series of revelations of government ministers' extra-marital affairs, illegitimate offspring and seeming disregard for their party's own standards of morality.)

Even the apparent bastion of traditional British values – the Royal Family – conforms to these general trends. Of the Queen's four children one is divorced and remarried, two are separated and the last is, for the moment, a bachelor. Of her six grandchildren, four are being brought up by lone parents and two are in a reconstituted family with their mother and stepfather.

A glance at some contemporary media forms also reflects awareness of the transition. In most popular television soap operas, for example, how many families fit the nuclear model of once-married parents living happily with their two children under one roof? (It is however argued later in this chapter that a more comprehensive analysis of the media shows that an ideological model of the family is still portrayed as the desirable norm.)

Clearly then the family is an exciting area of sociological study, particularly when set in a comparative context over time and culture. Research has shown that all societies exhibit some form of family and marriage arrangements. At the same time however, while it can be argued that the family is universal, the form that it takes is subject to enormous variation. Even if we take a single multicultural society such as Britain, it is evident that there are many forms of family life and that the nature of the family has changed over the years. These forms of family are examined in this chapter.

## Defining the family

It is inappropriate to talk about '*the* family' as if there is only one universal type; although it is more appropriate to talk about 'family life' and to explore the many variations of family life in contemporary society, let us try to give a preliminary definition of what we mean by 'the family'. While we all operate with a common-sense understanding of what we mean by the family, once we try to define the family it soon becomes obvious that it is not so straightforward. Such an exercise highlights the enormous cultural variation in the forms of family life.

Q Complete this sentence. The family can be defined as . . .

What difficulties arise in attempting to come up with a definition of the family?

Most sociological textbooks give a definition of the family. Here are two examples:

**A family is a kin-based co-operative** *(Broom et al. 1981: 324)*

**A group of people directly linked by kin connection, where the adult members take responsibility for caring for children.** *(Giddens 1989: 384)*

Behind such definitions lie some common assumptions of the family. Giddens' definition stresses the idea of parental responsibility. Traditionally this was broken down by gender such that the father was seen as the main breadwinner while the mother was expected to take on the main role in child-rearing and running the home. Aspects of social policy have reinforced the idea of fathers taking responsibility for supporting the family (for example the Child Support Agency: see pp.406–7). Over time this cultural expectation has been challenged and many women take on a dual role.

A cross-cultural perspective shows that definitions of childhood and adulthood are not universal, with consequences for assumptions about roles and responsibilities within the family. In Britain the age of majority is18, in Austria children are not legally independent from their guardians until the age of 19; in Switzerland it is 20 and in Malaysia 21. Assumptions about parental responsibility and relationships between members of the family tend to vary across different societies and even within different cultural groups within society. The social construction of age-related behaviour also extends to the other end of the life cycle in terms of expectations about retirement, pensions and the status of elderly people.

Q In Britain at what age can you (a) vote; (b) watch a PG category film unaccompanied; (c) be convicted of a criminal offence; (d) open a bank account; (e) leave school; (f) marry without parental consent; (g) buy a firearm; (h) become an MP; (i) qualify for a pension; (j) qualify for cheaper fares on public transport?

How do these ages vary in different countries?

The nature of marriage has changed in Britain in terms of the increase in divorce. We now talk about 'serial monogamy' referring to patterns of marriage, divorce and remarriage. There has also been a decline in the overall number of marriages and a rise in the number of births taking place outside of wedlock.

*Social Trends* (1994: 37– 8) analysed marriage and divorce rates in Britain since the 1970s. The number of marriages has fallen by almost 16 per cent, while divorces have more than doubled over the same period (see pp. 402–5). In 1981, 1.5 per cent of divorces in Britain occurred within the first two years of marriage. Following the Matrimonial and Family Proceedings Act 1984, this proportion multiplied sixfold to reach nearly 10 per cent in 1991. Over a quarter of divorces in 1991 occurred after five to nine years of marriage, but one-fifth occurred after twenty or more years.

**Fig 10.1** Grooms wanted for ... In societies like India, where arranged marriages are common, people use a wide range of methods to find suitable spouses.

WANTED FOR 28 years old Sindhi girl B.Com. DBM slim fair employed healthy diabetic under control physically handicapped diabetic also preferred. Broad-minded. Reply to Post Box No. 8493, Times of India, Madras 600034. (MDBR054450)

ALLIANCE FOR slim smart looking convent educated post graduate Sindhi girl 26/153 with independent source of income from well settled Bombay based boys Profession service business. Write to Box H 679-I, Times of India, Bombay 400001. (BYDR052975)

ALLIANCE INVITED for homely good looking graduate innocent issueless divorcee belonging to well to do family 30/5'4", from Bombay based boys. Write to Box H 790-I, Times of India, Bombay 400001. (BYDRO53970)

ALLIANCE INVITED for fair attractive Sindhi girl 24/164 cms, B.Sc. (Genetics) from U.K. coming from respectable family settled in Gulf, groom from highly educated, tall, handsome well settled business/ professional Hindu family, send bio data and horoscope and photograph returnable to Box G 674-I, Times of India, Bombay 400001. (BYAGO46826)

ALLIANCE FOR good looking, Sindhi girl 30/5'3", non working, from respectable family, from boys of business community of decent respectable families. Write to Box H B57-1, Times of India, Bombay 400001. (BYDP054286)

ALLIANCE INVITED for 24 yrs, 5'4" B Com. good looking Sindhi girl from decent cultured, well settled boys. Caste no bar. Contact 2622595/2622596 (Rita). (BYDR052903)

MATCH REQUIRED for 5'4" B.Com. South Indian Brahmin Vadama girl, 25, married and separated within a month. Now employed in Delhi and living with mother. Subsect no bar. Broadminded parents and boys contact Box 46473, Times of India, New Delhi 110002. (C80051946)

WANTED HINDU Tamilian tall wheatish complexioned educated well settled with clean habits between 30-35 for tall good looking respectable girls. Apply with photo to Box CC-863-S, Times of India, Bangalore- 560 001.

A SUITABLE match for a Telugu Mudiraj girl 26/163, B.A. passed having own beauty parlour. Write to Box H872-1, Times of India, Bombay 400001. (THBRO54371)

FOR 6000 Niyogi Andhra girl, 23/160, appearing final Chartered Accountancy, professionally qualified boy from decent family. Apply to Box H 767-1, Times of India, Bombay 400001. (BYDRO53738)

PROPOSALS INVITED for Aryavysya girl, B.Com. 23/155, white complexion, slim, beautiful from Aryavysya professionals, CAs/engineers/ doctors/ graduates well placed in job/business. Write to Box H 487-K, Times of India, Bombay 400001. (THBRO52017)

(Extracts from **Sunday Times of India** 24 April 1994)

**Q** Define (a) monogamy; (b) polygamy; (c) polyandry.

Why do some societies practise polygamy?

What do you think are the advantages and disadvantages of monogamy, polygamy and arranged marriages?

## European birth rates

*Social Trends* also highlights a dramatic rise in the number of births outside marriage since 1960. In the UK in 1992 this was almost one in every three births. The UK trend compares with other European states in this respect since in all European countries the proportion of births outside marriage doubled in the thirty years up to 1991. At the same time, however, the evidence suggests that more of these births were occurring in stable relationships. Three-quarters of the births outside marriage in the UK in 1992, for example, were registered by both parents in contrast to only 45 per cent in 1971 (*Social Trends* 1994: 40).

*Social Trends* details not only established patterns but also family-building projections, estimating the number of children that women are likely to have and the size of families based on current trends. For instance, more women are deciding not to have children at all or to have them later on in life and to have fewer. The average number of children per woman fell in all European countries from 2.4 in 1970 to 1.48 in 1992. The Irish Republic had the highest fertility rate in both years (3.93 in 1970 and 2.11 in 1992), while the UK average fell from 2.43 to 1.8 over the same period. Obviously such changes in child-bearing trends may be due to a variety of factors and are likely to have an impact in the future on the structures and patterns of family life. In China the impact of government policy restricting families to one child only is being felt. It is now being predicted that the concept of 'aunts' and 'uncles' (as blood relatives) will be meaningless to the next generation.

A common assumption about the family is that marriage involves having children. Young married couples are often asked when they are planning to 'start a family'. In some societies and communities the expectation and pressure to procreate can be more explicit, with child-bearing regarded as a couple's duty and a part of their responsibility to the community or state. In France child-bearing is encouraged through legislation, while in Singapore tax incentives have been used to encourage graduates to marry and start families. Many traditional religious and ethical codes regard child-bearing as a natural consequence of marriage and include prayers in wedding ceremonies that the couple will be blessed with offspring.

Many people see having children as not so much an obligation or even a choice but as a right. Archard (1993: 97) discusses how human rights charters have recognized the right of adults 'to found a family' as referring to both bearing and bringing up children. (Archard examines the limits and contingencies regarding this right, including concern for the well-being of the child and the consequences for society of any birth – 1993: 98.) Partly as a result of this view of child-bearing as a right, there continues to be extensive research and development in the field of biological and genetic engineering.

**Case Study**

### Foetal eggs: a fertile ground for debate

**These extracts are taken from the letters page in the *Guardian* on 6 June 1994. They illustrate public concerns about the use of genetic engineering and parenthood.**

Recent advances in reproductive technology have done much to enable some of those hitherto unable to have children to become parents. These developments have given hope to some, while causing many to consider the ethical and moral dilemmas created by our newfound ability to control aspects of our reproductive potential. . . .

Clearly there is a need for a wide ranging and informed debate. . . . However we must take care to ensure debate is not clouded by excessive anxieties about the possibility of abuse by a few at the expense of significant benefits for many others.

*(box continued)*

*(box continued)*

The debate on the ethics of genetic engineering is taking place with too narrow terms of reference. The reason why the concept of eugenics is unacceptable . . . is that it means making decisions for other people about their procreation – people without power to object. . . .

Overpopulation, defined as too many poor people, means that we in the North, who have our fertility checked by sheer consumerism, applaud sterilisation programmes and condoms galore (megabusiness!) for states which are still in fact colonies and cannot afford to listen to their own indignant populations. . . .

Genetic engineering is the latest focus for capital investment. Its application involves the need for control by laws and the state . . . but not by the millions of women who are never consulted when patriarchy acts 'for their good', 'to give them choice' and divide them into wombs, foetuses, eggs, each with a claim to life which sets the woman's rights against the 'properties' in her own body. . . .

We are back to eugenics: imposing a reductionist, patriarchal view of procreation and scientific 'progress' on an earth full of powerless people, when all that is needed to improve the human stock is food, shelter, freedom from want and war.

### Questions

**What ethical and political viewpoints are being put forward here?**

**How are traditional views about parenthood being challenged?**

Cross-cultural comparisons of family legislation, religious customs and kinship patterns show the significance of social context for different types of family structures. In analysing the different forms of family within society, sociologists make the distinction between the nuclear and extended type of family. The *nuclear family* is often referred to as 'immediate family' – parents and children living in the same household. The *extended family* goes beyond this to include wider kin such as aunts, uncles and grandparents. One feature of industrialization is the weakening of extended family ties as younger members of the family become socially mobile and move away from home for work and to set up their own nuclear family (see pp. 399–400).

Sociological research has shown that as societies change and evolve, so does the nature of the family. Expectations and assumptions about the family are constantly changing and it is impossible to study the family as a unit in isolation from wider developments in the nature and structure of society. Politicians recognize this when they use the welfare of the family as an indicator of the general health of society and express concern over figures that seem to suggest that the family as we know it is in decline. Those who mourn the apparent demise of the family tend to work with two further assumptions about the family: first, that the family is a positive and desirable part of society and that it is good for its members, and second, that where there is evidence of the negative side of the family this is a relatively new phenomenon and the traditional family did not experience it. Both of these assumptions have been challenged by sociologists.

## The ideology of the family

'Family ideology' in contemporary society is the idealized image of the family that tends to be the basis of our common-sense understanding of what the average family is or should be:

**Family boundaries and family relationships are shaped not merely by concepts or constructions as to what is but also by normative conceptions of what ought to be. By using the label 'ideology' in this context (rather than 'norms', 'values', 'mores' etc) we hope to convey the possibility that certain agencies are more specifically concerned with the generation of familial ideology . . . and the possibility of there being 'deviant' or counter-ideologies.** *(Morgan 1975: 210–11)*

The agencies that Morgan refers to may include the state (in terms of the assumptions about the family conveyed in welfare or educational arrangements), political parties (in terms of political structures and policies), legal systems (in terms of the structures and assumptions behind family law) and the media (in terms of its portrayal of family life).

The influence of ideology can be illustrated by a closer examination of media projections of the family. Abercrombie and Warde (1994) refer to commonly accepted media stereotypes of the 'cereal packet family' as the 'typical' normative family: two fairly young parents and their two children (a girl and a boy). The family is seen as a harmonious refuge, a unit of consumption, a 'good thing'. The ideology of the family corresponds to a functionalist model in that it is regarded as a positive social influence, beneficial both for its members and for society as a whole.

Marxists have criticized the ideology of the family as being distorted and biased and raising false expectations:

**The ideology of the family would have us believe that there is one type of family, one correct way in which individuals should live and interact together. . . . An ideology that claims there is only one type of family can never be matched in reality, for it represents an ideal to which only some can approximate, and others not at all.** *(Gittins 1985: 167)*

Find examples of the 'typical' family in, for example, adverts, holiday brochures, Christmas ads, women's magazines, including exceptions that prove the rule.

What are the typical roles of adults and children, women and men in these representations?

In your view how close is this image to reality?

The power of the concept of the ideology of the family lies in the fact that it is taken for granted rather than being subjected to constant reappraisal. Morgan suggests that even within sociology the ideological dimension is 'an important, yet often absent, part of the analysis of family relationships' (Morgan 1975: 213). What makes it all the more important to consider the ideology of the family is the fact that it often does not represent the reality of how individuals interact together. However,

> **it manifests just enough similarity to people's life situations to make it seem tangible and real to most. Thus the never-married, the divorced, and the childless can at least identify part of the 'ideal family' with a past childhood or family distorted in memory, and feel that their own 'failure' has been an individual failing rather than an unrealistic ideal.** *(Gittins 1985: 165)*

## Changing family patterns

### The role of the extended family

We tend to accept that the nuclear type of family is both a natural and normal arrangement for society. It is the yardstick against which 'abnormal' or 'alternative' types of families (such as one-parent families) are measured. However, sociological research reveals that the patterns of family life are far from constant and are subject to changes in line with changes in wider society. While it is true that today most people live in a household of three or more people, there has been a rapid increase in the number of people living either alone or with one other person (*Social Trends* 1994).

One of the best known studies of changing family patterns in Britain was carried out by Young and Willmott (1957) on working-class communities in east London in the 1950s. Like other family and community studies in the 1950s (for example Firth 1956; Kerr 1958), this classic study highlighted the strength of kinship networks. Young and Willmott found that the traditional extended family kin network weakened as younger members of the family moved from Bethnal Green to housing estates like Greenleigh in outer London and set up their own nuclear form of family. ('Kinship networks' covered all the relatives whom a person knows to exist, in all the families to which they are linked, such as through marriage as well as family of origin.) In Bethnal Green Young and Willmott found that traditionally most married couples had lived close to their parents-in-law and maintained virtually daily contact, particularly mothers and daughters whose relationship tended to be strong and vital. In this way the extended family had functioned as a mutual reciprocal support service, an arrangement threatened by change:

> **In a three-generation family the burden of caring for the young as well, though bound to fall primarily on the mothers, can be lightened by being shared with the grandmothers. The three generations complement each other. Once prise out two of them, and the wives are left without the help of grandmothers, the old without the comfort of children and grandchildren.** *(Young and Willmott 1957: 197)*

The effect of increasing levels of occupational and geographical mobility was to erode close-knit networks. It brought the transition from the characteristic extended family to the smaller nuclear pattern. This type of nuclear family was more self-contained with greater emphasis placed on conjugal relationships (the relationship between husband and wife).

## The family and industrialization

Young and Willmott's study illustrated, as later research has borne out, that changes in the physical and social environment can have enormous impact on patterns of kinship. Their final passage in 1957 sent out warning signals to town planners designing new housing and aiming to create new communities:

**Even when the town planners have set themselves to create communities anew as well as houses, they have still put their faith in buildings, sometimes speaking as though all that was necessary for neighbourliness was a neighbourhood unit, for community spirit a community centre. If this were so, then there would be no harm in shifting people about the country. . . . But there is surely more to a community than that. The sense of loyalty to each other amongst the inhabitants of a place like Bethnal Green is not due to buildings. It is due far more to ties of kinship and friendship which connect the *people* of one household to the *people* of another. In such a district community spirit does not have to be fostered, it is already there. If the authorities regard that spirit as a social asset worth preserving, they will not uproot more people, but build the new houses around the social groups to which they already belong.** *(Young and Willmott 1957: 198–9)*

Many out-of-town overspill estates and high-rise housing blocks in the 1960s came under severe criticism for having destroyed family and community life by failing to acknowledge the significance of geography and environment for family networks.

Taking a longer term historical perspective, historians such as Laslett (1972) and Anderson (1971) have carried out research which reinforces the effect of external environmental changes on family life. Their research suggests that before industrialization kinship was much less strong and that the onset of industrialization may well have helped to bring about the growth of the extended family pattern. By comparing family size and composition in pre-industrial England, Laslett (1972) suggests that the nuclear family may have been a significant factor in helping to bring about and accommodate the development of industrial society. Anderson (1971) analysed later nineteenth-century family life in Preston, finding evidence by then of the importance of kinship ties and exchange relationships in meeting the challenges of industrializing society. Thus in contrast to the popular myth that the changes accompanying industrialization are inevitably harmful to family networks, the research suggests that in Britain the opposite was historically true. Indeed Willmott (1988) has since commented that the strong extended family bonds found in Bethnal Green did not exist a hundred years earlier but rather emerged as a result of changes in the economy and housing patterns.

Since the 1960s the traditional urban kinship pattern in Britain has continued to weaken:

**A number of changes have broken the old order: high levels of geographical mobility, redevelopment of the inner areas of Britain's cities and industrial towns, changes in the family and marriage, and the increase in the number of wives going out to work (reducing their contacts with their mothers).** *(Willmott 1988: 44)*

Willmott points out, however, that while families may no longer live physically close to one another there is still close contact between them and relatives continue to be the main source of informal support and care. In follow-up research based on families in north London, Willmott (1988) found that families helped each other in areas such as child care, babysitting, lending money and supporting elderly relations and that class differences were not marked in this. High contact is facilitated by the car, the telephone and public transport systems.

Willmott concludes that although western kinship systems are based on choice – such that individuals can choose whether or not or the degree to which they maintain contact with wider kin – what is significant in British society is the fact that the family continues to survive, indeed to flourish. In support of a functionalist approach, Willmott implies that this is because the family continues to fulfil an important role within contemporary society.

**The most striking feature of British kinship, now and in the past, and in both urban and rural environments, is its resilience . . . kinship has continued, as it still continues, to supply the ties and support that people need. Throughout British history it has proved to be a national resource of great value. This has been possible because of its power to adapt to greater mobility and to the demands and opportunities of an increasingly urbanised world.** *(Willmott 1988: 46)*

**Case Study**

## Family life in an industrializing society: Malaysia

**This extract is taken from a Malaysian daily newspaper.**

**PM: Don't ape West blindly**

Malaysians must be discerning when imitating the West so as not to be caught in the social decay of the society, Datuk Seri Dr Mahathir Mohamad said today. The Prime Minister said . . . Malaysia too wanted to develop like the West so as to achieve a higher standard of living and to avoid being oppressed by other countries. 'But there are many flaws in Western societies, one of which is the decay of the family institution' he said when launching the first National Family Day celebrations at the Bandar Tun Razak Football Stadium here.

Dr Mahathir said once the family institution was destroyed there would be no meaning to progress. . . . He said the family institution had almost ceased to exist in the West. 'There are Westerners who place so much importance on independence and self-interest that they refuse to get married. They live alone and have temporary relationships'. Dr Mahathir said many Western couples also refused to have children or abandoned their responsibility once their children became teenagers.

'In the West there are nuclear families comprising just the parents and the children. Grandparents and other relatives are regarded as strangers' he said, adding that they did not accept responsibility for what happened to their relatives. The aged, he said, were dumped in old folk's homes where they were left to live out their days. 'Very often the government was held responsible for the welfare of the aged' he said.

He also spoke of the lack of parental control in Western societies where teenagers took drugs and committed crimes. Dr Mahathir said there were signs of decay in the

*(box continued)*

(box continued)

social fabric of Malaysian families as the nation entered the era of second generation societies where people were born and bred in urban surroundings. . . . Previously 'newly-weds lived with their parents or in-laws but now young couples move into their own houses after marriage' he said, adding that this trend would erode the family institution system if left unchecked. (*The Star* (Malaysia) 12 November 1990)

### Questions

**As a rapidly industrializing nation Malaysia is experiencing rapid changes in family life. Compare and contrast features of Malaysian and British families as portrayed in this article.**

**How would you respond to Mahathir's criticisms of family life in the West?**

## Marriage, divorce and cohabitation

Family breakdown and divorce are a significant part of contemporary family life, and affect all levels of society. Despite the increasing rate of divorces and the greater social acceptance of the vulnerability of relationships, the breakdown of marriages among rich and famous people regularly attracts sensational media attention. This suggests that there is still a certain amount of stigma associated with the break-up of a family even where a split may be seen as being in the best interests of all concerned. Nevertheless the increase in divorce has not detracted from the popularity of marriage, cohabitation and the attraction of family life, which seems to reinforce the view that the ideology of the family is as strong as ever. Here we shall examine trends in marriage, cohabitation and divorce and consider the sociological explanations behind them.

Case Study

### Royal attitudes to marriage and divorce

**Henry VIII** broke away from the Roman Catholic Church in order to divorce his first wife, Catherine of Aragon, his older brother's widow; he married a further five times.

**George IV** had two wives at once; he separated from the second, Caroline of Brunswick, and went back to the first, Mrs Maria Fitzherbert, a Roman Catholic.

**Victoria** had nine children with Prince Albert, most of whom married into other European royal houses.

**George V** married May of Teck after her original fiancé, his older brother, died.

**Edward VIII** relinquished the throne after 325 days in order to marry divorcée Wallis Simpson, saying ' I now quit altogether public affairs and I lay down my burden'.

**Princess Margaret** was prevented from marrying a divorcé, Group-Captain Peter Townsend, but later divorced Antony Armstrong-Jones.

**Princess Anne** married and divorced Mark Phillips, then married Tim Laurence.

**Prince Charles** married Lady Diana Spencer, who was descended from the Stuarts via an extra-marital liaison of Charles II; they separated after revelations about his relationship

(box continued)

*(box continued)*

with Camilla Parker-Bowles. This led to debates about his future as king and head of the Church of England. The Royal Marriage Act 1772 limits the monarch's freedom to marry, divorce or remarry (for example the monarch may not marry a Roman Catholic).

**Prince Andrew** married, then separated from, Miss Sarah Ferguson.

**Public opinion** In a *Daily Mail* opinion poll (12 December 1993), 70 per cent polled said they would oppose Prince Charles being king if he stayed married and kept Camilla as his official mistress. However, if he divorced Princess Diana and married Camilla then 64 per cent would oppose his succession.

### Question

How closely do you think changing royal attitudes towards marriage and divorce reflect those of the general public?

## The rise in divorce

In Britain there has been a steady increase in the rate of divorce since the Second World War. Between 1971 and 1991 it more than doubled while the number of marriages fell by almost 16 per cent (*Social Trends* 1994: 33). This rise is not unique to Britain but is matched by rising divorce rates in other European countries and in the USA. Statistics suggest that the prevalence of divorce and cohabitation has risen in most European countries while marriage rates have declined (*Social Trends* 1994: 37).

**Definition**

### Divorce terminology

It is important to adopt a careful and critical approach to any statistics presented on divorce and the terms used.

**Divorce rate** number of divorces compared to the number of marriages in any one year.

**Divorce petitions** number of requests for divorce.

**Divorce absolutes** number of marriages fully terminated by law.

As Nicky Hart (1976) points out, the statistical rate of divorce in England and Wales is not a full measure of the incidence of marital breakdown since not all separated couples seek legal termination through the courts. Others may separate without recourse to the law or else maintain an 'empty-shell' marriage, continuing to live as husbands and wives but with no real quality of relationship left.

Are some couples more prone to divorce than others? On the basis of present trends it is estimated that four in ten marriages will end in divorce (Gibson 1994: 30). Some marriages are statistically more likely to end in divorce, including teenage marriages, couples who start their child-bearing early, couples with four or more children, local authority tenants and couples with relatively low income. The rising divorce rates have affected all age groups, with the 25 to 29 age group having the highest divorce rate among both men and women in 1991 (*Social Trends* 1994: 38).

**Table 10.1** Marriages: by type.

| United Kingdom | Year of marriage | | | |
|---|---|---|---|---|
| | 1961 | 1971 | 1981 | 1991 |
| **Marriages (thousands)** | | | | |
| First marriage for both partners | 340 | 369 | 263 | 222 |
| First marriage for one partner only | | | | |
| Bachelor/divorced woman | 11 | 21 | 32 | 32 |
| Bachelor/widow | 5 | 4 | 3 | 2 |
| Spinster/divorced man | 12 | 24 | 36 | 35 |
| Spinster/widower | 8 | 5 | 3 | 2 |
| Second (or subsequent) marriage for both partners | | | | |
| Both divorced | 5 | 17 | 44 | 45 |
| Both widowed | 10 | 10 | 7 | 4 |
| Divorced man/widow | 3 | 4 | 5 | 4 |
| Divorced woman/widower | 3 | 5 | 5 | 4 |
| Total marriages | 397 | 459 | 398 | 350 |
| Remarriages as a percentage of all marriages[a] | 14 | 20 | 34 | 36 |
| Remarriages of the divorced as a percentage of all marriages[a] | 9 | 15 | 31 | 34 |

*Note:* [a] Remarriage for one or both partners
*Source:* Office of Population Censuses and Surveys

**Table 10.2** Divorce: by duration of marriage.

| United Kingdom | Year of divorce | | | |
|---|---|---|---|---|
| | 1961 | 1971 | 1981 | 1991 |
| **Duration of marriage (percentages)** | | | | |
| 0–2 years | 1.2 | 1.2 | 1.5 | 9.3 |
| 3–4 years | 10.1 | 12.2 | 19.0 | 14.0 |
| 5–9 years | 30.6 | 30.5 | 29.1 | 27.0 |
| 10–14 years | 22.9 | 19.4 | 19.6 | 18.3 |
| 15–19 years | 13.9 | 12.6 | 12.8 | 12.8 |
| 20–24 years | | 9.5 | 8.6 | 9.5 |
| 25–29 years | 21.2 | 5.8 | 4.9 | 5.0 |
| 30 years and over | | 8.9 | 4.5 | 4.1 |
| **All durations (= 100%) (thousands)** | 27.0 | 79.2 | 155.6 | 171.1 |

*Source*: Office of Population Censuses and Surveys; General Register Office Scotland

Q

What do these statistics tell us about divorce and remarriage?

What factors do you think might help to explain recent trends in marriage and divorce in Britain?

In explaining divorce rates, sociologists examine the wider social, economic and legal context of marriage and divorce. Such factors help to explain why the rates have risen as much as they have. A more complex analysis also challenges simplistic conclusions such as the view that marriage is entered into less seriously or is no longer highly regarded.

One factor that has contributed to the increase in divorce is that legal changes have made divorce easier. This suggests that the rise in divorce may not reflect the breakdown of marriage so much as the opportunity for broken marriages to be officially terminated. Following the Matrimonial Causes Act 1923, under which women were given equal access to divorce, the number of petitions rose from 2,848 per year to 4,784. The number of petitions rose dramatically after the Legal Aid Act 1949, which made divorce accessible to larger numbers of people by introducing financial aid for paying solicitors and court fees.

The Divorce Reform Act 1969 altered the concept of and grounds for divorce; there is no longer in law the idea of guilty parties but rather marriages can be terminated on the basis of irretrievable breakdown. Provision was also made in this Act for divorce after specified periods of time (two years with the agreement of both parties, five years where only one agrees). Fletcher (1988) points out that the aim of this legislation was not only to bring the law into closer touch with the social realities of marital breakdown but also to serve and support the family in society. According to the Law Commission the aim was

> **to buttress rather than undermine the stability of marriage, and, when regrettably a marriage has broken down, to enable the empty legal shell to be destroyed with the maximum fairness and the minimum bitterness, distress and humiliation.**
>
> *(Fletcher 1988: 2)*

The number of divorces also rose dramatically between 1984 and 1985 following the introduction of the Matrimonial and Family Proceedings Act 1984. Couples no longer have to be married for at least three years before they may petition for divorce, but may do so after their first anniversary. Thus while in 1981 1.5 per cent of British divorces occurred within the first two years of marriage, by 1991 this proportion had multiplied sixfold to nearly 10 per cent (*Social Trends* 1994: 38).

**Q** While changes in the law are significant, the rise in divorce cannot be attributed solely to this. Legal changes only make it possible to end a marriage which has already failed. What changes in social and religious attitudes can help explain the increase in divorce rates?

Another factor which may help to explain the increase in divorce is the changing status and attitudes of women. Women are more independent economically and socially and the increase in the number of wives petitioning for divorce shows that they are more able and willing to take steps to end dissatisfactory relationships. Some analysts suggest that women now expect more from marriage and are less willing to accept relationships with men who are unwilling to participate in household tasks and responsibilities.

Rates of remarriage suggest that marriage is as popular as ever. Indeed the rates of remarriage represent 'one of the most striking trends in family patterns in the last thirty years or so' (Morgan 1994a: 108). Although rates of cohabitation have increased, this generally tends to be, in Britain at least, 'a prelude to marriage rather than a substitute to it' (Morgan 1994a: 109).

## Increasing cohabitation

Just as divorce and remarriage have increased, so has cohabitation. A survey into the history of marriage in more that thirty European nations since the Second World War (Lord 1992) (carried out by the charity One Plus One: Marriage and Partnership Research) found that half of couples marrying in England and Wales live together first. The report predicted that the rest of Europe may increasingly follow the Swedish and Danish model where

> **the vast majority of people live together before marriage, nearly half of those aged thirty are not expected to marry at all, one in two marriages end in divorce and half of all births occur outside marriage.** *(Lord 1992: 2)*

While cohabitation tends to be less stable than marriage and most cohabitees eventually marry, there is evidence in Scandinavia that cohabitation is becoming more popular than marriage and that in Sweden cohabiting resembles marriage more closely, exhibiting 'greater permanency and childbearing' (Lord 1992: 2). The implication of this, as the report predicts, is that more children in Europe will in future be brought up in single-parent families, predominantly by their mothers.

> **In countries with high rates of relationship dissolution, a substantial proportion of children will be brought up by mothers alone for much of their childhood. If this trend continues the only indissoluble relationship will be between mothers and their children.** *(Lord 1992: 2)*

This emerging trend along with rising divorce rates raises the question of the welfare of children and the effects on them of marital break-up and single parenthood. Studies on the effects of divorce have found that compared to children in unbroken families, children involved in divorce perform less well at school and have more behavioural problems. The damage done to children by marital conflict occurs long before divorce and lasts long after it. Kathleen Kiernan found this in analysing the

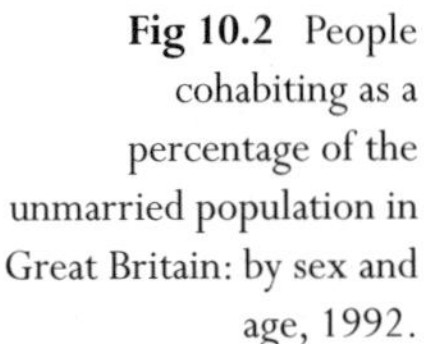

**Fig 10.2** People cohabiting as a percentage of the unmarried population in Great Britain: by sex and age, 1992.

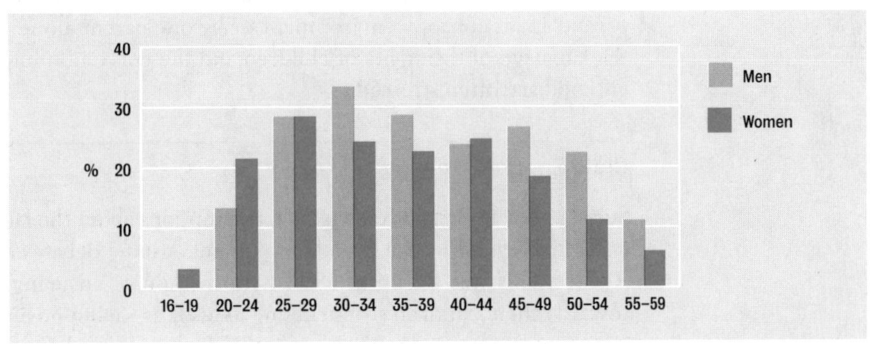


*Source*: Genral Household Survey, *Social Trends* 1994:38

findings from the National Child Development study of 11,000 children born in 1958. At a conference on young people and divorce in 1993 she reported:

**Evidence is beginning to accrue which suggests that children from lone-parent families and particularly step-families are more likely to leave home at a young age and for negative reasons, such as conflict and friction.**

***(Kathleen Kiernan, quoted in The Times 9 October 1993)***

## Single parent families

One of the most dramatic changes in the nature of families in Britain since the 1960s has been the increase in the number of single parent families and associated social concern about the welfare of family members. This means that organizations such as Social Trends have to operate with a wide definition of the family: 'A family is a married, or cohabiting, couple with or without children, or a lone parent with children' (*Social Trends* 1994: 35). The proportion of the population living in single parent families quadrupled between 1961 and 1992. While most people still live in the 'traditional' nuclear family, the proportion of these is declining (*Social Trends* 1994: 35).

A number of factors help to account for the increase in single parent families, including the rise in divorce and births outside marriage. There has been a lessening of the stigma associated with births outside marriage, partly as a result of secularizing influences. Between 1979 and 1989 the percentage of conceptions outside marriage increased almost 80 per cent to 42 per cent of conceptions in England and Wales in 1989 (*Population Trends* 1991). Younger parenting is also a feature of single parenthood; about one-fifth of lone parents in Britain were aged under 25 between 1989 and 1991(*Social Trends* 1994: 35).

The increase in single parent families not only challenges the stereotype of the 'normal' family, but also generates much discussion about the roles of parents and the moral welfare of children within different family arrangements. Some see the decline in marriage and the rise in the proportion of single parents as symptomatic of a diminishing sense of parental responsibility, particularly on the part of fathers given that most single parents are women. The concern centres especially on the well-being of children growing up in the absence of two parents and raises again the important issue of the primary function of the family in nurturing children. The implication is that where the influence of one or both parents is missing, children are in some sense deprived. The question is: is it better to be brought up by both parents in an unhappy environment or by one parent alone? It is in this context that the language of the rights of children and the corresponding responsibilities of parenthood are often stressed.

### Child Support Agency

Social policy in Britain reflects such assumptions about the family and has been graphically highlighted by the foundation of and ensuing debates about the Child Support Agency. This was set up in 1993 with the aim of ensuring that fathers contribute towards their children's upbringing as well as saving government expenditure on income support to lone parents (this had increased from £322,000 in 1979 to

£895,000 by 1991).The launch was seen as 'a recognition that the traditional family structure is breaking down and mark[ed] a break with the permissive attitudes over parental obligations towards their children' (*The Times* 10 February 1995).

However, the establishment of the agency brought widespread and vigorous reaction. Within a matter of months it was accused of insensitivity and inefficiency in the way it conducted and followed up its calculations. Groups representing single mothers were unhappy about being forced to claim maintenance from absent fathers from whom they wished to break contact, while groups representing fathers claimed that the agency failed to take account of men's financial circumstances in assessing contributions. It soon became apparent that in order to achieve its targets the agency was focusing on those fathers who were already keeping up payments rather than pursuing the vast majority of absent fathers who never paid at all.

The effects of the foundation of the Child Support Agency were far-reaching. It was blamed for a number of male suicides and the break-up of several second marriages, all of which eventually led to demands for a review. To this end an active campaign of lobbying and demonstrations was supported by mushrooming pressure groups such as The Campaign Against the CSA, Families Need Fathers, Absent Parents Asking for Reasonable Treatment (APART) and The National Campaign for Fair Maintenance. Eventually modifications were introduced, including the phasing in of new payments over a longer period.

An interesting aspect of the public debate around the Child Support Agency was its focus on fathers' abdication of responsibility and the reaction this generated in relation to fathers' sense of rights and needs in relation to parenting.

**Case Study**

**Effects of family breakdown**

**Man loses fight to prove child is his**

The Court of Appeal yesterday refused to order blood tests to determine the father of a young child, saying it was better to let her live in ignorance than risk upsetting her family life.

The tests were being sought by a man attempting to prove the girl, born after his affair with a married women, is his child.

The woman, named only as Mrs F, said her husband was the father, although she accepted that, at the time of conception, she was also having a sexual relationship with the other man. She and her husband are bringing up the girl, the court was told.

In an appeal against an earlier High Court ruling, the applicant, known as Mr B, argued it was best for the child to know the identity of her natural father. . . . He argued that in the future, the girl could unwittingly marry a blood relation. Further, he said that she could develop a disease for which treatment depended upon knowledge of her genetic make-up. . . .

But Lord Justice Balcombe, sitting with Lord Justice Nolan and Lord Justice Kennedy, dismissed these arguments, pointing out that the girl had been brought up 'as a child of the family of Mr and Mrs F.' Lord Justice Balcombe said: 'Now, and for the first few years of her life . . . [the child's] physical and emotional welfare are inextricably bound up with the welfare of the family unit of which she forms a part: any harm to the welfare of that unit, as might be caused by an order for the taking of blood tests, would inevitably be damaging to [the child].'

*(box continued)*

*(box continued)*

Afterwards, the applicant . . . said: 'My argument . . . is to do with the truth. What the court is saying is that it is all right for this child to go on being told things about her origins which those telling her know are almost certainly untrue.' He had started the action because 'I feel I'm being deprived of my daughter and . . . my daughter is being deprived of me'.

The Children Act had appeared to ensure that a child would be brought up by 'two natural parents', but in practice 'it still seems to be so much in favour of the mother', he said. In future, mothers would be able to say 'I don't want this man to be declared the father.'

(*Independent* 6 February 1993)

### Questions

**What assumptions are illustrated in this article in relation to (a) the needs of children; (b) the needs of fathers?**

**What are your views on these assumptions?**

## Homosexual families

Research into homosexual families illustrates the diversity of styles of relationships that can be described as constituting an alternative to the family and, as O'Donnell (1993: 191) points out, shows the danger of simplistic stereotyping of homosexual couples.

There are, for example, differences in the way in which male couples organize their relationships. Plummer (1978) describes how some couples may go through a set of marriage rituals similar to a heterosexual couple involving a period of engagement, a wedding ceremony and a honeymoon. Here the marriage may mirror a heterosexual one in terms of one partner being the main breadwinner. Plummer contrasts the homosexual marriage with the boyfriend relationship where the couple live apart and may conceal their relationship. A third arrangement is the homosexual partnership in which the couple's lifestyle is adapted to their particular needs and interests. This type of partnership rejects the model of marriage and distinctive roles as apparent in the other two models.

Lesbian couples also have different types of relationships, some again being based on a traditional type of gendered role distinction, others being more complementary or egalitarian. Tanner (1978) carried out research into lesbian couples in the USA and like Plummer came up with three categories of relationship, thus calling into question generalized assumptions about the nature of homosexual lifestyles.

The subject of homosexual families tends to become contentious when children are involved and questions are raised about their welfare. Some homosexual partners (particularly women, who are more likely to gain custody than men) may previously have been married or have children either from unmarried relationships or from artificial insemination. Reflecting the dominant ideology of the family, many people instinctively feel that children will suffer from being raised in the absence of either a father or mother. This remains an area for ongoing research and feeds into the wider debate about the ideal family and the most desirable social arrangement for the socialization of children. It also relates to the question of whether it is preferable for children to grow up in the company of two parental figures as opposed to one, as in the case of single parent families.

This brief overview of changing kinship arrangements has indicated how very varied are the forms of modern family life and how changes in the wider economic, moral and social structures of society continue to shape family patterns. As Morgan (1994a) states:

**Older sociologies of the family, based around the model of the traditional nuclear family, are becoming less and less appropriate. This is not to say that, in the light of these trends, the family is 'dead'. Indeed most people will continue to spend part of their lives within a nuclear-family based household. Yet these other trends can no longer be taken as minor departures from the norm but as signifying the complex strands of family and domestic life in modern society.** *(Morgan 1994a: 113)*

## Elderly people

If we look at the sociology of the family in the context of social change we cannot ignore the changes that occur within individual families and the way in which all members of the family go through their own life cycle. The distinctions between different age groups in relation to legal rights and responsibilities are reflected by sociological interest in the phenomenon of ageing, particularly since demographic changes have led to a sharp increase in the proportion of elderly people in western societies. There are implications not only for elderly people themselves, but also for wider society in terms of future policy and the role of the family in supporting its older members.

Across the world the expectation that people will live longer, and that an increasing proportion of the population will be older, is having repercussions on demographic, economic, medical and social frameworks. In Britain the average life expectancy has increased by twelve years for men and fourteen years for women since 1900 (Giddens 1989: 598)). While in 1850 less than 5 per cent of the population in Britain was over 65, it is projected to increase from 15 per cent in 1995 to 19 per cent in 2035 (D Field 1992).

Demographic analysis (the study of population changes) helps to explain the predicted increase in the number of older people. Researchers have focused on the effect of baby booms after the two world wars and declining mortality rates in general as significant factors, together with medical advances, better nutrition, improved health education and standards of living.

While we tend to generalize about 'the elderly' in society, there are important distinctions to be made in terms of age, class, ethnicity, marital status and gender; however, negative attitudes and images of elderly people prevail in society.

**Ageism means discrimination against people because they are no longer young. Ageist attitudes persist in the newspapers, on radio and television, in the world of work and in advertisements.** *(Jenkins 1988: 86)*

Although the majority are women (about 60 per cent of the over 65s in Britain), Field suggests that the differential will decrease in future as the current rates reflect the effect of the Second World War on males in the armed services (D Field 1992: 16).

Case Study

## Bungee jumping granny, aged 78

Nanaimo (British Columbia) – A 78-year-old grandmother of eight flew in the faces of her doctor and children and went bungee jumping on Sunday off an unused railway bridge near this Vancouver Island town. Wearing a cap emblazoned 'Eat Well, Stay Fit, Die Anyway', Norma McLean jumped from a trestle 42 metres above the Nanaimo River after removing her false teeth. McLean said the idea started as a joke when she went river rafting as part of a local festival two years ago.

'They teased me if I could river raft, I could bungee jump, and that's how it started', McLean said. The daredevil said she was not afraid to jump, but was a bit tired by the walk up to the jumping platform. 'The ligaments in one of my legs hurt a bit, but I think that was all the stairs I had to climb' she said.

A spokesman for Bungee Zone, a bungee-jumping company in Nanaimo, said McLean was the oldest woman to jump from their platform. 'I had to phone my doctor to see if I had a heart condition, and he said "No, but you're crazy",' McLean added

(Reuter, reported in the *New Straits Times* 30 March 1994)

### Questions

**What factors account for the rising proportion of older people in society?**

**What social and political implications follow from these changes?**

**What common stereotypes exist about old people?**

While the personal and social consequences of ageing vary, most old people live either with their spouse or on their own, but near to other family members. Women over pensionable age make up, and will continue to form, the largest group of one person households, at around 11 per cent all households in 2001 (*Social Trends* 1994). The proportion of old people in residential care increases with age (D Field 1992: 16).

For many people, growing old can be a time of social withdrawal and loss – loss of job, income, health, independence, role, status, friends and relatives. It is unsurprising that this can be a period of loneliness and social isolation.

**Entry to old age is unlike many other important status changes, such as graduating or getting married, in a number of ways. It is not generally a valued status, and there are few 'rites of passage' to signal entry into it, especially for those not previously in full-time paid employment. There is little prior socialisation for the role, which is amorphous and unstructured: there are very few social roles for 'being old'.**

***(D Field 1992: 17)***

**Fig 10.3** The proportion of old people in residential care increases with age: residential house for the elderly, Christmas lunch. (Courtesy of Robert Harding Picture Library Ltd.)

Giddens (1989) points out that in Britain respect for elderly people's experience and knowledge is often lacking in comparison to more traditional cultures where one reaches the elevated status of an elder. The increasing proportion of elderly people is often seen as problematic, partly because elderly people are regarded as dependent on medical and social services. Abercrombie and Warde refer to the economic 'burden of dependency':

> **They take up a disproportionate share of health and social security resources and they are also a non-earning sector of the population, thus dependent on those at work.** *(Abercrombie and Warde 1994: 285–6)*

However, while the cost to the National Health Service and local authorities is high, Field points out that the majority of care and social support for sick and disabled elderly people is provided not by the state but by 'informal' carers, such as families and neighbours. Since the 1980s the role of carers has increased in a political climate emphasizing a return to 'community' care. In reality this responsibility falls largely on women. However, the increasing proportion of older members within society will inevitably have implications for family structures and roles as a whole.

It is important to recognize the potentially positive benefits of an ageing society, both in terms of older people's contributions to society and within the family. Thane (1982) emphasizes this in relation to the rather negative generalizations often made about such a very varied population.

**It is essential to work with a more complex picture of who the elderly are and of their role in society than the simple, depressing picture of a costly burden.**

*(Thane 1982: 71)*

Thus it is important to take account of the contributions to society made by those older people who still work, still learn (many embark on Open University courses) and still provide material and emotional support within their families and communities through voluntary and unpaid services. Giddens (1989) points out that in many spheres of social responsibility in Britain leading figures remain prominent beyond normal retirement age.

Q Give examples of elderly people who continue to play leading roles in areas such as the arts, politics and law in contemporary society.

In what ways do they challenge negative stereotypes about elderly people?

This brief overview of elderly people sets the sociology of the family in the context of social change and illustrates the changes in status experienced by individual members within the family as they adjust over time to new roles and relationships.

## Theoretical perspectives on the family

Two contrasting approaches to the family are provided by the consensus and conflict approaches within sociology. Both schools of thought regard the family as a central institution within the structure of society, but they differ in so far as one focuses on the more positive aspects of the family and the other concentrates on its negative features.

### Functionalist views of the family

A functionalist approach tends to assume that any institution that exists in society plays a positive part in maintaining the social equilibrium and harmony in society. Functionalists ask what functions are provided by the family and how these are beneficial both for individual members of the family and for wider society.

At the most basic level the family functions to provide new members for society through reproduction. It is seen as the initial stable environment in which to rear children, who learn through the process of socialization to become acceptable members of society. Parsons (1954; Parsons and Bales 1955) has described this as being one of the main functions of the family in modern society. Chapter 1 described the significance of the family in providing a developmental framework by illustrating the deprivation associated with the denial of such an environment (see also pp.27–31). Parsons sees the family as also functional for adult members in that it stabilizes adult personalities. By this he means that wives and husbands give each other emotional support and work together in a mutually complementary relationship. Writing in the 1950s, Parsons reflected traditional assumptions about husbands being the breadwinner and wives chiefly taking on the domestic role (Parsons 1954; Parsons and Bales 1955).

Sociological research on the family examines the roles and relationships between wives and husbands within the family and how those roles have been affected by wider social changes such as industrialization, the increased involvement of women in the workforce ('feminization' of labour) and unemployment among male workers. Some functionalists, including Willmott and Young, argue that as families move from being extended to being more isolated, nuclear and privatized the relationship between wives and husbands adapts to become more egalitarian with both partners working and sharing household tasks. Young and Willmott (1975) call this the 'symmetrical family'.

Q Give examples of the complementary domestic roles fulfilled by women and men within the family.

How far in your experience is it true to say that as families change the relationship between wives and husbands has become egalitarian?

Despite changes in the nature of society that accompany social processes such as industrialization and modernization, functionalists believe that the family is as important as ever today. They resist suggestions that it is in danger of decline or dying out and focus rather on the way in which it is able to adapt and accommodate itself to the requirements of contemporary society.

**Functionalist accounts of historical change . . . assume that, whatever the struggles and false trails along the way, the social pattern finally arrived at will be the best adapted to the new situation.** *(Worsley 1987: 148)*

Given its predominance within sociology up until the early 1960s the functionalist approach to the family has been very influential. Thus in the 1950s and early 1960s public sentiment was dominated by the assumption that 'society rested on the basic domestic group of the family' (Fletcher 1988: 3). Indeed the sense that the family and marriage might be in a state of moral decline and decay was interpreted as a serious threat to the security and survival of society in general:

**The family [was regarded as] the very foundation of society, and since the family was now in dangerous disarray, so was the entire moral order of society.**

*(Fletcher 1988: 3)*

While functionalists today would recognize that the family has seceded many of its traditional roles which have been taken over by agencies of the state such as schools, health and welfare services, they would still maintain that it is a fundamental and desirable feature of society. This sentiment is echoed in public debates and calls for a return to 'traditional family values'. Changes in the 1990s in health and welfare systems in Britain which favour a minimal role for the state and stress a greater role for the community have shifted the responsibility for many of the traditional functions back on to the family. As Worsley's quotation illustrates, in view of continuing social change functionalists see the family adapting and modifying its structure to the needs of society. Thus while its form continues to change, its necessity does not.

Case Study

## Changing functions of the family

| Traditional functions of the family | How these functions were fulfilled | Are these functions still fulfilled today? |
|---|---|---|
| Procreation and regulation of sexuality | Reproduction of family members. Ensures continuity of society and constrains sexual desires within the context of marriage. Reinforces heterosexual norms. | Changing sexual attitudes and behaviour. Increase in cohabitation and pre-marital sex as well as alternative sexualities. More women deciding to limit family size or not to reproduce at all. |
| Affectional/emotional function | Marriage exists primarily for companionship as lifelong emotional tie. Parent–child relationship regarded as basis for other relationships in life. Family relationships seen as basis of emotional security and bonding in contrast to competitive contractual relationship in wider society. | Many relationships today are short term, e.g. rising divorce rate, more serial relationships. Nature of relationship between parents and children changing in context of emphasis on children's rights. Although relationships are changing, the need for affection/emotional security remains an important function. |
| Economic function | Family traditionally a unit of production in pre-industrial society – largely a self-sufficient unit sharing work tasks and the benefits of labour. Economic production has moved from home to factory/outside services. Family becomes unit of consumption; emphasis on family consumer items such as family car, TV, holidays, etc. | Growth of welfare state seen as taking over some of the economic function through provision of benefits, e.g. income support. However, recent dismantling of the welfare state means that the family is again becoming an important resource for economic survival, e.g. parents funding children through education; family members as carers. |
| Welfare/protective function | Linked with the economic function; family traditionally seen as source of protection and support for dependants, e.g. the young and the old. With the expansion of the Welfare State and the decline of the extended family this appeared to be a declining function. | Even within the welfare state many benefits and services assume the primary role of the family as the basis of support. Such expectations have increased as funding has been reduced since the 1980s and the focus shifted on to 'community' care (i.e. the family and mostly women). |
| Socialization | Traditionally the family was seen as the key agent in passing on basic skills and knowledge. Psychologists emphasize the primary role of parent–child relationship as providing the basis for other relationships in society. Education and media systems reinforce and sustain this function, which continues throughout the individual's life. | Functionalists still stress this as the basic function of the family in contemporary society. Political and religious affiliation are still influenced by family socialization, though there is more emphasis on individual choice and flexibility. |
| Social status | Family ascribes several aspects of social status – age, sex, birth order, ethnicity, religion, class. However, in modern society emphasis is on achieved status rather than ascription. There is scope for individuals to be socially mobile and change from their family status of origin. | While the emphasis on individual growth and achieved status remains important, ascription, heredity and 'who you are' is still influential in many political, occupational and social circles (e.g. 'old boy network'). |
| Recreation and leisure | Leisure pursuits within the family can influence children's development. The increase in leisure time brought recognition of the family as a unit of recreation and consumption, e.g. DIY, home videos and holidays. | Although the family leisure industry has grown, many recreational activities still take place outside the home and family, e.g. with the peer group. |

## Critical views of the family

In the late 1960s a range of alternative ideological positions on the family rose to prominence. Though each was distinctive they shared in common a radically different perspective on the family to that of the functionalists. Radical/critical sociologists challenged traditional functionalist assumptions about what they regarded as an over-idealized image of the family. They focused instead on the more constraining and oppressive features of family life. Their analysis may appear at first sight to be quite extreme in that it challenges many of the basic assumptions about the family that we tend to take for granted. A Wilson (1986) makes the point that in our society we are used to seeing the family as basically a good thing and this makes it harder to step back and question what we have always taken for granted:

**The family is one of our ideological blind spots. We become used to what was normal in our own upbringing in our own home.** *(A Wilson 1986: 217)*

The scope of the conflict perspective in sociology is very broad and a critical approach to the family encompasses a variety of approaches including Marxism, radical psychiatry and feminism. What all these approaches share in common is a focus on the more negative aspects of family life and the idea that the family may not be beneficial for all its members. This has led some to advocate the break-up of the family. While this may seem a rather extreme conclusion based on exceptional cases rather than the norm, these alternative approaches have helped to provide a balance to the rather over-optimistic, conservative and biologically deterministic approach that dominated functionalist sociology of the family up until the 1960s.

## Marxist approaches

In keeping with the emphasis on dominant and subordinate groups in society and the location of conflict within the structural composition of society, Marxists regard the family as yet another institution promoting dominant societal values and perpetuating the exploitation of subordinate groups by upholding the norms and values of capitalist society.

**Most Marxist analyses draw attention to the ways in which families tend to encourage and reproduce hierarchical, inegalitarian relationships and act as a safety valve, dampening down discontent so that it is robbed of revolutionary content.**
*(Bilton et al. 1987: 292)*

In the *Communist Manifesto* (1848), Marx and Engels outline their views of the family as a reflection of bourgeois interest and control.

**On what foundation is the present family, the bourgeois family based? On capital, on private gain. In its completely developed form this family exists only among the bourgeoisie. . . . The bourgeois claptrap about the family and education, about the hallowed correlation of parent and child, becomes all the more disgusting, the more, by the action of modern industry, all family ties among the proletarians are torn asunder, and their children transformed into simple article of commerce and instruments of labour.** *(Marx and Engels 1848, quoted in Fletcher 1988: 54)*

**Q** Do you agree with Marx and Engels that family relationships are determined by class and economic situation?

In defending the family Fletcher (1988) is keen to add that Marx and Engels were not advocating the abolition of the family *per se*, but rather the improvement of the monogamous family:

> **[Marx] was certainly not 'anti-family' in his personal life, and . . . this was no inconsistency with his own and Engels' view of the family in society in general. It was the bourgeois family – and all those traditional family-types in societies of the past which entailed the exploitation of women as property – to which they were opposed.**
> *(Fletcher 1988: 79)*

In other works Engels took an evolutionary view of the family, arguing that the form of family life changed as the mode of production did. In early communism property was collectively owned and the private family as such did not exist. There were no rules restricting promiscuity. It was only when private property developed that the monogamous nuclear family emerged to protect men's inheritance by ensuring their rightful heirs. Engels thus traces the subordination of women back to the emergence of private ownership, whereby women became economically dependent on men and thus subject to them within marriage.

Engels believed that the end of exploitation within the family would be guaranteed only in a truly communist society where individuals would return to living arrangements that existed before private property developed. True equality between the sexes would come where tasks were communally shared.

The Marxist view of the family was further developed and applied to modern capitalist societies in the 1960s and 1970s by such writers as Louis Althusser, who sees the norms and values of family life as part of the ideological state apparatus being used to further reinforce the exploitative nature of capitalist society. In the interests of capitalism other institutions such as the media encourage ever greater consumption by the family, setting up ideals of the modern family as one equipped with the latest consumer goods – the washing machine, video, mobile phone. Marxists see these as false needs created to serve the interests of producers and keep the capitalist economy ticking over rather than being in the genuine interest of consumers.

**Q** Examine examples of current advertisements in different forms of media (magazines, television, radio). What consumer goods are being promoted and how far do the adverts reflect or challenge stereotypes about the family?

In what ways do the norms and values of the education system reinforce the ideology of the family?

Within a Marxist perspective Gittins (1985) states that the ideology of the family is pervasive in modern industrial society:

> **Organisations are said to be run 'like a family', the highest compliment a man can receive is that he is 'a good family man' (women are never accrued the compliment of being 'a good family woman', as by definition they are assumed to be just that). The notion of the family informs the education system, the business world, asylums, the media and the political system.**
> *(Gittins 1985: 155)*

Yet she adds that this conceptualization of the family evolved historically only as part of the development of the industrial bourgeoisie during the late stages of capitalist development. Despite its appeal as a universal ideal achievable by all, Gittins argues that the ideology is a false one since it is rooted in a class-specific, patriarchal outlook.

**Family ideology has increasingly purported to be egalitarian, yet it remains based on notions of gender, age and authority that are by definition unequal. The ideal that families are egalitarian, like the ideal that class no longer divides society, has enjoyed considerable support, even if it seldom tallies with reality.**

*(Gittins 1985: 159)*

Gittins' analysis provides a good illustration of the Marxist notion of false ideology; the 'ideal' family is used to distort and disguise the real economic basis of exploitation:

**Family ideology implicitly presupposes a relatively secure economic base: the husband should be able to support the family by his income alone, the household income should provide adequate shelter, food, comfort, space, and consumer durables, the wife should be able to cease paid work when she has small children . . . everyone is supposed to aspire to a certain kind of family life, while the realities of economic inequality make it virtually impossible to achieve the ideal.**

*(Gittins 1985: 161)*

The value of the Marxist approach is that it emphasizes both the powerful ideology of the family in society and the structural relationship between the economy and family life, a consideration that has not been ignored in the development of sociological (particularly feminist) approaches to the family. Morgan (1994a) describes how changes in the formal paid economy have impacted on the family (in terms of the repercussions of more women working and high male unemployment) while the definition and measurement of family life has started to recognize labour within the home.

**The increasing tendency to write of 'the household' rather than the 'family' reflects an increasing willingness to see family relationships as having economic, and not simply emotional significance. Put another way, economic life is not simply what takes place in the sphere of paid employment outside the home. It is also within the household that economic activity takes place, in the unpaid labour of housewives and mothers, of fathers and husbands and, indeed, of children. The use of the term 'emotional labour' in relation to caring work is indicative of this growing recognition of the work which often takes place unnoticed within the home.**

*(Morgan 1994a: 122)*

### Feminist approaches

Marxist themes of exploitation within the family and society are taken up by feminists who highlight the continuing exploitation of women in capitalist societies, not least in terms of the way in which their contribution to the bulk of private domestic work remains unrecognized, unrewarded and undervalued labour. Sheeran (1993) points out the overlap between Marxist and feminist approaches:

**Marxist and radical feminists argue that the family is both an 'ideological construct' and a repressive, socially-produced reality, which helps to perpetuate capitalism and/or patriarchy. Such criticisms are overtly anti-family, and argue that women have been forced into taking responsibility for child care by that 'agent' of the state, the patriarchal family.** *(Sheeran 1993: 29)*

More fundamentally, feminists challenge the idea that the sexual division of labour within (and indeed outside) the family is based on biological and genetic predispositions so that women are 'naturally' more domesticated and men are 'natural' providers. Feminists and many others would argue that this sexual division is culturally determined (and hence, in this case, exploitative), as are many of the assumptions about relationships between women and men which are institutionalized within marriage or less formally through cohabitation arrangements. Traditional prescriptions about gender-related behaviour within the family and marriage are often supported by religious beliefs and customs. For example, in some Muslim communities men are permitted more than one wife (the condition being that they treat them all equally) and have easier access to divorce.

Feminists argue that in western societies, despite secularization and legislation giving women equal access to divorce and the ownership of property, the family and marriage are still arenas for the exploitation and subordination of women. In Britain many couples still opt for a ceremony in which the bride is 'given away' (symbolically from the property of one man to another) and choose to pledge vows in church based on the traditional assumption that the husband is the head of the family and that the woman's duty is to obey.

Examine the rituals, prayers, blessings and hymns of different Christian marriage ceremonies. What assumptions about the roles of women and men within marriage are implied?

Compare these with the procedures in a registry office marriage and in marriage ceremonies practised by different religions.

Oakley (1974a) has analysed the traditional role of the housewife as a feature of women's exploitation within the family. Despite the socialization of women as homemakers, Oakley reported that as well as being unpaid labour, women found housework dull, monotonous and unfulfilling. It provided little job satisfaction and was attributed low status ('I'm "just a housewife"'). This sort of analysis led to calls for housework to be recognized as a form of labour by being paid.

Women increasingly opt for a career resulting in their having a 'dual role'. This often generates a need for child-care support outside the home with associated financial implications. However, the increase in the number of women going out to work has not resulted in the sharing of domestic responsibility. Feminists have described the role that women have continued to play as the major provider of care within the family regardless of the diversity of forms that the family may take. Sheeran (1993) points to the centrality of this 'female-carer core unit' today, historically and across different cultures.

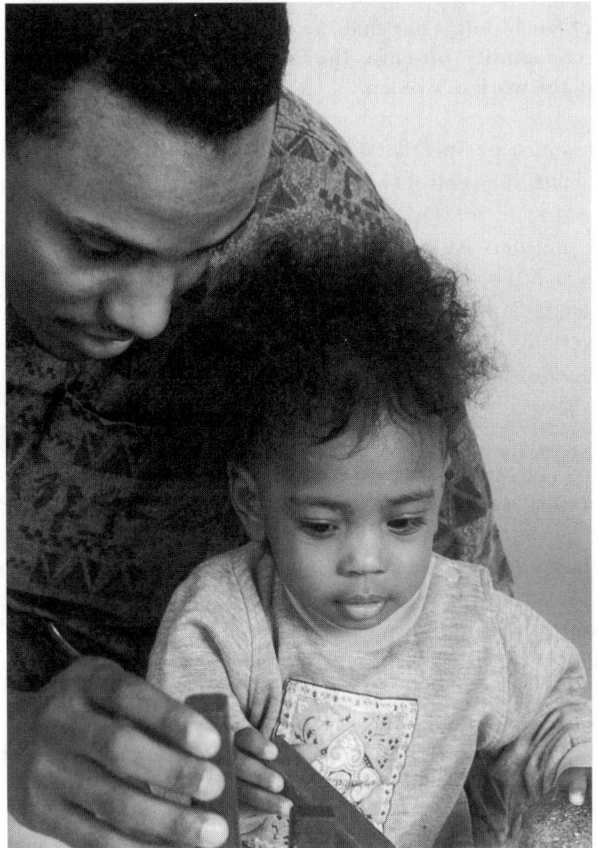

**Fig 10.4** Feminists have pointed out that men tend to 'help' with the more enjoyable aspects of child care: father playing with 14-month-old-baby. (Courtesy of Robert Harding Picture Library Ltd.)

**In households with male and female partners, most males have a relatively small amount of interaction with the children, even when both partners work. Many female partners only work part-time so that they can look after the children. Making child care arrangements, and staying off work when children are sick is also largely the woman's responsibility. Men tend to 'help' rather than assume full responsibility, and then only with the more enjoyable aspects of child care.**

***(Sheeran 1993: 30)***

Research into the phenomenon of the 'new man' and into roles within the changing nature of the family has found that it is still women who are doing the housework and providing child care. Women's jobs still tend to be regarded as secondary within the family and women are more likely to give up their jobs to rear children.

This role of women as chief providers of care has become more significant in view of recent developments in the field of social policy which have re-emphasized the importance of the family as a source of care and support. There has been a reversal of the trend towards state support for sick and disabled people through the provision of institutional care and the welfare state and calls for the community to become the basis of support. 'Community' tends to mean in practice 'family', which generally means women:

**Janet Finch points out that the increasing use of terms such as 'caring' and 'care in the community' obscures the fact that caring involves work and, in many areas at least, the work of women.** *(Morgan 1994a: 119)*

A feminist perspective is particularly significant to the sociology of the family. It highlights the centrality of women within the core domestic unit, the changing attitudes to and roles of women in the spheres of marriage, divorce and cohabitation and the increasing significance of their role as carers within the community. Although the central female carer role is not inevitable (rather it is a cultural construct as opposed to being immutably biologically determined), its virtual universality is such that the sociology of the family cannot proceed without taking account of the roles and experiences of women.

### Interpretive approaches

In keeping with an interpretive approach some radical psychiatrists have examined the micro-level relationships between children and adults within the family. The advantage of their contribution to the sociology of the family, particularly in the 1960s and 1970s, was their focus on the individual experiences and face-to-face relationships of members within the wider family group. Even functionalists such as Fletcher, though critical of their conclusions, acknowledge the value of this perspective:

**One fundamental significance of the Laing, Cooper, Esterson school . . . was that they had validly seen the importance of the sociological perspective for the understanding of individuals and their problems.** *(Fletcher 1988: 29)*

These writers agree with critical approaches that challenge the positive assessment of socialization within the family (as argued by functionalists) and focus on pathological situations where the family prevents individuals from achieving personal freedom. Laing and Esterson (1970) and Cooper (1972) argue that parents can over-protect the young and smother individuality. Love can be used as an emotional weapon to manipulate children or partners. The family sometimes creates barriers between itself and the outside world – a kind of 'us and them' mentality. Such authors condemn the institution of the family and the socialization process which trains children to accept indoctrination and subordination in later life. They would probably sympathize with the sentiment expressed by Edmund Leach in his Reith lecture in 1967:

**Far from being the basis of the good society, the family, with all its narrow privacy and tawdry secrets, is the source of all our discontent.** *(Leach 1967)*

## Current issues in the sociology of the family

The shifting focus provided by radical analysts of the family since the 1960s has shed light on what many have referred to as the 'dark side' of the family. Many cases of violent crime, and statistically most murders, take place within the home. Domestic violence and child abuse have both been underestimated and 'brushed under the carpet' in the past.

## Domestic violence

Domestic violence began to be recognized as a serious social issue in the 1970s: while the phenomenon of battered women was not a new one, its recognition as a social problem requiring a political response was (Johnson 1985). The term 'domestic violence' covers a variety of behaviours ranging from verbal and emotional abuse to physical attack, including sexual assault and rape. It is more commonly, though not exclusively, inflicted by men on women and often includes behaviour referred to as 'wife-beating' or 'wife-battering'

Domestic violence is a widespread form of crime which is notoriously under-reported and thus underestimated in official statistics. Stanko cites one estimate that only 1 out of 270 incidents of wife abuse is ever reported to the authorities (1992: 187). Many victims are afraid or too ashamed to report it. Some victims may blame themselves, an attitude reinforced by suggestions that domestic violence is part and parcel of marital life and a private family matter that should not be interfered with by outsiders. 'To hear battered women recount these experiences is to hear stories of abuse which are often characterised as the "normal" interaction of intimate couples' (Stanko 1992: 186).

Research commissioned by the Home Office in 1990 found that in the past cases of domestic violence (referred to as 'domestics') were not always taken seriously by the police. As one woman police constable stated:

**In the old days you would go to the call, tell them to quieten down and that would be that. Husband and wife rows were taboo: it was down to them.**

***(Guardian 12 December 1990)***

In response, police have set up special Domestic Violence Units to support victims and issue 'deferred cautions' to perpetrators in an attempt to prevent reoffending. This reflects the recognition previously lacking that domestic violence is a serious crime. Researchers have suggested that other key members of society – doctors, social workers, neighbours, parents and so on – have played a part in perpetuating the cycle of domestic violence by failing to confront it or by shifting responsibility back on to the victim. Johnson (1985) concludes from his research into marital violence:

**The failure to respond adequately has the effect of diminishing the importance of the problem. In this way the statutory services both reflect and reinforce the view of women as 'appropriate victims' of violence. The services do not present a serious challenge to the legitimacy of male violence as a means of socially controlling women.** ***(Johnson 1985: 122)***

While some people believe that the victims of domestic violence must be weak individuals who allow abuse to take place, many recognize the wider environment is significant in explaining the sort of behaviour involved and see the problem as being based on the power relationships between men and women in society as reflected in family structures:

**Both lawyers and sociologists agree that the problem of violence against women is a deep societal one, arising out of a patriarchal family system in which husbands' 'authority over their wives' creates a particular 'marriage power relationship' and a 'subordinate status to wives and mothers'.** ***(Maidment 1985: 22)***

## The role of children

An examination of the sociology of the family would be incomplete without focusing on the expectations and experiences of children. Here interpretive approaches are valuable in that they shift the focus of attention on to the micro relationships between members of the family and thus complement the more macro, structural approach of functionalist and conflict perspectives. By focusing on the dynamics within the family we have become much more aware of individuals' experiences and emotions. While psychologists have analysed aspects of child development within this context, sociologists have become more interested in the social construction of age-related behaviour and since the mid-1980s attention has shifted to the role of children. This reflects increasing recognition in society of the rights of children both in general and in relation to the family.

On 20 November 1989 the United Nations General Assembly unanimously adopted the Convention on the Rights of the Child. T David (1993) reports the significance of this action: 'the most important aspect of the Convention may be the fact that at last children are recognised as human beings with rights' (1993: 3). The Convention has 54 Articles covering the following broad areas of rights: survival, protection, development and participation. As well as defining the social, economic, cultural, civil and political rights of children, the Convention outlines the duties and responsibilities of governments and other adults to children and their families.

From a sociological point of view the behaviour of children and adults is socially constructed, that is, our expectations of age-related behaviour are determined by the culture in which we live.

**Childhood is a social construction. It isn't natural, and should be distinguished from biological immaturity. Childhood varies, both in relation to class, gender and ethnicity and across national cultures. There's no single universal childhood.**

*(Wagg 1992: 10)*

Aries (1973) studied the social construction of childhood in industrial societies and found that the modern notion of childhood dates back to the fifteenth century. Before then young people were treated as miniature adults; they were integrated into the adult world of work and leisure rather than being separated from the adult world. Gradually through the introduction of restrictions on child labour, the development of education and legislation which brought a separate criminal justice system for the young, the social category of the child became established. Norms and values about expected forms of behaviour for children developed. In modern Britain we assume that children are and should be dependent on adults. We adopt an adult reference point seeing children through adults' eyes and expecting them to behave in a submissive manner. We tend to make decisions about children's welfare and their role within the family and society without consulting children themselves.

**Q** In what ways and to what extent are children's interests represented in these social institutions: (a) the family; (b) different forms of media; (c) religion; (d) politics; (e) education; (f) the law?

In discussing this you may find it useful to compare and contrast possible responses from adults and children and compare these institutions across time and cultures.

The 1990s have seen a shift in favour of promoting the rights of children and in recognition of the fact that the interests of children may not always coincide with keeping families intact. A fundamental piece of legislation in Britain was the Children Act 1989 which represented a major shift in thinking about children and their relationships with adults. Its recognition of the need for action in accordance with children's wishes and feelings is very different from the traditional assumption that children should be 'seen and not heard'.

Definition

### The Children Act 1989

In 1989 the Children Act was passed. It was regarded as the most important law reform affecting children for many years. It deals with the care, bringing up and protection of children. It also covers children's welfare in the event of parental separation and divorce and the intervention of local authorities if a child suffers or is in danger of suffering significant harm.

A central principle of the Act is the view that in court proceedings **'the child's welfare must be paramount'**. To this end children's wishes and feelings are taken into account in deciding their best interests. A further principle behind the Act is that **parents have responsibility for their children until they are 18.** Where possible local authorities aim to keep families together and work with children, parents and relatives.

In pursuing children's wishes, the Act **enables children to bring proceedings** on their own behalf, though a court must approve such an application first. Areas of dispute predicted to come under the courts' jurisdiction include education, medical needs and religious questions.

Other areas covered by the Act include provision of services for children in need, the administration of children's homes, adoption and fostering and childminding.

Some of the more radical changes introduced through the Children Act have been seen in the area of divorce proceedings. Where previously the courts (in the event of divorce) decided which parent would have custody of the children and which would have access to visiting, children now have a say in decisions about where and with whom they should live and forms of contact. In exceptional cases children have even had recourse to the law in taking action to 'divorce' their parents. Here the law allows for children to bring to the attention of the courts issues relating to dissatisfaction with aspects of their parents' responsibility. While such cases are extremely rare, they illustrate a fundamental change in thinking about the roles and rights of children who are no longer regarded as passive members of society for whom decisions are made. Rather their role within the family and in society may increasingly be seen as an active one at least with respect to family decisions.

Case Study

**Children exercising their rights**

In 1990 the Children's Legal Centre had received enquiries from ten children about moving from one divorced parent to the other. By 1991 it was predicted that under the Children Act children may bring 'a wide variety of proceedings, over schooling, medical treatment, money and contact with absent parents or other relatives' (*Guardian* 31 October 1991). Here are some examples of children exercising their rights in the first few years of the Act.

- A 15-year-old Birmingham girl won the right to stay with her grandparents after leaving her father's home
- A 14-year-old girl from Surrey divorced her father and new stepmother and won the right to move into her boyfriend's home
- A 14-year-old London boy won the right to live with his father after custody had been given to his mother when he was a baby
- In 1993 children were reported to be taking advice about suing parents after legal claims were made against employers over passive smoking
- Teaching unions claimed that more pupils were realizing they could intimidate teachers by making false allegations under the Children Act
- In 1993 six children aged from 2 to 4 years, acting through their mothers, failed in the High Court to save their nursery from closure. They were the youngest children to date to seek a judicial review under the Act.

Despite this changing view of the role of children it is interesting to note that legislation such as the Children Act 1989 still recognizes the primacy of the family and the importance of family life. Examples of where parenting and relationships have broken down are regarded as exceptions rather than the rule. Thus politicians and the law still place a priority on parental responsibility and on the fundamental belief that the family is inherently a positive environment for the healthy socialization and support of the young.

However, there is evidence of significant mental illness among children in Britain, estimated at 3 million of those under 16 according to a report by the Mental Health Foundation (1993). The report highlights symptoms such as sleeplessness, anorexia, depression and school phobia as the effect of young lives marred by poverty, breakdown in parental relationships and the stresses of the modern world.

## Child abuse

Today society has become more open and responsive to the phenomenon of child abuse. Some sociologists refer to this as one feature of the 'dark side' of family life, which 'belies the rosy images of harmony with which we are relentlessly bombarded in TV commercials and elsewhere in the popular media' (Giddens 1989: 405). The acknowledgement of the more sinister side of family life has brought a shift of emphasis in favour of listening to children and taking account of their experiences within the family.

In previous eras children were not regarded as vulnerable members of the community but treated as adults and only gradually did a sense of their needs and rights come to be identified as an issue of social concern. T David (1993) records the historical foundations of legislation and organizations specifically focusing on children:

> **When one considers the difficulties working class men – and then women – had in gaining the vote and in gaining rights as human beings and citizens, it is hardly surprising that children's rights have been neglected. In fact, child abuse was first brought to the headlines in 1874 under the auspices of an animal protection campaign in New York. A young girl named Mary Ellen, who lived with her adoptive parents, was regularly beaten and neglected by them. Her neighbours became concerned, though the adoptive parents saw no fault in their actions, as they 'owned' the child. The case was eventually brought to the attention of Henry Bergh, the founder of the Society for the Protection of Cruelty to Animals who brought a court action against the parents. Although there were more laws relating to the protection of animals than children at the time, the case was won on the basis of Mary's human rights, not – as is sometimes thought – because Mary Ellen was a member of an animal species. The lawyer who was hired by Henry Bergh subsequently precipitated the development of a new movement, the Society for the Prevention of Cruelty to Children, in December 1874.** *(T David 1993: 10)*

It was this that led to the foundation of the equivalent National Society for the Prevention of Cruelty to Children (NSPCC) in the UK.

In examining concepts of childhood and children's rights, Archard (1993) shows the problem of detecting and dealing with child abuse rests on the link between the discovery and definition of abuse:

> **In all the talk of child abuse as a new problem, two related mistakes are often made. The first is to think that child abuse itself, rather than its recognition and description, is a modern phenomenon. The second is to believe that child abuse is more extensive than in the past, whereas what, in fact, has increased is the reporting of abuse. This in turn may be ascribed to the explicit acknowledgement by society that child abuse does exist and that an account of it can be rendered.**
>
> **Significantly, what has been 'discovered' is a certain kind of abuse, and this has helped to determine the ways in which 'abuse' is defined, explained and dealt with. The standard case of abuse, at least in the 1960s and 1970s, was that of a child's physical maltreatment, most often leading to serious injury, by an adult within the child's family. What may probably not be considered abuse is, for instance, that a child is brought up within a significantly poorer household than its contemporaries.**
>
> **Consequently, everything depends on how 'abuse' is defined and this depends on what the definition is required to do.** *(Archard 1993: 147–8)*

As the quotation from Archard implies, there are many different interpretations of child abuse, reflecting both the variety of perspectives on this subject and the range of behaviour which is regarded as constituting forms of abuse. The NSPCC and the National Children's Homes (NCH) recognize and keep statistics on four types of abuse physical abuse, sexual abuse, emotional abuse and neglect. *Working Together* – official guidelines encouraging inter-agency cooperation (DHSS 1988) – adds a further definition based on 'grave concern':

**Children whose situations do not fit the above categories, but where social and medical assessments indicate that they are at significant risk of abuse. These could include situations where another child in the household has been harmed or the household contains a known abuser.**

*(DHSS 1988: para 5.31, as reported in T David 1993: 18)*

In the 1990s cases of child abuse along with child neglect have become familiar news stories covered in the media. The public recognition that child abuse takes place, the lifting of the 'taboo' against open discussion and the move in favour of listening to children all help to account for the dramatic increase in the rates of recorded child abuse, not only in Britain but also internationally. The extent of the problem in Britain is illustrated by official statistics, though these are likely to give only a partial picture:

**Department of Health (DoH) statistics for the end of March 1990 indicate that around four children in every 1000 aged under 18 in the UK were on child protection Registers. Furthermore, according to the NSPCC (1989), the number of cases of child abuse registered by them doubled during the mid-1980s, from 1115 in 1985 to 2307 in 1987. Those who work in the field know that this may represent only the tip of the iceberg, ie those cases where concern had become so great and the evidence so certain that the children in question were registered.** *(T David 1993: 4)*

It is likely that many cases remain unrecognized and unrecorded due partly to a misplaced sense of shame or embarrassment on the part of the abused or even due to threats made by the abuser in the event of the facts becoming public.

Statistics imply that levels of abuse are higher in poor and working-class areas. However, David suggests that this may be due to higher detection rates as a result of close monitoring rather than real incidences (1993: 13). It is more significant to note that abuse occurs in all strata of society, and that increasingly, older children are being found to be abusing younger ones (T David 1993: 5), a shocking recent example being the James Bulger case in 1993. Teachers and other professionals working closely with young people can potentially monitor children's behaviour for signs of distress.

Theories seeking to explain child abuse can be categorized broadly as biological, psychological, sociological and political (T David 1993: 38–9). In a paper examining the relationship between child abuse and the battering of women, Stark and Flitcraft (1985) suggest that the battering of women may be a major precipitant of child abuse.

**Marital violence frequently provides the context within which child abuse occurs, ether because the male batterer is also the child's assailant or because the mother abuses the child after her own battering is firmly established.**

*(Stark and Flitcraft 1985: 3)*

Stark and Flitcraft suggest that their findings have important implications for policy, and that those concerned with child abuse 'would do well to look toward advocacy and protection of battered mothers as the best available means to prevent current child abuse as well as child abuse in the future' (1985: 147).

Public concern over the phenomenon of child abuse has expressed both the sense of moral outrage and perhaps the community's awareness that it bears some sort of responsibility for allowing such behaviour to persist. David asks: 'If children feel that no-one close to them can be of help, that they need to resort to phoning someone they do not know on a helpline, what kind of a society do we live in?' (1993: 4) Some commentators, such as the late Conservative MP Geoffrey Dickens, have called for child abusers to be castrated, reflecting the high degree of public anger, though such extreme solutions are contentious. Others have stressed that both preventive action and collaborative cooperation between those in the fields of health, social services and education (T David 1993: 6) are important if family life and the most vulnerable members of the community are to be supported.

Other commentators suggest that the protection and reinforcement of family values is problematic in that it reinforces the very institution which is the source of conflict:

**It is not the breakdown of family life which causes violence, but the endless protection of what goes on within it.** *(Burchill 1985)*

However, perhaps because people have higher expectations than ever of family life, the family in all its forms continues to play a vital part in society.

**Perhaps the biggest change in families and family ideology is that now more is expected from marriage, childrearing and sexuality than in the past. Moreover, as family ideology has become stronger over time, by definition the reality and the ideal become further and further apart. . . .Without family ideology it would be possible to reconsider and reconstruct the realities of relationships between men, women and children and to work towards more equal and more caring ways of living and working together.** *(Gittins 1985: 166–8)*

## The ever-changing family

This chapter has illustrated how difficult it is to provide a straightforward definition and analysis of the 'family' given its ongoing modification in the context of social change.

**We cannot speak of 'the family' as if it were a static and unchanging thing. Rather, it is better to use the word as signifying the character of a complex series of processes over time. Thus, instead of talking of 'the family' we should speak of 'family processes', 'family living' or 'family life courses'. In this way we will come to recognise that family life is always subject to change and variation, that change is at the very heart of family living.** *(Morgan 1994a: 124)*

Morgan's statement shows that diversity is as important a feature of family life today as any other. Within this diversity it is important to take account of the experiences of family life through a range of perspectives. You may research further into the distinctions between and within households based on gender, age, ethnicity and class. A cross-cultural approach broadens the possibilities even more in an age when we are increasingly exposed through the media and technological advance to alternative value-systems and lifestyles.

This chapter has stressed the more negative features of the family and the prevalence of extreme violent forms of behaviour such as child abuse and domestic violence. Such awareness counterbalances naive views of the family which focus simply on its positive attributes. An alternative focus also challenges the pervasive ideology of the traditional nuclear family, 'a social construct which is often held up as both the norm and the ideal, perpetuated by many media, from television dramas and advertisements to children's reading schemes' (T David 1993: 27). The realities of family life demand that we weigh up carefully arguments on both sides of the debate about whether the family is a good or bad thing and in fact demonstrate that the complex and various nature of family life in modern society precludes any simplistic conclusions.

**Summary**

- While all societies exhibit some form of family arrangement, norms and values vary widely across and within generations and cultures. Defining the meaning and expectations associated with concepts such as 'family', 'marriage','childhood' and 'old age' is less straightforward than we often assume.
- Research into the transformation of family patterns within Britain clarifies the influence of changing social and physical environments. The processes of industrialization and urban development, for example, have been associated with the evolution from nuclear to extended families and later the relinquishing of close kinship ties.
- Despite these changes, theorists within the functionalist school maintain that the institution of the family remains a fundamental feature of society that is able to adapt and evolve in function according to societal needs. Conflict theorists tend to focus on more negative interpretations of the family as an arena of power relationships and social control stifling the individuality of members.
- Trends in marriage, divorce and cohabitation illustrate the continuing dynamism of family patterns. Despite evidence of rising divorce rates and the increasing popularity of cohabitation in Britain and beyond, the evidence suggests that this does not signify the declining popularity or expectations of marriage. Debates about the rise in lone parenthood have triggered further public debate and policy regarding the most beneficial family arrangements for the welfare of children and parents.
- Social policy is also addressing the health and welfare implications of an increasing proportion of elderly members of the family and society. Examination of the various expectations and consequences of ageing challenges traditional stereotypes which necessarily see ageing as a negative feature of the family and wider society.
- Current issues in the sociology of the family include ongoing research into the phenomena of domestic violence and child abuse. The latter is set within a wider context of the sociology of childhood and the changing conceptions and actions relating to the rights of children. This has been most graphically illustrated in the passing of the Children Act 1989.

## Further reading

Archard, D (1993) *Children: Rights and Childhood*, London: Routledge.
This examines children and their rights. It includes a focus on concepts of childhood, traditional and modern, as well as an analysis of the rights of children in relation to parents, the family and the state. The discovery and definition of child abuse is also covered.

Bond, J, Coleman, P and Peace, S (1993) *Ageing in Society: An Introduction to Gerontology*, London: Sage.
For those wishing to study further the ageing process in society, this book includes differing perspectives on ageing, the sociology of retirement and a focus on death, dying and bereavement.

Fletcher, R (1988) *The Abolitionists: The Family and Marriage under Attack*, London: Routledge.
This addresses criticisms of opponents to functionalism which Fletcher sees as undermining the family and marriage. Good overview and discussion of new and radical criticisms set in the context of public debates.

Miller, A (1983) *For Your Own Good: The Roots of Violence in Child-Rearing*, London: Virago.
Not strictly a sociological text but this is an eye-opening insight into how orthodox child-rearing practices can cause damage to children which lasts into adulthood. Clear implications arise for family relationships and social consequences.

Tinker, A (1996) *Elderly People in Modern Society*, 4th edn, London: Longman
A classic text which brings together research, policy and practice relating to older people in a clear and accessible style.

Wellings, K, Field, J, Johnson, A and Wadsworth, J (1994) *Sexual Behaviour in Britain: The National Survey of Sexual Attitudes and Lifestyles of the British Population*, Harmondsworth: Penguin.
This is the first and largest national survey on sexual attitudes and practices in Britain. It will be of interest to those studying fertility rates, family life, contraception and sex education. There is a full appendix including the survey used which will be of interest to those studying or applying research methods.

## Activities

### ■ Activity 1 Social policy and the family

Sommerville (1982) claims that in those countries in which the government encourages a variety of social bonds by offering some support to families, sharing child-rearing and presumably also the care of the elderly, life in families is thriving in a way which is not happening in those societies where support is haphazard. (T David 1993: 35)

**Social policy in Britain reflects certain assumptions about the family and members' roles and responsibilities. Collect information on current legislation and welfare benefits and analyse the assumptions that underpin them in the light of the discussions covered in this chapter. You may wish to discuss what amendments, if any, you would make were you in a position to influence policy.**

**Useful sources will include advice leaflets and benefit forms available from the local Department of Social Security and details of current legislation from the media.**

### ■ Activity 2 Family breakdown

**Breakdown of family can lead to life of crime, says Bottomley**

The community and the family must first look to themselves when society breaks down, Virginia Bottomley, the only woman member of the Government to address the Tory conference, said yesterday.

Mrs Bottomley, the Health Minister, was winding up a debate on the family, during which Geoffrey Dickens MP received loud applause when he called for the castration of rapists and child abusers.

Mrs Bottomley said: 'Time and again, from so-called joyriders to horrific instances of child abuse, when the basic cohesiveness of the family unit breaks down, crime, degeneracy, violence and horror break to the surface of our society. When parents give up caring, children, sometimes literally, run riot. Too many young people drift easily into a life of crime'.

She said the family was the basic building block of society, and the Government would go on producing policies to support it. . . . Mr Dickens, MP for Littleborough and Saddleworth, called for the recruitment of more experienced people into social work – 'grannies who would stand no nonsense'. He also called for legislation to castrate child abusers and rapists on second conviction. (*Guardian* 12 October 1991)

Public and political concern about the single family is associated in the minds of many with concern about the ultimate welfare of society. Those who interpret the single parent family as symptomatic of the breakdown of the family and communal values are more likely to see a link between changing family forms and the increase in society's crime rates, particularly in the area of juvenile delinquency. The views expressed by a Conservative minister at the party's annual conference reflect this sentiment.

## Questions

The statements quoted from Virginia Bottomley's speech indicate the view that there is a very clear and direct relationship between the changing nature of the family and rising crime rates. What evidence is there of this if you examine recent crimes which have been featured in the media?

What effect do you think recruiting 'grannies who would stand no nonsense' to the social services would have on those who used these services?

Chapter 11

# Education

**Chapter outline:** Introduction • Schooling in Britain • Origins of the current schooling 'system' • Development of sociological explanations and theories • Sociological approaches to education policy • Social groups and education • Summary • Further reading • Activities

**Learning objectives**

When you have studied this chapter you should be able to address these key questions:

- How has the provision of schooling in Britain developed over time?
- What are the main sociological approaches to the study of education and what problems do they identify?
- How has the sociology of education helped to inform education policies?
- In what ways do social class, gender and race affect educational achievement?

## Introduction

**For a long time, from babyhood through young adulthood mainly, we grow, physically and spiritually (including the intellectual with the spiritual) without being deeply aware of it. In fact, some periods of growth are so confusing that we don't even recognize that growth is what is happening. We may feel hostile or angry or weepy and hysterical, or we may feel depressed. It would never occur to us, unless we stumbled on a book or person who explained it to us, that we were in fact in the process of change, of actually becoming larger, spiritually, than we were before. Whenever we grow, we tend to feel it, as a young seed must feel the weight and inertia of the earth as it seeks to break out of its shell on its way to becoming a plant. Often the feeling is anything but pleasant.** ***(Walker 1988: 70)***

These words from Alice Walker serve as a reminder that we can easily become so absorbed in criticisms of the negative aspects of education that we forget our ultimate concern with this process of personal growth. Even if our personal experiences of education have been 'anything but pleasant', and if that negative impression is reinforced by what we read in the sociology of education, it is still possible to be interested in the problems unearthed and even more fascinated by debates about the possible solutions. to those problems.

This balance between negative and positive aspects of education is used in the structure of this chapter. We shall start by looking at how sociologists have used various perspectives in their critical analyses of education. Here we get a largely negative impression of some of the problems associated with education, and often the sociology of education has stopped at this point. These theorists have felt that their role was to describe what existed, and not to concern themselves with what 'could be'. However, contemporary studies of education are concerned just as much with prescription as description. Debates about how many of these problems could be tackled via educational policies are in many ways more constructive and positive, but they do tend to highlight even more difficulties than those initially identified.

To return to personal experiences, Walker suggests that the learning process is confusing and anything but straightforward. It could even be perceived as involving 'one step forward and two steps back'! Our formal education does not simply teach us uncontroversial 'facts'; schooling also includes hidden messages or unofficial rules that must be understood if we are to succeed in education. Jackson (1968) called this unofficial learning the 'hidden curriculum' and Hargreaves (1978) described it as the 'paracurriculum'. Aspects of this unofficial learning and personal experiences of education can teach us that we are valuable, intelligent individuals, or that we are worthless and 'dim'. Sociologists sometimes talk about personal aspirations being 'warmed-up' or 'cooled-down'. This can be seen, for example, in the experiences of some Black girls, whose aspirations could have been 'cooled-down' by the force of their negative school environment.

**Children were presented with a world view in which blackness represented everything that was ugly, uncivilized and underdeveloped, and our teachers made little effort to present us or our white classmates with an alternative view. Having been raised on the same basic diet of colonial bigotry themselves, they simply helped to make such negative stereotypes and misconceptions about us more credible.**

**According to them, we 'could not speak English' and needed 'special' classes where our 'broken' version of the language could be drilled out of us. We were quiet *and* volatile. Best of all, we were good at sports – physical, non-thinking activities – an ability which was to be encouraged so that our increasing 'aggression' could be channelled into more productive areas.** *(Bryan et al. 1987: 93)*

Notice the suggestion that this could discourage *some* Black girls! It is not simply a case of a certain cause having a predictable long-term or short-term effect, as we respond to our experiences in a variety of ways. Bryan and colleagues entitled their article 'Learning to Resist' because they found that many Black girls were not prepared to accept this negative conditioning, and instead used education as a source of personal liberation. Further support for their findings is provided by national data indicating that, in general, Black women are now achieving better qualifications than Black men (*Social Trends* 1994: Graph 3: 23) and that it is 'Asian' girls who are currently making the greatest strides in improving their academic performance (see p. 466).

Think of illustrations of your personal 'growth' or 'regression'. Do you perceive your own experience of schooling mainly as a process of 'warming-up', 'cooling-down', or neither? Was this process straightforward?

Interview another student about his or her experiences.

To what extent can we associate the roots of these positive and negative educational processes with individual action or with the social structure?

In considering whether someone is 'bright' or 'dim', we should be aware that there are many types of intelligence (for example, a quiz champion who cannot cook a meal, an autistic child who can make rapid mathematical calculations) and a wide variety of educational experiences and outcomes. There are also a variety of ways of assessing abilities.

**If we take the notion that intelligence is not an intrinsic quality of the child but is imputed to him by others then we can ask questions like how does the teacher define an intelligent child? What is the implicit concept of intelligence used by the teacher and where did he acquire it? Are the teacher's judgements about intelligence linked to his belief about social class?** *(Gorbutt 1972: 8)*

**Definition**

### Assessment

In sociology the use of concepts such as 'intelligence', 'knowledge' and 'ability' is regarded as problematic. Our 'common sense' may tell us that such things can be identified and measured (and we may see this as a prime function of our own education) but those professionals with a responsibility for their measurement are often acutely conscious of the practical problems involved. A brief consideration of how the purpose of assessment influences the methods that are used demonstrates how complex this topic is.

*(box continued)*

*(box continued)*

To start we could ask if the purpose of the assessment is summative or diagnostic. **Summative assessment** aims to describe an individual's current intelligence/knowledge/ability. This may lead to a grading, or some other type of summary or label (for example, a second-class honours degree). Yet, even a descriptive assessment of this kind can lead to a variety of results. Objectivity is very difficult to achieve, and examiners may disagree about what questions should be asked, what skills should be tested, and how results should be interpreted. **Diagnostic assessment** is likely to include a summative assessment, but will go further by providing an indication of what the next stage of the learning process should be (for example, by identifying special educational needs). Positive action can be taken, but again we can reasonably ask how objective the assessor's recommendations can be.

The degree of objectivity must also be considered in the selection of a standard, or standards, against which individuals are to be judged. When **criterion-referencing** is used there is some sort of list of criteria available to provide guidance concerning the standard that has been reached. An individual is assessed according to how the criteria have been satisfied, and the assessment can be made by a tutor or by the student (e.g. self-assessment using a tutorial on computer). When **norm-referencing** is used the performance of one individual is ranked in comparison to that of others. Usually the aim of this approach is to ration the number of 'passes' or qualifications (for example, in the use of an 11+ examination to allocate children to a limited number of grammar school places).

## Questions

What type of assessment is most likely to be used for the following:

(a) a driving test;
(b) admission to university:
(c) music grades;
(d) GCSE;
(e) assessment of students' knowledge of sociology?

Give reasons for your answers.

Do you think the types of assessments are fair?

The sociology of education shows us that individual 'failures' or 'successes' are socially as well as personally constructed, that knowledge is socially constructed and that the identification of intelligence is a social and subjective process. Returning to Alice Walker's imagery, you could say that we are interested in the 'weight and inertia of the earth' as well as the behaviour of the 'seed'.

**I regard as the prime postulate of all pedagogical speculation that education is an eminently social thing in its origins and in its functions, and that, therefore, pedagogy depends on sociology more closely than any other science.** ***(Durkheim 1956: 114)***

Sociologists commonly use a wide definition of education, to include informal education in the home and elsewhere. As education is part of the process of socialization, and influenced by other agencies of socialization, studies that separate it from other parts of society are severely limited. In Chapter 10 we saw how important the family is to our whole experience of life, and the influence of the family on our educational experiences can hardly be overestimated. However, sociologists are likely to reject claims that intelligence is primarily innate and inherited biologically from our parents. Instead they will emphasize the ways that families influence educational achievement after birth and the social labelling of children according to their background.

## Schooling in Britain

In this chapter we are concentrating on formal education in schools, colleges and universities. While this is a large enough area in its own right, it is important to bear in mind that we learn a great deal outside formal education – from parents, friends, the television, and so on. We shall look at the kinds of schools provided in Britain and the origins of that provision, then consider some of the problems sociologists have identified and debates about how those problems should be dealt with.

**Fig 11.1** Education in the early years. (Courtesy of Robert Harding Picture Library Ltd.)

Definition

## Maintained schools

The following are state schools, financed (maintained) by public taxation.

### Primary schools

These schools are attended by children aged 5 to 10 or 11. Primary provision could consist of one school covering the whole age range, or children may be split into two schools; an **infant school** for children aged 5 to 7, and a **junior school** for children aged 7 to 11. In some areas children leave primary school early (e.g. aged 8) and move to secondary school late (e.g. aged 13). The intervening years are spent at a **middle school**.

### Tripartite secondary system

The Education Act 1944 aimed to introduce a tripartite system. This involved selection of children at the age of 11+ for one of three types of schools. Those who were deemed to be 'academic' went to **grammar schools**, those with 'technical' abilities went to **technical schools** and those with more general, or practical, abilities went to a **secondary modern school**. Few technical schools were ever introduced and, in effect, most local authorities provided a bipartite system.

### Bipartite secondary system

This was the most common form of secondary provision between 1944 and the 1960s and still exists in Northern Ireland and some areas of Britain. Children are assessed during their final year of primary education and allocated to a **grammar school** or **secondary modern school** on the basis of their results.

### Comprehensive schools

It was originally hoped that comprehensive schools would be attended by children with the widest possible range of abilities and socio-economic backgrounds. The aims were (and still are) to generate more social mixing and more opportunities for children to pursue a diverse range of educational paths. However, it was found that some of the more academic children were sent by their parents to more prestigious schools.

### High schools

This label can be given to almost any type of school providing a secondary education (i.e. for children over 11).

### Grant maintained schools

These schools are supported by a central government grant instead of funding from a local education authority (LEA). Conservative governments have encouraged schools currently maintained by LEAs to apply for grant maintained status (i.e 'opt-out' of LEA control). In theory a grant maintained secondary school can still have the characteristics of a comprehensive, grammar or secondary modern school.

### City technology colleges

These schools were introduced during the 1980s for pupils aged 11 to 16 or 18. Although the National Curriculum is taught, each city technology college offers a particular specialism. Most emphasize science and technology but some emphasize other areas, such as the performing arts. Conservative governments expected these new schools to be financed by private sources but had to step in to provide most of the funding when private finance was not forthcoming.

*(box continued)*

*(box continued)*

**Voluntary aided (church) schools**

These schools are partly financed by the state and partly by a church.

**Special schools**

These are schools attended by children with special educational needs (SEN), i.e. physical or mental disabilities. The Education Act 1981 had a commitment to integrating most children with SEN into mainstream schools ('mainstreaming'). However, thousands of children still attend special schools.

**Integrated schools (Northern Ireland)**

Most schools in Northern Ireland are either Roman Catholic or Protestant. However, there are a few integrated schools which aim to break down sectarian differences by educating children of different faiths together. The Department of Education and Employment has a statutory duty to encourage the creation of more integrated schools.

## Non-maintained (or independent) schools

Although some of the schools listed above may be partly funded by private sources, parents are not officially required to pay fees for their children to attend. Independent schools are, to a large extent, financed by fees charged to families who 'buy' their children's education. Some 'academically able' children from less affluent background are granted an 'Assisted Place' which at least partly finances their education at a suitable independent school.

**Private schools**

This is a general label that may be attached to any school that is not financed by either LEA funds or a central government grant (although they may receive some government subsidies, such as tax concessions). The quality of these schools can vary, as they are often not subject to the sort of inspection that maintained schools now expect. Private **preparatory schools** are for pupils in the primary or middle school age range. Some private schools are intended to serve the needs of specific religious beliefs.

**Public schools**

This label is attached to an elite number of high-status, non-maintained secondary schools (e.g. Eton, Harrow, Winchester). Some can be identified by their head teacher's membership of the prestigious Headmasters' Conference. Unlike other private schools, public schools are not profit-making.

**Q**

Give some examples of how the school systems in Scotland, Northern Ireland and England and Wales differ.

Find out what kinds of schools were attended by other students in your group.

Do any of these schools not fit the above descriptions?

In what ways do they differ?

What is the most common type of schooling among the group?

Does the group favour any one type of schooling in particular, and why?

How much influence does the type of school attended have on educational outcomes?

## Origins of the current schooling 'system'

Such a diverse range of schools exists in Britain that the term 'school system' no longer seems as appropriate as it was in the 1950s (when most children were educated in a bipartite system) or 1960s (when comprehensive schools were more common). During the 1940s and 1950s the one point on which most politicians and educationalists were agreed was that social origins could have a profound, and often negative, effect on educational achievement. To tackle this problem some favoured the sort of competitive access to secondary education offered by the tripartite system, and this was the system that was originally promoted by the Education Act 1944. This Act was introduced in wartime, by a coalition government and with wide-scale public support. For the first time it provided free secondary education for all and therefore created a 'ladder' of educational opportunity for working-class children. The three types of schools planned for a tripartite system were originally presented as being of equal value but offering different types of education to suit different abilities. Planners aimed to provide 'parity of esteem' for all children but, partly because few technical schools were provided, the reality was that children were seen as 'passing' the 11+ examination and going to a grammar school or 'failing' and going to a secondary modern school.

Criticisms of what was largely a bipartite system gradually gained strength during the 1950s and 1960s. These were mainly concerned with two assumptions, first, that intelligence could be assessed accurately at the age of 11, and second, that abilities would be fixed for life. It was found that relatively few children from working-class backgrounds were 'passing' the 11+ to find a place on the 'ladder' of educational opportunity and that girls were often discriminated against in the allocation of grammar school places. There were also regional disparities in the provision of grammar school places, making it more difficult to 'pass' the 11+ examination in some areas than in others. During the 1960s increasing numbers of secondary modern school pupils passed GCE O Level examinations. This meant that some 11+ 'failures' left school better qualified than some grammar school pupils.

During the 1960s the tone of sociological research seemed to become more radical and egalitarian as educationalists grew more persistent in their claims that changes in the school system were not enough to improve working-class opportunities. Among others, work by Douglas (1964), Halsey *et al.* (1961) and Jackson and Marsden (1963) emphasized the need to make schools more accessible to working-class parents and to involve parents more fully in their children's education. This coincided with a period of Labour government and political initiatives aimed at generating greater equality: for example, Circular 10/65 (Department of Education and Science 1965) instructed LEAs to replace a bipartite system with comprehensive schools and the Plowden Report (Central Advisory Council for Education: CACE 1967) recommended the introduction of Educational Priority Areas (to provided compensatory education for children living in poor areas).

By the mid-1970s economic issues had become uppermost in political debates, as economic crisis followed economic crisis. This was reflected in a new emphasis on the role of education in serving the needs of the economy; this emphasis was labelled the 'Great Debate', and continues in the 1990s. The starting date is generally cited as a speech by the then Labour Prime Minister James Callaghan at Ruskin College, Oxford, in October 1976. To say that one speech was solely responsible for the Great Debate would be a gross simplification, but it was followed by a period of intense political activity around a theme of 'vocationalism', that accelerated throughout the 1980s and until the present day. Some educationalists have noted in particular the way that politicians have criticized education for in some way 'failing' the nation – Ball (1991) called it a 'discourse of derision' – and we can see signs of this discourse emerging in Callaghan's speech.

**Case Study**

### Extracts from the speech made by James Callaghan, Ruskin College, 1976

I am concerned on my journeys to find complaints from industry that new recruits from schools sometimes do not have the basic tools to do the job that is required.

I have been concerned to find that many of our best trained students who have completed the higher levels of education at university or polytechnic have no desire to enter industry. . . .

There is no virtue in producing socially well-adjusted members of society who are unemployed because they do not have the skills. Nor at the other extreme must they be technically efficient robots. Both of the basic purposes of education require the same essential tools. These are basic literacy, basic numeracy, the understanding of how to live and work together, respect for others, respect for the individual. This means acquiring certain basic knowledge, and skills and reasoning ability. It means developing lively inquiring minds and an appetite for further knowledge that will last a lifetime. It means mitigating as far as possible the disadvantages that may be suffered through poor home conditions or physical or mental handicap.

(quoted in *Education: Journal of Educational Administration Management and Policy* 22 October 1976: 333)

Until the 1980s a rather fragile process existed by which education policy was generated via negotiations between three groups: local councils and their local education authorities (LEAs), central government, and teachers' representatives. This came to be known as the 'triangle of tension' (Briault 1976). Teachers also had considerable freedom to decide what should be taught in class; so much so that the curriculum was often described as a 'secret garden'. Local education authorities had the main responsibility, and some freedom, in deciding what kinds of schools should be provided in their areas. They had always been influenced by directives from central government, but maintained some flexibility in their responses. For example, after a Labour government issued Circular 10/65 in 1965 some Conservative LEAs were so effective in stalling the move to comprehensive secondary education that their areas still have a largely bipartite system in the 1990s.

However, a major shift of influence has taken place as the previous 'triangle of tension' has gradually been replaced by the allocation of more power to central government, at the expense of LEAs and teachers. This shift has been sustained by the 'discourse of derision' (Ball 1991) and its allocation of blame for educational 'failures' to LEAs and teachers. Conservative governments have gradually reduced the amount of influence that LEAs have on the types of schools provided in their areas (for example, by promoting grant maintained schools and city technology colleges) and have acquired a tighter control of LEA spending. To a certain extent the influence of Labour-controlled LEAs could be seen as incompatible with the policies of

**Table 11.1** Milestones in education.

| Political events | Developments in the study of education |
|---|---|
| 1944 Education Act (tripartite system) | **1940s** Sociology mainly about behaviour in class, social control, knowledge and IQ |
| 1954 Gurney-Dixon Report (*Early Leaving*)<br>1959 Crowther Report (*15–18*)<br>1963 Newsom Report (*Half our Future*)<br>1963 Robbins Report (*Higher Education*)<br>1965 Circular 10/65 (*The Organization of Secondary Education*)<br>1967 Plowden Report (*Children and their Primary Schools*)<br>1969/70 Three Black Papers published | **1950s and 1960s** Two types of sociology of education emerging: structural functionalist emphasis on equal opportunities and school as a social system; education courses mainly for the training of teachers<br>Growing interest in home–school relations and compensatory education |
| 1975 Sex Discrimination Act<br>1976 Race Relations Act<br>1976 Callaghan Speech<br>1978 Warnock Report (*Special Education Needs*) | **1970s** British Sociological Association conference on education associated with start of the 'New Sociology of Education'; Young presented a paper on which his book *Knowledge and Control* (1971) was based (about cultural reproduction)<br>Increasing influence of feminism, anti-sexist and anti-racist approaches; Bowles and Gintis (1976) and Willis (1977) on the correspondence between education and social class inequality; the Great Debate; increased emphasis on vocationalism interpretative/micro-approaches |
| 1980 Education Act (introduced assisted places, removed LEA obligation to provide school meals and milk)<br>1981 Education Act (special needs)<br>1981 Rampton Report (*West Indian Children in our Schools*)<br>1985 Swann Report (*Education for All*)<br>1985/6 Teachers' 'strikes'<br>1986 Education Act (school governors)<br>1987 Teachers' Pay and Conditions Act<br>1988 Education Reform Act (National Curriculum, grant maintained status)<br>1988 Local Government Act (Clause 28 about homosexuality)<br>1988 Elton Report (*Discipline in Schools*) | **1980s** Ongoing politicization of sociological studies of education; considering implications of parental 'choice', 'rolling back the state', the continuing Great Debate about vocationalism, anti-racism, anti-sexism, the reduced influence of teachers and LEAs, the introduction of a National Curriculum<br>1988 Macdonald Report into the murder at Burnage High School<br>Ongoing interest in the relationship between gender, sexuality and educational experiences |
| 1990 Abolition of the ILEA<br>1991 School Teachers' Pay and Conditions Act<br>1992 White Paper (*Choice and Diversity*)<br>1992 Further and Higher Education Act (removed binary divide)<br>1992 Education (Schools) Act (school inspection)<br>1993 Education Act (grant maintained schools, school standards)<br>1993 Education Act (special educational needs) | **1990s** Educationalists producing critical alternatives to Conservative education policies<br>1993 Institute of Public Policy Research, *Education: A Different Vision*<br>1993 National Commission on Education Report, *Learning to Succeed*<br>1993 Start of more school-based system of teacher training |

Update the table.

What relationships can you identify between political developments and developments in the study of education?

central government. For example, the policies of the Labour-run Inner London Education Authority (ILEA) were seen as a major challenge by the Conservative government, which abolished it. During the mid-1980s teachers' unions took industrial action, in protest not only about their pay, but also about conditions of work and changes in the education system. The government responded by withdrawing their negotiating rights. Efforts by LEAs, teachers' unions and other interest groups to promote stronger versions of equal opportunities have been suppressed by government policies favouring a diverse range of opportunities. What has emerged in the 1990s is an ever-increasing range of different types of schools in Britain.

## Development of sociological explanations and theories

We shall now consider the main sociological approaches to the study of education and the problems they identify. Sociological perspectives (see Chapter 2) can help to make sense of educational provision and processes, but critical analyses of education have often limited themselves to describing problems, without concerning themselves with solutions. We shall follow this application of familiar sociological explanations and theories with a short analysis of themes that are more particular to the study of education policies.

As the aim here is to follow a basically developmental approach, we shall start, as early sociologists tended to start, with an emphasis on the social structure. Writers such as Durkheim were concerned with establishing the relatively new study of society and with arguing the merits of a sociological study of education at a time when education was largely seen as a matter for individuals only. This structural approach emphasizes the role of education in maintaining consensus and continuity in society, and is often primarily descriptive. However, other writers, such as Karl Marx, have emphasized the use of education as a means of perpetuating or shifting structural inequalities within society, focusing their attention on education as a source not only of continuity but also of conflict and change.

These structural concerns could be viewed as over-deterministic if they ignore the reactions of individuals to their educational experiences. We have already noted that some individuals can 'learn to resist' the negative influences within education. This emphasis on interaction will be considered in more detail when we look at interpretive approaches. The dynamic relationship between structural and interpretive approaches will be acknowledged when we look at recent movements towards a synthesis of these theoretical positions.

### Structural explanations: consensus and continuity

Consensus perspectives emphasize the important role of education in socializing the individual to fit into, and perpetuate, the social system. Although society has been created by people, individuals are seen as being born into a society which already has an identity of its own, and education as serving the function of passing on the collective consciousness, or culture, of that pre-existing society. This approach is most commonly associated with functionalist perspectives and Emile Durkheim. In the extract below we can see Durkheim urging his readers to accept what was a relatively unorthodox idea at the time, that education had a social, rather than just an individual, reality.

Case Study

## Durkheim: Education and Sociology

In sum, education, far from having as its unique or principal object the individual and his interests, is above all the means by which society perpetually recreates the conditions of its very existence. Can society survive only if there exists among its members a sufficient homogeneity? Education perpetuates and reinforces this homogeneity by fixing in advance, in the mind of the child, the essential similarities that collective life presupposes. But, on the other hand, without a certain diversity, would all co-operation be impossible? Education assures the persistence of this necessary diversity by becoming itself diversified and by specializing. It consists, then, in one or another of its aspects, of a systematic socialization of the young generation. In each of us, it may be said, there exist two beings which, while inseparable except by abstraction, remain distinct. One is made up of all the mental states which apply only to ourselves and to the events of our personal lives. This is what might be called the individual being. The other is the system of ideas, sentiments, and practices which express in us, not our personality, but the group or different groups of which we are a part; these are religious beliefs, moral beliefs and practices, national or occupational traditions, collective opinions of every kind. Their totality forms the social being. To constitute this being in each of us is the end of education.

(Adapted from Durkheim 1956: 114–16)

### Questions

Can you find any examples of education policies that have as their 'principal object the individual and his [*sic*] interests' ?

Why did Durkheim regard diversity (and the provision of diversity via education) as necessary in order to promote social cohesion? (See Chapter 2 for guidance.)

As a socialist Durkheim was concerned about social inequality, but as a positivist he also believed that the role of sociology was to describe society without aiming to change it. Functionalist approaches to education have therefore been portrayed by their critics as being rather conservative: analysing the functions of education in maintaining an efficient and stable social order. They have also tended to adapt to the context of the time, more recent writers focusing on the study of classrooms and schools as social systems.

Parsons, for example, was primarily concerned with the problem of

**how the school class functions to internalize in its pupils both the commitments and capacities for successful performance of their future adult roles, and second of how it functions to allocate these human resources within the role structure of the adult society.** *(Parsons 1959: 297)*

Parsons was aiming to integrate structural and interpretive approaches by emphasizing how the social structure influences the roles of individuals within the education system. His work is relevant in both sociology and psychology, and is an example of how unrealistic it is to make sharp distinctions between structural and interpretive approaches. Nevertheless Parsons' work is more often cited in the sociology of education as a 'structural functionalist' approach simply because he does not emphasize the routine small-scale classroom interactions that provide a focus for interpretive approaches. He was interested in the 'patterned expectations' (rules and regulations) that have developed, governing how individuals should behave in order to maintain social order and continuity. More specifically, education is seen as serving the four functional requirements that all societies have in order to survive.

Definition

### Four functional requirements of society

**Adaptation**

Education adapts itself and individuals to changes in the cultural, technological and physical environment. It helps to emancipate the child from dependence on the family.

**Goal attainment**

Education helps individuals to identify and realize their personal and collective needs. Differentiated achievements can contribute to an effective division of labour.

**Integration**

Education provides some coherence between the relative influences of, for example, family, legal system, church, employment and the wider economic system. It helps individuals to identify themselves within a wider social system.

**Latency or pattern maintenance**

Educational processes lead to the reproduction of common values and social norms. It teaches us, not only how to conform, but also how to think.

Here we can see a continuation of Durkheim's positivist approach, with its emphasis on description, rather than criticism. Its implication that education contributes towards a meritocratic system (in which pupils' educational achievements are based only on ability and effort) has been severely challenged as research has repeatedly highlighted the profound effects of social inequalities on educational outcomes. Critics have also argued that education can contribute to both social cohesion and social conflict, and that education does not necessarily serve the needs of either the economy or the individual. There are, moreover, no clear and agreed sets of 'needs' that can be functionally fulfilled. In general, functionalist images of society have been seen as being so unrealistic that they should either be dismissed or be adapted to suit reality.

It would, however, be wrong to assume that functionalist approaches to education are no longer influential. Some aspects have indeed been adapted or developed more fully to incorporate criticisms. For example, theories about social dysfunction (Merton 1938) help to explain how education can not only fail to serve the needs of society, but also actually work against the interests of society. It can also reasonably be claimed that it is just as important to observe the role of education in maintaining society as to observe the manifestation of conflict within education.

Conflict perspectives emphasize inequalities of educational opportunities and the need for social change. These have varied from the revolutionary writings of Marx and Engels to more moderate appeals for reforms within the existing social system. Classical Marxists have emphasized the primary influence of the capitalist economic infrastructure and the secondary role of education in perpetuating the necessary supportive ideology. In the box we can see Marx and Engels' condemnation of education as a means by which the state maintains a capitalist system and its associated inequalities.

Definition

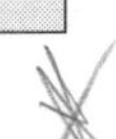

### Marx and Engels: education and the state

The communists have not invented the intervention of society in education; they do but seek to alter the character of that intervention, and to rescue education from the influence of the ruling class.

The bourgeois claptrap about the family and education, about the hallowed co-relation of parent and child, becomes all the more disgusting, the more, by the action of modern industry, all family ties among the proletarians are torn asunder and their children transformed into simple articles of commerce and instruments of labour.

(Marx and Engels 1976 vol. 6: 502)

Equal elementary education? What idea behind these words? Is it believed that in present-day society, (and it is only with this one has to deal) education can be equal for all classes? Or is it demanded that the upper classes also shall be compulsorily reduced to the modicum of education – the elementary school – that alone is compatible with the economic conditions not only of the wage workers but of the peasants as well? . . .

'Elementary education by the state' is altogether objectionable. Defining by a general law the expenditures on the elementary schools, the qualifications of the teaching staff, the branches of instruction, etc., as is done in the United States, supervising the fulfilment of these legal specifications by state supervisors, is a very different thing from appointing the state as the educator of the people! Government and church should rather be equally excluded from any influence on the school.

(Marx 1891, *Critique of the Gotha Programme*, quoted in Feuer 1969: 170–1)

#### Questions

**How could education transform children into 'simple articles of commerce and instruments of labour'? Could aspects of your education be interpreted in this way?**

**Compare these views with those of Durkheim. What are the similarities and differences?**

Marxist influences continue today but have (like functionalism) been developed and adapted to the changing historical context. They have probed more deeply into the processes by which inequality is perpetuated through education. For example, writing about *Schooling in Capitalist America*, Bowles and Gintis (1976) analysed the correspondence between children's experiences in school and the inequalities they encounter as adults in the workplace. In this way the school is seen as introducing and reproducing the inequalities of social class that are perpetuated in a capitalist system, normalizing them in the process so that the working class are hardly aware of them (and therefore in a state of false consciousness).

**Alienated labor is reflected in the student's lack of control over his or her education, the alienation of the student from the curriculum content, and the motivation of school work through a system of grades and other external rewards rather than the student's integration with either the process (learning) or the outcome (knowledge) of the educational 'production process'. Fragmentation in work is reflected in the institutionalized and often destructive competition among students through continual and ostensibly meritocratic ranking and evaluation. By attuning young people to a set of social relationships similar to those of the workplace, schooling attempts to gear the development of personal needs to its requirements.**

*(Bowles and Gintis 1976: 131)*

Q

What influences have you had on the content or style of your education (a) at the age of 8; (b) at the age of 12; (c) now?

List any aspects of schooling that are essentially (a) cooperative; (b) competitive.

Yet even in what is often defined as a structural approach, Bowles and Gintis (1976) were looking not only at the social structure, but also at the way that small groups and individuals related to each other in schools. This makes it difficult to see where a structural approach may end and an interpretive approach start, and divisions between these approaches become even more spurious when we consider the work of Paul Willis. Willis (1977) analysed the attitudes of a group of working-class 'lads' during their last year at secondary modern school and their first year in the workplace and, in the process, greatly enhanced our understanding of how the 'correspondence principle' identified by Bowles and Gintis could work in practice.

The focus of writers working within a Marxist tradition (and critical theorists in particular) has also shifted to an emphasis on hegemony and the role of the ideological superstructure in perpetuating social inequalities. For example, Althusser (1972) saw education as playing a vital role within the ideological state apparatus, perpetuating inequalities by conditioning the masses to accept the status quo. Similarly, feminists have examined the features of education that perpetuate and legitimize gender inequalities (see e.g. Arnot 1986; Byrne 1978; Deem 1978; Kelly 1981; Kenway and Willis 1990; Stanworth 1983).

One feature that many of these new theoretical developments have in common is an emphasis on the use of education as part of a process of liberation. This can be seen in the earlier quote (p.433) from Bryan *et al.* (1987), where we saw that Black girls described their educational experiences as being primarily defined by their Blackness in a negative way. The title of their article, 'Learning to Resist', suggests that children do not automatically accept this sort of labelling. They (and their teachers) may resist negative influences and not only use education as a source of personal empowerment, but also bring about minor or major changes in educational processes. In order to really achieve any depth in our understanding of education we must therefore look at how individuals relate to structural constraints and at their experiences of small-scale interaction.

### Interpretive influences

From the late 1970s onwards the influence of Weber and other action theorists was becoming more noticeable in educational research. More sociologists started to present findings based on classroom observation and interview data, the best known of these being provided by Ball (1981), Hargreaves (1967), Lacey (1970) and Willis (1977). They were trying to understand the meanings that individuals and groups attached to their behaviour, and to interpret their findings at a theoretical level. However, it would be a simplification to depict these as just interpretive studies, when often they have been motivated by an interest in how structural inequalities are maintained by educational processes. This interest in showing how many 'interpretive' studies of classroom interaction incorporate 'structuralist' issues could be seen as a natural progression from the work of Weber (1964: 88–120) and part of a general move towards the triangulation of methodological and theoretical perspectives.

Paul Willis' (1977) research has already been mentioned as it relates quite closely to the 'correspondence principle' described by Bowles and Gintis (1976) (notice that his book was published a year after theirs). Willis acknowledged the use of both structuralist and interpretive approaches at the very beginning.

> **The difficult thing to explain about how middle class kids get middle class jobs is why others let them. The difficult thing to explain about how working class kids get working class jobs is why they let themselves.** *(Willis 1977: 1)*

However, you can see the essential features of interpretive sociology, as he uses 'the lads'' own words and tries to communicate their own sense of reality (see box).

**Case Study**

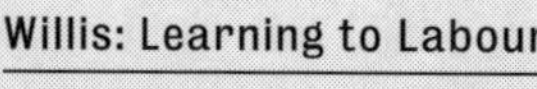

#### Willis: Learning to Labour

It is essentially what appears to be their enthusiasm for, and complicity with, immediate authority which makes the school conformists – or 'ear 'oles' or 'lobes' – the second great target for 'the lads' [the first target is the teachers]. The term 'ear 'ole' itself connotes the passivity and absurdity of the school conformists for 'the lads'. It seems that they are always listening, never doing: never animated with their own internal life, but formless in rigid reception. The ear is one of the least expressive organs of the human body: it responds to the expressivity of others. It is pasty and easy to render obscene. That is how 'the lads' liked to picture those who conformed to the official idea of schooling.

Crucially, 'the lads' not only reject but feel superior to the 'ear 'oles'. The obvious medium for the enactment of this superiority is that which the 'ear 'oles' apparently yield – fun, independence and excitement: having a 'laff'.

[In a group discussion]

| | |
|---|---|
| PW | ... why not be like the 'ear 'oles', why not try and get CSEs? |
| – | They don't get any fun, do they? |
| Derek | Cos they'm prats like, one kid he's got on his report now, he's got five As and one B. |
| – | Who's that? |
| Derek | Birchall. |

*(box continued)*

*(box continued)*

**Spanksy** I mean, what will they remember of their school life? What will they have to look back on? Sitting in the classroom, sweating their bollocks off, you know, while we've been . . . I mean look at the things we can look back on, fighting on the Pakis, fighting on the JAs [Jamaicans]. Some of the things we've done on teachers, it'll be a laff when we look back on it.

(Willis 1977: 14)

**Questions**

Most of 'the lads' got jobs when they left school in the early 1970s. Consider the implications of Willis' findings in view of the high level of unemployment today.

Were there similar groups to 'the lads' in your school? Were any of these groups, or members of these groups, female?

Willis' interests reflect common sociological interests in pro- and anti-school subcultures, the self-fulfilling prophecy and the 'hidden curriculum'. Put simply, teachers' expectations about how well or how badly individuals will behave are likely to influence that behaviour. Pupils are likely to internalize their teachers' expectations and make them their own, eventually matching their behaviour to the predictions made. Expectations may be derived not only from teachers, but also from families, friends and society in general; in this way, social inequalities can be perpetuated by low self-esteem.

Willis, however, adds depth to this sort of scenario by illustrating 'the lads' ' creative interaction with social constraints as well as the processes by which they reach a predictable structural location. (Other well-known studies of the self-fulfilling prophecy include Holt (1969), Rosenthal and Jacobson (1968) and Spender and Sarah (1980).)

Willis' 'lads' may be seen as taking a rather predictable route but what about the Black women interviewed for 'Learning to Resist'? Fuller (1980) also found that a group of Black girls in comprehensive school created an anti-school subculture but still valued academic achievement as a form of resistance.

## Unity and diversity in the study of education

Developments in sociological theories about education seem to have moved towards a synthesis of structural and interpretive perspectives. For example, critical theory has Marxist origins but emphasizes the ways that language reproduces or transforms culture. Like classical Marxist approaches it advocates changes in education to reduce social inequalities, but it also emphasizes individual, rather than social class, empowerment in recognition of the increasingly diverse nature of society and the fragmentation of social classes.

Similarly, post-modernist and feminist approaches to the study of education often mix theories and techniques. Feminists share a common concern about gender inequalities in society (i.e. a structural emphasis) but the diverse range of, sometimes competing, feminist theories often seem to share little else (see pp. 77–88).

This blend of common and diverse features also corresponds with current developments and themes in the study of education policy. A wide range of approaches to the study of education remain, but there is also an element of consensus in academic responses to political developments within education. Universities have been subject to control by a government that does not approve of sociology, and the status of the sociology of education as a fundamental part of teacher education has been challenged by New Right ideology. Sociologists are now concerned with defending the status of the subject and justifying their concern about educational inequalities. For example, in her presidential speech to the British Educational Research Association, Patricia Broadfoot outlined inherent conflicts between the values of the New Right and those of educational researchers.

**The world of academe is quite literally another world, or . . . another culture. It is characterised by values, goals, ways of working and rewards which are fundamentally at odds with those of laissez-faire individualism and profit, market forces and competition. It cannot . . . be squeezed into a conformity with the prevailing political culture.** *(Broadfoot 1988: 4–5)*

## Sociological approaches to education policy

We have seen how educational studies have become more 'political', encompassing not only their traditional interests in educational problems but also increasingly emphasizing debates about how those problems should be tackled. In order to clarify current political debates about educational issues we shall consider the two main themes of equality/inequality and uniformity/diversity. The theme of equal (or rather *un*equal) opportunities is already well established in educational studies and, although debates about uniformity/diversity are certainly not recent, they currently have particular relevance in view of New Right education policies and post-modernist ideas.

### Equality or inequality?

There seems to be an almost universal assumption that 'equal opportunities' are a 'good thing' much in the same way that 'democracy' is regarded as a 'good thing'. Yet if we try to clarify these concepts it is likely that individual interpretations of these terms will differ. In educational studies there is a wide range of views as to what 'equal opportunities' means based on different assumptions about human nature (e.g. that we are basically competitive or basically cooperative) and the purpose of formal education (e.g. to emphasize the needs of the child and/or of the economy).

### Egalitarian approaches: equal outcomes

At one end of this range are views often described as 'egalitarian', emphasizing equality of outcomes, in which identifiable social groups are not over- or under-represented among high or low achievers. This means that the proportion of a social group represented among university graduates (and also among those without qualifications) should correspond with the proportion of that group in the whole population; for example, if 50 per cent of the population is female, about 50 per cent of all graduates should be female. In the sections on social class, gender and race we shall see how far we are from such equal outcomes (pp. 455–70).

Egalitarian arguments have supported the need for compensatory education, such as the Educational Priority Areas promoted by the Plowden Report in 1967. In other words some children are seen as needing extra resources and extra help in an effort to compensate for wider social inequalities. However, according to egalitarian approaches, social inequalities cannot be tackled by education alone. A new educational power base and other changes in education (such as anti-racism, anti-sexism and anti-heterosexism) are promoted, but egalitarians present these as just part of the necessary shift towards a more equitable and caring society in general. The use of education for personal empowerment fits egalitarian images of enlightenment and emancipation.

---

**Education has also been seen as a means to social emancipation. It is through education that socialists and feminists, for instance, have come to know their everyday unhappinesses aren't the fault of personal inadequacies but are common experiences, shared by others, and produced by particular social arrangements.**

*(Johnson 1983: 20)*

---

Critical theorists and action researchers have encouraged individuals not only to acknowledge but also to challenge the forces that oppress them, and nowhere can this be seen more forcefully than in the writings of Paulo Freire. Freire worked among poor farmers in northern Brazil during the 1960s. In *The Pedagogy of the Oppressed* he said that they were trapped in a 'culture of silence' by being in an economic and social situation in which critical awareness and responses were virtually impossible. What was needed was teaching as a partnership and dialogue through which people could 'achieve significance as people' (Freire 1972: 61).

---

**Conscientization is a permanent critical approach to reality in order to discover it and discover the myths that deceive us and help to maintain the oppressing dehumanizing structures.** *(Freire 1976: 225)*

---

Case Study

## Education for liberation

**In Britain Freire's approach was adopted by Doreen Grant (1989) when she worked with parents and children in a Glasgow slum. Here she explains why her emphasis is on a dialogue between participants.**

Presenting information is not the main task in such a dialogue. The learners, not the subject matter, are the focus. Information only has impact, Freire maintains, when a question has already been raised, at least implicitly. In an area such as schooling where people only have experience as recipients, not as providers, many questions are submerged and surface merely as muffled reactions. The first task, then, is to identify the main concepts within these inchoate responses.

*(box continued)*

*(box continued)*

Once the themes have been identified, the group leader's task is to find 'codes' which will epitomize the themes and so re-present them for focused dialogue. A Freirian code is an arrangement of the theme in some evocative form – tape-recording, picture, activity, or role-playing. This detached form of presentation frees the participants to speak their hidden and often unconscious thoughts, instead of automatically regurgitating some learned or expected response.

In the context of under-achievement in school, the ultimate goal of such dialogue is an improvement in children's learning. But there are intermediate goals. Parents need to work through hidden fears and feelings which block successful involvement in their children's education. Positive feelings have to be strengthened in two areas; pride in their role as educators of their own children, and interest in widening their own knowledge base and personal scope. The parents are, therefore, the central participants with their own children, with each other and with professional educators.

(Grant 1989: 132)

### Questions

**Is Grant right to claim that people have experience of education only as recipients?**

**What practical constraints could there be on adopting this approach in schools?**

**How does the role of parents differ from their conventional role in contemporary schooling?**

## Equal access

A second interpretation of equal opportunities describes a cooperative system in which equal access to a high quality education, with equal resources, is be provided for all. The image is of a broad staircase to which all should have access; it is this sort of definition that supported the provision of comprehensive schools attended by children of all abilities and (in theory) all social backgrounds.

In the past this approach was seen as quite radical because of its emphasis on equal treatment for all, irrespective of social origins. It is still popular in the 1990s, but is limited in its application to social class inequalities by the existence of a diverse range of schools, and its success is more noticeable in policies relating to gender and racial issues. For example, efforts to ensure that individuals are not discriminated against on the grounds of gender or race include the Sex Discrimination Act 1975 and Race Relations Act 1976. Proposals such as these, couched in terms of equal access, were able to gain more popular and political support than some of the more radical (egalitarian) action promoted by the Equal Opportunities Commission and Commission for Racial Equality. The 'discourse of derision' helped to generate a climate that was generally disparaging of anti-sexist and anti-racist ideas, but could tolerate 'weaker' versions espousing equal access.

Legislation has therefore been more successful in generating less discriminatory practices than in changing public attitudes. It is more difficult to foster fundamental changes in public attitudes and the educational culture as a whole (such differences being seen in Activity 2). In Britain there have been many other initiatives since the 1970s in which the aim of changing attitudes had to take a back seat to the achievement of equal access. For example, the Girls Into Science and Technology initiative aimed to encourage more girls to take science and technology courses, and had some success, but was less successful in challenging the high status often associated with 'male jobs' or the low status associated with 'female jobs'(Kelly 1981).

### Competitive access

A third approach involves the idea of a competitive system in which only a few children can find a place on the narrow ladder to success. Superior educational provision is seen as being rationed according to ability, the less able being provided with the sort of education that will equip them for relatively undemanding working lives. This sort of approach has supported the provision of scholarships, or the 11+ examination for entry into grammar schools, and rests on two assumptions – that intelligence can be identified at an early age and that basic aptitudes do not change considerably over the years.

We have already considered assessment by norm-referencing as a form of selection for places on this narrow ladder and the criticisms of the bipartite system that eventually lead to the introduction of comprehensive schools. The next move is to consider the market-led form of competitive access associated with New Right political policies.

### Parental choice

A long period of Conservative government in Britain (since 1979) has brought with it a new emphasis on parental 'choice', and an uncritical approach to inequalities in education. From this perspective more egalitarian approaches to equal opportunities are unrealistic and impractical. They are unrealistic because they do not accommodate our competitive natures, and they are impractical because they demand too much action from the state via the education system. Margaret Thatcher's criticisms of the 'nanny' state were supported by her conviction that the state, and therefore education, can and should do very little that interferes with individuals' private lives.

> **The government views inequality as being helpful to incentives at both ends of the income distribution and does not regard gross inequalities in income and wealth as a problem.** *(Walker and Walker 1987)*

Although similar to the third approach (competitive access) because of its emphasis on competition, this fourth approach no longer sees competition as being only among children, but also among parents, who are expected to act in their children's best interests by sending them to the best possible schools. The ultimate aim is to provide a free market education system in which only those high quality schools that attract parents will survive. As schools and families become more self-sufficient, the pressures of education on the state should decrease and consumer-led education should lead to optimum consumer satisfaction:

**the 1944 Act was profoundly alien to Conservative philosophy. The idea that state officials should allocate children to different kinds of school, on the basis of the decisions of experts about what kind of occupation they are best fitted for, is part of the philosophy of socialism and the planned society. The Conservative tradition is surely one of individual families making decisions for themselves.** *(Lynn 1970: 32)*

Brown (1989: 42) called this perspective the 'ideology of parentocracy'. However, an emphasis on competitive access does not allow parents complete freedom of choice, or eliminate selectivity on the part of the school. Some popular schools have had to adopt stringent criteria for the selection of pupils, and 'parental choice' raises uncertainties about who is really being selected in this sort of competitive system: is it parents or their children? Choice is also limited by practical and economic factors.

### Inequality: biological determinism

Our earlier extract from Durkheim presented criticisms of the then orthodox view that educational achievement was entirely based on individual ability, and that this ability was determined at birth. However, Jensen (1969) and Eysenck (1971) claimed that educational attainment was heavily influenced by biology. Many (perhaps most) people regard themselves as naturally 'bright' or 'dim'! This sort of approach often appeals to our common-sense assumptions and provides a simple explanation of, and justification for, social inequalities. However, sociology challenges common-sense assumptions and, although accepting that some aspects of educational ability may be biologically determined (for example, the abilities of autistic children), it is clear that sociologists would reject the sort of biological determinism illustrated by Lynn.

**No amount of money poured into the 'Educational Priority Areas' enthusiastically espoused in the Plowden Report, is likely to bring any appreciable proportion of slum children up to the standards of university entrance.**

**The suppression of these truths by progressives leads to a whole series of false deductions. One of the most serious is that it is the fault of society that slum dwellers are impoverished and their young do so badly at school. To the young red guards, it follows that society is unjust and must be overthrown. They do not realise that slum dwellers are caused principally by low innate intelligence and poor family upbringing, and that the real social challenge is posed by this.** *(Lynn 1970: 30)*

Notice the date of this quote. Academics and politicians are unlikely to articulate such ideas today. Why? Does this mean that this perspective is no longer influential?

### Uniformity or diversity?

Although the theme of equal opportunities is well established in the sociology of education, debates about uniformity and diversity reflect a growing emphasis on policy issues. We have seen that many different types of schools are currently provided in Britain, and that this provision is likely to become more diverse. Yet the fragmentation of educational provision is in keeping with current post-modern the-

ories about the fragmentation of society in general. In other words, it would be wrong to associate educational diversity only with Conservative policies without also acknowledging other social trends. One of these trends is the common concern of politicians and academics from many perspectives that ever-increasing demands on the state leave it overburdened or overloaded. Efforts to reduce government responsibilities for education are in keeping with New Right policies favouring greater self-sufficiency and the 'rolling back of the state'. Yet, writing from a left-wing perspective, Habermas (1971) observed the problems of an overburdened state and associated them with a legitimation crisis in capitalist societies. All of this might suggest that a shift towards the fragmentation of educational provision is inevitable but, again, it is not as simple as that.

In the 1980s and early 1990s there have been concurrent moves towards both diversification and uniformity in education. For example, the Education Reform Act 1988 included elements of diversity and uniformity: provisions for schools to apply for grant maintained status and 'opt out' of LEA control; details concerning the reorganization of education within the Inner London Education Authority area after its abolition in 1990; limitations on the influence of LEAs on further and higher education; the introduction of a centrally determined National Curriculum, and a requirement that all children in maintained schools should attend an act of collective worship. We have seen the wide range of schools already existing in Britain. Yet the school curriculum is constrained by central directives and the educational power base has shifted away from LEAs to central government control. In theory Conservative governments have been committed to reducing state involvement in education but in practice they have been increasing central government control in many ways.

**Definition**

### The National Curriculum

The National Curriculum sets out what must be taught to children between the ages of 5 and 16 in all state schools in England and Wales. It does not apply to independent schools or city technology colleges. Schools in Scotland and Northern Ireland have their own versions of the National Curriculum.

#### What is it and how does it work?

The National Curriculum specifies ten subjects which must be studied and sets out what children must learn in each one. Originally it was designed for all children in state schools between the ages of 5 and 16 but recent developments mean it has all but been abandoned for 14–16 year olds.

These ten subjects are

| | |
|---|---|
| English | design and technology |
| mathematics | music |
| science | art |
| history | physical education |
| geography | a modern foreign language, e.g. French or German |

In addition, all pupils must study religious education.

*(box continued)*

*(box continued)*

Some subjects are considered more important than others, particularly English mathematics and science. These are called the **core subjects**. They must be studied by all children to GCSE level. The other seven subjects are called **foundation subjects**.

**Key Stages**

The end of each Key Stage marks the point at which children will be formally assessed:

Key Stage one: ages 5–7
Key Stage two: ages 7–11
Key Stage three: ages 11–14
Key Stage four: ages 14–16

**Attainment Targets**

The content of each of the ten National Curriculum subjects is broken down into a set of Attainment Targets. They are simply statements of what children are expected to know or be able to do at each Key Stage.

**Levels of Attainment**

Each Attainment Target is further divided into ten levels. Each level becomes progressively more demanding. At the age of 7 most children are expected to have reached level two; the brightest children will have reached level ten by the age of 16.

In theory, a child of any age can perform at any level. A child with difficulties in, say, maths or English, may never achieve more than level three or four. Exceptionally able children might be working towards level eight by the time they are 11.

**Standard Assessment Tasks (SATs)**

These are set tasks used teachers for formal assessment at the end of each Key Stage.

(Adapted from Mason and Ramsay 1992: 146–8)

## Questions

How is the National Curriculum managed in the school timetable and classroom?

What are the cross-curricula themes?

How does the National Curriculum apply to children with Special Educational Needs?

What sort of assessment is used in the National Curriculum: descriptive or prescriptive, criterion-referencing or norm-referencing (see pp. 433–4)?

Can the National Curriculum be politically neutral?

Shifts in educational policy have been so fundamental that it is not clear that a total reversal would occur if a more left-wing government came to power. There is, for example, much support within the Labour Party and among educationalists for some sort of National Curriculum, even if it only encompasses ‘core’ subjects. As far back as 1976 James Callaghan voiced his support for a national core curriculum in his Ruskin speech. It is also unlikely that grant maintained schools would simply be returned to LEA control with the election of a Labour government.

Nevertheless, there are certain fundamental distinctions between left-wing and right-wing perspectives on education; you should consider how they relate to wider sociological theories and findings. Left-wing politicians (in both central and local government) are likely to emphasize stronger definitions of equality, but are still faced with decisions about uniformity or diversity. An emphasis on egalitarianism and uniformity may lead to the state being overburdened by its responsibilities, but an emphasis on egalitarianism and diversity may have inherent contradictions or may just be a Utopian dream.

Decisions about the segregation or integration of children within and between various schools also have to be made, and it is often difficult to identify the perspectives on which such decisions are based. For example, arguments about coeducational or single sex education, schools for separate religious faiths, and the integration (in mainstream schools) or segregation of children with special educational needs are not clearly delineated along political lines. Pressure groups associated with any one of these issues could include members of all political hues and various sociological perspectives.

**Q** Consider the arguments for and against (a) single sex education (either within individual schools or via separate schools); (b) the granting of voluntary aided status to Muslim schools; (c) the integration of children with special educational needs within mainstream schools (for ways in which this could be done see the Warnock Report (1978) and the provisions of the Education Act 1981).

## Social groups and education

If you were asked to explain which social characteristics most influenced your educational experiences and achievements you would probably be rather baffled. Which was most significant: your gender, social class, racial identity, religion, physical handicap, geographical location? There is no simple answer; it is the same when sociologists study the relationships between social characteristics and education in general. The search for indicators of social class or race has to be combined with a sense of realism and an appreciation that individual experiences of social class or race may be very different. For these reasons, by the end of the twentieth century, sociological studies of education had become more concerned with the cumulative effects of social characteristics than with discrete social groupings. For example, the experiences of working-class, Black girls may be so different from the experiences of middle-class, white girls that it would be unrealistic to suggest that 'gender' has had the greatest influence on their educational outcomes.

Why then are we providing an overview of findings concerned with the *separate* categories of social class, gender and race, especially when we have already considered them under other headings? This is partly in recognition of the sheer mass of data now available from studies in those three areas. Sociologists have also been able to provide valuable insights into the social labelling of individuals, continuous social trends (for example, the socio-economic origins of graduates) and dramatic shifts of direction (for example, gender differences in educational achievement). However, they are merely scraping the surface of the complex social influences on educational experiences.

## Social class

We have already looked at conflict theorists' criticisms of the role of education in supporting social class inequalities and at functionalists' concern about the maintenance of a true meritocracy. Some interpretive/structural explanations of how inequalities have been legitimized and reproduced have also been considered. Different definitions of equal educational opportunities have also provided some understanding of how relative are ideas about inequality. It really is in the eye of the beholder!

More empirical data are therefore needed in order to evaluate the theories provided. The 1950s and 1960s produced a series of official reports – e.g. Gurney-Dixon (CACE 1954); Crowther (CACE 1959); Newsom (CACE 1963); Robbins (1963); Plowden (CACE 1967) – which provided cumulative evidence of the relationship between father's occupation and educational outcomes. Concurrent support for official findings about social class inequalities was provided by sociologists (e.g. Bernstein 1971; Bourdieu and Passeron 1977; Bowles and Gintis 1976; Douglas 1964; Goldthorpe *et al.* 1980; Halsey *et al.* 1961, 1980; Jackson and Marsden 1963; Rutter *et al.* 1979; Willis 1977) and by the end of the 1970s the evidence had become overwhelming. From the 1970s onwards we can see a long list of sociological findings in which the focus is more sharply placed on educational policy-making, with an emphasis on social inequalities (e.g. Flude and Ahier 1974; Institute of Public Policy Research 1993; Karabel and Halsey 1977; Kogan 1975; Lodge and Blackstone 1982; McKenzie 1993; National Commission on Education 1993).

Yet, despite such activity and noticeable changes in class composition over the years it is remarkable how consistent some findings still are. For example, the survey carried out for the Robbins Report (1963) found that 33 per cent of all respondents with fathers in the 'Professional' group had a degree, compared to 1 per cent of respondents with fathers who were 'Semi/unskilled manual' workers. Only 7 per cent with fathers in the 'Professional' category had no qualification, compared with 65 per cent with fathers in the 'Semi/unskilled manual' category (Robbins 1963: Table 2, p. 40).

**Table 11.2** Highest qualification held, by socio-economic group in Britain, 1992–3 (%).[a]

| | Professional | Employers and managers | Intermediate non-manual | Junior non-manual | Skilled manual and own account non-professional | Semi-skilled manual and personal service | Unskilled manual | All persons |
|---|---|---|---|---|---|---|---|---|
| Degree | 61 | 19 | 21 | 3 | 2 | 1 | – | 12 |
| Higher education | 16 | 19 | 29 | 6 | 9 | 4 | 2 | 13 |
| GCE A level[b] | 7 | 16 | 12 | 13 | 14 | 7 | 3 | 12 |
| GCSE grades A–C[b] | 7 | 21 | 20 | 35 | 23 | 21 | 12 | 22 |
| GCSE grades D–G[b,c] | 1 | 7 | 5 | 16 | 15 | 12 | 10 | 10 |
| Foreign | 4 | 3 | 3 | 3 | 2 | 4 | 3 | 3 |
| No qualifications | 3 | 15 | 10 | 24 | 36 | 51 | 70 | 28 |

*Notes:*
(a) sample aged 25–69 and not in full-time education
(b) or equivalent
(c) includes commercial qualifications and apprenticeships

*Source: Social Trends* 1995 25 (Table 3.24 p.57)

When these findings are compared with information for the year 1992/3 it seems that the imbalance remains (see Table 11.2).

This imbalance has not been helped by the freezing and gradual reduction of student grants. It has long been claimed that children from working-class families are less willing to 'defer gratification' and want to start earning a wage as soon as possible rather than stay longer in education. Yet, the route to higher education has for a long time been effectively blocked for some by the lack of LEA grants for A Level students. Sociologists have observed a tendency to split young people into 'sheep and goats', with some being able to take the route to a high-status qualification, others resigning themselves to low-grade training for low-status jobs or long-term unemployment.

**Case Study**

### Young 'forced into FE to avoid poverty trap'

**Taking their Chances**, published by the Coalition for Young People and Social Security [COYPSS], said the transition from school to the labour market was no longer a period of opportunity and potential leading to a desired career, nor a way to increase the skills of the workforce for the economy's benefit.

Ian Sparks, chief executive of the Children's Society, which currently chairs COYPSS, said: 'Urgent action needs to be taken to improve training, employment and income for 16 and 17-year-olds leaving school. The current situation will result in grave consequences for the future of young people and the national economy.'

The report is calling for the Government to introduce a further education subsistence allowance and to increase the youth training allowance to a minimum of 50 a week. It also wants the return of the benefits for unemployed school-leavers abolished in 1988.

Last year around a quarter of school-leavers ended up unemployed. Of these, 85 per cent had no income because they were not eligible for income support. The Government's intention to cut £56 million from training programmes for 1995/6 will reduce their prospects further.

Sixty per cent of those who do get on to training schemes leave early. The report said that this was usually because they were unhappy with the way their schemes were run, but also because they did not receive appropriate training or enough money. Over the past few years, youth training allowances have been frozen at £29.50 for 16-year-olds, and at £35 for 17-year-olds. (Malik 1995)

### Questions

**What are the strengths and weaknesses (for individual trainees and for the state) of recent youth training schemes and of the long-term apprenticeships that they have replaced?**

**Look at the extracts from James Callaghan's speech (p. 439). To what extent have his concerns been satisfied by vocational education since the 1970s?**

Education in Britain has never been widely based on egalitarian ideals (see pp. 448–55). Some schools have been able to thrive due to their popularity with parents and their position in published 'league' tables. A growing dependence on fund-raising by parents for school resources also means that where a large proportion of pupils come from affluent backgrounds the school is more likely to prosper. Some schools in less affluent areas have become what are popularly known as 'sink' schools (i.e. unable to afford proper maintenance and with facilities that are barely adequate), with an intake of children whose parents cannot compete in a market system. Success in a market system therefore relies more heavily on family background than do even the more moderate forms of competitive access.

This diversity of provision obviously means a diversity of educational experiences. At one extreme a larger proportion of children are now attending non-maintained schools (7 per cent in 1991/2 compared to 5 per cent in 1975/6: *Social Trends* 1994) but government support for private education has been balanced by a lack of support for social provision at the other extreme. The Education Act 1980 introduced the Assisted Places Scheme (which provides money from central government for part or all of the fees for some children to attend private schools), but the same Act withdrew the statutory duty of LEAs to provide school dinners and milk.

Unequal educational opportunities have apparently been legitimized by the dominant political ideology, but what about the reactions of working-class children and their families to growing educational inequalities. Many interpretive sociological studies have focused on the jarring of working-class culture and language with an education system that is often regarded as alien. We have already looked at Willis' theory of why working-class boys got working-class jobs and at egalitarians' efforts to use education as a form of liberation. Yet interpretive studies of social class and education have far more to offer than can be covered in this section (see Lee 1989).

**Case Study**

### Social class and schooling

The only way in which the children of the working classes can then succeed in the present schooling system is to acquire the language, procedures, rules, expectations, etc. of the middle classes. They must do this not because these forms are in any way inherently superior but because they are perceived as natural or universal by middle class teachers who, in general, have not acquired the intellectual attributes of critical consciousness which most working class children appear to have acquired at a very early age. This may well be due to the lack of disjuncture, contradiction and conflict experienced by the middle classes particularly in relation to home and school environments. Their 'weltanschauung' or world-view has never been seriously jolted, whereas on transition to school, if not before, many working class children will experience severe discontinuities and conflicts. Many children who are capable of taking on these forms recognize the schooling process for what it is, a middle class institution where working class values and skills are unwelcome. (Lee 1989: 102)

*(box continued)*

*(box continued)*

**Questions**

**What do you think Lee means by the 'procedures, rules, expectations, etc. of the middle classes' and 'working class values and skills'?**

**How could the differences between middle-class and working-class language affect education? (A useful source would be Bernstein's (1971) analysis of restricted and elaborated language codes and family role systems. You could also read debates about the use of Standard English in schools and in the English curriculum.)**

**Can you find any support for, or criticisms of, Lee's criticisms of teachers?**

## Gender

There has been an increasing influence from feminist and anti-sexist approaches since the 1970s. Although many feminists will argue that not enough progress has been made, research into gender inequalities does seem to have had a greater influence on education policies than has research into social class inequalities. Apparently policy-makers were prepared to accept stronger definitions of gender equality than of social class equality.

The Sex Discrimination Act 1975 can be clearly associated with an equal access approach to equal educational opportunities. It prohibited sex discrimination in admission to schools, in the appointment of teachers (with some exceptions for single-sex schools) and in careers advice. It also stipulated that neither boys nor girls should be refused access to 'any courses, facilities or other benefits provided solely on the grounds of their sex'. The National Curriculum also emphasized equal access, by tackling the problem of gendered subject choice – the tendency for girls to favour languages and boys to favour science subjects (except for biology, which has been more popular with girls). All boys now have to take a language and all girls a science subject.

A stronger, egalitarian approach to equal opportunities places more emphasis on equality of outcomes. Using this approach it is important not only to look at access, but also to see whether males and females are equally represented at all levels of educational achievement. Even applying this sort of definition there are indications that, in education at least, gender inequalities are being transformed.

Tests of 7 year olds have, since 1992, shown that girls achieve better grades than boys in English, maths, science and technology (*Social Trends* 1994: Chart 3.16). However, these findings have not come as a surprise to many educationalists. It has long been claimed that, in general, girls mature at an earlier age than boys and therefore achieve more during their early years at school. Boys have been expected to catch up at a later age. Girls often had to get better results than boys to 'pass' a norm-referenced 11+ examination. The problem with the 'catch-up' argument is that girls also achieve better results at the age of 16, and by 1995 had overtaken boys at A Level standard.

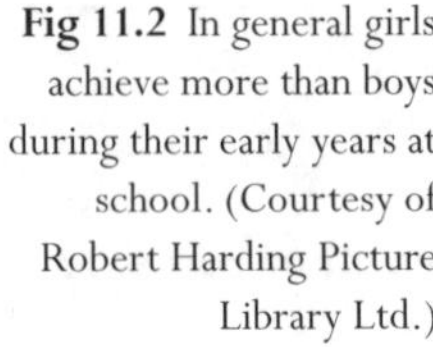

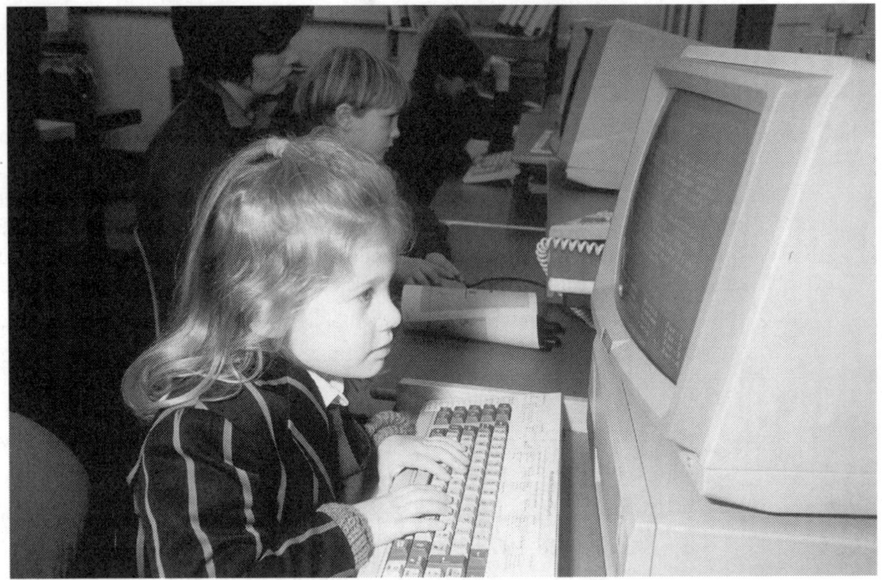

**Fig 11.2** In general girls achieve more than boys during their early years at school. (Courtesy of Robert Harding Picture Library Ltd.)

Since the mid-1970s more girls than boys have been achieving five or more GCSE passes in grades A to C (or O Level grades A to C, or CSE grade 1). In 1975/67 per cent of boys and 10 per cent of girls had five or more high-grade passes but by 1990/1 the corresponding percentages were 12 per cent and 16 per cent. Changes at A Level have been more of a reversal, with fewer girls than boys achieving A Levels in 1975/6 (16 per cent of girls to 18 per cent of boys) but a larger percentage of girls achieved A Levels in 1990/1 (29 per cent of girls to 25 per cent of boys).

These inequalities among school-leavers are now making their way into further education (FE) and higher education (HE). Between 1980/1 and 1991/2 the number of students taking FE courses increased by a quarter to just over 2 million and female students accounted for 84 per cent of the increase. In 1980 there were fewer females than males taking further education courses, but by 1991 there were more females, both in part-time and full-time courses.

The gender distribution of higher education students is also changing, although not quite so dramatically at the highest levels. Between 1970/1 and 1991/2 the total number of students in higher education more than doubled, and the number of females tripled (the Conservative government's intention being to double the number of students in HE by the year 2000). Although the gap has narrowed over time, in 1992/3 there were still more male than female full-time undergraduates (approximately 436,000 male and 416,000 female) and many more male full-time postgraduate students (approximately 61,000 male and 44,000 female: *Social Trends 1995*).

These developments seem rather surprising to sociologists who have tended to assume that 'gender' inequalities really meant 'female' disadvantage. So what do we now mean by 'gender inequalities' in education and are boys now the disadvantaged ones? Developments must be set into a wider context by considering the educational achievements of all ages, and not just of the rising generation. Figure 11.3 shows that the proportion of school-leavers in Britain without graded GCSEs or their equivalent has been dramatically reduced since 1975/6.

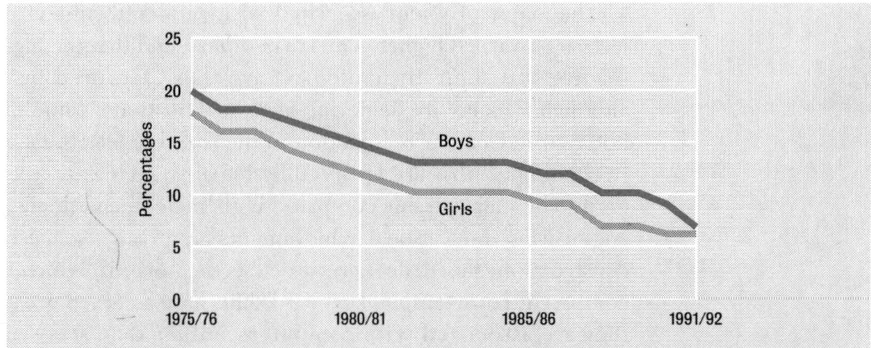


**Fig 11.3** School-leavers with no GCSE or equivalent qualifications.[a]

*Note* : [a] Includes GCE, SCE and CSE. Some of these pupils will have achieved passes in other examinations, eg BTEC, RSA, Certificate of Education (in Wales) and SCOTVEC (in Scotland).

*Source*: *Social Trends* 1995: Chert 3.16.
*Original sources*: Department for Education, Welsh Office and Scottish Office Education Department

Nevertheless, when these results are compared with the qualifications of the whole population (including all age ranges) it is clear that, overall, men are still more highly qualified than women. It will take a long time for the improved performance of female school-leavers to make an impact on the dispersion of qualifications among the whole population.

The impact of these changes on gender inequalities in general will also be moderated by access to, and conditions in, the workplace; sociologists have found that there is no perfect link between educational achievement and advancement in employment (Maguire and Ashton 1981). The extent of the problem can be illustrated if we look at occupations in the field of education. Gender inequalities in the teaching hierarchy are long established; the educational achievements of women and girls may not lead to any dramatic improvement. Women teachers and lecturers have held few of the top jobs in education and tend to be clustered around the lower grades. For example, in 1985, 78 per cent of all primary school teachers were female, but only 60 per cent of deputy heads and 46 per cent of heads were women (Statham *et al*. 1991: Figure 7.3). In 1985, 46 per cent of all secondary school teachers were female, but only 29 per cent of deputy heads and 16 per cent of head teachers were women. Inequalities in higher education are even more noticeable. In 1990 approximately 30 per cent of lecturers in the 'new' universities were women; this fell to 10 per cent or less at grades above senior lecturer level (DES 1992). In the 'old' universities approximately 6 per cent of senior lecturers were women and only 3 per cent of professors (Hart and Wilson 1992).

The impact of changes in educational achievement will also be influenced by the way that qualifications are dispersed between subject areas. Despite efforts via the National Curriculum to encourage pupils to make non-gendered subject choices, in 1990/1 more girls got A–C grades in arts subjects (e.g. English, French, history) and biology in GCSE and more boys got A–C grades in maths and other sciences (physics, chemistry, geography). It is possible that, as the National Curriculum becomes more established, subject choice will become less gendered – but this is to evade the main issue.

The major problem associated with gendered subject choice is that some subjects are awarded higher status than others, and that the high-status subjects (maths, science and some technologies) are those favoured by boys. This means that, although females are achieving *more* qualifications, some of their qualifications are not awarded similar recognition to the *fewer* qualifications achieved by males. Those 'technologies' that are favoured by females, such as textiles and home economics, tend to be unfavourably compared with 'male' technologies, such as electronics and engineering. Educational achievements are given a social rather than an individual construction: the 'male' is regarded as the norm to which female achievements are compared. For example, keyboard skills have assumed greater importance now that they are associated with computers, rather than secretarial work. Yet, as more women have gained word processing skills, that particular application of information technology has also lost its relative status.

There has, nevertheless, been a shift in subject choice at A Level standard. From 1970 to 1985 the most common A Levels taken by boys were maths, physics and chemistry (Statham *et al.* 1991: 151), but during that period girls' subject preferences changed. In 1970 the most common A Levels taken by girls were English, history and French but by 1985 these had changed to English, biology and maths (Statham *et al.* 1991: 151). These were, however, their most frequent choices and do not reflect the spread of subject areas. The gender gap in subject choice in higher education remains, with more men taking science, engineering and technology courses and more women taking language and literature courses.

Gaby Weiner's (1985) summary of relevant gender-related strategies may provide a useful overall view of changes in the relationship between gender and education and how they relate to theories about equal opportunities. The 'Equal opportunities/girl friendly' approach is similar to what we have described as an equal access approach to equal opportunities. It reflects a fairly moderate interpretation of equal opportunities, compared to the stronger egalitarian outlook of the 'Anti-sexist/girl centred' approach.

Despite the statistical data illustrating changes in achievement, structural approaches have to be supplemented by interpretive approaches to provide a comprehensive understanding of the nature of gender differentiation in education. Both girl-friendly and girl-centred approaches emphasize the importance of monitoring the images of women provided by textbooks and other resources. Stereotypical images of women and men have been normalized by textbooks so that readers have often been unaware of the gendered messages transmitted. For example, when one mother tried to make all her own changes to a book her 5-year-old son was reading she was met with an angry response.

**In fact he was a bit upset when I went through a book which has a boy and girl in very traditional roles, and changed all the he's to she's and the she's to he's. When I first started doing that, he was inclined to say 'you don't like boys, you only like girls'. I had to explain that that wasn't true at all, it's just that there's not enough written about girls.** ***(Statham 1986: 46, 67, cited in Giddens 1989)***

Nilsen (1975) analysed fifty-eight award-winning children's picture books and found that twenty-one of them included a picture of a woman in the home, while men were pictured at work or in various adventures, their image being associated

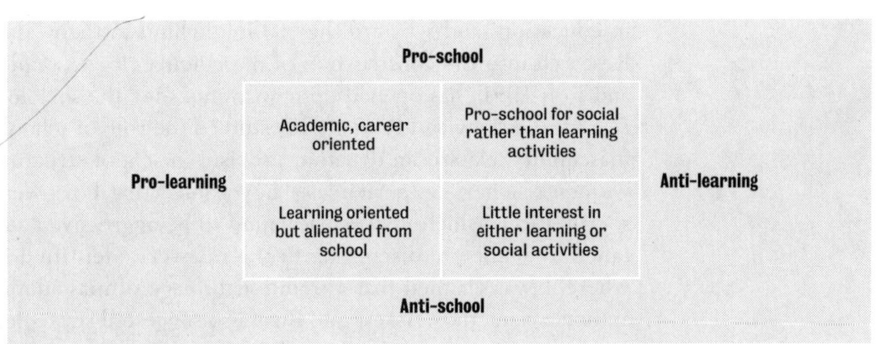


**Fig 11.4** Girls' attitude to schooling.

**Q** What factors could influence pupils (female or male) to adopt each of the four types of attitudes described in Fig 11.4?

with the public world of work and outside the home. She christened this domesticated representation of women the 'cult of the apron'. Yet, where is the 'cult of the apron' today? Although there is no room for complacency (and sexist images are still common in the wider media) continuous monitoring of resources by sociologists and educationalists has helped to promote more positive images of women in school textbooks.

Feminist studies have also raised awareness of sexism in classroom interaction and an understanding of how girls and women perceive themselves in education. For example, Stanworth (1983) and many others observed that boys tended to demand, and get, more of the teacher's attention in class and that girls tended to have unrealistic ideas about their own capabilities. Boys tended to overestimate their own capabilities while girls tended to underestimate their capabilities.

Lees (1986) studied the attitudes of 15–16-year-old girls, from various social class and ethnic backgrounds, in three London schools. Her interpretive approach elicited the terms on which they described their sexuality and managed their social world and helped to explain how some girls rationalized their lack of achievement. Yet this now rather dated research still offers a possible model for the analysis of girls' achievements in the 1990s. She categorized the main attitudes of the girls she studied into four main groups (see Fig 11.4).

The growing numbers of mature women students since the 1970s (see R Edwards 1993: 6) has also meant that sociologists have become more absorbed in the educational experiences of women as well as girls. Using feminist methods this research has often been used as a source of empowerment for the subjects, rather than straightforward academic analysis. For example, the Taking Liberties Collective (1989) published accounts of the educational experiences of over fifty women, recording how they had encountered 'oppression in men's education'. One of the themes emerging from this and other studies (e.g. Pascall and Cox 1993) is that mature women have perceived education as playing a dual role: their schools encouraging domesticity and low-status jobs, but further and higher education providing an escape route from traditional roles and into more rewarding jobs.

This emphasis on the empowerment of women through education has tended to dominate feminist research, but what of the gendered experiences of boys and men in education, and why are they falling behind in their educational achievements? Research into the construction of masculinity (for example, Morgan 1992; Roper and Tosh 1991) has opened up new avenues for the sociology of education. In *Boys Don't Cry*, Askew and Ross (1988) studied the role of schools in the construction of masculinity, classroom dynamics, sexism in school structure and organization and women teachers' experiences. They argued that boys were victims of their own socialization, which involved learning to be aggressive and attaching little importance to academic discourse. Problems were identified in some boys' schools, where it was claimed that a traditional image of masculinity was reinforced by an authoritarian ethos. Askew and Ross also suggested strategies for working with boys and for in-service work with teachers, including the use of workshops, the adoption of anti-sexist initiatives and strategies for persuading boys to talk more openly and honestly.

Some remaining problems and policies regarding gender and education centre around the theme of uniformity and diversity. For example, we have already briefly considered the question of whether or not education should be coeducational, but this debate is too large to be probed in depth.

Debates about uniformity and diversity have also encompassed concerns about how attitudes to sexuality are influenced by education. Clause 28 of the Local Government Act 1988 forbids local authorities from promoting the 'teaching in any maintained schools on the acceptability of homosexuality as a pretended family relationship'. Critics have argued that this could encourage homophobia and the presentation of heterosexuality as a norm from which individuals must not deviate. Not only does this also have implications for the social construction of knowledge but also interpretive sociologists have generated accounts of the experiences of homosexuals in academic environments. For example, Trenchard and Warren (1984) found individuals who had been expelled or referred to a psychiatrist when they 'came out'. Jones and Mahony (1989) provided an analysis of the historical background to this debate, including criticisms of the sociology of education for the way it had ignored the promotion of heterosexuality in the past.

The study of gender and education is not only wide ranging and confusing but also quite fascinating when we look at findings about the achievements of males and females (see Fig 11.3). When the cumulative effects of social class, gender and race are considered we shall get a clearer impression of current debates within the sociology of education.

## Race

'Ethnicity' and 'race' are confusing concepts (see pp. 321–3, 350–2). In general, too many studies of education and race could be justifiably accused of gross simplification because they have forced individuals into inappropriate, homogenous categories and thus misrepresented the unique nature of our ethnic backgrounds. Despite the wide range of ethnic backgrounds in Britain, educational research has tended to categorize individuals into three main, and largely incomprehensible, groups – 'West Indian', 'Asian' and 'Other'. It is easy to see why this has happened. Sociologists study group behaviour and are, by the nature of their subject, obliged to allocate individuals into groups. They are also concerned about inequality in education and make such distinctions in order to identify and measure inequality.

Sociologists have also labelled people as 'Black' or 'white' in order to identify racism in education as being primarily based on skin colour, rather than cultural or ethnic identity. However, this raises the possibility that sociologists themselves could be accused of racism because of their tendency to use the categorization of 'Black' to override any other personal characteristic and to label Black children (and 'West Indian' children in particular) negatively as 'under-achievers'.

Research into race and education is therefore fraught with difficulties, first because of the problem of finding suitable ways of labelling groups, second, because there is a temptation to generalize from small samples, and third, because an emphasis on statistical data often means that qualitative differences in educational experiences are ignored. These reservations help to explain why figures relating to various ethnic groups have been included in official, national statistics on education only since 1990–1.

We are left then with the central question: are educational outcomes most influenced by social class, gender or race?

In view of Britain's history of racial discrimination and prejudice we could reasonably ask whether race affects social class and, if so, whether research that intends to study 'race' is actually studying social class. For example, continuous research into school-leavers for both the Rampton Report (1981) and Swann Report (1985) was carried out in five inner city LEA areas where the educational attainment of *every* ethnic group in the study was lower than the national average. The reports nevertheless confirmed earlier findings (e.g. Tomlinson 1980) that the performance of 'West Indian' children at O Level/CSE and A Level was markedly lower than that of 'Asians' and 'Others'. The Swann Committee also found that in the time between its fieldwork (1981–2) and the fieldwork for the Rampton Report (1978–9) the performance of 'West Indian' children had improved but was still lower than that of the other groups (Rampton 1981; Swann 1985; see also Fig 11.5).

This obviously leads us to ask whether there were differences in the social class background of 'West Indian', 'Asian' and 'Other' children and some evidence of this was provided in 1986 by Eggleston *et al*. According to these findings 87 per cent of children from 'Afro-Caribbean' backgrounds had fathers who were manual work-

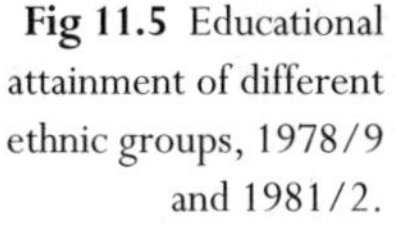

**Fig 11.5** Educational attainment of different ethnic groups, 1978/9 and 1981/2.

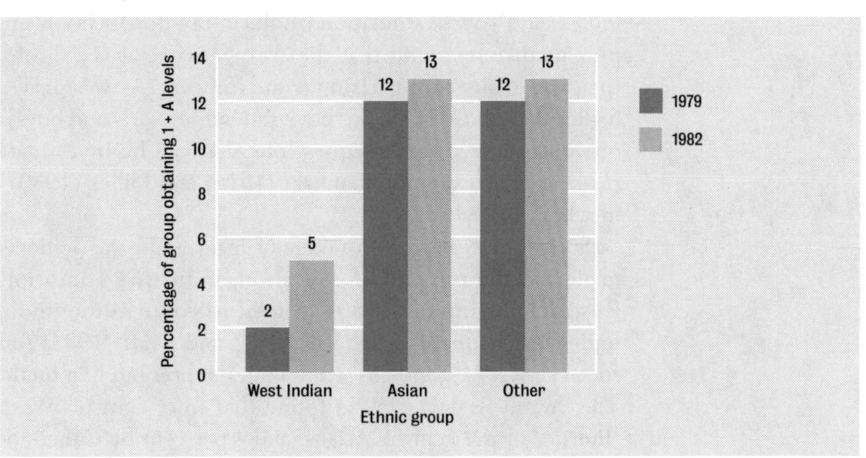


*Source*: Statham *et al.* 1991: Figure 11.13. Adapted from Rampton 1981: ch. 1, Table D; Swann 1985: ch. 3, Annex B

ers, compared to 73 per cent of 'Asian' children and 69 per cent of 'white' children. This might suggest that some children were more disadvantaged by social class but, yet again, we encounter the problem of labelling children. Do 'Afro-Caribbean' and 'West Indian' mean the same thing and are the samples comparable?

In 1985 the first national study (of England and Wales: Drew and Gray 1989) of the achievements of Black young people found that the performance of 'Afro-Caribbeans' was better than in earlier studies, but still concluded that the results of this group had changed little between 1972 and 1985. However, the study went further by considering the relative influences of race, social class, and gender. Drew and Gray (1989) found that social class explained more variation in examination performance than did ethnic group or gender, but the combined effects of social class, gender and race still left the larger part of the variation in performance unexplained. This suggests that other, unknown factors were also significant.

**Q** What factors, other than social class, gender and race, could be particularly significant influences on educational achievements?

We have seen that girls have moved ahead of boys in their educational achievements and this raises questions about the comparative influences of gender and race. Driver (1980) studied five multiracial schools and found that 'West Indian' girls did better than 'West Indian' boys but that, among 'whites', boys did better than girls. It was also found that in these five schools 'West Indian' children performed better in their 16+ examinations than did 'whites'. This raises the possibility that individual school factors might have a significant influence on educational outcomes.

Further evidence of the academic achievements of Black women can be found when we look at the working age population as a whole. Here we can see that there are marked variations according to ethnic groupings and that the 'Black' population is the only group in which women are better qualified than men (Fig 11.6).

The achievements of Black women have been established long enough to feed through to statistics covering a wide age range. It is therefore reasonable to ask if there are more developments waiting to make a similar impact, and one possible trend has already been identified. Reid (1993) carried out a study of socio-spatial indices and 16+ examination results in Bradford schools in 1991. From a very complex picture he found that the average score at GCSE of 'Asian' girls' was higher than for 'white' boys. Using some indices, 'Asian' girls' achievements were also higher than those of 'Asian' boys and 'white' girls and boys. This structural approach obviously raises various questions that can be investigated only by interpretive research. For example, Lambart (1976) and Fuller (1980) both studied Black girls in school subcultures.

Sociologists have also taken an interest in the achievements of various racial groups at the top end of education, in further education and higher education. Research during the 1980s seemed to confirm the findings about 'West Indian' under-achievement in schools. Craft and Craft (1983) found that, irrespective of social class, 'West Indians' were under-represented in further and higher education. The Swann Report (1985) found that l per cent of 'West Indians', 4 per cent of 'Indians', 4 per cent of 'Asians' and 4 per cent of 'Others' went to university. However, the report also found that a larger percentage of 'Asians' and 'West Indians'

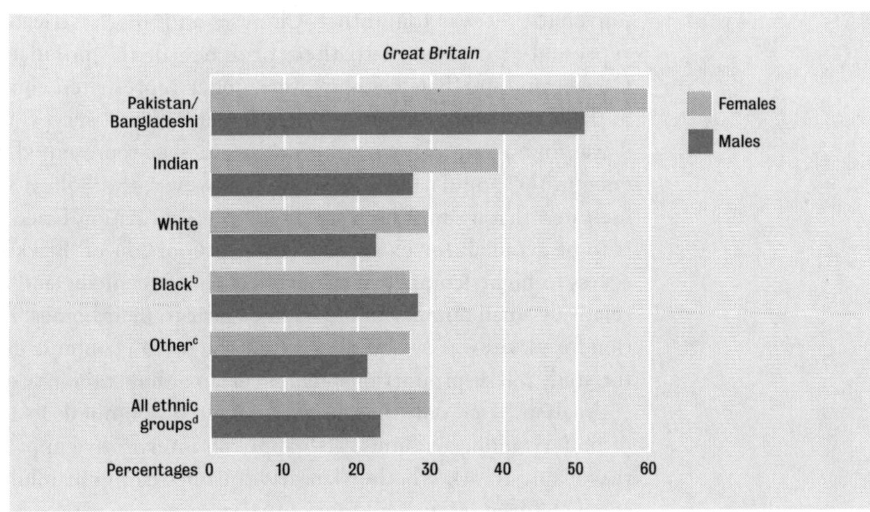


**Fig 11.6** Percentage of the working age population without a qualification: by ethnic origin and sex, Spring 1993.[a]

*Notes*: a Men aged 16–64 and women aged 16–59.
b Includes Caribbean, Afican and black people of non-mixed origin.
c Includes Chinese, other ethnic groups of non-mixed origin and people of mixed origin.
d Includes ethnic group not stated.

*Source*: *Social Trends* 1994: Graph 3.23
*Original source*: Employment Department

took some sort of further education course than was general for the whole population. This finding has been supported by more recent research which seems to strongly contradict earlier negative images of the achievements of 'West Indians' or 'Afro-Caribbeans'. Labour Force Surveys between 1988 and 1990 found that not only have the numbers of young people taking some sort of further education increased, but also 'Afro-Caribbeans' and 'South Asians' have maintained a tendency to be over-represented compared to 'whites'. If we extend our interest to all age ranges in further education we can see that it is 'whites' who are under-represented in further education (Table 11.3).

In 1994 the Policy Studies Institute published its findings about the different rates of entry of ethnic minorities into higher education in 1992. It considered the percentages of successful applicants from various groups and found radical differences in access to universities and polytechnics. When looking only at success in access to

**Table 11.3** Full-time participation rates in further education by ethnic community and age, 1991–2, England.

| | Percentage of relevant population | | | | |
|---|---|---|---|---|---|
| Age | White | Black Caribbean/ African/other | Indian | Pakistani/ Bangladeshi | Other |
| 16–19 | 12.6 | 29.3 | 24.0 | 21.0 | 17.2 |
| 20–24 | 0.8 | 4.3 | 1.0 | 1.6 | 2.4 |
| 25+ | 0.1 | 0.9 | 0.1 | 0.2 | 0.5 |
| All over 16 | 0.9 | 3.7 | 2.2 | 3.3 | 2.6 |

*Source:* National Commission on Education 1993

universities it was found that 'Chinese' and 'Black African' applicants were over-represented compared to their presence in the population as a whole. 'Black Caribbeans' and 'Bangladeshis' were under-represented compared to their presence in the population as a whole. When looking only at success in access to polytechnics it was found that 'Black Caribbeans' were over-represented compared to their presence in the population as a whole. However, the Policy Studies Institute (1994) indicated that a simplistic cause/effect interpretation based on racial categorization is to be avoided, for example a larger proportion of 'Black Caribbeans' applied for access to highly competitive courses (such as medicine and law) and to courses in a relatively small number of universities near to their homes. This meant that competition for places was not evenly spread. The socio-economic inequalities highlighted in the study fell disproportionately on certain ethnic minority groups.

Analysis based only on statistical data is very limited. To achieve any sort of depth of understanding we must also apply an interpretive approach. For example, it is reasonable to ask whether language problems might inhibit the achievements of some children. Many children of 'Asian' origin appear to have thrived in education despite the fact that many of them have English as their second language; in comparison, earlier claims that 'West Indians' were under-achieving seemed peculiar when so many of them had been raised with English as their first language.

Various writers have claimed that the language problems of 'Asian' children have been more easily recognized and treated more sympathetically than the language problems of 'West Indian' children. Children are expected not only to speak English in British schools, but also to speak standard English or, even more specifically, what Bernstein (1971) called an 'elaborated code'. When children learn English as a second language they are taught the 'correct' grammatical constructions; when English is a child's native language, it may be spoken with a wide range of dialects and grammatical constructions. Labov (1969) maintained that non-standard English was different, rather than inferior, that it could have its own logical structure and could be very effective as a means of communicating complicated arguments. V Edwards (1976, 1979) argued that Creole played an important role in the under-performance of West Indian children. Although the Creole spoken by many West Indian children (and children of West Indian parents) includes English vocabulary, it has different grammatical constructions and sound systems. These children are at a disadvantage not only because their Creole 'interferes' with their use of standard English, but also because they have to endure the commonly held view that they are inarticulate: children who speak Creole are assumed to be speaking 'poor' English.

Little (1981) and Mabey (1981) studied literacy in Inner London Education Authority schools and found that 'Black British' pupils achieved very low scores compared with other groups. Their attainment was only marginally affected by the length of education they had received in Britain. Yet 'Asian' children who had been fully educated in Britain scored as well as indigenous 'white' children. This does seem to support Edwards' (1976, 1979) claims, although Mabey (1981) also found that social deprivation accounted for about half of the difference in the scores of Black and white children. The influence of racist attitudes is more difficult to gauge, but one of the women interviewed by Bryan *et al.* (1987) provides an indication of other factors that could affect the literacy of Black children.

**I had always liked reading, and could have really enjoyed literature at school. I suppose I liked the strange and different world I found in books, especially the ones about life as it was supposed to have been in Britain. This couldn't last though, because reading often became a nasty, personal experience. You would be getting deep into a story and suddenly it would hit you – a reference to Black people as savages or something. It was so offensive. And so wounding. Sometimes you would sit in class and wait, all tensed up, for the next derogatory remark to come tripping off the teacher's tongue. Oh yes, it was a 'black' day today, or some kid had 'blackened' the school's reputation. It was there clearly, in black and white, the school's ideology. The curriculum and the culture relies on those racist views.**

***(Bryan et al. 1987: 93)***

In a review of thirty-three studies of the performance of ethnic groups in schools, Tomlinson (1980) noted that twenty-six of them showed that West Indians were scoring lower than whites on individual or group tests, they were over-represented in the category of Educationally Sub-Normal (ESN) and under-represented in the higher streams of schools. However, Tomlinson's review is now rather dated; more recent studies (see pp. 466–7) no longer support this pattern of under-achievement. As with gender, there have been efforts to attack racial discrimination within the system and to mobilize education as a source of personal liberation. This is particularly noticeable in the achievement of Black women.

Political perspectives on race and racism tend to encompass all of the approaches we have already encountered, ranging from egalitarianism to biological determination and including debates about uniformity, diversity, integration and segregation. Some right-wing perspectives take a 'colour-blind' approach, assuming that children from a wide range of backgrounds will be incorporated into the existing British 'culture', submerging their own cultural heritage in the process. A New Right emphasis accepts individual diversity but assumes that social cohesion can be maintained and promoted by the sound operation of market forces, without government intervention. However, the most extreme right-wing approach is obviously in favour of negative racial discrimination and enforced segregation of some sort.

Centre-ground and left-wing perspectives tend to involve more concern about racism and the negative effects of racial inequalities, but vary in their proposed solutions. A multicultural approach tends to assume that, if children can learn about cultures other than their own, a greater degree of tolerance will be cultivated, not only in the individual, but also in society as a whole. This approach has been criticized for being naive in its understanding of the true nature of racism (caricatured as just being about 'saris and samosas'). It ignores the fact that many children who are born to indigenous 'British' families and in a British 'culture' (if that could be defined) suffer from covert or overt racism simply because they have black or brown skin. Anti-racists therefore argue that it is racism, rather than cultural diversity, that must be confronted. The role of education is to challenge racism in society as a whole by, for example, providing children with positive images of 'Blackness' (Bryan *et al.* 1987). However, a third (and there are probably more) approach tries to assimilate multicultural and anti-racist approaches. Interculturalism promotes a recognition and acceptance of the uniqueness of the individual and the superficiality of labelling anyone simply by skin colour, 'culture', social class, gender, disability, and so on.

It seems that, despite the problems involved in studying race and education, racism must be acknowledged as a fundamental problem and the role of education in the transmission or amelioration of racism must be considered. Studies of racism in schools are still beset with difficulties due to its often covert nature. There are, however, many 'victim reports' of the sort furnished by Bryan *et al.* (1987) and other studies into the nature of racist bullying and name-calling (e.g. Cohn 1988). Some of these were inspired, or commissioned by Macdonald *et al.* (1990) into one particularly horrific racist incident in a school (see Activity 1).

If we try to simplify the findings of the Macdonald Report and allied research we are sure to fail, and this is a problem for the sociology of education in general. There seem to be no easy answers to our earlier question of whether educational outcomes are most influenced by social class, gender or race.

**Q** It is easier to identify and categorize an individual according to sex than according to social class or racial group. How has this affected the introduction of education policies that (a) are egalitarian; (b) emphasize equal access; (c) promote inequality?

Compare the policies of central government (on social class, gender and race) with local or independent initiatives that aim to reduce educational inequalities. How effective have local initiatives been and what challenges have they faced?

We can identify some themes and trends at a structural level, and can see some patterns emerging in small-scale interactions, but must still acknowledge education as a unique experience. Race, social class and gender must be recognized as sources of educational inequalities, but their effects and interrelationships must not be distorted by oversimplification. Even the improved educational performance of girls and women does not provide a regular pattern of educational achievement and more equal opportunities. For example, the Policy Studies Institute (1994) found that in 1992 (holding all other variables constant) women were still significantly less likely to be admitted to universities than men.

We have already briefly considered some educational policy options related to social class, gender and race as separate issues – but what can we learn if we compare policies regarding all three? As an acknowledgement of constantly changing education policies and transformations in the achievements of some social groupings we end with more questions, rather than answers. Develop your own theories!

**Summary**

- Positive or negative educational experiences of education do not stem entirely from individual actions and abilities but are filtered through a socially constructed education system. Personal growth and learning processes are confusing, in the messages communicated by the curriculum, the 'warming-up' or 'cooling-down' of aspirations, and in fundamental problems associated with the assessment of intelligence.
- Developments in educational provision and in sociological studies of education have been explored in order to identify trends and to understand the origins of diversity within the current 'system'.
- In the development of sociological explanations and theories about education there has been a movement towards the integration of structural approaches (emphasizing consensus and continuity and/or conflict and change) and interpretive approaches (in which the emphasis has been on interaction within educational institutions). This

blend of diverse thought has been combined with a common concern among sociologists about a perceived conflict between the values of the academic community and those of the prevailing political culture. They have therefore moved beyond the descriptive analysis of educational 'problems' and have interested themselves in debates about how these issues could be tackled.

- Sociological approaches to the study of education policy include two important themes. Pupils and students experience 'equal' or 'unequal' educational opportunities: there are various definitions of equal opportunities, with their relevant policy implications. When educational decision-makers aim for uniformity or diversity in the provision of education, there are questions about types of schools and the curriculum.
- The various themes and theories were combined with research data in order to study the influences of social class, gender and race on educational outcomes. There are problems of labelling and difficulties involved in assessing the relative, or cumulative, influences of social class, gender and race.

## Further reading

Educational processes are constantly changing; recent textbooks and edited books of readings can provide valuable insights into fresh developments, but even the most recently published books will be out-of-date in some respects. Many educational statistics provided by the Department of Education and Employment can be found in university libraries.

Educational journals and magazines provide a useful resource for updating and expanding your existing knowledge. Weeklies include the *Times Educational Supplement, Times Higher Educational Supplement* and *Education*, the journal of educational administration and management. Academic journals provide the best source of recent research findings, and sometimes focus on one aspect of education: these include the *British Journal of Sociology of Education, British Educational Research Journal, Educational Review, Educational Studies, Educational Theory, Journal of Educational Studies, Educational Theory, Journal of Education Policy, Gender and Education*, and many more.

Longman Community Information (1995) *Education Yearbook*, London: Longman. Provides guides to educational terminology and abbreviations, reports, legislation, statistics, publications, central and local government services, and educational establishments.

Mason, H and Ramsay, T (1992) *A Parents' A–Z of Education*, London: Chambers. Provides relatively comprehensive explanations of educational terms.

Office of Population Censuses and Surveys (annually) *Social Trends*, London: HMSO. Particularly useful for fairly up-to-date information on education.

Statham, J and Mackinnon, D, with Cathcart, H and Hales, M (1991) *The Educational Fact File*, 2nd edn, London: Hodder & Stoughton.

Provides statistical data in an easily digestible form, together with useful explanations. Further editions may be published.

## Activities

### Activity 1 Murder in the Playground

*Murder in the Playground* is the title of the report (Macdonald *et al.* 1990) of a committee headed by Ian Macdonald QC, which investigated the murder of 13-year-old Ahmed Iqbal Ullah in the playground at Burnage High School, Manchester, in 1986. Ahmed was stabbed by a 13-year-old white pupil, who was later heard by fellow pupils to be shouting, 'I've killed a Paki'. Subsequent investigations examined not only the actions of the boy who committed the murder, but also the wider social context in which the murder took place.

Perhaps one of the most probing attempts to understand the circumstances which led to the murder was provided by Gill *et al.* (1992: 195–8), who adapted Waddington *et al.*'s (1989) Flashpoints model. The original model illustrated various levels of analysis, surrounding the individual, who is represented at the central, interactional level. It was originally intended to act as an aid in identifying multicausal influences that could trigger an incident of public disorder. Gill *et al.* adapted these levels to provide a lens through which we might specify and interpret the events which led to the murder of Ahmed Iqbal Ullah'. Gill *et al.* explained the analytical levels as follows:

- **Structural** Refers to differential relations of power and structurally induced conflict between groups perceived as racially different in society.
- **Political** Refers to prevailing systems of ideas in play.
- **Ideological** For instance, racism justified in terms of the prevailing Zeitgeist; anti-racism defended in egalitarian terms.
- **Cultural** Refers to the level of lived experience and common sense understandings within the locality and community, especially as refracted through family and family networks.
- **Institutional** Refers to the ideologies, procedural norms and practices which are promoted, sanctioned and transmitted by the school.
- **Subcultural** Refers to the children's subcultures.
- **Biographical** Refers to factors and characteristics which are specific to the individuals involved.
- **Contextual** Refers to the immediate history of a racist incident.
- **Interactional** Refers to the actual event or incident, what was done; what was said.

When some of the right-wing tabloid press apportioned blame to the school's anti-racist policies they not only ignored the many other contextual influences, but also distorted the Macdonald Report's criticisms of a certain type of 'doctrinaire anti-racism' that does not integrate the problems caused by other forms of social inequality:

> ostrich-like analysis of the complex social relations which leaves white working class males completely in the cold. They fit nowhere. They become all-time losers. That surely is a recipe for division and polarization, particularly in the area of anti-racist policies. (Macdonald Committee, quoted in *Guardian* 29 June 1988)

The committee wanted to emphasize the importance of effective implementation of anti-racist policies:

> anti-racist policies do not produce racism. . . . Badly thought-out and implemented policies may well be counter-productive but certainly no more so than policies that pretend that race does not exist as an issue. (quoted in *Guardian* 29 June 1988)

## Questions

Does this analytical framework absolve individuals of responsibility for their own actions?

Consider the question asked in the Runnymede Trust's summary of the Burnage Report: 'Did Ahmed Ullah die at the crossroads where the power of masculinity, male dominance, violence and racism intersect?'

Why did the press respond so negatively to anti-racist policies and what are the implications of their distorted reports?

## ■ Activity 2 Education in Denmark and Japan

### 'Liberal studies for life': education in Denmark

Denmark's reputation for liberal attitudes is well earned when it comes to education, where experimentation is encouraged and participation in decision-making is the norm rather than the exception. The education system enjoys a broad consensus of support among the population and politicians across the spectrum of opinion.
Nevertheless, it is now undergoing reforms designed to inject a greater degree of parent-power, a market-orientated philosophy and greater autonomy for individual schools. Opponents charge that the government is modelling reforms too closely on those in England.

The school system is radical in the way it prepares and shapes young people for future life. It rejects the notion that a child is to be taught to take its place in a society where too much questioning of those who 'know best' is discouraged and going against the herd is seen as subversive.

'In Denmark we get children to understand that to learn something and become wiser are two different things. It's more incidental in England,' says Yvonne Haakonsson, a 50-year-old teacher who spent last year teaching in a middle school at Leamington Spa. 'In Denmark children are asked what they think and asked to take responsibilities. In England it is hard to tell if pupils work well because they want to or because they are afraid of being punished.'

Danish education legislation states that school 'shall prepare the pupils for active decision making in a democratic society and for sharing responsibility for solving common problems. The education activities of the school and its daily life as a whole must therefore be based on intellectual freedom and democracy.'

Jette Kammer Jensen, chairwoman of the education committee of Albertslund municipal council, says a basic attitude of most Danes is that it does not matter whether a child is the offspring of a factory labourer or a bank manager; all will be equally valued, their point of view respected and encouraged, with the same opportunities as anyone else.

Even young children are helped to form opinions on their education and tell their teacher what they think is good or bad about it. Teachers note that when they meet parents the first question asked is about the well-being of their child and how he or she is getting on with the other children. 'If they get on well with other children and are happy, they will learn well,' says Kammer Jensen.

Social class differences do not exist here to the same extent as in Britain. Buying an education for social reasons by selecting the best and most exclusive private schools is alien to Danish mentality.

The school system is a mix of private and state institutions, but with the crucial difference that the state heavily subsidises private schools as a means of extending individual choice. Around 10 per cent of children attend private 'free schools', but Jette Kammer Jensen says this is not from any desire for academic or social betterment but for something which is different.

The state pays up to 85 per cent of running costs and offers cheap loans to help start such schools. 'If a group of parents is dissatisfied with the school their children go to, there is nothing to stop them deciding to create something alternative,' she says. So long as educational criteria are met they will receive the state's blessing and money. Private school fees average £53 a month.

Schools have been started under these circumstances by parents with religious, political and social norms which differ from those of the state. Even private socialist schools exist.

The Danish government boasts that it spends more than any other country in the world on its education system. It currently allocates 7.3 per cent of Gross National Product each year on educating its 5 million people. By comparison, Britain spends 4.8 per cent of its GNP for a population more than ten times as large.

A substantial proportion of Danish spending goes on adult education, an area where once again Denmark claims a world record. Each year more than 1 million adults undertake some form of education or training.

Kammer Jensen says: 'If Denmark is to survive, it's important we have something useful between our ears. We don't have any exciting minerals in the earth like coal, so we depend on our know-how to get on.'

(Adapted from A Draper, 'Liberal Studies for life', *Guardian* 13 August 1991)

**'Too high a price for excellence?' Education in Japan**

Japan's great achievements have been won at considerable cost. They may have the highest literacy rates in the world and 50 per cent of all schoolchildren may go to higher education in contrast to our lowly 20 per cent. But would you ever in Britain hear, as happened in Japan, of a schoolgirl being accidentally crushed to death by a teacher closing the school gates on her when she was ONE SECOND late?

Teaching methods in Japan are so traditional they're close to medieval. Chalk and talk, followed by tests. Children are not encouraged to ask questions, and any expression of disagreement with the teacher's views would probably draw a punishment for impertinence.

Huge chunks of knowledge have to be memorized; a Japanese high schooler is more likely than a British one to know the difference between a participle and a gerund in the English language. But ask him to say hello to an English-speaking foreigner and he'll get nowhere: he can't use the language creatively any more than his teacher can.

Even essays and stories, hardly radical methods in British terms, are generally considered frivolous luxuries in Japan. They're just too far from the serious business of memorizing facts.

The British national curriculum proposes exams for pupils at ages 7, 11 and 14 – but that's nothing by Japanese standards. There, they are tested by their schools five times a year, with each exam period lasting a week. Ninety-five per cent of all Japanese exams consist of multiple choice questions or one-word answer questions, for such is the Japanese view of knowledge: something that is right or wrong, with nothing in between.

That's why there has never been a prominent Japanese economist: in life sciences there are no black and white solutions of the kind Japanese schoolchildren are expected to memorize. Meanwhile, the hothouse exam environment is blamed for a distressingly high level of schoolchildren suicides.

History textbooks in Japan are notorious for their thorough whitewashing of all unpleasant aspects of the nation's past. I know no history book is perfect. But there's no question that the humanities are presented here in Britain with far greater intellectual honesty than in Japan. And I believe that children should be told the truth – even when it's ugly.

But the highest price of all is exacted through discipline. It is the cornerstone of Japanese education and undoubtedly stamps the character that has made the country so brilliant. The fanatical application of school rules in Japan sometimes amounts to little more than a systematic obliteration of the child's individuality. Some rule books even specify the number of pleats in a girl's skirt and the length of toilet paper to be used at one sitting in the school lavatory. Uniform codes are frequently enforced outside school hours and school premises: you can be punished if a teacher spots you walking down the street in jeans on a Friday evening.

Corporal punishment is supposed to be illegal, but is frequently used. A common punishment in Japanese schools is to shave off all the hair of the offending pupil: a humiliating public mark of disgrace.

And finally when these perfectly-behaved, responsible if emotionally battered children graduate, it is as though they have been let out of a pressure cooker. Universities are little more than holidays to most students: academic standards are poor and even the most prestigious of the lot, Tokyo University, has only two Nobel prize-winners to boast of.

Interestingly, for all its industrial and technical prowess, Japan has picked up only four Nobel prizes in the last 20 years compared to 25 in Britain with half the population – and a poorly educated half at that.

(Adapted from T Gill, 'Too high a price for excellence?', *Daily Mail* 28 July 1990)

## Questions

What do you think Danish legislation means by intellectual freedom and democracy?

What is the difference between learning something and becoming wiser?

What does Gill mean by 'excellence' and the 'price' paid for excellence? Comment on both articles from approaches emphasizing (a) consensus/continuity; (b ) conflict/change.

What do these accounts tell us about the way that the Danes and Japanese tackle the problems of (a) equality/inequality; (b) uniformity/diversity?

What would you say are the advantages and disadvantages of the different educational cultures in Japan, Denmark and Britain?

# Chapter 12

# Religion

**Chapter outline:** Introduction • The sociological approach to religion • Defining and measuring religion • Types of religious organizations • The role of religion in society • Is religion dying out? • Summary • Further reading • Activities

**Learning objectives**

When you have studied this chapter you should be able to address these key questions:

- How should religion be defined and measured?
- What explanations have been given for the role of religion in society?
- How does religion affect our daily lives?
- What are the main debates about the decline and future of religion?

## Introduction

> Whatever any individual's religious beliefs may be, or even if there is some antagonism towards religion, it is difficult for anyone to deny that religions have had considerable impact on societies in all continents. (Hinnells 1984: 11)

We live in a world which has been and continues to be widely influenced, for good or ill, by religion. A glance at any week's newspapers and television news confirms that world-wide events are influenced directly or indirectly by religion. Religion is not just about churchgoing or Christianity, although early sociologists reflected their predominately western Judaeo-Christian heritage in their writings. Religion affects virtually every area of social life, including dress, dietary habits, marriage customs, the types of schools and hospitals attended and the services provided therein, as well as attitudes to moral issues. It is therefore unsurprising that early sociologists were fascinated by religion and it was a central concern of early sociological research.

> **Sociology has always had a strong interest in analysing the nature of those shared beliefs to which men [*sic*] attach some kind of priority of sacredness, and which provide the basic perspectives around which groups of individuals organise their life.** *(Thompson and Tunstall 1971: 363)*

Today there is as much interest as ever in exploring the centrality of religious beliefs in many communities and their pervasiveness across time and culture. Though the social context of beliefs has changed, the questions are similar: under what circumstances do religious beliefs arise, develop, and decline? Do the social structures of different communities help us to understand the diversity of religious forms and experiences? The approaches of Marx, Durkheim and Weber to these questions are examined in this chapter. Although these writers predicted the gradual decline of religion in advanced industrial societies, religion appears to be surviving and reviving in many areas of the world in various forms and degrees of intensity.

## The sociological approach to religion

Given the sociological aim to avoid bias and prejudice in the study of society, it is important to be aware of one's own attitudes towards religion and how these may impinge upon its study. For many people religion can be a sensitive, personal and emotive subject about which value-neutrality seems inappropriate.

The sociology of religion is not so much interested in weighing up the validity of particular doctrines, but rather focuses on the social context and consequences of belief systems. Sociologists are interested in the ways in which beliefs are translated into social action.

> **Sociological researchers set aside, for the purposes of the study, their personal opinions about religion and try to be as objective as possible in observing and interpreting the religious phenomena under study. From a sociological perspective, one religion is not superior to another.** *(McGuire 1992: 8)*

Q What assumptions or beliefs do you bring with you to the sociology of religion? Would you describe any of them as prejudices?

How do your own beliefs differ from those of (a) your family; (b) your closest friends? Would you describe any of their beliefs as prejudices?

The ongoing sociological debate about whether it is possible and/or desirable to be value-free (see pp. 113–14) applies to the sociological study of religion. A preconceived understanding of what is or is not 'religion' may be brought to bear in an assessment of the following sociological approaches to the definition and measurement of religion.

## Defining and measuring religion

Sociologists acknowledge the inherent complexities in attempting to define and measure religion. Some researchers focus on adherence to particular beliefs or attending a place of worship in determining levels of religiosity. However, 'being religious' means different things to different people. This can become problematic for the social scientist attempting to quantify and compare religiosity within and across societies.

In a book examining forms of religious life, Durkheim (1976) argues that all religious beliefs share an important criterion, namely the clear distinction they make between two realms: the sacred and the profane. The sacred is not limited to gods and spirits, but includes anything considered superior in dignity and power, protected and isolated through a sense of awe and thus treated with special respect. Durkheim elaborates on the sacred and profane in relation to religious beliefs and behaviour:

> **The real characteristic of religious phenomena is that they always presuppose a bipartite division of the whole universe, known and knowable, into two classes which embrace all that exists, but which radically exclude each other. Sacred things are those which the interdictions protect and isolate; profane things, those to which these interdictions are applied and which must remain at a distance from the first. Religious beliefs are the representations which express the nature of sacred things and the relations which they sustain, either with each other or with profane things. Finally, rites are the rules of conduct which prescribe how a man [*sic*] should comport himself in the presence of these sacred objects.** *(Durkheim 1976: 40–1)*

Durkheim proceeds to this definition:

> **a religion is a unified system of beliefs and practices relative to sacred things, that is to say, things set apart and forbidden – beliefs and practices which unite into one moral community called a Church, all those who adhere to them.**
> *(Durkheim 1976: 47)*

A key feature is Durkheim's identification of religion with society. He sees a parallel between dependence of the individual on the community and on the sacred, the gods being an expression of society itself.

> **This reality, which mythologies have represented in so many different forms, but which is the universal and eternal objective cause of these sensations *sui generis* out of which religious experience is made, is society. . . . If religion has given birth to all that is essential in society, it is because the idea of society is the soul of religion. Religious forces are therefore human forces, moral forces.** *(Durkheim 1976: 418–19)*

Durkheim stresses that in seeing religion as something essentially social he does not regard it as a mere epiphenomenon, an unreal reflection of real material conditions (this is more the case with Marx's theory of religion and historical materialism). Rather, Durkheim sees religious sentiments, ideas and images as having an independent existence and life of their own. Once born of society, they develop laws of their own:

> **They attract each other, repel each other, unite, divide themselves and multiply, though combinations are not commanded and necessitated by the condition of the underlying reality.** *(Durkheim 1976: 424)*

It is for this reason that there is such a dynamic and varied pattern of religious life.

This emphasis on the real, autonomous existence of religion is a departure from Marx's definition of religion which, though also seeing religion as socially grounded, attributes much more limited scope to it. For Marx religion has no independent existence but is simply a fantasy (see pp. 495–7). By taking the individuals out of themselves religion forces them into self-alienation. Hence the task of explaining religion is the task of explaining social reality:

> **Religion is only the illusory sun which revolves round man [*sic*] as long as he does not revolve round himself. . . . Thus the criticism of heaven turns into the criticism of the earth, the *criticism of religion* into the *criticism of right* and the *criticism of theology* into the *criticism of politics*.** *(Marx and Engels 1955: 42)*

It is neither easy nor appropriate to consider Durkheim and Marx's understanding of the essence of religion without examining the way in which they both locate their views in the social context and role of religion. This aspect of their writings is discussed on pp. 487–98.

**Q** How would a society without any religion at all differ from your own?

Weber (1963) provides an alternative definition of religion. He departs from an exclusive emphasis on the *social* grounding of religion, and highlights the meaning of religion for *individuals*. Weber wrote far more about religion than Marx or Durkheim and his emphasis on meaning has inspired many theoretical contributions to our understanding of religion. In the sociology of religion his legacy is illustrated in the work of Berger (1967b) and Luckmann (1967), while researchers in the field of religious studies (for example Smart 1978) also refer to the phenomenological origins reflected in Weber's approach.

Weber stated that 'to define "religion", to say what it *is*, is not possible at the start. . . . Definition can be attempted, if at all, only at the conclusion of the study' (Weber 1963: 1). For him the concern of the sociologist should not be the essence

**Fig 12.1** Bhuddist monks, Thailand. (Courtesy of Robert Harding Picture Library Ltd.)

of religion; rather the task is to understand religion as part of meaningful human behaviour and explain its influence on other spheres of activity such as ethics, economic and politics. (Chapter 2 described how Weber's (1974) study of Protestantism is part of a wider analysis of capitalist ethical and economic behaviour.)

Weber's concentration on both the social context and the significance of meaning systems in the sociology of religion is illustrated in a broad range of works on the religions of China (Confucianism and Taoism), India (Hinduism and Buddhism) and ancient Judaism. Weber also studied Calvinism in *The Protestant Ethic*, which was more than simply a response to Marx's seemingly deterministic view of religion as being dependent on economic factors. Weber's study was part of a much broader analysis giving emphasis to the nature and significance of religious motivation; he concluded that religion can play a key part in helping to shape economic attitudes and behaviour.

Berger and Luckmann (1963) take up this interpretive approach linking the study of religion to the broader field of the sociology of knowledge. They see religion as an attempt to make sense of reality through the development of a subjective world-view. Luckmann (1967) reflects both Durkheimian and Weberian influences when he suggests that religion plays an important function in helping individuals to make sense of the world around them. Berger (1967b) outlines his thesis of religion as the means by which a sacred external cosmos is constructed:

> **Religion has played a strategic part in the human enterprise of world-building. Religion implies the farthest reach of man's [*sic*] self-externalization. . . . Put differently, religion is the audacious attempt to conceive of the entire universe as being humanly significant.** *(Berger 1967b: 37)*

Definitions of religion tend to be either substantive or functional. *Substantive* definitions try to uncover the essence of religion – what religion *is*. *Functional* approaches place more emphasis on the effect of religion – what religion *does*. Such distinctions become significant when discussing whether religious ideas and practices are inevitable in society and in debates about secularization. For those operating with more inclusive definitions of religion – seeing, for example, apparently secular ideologies as functional equivalents of religion where they have the same effect – secularization is a limited possibility. Those examining the extent to which religion has declined, and areas where it competes with non-religious conceptions of the social order, are more likely to prefer exclusive definitions.

Linked in with these debates are discussions about measuring religiosity. Glock and Stark (1968: 253–61) differentiated five dimensions of religiosity. These are indicators by which it might be possible to measure degrees of religiousness. Particular indicators may apply more to one individual, group or religion than others at any particular time. The five dimensions are belief, practice, experience, knowledge and consequences.

Case Study

## Five dimensions of religiosity

The *belief* dimension refers to the core beliefs of a religion. *Practice* refers to acts of worship carried out either publicly through formal rituals (such as taking communion or attending prayers at a mosque) or privately (such as personal prayer or meditation). The *experience* dimension refers to the expectation that religiosity involves subjective feelings and perceptions, some personal sense of communication with the transcendental. This again varies within and between religions. Members of a Pentecostal Christian group, for example, may be encouraged to express personally the power of God through speaking in tongues, singing or crying aloud. By contrast, the kind of religious experience associated with those who have claimed to see apparitions of the Virgin Mary has often been discouraged by authoritative figures within the Catholic Church.

The *knowledge* dimension refers to the extent of understanding the basic tenets of a religion. This need not align with the belief dimension: one may study the teachings of a religion without believing them, or one may have faith without deep knowledge. The *consequences* dimension extends the idea of religious commitment beyond the first four criteria and focuses on their effects in everyday life. Muslims, for example, may be recognizable outside the mosque by the way they dress, their diet, the type of school they attend and their social and moral codes.

### Questions

Consider one religion. Give an example of each of Glock and Stark's five dimensions of religiosity.

How might each of these dimensions be measured?

What difficulties would arise in measuring these dimensions?

## Types of religious organizations

All religions involve a community of believers but there may be variations in members' commitment, or in the way the community is organized. Like other organizations, religious institutions are constantly changing, in terms of both their internal structure and their relationship and status *vis-à-vis* the secular environment. At the same time there are clearly differences between the size, constitution and status of bodies such as the Anglican Church in relation to organizations like the Unification Church (sometimes referred to as 'The Moonies' after their leader Revd Sun Myung Moon).

Sociologists have devised a number of ways of classifying religious organizations. As well as being of academic interest, this has important legal and political implications. Barker (1989: 146) points out that many organizations actively seek either to attain or to avoid religious status in order to qualify for certain social advantages. In Britain, for example, religious bodies may qualify for tax exemption, so groups such as the Unification Church have actively claimed religious status. In the United States, however, where religious beliefs have traditionally not been taught in public (i.e. state) schools, some groups have sought to avoid the religious label so that their teachings can be communicated through the curriculum.

There are four main categories of organization: *church*, *denomination*, *sect* and *cult*. Within the sociology of religion Weber (1963) made the original distinction between church and sect and inspired further research into the social characteristics of different types of religious organizations (for example Troeltsch 1931).

The sociological terms such as 'sect' and 'church' may differ from everyday usage and meanings of these terms, which may not be referring to the social characteristics defined in the box (p. 484).

### Church

In sociological terms a '*church*' is a well-established religious body. It maintains a bureaucratic structure (including a hierarchy of paid officials) and a formal distinction between religious officials and the laity. (In the Christian tradition this is illustrated by the authority of the priesthood in celebrating the sacraments and in Islam by the legal authority of the imams.) Through its links with the establishment, the church is generally integrated into the wider economic and social structure of society: its beliefs and values are widely accepted by the population. It is part of the status quo and tends to be conservative, with an interest in maintaining traditions and its privileged position within the system. Although all sections of the population may be represented in its membership, the higher status groups in society tend to be over-represented. The saying that the Church of England is 'the Tory Party at prayer' reflects this association between the Church of England and the establishment.

**Q** **Give examples of how the Church of England and other national churches have (a) supported governments and/or political leaders; (b) criticized them.**

Definition

### Troeltsch's church-type and sect-type

**A theologian and church historian, Troeltsch developed Weber's typology for the purposes of historical comparative analysis. Troeltsch (1931) was focusing specifically on church and sect types within Christianity, so it is harder to apply the typology to traditions such as Hinduism and Buddhism. His distinctions were also based on societies much more polarized and differentiated than today:**

| Church-type | Sect-type |
|---|---|
| Large and universal; aims to embrace everybody | Small and particularist; fellowship with members but not outsiders |
| Individuals born into church; infant baptism | Members join voluntarily; conscious conversion |
| Grace through intervention of priest and sacraments | Grace through individual personal effort |
| World-accepting; stabilizes social order/established institutional set-ups | World-rejecting; avoids wider society |
| Top-down; develops from upper classes | Bottom-up; connects with those opposed to state and society |
| Asceticism seen as preparation for afterlife; means of acquiring virtue | Asceticism seen as means of direct union with God; expresses detachment from the world |

### Question

**Troeltsch's typology is located within a Christian theological and historical context. How helpful is this classification for understanding different types of religious organizations today? (See also the work of Neibuhr 1957, Yinger 1946 and Beckford 1975.)**

## Sect

Sociological research into *sects* and sectarianism has identified social characteristics contrasting with those of a church. Sects tend to be much smaller, more insular and more in conflict with, or even overtly rejecting, the values and behaviour of the church and wider society. A sect is usually a breakaway movement from a church, formed in protest to the established or orthodox traditions. Disputes may be centred on official doctrines, the interpretation of teachings, or questions around leadership and succession. Christian sects include Jehovah's Witnesses, Christadelphians and the Branch Davidians. Islamic sectarian movements include Shiism and the Bahais. In Judaism examples include the Hassidim, while in Buddhism there are followers of the Pure Land sect. Although these examples may be regarded as sectarian responses, they might not maintain all the features listed here; caution must be exercised in applying categorical labels.

Unlike churches, sects are more likely to require strict discipline and control of members and to perceive themselves as part of an exclusive community. They may withdraw from the surrounding society, thus reinforcing their marginality and sense of being set apart.

When attempting to define a typology of religious organizations such as sects, there may be a tendency to over-generalize and to ignore the enormous diversity between groups that fall into the category of sect. Wilson (1963) outlined a sevenfold typology of sects, which he hoped could also be applied to sects beyond the western and Christian world. He classified sects in relation to *their response to the world*. The seven types of responses were conversionist, revolutionary, introversionist, manipulationist, thaumaturgical, reformist and utopian. Wilson illustrates how important it is to analyse religious organizations in social context: when sects persist they always undergo processes of change and face challenges to their organizational features. Social realities to be faced may include changes in leaders and followers, the disappointment of eschatological hopes (see for example Festinger *et al*. (1956) on pp. 126–7, 145) and declining commitment to original values, especially in protest movements.

## Denomination

As sociologists of religion developed the original church–sect typology, they introduced the term *denomination* to refer to the advanced state of the sect once it loses its original fervour (Becker 1932) and becomes more world-accommodating (Neibuhr 1957). Denominations are a more established part of society without the conflictual characteristics of the sect. Sects are likely to be valid for one generation only; if they survive longer their organization adapts in order to maintain a routine existence within mainstream society. The relationship between the norms and values of the denomination and the majority religion of society tends to be one of coexistence and cooperation rather than conflict and challenge. However, denominational representatives may actively challenge the moral norms and values of mainstream society and urge their followers to re-examine their own beliefs, and practices. Examples in Britain include pronouncements by the Roman Catholic Church about the teaching of sex education in schools and opposition by some Christian groups to Sunday trading.

## Cult

While these examples are exceptions to the mostly peaceful coexistence of religious denominations in multicultural Britain, one type of religious organization generates consistent public hostility – the *cult*. While the term 'cult' is often interchanged in everyday conversation with terms such as 'sect' and 'new religious movement', within sociology there has been much discussion of the appropriateness of labels. The term 'cult' should be used cautiously because of its negative connotations. Cults contain some similarities with 'sects' in terms of size, leadership and lifespan, but the term embraces a large variety of groups outside the main religious traditions. Sociologists originated the category of 'new religious movement' (Barker 1989) to refer specifically to the spate of religious groups that grew very rapidly in North America and western Europe in the post-war period. However, it is a broad term used to cover a wide range of different religious groups, some more deserving of the negative reputation attributed to them than others.

Q Why did so many new religious movements gain popularity in the western world in the 1960s and 1970s?

How do you think such movements have had so much media attention and why?

Case Study

## The Soka Gakkai in Britain

In the 1990s there appears to be renewed public interest in the dangers of new religious movements in view of the events surrounding groups such as the Aum sect, the Order of the Solar Temple and the Branch Davidians following David Koresh at Waco. In these cases commitment to certain ideals led to tragic consequences, but it would be wrong to make generalized assumptions about the appeal, conduct and followers of all new religious movements. In 1990 one such movement in Britain, the Soka Gakkai, was studied by questionnaires and interviews. Wilson and Dobbelaere's study, *A Time to Chant* (1994), examines the social characteristics of British members of the movement, their beliefs and practices and the location of the movement in the wider social structure.

Soka Gakkai International was founded as a lay Buddhist organization in Japan in 1930. It was affiliated to Nicheren Shoshu, the largest sect in Japan, which followed the teachings of a thirteenth-century Buddhist monk. In 1991, however, while the research was being conducted, Soka Gakkai broke away from its parent body. Wilson and Dobbelaere were interested in the reasons for its impressive growth in western secular society (it has around 5,000 followers in Britain). They concluded that part of the appeal of this religion was its practical, world-affirming and life-enhancing orientation rather than any sense of retreat from the world affairs. The main form of religious practice is chanting, which is supposed to bring about tangible benefits, whether these be spiritual, material or communal.

Soka Gakkai in Britain is a largely urban movement of followers integrated into wider secular society, fulfilling their own careers and not segregated from wider family and friendship networks beyond the movement. Many members were in professional, cultural and caring occupations. They tended to have a high degree of educational attainment and to be slightly older on average than followers of some other new religious movements (members tended to be aged between 24 and 45).

Wilson and Dobbelaere concluded that the practical nature of this religion, with its endorsement of tangible rewards and a world-affirming lifestyle, helps to explain its success in contemporary western society. In contrast to the moral economy of sinfulness, suffering and penitence associated with the work ethic and lifestyle of traditional religions such as Christianity, Soka Gakkai embraces the consumer society of spending, hedonism and individualism. While emphasizing personal responsibility, Soka Gakkai also encourages personal positive thinking and achievement in line with the enterprising culture of wider society.

As well as being of intrinsic interest as a social movement, the case of Soka Gakkai serves to warn us of simplistic over-generalizations about the nature and conduct of new religious movement. While it is sociologically useful to distinguish broadly different types of religious organizations, it is important to avoid stereotyping as, for example, the media often tend to do when covering sensationalist news stories relating to cults.

(Adapted from Beckford 1985)

## The role of religion in society

Following on from their interest in the structure of society and the problem of social order, Marx and Durkheim tended to generalize about the universal role of religion in maintaining and reinforcing the status quo. However, there are important differences in their analyses and consequently in the way modern sociologists have developed their ideas. Today sociologists are less interested in looking for one all-embracing role that applies to all manifestations of religion in any time or place. Rather it is recognized that just as the form of religion varies, so does its role both within and across different social settings. Religion has a dual function both to bind and divide, to contribute both to social integration and to social conflict.

### The integrative role of religion

Durkheim was one of the first sociologists to describe the function of religion in binding communities together. His main emphasis was on the level of the social structure and how religious beliefs and rituals bring people together, giving them a sense of unity and shared values. Durkheim's identification of religion with society focuses on its integrative effects. Religion's affirmation of collective ideals has been taken up by later analysts such as Bellah (1975) and Parsons (1971), who have applied a functionalist approach to the study of religion in contemporary societies.

Functionalist theorists assume that since most people in society follow religious beliefs and practices, and since societies on the whole function cohesively, religion must be playing a significant role in reflecting, sustaining and legitimizing the social order. As a key socializing agent religion transmits norms and values that help hold society together. While the style and content of different religions may vary, what they share in common is a coherent system of beliefs and practices serving universal human needs and purposes.

**To what extent do you think such things as football and music have taken the place of religion in fulfilling people's needs for a coherent system of beliefs and practices?**

Religious beliefs and ceremonies integrate individuals into social groups or communities in several ways by

- providing identity
- expressing shared meanings and understanding
- physically bringing worshippers together
- prescribing moral norms
- sanctioning changes of status
- dealing with emotional stress or life crises.

First, religion helps by *providing identity*, a sense of who we are both in this world and in relation to the next. Wilson refers to how religion has 'answered the question "who am I?" for individuals and "who are we?" for groups' (1982: 34).

Many people inherit affiliation to a religious group through their family, just as they inherit a sense of belonging to a kin group. Formal identification often takes place through a religious naming ceremony whereby an individual becomes formally accepted as a member of the community. In Christianity, for example, the first stage of membership is baptism or christening when an individual traditionally adopts a Christian name (perhaps that of a saint). In Islam, although babies born of Muslims are automatically regarded as Muslims, membership of the *ummah* (the Muslim community) is signified by the name Muhammad (the name of the Prophet) or by the adoption of one of ninety-nine names used to describe God, e.g. Rahim ('Kind') or Hafiz ('Protector').

As well as marking an individual's identity in this life, many belief systems include a strong sense of the past in terms of heritage and ancestry. This reinforces the uniqueness of both the individual and the group which, through commemorative rituals, further enhances social solidarity. For Jews the Hebrew Scriptures and regular festivals and ceremonies such as Passover and Hannukah, recalling events in Jewish history, reflect the belief that they are a chosen people whose special relationship with God marks them out from other communities.

Religious beliefs and practices can affect social behaviour in relation to customs associated with life after death. Both Marx and Weber were interested in how Christian beliefs about the afterlife affected the behaviour of people on earth, albeit to produce either apathy or activity within the social and economic system. It is not only the various Christian concepts of heaven and hell which affect people's sense of destiny and social behaviour. Both Hinduism and Buddhism include the concept of reincarnation or rebirth, which helps to explain people's social situation and also functions to modify behaviour. Many Chinese communities believe that paying proper respect to their ancestors will secure their prosperity and welfare and bode well for the future. Beliefs about the continuity of life beyond physical death reinforce identity in the family group and can also strengthen social solidarity and social order.

Second, an interpretive approach to religion highlights the importance of religious symbols in *expressing shared meanings and understanding* among believers. Religious language, gestures, images and icons all have special significance to members partaking in rituals and ceremonies. This sense of mutual understanding and adoration unites worshippers and sets them apart from non-believers. Indeed it is the spiritual meaning and sacred significance bestowed by believers on to symbolic forms and actions which makes them 'religious'. Lighting a joss stick, kneeling in front of a statue or wearing particular clothes are actions that could have either secular or religious connotations depending on their context and the meaning attributed to them by participants.

Third, religious meanings and feelings cannot be directly observed. They can be 'seen' only in the physical actions of those translating beliefs into action. *Physically bringing worshippers together* in regular rituals and ceremonies binds members of a religious community together. Examples of annual occasions include Christmas, Divali, Eid, Passover and Visakha.

Definition

## Religious festivals

**Christmas** is a Christian festival celebrating the birth of Jesus, regarded as the Messiah (the 'Christ'). It extends from Advent through to the Epiphany, celebrating Jesus' revelation to the Gentiles. This festival is based on the Pagan calendar and customs of present-giving and feasting at the winter solstice.

**Divali** is the Hindu festival of light held at the onset of winter, when Hindus honour Lakshmi, the goddess of wealth. As with many other religious traditions, the lighting of candles and oil lamps has symbolic significance and, with other aspects of celebration, draws together Hindu families and communities.

**Eid or Id** is an Islamic term for 'religious festival' and refers to two great feasts: Id al-Adha ('of sacrifice'), associated with Abraham's attempt to sacrifice his son, and Id al-Fitr ('of breaking fast') celebrating the end of Ramadan, the fasting month. Both are periods of rejoicing, the latter involving much communal festivity.

**Passover (Pesach)** is celebrated by Jews marking the historical Exodus from Egypt. A Seder meal is held during which four cups of wine are drunk and the Exodus story recited. The Passover is an important family occasion and reinforces members' roles in the preparation and conduct of the ritual meal.

**Visakha** is the name of an Indian month and refers to the annual Buddhist festival celebrating the birth, death and enlightenment of the Buddha. In Buddhist communities social and religious values are reinforced through visits to the temple where prayers and gifts are offered.

The fourth way in which religion contributes to social cohesion is in *prescribing moral norms*; this refers to the role of religion in providing a sense of right and wrong. (This is explicitly recognized in the British education system which emphasizes the teaching of religious education in schools as part of young people's moral education.) A belief in the afterlife is one factor influencing social behaviour. Some societies also develop legal codes incorporating systems of punishment for behaviour regarded as contravening God's law. In Islamic states the religious and civil law coincide and punishment is administered according to the strictures of the Koran. Most societies do not have a complete overlap between religious and secular law; the number of Islamic states where this is so is small. (Although the Organization of Islamic Conferences lists forty-three member countries as Islamic states, the majority of these would feature secular influences in areas such as the law: Zakaria 1988.) However, even in largely secular societies such as Britain there are legacies of a religious heritage in the legal system with many examples of laws and custom based on and still reflecting Christian interpretations of right and wrong.

Q Is it fair to conclude that in prescribing moral codes religion contributes to social cohesion? Or are there some instances in which this could lead to conflict?

Fifth, religion often plays an important part in rites of passage which alter sets of social expectations and responsibilities of individuals. Examples of such transitions include coming of age and marriage, which religious ceremonies mark by publicly

**Fig 12.2** A Bar Mitzvah ceremony makes the transition from childhood to adult status. (Photograph © Chris Ridley, courtesy of Robert Harding Picture Library Ltd.)

*sanctioning changes of status* for the individual and reinforcing the norms and identity of the whole group. Rituals recognizing the change from childhood to adult status are ceremonies such as Confirmation within Christianity, Bar/Bat Mitzvah within Judaism and the Sacred Thread ceremony (*Upanayana*) within Hinduism.

Finally, given the functionalist emphasis on social order, this approach recognizes the important role that religion can play at times of social disorder, by *dealing with emotional stress or life crises.* Periods of social upheaval or uncertainty such as a death in the family, large-scale disaster or war may be anomic situations when individuals or communities question social norms and ask ultimate questions about the meaning of life and death. Religious beliefs may provide answers for those who believe that all events are part of God's will. Anthropologists (such as Malinowski 1926) argue that funerary and commemorative rituals function to restore social balance and gradually reintegrate bereaved individuals back into normal life.

Since the 1980s, while there have been more 'secular' funerals featuring less traditional religious symbolism, there has also been a growth in symbolic ritualism in response to local tragedies. The laying of flowers at the scene of accidents, murders or disasters is an example of the continuing need to express loss and seek answers at a time of social distress, be it in traditional or quasi-religious terms. The response of the public after the Hillsborough football disaster in 1989 illustrated this most graphically.

Case Study

## You'll never walk alone

The most visible response in this first week was the visit of over a million people to Anfield, Liverpool's home ground. Large crowds had already gathered outside the ground when club officials opened the gates at noon on Sunday and began admitting people. By five o'clock the Kop end of the ground, where home supporters always stand, had become a shrine bedecked with flowers. The visitors continued to arrive from all over the country over the seven days of official mourning, queuing for hours in silent solemnity. The field of flowers gradually grew towards the centre of the pitch, whilst the concrete steps behind the goal were transformed into a carpet of scarves, pictures and personal messages. Scarves were also hung on the metal barriers, many of which became dedicated to the fans who had stood behind them week after week. School friends penned the names of their lost classmates on the walls outside the stadium. These messages expressed personal and communal grief as much, if not more than, any of the official ceremonies could have. For many people, visiting Anfield – Liverpool's home ground – brought their grief to the surface. (Eyre 1989)

### Questions

How far do you think traditional religious beliefs, rituals and codes function to integrate members in modern society?

To what extent do public mourning rituals replace the role of traditional religion in fulfilling individual and social needs?

Religious beliefs, rituals and codes can uphold social solidarity and consensus, depending on the extent to which all members of society share the same values and belief systems. If this idea of consensus is questioned, however, religion may instead be interpreted as a negative force of social control with its beliefs, rituals and codes part of an imposed system of norms and values. Critics have suggested that a functionalist analysis is more appropriate to smaller-scale, less complex societies where the majority adheres more strongly to a unitary religious system. Where such consensus does not exist or is questioned, social expectation and pressure to participate in prevailing cultural norms might be regarded by individuals as an unwelcome imposition. Questioning particular beliefs or customs might even be interpreted as a rejection of all the wider community stands for. In modern or post-modern societies, characterized by a vast range of competing beliefs and practices, traditional functionalist analysis might seem less appropriate. However, functionalist theory has had a strong impact on the development of the sociology of religion. The main impetus for the development of this perspective was Durkheim.

### *Durkheim's study of religion*

Durkheim's central concern in studying religion was the role it played in keeping societies ordered (see also pp. 47–9). He believed that just as cohesion was a basic requirement of all societies so was religion, operating as a kind of social cement binding individuals within the social system. Durkheim sought to discover the essence of religion by examining what he regarded as its most elementary form: the totem religion of Australian aborigines. Once he understood the essential characteristics of this religion he believed he could generalize about the religious character of any society.

Drawing on anthropological data of aboriginal society, Durkheim concluded that by regularly gathering together to worship the totem, the rituals reminded aborigines of their sense of unity, obligation and interdependence, all of which were imperative for the group's survival. The sacred significance attributed to the totem represented to Durkheim not so much the supernatural quality of the totem itself, but rather the worship of the group's collectiveness. Through the tangible worship of the totem the more abstract quality of society was being essentially worshipped and reinforced.

While the aborigines did not think in terms of worshipping society, Durkheim believed that as a distanced observer he was able to make a more objective evaluation of the underlying significance of totem worship. As a positivist, Durkheim's sociological interest lies less in the subjective personal experiences of the individual or in the theological essence of religious belief; rather he is interested in the wider social context and general effect of collective religious behaviour. For him religion can be understood in terms of its sociological effect as the most basic 'collective representation' in society:

**The general conclusion . . . is that religion is something eminently social. Religious representations are collective representations which express collective realities; the rites are a manner of acting which take rise in the midst of the assembled group which are destined to excite, maintain or recreate mental states in these groups.**
***(Durkheim 1976: 10)***

Following on from this understanding about the real nature of religion Durkheim looked for examples of beliefs, values and rituals in modern society functioning in the same way as traditional religion.

**There can be no society which does not feel the need of upholding and reaffirming at regular intervals the collective sentiments and ideas which gave it its unity and individuality.** ***(Durkheim 1976: 427)***

Durkheim regarded the national flag of a modern society as an equivalent of the totem in that it too represents the sum of a nation, a reality over and above all the individuals comprising a society and a symbol of national values given special or 'sacred' qualities. Durkheim reflected the rise of nationalism in his own country after the French Revolution in which the ideals of liberty, equality and fraternity had been held up as national ideals. This reminds us that authors of sociological studies will to some extent be influenced by the cultural developments, norms and values around them. It also leads us to ask how applicable Durkheim's ideas are in contemporary societies.

### *The civil religion thesis*

In 1967 the US sociologist Robert Bellah applied Durkheim's ideas to the United States and developed the sociological concept of 'civil religion'. The term had first been used by Rousseau in 1762 to refer to the religious dimension underlying the political order. Bellah extended it to the fundamental, universally accepted moral beliefs and values of a nation, in this case the United States. He argued that national values such as the ideals of freedom, justice, equality and democracy are given 'sacred' status in the Durkheimian sense in American civil life in the way that they are esteemed principles augmented within the national psyche and regarded with special respect. Just as the aborigines effectively worshipped their unity through regular rituals and ceremonies, so civic rituals in the United States function to bind together the nation through the celebration and commemoration of key national events.

Religious language and imagery have been applied to the sense of history and heritage of the American people with biblical analogies of a chosen migrant people settling in the promised land of their ancestors – the 'pilgrim fathers'. Bellah (1967) analysed the content of presidential speeches and observed the frequent references to God in such statements as 'God bless America'. Contemporary examples of civil religion in symbols and action include the celebration of Independence and Thanksgiving Day, the Declaration of Independence, the Statue of Liberty and national shrines such as Mount Rushmore and presidential birthplaces.

Thus the nation's flag and other national symbols and ceremonies upholding American ideals serve to remind civilians of their loyalty to the nation, of their interdependence and reliance on basic standards and responsibilities within the community and of the fact that the nation stands as a collective ideal over and above the individual. Irrespective of ethnic, religious and other distinctions individuals are all part of the greater unity which is the United States nation.

---

**Civil religion is the expression of the cohesion of the nation. It transcends denominational, ethnic and religious boundaries.** ***(McGuire 1992: 179)***

---

**Q**

Civil religion refers to 'any set of beliefs and rituals, related to the past, present, and/or future of a people ("nation") which are understood in some transcendental fashion' (Hammond 1976).

Which activities, rituals and emblems illustrate the United States' civil religion? In order to qualify as examples of civil religion they should fulfil these criteria:

- The symbols and rituals operate at a national level uniting the nation.
- The symbols and rituals are set apart and treated with special respect: they are given 'sacred' significance.
- There are regular rituals and ceremonies which bring people together and function to remind people of their collectivity as a nation.

In countries undergoing rapid social, economic and political change there is often increased potential for social dislocation and division at a time when traditional religious ties are being challenged by secular norms and ideals. Many countries in the east, and in South East Asia in particular, face just such a situation as they undergo capitalist development. In Malaysia, Singapore and Indonesia, for example, governments have tried to mitigate what they see as potentially threatening effects of development by introducing ideologies and customs stressing national values and norms. In Malaysia the *Rukunegara* – a statement of national ideals – has been formulated and is regularly recited, while at the same time the celebration of independence day (National Day) and the construction of a national culture are examples of attempts to bind this multicultural nation over and above communal differences (Eyre 1995).

### *Civil religion in Britain*

How appropriate is the concept of civil religion for Britain? Are there regular rituals and symbols associated with national values which function to bind together the disparate elements of British society? One obvious difference between Britain and the United States is that in Britain there is an established Church; in the coronation service the monarch becomes head of the Church and Defender of the Faith. In the United States no particular traditional religion is identified with the civil religion, but in Britain there has traditionally been a close association between the Church of England and expressions of nationalism; an illustration of this is the controversy caused by Prince Charles's statement (during a BBC television interview with Jonathan Dimbleby, 29 June 1994) that he would want to be Defender of *Faiths*. This 'church-sponsored' civil religion (Gehrig 1981) also embraces the royal family as part of the historical relationship between church and state.

Analysts of civil religion in Britain have identified ceremonial events such as the coronation, royal weddings, the Queen's speech on Christmas Day and other civic events involving a royal presence as examples of civil religion. Shils and Young (1956) studied the coronation of Queen Elizabeth II in 1953 and concluded that such an event not only expressed national values and sentiments but also united the British people in an act of national communion. They suggested that there was an underlying respect among the British people for the symbols of society and for the royal family as upholders of national values.

This perception may no longer be appropriate in view of the declining respect for the royal family reflected in increased media criticism and calls for disestablishment. Although this suggests that the content of civil religion might be changing, functionalists would look for alternative national rituals and symbols which continue to uphold national values and fulfil the necessary function of binding the community.

### *Evaluating the concept of civil religion*

While civil religion is a useful notion for measuring integration in contemporary societies, the vagueness of the concept makes it difficult to limit the various elements that could be included in a list of civil religious rituals. Hughey (1993) sums up further difficulties involved in trying to accurately understand and measure civil religion:

> **The Durkheimian analysis excludes from consideration the possibility that different groups may be differently committed even to orthodox values and that, therefore, the substantive grounds on which particular groups respond to these values may also be different. If a more empirically adequate understanding of the relationship between values and social order is to be attained, one must know not only that certain values and symbols have attained orthodox stature, or that they have been ceremonialised, but also which groups are most committed to those values, who controls the rituals, and what, if any, other institutionalised mechanisms for their support exist. One must also explore the substantive grounds on which particular groups respond to those values or participate in their ritual celebration.**
>
> ***(Hughey 1993: 172)***

This sort of evaluation forms part of a more general criticism of the functionalist approach to defining religion in terms of its effects. It has been suggested that the label of religion is too inclusive and should be restricted to those beliefs and rituals associated with a sense of the supernatural. A further criticism of the functionalist approach to religion is that it tends to overemphasize consensus and to underestimate it as a potential source of conflict. Within the sociology of religion a useful balance is provided by a Marxist analysis of religion.

## The divisive role of religion

Marxist analyses of religion form part of a wider critique of social structures regarded as tools of control and manipulation used by dominant groups. It will come as no surprise to a student of sociology that Marx did not regard religion within capitalist society as redemptive in any way. Rather he believed it to be a powerful ideology used to express and reinforce class divisions within capitalist society. For Marx salvation could be achieved only by individuals taking action within this world, not by continuing to depend on and give credibility to institutional structures or beliefs that try to explain and dismiss worldly experiences of oppression.

However, this interpretation of Marxism is by no means the full picture. In order to do justice to a conflict approach to religion it is necessary to look at how Marxist themes have been adopted by later scholars, including those focusing on the revolutionary potential of religion as an agent of social change and not merely seeing it as an ideology supporting and reinforcing the status quo. Here it is helpful to remember that the twin themes of consensus and conflict are inevitable features of society and that something as complex as religion is likely to fulfil both integrative and divisive functions in contemporary contexts.

**The aspect of conflict is basically the obverse of social cohesion; a certain amount of conflict is part of the very structure that holds groups together. And because religion is an important way by which groups express their unity, it is also a significant factor in conflict.** *(McGuire 1992: 175)*

**Q** Is there a relationship between religion and social class? Do you think people from one class are more likely to be attracted to religion than those from another?

### *Marx's views on religion*

Karl Marx not only shared with Durkheim a Jewish family background, but also applied a top-down approach to the study of religion in so far as he felt it appropriate to consider religion's general contribution to the perpetuation of social order. However, whereas Durkheim's analysis seems to accept uncritically the role of religion in maintaining the status quo, Marx did not. Religion was seen as a distraction from the struggle towards the Utopian new world of the communist order. Marx believed that a new society truly based on equality, fairness and freedom would have no use for the sort of exploitive ideas and belief systems encapsulated in religion. There would be no need of any such human ideologies to manipulate, pacify and control the masses.

It is important to be aware of the fact that most of Marx's writings were not directly related to religion. Unlike Weber and Durkheim he did not devote special attention to a study of religion or develop a coherent treatise on it. However, as Elster (1985: 504) points out, there are brief passages about religion scattered throughout his writing over twenty-five years in which he discusses his views on the nature, causes and consequences of religion. It is also important to appreciate that unlike Durkheim, and even more so Weber, Marx did not give credit to the many forms and varieties of religion across the world, tending rather to generalize from his own experience of religion in western, capitalist societies based on a Judaeo-Christian heritage.

Marx's basic premise was that religion is a human phenomenon rather than a supernatural one. Religion arises in society out of human or social need, either as a spontaneous invention by the oppressed to make sense of their condition or as an ideology developed by the ruling class. Marx was influenced by the writings of Feuerbach (1957) and saw religion as a way that individuals could satisfy their needs in this world by imagining their fulfilment in a future world. Such an imaginary world is ruled over by a supernatural being in whom is realized humanity's supreme potentialities:

**The basis of irreligious criticism is: man [*sic*] makes religion, religion does not make man. Religion is indeed the self-consciousness and self-feeling of man who has not yet gained possession of himself or has already lost himself again. But man is not an abstract being lurking outside the world. Man is the world of men, state, society. This state, this society produces religion, an inverted consciousness of the, world, because it is an inverted world. . . . Religion is the realisation of the essence of man in the imagination because the essence of man has no true realisation. The battle against religion is thus indirectly the battle against that world whose spiritual aroma religion is.** *(Marx and Engels 1976 vol. 3: 175)*

For Marx, religion cannot be divorced from the social context in which it is found because the social context is the basis of both its origin and its form.

**If therefore we investigate the religion of a people, we are not really exploring a world beyond this world, but are examining symptoms that reveal the social diseases from which the people are suffering.** *(Acton 1967: 26)*

Here again there are similarities with Durkheim in the sense that Marx seems to be explaining away religion by regarding it as purely of social origin. Many sociologists of religion today would challenge such an extreme and dismissive position.

Marx elaborates on the idea of religion as a reflection of and protest against distressing social conditions in what has become a well-known summary of his thought:

**Religious want is both the expression of and the protest against real want. Religion is the sigh of the oppressed creature, the heart of a heartless world, the soul of soulless circumstances. It is the opium of the people.** *(Marx and Engels 1976 vol. 3: 175)*

While the term 'protest' tends to conjure up images of engaged action and demonstration, in Marx's analysis the form of protest engendered by religion is more passive, a process of withdrawal from worldly involvement. He suggests that, just like a drug, religion can give the user temporary relief and even a temporary 'high', but in the long run the prognosis is not good.

Q In what ways might the effects of religion be comparable to those of taking drugs? How appropriate do you think this analogy is in terms of the following:
(a) Gives an emotional and physical high; release from reality.
(b) Affects consciousness either through hallucination or distortion of reality.
(c) Leads to long-term effects of apathy, lethargy, inaction.
(d) Results in physical and psychological dependency.

Marx argues that religion not only has a narcotic effect on the masses but also functions for the dominant class in sustaining the status quo. Religion justifies for them their social and political status as well as maintaining their position by diverting the revolutionary potential of the oppressed.

**The social principles of Christianity justified the slavery of antiquity, glorified the serfdom of the Middle Ages and are capable, in case of need, of defending the oppression of the proletariat, even with somewhat doleful grimaces. The social principles of Christianity preach the necessity of a ruling and an oppressed class, and for the latter all they have to offer is the pious wish that the former may be charitable. . . . The social principles of Christianity declare all the vile acts of the oppressors against the oppressed to be either a just punishment for original sin, and other sins, or trials which the Lord, in his infinite wisdom, ordains for the redeemed. The social principles of Christianity preach cowardice, self-contempt, abasement, submissiveness and humbleness, in short all the qualities of the rabble, and the proletariat, which will not permit itself to be treated as rabble, needs its courage, its self-confidence, its pride and its sense of independence even more than its bread. The social principles of Christianity are sneaking and hypocritical and the proletariat is revolutionary.** *(Marx and Engels 1976 vol. 6: 231)*

Marx was hopeful that the oppression of the masses would end. He predicted that capitalism would be overcome along with its unjust ideologies and false hopes. Once the social conditions of capitalism were overthrown there would be no need for false ideologies such as religion to compensate for social reality.

**To remove religion as the people's illusory happiness is to demand real happiness for the people. The demand for the abandonment of illusions about one's condition is the demand to give up a condition that needs illusion. The criticism of religion is thus in embryo the criticism of the vale of sorrows whose halo is religion.**
*(Marx and Engels 1976 vol. 3: 176)*

His views of communism appear rather naive now that we have the advantage of historical insight into the limits of communism and the sweeping changes in eastern Europe. However, this is not to set capitalist systems above criticism; indeed religious leaders continue to speak out about what they regard as the evils of modern economic systems. In 1993 Pope John Paul II gave an interview in which he criticized the extremes of both communism and capitalism. He also highlighted those strands of Catholic thought compatible with Marx's views:

**Communism has had its success in this century as a reaction against a certain type of unbridled savage capitalism which we all know well. One need only take in hand the social encyclicals, and in particular the first, Rerum Novarum, in which Leo XIII describes the condition of the workers of that time. [This powerful encyclical, issued in 1891, asserted the right of labour to just rewards and endorsed legislation, trade unions and co-operative organizations having this purpose.] Marx, too, described it in his own way. That's what social reality was like, without a doubt, and it was a consequence of the system, of the principles of ultra-liberal capitalism.**

*(Pope John Paul II, quoted in 'States of Savagery; Seeds of Good', Guardian 2 November 1993)*

Later in the interview he said:

**Of course, it was legitimate to fight against the unjust, totalitarian system which defined itself as socialist or communist. But it is also true what Leo XIII says, that there are some 'seeds of truth' even in the socialist programme. It is obvious that these seeds should not be destroyed. . . . The proponents of capitalism in its extreme forms tend to overlook the good things achieved by communism: the efforts to overcome unemployment, the concern for the poor.** *(Ibid.)*

### *Neo-Marxist approaches to religion*

The statements from Pope John Paul II show that the relationship between religion and Marxism is a surprisingly complex one. Making simplistic generalizations about religions in historical or contemporary context, therefore, would be highly misleading. However, it would be equally misleading to leave a Marxist analysis here since the classic interpretation of Marx's views on religion outlined so far has itself been subject to substantial reinterpretation. Neo-Marxists today defend Marx's views on religion against misrepresentation and an overemphasis on religion's opiate effects. They suggest that Marx balanced this analysis by acknowledging a dynamic role for religion as a powerful agent of challenge and social change in society.

**The fact that religion is far from being in all cases a drug administered by the oppressors for the purpose of inducing resignation and inaction among the oppressed has long been clear to Marxists as well as to others . . . . Thus repetition of a crude opium-of-the-people thesis has no scholarly justification, least of all if presented as *the* Marxist view of religion.** *(O'Toole 1984: 189)*

Using Marxist themes, contemporary analysts focus on situations where religious and cultural ideologies are developed and applied as part of revolutionary struggle of the oppressed against injustice, using both violent and non-violent means. In South Africa, Latin America and Poland, for example, activists in the Catholic Church have mobilized the poor and oppressed against the authorities. These activists combine Marxist and Christian strands in *liberation theology*, invoking the Christian Gospels to justify their resistance against poverty and exploitation in the name of human rights.

**Case Study**

## Liberation theology

When I feed the poor they call me a saint; when I ask why they are poor they call me a communist. (Dom Helder Camara, quoted on a CAFOD poster)

Liberation theology represents a radical engagement of Christianity with the world, with the intent to represent human freedom and God's gratuitous activity in the questions and issues of the day. As a radically new paradigm and departure from modern theology, liberation theology reflects and guides a Christianity that is identified with those who suffer, that represents a freedom of transformation, and that proclaims a God whose love frees us for justice and faith. (Chopp 1986: 153)

In prefacing a documentary history of liberation theology, Hennelly (1990: xv) states that its development sprang not from First World scholars in great universities, but from small communities of the poorest and least literate men and women, first in Latin America and later in other parts of the Third World. Latin American theology first started to be identified as a 'theology of liberation' in the 1960s and has been inspired by the writings and actions of individuals such as Leonardo Boff (1987) and Gustavo Gutierrez (1973; 1990). Many lay churchworkers, nuns and priests have given their lives fighting oppressive systems as part of their Christian vocation. They include Archbishop Oscar Romero, shot through the heart as he preached at mass in San Salvador in 1980.

Liberation theology illustrates how a conflict approach to understanding and evaluating social reality can be compatible with a religious outlook and can actively bring about social change. Indeed 'the ideals and ideas of Liberation Theology specifically point[ed] to a transformative approach to religious action' (McGuire 1992: 241).

Hennelly (1990) gives a full history of liberation theology and McGuire (1992: 239–45) contains an extended analysis of religion and social change in Brazil as an example of liberation theology in action.

An interpretation of the Gospels as demanding a 'preferential option for the poor' has also been promoted in Britain by leading clergy challenging injustices in the inner city. In Liverpool, for example, Bishop David Sheppard has written about the *Bias to the Poor* (1983) and, together with his Catholic counterpart the late Derek Worlock, has frequently attacked government policies favouring 'comfortable Britain'. A further example of this politically active role of the churches was the publication of the Church of England's report *Faith in the City* (ACUPA 1985), which described the plight of poor people living in urban priority areas (UPAs) and challenged the government and nation to activate social change. It caused a heated public debate and was labelled by members of the government as 'Marxist' and the Church was criticized for meddling in politics.

Case Study

## Faith in the City

In 1983 the Archbishop of Canterbury set up the Archbishop's Commission on Urban Priority Areas (ACUPA) with the aim of examining the strengths, insights, problems and needs of the Church's life and mission in UPAs and making recommendations to appropriate bodies within the Church and nation.

> If our Report has a distinctive stance, it arises from our determination to investigate the urban situation by bringing to bear upon it those basic Christian principles of justice and compassion which we believe we share with the great majority of the people of Britain. (ACUPA 1985: xiv)

The commission membership included individuals with a wide range of experiences, qualifications and backgrounds. It included both clergy and laypeople and invited other interested parties to submit evidence. Visits were undertaken to UPAs to reinforce the report's validity

The main finding of the report was that UPAs are characterized by a vicious circle of continually declining quality of life, acute human misery and powerlessness. Underlying causal factors included unemployment, decayed housing, substandard educational and medical provision and social disintegration.

> It is our considered view that the nation is confronted by a grave and fundamental injustice in the UPAs. The facts are officially recognised, but the situation continues to deteriorate and requires urgent action. No adequate response is being made by government, nation or Church. There is barely even widespread discussion. (ACUPA 1985: xv)

Davie (1994) suggests that the political repercussions of the report were considerable:

> For an established church can, it seems, still create an impact denied to other denominations and bring to the attention of the nation as a whole the plight of those living in the most deprived areas of Britain's larger conurbations. The Church of England had in fact achieved what the Labour Party had so conspicuously failed to do; that is, to push issues of deprivation – and in particular urban deprivation – to the top of the political agenda. (Davie 1994: 152)

At the same time though, she adds that it is important not to exaggerate the effectiveness of the churches during this period:

> They were successful . . . in some respects, for the concept of 'UPA' became current in political circles and grave injustices had to be acknowledged. But acknowledging injustices did not remove them, a point all to evident to anyone with first hand experience in the inner-city. Nor, it must be stressed, were all those in the churches equally enthusiastic about what was going on. . . . The Faith in the City debate simply reveals a more persistent trend in Church life in the later postwar decades; namely that the Anglican laity were proving themselves considerably more cautious, more conservative and indeed more Conservative than their clergy. (Davie 1994: 154)

### Questions

Do you think that it is right that religious leaders should be involved in political debates?

Or should they confine themselves to quietly getting on with good works and leave politics to others?

While it is important to recognize alternative strands in the Marxist analysis of religion, it is true to say that the 'opium-of-the-people' interpretation appears to be the strongest and most consistent element in Marx's writing. However, this has not prevented modern analysts from developing the emphasis throughout his work on the significance of differing interest groups and the power of ideologies in trying to understand and interpret the role of religion in contemporary situations of social conflict.

### *Religion and social conflict*

Media coverage of religion in contemporary world affairs usually highlights its role in social and political struggle. Religion is more 'newsworthy' when it is part of conflict than when it fulfils its expected role of integrating communities through rituals, worship and festivals. Even in situations where religion enhances community and belonging, it engenders a sense of insiders and outsiders, of 'us' and 'them'. In some social and political contexts these lines of division may be made explicit. The war in former Yugoslavia illustrates that even where religious communities have existed alongside each other relatively peacefully for many years, circumstances may combine to ignite a confrontation.

Conflict within and between groups may be based not only on religion but also on economic, political, ethnic and cultural lines of social division. These factors overlap and it is difficult to isolate the extent to which any one is the main cause or influence. Indeed, different individuals involved in such conflicts may disagree about the significance of particular factors, whose significance may vary over time.

Q

Examples of twentieth-century conflicts involving religion include the Holocaust, the 1950s Civil Rights movement in the United States, the Iran-Iraq war in the 1980s, the Gulf War 1990–1, Arab–Israeli conflicts and the civil wars in Northern Ireland and former Yugoslavia. To what extent were these conflicts based on theological, religious, racial, political or other grounds?

How far does religion overlap with other lines of social division and to what extent is it possible to distinguish between them?

In the above examples complex factors are involved and it is difficult to isolate the precise role and significance of religion. In other situations, however, religion appears to be the most central factor in a conflict based on specific theological, ethical or organizational questions. Where a religious belief system includes an exclusivist or particularist world-view (that is the idea that its own religious outlook is the only legitimate one), it is likely that conflict with outsiders may arise. Examples of movements attempting to convert outsiders to particularist religions are the medieval crusades and some missionary movements. In extreme cases refusal to convert ends in death (or martyrdom depending on your point of view).

Within any religious community disagreements may arise over questions of doctrine, ethics or leadership. Individuals who openly challenge officially defined doctrines may be labelled as heretics. They may be excommunicated from the official structures or break away from the main tradition to set up sectarian alternatives (see pp. 483–6). Schism occurs throughout the history of religion and might be seen as an inevitable consequence of institutions trying to reconcile competing demands of tradition and change. In the Church of England the debates and consequences relating to the ordination of women illustrate themes of religious and social conflict. Leaders of the main religious institutions expect to be challenged by grassroots members – within the priesthood or the laity – over issues of doctrine and ethics. In smaller religious groups, such as new religious movements, questions of succession may arise once the charismatic founders pass away. Resolving leadership challenges are crucial in determining the long-term survival of a movement.

In the wider arena of ethics, there are also many examples of religiously prescribed codes of behaviour being subject to negotiation, disagreement and difference. In contemporary societies standards of public morality are dynamic, constantly facing reassessment in response to the challenges provided by developments in the fields of science and technology. In the area of medical and sexual ethics, for example, there are ongoing debates about genetic engineering, euthanasia, contraception and abortion. Religious bodies often subscribe to particular ethical codes in relation to such dilemmas though these may give rise to conflicting opinions and actions both within and between denominational boundaries. The media often give coverage to such controversies, particularly when religious authorities are being called on to inform public debates about ethical and moral standards.

Q Think of examples of recent press coverage of public moral and ethical debates. How much space is given to religious perspectives? Are they presented in a predominately positive or negative way?

This overview of religion and social division illustrates the various ways in which religion is associated with social conflict. It is important to develop beyond a classic Marxist interpretation in order to understand the rich complexity of religions in social context. The sociology of religion, having evolved beyond its founding theories, defies any simplistic deduction about the ideological function of beliefs. Both consensus *and* conflict are important features of religious life and any analysis that underplays the significance of either can be only partial.

## Is religion dying out?

Many people today query whether religion can survive the onslaught of secularism. A hundred years or so ago, sociologists predicted the gradual decline and even disappearance of religion. While their ideas have received much support within the sociology of religion, it seems less appropriate in the 1990s to talk of the demise of religion given its persistence as a political and cultural force in a rapidly changing world. We shall consider and evaluate the secularization thesis.

The term *secularization* carries many meanings, some of which imply a value-judgement. Originally 'secularization' referred to the transfer of church property from ecclesiastical to secular state control during the Reformation. In Roman Canon law it denotes the return of a person from a religious order to the world. In some theological circles it may refer to 'deChristianization' and carry a negative sense of loss, whereas critics who see religion as a false or harmful ideology (radical Marxists for example) may regard secularization as a positive process in the sense of enabling the liberation of humanity's rational intellectual potential.

In sociological terms secularization is not intended to carry any prescriptive judgements, but rather refers to a variety of processes associated with the gradual decline of religion in society. It has been succinctly defined as 'the process whereby religious thinking, practice and institutions lose their social significance' (Wilson 1969: 14).

Secularization is often identified with a more general process which includes features such as industrialization, modernization and rationalization. Thus while being part of something greater, and involving many sociological features beyond the manifestation of religion *per se*, the secularization process refers specifically to the transition from a society dominated by religious forms to one marked by the increasing absence of religious influence in social life (Berger 1967b: 113). Secularization has been related to wider processes of 'modernization' though current debates about 'post-modern' living have modified theories of secularization.

Defining and measuring secularization in relation to religion are hampered by similar problems as those that beset attempts to define religion. While 'secular' tends to be referred to as the opposite of 'religious', as with the dichotomy sacred–profane, it is questionable whether the distinction is so rigid: at what point does the secular become the religious?

**Q** How would you measure the extent of secularization in your own community?

What problems might there be with attempts at measurement?

## The myth of secularization?

Critics have questioned the value of the secularization thesis for implying that we have moved from a religious 'golden age'. Glasner (1977) suggests that it is misleading to assume either that the historical past was one in which people were more religious or that any decline that has taken place has been uniformly spread throughout society or the world. This brings us back to how we define and measure religiosity in society. Statistics on church attendance show that fewer people attend services than in the past, but this does not mean that our ancestors were more religious. In Victorian times, churchgoing was strongly associated with respectability and people were under considerable social pressure to attend church. Campbell (1971) suggests that if public standards of morality are referred to as the yardstick for measuring religiosity, we should query designating the Victorian period as a golden age of religiosity given its moral attitudes to prostitution, for example.

Various phases in history such as the last years of the Roman Empire and the Reformation can be identified as 'irreligious' to the extent that they were characterized by much scepticism and heresy. Consequently, the implication within the secularization thesis of a past golden age of religion has been seen by some as a myth. Glasner (1977) argues that the myth has been used out of context by those looking for an all-purpose explanation for the supposed ills of contemporary society. In challenging the idea that there has been a steady and irreversible fall in moral standards, these critics suggest that a linear conception of religious decline may be too generalistic and warn against oversimplification in any analysis of religion and social change.

Although there has been much debate about the difficulty of both defining and measuring secularization, as well as controversy about the extent of its impact, few would doubt that secularizing processes have been at work, not just in the west but increasingly as a global phenomenon. Since secularization can be seen as a multidimensional concept, the main aspects of this process will be examined.

## The institutional decline of religion

As an institutional process, secularization includes the *decline in church membership and practice*; there has been decreasing participation in most forms of religious ceremonies. The *UK Christian Handbook* (Brierley and Hiscock 1993) provides up-to-date figures on church membership. Between 1975 and 1992 church membership in the United Kingdom fell from an estimated 8 million (one in five of the adult population) to 6.7 million (one in seven). Given that the majority of churchgoers tend to be older, demographic changes suggest that the proportion of churchgoers will decline to around one in eight after the 1990s: 'Britain's Christian congregations are shrinking by almost 1500 people a week – the Church of England being the worst hit' (Denscombe 1994: 23).

More indepth research has shown that the decline has been far from uniform; while some religious groups have declined rapidly, others have experienced periods of stabilization or even growth. Davie (1994) gives a good critical overview of religious constituencies.

Religious membership and attendance may not be accurate reflections of the religiosity of individuals: difficulties in using these criteria as accurate measures include the accuracy, reliability and interpretation of such data in terms of methods of collecting statistics and the relative importance within different belief systems on attendance at a place of worship. There are also problems in defining 'membership' of a religious organization. A one-off attendance at a meeting could be evidence of 'membership' for some religious groups, while irregular attendance indicates personal disaffiliation for other groups. The tenth British Social Attitudes survey in Britain provided data on the proportion of people describing themselves as regular worshippers; only one in five would describe themselves as a regular Christian worshipper, while over one-third said they had no religion. The statistics suggest that compared internationally, Britain is 'particularly low in terms of religious commitment' (Denscombe 1994: 23).

While the evidence suggests that there has been a decline overall in what is referred to as 'church-oriented' religiosity in Britain, this does not necessarily mean that people are no longer 'religious'. Indeed there remains a relatively high rate of belief in God among the general population, which Davie (1994) describes as 'believing without belonging'.

In institutional terms, secularization in Britain refers to the decreasing *social and political influence of the Church of England*, including the Church's declining wealth

**Table 12.1** Religious affiliation (per cent).

| | Regular Catholic | Irregular Catholic | Regular Protestant | Irregular Protestant | Other religion | No religion |
|---|---|---|---|---|---|---|
| Great Britain | 6 | 5 | 14 | 36 | 3 | 36 |
| N Ireland | 32 | 4 | 35 | 21 | – | 9 |
| Ireland | 77 | 16 | 2 | 2 | 2 | 2 |
| USA | 15 | 12 | 34 | 27 | 4 | 7 |
| Poland | 78 | 19 | – | – | 1 | 3 |
| W Germany | 17 | 26 | 6 | 38 | 2 | 11 |
| E Germany | 3 | 3 | 3 | 26 | 1 | 64 |

*Source: International Social Attitudes: The Tenth BSA Report* 1993, quoted in Denscombe 1994: 24

**Table 12.2** Indicators of religious commitment, Britain compared with European average 1990.

| Indicators of religious disposition | Britain | European average * | Indicators of orthodox belief | Britain | European average * |
|---|---|---|---|---|---|
| Often think about meaning and purposes of life | 36 | 33 | Believe in personal God | 32 | 39 |
| Often think about death | 19 | 20 | Believe in a spirit or life force | 41 | 30 |
| Need moments of prayer, etc. | 53 | 60 | Believe in: | | |
| Define self as a religious person | 54 | 63 | God | 71 | 72 |
| | | | Sin | 68 | 54 |
| | | | Soul | 64 | 61 |
| | | | Heaven | 53 | 42 |
| Draw comfort/strength from religion | 44 | 48 | Life after death | 44 | 44 |
| | | | The devil | 30 | 26 |
| | | | Hell | 25 | 23 |
| God is important in my life | 44 | 52 | | | |

*Note*: * Figures for equivalent countries provided by Dr D Barker, European Values Group

*Source*: Table adapted from Abrams *et al.* 1985: 60 and further adapted from Davie 1994: 78

and influence over areas of social and political life that in the past came under its jurisdiction and authority. With the development of the welfare state, the public sector increased its control over areas of social provision such as education, welfare and patronage of the arts, while the Church's involvement diminished. However, the Church's influence has not altogether disappeared. Indeed since the 1980s the state's role in the public sector has been markedly reduced with the effect that the voluntary sector (including religious bodies) has increasingly re-emerged to try to fill the gaps in services that have accompanied the dismantling of the welfare state. Though the Church is unlikely to regain the wealth and range of influence that it once had, the renewed need for its role as a provider of care within the voluntary sector is in part a response to the secularization process.

**Definition**

**Differentiation**

**The process whereby the Church has become disengaged from these different institutions of society and has become more specialized in relation to its main function of 'hatching, matching and dispatching' is known as 'differentiation'. Differentiation has been defined as 'the development of increasing complexity within organic systems or societies' (Giddens 1989: 738).**

### The decline of religious thinking

Referring back to Wilson's definition (p. 503), secularization reflects the decline of religious thinking in society. This has been related to the rise of scientific and rational modes of thought in advanced societies which gradually replaced non-rational systems of belief such as religion. For some of the early sociologists this was seen as the logical conclusion to the Age of Enlightenment; religious ideas, symbols and values would gradually be replaced by instrumental values, rational procedures and technical methods (Wilson 1982). A clear parallel was drawn between the increasing secularization of society and processes of modernization; a modern advanced society would have no need for the irrationality of religion and reference to a supernatural God. Rather in time all would be subject to human influence and control. In such an advanced (and by implication superior) society, science would provide the explanations of the way the world functions, so enabling humanity to control all events within it.

To a limited extent this has happened: many natural and social events are explained by reference to scientific phenomena. Our ability to understand and control environmental, technical and medical developments has never been greater; most of the time we find no need to refer to supernatural explanations.

However, there is clearly a limit to the extent to which all phenomena are explicable in scientific and rational terms. The realities of death, war, world famine, earthquakes and environmental destruction bear witness both to the unpredictability of human behaviour and our inability to control all events. In terms of secularization both sociologists and theologians have pointed out that there are still fields of human action and inquiry which go beyond science in offering explanations for ultimate questions of human existence. There is continuing reference to religious and spiritual authorities for guidance in addressing moral dilemmas generated by a changing world. These factors help to explain the continuing need and survival of religious modes of thinking and expression.

In thinking about the future of religion, sociologists no longer assume that it might well die out, but ask rather what form and role religion might take in the twenty-first century. Questions about the fundamental nature of religion and reasons for its existence were raised by the first sociologists, knowing that they were on the brink of unprecedented social and economic change. As we move towards the next millennium, the uncertainties surrounding global religious, political and economic transformation make the search for meaning, identity and destiny as relevant as ever.

## Summary

- The sociology of religion focuses on the social context and consequences of belief systems. It attempts to define and measure religiosity but this can prove problematic across time and culture. Glock and Stark (1968) differentiated five dimensions of religiosity: belief, practice, experience, knowledge and consequence.
- Durkheim made a clear distinction between the sacred and profane and defined religion as 'a unified system of beliefs and practices relative to sacred things' which united its followers into a moral community or church. Once these beliefs had been created by society they acquired an autonomous existence of their own.
- Weber emphasized not only the nature and significance of religious motivation but also the influence of religion on other aspects of society including ethics, economics and politics.
- There are four main categories of religious organization: church, denomination, sect and cult.
- Religion can contribute both to social integration and to social conflict. Functionalist approaches have tended to emphasize religion's integrative effects and these ideas were developed further by Robert Bellah (1967) into the concept of civil religion. In

contrast, the conflicts in the former Yugoslavia, Northern Ireland and the Middle East all illustrate instances where religion has played a divisive role.

- Marxist analyses of religion traditionally present it as a powerful ideology which expresses and reinforces class division and oppression, the 'opium of the people'. However, some neo-Marxists have recognized the revolutionary potential of religion as an agent of social change as illustrated by the impact of liberation theology in parts of Africa, Latin America and eastern Europe.
- Despite predictions of the decline and eventual disappearance of religion it still remains a powerful political and cultural force on a global scale and has resisted the forces of creeping secularization.

## Further reading

Davie, G (1994) *Religion in Britain since 1945: Believing without Belonging*, Oxford: Blackwell

A significant contribution to the sociology of religion in Britain, tracing post-war patterns of religion. A key theme is 'believing without belonging' – the growing discrepancy between high indicators of religious belief in Britain and low statistics on membership and practice. This is a very readable book integrating both theoretical and empirical strands.

Lion (1988) *The World's Religions: A Lion Handbook*, Oxford: Lion

A very useful complement to sociological sources, this is a comprehensive, illustrated guide to the major world religions. It overviews the historical development of religion as well as depicting faith and practice as lived today

Roberts, R H (ed.) (1995) *Religion and the Transformations of Capitalism: Comparative Approaches*, London: Routledge

A collection of essays addressing the interaction of religion and contemporary forms of capitalism. This book applies classic Weberian approaches to contemporary societies such as India and Japan. It also covers themes such as globalization and post-modernity and includes case studies on Africa, East Central Europe, Israel, Malaysia and China.

*Social Compass* (Sage Publications)

This regular journal is the international review of the sociology of religion. It includes contributions from top analysts in the field and from all over the world. Recent editions have focused on the following themes: 20 Years on: Changes in New Religious Movements; Durkheim: The Sacred and Society; Religion, Culture and Identity; The Sociology of Christianity's Beginnings.

## Activities

### ■ Activity 1 New religious movements

To highlight one aspect of the variety of groups within *the category of new religious movement*, group the following organizations in relation to their theological roots: western (i.e. Judaeo-Christian), eastern (i.e. Hindu or Buddhist) or other (e.g. satanic, New Age). You will need to do some library research in order to find out more about the beliefs of these groups and their activities. It is important to be critical about your sources and the perspectives they engender:

(a) Unification Church (Moonies); (b) Scientology; (c) International Society for Krishna Consciousness (ISKCON or Hare Krishna); (d) Soka Gakkai International; (e) Children of God (also known as The Family of God or the Family); (f) Bawan Shree Rajneesh; (g) Branch Davidians (followers of David Koresh at Waco, Texas); (h) Church of Satan; (i) Findhorn Community.

Add to this list and discuss other similarities and differences between these groups in terms of their beliefs and practices.

The three classifications (western, eastern, other) are not the only ones which have been applied to religious organizations. Consider the application and methodological issues associated with the following ways of classifying religious forms: 'world religion'; 'established religion'; 'traditional religion'; 'messianic and millenarian movements'; 'official and unofficial religion'; 'popular/folk religion'.

### ■ Activity 2 Religious ceremonies

Observe a religious ceremony and give an account of the symbolic behaviour and its meaning for believers. You may choose one of the ceremonies referred to in this chapter or else a more regular religious gathering such as weekly worship or one relating to birth, marriage or death.

What norms are involved? (Describe observable forms of behaviour such as ritual, gestures, dress, speech and song.)

What values underpin these norms? (Investigate the symbolic meaning attached to forms of behaviour. Your research may involve asking participants or researching second-hand sources.)

How far do these ceremonies function to bind the community? Discuss whether such functions are more or less important in secular society.

Chapter 13

# Crime and punishment

**Chapter outline:** Introduction • The sociology of crime • The relationship between crime and deviance • The sociological study of crime • Explaining crime • The extent and pattern of crime • Controlling crime: law enforcement and the role of the police • The sociology of punishment • The aims of punishment • The sociological theory of punishment • Summary • Further reading • Activities

## Learning objectives

When you have studied this chapter you should be able to address these key questions:

- How has crime been defined and measured?
- How have sociologists tried to explain crime?
- To what extent is crime characteristic of particular social groups?
- What are the main aims of punishment?
- How have sociologists explained the role of punishment in society?

## Introduction

The study of crime begins with the knowledge of oneself. (Miller 1945)

The standards of a nation's civilisation can be judged by opening the doors of its prisons. (Dostoevsky 1860)

Unconventional and criminal behaviour fascinates people. Many popular TV programmes, successful films and bestselling books are about crime and criminals, both 'real life' and fictional. Our interest is in criminal behaviour – what it involves and how it is done – and in what happens to the criminals – whether they 'get away with it' and what happens to them if they do not. However, while we like to watch and read about crime, and many of us break laws from time to time, relatively few of us will have been caught and prosecuted for our lawbreaking behaviour and even fewer will make crime a way of life and become professional murderers, smugglers or fraudsters.

This chapter looks at both crime and punishment, at the extent of crime, why some people and social groups are more likely to engage in criminal behaviour than others, how society controls crime and how it deals with those people who are caught. The role of the police in enforcing the law and the debates surrounding punishment of offenders are discussed. Punishment is examined as a key element of the sociology of crime; this is evident in the work of Durkheim, the major 'classical' theorist in this area. Durkheim highlighted the importance of crime for maintaining the collective conscience of society and emphasized how punishment exemplified this collective conscience at work. The first section of the chapter focuses on the sociology of crime and the second section centres on the sociology of punishment.

Why do you think that there is so much interest in all aspects of crime in the mass media?

What are the differences and similarities between the depiction of fictional and real life crime on television?

# The sociology of crime

## The relationship between crime and deviance

Before looking at sociological work on crime, we need to define and clarify our subject matter, particularly as crime is often examined as part of the broader field of the sociology of deviance and the terms crime and deviance are sometimes used interchangeably. Unconventional behaviour fascinates people; such behaviour might involve breaking the law or just fall outside the commonly held definition of what is normal and reasonable. This distinction helps us to distinguish crime from deviance.

*Crime* may be defined as an act that breaks the criminal law; it can be followed by criminal proceedings and formal punishment.

*Deviance* is a less precise concept than crime: deviance means any behaviour that differs from the normal. Thus deviant behaviour could be uncommonly good or brave behaviour as well as unacceptable behaviour, such as theft or vandalism. It could also be eccentric or bizarre behaviour, such as talking loudly to oneself or to no one in particular in public places. However, deviance generally refers to behaviour that is disapproved of and subject to some form of punishment; behaviour that is outside the rules of society and leads to hostile and critical response from 'conventional society'. These rules might be legal rules – laws that have specific penalties established to punish those who break them – or social and moral rules – rules about how people should behave in public, for example.

In distinguishing between crime and deviance we have talked about breaking laws and not following conventional standards of behaviour or norms. *Norms* are the unwritten rules that influence people's behaviour. They are the ideal standards of behaviour that members of a social group share and form part of the culture of that society, such as the manner in which parents should treat their children and children their parents. Different groups within a society may have their own norms. While it is the norm in the UK to eat meat, being a vegetarian is not generally seen as unacceptable behaviour. Young people may hold quite different norms from older people and particular youth groups have norms that are distinct from other groups.

The definitions of crime and deviance as behaviour that is outside the laws or norms of society emphasize the importance of the reaction of others; such behaviour will usually produce some form of critical or hostile response from the wider society. However, laws and norms are not fixed; they vary from time to time and from place to place. Therefore behaviour which breaks them will also vary. So crime and deviance are *relative concepts*, which vary according to the particular social situation. Behaviour which is criminal in one country can be acceptable in another, for example drinking alcohol or having several spouses at the same time. Certain types of behaviour have been criminal at one period of time but not at others; homosexuality, for instance, has been decriminalized in many countries but carries the death penalty in Iran.

*Social reaction* is of central importance in determining whether behaviour is categorized as criminal or deviant. No action is criminal or deviant in itself; it becomes so only if the society defines it as such, through the legal system or through the general acceptance of certain norms of behaviour. In modern societies killing is usually seen as the most serious of offences, but in the context of war killing can be seen as heroic and people may even be punished for not wanting to take part in killing, as happened to the conscientious objectors who were imprisoned in the First World War.

Crime is behaviour that deviates from conventional, accepted behaviour and can lead to formal punishment. Many other forms of behaviour contravene norms without actually breaking the law and becoming criminal. Transvestism is not a crime but may be considered deviant. While deviance is a broader concept that encompasses crime, criminal behaviour is not always seen as deviant. Making private phone calls on an office telephone is, strictly speaking, theft, yet may be widely accepted as a 'perk' of the job.

**Case Study**

### Crime and deviance: cultural and historical relativity

It is easily observable that different groups judge different things to be deviant. This should alert us to the possibility that the person making the judgement of deviance, the process by which the judgement is arrived at, and the situation in which it is made will all be intimately involved in the phenomenon of deviance. . . .

Deviance is the product of a transaction that takes place between a social group and one who is viewed by that group as a rule breaker. Whether an act is deviant, then, depends on how people react to it. . . . The degree to which other people will respond to a given act as deviant varies greatly. Several kinds of variation are worth noting. First of all, there is variation over time. A person believed to have committed a given 'deviant' act may at one time be responded to much more leniently than he would at some other time. The occurrence of 'drives' against various kinds of deviance illustrates this clearly. (Becker 1963: 4–12)

#### Questions

**Alcohol drinking and bigamy illustrate the relative nature of crime and deviance.**

**List other types of behaviour that have been categorized as criminal or deviant in one society but not another.**

**Give examples of behaviour that has been criminal or deviant at different periods of time in the same society.**

**In looking at responses to crime and deviance Becker refers to 'drives' against certain types of behaviour. What types of crime or deviance have been subject to such drives in recent years in the UK?**

## The sociological study of crime

Crime encompasses such a vast range of activities that its sociological study is a massive and uncertain task. An unquantifiable, but clearly large, amount of crime is not generally known about. Burglars and fraudsters may not be caught; assaults, prostitution and illegal drug use occur on a far wider scale than is officially recorded. People who break the rules of society tend not to advertise themselves, which makes the study of this sort of behaviour more problematic than many other areas of sociological study. Some criminals do appear to enjoy publicity but the majority of those who commit criminal actions attempt to conceal themselves.

The secretive nature of crime raises a number of problems for those wishing to study it. First, the researcher needs to find the subjects for study. How does one go about locating a group engaged in forgery, for example? Crime often occurs in conventional situations and the researcher has to be alert to this. In *Cheats at Work* Gerald Mars (1982) studied the variety of crime in everyday work situations and found that fiddling and thieving was accepted practice in many occupations. One example that Mars cites involved 462 watch repairers being presented with an identical problem, a watch in perfect condition except for a small fault, a loose screw that could be easily tightened and that would be obvious to a scarcely trained repairer. Nearly half the sample (226 repairers) responded to this 'problem' with diagnoses that lied, overcharged or suggested extensive and unnecessary repairs; many of the repairers suggested that the watches needed a clean and overhaul, in spite of their pristine condition. Mars called this the exploiting of expertise, when one person (the expert) has knowledge that others (the customers) do not have access to. Although not rare, employee theft is usually hidden, which raises problems for research.

Second, once a group or individual has been located it is necessary to convince them that they can safely discuss their criminal behaviour with the researcher. Their confidence has to be gained and it can take months to gain the trust of a professional criminal. Research into crime is thus likely to take comparatively longer and be more expensive than research into other areas of social behaviour.

Third, the behaviour being studied is often widely condemned, which can cause moral dilemmas for the researcher over whether to reveal information that might help the authorities and could, perhaps, help prevent others from getting hurt. This problem is faced by other people who are entrusted with confidential information, such as doctors, lawyers and priests. Fourth, it is not always easy for researchers to remain neutral and objective; they may feel sympathy or disgust depending on the particular topic being studied.

Q

In view of the problems that the sociological study of crime faces, which methods of research might be most appropriate for investigating such behaviour? Why would they be appropriate?

What particular problems would be faced by the different methods?

---

## Why do most people conform?

Although people sometimes break the law, few become regular offenders and most people never commit criminal offences. So why does the majority conform? There are two basic types of social control or restraint:

- *Informal mechanisms of control* centre around the socialization process: children learn that stealing, cheating and so on are wrong.
- *Formal mechanisms of control* involve legal and formally established sanctions, such as the law, the police and punishment system.

These control mechanisms do not exert a uniform influence on all individuals or groups. This can be illustrated by considering your own behaviour. Why do you follow the laws of society? If you follow laws because you agree with them and feel them to be right, this indicates the influence of informal control mechanisms. If you follow laws because of a fear of being caught and punished, the influence of formal control mechanisms is greater. Would you steal from shops if it could be guaranteed that you would not get caught? Answers of 'yes' to this question would suggest that formal control mechanisms are the major determinant with regard to shoplifting, rather than a belief that the behaviour is wrong in itself.

Clearly it is not always easy to pinpoint exactly why we do or do not follow any particular action. Often the reasons reflect a mixture of informal and formal social controls, their relative importance varying with different circumstances. It might be very easy to steal from a friend and not get caught, but most people would feel this to be wrong. Such feelings of disapproval would perhaps not exert such a strong influence over decisions as to whether to steal from less personal, larger victims. Stealing from a small corner shop may seem more personal than stealing from a supermarket which makes vast profits and expects a certain amount of theft or 'stock shrinkage'. However, it is more 'dangerous' to steal from a supermarket in that the chances of getting caught and prosecuted will be greater in the larger store.

## Explaining crime

Explanations for why people break laws are of great public interest and over time a vast array of possible causes of crime have been suggested, such as inherited personality traits, poor housing, getting in with the 'wrong crowd' and inadequate parental control. More recently, there has been considerable controversy over the possibility raised by some scientists that individuals might have a genetic or inherited predisposition to certain types of behaviour and feelings that are more likely to result in criminal acts. But even these deterministic approaches do not deny the importance of environmental factors such as nutrition and deprivation.

Sociological theories of crime emphasize the importance of the social context: crime and criminals are viewed in relation to specific social conditions and opportunities. The review of theories in this section follows the conventional division of functionalist, interactionist and conflict-based approaches; these are broad schools of thought containing many variations and particular studies may not fall neatly into one perspective. None the less, this division does enable sociological theories to be discussed in a chronological sequence. At the risk of oversimplification, functionalist approaches were taken issue with by interactionist and conflict theories in the 1960s and 1970s. More recent theoretical approaches have included elements of the interactionist and conflict perspectives, in an attempt to avoid the limitations of one particular theoretical position.

### Functionalist theories

#### *Durkheim*

The underlying characteristic of all functionalist-based theory is the importance of shared norms and values which form the basis of social order. Durkheim argued that deviance, and crime in particular, was a normal phenomenon in society, an 'integral part of all healthy societies'. Given that crime involves breaking laws, it might seem odd to argue that it is necessary for society. The emphasis of Durkheim's argument is that crime is inevitable and can be functional. His work is looked at in more detail in relation to the punishment of crime (pp. 541–3). The box illustrates how crime can not only encourage social change but also strengthen the generally held values and rules of a society.

**Case Study**

## Crime and the collective conscience

In the first place crime is normal because a society exempt from it is utterly impossible. Crime consists of an act that offends certain very strong collective sentiments. . . . Imagine a society of saints, a perfect cloister of exemplary individuals. Crimes will there be unknown; but faults which appear venial (trivial) to the layman will create there the same scandal that the ordinary offense does in ordinary consciousness. If this society has the power to judge and punish, it will define these acts as criminal and treat them as such. For the same reason, the perfect and upright man judges his smallest failings with a severity that the majority reserve for acts more truly in the nature of an offense. . . .

Crime is, then, necessary; it is bound up with the fundamental conditions of all social life, and by that very fact it is useful, because these conditions of which it is a part are themselves indispensable to the normal evolution of morality and law. . . .

Crime itself plays a useful role in this evolution. Crime implies not only that the way remains open to necessary changes but that in certain cases it directly prepares these changes. According to Athenian law, Socrates was a criminal. However, his crime, namely, the independence of his thought, rendered a service not only to humanity but to his country. . . .

Nor is the case of Socrates unique; it is reproduced periodically in history. It would never have been possible to establish the freedom of thought we now enjoy if the regulations prohibiting it had not been violated. At that time, however, the violation was a crime. . . .

From this point of view the fundamental facts of criminality present themselves to us in an entirely new light. Contrary to current ideas, the criminal no longer seems a totally unsociable being, a sort of parasitic element. On the contrary, he plays a definite role in social life. (Durkheim 1964: 67–72)

### Questions

**What are the positive and useful functions of crime suggested by Durkheim?**

**Suggest any other social functions that crime might perform.**

**Look at press and/or television reports of a recent criminal trial and suggest (a) the values reinforced by the crime; (b) the possible social changes that might follow from that case.**

### *Structural and subcultural adaptations*

Durkheim's argument that crime is inevitable and functional does not explain the causes of crime or why certain people are more likely to engage in criminal activities than others. More recent functionalist theories, based on the notion of there being a general consensus of values and norms, have focused on and tried to explain the *causes* of criminal behaviour.

Robert Merton (1938) suggested that in situations where there is a strong emphasis on particular goals but the means for achieving these goals is not available for certain groups or individuals, *anomie* will result. This means that the rules that normally govern behaviour lose their influence and are liable to be ignored: the shared values and norms no longer determine behaviour. Merton explains criminal behaviour as resulting from a contradiction between the aspirations into which society has socialized people (the goals – in western society material success is a generally held goal) and the ways that are provided for the realization of these aspirations (the means). In devising ways of adapting to this contradiction between what they want from society and the means they have available to get it, some people will turn to criminal behaviour, such as theft. This approach explains crime in terms of the structure and culture of society, rather than in terms of the individual; it laid the ground for explanations based on the notion of subculture and the argument that certain groups will be more liable than others to engage in criminal behaviour.

Albert Cohen's (1955) study *Delinquent Boys* is generally seen as the starting-point for subcultural theories. Cohen takes issue with the view that delinquent behaviour is directly caused by the desire for material goals. Although some forms of crime and delinquency are centred on acquiring goods or money, a large amount of it is expressive (e.g. vandalism) rather than concerned with materialistic gain.

Cohen's explanation turns to the educational system. Schools, he argues, are middle-class institutions that embody middle-class values and goals. Individuals brought up in a working-class environment will be likely to desire the generally held goals, but will have less opportunity to achieve them due to educational failure. Seeing the avenues to success blocked will lead to working-class boys suffering from what Cohen termed 'status frustration'. They will be likely to reject the school system and form a delinquent subculture. Delinquent subcultures, according to Walter Miller (1958), are based on a number of 'focal concerns' that reflect the values and traditions of 'lower-class' life; these focal concerns include 'toughness', 'excitement' and 'smartness'.

The subcultural approach stresses the collective response as crucial, rather than seeing criminal behaviour as an individual response to failure, as Merton argued. As Cohen puts it:

> **Delinquency, according to this view, is not an expression or contrivance of a particular kind of personality; it may be imposed upon any kind of personality if circumstances favour intimate association with delinquent models. The process of becoming a delinquent is the same as the process of becoming, let us say, a Boy Scout. The difference lies only in the cultural pattern with which the child associates.**
> ***(Cohen 1955: 13–14)***

Another subcultural theory that stresses deprivation and develops from the work of Merton and Cohen is that of Cloward and Ohlin (1961). They argue that there is greater pressure to behave criminally on the working classes because they have less opportunity to 'succeed' by legitimate means. Working-class boys are liable to form and join delinquent subcultures, but there is more than one type of subculture. Cloward and Ohlin define these as:

- a criminal subculture where delinquency is closely connected with adult crime
- a conflict subculture which develops where links with adult crime are not well established
- a retreatist or escapist subculture.

Subcultural theories suggest that crime and delinquency can, ironically, represent conformity. In modern society there are a range of subgroups with their own subcultures that include norms, values and attitudes that differ from and conflict with those of the rest of society. Conformity within such subgroups will involve some form of deviance from and conflict with the wider society.

**Q** Delinquent subcultures are typically described as male and working class.

Can you think of examples of criminal, delinquent subcultures that do and do not fit this stereotypical picture, in terms of both class and gender?

Cloward and Ohlin refer to criminal, conflict and retreatist subcultures. Give an example of each type..

Functionalist theories can be criticized for offering explanations of crime that are too generalized. Characteristics that are common to the working class as a whole are used to explain crime. Merton (1938) highlighted the importance of restricted opportunities to achieve material goal; however, restricted opportunities are very common and most people who suffer from them do not turn to crime. A similar point can be made with regard to Cohen's (1955) notion of status frustration and Cloward and Ohlin's (1961) explanation of delinquent subcultures.

## Interactionist theories

Functionalist theories of crime tend to assume that there is a general consensus within society over what is right and wrong behaviour. The interactionist approach questions this assumption; it does not see criminals as essentially different from so-called 'normal' people. Many people commit criminal actions and it is therefore not easy to maintain a clear distinction between the criminal and non-criminal in terms of particular personal characteristics.

### *Labelling*

Labelling theory is perhaps the key aspect of the interactionist perspective. The criminal is an individual who has been labelled so by society and interactionist theory centres on the relationship, or interaction, between criminals and those bodies or individuals who define them as such.

Howard Becker's (1963) study of deviance, *Outsiders*, contains one of the most quoted statements on the labelling perspective:

> **Social groups create deviance by making rules whose infraction constitutes deviance and by applying those rules to particular people and labelling them as outsiders. From this point of view deviance is not a quality of the act a person commits, but rather a consequence of the application by others of rules and sanctions to an offender. The deviant is one to whom that label has been successfully applied; deviant behaviour is behaviour that people so label.** *(Becker 1963: 9)*

Thus labelling is a process by which individuals or groups categorize certain types of behaviour and certain individuals. A deviant or outsider is a person who has been labelled as such, which raises the question of 'Who does the labelling?' The actions and motives of those doing the labelling are of as much, if not more, concern as those of the labelled. The focus on the process of labelling raises the issue of who has the power to define and impose their definitions of right and wrong on others. Giddens (1993) puts the interactionist position succinctly:

**The labels applied to create categories of deviance thus express the power structures of society. By and large, the rules in terms of which deviance is defined, and the contexts in which they are applied, are framed by the wealthy for the poor, by men for women, by older people for younger people and by ethnic majorities for minority groups.** *(Giddens 1993: 128)*

The emphasis on labelling is due, in part, to the interactionist interest in the political nature of crime and deviance. Laws are essentially political products that reflect the power some groups in society have, a power that enables them to impose their ideas about right and wrong, normality and the like on the rest of society. Although the law applies to everyone, including the powerful, interactionists suggest that it is less frequently and vigorously applied to some people and groups: there is a selective enforcement of the law and a selective application of criminal labels.

The selective enforcement of the law was examined by Cicourel (1976) in his study of the way in which juvenile justice is administered in the USA. Cicourel found that particular groups are selected, processed and labelled as delinquent. White, middle-class youths are less likely to be identified by police and probation officers as being potential delinquents. The police are more liable to react toward those groups and individuals whom they see as being especially prone to engage in delinquent behaviour, often labelling such individuals before the actual committing of any act.

Case Study

### High jinks and hooliganism: having a smashing time

It was a lovely evening. They broke up Mr Austen's grand piano, and stamped Lord Rending's cigars into his carpet, and smashed his china, and tore up Mr Partridge's sheets, and threw the Matisse into his water-jug; Mr Sanders had nothing to break except his windows.

Evelyn Waugh's account of the activities of the Bullingdon Club at Oxford University was written in the 1920s. The recent antics of James Sainsbury and other Oxford undergraduates suggest that little has changed since then. Sainsbury, heir to £124 million-worth of his family's grocery business, went out to dinner in June at Thatcher's restaurant, near Oxford, with fellow members of the Assassin's Club. They set fire to the table cloths, smashed crockery, threw food at the walls, vomited on the carpet and tore curtains down. Sainsbury was fined £25 last week.

If James Sainsbury's hooliganism was in keeping with the traditions of his university, so was the gentle punishment which he received for his misdeeds. (When asked if he could afford the £25 fine and £25 prosecution costs, he replied: 'I expect I can manage it'.) Sean Paton, co-editor of the student newspaper *Isis*, thinks that too much fuss has been made about the Sainsbury case. 'James Sainsbury's a pretty harmless bloke,' he told me. 'He just does silly things when he's drunk. To his friends he's a pretty reasonable bloke.' Paton adds: 'I think it's all high jinks.'

Indeed, some upper-class and upper-middle-class parents actually approve of 'horseplay' (a word which is applied only to their class; when working class youths behave in a similar manner they are called juvenile delinquents). (Wheen 1982: 9)

*(box continued)*

*(box continued)*

Rules tend to be applied more to some persons than others. Studies of juvenile delinquency make the point clearly. Boys from middle class areas do not get as far in the legal process when they are apprehended as do boys from slum areas. The middle class boy is less likely, when picked up by the police, to be taken to the station; less likely when taken to the station to be booked; and it is extremely unlikely that he will be convicted and sentenced. (Becker 1963: 12–13)

### Questions

**Why might upper-class hooliganism be responded to in a different manner from working-class hooliganism, and by whom?**

**Becker and Cicourel highlight social class as a factor which influences whether or not a person is defined as criminal. What other social factors might influence such definitions? How might they do so?**

Labelling individuals will tend to mark them out. The knowledge that someone has been convicted for a violent crime, for instance, might well influence how you react to that person. Furthermore, individuals who have been labelled tend to view themselves in terms of the label and act accordingly. This produces an amplification or snowballing effect: the label becomes more firmly fixed and the person more attached to it. Interactionists argue that the social reaction, in terms of labelling, can actually increase or 'amplify' the criminal behaviour of the labelled individual.

Interactionists place great stress on social reaction; however,they do not really attempt to explain why certain actions are labelled as crimes and not others. There is little examination of who makes the rules. The relationship between power and crime is raised with regard to the selective nature of labelling, but is not really explored. Interactionism concentrates on the specific interactions between people, on the 'drama' of the police station and courtroom, without investigating the importance of the social system itself. Interactionists look at criminals, the police and the legal system without examining the power underlying the system, without examining how power and decision-making are distributed. These issues are central to the conflict explanations of crime.

## Conflict theories

### *'Classic' Marxism*

Marx did not write in detail or theorize about crime; later writers working within a Marxist framework have developed a Marxist theory of crime. From this perspective crime is seen largely as the product of capitalism, with criminal and anti-social behaviour indicative of the contradictions and problems inherent in the capitalist system. The basic motivations of capitalism, such as the emphasis on materialism and self-enrichment, encourage self-interested, anti-social and, by implication, criminal behaviour.

With regard to the control of crime, Marxists argue that the law expresses and reflects the interests of the ruling classes. Furthermore, there has been a great increase in the range of behaviour that has come under the control of the law. In their introduction to *Critical Criminology*, Taylor, Walton and Young (1975) point out that old laws have been reactivated and new laws created in order to control and contain an increasing range of behaviour seen as socially problematic. The legal system is seen as reflecting economic interests; it is seen as an instrument that supports the powerful groups in society against behaviour that threatens or interferes with their interests.

**Case Study**

**Criminal Justice and Public Order Bill 1994**

This Bill has brought massive changes to the criminal justice system. The extent of the Bill is vast. Among other things, the principle of a defendant's 'right to silence' has been withdrawn. Part five of the Bill deals with public order offences and has led to a concerted campaign of opposition. A series of clauses in the Bill will effectively criminalize sections of the community which the government feels to be 'anti-social'. It has become an offence to take part in a gathering of more than twenty people on a highway or on any land without the owner's permission. Hunt saboteurs and squatters have been criminalized, raves banned and New Age Travellers have had their sites taken away.

The Bill is a central plank of the government's policy on crime; the Conservative Party's Campaign Guide 1994 talks directly about a 'crackdown on squatters, "ravers", "New Age Travellers", and hunt saboteurs'.

An example of the way that the law reflects the interests of the powerful is the way in which the 'crime problem' tends to be equated with working-class crime, often of a fairly trivial nature, rather than the more significant, at least in financial terms, business and white-collar crime. Marxists argue that business crime is largely ignored by the legal system. There are some well-publicized exceptions, but these tend just to reinforce the impression that criminals are mainly from the working classes and that business criminals are not 'real' criminals – they are just doing 'what everyone else does'.

The way in which the legal system reflects economic interests is also illustrated by the relative power that different groups have to impose rules and their own definitions and interpretations of them on others.

> **When, for example, is a particular behaviour – like drinking liquor or smoking pot – defined as deviant or illegal and when is it viewed as an 'alternative life-style' that individuals are free to accept or reject? Formal and informal social power play major roles in this definitional process.** ***(Persell 1990: 159)***

The Marxist argument that the legal system works in the interests of the powerful and against those of the working classes is returned to in our examination of theories of punishment (pp. 544–7).

Case Study

## White-collar crime

The term white-collar crime is usually associated with scandals in the business world and sophisticated frauds. Croall (1992) adopts a broad definition of white-collar crime as 'the abuse of a legitimate occupational role which is regulated by law'. This includes occupational crimes committed by employees and corporate crime, where businesses or corporations exploit consumers and workers .

There are regular examples of notorious white-collar crimes such as the Guinness takeover in 1990, the collapse of the Bank of Credit and Commerce International in 1991 and the 'breaking' of the City of London's oldest merchant bank, Barings, in 1995. The Barings case involved Nick Leeson, one of the bank's general managers and the head of its futures operation in Singapore, allegedly entering into a series of fraudulent trades involving fictitious client accounts to try and cover up for substantial losses he had made on behalf of Barings. White-collar crime can also encompass 'accidents' like the sinking of the ferry, the *Herald of Free Enterprise*, in 1987. The ferry had sailed from Zeebrugge with its bow doors open – something that should have been checked before the ship left port – and over 100 people were drowned when it sank. The ferry's owners, Townsend Thoreson, had a poor safety record. Although it could be argued that these kinds of crimes are more serious and damaging to society than conventional crimes like burglary, white-collar crime tends not to be seen as part of a 'crime problem'. The public are more concerned about and afraid of being mugged or burgled than they are of being misled by bogus adverts or killed on a ferry. This is not to say that white-collar crime is ignored, but the media and public focus tends to be on the more spectacular frauds involving millions of pounds or on cases involving well-known personalities (Ken Dodd or Lester Piggot, for example).

Croall (1992) describes the considerable scope of fraud:

- *Tax evasion* commonly referred to as a perk. Often law-abiding taxpayers condone tax evasion by paying for services 'cash in hand'.
- *Trade description offences* the false description of goods, misleading bargain offers and other deceptive practices.
- *Weights and measures offences* including deceptive packaging and short measures.
- *Food and drugs offences* selling 'unfit' food.

Although unaware of it, most of us are probably multiple victims of white-collar crime. Many offences are commonplace and there is a thin line between normal trading and fraud and deception.

## Questions

How does the relative power of different groups in society influence the way in which the following activities are viewed: (a) prostitution; (b) social security fraud; (c) providing false information to tax inspectors.

Why might business crimes and criminals be treated differently from other forms of crime?

Give an example of each type of fraud listed by Croall: (a) tax evasion; (b) trade description offences; (c) weights and measures offences; (d) food and drugs offences.

How often have you or your family been victims (or perpetrators) of these frauds?

### *New criminology and recent conflict approaches*

Marxist explanations suggest that capitalism produces the conditions that generate criminal behaviour. Crime occurs because of economic deprivation and because of the contradictions that are apparent in capitalist societies. Working-class crime is a 'rebellion' against inequality and against a system that uses the legal process – including the law, the police, courts and prison – as weapons in a class war.

A number of writers who adopt a broadly conflict perspective have criticized the 'left idealism' of the basic Marxist approach and have developed a realistic approach to law and order. Lea and Young (1984) argue that, in contrast to the left idealist view, crime really is a problem for the working classes. This is not to deny the impact of crimes of the powerful, but to suggest that the working classes are most often the victims of crime – both crimes of the powerful and working-class or 'street' crime. In street crime there is an overlap between victims and offenders with the working class forming the great majority of both groups. As Young (1992: 146) suggests, 'it is difficult to romanticize this type of crime as some kind of disguised attack on the privileged'. The 'left realist' approach also highlights the widespread consensus there is about crime. Most people of all social classes are offended by rape, robbery, drug smuggling and so on; there is little evidence that the working classes see crime as a rebellion against the inequalities of capitalism.

Young and Mathews (1992) distinguish between what they term the realist and the radical positions. The classic Marxist approach is linked with radical notions that the criminal justice system does not work in the interests of the mass of working people and should therefore be abolished. A more accountable and efficient system of justice is not possible nor is it really desirable; the legal system is just another aspect of ruling-class domination that should be smashed.

This left radical view has been attacked by sociologists and criminologists writing from the left realist position. Left realists point to the injustices that marginalize sections of the population and encourage crime. However, they realize that there are no magical solutions. Only socialist intervention will reduce the causes of crime fundamentally as these causes are rooted in social inequality; only a genuinely democratic police force will provide greater safety in the community. Young and Mathews (1992) point out that poor people pay dearly for inadequate protection; there is a need for an adequate criminal justice system that works in the interests of all social groups. Left realism is advocated as a social democratic approach to the analysis of crime and the development of effective policies to control it.

**Q** **How might left realists and left radicals respond to initiatives such as neighbourhood watch schemes and community policy?**

We have introduced a number of theories which have attempted to explain criminal behaviour. All of them contain important insights and elements of 'truth', but it is unrealistic to expect to discover an ultimate explanation for such behaviour given the diverse range of activities encompassed by the term crime. Why should an explanation for fraud by wealthy business people also provide an explanation for football hooliganism or burglary committed by drug addicts, for example?

## The extent and pattern of crime

Official crime statistics in Britain are published by the Home Office and provide data on criminal offences recorded by the police. They play an important part in influencing government policies toward crime and its treatment. This section begins with a brief review of the trends in officially recorded criminal behaviour and then examines some of the problems associated with the use of crime statistics.

### What do official crime statistics measure?

There are hundreds of possible offences ranging from murder to not paying one's TV licence. Recorded offences generally include only *notifiable offences*. These are the more serious offences; illegal parking, minor assaults, licence evasion and speeding, for example, are not notifiable. Notifiable offences are a measure of the number of crimes that are recorded by the police. It is not a measure of the real level of crime: many offences are not reported to the police, while others are not recorded if the police do not feel that there is enough evidence that a crime has been committed. Unrecorded crime is known as the 'dark figure of crime'. So official crime statistics provide only a partial picture of crime committed. Crime recording can start only when someone reports an offence to the police or when the police themselves discover an offence.

The official statistics indicate that there is an ever increasing rate of crime. Recorded offences in England and Wales rose from around 3 million in 1981 to over 5.5 million in 1993 (*Social Trends* 1995). However, the rate of increase did slow down in the 1992–3 period; the increase of 3.8 per cent was the lowest in four years. Over half of all recorded crimes were burglaries or car-related thefts. About one in twenty were violent offences with robberies (theft from a person, like mugging) amounting to just under 1 per cent of crime (Denscombe 1994).

The increase in recorded crime is not a recent trend. Radzinowicz and King (1977) found that the police in England and Wales recorded fewer than three crimes per thousand of the population in 1900; by 1974 they recorded four crimes per hundred of the population – a thirteen-fold increase in just over seventy years. Although the increases in crime appear startling, it is important to bear in mind that concerns over 'crime waves' are not new. The streets of London and other cities in the mid-nineteenth century were not havens of safety, ideally suited for a night-time stroll. Robbery and violence were commonplace, as the stories of Charles Dickens and other writers illustrate. Although official statistics demonstrate a rapid increase in crime, violent crime is not a modern problem.

### Problems with crime statistics

Although official crime statistics do not measure the real amount of crime, they are the basis for people's ideas about crime and criminals. The 'facts' about crime quoted in the media are assumed to provide an accurate picture of the extent of criminality.

The official statistics are the end result of a series of decisions by victims, the police and the courts about what action to take in particular situations; they are 'socially constructed'. The relationship between the real and recorded rates of crime is complex. Some indication of the gap between them can be seen by contrasting the official figures with those provided by the British Crime Surveys, which ask people, among other things, whether they have been victims of crime and if so what crimes. The British Crime Survey (Hough and Mayhew 1993) estimated that the amount of crime is at least three times as great as the figure from police records. While this might seem alarming the main reason people gave for not reporting offences to the police was that they considered them too trivial to waste police time. It is reasonable to assume that a much higher proportion of serious offences is known about by the police and included in the official statistics. The degree to which official statistics underestimate the actual level of crime depends, therefore, on the particular category of crime. Virtually all stolen cars are reported for the simple reason that this is the only way owners will get insurance compensation.

Reasons why the official statistics underestimate the amount of criminal activity include

- victims being unaware that they are victims of specific crimes
- victims feeling that there is no point in informing the police
- victims dealing with the matter informally, outside of the legal system
- victims' embarrassment
- victims (or witnesses of a crime) not liking or trusting the police
- crimes without victims – all parties involved in a crime not wishing the police to know about it.

Give an example of a criminal activity which is liable to be unrecorded for each of these six reasons.

Why are these offences unlikely to become official statistics: (a) fraud; (b) drug dealing; (c) incest?

What problems might there be with the use of crime surveys to find out about rates of crime?

## The social incidence of crime

Official statistics indicate that criminal behaviour is not randomly distributed throughout the whole population; some social groups commit more crime than others. Two aspects of the social incidence of crime are the relationship between crime and gender and that between crime and ethnicity.

### *Crime and gender*

There is a strong link between gender and both the rate of recorded crime and crime survey data. All the data indicate that crime is an activity carried out mainly by males. Over 80 per cent of those convicted of serious offences in England and Wales are males: in 1992 close to 438,000 male offenders and 101,000 female offenders were convicted (*Social Trends* 1994). The proportion of men and women offending varies according to the offence. The most common offences for both sexes are thefts. Shoplifting is often thought of as the 'typical' female crime but more males than females are convicted of it: '40 per cent of the convicted are female [but] many more women than men are shoppers, so that the proportion of women shoppers who shoplift is smaller' (Hart 1985: 299). Women commit fewer crimes of violence. In 1993 just over 34,000 man aged 21 or over were found guilty of, or cautioned for, crimes of 'violence against the person', compared to just over 4,500 women (*Social Trends* 1995: 160). In Britain, out of a prison population of around 50,000, fewer than 1,500 (3 per cent) are female.

With regard to the control of crime, women are also under-represented in the criminal justice system. In 1991 they made up one in four of the recruits to the police forces in England and Wales and out of 1,736 full-time and part-time judges, only 92 (5.3 per cent) were women (Denscombe 1992, 1993).

*Why do women commit less crime?*

Heidensohn (1989) points out that in spite of the clear and persistent differences in rates of male and female criminality, it is only since the 1970s that sociological and criminological attention has turned to this issue.

Prior to this, explanations focused on the biological and/or psychological make-up of women. These studies, often written by men, argued that female biology determines their personality and makes them more passive and timid and therefore less likely to commit crime, which is an aggressive activity. The relatively few female criminals were seen as suffering from some sort of physical or mental pathology. In 1895 Lombroso and Ferrero argued that women were naturally less inclined to crime than men, and that those who did commit crimes were not 'really' feminine. Explanations emphasizing the physiological bases for females criminality remained popular up to the 1960s (Cowie *et al.* 1968).

Sociological explanations have focused on the expectations and constraints that are placed on women by society. The different role expectations for women and men lead to different patterns of socialization. Men, rather than women, learn the skills that are usually connected with certain types of criminal activities. Boys play with guns, learn how to fight and are more likely to be socialized for active and aggressive behaviour. Burglary, for example, is an untypical female crime. It requires the crimi-

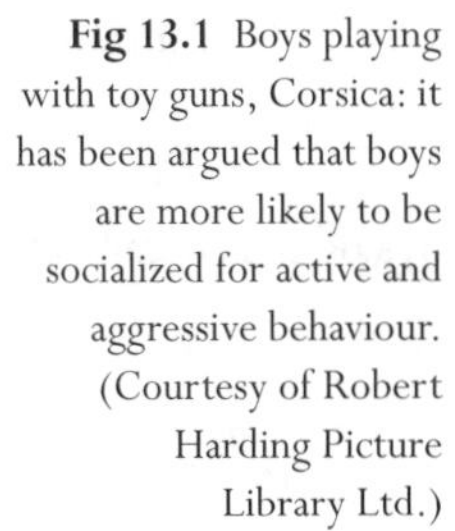
**Fig 13.1** Boys playing with toy guns, Corsica: it has been argued that boys are more likely to be socialized for active and aggressive behaviour. (Courtesy of Robert Harding Picture Library Ltd.)

nal to be out alone on the streets at night, and to possess 'masculine skills' associated with being able to force an entry. However, 'women have got sufficient strength and skills to commit all sorts of offences which they hardly ever do commit. One does not need much strength to mug a small and frail old lady' (Hart 1985: 299).

It has been argued that women, and girls in particular, are subject to stronger social control than are men and boys. Girls are 'taught law-abiding behaviour and are expected to be non-violent, cooperative and docile' (Hart 1985: 300). Girls are expected to conform to a stricter morality by their parents and also by their peers (girls have to keep their 'reputations' in a way that does not apply to boys). Adolescent girls are likely to be allowed less freedom to go out and stay out than are their male peers. This will limit the opportunities they have to become involved in criminal and delinquent behaviour.

Heidensohn (1989) summarizes the impact of feminist criminology on the study of women and crime. A major area of interest has been the criminal justice system and the alleged bias in favour of women – the 'chivalry' idea that male police officers and judges treat female offenders more sympathetically than they do male offenders. Heidensohn dismisses this idea and suggests that women offenders are more stigmatized than men. Courts treat them as doubly deviant, as being both unfeminine and criminal by breaking laws. The social consequences of this can be women offenders losing their children, homes and partners. In examining reasons for the low rate of female crime, feminists have warned of the dangers of looking for all-embracing explanations. Women's criminality, like men's, is mainly instrumental and related to economic goals; women can and do commit all crimes, including very serious, sometimes horrific, crimes such as terrorism and child murders.

On the whole, domestic violence is perpetrated by men against women and children. Awareness of the problems of wife battering, child abuse and sexual assault has grown in the 1990s due in part, to the work of feminist sociologists (see p. 421). There has also been concern about the different ways that women and men are treated by the courts, for example men who kill a 'nagging' wife have been given derisory sentences in comparison with women sentenced to life imprisonment for killing long-term violent husbands.

**Q** **Do you agree that girls are subject to stricter social control than boys by their families?**

**Give examples from your own experiences.**

**Does this continue into adulthood?**

### *Crime and ethnicity*

Black males are much more likely to go to prison than white males; although 6 per cent of males over 21 are from ethnic minority groups, 17 per cent of male prisoners over 21 are from these groups. This over-representation in prison does not apply to all ethnic minority groups but is particularly the case for those of Afro-Caribbean origin.

With regard to policing and the criminal justice system, ethnic minorities are even less represented than women. In 1991 just over 1,000 of the 128,000 police in England and Wales (0.8 per cent) and only 6 out of 1,736 judges (0.3 per cent) were from ethnic minority backgrounds (Denscombe 1992, 1993). Similarly, only 0.1 per cent of senior

**Table 13.1** Prison population rates in England and Wales by ethnic origin (rate per 10,000 population).

| | Males | Females | All |
|---|---|---|---|
| White | 19.4 | 0.5 | 9.6 |
| West Indian, Guyanese, African | 144.0 | 9.9 | 76.7 |
| Indian, Pakistani, Bangladeshi | 24.3 | 0.4 | 12.4 |
| Other/not disclosed | 72.1 | 5.4 | 38.3 |
| All ethnic origins | 22.0 | 0.7 | 11.0 |

*Source: Social Trends 24* 1994: 162

barristers are Black (*Labour Research*, August 1992). In the USA, 36 states have executed people since the ban on the death penalty was overturned in 1976. Black people are much more likely to be executed than whites. Only 12 per cent of the US population are Black, but 39 per cent of those executed have been Black (*Guardian* 23 July 1994).

**Case Study**

### Crime and different ethnic minority groups

The sociological study of crime and ethnicity should acknowledge that different ethnic minority groups have varying propensities to offend and differing relationships with the criminal justice systems. Most discussion of the crime and race issue has concentrated on Afro-Caribbeans and ignored other ethnic minority groups. Moore (1988) summarizes explanations for the low levels of criminality in Asian groups:

1 *Greater economic success* Asians, particularly Indians, have been relatively successful in business and commerce and are more likely to be in employment. Therefore, they suffer less from the marginality experienced by other young Blacks.
2 *Stronger family and community* Asian families exert strict control over family members, which can limit the opportunities for criminal activities. In contrast, West Indian youths are more likely to leave their homes earlier and be free from the influence of close family ties.
3 *Different cultures* Asian cultures are clearly distinct from mainstream British culture and Asians are perhaps less likely to feel resentful about the difficulties they face in becoming part of this mainstream culture. Lea and Young (1984) argued that young West Indians feel more bitter when they are not accepted by the wider culture and are consequently more likely to turn to crime.

*Explanations for the relationship between crime and ethnicity*

First, some of the difference in crime rates between whites and Blacks may be due to *demographic factors*: there is a greater proportion of young people among ethnic minority populations and Black people are more likely to live in poor inner city areas. However, research which has isolated age and socio-economic variables has indicated that such factors cannot be used to explain the higher rate of crime among West Indians (Stevens and Willis 1979, cited in Moore 1988).

Second, there may be some *racial prejudice within the police*, but this could not completely explain differences in police arrest rates. The fact that the vast majority of serious crimes are reported by the victims rather than initiated by the police will limit the police's influence on reported crime rates.

Third, *race and political struggle* are rooted in Britain's colonial history. Britain controlled its colonial populations through force, slavery and 'education'. When immigrants from the former colonies were recruited to work in Britain in the 1950s, the conditions of the colonies were reproduced in the British inner cities. Black crime is seen as a continuation of the struggle against colonialism; the activities of young Blacks are a form of rebellion. Crime is, then, a form of politics, a form of organized resistance (Moore 1988). However, there is little evidence that Black people commit crime as a form of political struggle. Black youth appear to be as conformist to the values of the wider society as other young people. As Moore (1988) puts it, 'One must be suspicious when "experts" can read meaning into behaviour that the actual participants are totally unaware of'.

Fourth, Black people have been *marginalized* due to their lack of opportunities to achieve financial success; this encourages some of them to turn to crime. Cashmore (1984) argued that young Blacks faced a situation where their aspirations (for consumer goods) were not matched by the reality of their economic situation (high unemployment rates). The outcome is that they are drawn into criminality. Again, this explanation lumps all young Blacks together and does not take account of the variety of responses; only a small proportion of those who cannot achieve financial success turn to crime.

Having looked at possible explanations for crime and the extent and distribution of recorded crime we shall now focus on the control of crime; we shall look briefly at the role of the police before examining in greater detail the punishment of crime.

## Controlling crime: law enforcement and the role of the police

In looking at why most people conform, we discussed two basic types of social control – informal and formal social control (see pp. 513–14). The police are part of the formal control mechanisms of modern society. They are not the only agency of formal control; customs and excise, private security firms, store detectives and regulatory bodies such as factory inspectorates are all able to exert formal control over others. However, the police have a decisive role as the 'last resort' in the process of social control. The police tend to be seen, and to see themselves, as the 'thin, blue line' protecting the majority of respectable citizens. The division between informal and formal social control is not absolute; although the police are the most visible agent of formal social control, much of their work is carried out in an informal manner. There is a considerable degree of flexibility and discretion in police work.

### The police and the public

The police are a segregated group in society. Public opinion varies from suspicion to hostility, and a major police problem appears to be relations with the public. The Policy Studies Institute (PSI) report *The Police and People in London* (1983) indicated that roughly half of the London population had serious doubts about the standard of police conduct. Everyday interaction between the police and public tends to do little to improve relations. Traffic patrol, for instance, provides many people with their only direct contact with the police; the attitude that 'they should be catching criminals not bothering me' would seem to be widely held.

Definition

### The clearance rate

**The clearance rate is the percentage of crimes solved out of those reported. It is the main official means of measuring the success and efficiency of the police and of comparing different police forces. If a particular police force or division had a 50 per cent clearance rate it would be solving ('clearing up') 50 per cent of the crimes reported to it. Thus, the higher the clearance rate the more efficient that police force is seen to be.**

### Questions

**The clearance rate varies from offence to offence. What kinds of offences will have the highest clearance rates and what the lowest? Give reasons for your answers.**

**What problems are there with using clearance rates as a measure of police efficiency?**

Police officers' relative social isolation encourages strong inter-group solidarity and mutual dependence which tends to further their segregation. Occupational groups often mix together and have some measure of self-identification, but the police have a particularly high degree of occupational solidarity. This segregation encourages the development of a special code and subculture within the police, which we examine in our discussion of the PSI report (pp.530–1).

As well as conflict with the public, relations between the police and the legal system are not always easy. The British legal system depends on the rule of law and the supremacy of Parliament (which makes the laws), and the police are required to maintain order under the rule of law. There is, though, a basic tension between the concepts of order and legality. Criminal law presumes innocence until guilt is proved. The police, however, tend to presume guilt. When arresting someone, the police officer will believe the suspect to be guilty. Furthermore, the police are likely to feel that the legal process makes their task increasingly difficult. The presumption of innocence is the first in a series of restrictions: the police are interested in actual guilt, which they believe they can recognize, rather than legal guilt. Court decisions to dismiss charges are likely to especially annoy the police, who will have spent time and effort bringing the case to court. When in court police officers face something of a role reversal in that they are subject to cross-examination, whereas they are usually questioning suspects themselves.

## The organization of modern policing

Effective policing depends on receiving information: the vast majority of crimes are reported to the police by the public. The investigative policing common on TV portrayals is not the norm. However, the extent to which the police and public work together varies according to the style of policing; since the 1970s there have been two distinct styles that seem to pull in opposed directions.

Case Study

## The police and people in London

The Policy Studies Institute (1983) report into the Metropolitan Police force is a detailed examination of the world of the police officer in London. It highlighted various aspects of 'police culture'.

### A desire for action

In contrast to the image of police work as exciting and dangerous (an image which the police themselves tend to stress), for most police officers, patrolling was invariably boring and somewhat aimless. A considerable amount of police behaviour can best be understood as a search for some interest or excitement. Officers on patrol might spend whole shifts without doing any police work apart from providing simple information. Even car patrolling might involve hours of doing nothing while waiting for calls. Occasionally a patrol car will be rushing from one call to another, but such occasions are unusual. This boredom and aimlessness is not apparent in popular portrayals of police work in the media, where there is a natural concentration on the interesting bits. One result is that car crews compete with each other to answer calls that sound interesting. Car chases offer the kind of excitement which bored patrol officers are looking for.

The desire for action is illustrated by the comment of one young police officer:

> I liked [the Grunwick union dispute] best of all. It was such a fair, clean fight. The unions got all these blokes in from all over the country, they were a really tough lot, not rubbish mind you, but a good class of demonstrator. They had a go at us and we had a go at them. . . . When it was all over I felt like shaking hands with the opposition and thanking them for such a good contest.

Another officer recounted how much he enjoyed the Southall race riots of 1981:

> It was a great day out, fighting the Pakis. It ought to be an annual fixture. I thoroughly enjoyed myself.

While some of this talk might be exaggerated, many police officers do not appear to object to occasional violent confrontations. And the comment on Southall illustrates another aspect of police culture – racism.

### Racism

Racialist language was used by the police in a casual, almost automatic way and was commonly used over the personal radio. The report's authors heard one inspector say over the radio, 'Look I've got a bunch of coons in sight'. The report found that Black people (but not Asians) were much more likely to be stopped by the police than white people.

### Masculinity

The report describes a 'cult of masculinity' in the police force which has strong influence on police officers' attitudes to women and toward sexual offences. Most of the women police officers interviewed felt that there was a prejudice against them; they felt that the importance of physical strength in police work was greatly over-emphasized and that they were regularly excluded from more interesting kinds of police work. Many of the women officers have had to accept these attitudes. One recounted how an inspector at training school had said to her, 'Why don't you admit it, you're only here to get a husband, aren't you?' She had 'let it run off her back'.

*(box continued)*

*(box continued)*

**Solidarity**

There is a strong sense of solidarity among police officers and particularly among the small groups who work together. Calls for urgent assistance from police officers are always met with a massive and immediate response – all available cars would dash to answer such calls. However, this solidarity encourages officers to cover up for colleagues. On being asked whether he would 'shop' a colleague who had seriously assaulted a prisoner, one sergeant responded:

> No, I never would. If one of the boys working for me got himself into trouble, I would get us all together and I would literally script him out of it. I would write all the parts out and if we followed them closely we couldn't be defeated. And believe me, I would do it.

When questioned a bit further on his attitude, he said that the disciplinary system was unfair and he wouldn't stand by and let someone lose their job.

**Questions**

How might the sort of police culture described above influence (a) the way the police carry out their job; (b) their relations with the public?

Do you think police officers should be subject to stricter rules of behaviour than other people?

### *Community or consensus policing*

The community sees the police as doing a socially useful job and supports them. This style is characterized by foot patrols, juvenile liaison schemes, neighbourhood watch and a generally 'softer' approach from the police. Here the police are likely to receive useful information from the public.

### *Military or 'fire-brigade' policing*

Essentially this style of policing is without consent and with some hostility from the community. It is reactive and involves the use of guns, CS gas, surveillance technology and so on. The flow of information to the police is likely to be minimal and an important part of police activity will be random stopping and questioning. The police tend to concentrate on those people they feel to be 'typical criminals'; they make maximum use of stereotypes.

Heidensohn (1989) suggests that from the 1970s there has been a changed context of policing. A number of events have led to a distancing of the police from the public and have perhaps encouraged the spread of the military style of policing – events such as the inner-city riots of the early 1980s, the miners' strike of 1984–5 and various scandals and exposures of corruption within the police. Waddington (1993) points to the pressures that have tended to push contemporary policing toward the military style. It is difficult to prevent the continuation of 'fire-brigade' policing due to the subcultural emphasis on action and excitement; while 'the police persist in rushing from one reported incident to the next and spend little time in the proactive business of fostering links with the community' (Waddington 1993: 18).

**Fig 13.2** Police line at an anti-poll tax demonstration, Cheltenham. (Courtesy of Robert Harding Picture Library Ltd.)

**Q** We have suggested that the police tend to have a picture of the stereotypical criminal.

What sort of person do you think the police see as the 'typical criminal'?

What is your attitude to the police? Is it based on stereotypes?

## The sociology of punishment

In this section we shall look at the relationship between crime, punishment and society. The examination of punishment as a social phenomenon provides a broader approach than that of 'penology', which focuses on the workings of specific institutions of punishment. Although punishment occurs in various social contexts – in the family, at school and at work, for instance – our focus is on punishment in the legal system.

The legal punishment of offenders is a complex process that involves law making, conviction, sentencing and administering penalties. The sociological examination of punishment has, therefore, to be wide ranging. Legal punishment can have various aims although its major purpose is to reduce the rate of crime. Punishment is seen as a means to an end, of controlling crime. Given that crimes still occur, and in ever greater numbers, it could be argued that punishment has 'failed', but it is probably unrealistic to expect punishment to control crime.

Until the mid-twentieth century the main aim of punishment was to punish wrongdoers and there was little attempt to reform those who had offended. Punishments tended to be quick, harsh and public, with little pity wasted on lawbreakers.

During the 1950s and 1960s in Britain, reform and rehabilitation became key elements in what Garland (1990) has termed the 'ideological framework' of punishment. They provided a sense of purpose and justification for punishment, reflected in the introduction of a number of a new methods of punishment. Parole and suspended prison sentences were established by the Criminal Justice Act 1967 and community service orders and day training centres by the 1972 Act. These measures greatly extended the role of the Probation Service, which played a major role in many of the new initiatives that aimed to reduce and avoid custodial punishments: probation officers were responsible for supervising offenders on probation, parole, suspended sentences and community service orders.

In the 1970s optimism gave way to a general scepticism. Rising crime rates and the high percentage of criminals who reoffended raised doubts about the efficiency of 'modern' punishment. The emphasis moved away from reform; in 1980 'short, sharp, shock' sentences were introduced in detention centres and senior politicians advocated a hard-line approach to punishment. In 1991 51,083 males entered prison; information on previous convictions was not available for 31,348 of these prison 'receptions', but 12,443 of the remainder had served six or more previous sentences – over 24 per cent of the total figure (Home Office data, *Annual Abstract of Statistics*, 1994). These kinds of figures and concerns have reopened questions about the aims of punishment.

**Case Study**

## The politics of punishment: hard vs soft approaches

In the political arena, the debate about punishment has tended to polarize around the 'hard' versus 'soft' positions. Home Secretary Michael Howard was a strong advocate for the 'hard' position:

> Prison works . . . it makes many who are tempted to commit crime think twice. . . . This may mean that more people will go to prison. I do not flinch from that. We shall no longer judge the success of our system of justice by a fall in our prison population.
>
> (Michael Howard, Conservative Party Conference, October 1993)

As well as being out of line with his recent (Conservative) predecessors as Home Secretary – Kenneth Clarke, Kenneth Baker, David Waddington, Douglas Hurd, Leon Brittan and William Whitelaw all favoured a reduction in prison sentences, for minor offenders at least – Howard's comments have been criticized by those centrally involved in the running of our prisons. Lord Woolf, author of the government's prison reform programme, has said that sending more people to prison is the easy answer to concerns over increasing crime and would increase the likelihood of prison disturbances and riots. The former Director General of the prison service, Derek Lewis, criticized the Home Secretary's call for stricter, more austere prisons and stated that he would not abandon the rehabilitative role of prisons.

This hard-line approach tends to be popular with the general public and with certain sections of the mass media. Perceived 'softness' on crime tends to be seen as a sign of political weakness. In the face of the evidence (and reporting ) of horrific crimes it is easy to see how hard-line, 'hang them high' approaches to punishment gain considerable sympathy and support.

The hard-line approach to punishment was highlighted by Prime Minister John Major's comment on the supposedly lenient treatment of juvenile offenders serving custodial sentences, that 'we should understand a little less and condemn more.'

### Questions

Make a case for and against sending more offenders to prison.

What are the arguments for and against alternative methods of punishment?

Look at the quote from Dostoevsky (p.510). Do you think that the way in which lawbreakers are punished tells us something about a society? Give reasons for your answer.

## The aims of punishment

We shall discuss five aims of punishment:

- deterrence
- retribution
- rehabilitation
- incapacitation
- reparation.

### Deterrence

The utilitarian approach to punishment focuses on its 'usefulness' for society (utilitarianism is a doctrine that the value of anything is determined solely by its utility). If punishments deter offenders from reoffending or discourage other people from offending in the first place then their utility is apparent. There are two basic ways in which deterrence can work, described by Cavadino and Dignan (1993) as individual deterrence and general deterrence. *Individual deterrence* is when offenders find their punishment so unpleasant that they never repeat the offence for fear of that punishment. *General deterrence* is when offenders are punished not only to deter them from reoffending but also to encourage others not to commit similar offences. As the focus of deterrence is on frightening people into not offending, it is associated with severe penalties, such as long prison sentences.

While the theory of individual deterrence – that people 'refrain from action because they dislike what they believe to be the possible consequences of those actions' (Walker 1991) – seems plausible, it does not work well in practice. Offenders who have been subject to harsh punishments should, in theory, be less likely to reoffend than similar offenders who received a less severe punishment. In practice the reverse seems to occur. The introduction of much stricter regimes in detention centres in the early 1980s had no effect on the reconviction rates of young offenders. Cavadino and Dignan point to research that suggests that offenders who suffer more severe penalties are *more* likely to reoffend: 'harsher penalties . . . could help foster a tough, "macho" criminal self-image in the young men who predominate in the criminal statistics' (1993: 34). This is not to argue that no offender is ever deterred by a harsh punishment but that there are other effects of punishment which will have a greater influence on offenders.

Walker (1991) suggests that the notion of deterrence with regard to punishment is imprecise. Are individuals deterred if they refrain from committing an offence at one time but then commit the same offence later, or in another place? The sight of a police car might deter the burglar for that particular night or the burglar might move to another street. Whether this sort of 'displacement' could be classified as deterrence is, Walker argues, rather doubtful.

The potential punishment is not the only factor influencing the would-be offender. Walker suggests that 'on-the-spot deterrents' that pose practical difficulties, such as effective security, high walls, large dogs and the like, will have a greater deterrent effect. More remote consequences, such as the 'stigma' of being known as a shoplifter, may also be deterrents.

Deterrence involves the individual weighing up a range of possible consequences of committing an offence, but it would 'work' only if that individual was tempted to offend in the first place; a person who is not tempted cannot be deterred. Walker (1991) argues that the key factor in assessing the effectiveness of deterrent punishments is that the person believes in the deterring consequences; some people will be deterred by quite remote possibilities. Walker uses the example of many parents not immunizing their children against whooping cough because of a minimal risk of brain damage. The effectiveness of deterrence can vary as the individual's state of mind varies. Normally law-abiding people might become undeterrable when sufficiently angry, drunk or jealous, and commit offences from which they would usually be deterred.

The fear of being caught and stigmatized is enough to deter some people from committing any offence and the degree of harshness of the punishment attached to an offence is irrelevant. Others see punishment as part of the risk: 'if you can't do the time, don't do the crime'. Punishments can have some deterrent effect. If life imprisonment was the standard sentence for shoplifting or exceeding the speed limit, the rate of such offences would probably be significantly reduced. Cavadino and Dignan (1993) refer to the deportation of the entire Danish police force by the German occupiers for several months during the Second World War leading to a spectacular rise in rates of theft and robbery in Denmark. However, aside from such extreme examples *there is little evidence that the type or severity of punishment has much influence as a general deterrent*. This argument is supported by the example of a Birmingham youth receiving a twenty-year detention sentence for a mugging offence in 1973. This exceptional punishment attracted plenty of media attention, yet research comparing rates of mugging before and after that sentence, in Birmingham, Liverpool and Manchester, found that it had no effect on the rate of such offences.

**Q**

**Do exemplary sentences work?**

**Which of the following crimes have you committed?**

- theft of stationery or similar from the workplace
- using TV without a licence
- possession of illegal drugs
- buying goods that may have been stolen
- theft of a car
- drinking in a pub while under age

**What would deter you from committing such crimes?**

The old saying 'might as well be hanged for a sheep as a lamb' suggests that too severe a punishment for a relatively minor offence might drive the offender into committing more serious offences. Although offenders always run the risk of being caught, the chances of getting away with an offence (the amount of unrecorded and unsolved crime indicate these chances are pretty good) will greatly weaken the deterrent effect of any punishment.

The probability of conviction – offenders' own estimate of whether they will 'get away with it' – is a key influence on whether a particular offence is committed. The actual punishment seems to have less influence as a general deterrent than the offenders' estimation of the likelihood of detection.

### *Capital punishment*

Capital punishment is the ultimate form of deterrence. Those who advocate the reintroduction of capital punishment for murder have argued that the death penalty would have a deterrent effect and lead to a reduction in serious crime. The view that capital punishment must be a better deterrent than any other penalty presupposes that the potential murderer rationally calculates the advantages and disadvantages of murder and is therefore deterrable. However, an estimated three-quarters of murders are committed on impulse, perhaps in a fit of rage or during a fight. Furthermore, it is questionable whether the supposedly rational murderer – for instance, the terrorist or armed robber – is so easily deterrable. They will tend to think that they have a good chance of getting away with their crime, and, particularly in the case of politically motivated murderers, they will often have some form of organization to help them escape detection.

It is possible that capital punishment does act as a deterrent in some cases, but it is difficult to recognize when deterrence works. There is little evidence that long-term imprisonment deters would-be murderers any less than capital punishment. There are other arguments concerning capital punishment that have nothing to do with its deterrent potential, including the belief that murder is so wicked that the death penalty is the only proper response, which illustrates the retributionary aim of punishment (see pp. 538–9). These beliefs may account for the fact that in a MORI poll carried out in 1994, 72 per cent were in favour of reintroducing the death penalty, 24 per cent were opposed to it and 4 per cent unsure.

**Case Study**

#### Capital punishment: China and the USA

**Executions are still commonplace in many countries, as these findings from Amnesty International on China and the USA illustrate.**

**Chinese secrets**

Hundreds – possibly thousands – of people were executed in China in 1993. Official figures for death sentences and executions are regarded by the Chinese authorities as a 'state secret', making it impossible to know the true numbers. But from January to November 1993, Amnesty International recorded 1,249 executions. . . .

The actual number is certainly much higher. The number of death sentences and executions appears to rise during anti-crime campaigns and on key dates – such as 26 June, International Day against Drug Abuse and Trafficking, and in January as the Chinese New Year festival approaches – a warning to potential offenders.

. . . One third of all criminal offences in Chinese law carry the death penalty. Defendants are not presumed innocent and many prisoners sentenced to death are publicly displayed at mass sentencing rallies which take place at football grounds before they are executed, with rally tickets available in advance from selected Hong Kong outlets. Condemned prisoners are then put on open lorries, and driven straight from the rally to the execution grounds with placards around their necks which announce their crimes. Then they are shot.

(*Amnesty International Bulletin* March/April 1994)

*(box continued)*

*(box continued)*

**US state executions**

**1993 was a bumper year for executions. To the end of November, 35 people had been killed by the state, with at least three more executions scheduled for December. The total was the highest for any year since the death penalty was reintroduced in the US in the mid-1970s, beating 1992's record of 31 deaths.**

(*Amnesty International Journal* Jan/Feb 1994)

**Fig 13.3** US States that have the death penalty.

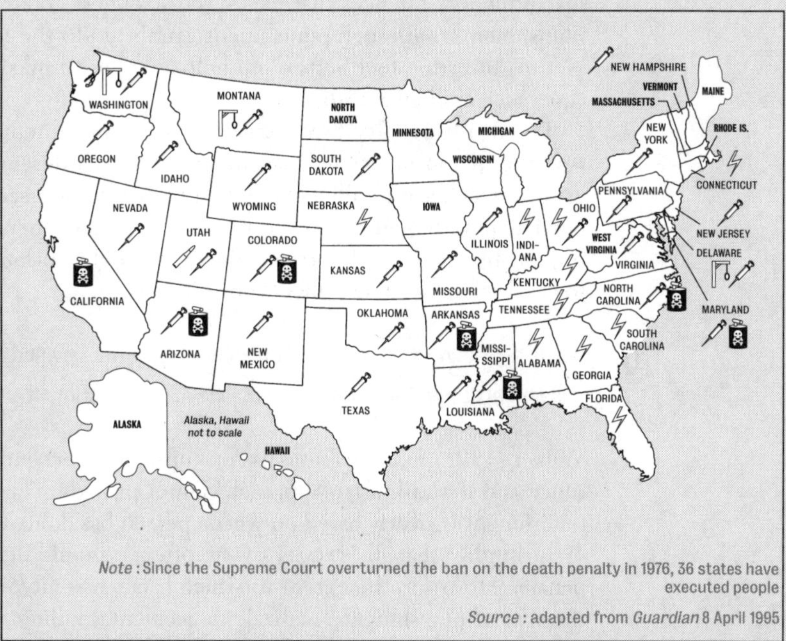


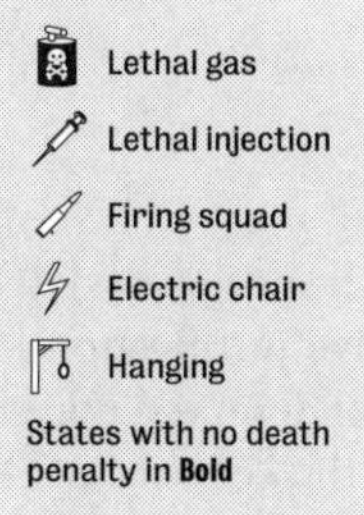


*Note*: Since the Supreme Court overturned the ban on the death penalty in 1976, 36 states have executed people

*Source*: adapted from *Guardian* 8 April 1995

**Fig 13.4** Executions per year in the US.

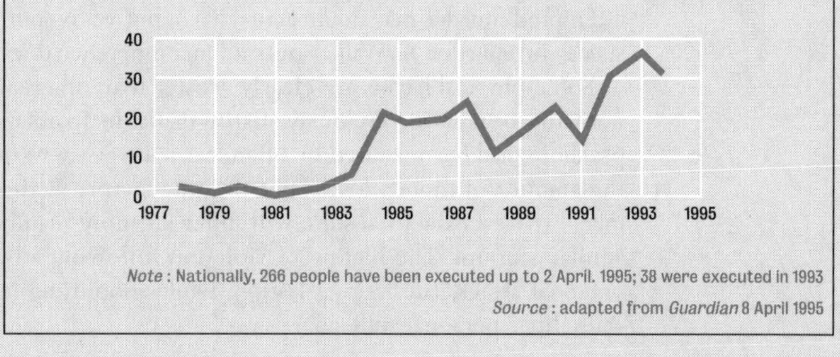


*Note*: Nationally, 266 people have been executed up to 2 April. 1995; 38 were executed in 1993

*Source*: adapted from *Guardian* 8 April 1995

### Retribution

Retribution is based on the revenge motive: 'an eye for an eye and a tooth for a tooth'. It originally meant the paying back of a debt and in the penal context refers to deserved punishment. It is often seen as the most important aim of punishment: certain offences deserve certain punishments and if criminals do not receive 'proper' punishment then law and order will break down. Linked with retribution is the belief that punishment should demonstrate society's condemnation of particular offenders offences that excite the strongest condemnation merit the severest punishments. Although punishment cannot undo the harm done, it can make the victims of crime feel better and helps people to make sense of the senseless (in cases such as child abuse).

The death penalty is a retributionary punishment that meets the desire for revenge. It can be argued that people who kill deserve to be killed themselves; crimes which are totally condemned by society are seen as requiring the severest possible punishment. However, retribution is not generally put forward as the most important argument for reintroducing capital punishment, rather the debate has focused on its deterrent effect (pp. 536–7).

**Q** Would a return to retributive punishment lead to televised executions?

Suggest arguments for and against televised punishments.

Walker (1991) sees retribution as promising the certainty which the notion of deterrence and the utilitarian approach cannot provide. The retributive justification for punishment is clearly based on what a person has done. The idea of deserved punishment implies that the gravity of the offence should determine the severity of the penalty. However, the extent to which harm was intended is a variable that affects the sort of punishment received: an accidental killing is not punished as if it were murder, even though the end result is the same. Furthermore, some offences might cause only a minimal degree of harm yet be seen to merit severe punishment: an attempted murder may do no actual harm but yet be punished almost as severely as a successful murder. As Walker puts it, 'incompetence does not mitigate'.

Some physical harms are clearly greater than others: injuries that lead to permanent disability are obviously distinguishable from minor cuts or bruises. The psychological harm caused by offenders is less easy to quantify. In the case of theft, the amount of money lost is not the sole factor: victims deprived of all their savings, whatever the total sum, will suffer far more than better-off victims who lose a similar amount. The feeling of violation following a burglary in one's home or a personal attack can be long-lasting, while shoplifting from large stores is liable to cause little personal suffering.

**Q** Although incompetence may not be seen as a mitigating factor (something that might be taken into account to lessen the normal penalty), there are other factors which influence the punishment received.

List as many factors as you can which you feel 'sentencers' should take account of when punishing offenders.

Suggest reasons for and against these factors affecting a sentence.

Harm done is not the only factor that causes difficulty in applying the retributive idea to punishment. Assessment of the offender's character is often problematic. Walker refers to a case where the Court of Appeal reduced the prison sentence given for a serious insurance fraud because the offender, while on bail, had jumped into a canal to save a drowning boy. He suggests that 'spectacular behaviour seems to influence courts more than unobtrusive decency'. We have seen that it is difficult to quantify the suffering experienced by victims. A by-product of punishment is that people other than the offender will often unintentionally suffer from that punishment. If the offender has a family, imprisonment or fines will usually cause distress and hardship for innocent partners and/or children.

### Rehabilitation

Rehabilitation is based on the belief that people can change: they are never beyond reform. Thus offenders can be taught how to be 'normal' law-abiding citizens; their punishment will make them less likely to reoffend. We shall use the terms rehabilitation and reform interchangeably, although strictly speaking *reform* refers to individuals being persuaded and given the space to change themselves, while *rehabilitation* involves a more planned and regulated treatment, for example a supervisor finds employment for offenders and monitors their progress. The focus is on how punishment can be used to 'correct' an offender's behaviour (indeed Walker uses the term 'correction' in preference to rehabilitation or reform).

Religious influence has usually emphasized the correction of the offender, but religiously motivated attempts at reform often caused as much hardship as the methods that they aimed to replace. Victorian reformers believed that prison should be a place where the offender might become a reformed person; they advocated long periods of solitary confinement during which time prisoners could examine their souls and consciences, spend hours in prayer and emerge purified; Bibles were made available in all cells

With the growth in the study of crime, there have been strong arguments for more constructive and humane punishments, supported by groups campaigning against unjust and inhumane punishments, such as Amnesty International and the Howard League. However, revenge and deterrence justifications for punishment are still widely supported and public anxiety is easily aroused about the supposed softness of modern punishments.

In practice there has tended to be a balance between reform and retributivist themes; one or other theme becomes fashionable at particular times. Cavadino and Dignan (1993) suggest that there has been a revival of the reformative approach, but that the claims made for rehabilitative punishments such as Intermediate Treatment are now more modest. The idea that methods of punishment could work almost independently of the offender has been replaced with an emphasis on punishment helping offenders improve their own behaviour. Intermediate Treatment programmes confront offenders with the consequences of their behaviour in the hope that they will choose to change their attitudes towards offending.

The contradiction between reform-based and retributive-based punishments is a basic problem that faces any system of punishment. The lack of success of harsh punishments encourages reform measures, but these are felt by many people not to be a proper response to the harm caused by offenders.

In assessing the extent to which rehabilitation 'works', Walker (1991) points to the difficulty of ever being sure why a particular offender ceases to offend. It may be the stigma, the unpleasant memory of the punishment, the influence of family, friends or social workers. Even offenders who appear to be successfully corrected may still be involved in crime but have not been caught again. The difficulty in assessing reform-based punishments does not mean that 'nothing works'; some approaches may work with some offenders but not with others.

Uncertainty over the extent to which rehabilitation works led to the emergence of a *justice model* of punishment in the 1970s. Rehabilitative, treatment-based approaches included indeterminate sentences, based on the notion that when the treatment worked the punishment could end. However, the justice model argued that this gave too much discretion to 'experts' working in the criminal justice system and that punishment should be based on the seriousness of the offence; the rehabilitative approach was inherently unfair in that it treated similar offences in very different ways. Cavadino and Dignan highlight the abolition in 1982 of the indeterminate borstal sentence for young offenders (who were released anytime between six months and two years according to how they had 'responded' to their punishment) and its replacement with a fixed-term sentence as evidence of the impact of the justice model on penal policy in Britain.

### Incapacitation

Incapacitation means that offenders are prevented from reoffending, either temporarily or permanently, by the punishment they receive. In some societies this has taken the form of preventive detention, whereby people who are perceived as potential offenders or a political threat are imprisoned. This is clearly opposed to the basic notions of individual freedom. Milder forms of incapacitation can result from a range of punishments. Banning people from driving should prevent them repeating motoring offences. Any form of detention or imprisonment ensures that the offender is unable to commit certain offences, at least for the duration of the sentence.

### Reparation

Another aim of punishment is *reparation* or *compensation*. If there is not an individual victim or identifiable victim for the offender to compensate, reparation could be made to society through some form of community service or by paying a fine into public funds. However, reparation is difficult to apply. Often the offender will not have the means to repay the victim; if a youngster commits an offence it is debatable whether the parents should be responsible for compensation. None the less, in a high proportion of offences the offender and victim know one another; if they are brought together to arrive at a settlement it can be better and quicker for all parties, as well as cutting down on court workloads. Such an approach might be particularly suitable for offences involving damage to property. This approach to punishment, like other new methods, is likely to be seen by many as too soft a response to crime.

## The sociological theory of punishment

Although punishment and justice have not been a major area of sociological inquiry, certain theoretical approaches provide the basis for the sociological study of punishment:

- punishment and social cohesion: Durkheim
- punishment and class control: Marxism
- punishment, power and regulation: Foucault

Sociologists have examined punishment in social terms rather than as crime control. Garland (1990) points out that institutions of punishment such as prisons or community service orders are social artefacts reflecting cultural standards. Just as styles of building or music cannot be explained solely in terms of their obvious purposes of providing shelter or entertainment, so punishment has to be considered in historical, cultural and social contexts.

Q What social purposes other than the control of crime might punishment have?

What specific penalties might achieve these purposes?

### Punishment and social cohesion: Durkheim

In Durkheim's sociological analysis, punishment represented the 'collective conscience' of society at work and the examination of punishment would provide an insight into the moral and social life of the society. Durkheim believed that social order was based on a core of shared values and moralities (see pp. 43–4). Punishment provides a clear illustration of the moral nature of social order; it is not just about controlling crime. In Durkheim's *The Division of Labour in Society* (1893), changes in the nature of punishment were seen as reflecting changes in the nature of social morality and social solidarity.

Durkheim emphasized the relationship between the punishment of crime and the maintenance of moral and social order. Crimes are moral outrages that violate a society's collective conscience; this violation produces a punitive reaction. As Durkheim puts it, 'crime brings together upright consciences and concentrates them'; crime provides an occasion for the collective expression of shared moral feelings (see pp.514–15).

The existence of social morality and social solidarity makes punishment necessary, in that it reaffirms moral and social bonds. Of course, punishment is not the only social institution that reinforces social morality and solidarity. Religion, education and family life all help to strengthen the collective conscience and to promote social cohesion; however, formal punishment enjoys a special place in Durkheim's work.

Durkheim acknowledges that the nature of punishment changes as society changes; he saw punishment as more important as a means of reinforcing moral and social order in less complex societies with a less developed division of labour. However, while methods change the functions of punishment remain constant. Although people are outraged by different activities over time, punishment as a social process has an unchanging character.

In contrasting simpler societies based on mechanical solidarity with modern societies based on organic solidarity, Durkheim suggests that the former are characterized by more severe and intense punishment. The intensity of the collective conscience in simple societies is reflected in the intensity of punishment. In modern, advanced societies, collective sentiments are less demanding; there is more scope for diversity and interdependence, so punishment for violations of the collective conscience is more lenient. The intensity of punishment reflects the nature of the collective conscience; as society develops the severity of punishment diminishes.

The link between punishment and morality is the key element of Durkheim's sociology of punishment. Punishment helps prevent the collapse of moral authority and demonstrates the force of moral commands; its primary function is the reassertion of the moral order of society. Punishment is not an instrument of deterrence; the threat of unpleasant consequences just presents practical problems that stand in the way of the criminal's desires. Although in practical terms punishment has to be unpleasant, Durkheim sees this as incidental. The essence of punishment is the expression of moral condemnation.

### *Rituals of punishment*

Durkheim believed that it was the rituals associated with punishment which specifically conveyed moral messages and helped to maintain social order. These rituals tend nowadays to centre around the courtroom drama. They include the wearing of wigs and gowns, the process of the trial, the passing of sentence (guilty or not) and the meting out of punishment. The focus on the courtroom is due in part to the decline in public, and therefore visible, punishments, such as public floggings or executions. Prisons and other institutions responsible for punishment tend to be closed to the public and the media. Of course there are rituals associated with imprisonment; in his famous study of total institutions Goffman (1968) highlighted the rituals of initiation that serve to 'mortify the self', including the replacing of prisoners' names with numbers, the issuing of prison clothing, the shaving of heads and the restrictions on contact with the outside world. However, these rituals are undertaken to maintain the institution itself; they are done for an internal audience. As a consequence of this decline in public punishment, the focus of public and media interest tends to be on the trial of offenders and on 'who gets what' rather than on the detailed workings of the processes of punishment. Durkheim's emphasis on the rituals of punishment can be compared with his study of religion; it doesn't matter if a particular doctrine is true or not, the importance is the faith and the rituals which have social functions (see pp. 47–9).

**Q**

Which criminal trials have received detailed media coverage recently?

How have the media reported these trials? How did it make you feel?

To what extent might such trials strengthen the 'collective conscience'?

Court cases and punishments can provoke a range of responses as well as social solidarity. What other responses might these trials have provoked?

### *Comment and criticism*

Just as Durkheim's description of simple societies, characterized by mechanical solidarity, and advanced societies, characterized by organic solidarity, has been criticized as oversimplistic so his history of punishment has been similarly criticized. Garland (1990) suggests that the historical transition from simple societies characterized by severe punishments to advanced ones characterized by lenient punishment is not really demonstrated by Durkheim; no account of any intermediate stages is given.

Garland also criticizes Durkheim's application of the notion of the collective conscience. A certain degree of order in society does not necessarily indicate a general commitment to shared moral norms; many people follow laws for practical reasons, to avoid punishments rather than because of moral commitment. This raises the question as to whether violations of the criminal law do really break genuinely held moral sentiments. Clearly there is some link between the law and popular sentiment; the laws protecting property and personal safety, for instance, are supportive of widely shared values. However, while there may be general agreement that rape and burglary are morally repugnant, there is considerable disagreement over the 'proper' punishment for such behaviour. And there is even less agreement over criminal offences which do not offend such strongly and widely held sentiments – crimes such as tax evasion or infringing copyright laws, perhaps. Punishments which deal with the most serious and shocking crimes – child murder for example – provoke the strongest feelings and the greatest moral outcry.

It seems clear that the punishment of crime produces emotive responses. Garland refers to the philosopher Nietzsche who suggested that positive pleasure can be gained from punishment; it can gratify impulses of sadism and cruelty. The fascination with crime and criminals – witness for example the popularity of films, books, magazines and TV programmes on serial killers – can be seen as a gratification of repressed aggression as well as a reflection of horror and repugnance.

**Q** Which crimes excite the greatest moral repugnance? Why do they?

What forms of punishment express this moral condemnation and repugnance?

To what extent, then, is punishment functional for society? Certainly it performs some functions – restraining some types of behaviour and legitimizing some forms of authority. However, what is functional from one point of view may be dysfunctional from another. This is a criticism that is often made of functionalist work which implies that there is a general agreement over what is functional or not and what should and should not be valued and appreciated. The emphasis on general agreement ignores the obvious power differentials in the maintenance of order in society. Garland also questions whether Durkheim's theory is relevant to modern, advanced societies with a complex division of labour and where the moral order is not necessarily universal.

Durkheim's work has encouraged examination of the social processes of punishment; his work introduced the symbolic and emotional elements of punishment rather than just the narrow technical side. In arguing that punishment was necessary and functional for society, Durkheim realized that it had only a very limited ability to control criminal behaviour. It was this apparent contradiction – that punishment was politically and socially functional yet had little effect on actual criminal behaviour – that Garland argues is the crucial characteristic of punishment:

> **This sense of being simultaneously necessary and also destined to a degree of futility is what I will term the *tragic* quality of punishment.** *(Garland 1990: 80)*

## Punishment and class control: Marxism

Neither Marx nor Engels analysed the practices and institutions for the punishment of offenders; they wrote very little on crime and criminals and did not develop a theory of crime. Thus we have to look at the writing of later Marxist writers to provide us with a Marxist analysis of punishment.

The basic Marxist approach sees the economy as the key locus of power in society. The economic system determines all other areas of social life, including the legal system. Those groups who have economic power are able to ensure that social institutions work in a way that is consistent with their interests. Thus the institutions of the law and punishment come to reflect the interests of the dominant economic groups. Marxist analysis of punishment has tended to focus on the way in which elements of the superstructure support ruling-class power. The law works in the interests of some groups more than others: 'there's one law for the rich and one for the poor'.

Garland suggests that the Marxist analysis of punishment centres on the notion of class struggle and the ways in which the relationship between social classes shapes the form of punishment in a particular society. He highlights the work of Rusche and Kirchheimer as the best example of the Marxist interpretation of punishment. Rusche and Kirchheimer's major text, *Punishment and Social Structure* (1939), was not widely read when first published and it is only since its reissue in 1968 that their work has been taken up by Marxist criminologists and become more widely known.

Rusche and Kirchheimer provide a detailed history of punishment which emphasizes how the economy and, in particular, the labour market influence the methods of punishment in society. An illustration of their basic argument is provided by their account of the development of punishments such as galley slavery, transportation and hard labour. These 'new' punishments emerged in the sixteenth and seventeenth centuries alongside the early developments of a capitalist economic system. Labour power increasingly came to be seen as a vital resource and the harsh physical punishments, such as whipping, branding and execution, were replaced by punishments that involved productive, hard labour, and particularly work that 'free' people were unwilling to undertake. At this period there were vast amounts of land in the colonies that needed to be worked and the penalty of transportation was used to develop these areas. Transportation was initially offered as a commutation of capital punishment but by the early 1700s was regularly used as a sentence for a range of minor offences. By the end of the eighteenth century the growing prosperity in the colonies led to the decline of this form of punishment; the free immigrants to Australia and elsewhere were not happy about criminal labour and convicts undercutting their wages, while the authorities felt that transportation was becoming little deterrent to criminals.

Case Study

**Rusche and Kirchheimer's theoretical approach to punishment**

- Punishments have to be viewed as historically specific phenomena that appear in particular forms at different periods. This principle of historical specificity distinguishes Marxist accounts from Durkheim's view of punishment as something that performed essentially similar functions in all societies.
- The mode of production is the major determinant of specific penal methods in specific historical periods. Different systems of production will produce different methods of punishment.
- The particular forms of punishment are, therefore, social artefacts or constructions.
- Penal policy is one element within a wider strategy for controlling the poor. Punishment is seen almost exclusively as aimed at the control of the 'lower orders'. Rusche and Kirchheimer suggest that there were clear similarities between the way criminals were treated and the policies aimed at controlling the labouring masses. In the early industrial period the regime and organization of prison life was similar to the way workers were treated in factories and beggars and vagrants in workhouses.
- Punishment is a mechanism deeply implicated within the class struggle: 'the history of the penal system is the history of the relations between the rich and the poor' (Rusche 1933).
- Although punishment is generally and conventionally seen as an institution which benefits 'society as a whole', for Marxists, in reality it supports the interests of one class against another. Punishment is (another) element and example of control that is hidden within ideological veils.

(Adapted from Garland 1990: 90–2)

### *Comment and criticism*

The priority given to economic explanations by Marxist writers such as Rusche and Kirchheimer has been criticized for understating the importance of political and ideological factors; religious and humanitarian influences on the development of punishment are accorded only secondary importance, for example. Furthermore, the emphasis given to class and class relationships tends to ignore popular attitudes to punishment. There is widespread support among the working classes for harsh punitive policies and little evidence that the working classes support criminals any more than other social groups, which Garland suggests casts doubt on a simple class conflict approach to punishment.

However, these comments do not refute Rusche and Kirchheimer's argument that economic relationships and the labour market can exert an important influence on penal policy and that the institutions of punishment can be seen as part of a wider strategy for managing the poor and working classes.

The essence of the Marxist approach is that the approach to and form of punishment is influenced by the strategies that the dominant, governing groups adopt towards the working classes. Punishment is not merely shaped by patterns of crime but by the perception of the working class, and the poor in particular, as a social problem. Rusche and Kirchheimer argue that the working classes have little commitment to the law or to the dominant moral order in general and that it is therefore important for the criminal law and the punishments associated with it to make sure that crime does not pay. Punishments have to be severe and institutions of punishment such as prisons have to be unpleasant; indeed they have to be more unpleasant than the conditions that the worst off 'free' people are able to live in.

In contrast to Durkheim's view that punishment expresses the interests of society as a whole, the fairly simplistic review of the Marxist approach to punishment that we have presented here sees punishment as expressing ruling-class interests only. Although the criminal law and punishment does provide protection for the working classes as well as the ruling classes – protection against assault and burglary, for instance – it does not, according to Marxists, 'protect' against economic domination and oppression.

**Case Study**

### Rich law, poor law

**The sociological study of white-collar crime lends support to the idea that the extent and severity with which the legal system is applied varies between different social groups. Dee Cook (1989) examined the different responses to tax and supplementary benefit fraud. She cited examples of judicial responses to defrauding the public purse by two different means – by defrauding the Inland Revenue by evading tax and defrauding the DHSS by falsely claiming supplementary benefit:**

Two partners in a vegetable wholesalers business admitted falsifying accounts to the tune of £100,000. At their trial the judge said he considered they had been 'very wise' in admitting their guilt and they had paid back the tax due (with interest) to the Inland Revenue. They were sentenced to pay fines. A chartered accountant who defrauded taxes in excess of £8,000 was sentenced to pay a fine as the judge accepted, in mitigation, that his future income would be adversely affected by the trial.

An unemployed father of three failed to declare his wife's earnings to the Department of Health and Social Security (DHSS). He admitted the offence and started to pay back the £996 he owed them by weekly deductions from his supplementary benefit. He was prosecuted a year later and sentenced to pay fines totalling £210, also to be deducted from his benefit. Magistrates told him that 'this country is fed up to the teeth with people like you scrounging from fellow citizens'. A young woman defrauded the DHSS to the tune of £58: she served three months in custody as magistrates said she 'needed to be taught a lesson'. (Cook 1989: 1)

**In looking at why the law does not treat white-collar crime in the same way as conventional crime, Hazel Croall (1992) points out that white-collar crime is subject to different regulatory arrangements and these tend to be more lenient than those of the criminal justice system; regulatory bodies are less worried about securing convictions and more keen on settling disputes with a minimum of fuss and, often, publicity. This point is supported by Steven Box's (1983) comments on the deterrents for would-be corporate criminals.**

For the most part corporate crimes are not/do not fall under the jurisdiction of the police, but under special regulatory bodies. . . . In the UK, there are numerous inspectorates, commissions and government departments. . . .

Although they all have powers either to initiate or recommend criminal prosecution, they are primarily designed to be regulatory bodies whose main weapon against corporate misbehaviour is administrative, i.e. (occasional) inspection coupled with (polite) correspondence.

*(box continued)*

*(box continued)*

Corporate executives contemplating the possibility of being required to commit corporate crimes know that they face a regulatory agency which for the most part will be unable to detect what is going on, and in the minority of cases when it does, it will have no heart and few resources to pursue the matter into the criminal courts. . . .

Criminal laws aimed at regulating corporate activities tend to refer to a specific rather than a general class of behaviour . . . they focus purely on the regulation broken and not on the consequences of that broken regulation. Thus the company responsible for the hoist accident at Littlebrook Dee power station were not prosecuted for the fact that five men died, but for the fact that the machinery was not properly maintained or inspected. For this they were fined £5000. In conventional crime . . . a person is charged with the consequences of his/her action; if someone dies as a consequence of being stabbed, the assailant is more likely to be charged with a homicide offence rather than 'carrying an offensive weapon'. The point of this fracture between the regulation broken and its consequences is that it facilitates corporate crime; executives need only concern themselves with the likelihood of being leniently punished for breaking regulations. (Box 1983: 44–58)

### Questions

**What are the key differences between corporate and conventional crime?**

**To what extent do they provide a justification for the differential treatment of white-collar and business criminals?**

## Punishment, power and regulation: Foucault

Foucault's (1975) *Discipline and Punish* has become one of the key texts in the sociology of punishment. Foucault sees punishment as a system of power and regulation which is imposed on the population; an analysis that overlaps with the Marxist approach and contrasts with Durkheim's argument that punishment is embedded within collective sentiments and therefore conveys moral messages. Foucault, however, focused on the specific workings of penal institutions – how they were structured and how they exercised control. This approach moves away from the examination of society as a coherent whole that can be analysed by structural methods and to that extent Foucault's work could be described as phenomenological rather than Marxist (see pp. 98–9 on post-structuralism).

The historical issue that Foucault sets out to explain in *Discipline and Punish* is the disappearance of punishment as a public spectacle of violence and the emergence of the prison as the general form of modern punishment – hence the subtitle of the book 'The Birth of the Prison'. This change in the basic form of punishment took place between 1750 and 1820 when the target of punishment changed, with an emphasis on changing the soul of the offender rather than just the body, on transforming the offender not just avenging the crime. Foucault sees these developments as reflecting how power operates in modern society with open physical force and ceremonies associated with it replaced by more detailed regulation of offenders; troublesome individuals are removed from society rather than destroyed, they are resocialized.

Foucault goes on to consider why imprisonment so quickly became the general method of legal punishment. He saw the development of the prison and imprisonment in relation to the growth of the human sciences. The prison practice of isolating and monitoring inmates ensured that they were studied as individuals with their own characteristics and peculiarities. To an extent, prison led to the discovery of the 'delinquent' – a person distinct from the non-delinquent – and, according to Foucault, to the rise of the science of criminology.

Foucault also argues that the creation of delinquency has been a useful strategy of political domination by dividing the working classes, enhancing fears of authority and guaranteeing the power of the police. Delinquency, which generally consists of relatively minor attacks on authority, is not a particular political danger and can, within limits, be tolerated by the authorities; furthermore it produces a group of known habitual criminals who can be kept under surveillance.

**Q** In spite of the problems with prisons, Foucault suggests that prisons have important political effects at a wider, social level. What do you think these effects might be and how might they work?

### *Punishment in modern society: the rationalization of punishment*

Over the last two hundred or so years, makeshift forms of punishment have been replaced by centrally administered arrangements, with greater uniformity in punishment and the development of a penal infrastructure, due in part to the growth in population since the eighteenth century and the rising rate of crime. The range of professional groups working in the penal system – social workers, probation officers, psychiatrists, prison officers and governors – tend to see prisoners in terms of whether they are good or bad inmates on account of their institutional conduct, rather than as evil or wicked on account of the crimes they are being punished for. The punishments are administered by paid officials rather than the general public or, indeed, those personally affected by the offenders' actions.

This 'professionalization of justice' (Garland 1990) has altered the place and meaning of punishment in modern society. The institutions of punishment have become less accessible and more secretive as specialized professions have become involved. This trend toward rationalization runs counter to Durkheim's emphasis on the emotional nature of punishment – as reflecting an outrage to generally held moral sentiments. Indeed this may help explain why the public often feel frustrated by moves to release criminals 'early' – as evidenced by the campaign to ensure that the two 10-year-old boys who abducted and killed toddler James Bulger in 1993 remain in prison for many years and the opposition to periodic suggestions that Moors murderer Myra Hindley (imprisoned in 1965) be considered for release on parole.

### *Punishment as a social institution*

No method of punishment has ever managed to control crime or to achieve high rates of reform of offenders; it is unrealistic to hope that any methods will. Punishments fail because they can never be any more than a back up to the mainstream processes of socialization. A sense of duty and morality, acceptable standards of behaviour and so on have to be learned and internalized, they cannot be imposed.

'Punishment is merely a coercive back up to those more reliable social mechanisms, a back up which is often unable to do anything more than manage those who slip through these networks of normal control and integration' (Garland 1990: 289).

Garland suggests that we should expect less from penal policy. Although sometimes necessary, punishment is beset by contradictions and irresolvable tensions:

**However well it is organized, and however humanely administered, punishment is inescapably marked by moral contradiction and unwanted irony – as when it seeks to uphold freedom by means of its deprivation or condemns private violence using a violence which is publicly authorized.** *(Garland 1990: 292)*

## Summary

- Crime is behaviour that breaks the criminal law and, if detected, leads to criminal proceedings and formal punishment; it is distinct from the broader area of deviant behaviour.
- Those who commit crimes generally wish to keep their criminal behaviour secret. The methodological problems for the sociological study of crime include the difficulty of gaining access to such behaviour and of collecting reliable data from law breakers and the moral dilemmas that can face researchers who are confronted with behaviour which may, for instance, cause suffering to innocent victims.
- Crime has always fascinated people and explanations for it have been wide ranging. Sociologists emphasize the specific social conditions and opportunities that are available to different groups. However, there is no one sociological position on crime.
- Crime has been seen as a response to the frustration felt by those who cannot achieve the 'success goals' of society (Robert Merton and Albert Cohen, for example); as a consequence of society, and particularly the agencies of social control within it, labelling certain forms of behaviour and groups of people as criminal (interpretativist approaches); and as a result of the power of the ruling, dominant groups to impose their standards of appropriate and inappropriate behaviour on other, less powerful groups (critical, Marxist theories).
- Criminal statistics indicate that crime has grown spectacularly in the twentieth century. However, these statistics have to be treated with caution: the extension of formal control mechanisms, such as more and better equipped police and more laws, will clearly influence the amount of criminal behaviour that is known about. Criminal statistics also show that crime is a largely male preserve and that ethnic minorities, and especially Black males, are more likely to be convicted and punished for criminal behaviour than other social groups.
- The police are the most visible formal agency of social control; the relationship between the police and public is of crucial importance in the control and subsequent punishment of criminal behaviour. A 'police culture' has helped to segregate the police from certain sections of the wider public, particularly young Blacks.
- Legal punishment is the ultimate form of social control. There are different opinions over what should be the 'aims of punishment'. Deterrence, retribution and rehabilitation are three major aims that have been given more or less support and credibility by both governments and the public at different periods of time.

- There are various sociological explanations of the role of punishment in society. The Durkheimian approach sees punishment as helping to maintain social cohesion through strengthening the moral and social bonds of a society; the work of Foucault and the Marxist approaches have focused on punishment as a formal means for regulating the mass of the population and for supporting the power of the ruling classes.

## Further reading

Becker, H S (1963) *Outsiders: Studies in the Sociology of Deviance*, New York: Free Press.

Cohen, A K (1955) *Delinquent Boys: The Culture of the Gang*, New York: Free Press.

Pearson, G (1983) *Hooligan: A History of Respectable Fears*, London: Macmillan.

Young, J and Mathews, R (eds) (1992) *Rethinking Criminology: The Realist Debate*, London: Sage.

There is nothing like the 'real thing' and many of the original sources referred to in our examination of theories of crime are most accessible.

Cavadino, M and Dignan, J (1993) *The Penal System: An Introduction*, London: Sage.

As well as looking at justifications and explanations for punishment, this book examines the specific elements of the penal system of England and Wales, including sentencing practices, imprisonment, non-custodial penalties and issues of bias within the criminal justice system.

Garland, D (1990) *Punishment and Modern Society: A Study in Social Theory*, Oxford: Clarendon.

A comprehensive introduction to the sociology of punishment.

Heidensohn, F (1989) *Crime and Society*, London: Macmillan

Hester, S and Eglin, P (1992) *A Sociology of Crime*, London: Routledge

Two clear comprehensive introductions to the sociology of crime.

Maguire, M, Morgan, R and Reiner, R (eds) (1994) *The Oxford Handbook of Criminology*, Oxford: Clarendon.

Comprehensive and up-to-date readings by key writers and researchers on criminology and the criminal justice system. If we were to recommend one textbook that covers the sociology of crime and punishment this would have to be it.

Newburn, T (1995) *Crime and Criminal Justice Policy*, London: Longman.

A fully up-to-date overview of the penal system including coverage of future policy issues and implications of privatization.

Walker, N (1991) *Why Punish*, Oxford: Oxford University Press.

This short, thought-provoking book looks at the justifications for and aims of punishment, grappling with the moral issues and dilemmas that they raise.

## Activities

### ■ Activity 1 Explanations of crime

**Rather than focus on the individual characteristics of criminals, sociological theories of crime emphasize how the characteristics of the particular society play an important part in the explanations for crime. The following extract is from American sociologist, Jack Levin (1993), who describes how the sociologist's 'eye' on crime differs from biological, psychological and common-sense explanations.**

Watching the evening news on television, I learn that a 35 year old man has murdered 23 people at a Luby's Cafeteria in Killeen, Texas. I read in the paper that a 'cannibal killer' in Milwaukee has strangled and dismembered 17 men. Then, I discover that the cities are burning again. The city of Los Angeles has gone up in flames following days and nights of rioting, looting and killing. Everyone is eager to understand why. So they consult the experts.

Biologists and psychologists find their answers in the offenders themselves. Perhaps the mass murderer in Killeen had an undiagnosed tumour; maybe he had experienced severe blows to the head as a child. Perhaps the cannibal killer had been abused or neglected. He certainly had to be 'crazy', didn't he? And, the rioters must have been 'just plain rotten.'

. . . [Sociologists] look at the structure and changes in American society that are possibly responsible for our growing problem of discontent and violence – . . . the breakdown in rules and regulations concerning moral behaviour, the high divorce rate and residential mobility . . . a high unemployment rate and a stagnant economy, and a collective belief that the ordinary American is powerless to control his or her destiny.

Biological and psychological explanations are not necessarily incorrect. In fact, many serial killers may suffer from bad childhoods. Some rioters may have had brain disease. [But] someone looking only for psychological or neurological causes will focus on the perpetrator alone: Send him to prison, put her in the chair, give him surgery, treat her with anti-convulsant drugs, or see that he receives psychoanalysis or electro-shock therapy. From this viewpoint, only the perpetrator needs to change; the rest of us don't have to do anything.

The sociological eye sees things differently. It does not deny the need to punish or rehabilitate violent offenders, but it also focuses our attention on ourselves and, on so takes a much broader view. To reduce the level of violence, for example, we might consider changing laws, modifying the distribution of wealth, improving education, providing jobs that lead to upward mobility, reducing discriminatory practices, lowering the level of isolation in our major cities, improving our criminal justice system, or possibly even changing our values. As a society, as a community, as a group, we must make at least some changes, too. (Levin 1993: xvi–xvii)

#### Questions

**The notion of the 'criminal type' is still widely held. What sort of characteristics form the common perception of the 'criminal type'?**

**Take an example of one particular criminal activity. What kinds of explanations for this would be offered by the different theoretical perspectives we have looked at?**

### Activity 2 Crime and punishment

**The two extracts below illustrate in their different ways the fact that some aspects of prison life have changed very little since the nineteenth century when Dostoevsky was writing.**

#### First impressions

Those first few weeks, and indeed all the early part of imprisonment, made a deep impression on my imagination. The following years, on the other hand, are all mixed up together, and leave but a confused recollection. Whole periods, in fact, have been effaced from my memory. Generally speaking, however, I remember life as the same – always painful, monotonous and stifling. What I experienced during the first few days of my imprisonment seems to me as if it took place but yesterday. Nor is that unnatural. I remember so well in the first place my surprise that prison routine afforded no outstanding feature, nothing extraordinary, or, perhaps I should say, unexpected . . .

I experienced, moreover, one form of suffering which is perhaps the sharpest, the most painful that can be experienced in a house of detention cut off from law and liberty. I mean forced association. Association with one's fellow men is to some extent forced everywhere and always; but nowhere is it so horrible as in a prison, where there are men with whom no one would consent to live. I am certain that every convict, unconsciously perhaps, has suffered from this. (Dostoevsky 1962: 21–3)

#### Culture of self-destruction

Armley prison in Leeds where sixteen teenagers have hanged themselves since 1988 is unfit for the custody of young people, Judge Stephen Tumim said yesterday in the most critical report ever published by the prison inspectorate.

B wing was cramped, overcrowded, insanitary and so deprived that a subculture of self destructive behaviour took hold, said Judge Tumim, the chief inspector.

The wing's 337 inmates, youngsters under the age of 21 held mainly on remand prior to trial, should be moved to a more suitable establishment and a government task force established to bring the rest of the jail up to scratch.

Suicide verdicts were recorded on five teenagers who hanged themselves in Armley between May 1988 and February 1989. . . . A sixth died in August this year while Mr Waddington (Home Secretary) was considering the report.

'It was clear to us it was the absence of sufficient activities which provoked much of the self harm,' it says. There was no work and far too much 'lying on beds'. Youngsters were locked up two or three to a cell for approaching 23 hours a day.

(*Guardian* 6 November 1990)

### Questions

**What do you think may be the long-term effect on prisoners, prison warders and society as a whole of experiences and institutions such as these? How do you think they might affect you?**

**How might those who favour (a) retribution (b) rehabilitation respond to these extracts?**

Chapter 14

# The mass media

**Chapter outline:** The historical development of the mass media in Britain • The mass media and control • External influences on media content • Internal influences on media content • Perspectives on the mass media • Effects of the mass media • Summary • Further reading • Activities

## Learning objectives

When you have studied this chapter you should be able to address these key questions:

- How have the mass media developed and extended their influence in modern societies, particularly in Britain?
- What factors determine and constrain the content of the mass media?
- What are the major sociological explanations of the role of the mass media in society?
- How do the mass media influence social and cultural behaviour – in particular what is the relationship between the portrayal of violence in the media and violent behaviour?

## Introduction

> To understand day-to-day media use, it is necessary to take the whole ensemble of intersecting and overlapping media provision into consideration. Audiences piece together the contents of radio, television, newspapers and so on. As a rule, media texts and messages are not used completely or with full concentration. We read parts of sports reviews, skim through magazines and zap from channel to channel when we don't like what's on TV. Furthermore, media use, being an integrated part of the routines and rituals of everyday life, is constantly interrelated with other activities such as talking, eating and doing housework. In other words, media use is not a private, individual process, but a collective, social process. (Bausinger 1984: 349)

The importance of the media within society cannot be overestimated. We live in a media-saturated world where much of our social knowledge is gained through the channels of television, radio, cinema, video, newspapers, advertising, comics, and home computers. The media have become an accepted part of our urban way of life: they give us news and entertainment, sell us lifestyles and reinforce social identities; we use them to educate ourselves and spend much of our spare time and a lot of money on the media in one form or another, and much of it is taken for granted. 'The media are central in the provision of ideas and images which people use to interpret and understand a great deal of their everyday existence'(Golding 1974: 78).

**Q** Which of the following mass media do you use: daily newspapers; magazines; radio; television; video; home computer?

Why do you read the newspapers and magazines that you do?

What kinds of programmes do you listen to and watch? Do you consider alternatives?

How similar are your 'media tastes' to other members of your family?

It is clear from market research and social surveys that people in general depend heavily upon the media for information and entertainment. By looking at ownership of media hardware and the purchase of consumer items we can get some idea of the level of media saturation of modern society.

In 1992 99 per cent of households owned a television set, while a video recorder (VCR) is no longer regarded as a luxury item (60 per cent of households). There has also been a significant increase in the possession of home computers (19 per cent) and compact disc (CD) players (15 per cent: *Social Trends 22* 1992). The sales of related consumer goods represents a billion-dollar market which has seen an increase in video tape consumption and CDs (and the demise of the vinyl disc). The computer games market also continues to expand with major competitors like Sega and Nintendo spending millions on developing new products. In contrast with this drive towards a more privatized leisure culture, the cinema increased in popularity during the 1980s with 64 per cent of the population over 7 years of age attending at least once a year (*Social Trends 22* 1992).

The level of interest in newspapers and magazines has remained high with 64 per cent of adults in Britain being regular readers of a daily newspaper and 71 per cent reading a Sunday paper. The magazine industry in Britain remains very strong: at the beginning of 1993 there were 54 per cent more periodicals than in 1983 (Peak 1994). The *Radio Times* remains the top selling magazine with sales of around 1.6 million copies a week. Women's magazines also retain their popularity with market leaders *Take a Break* and *Bella* selling over a million copies a week and older titles such as *Woman's Own* and *Woman* still retaining large readerships.

Simply because people buy these products does not in itself tell us very much. Almost everyone owns a radio (or three) but how are they used and how many of us really listen? Social surveys reveal the hidden patterns in our viewing, listening and reading habits and they tend to confirm the fears of saturation suggested by the trends in media consumption. Not only do we rely upon the media as sources of up-to-the-minute information but also the media have come to dominate our leisure time.

**Q** How would your life change without the media, if you didn't have television, newspapers, advertising, radio and video? What would be the possible consequences for personal and social interaction? How often do you discuss films or TV programmes with your friends?

The point of such speculation is to emphasize the extent to which we depend on the media without really recognizing it. Consequently Masterman (1985) has argued that 'Media studies has become as important as reading' and identifies these reasons for its inclusion in the curriculum:

- high levels of media production, consumption and saturation within contemporary society
- ideological importance of the media and their influence as consciousness industries
- growth in the manufacture and management of information and its dissemination through the media
- increasing penetration of the media into our central democratic processes
- importance of visual communications and data handling in many areas
- increasing cross-media ownerships which concentrate power and influence in fewer hands
- increasing commercialization of the media environment, the privatization of information and the threat to public service obligations.

(Adapted from Masterman 1985: 2)

These issues are particularly relevant in a media-saturated world where the media have become so much part of our way of life that it is almost impossible to talk objectively about our relationship to them. As Postman has observed, the media are not only taken for granted but also mythologized into part of the natural order; the alphabet and the television set are no longer regarded as human inventions but, like trees and clouds, seen as elements of natural inheritance (Postman 1987: 167). Fiske and Hartley (1978) put their finger on it when they describe our problematic relationship to television:

**Everybody knows what it is like to watch TV . . . and it is television's familiarity, its centrality to our culture, that makes it so important, so fascinating and so difficult to analyse. It is rather like the language we speak: taken for granted but both complex and vital to an understanding of the way human beings have created their world.** *(Fiske and Hartley 1978: 16)*

This underlines the central place of the media within secondary socializing processes, to provide ideas and images which help to map out the contours of social reality, and to construct 'common-sense' meaning systems. Our main intention throughout this chapter is to provide a comprehensive grasp of the relationship between the individual, the media and society. Indeed, much of the necessary groundwork for this chapter has been achieved already, in that we are all media experts in our own right, with a personal appreciation of the importance of the media in our own everyday lives. We stress the everyday importance of the media because it underlies the theme of an interactive approach to media criticism. In this respect, the significance of media power can be related to arguments about how we *use* the media ourselves, and how it makes meaningful connections with our everyday experience and provides opportunities for significant social understanding.

The rest of this chapter will focus on the historical context of media development, the relationship between the media and society and the power of the media to influence the attitudes and behaviour of their audiences.

## The historical development of the mass media in Britain

Over time the mass media have come to play an increasingly important part in the everyday transmission of information and culture. These developments are largely due to technological inventions but are also influenced by social, economic and political factors. The invention of the printing press created the possibility of mass communication but it was only with the establishment of a free press and the right to a free education that an affordable daily newspaper became a reality. Similarly the world-wide potential of satellite or the Internet will remain unexplored for as long as the hardware can be affordable only by a minority or governments continue to practise official censorship. Nevertheless, there can be few people who have not been affected by the media; for many of us it is the main means by which we relate to one another. Knowledge based on direct experience and the oral transmission of culture are parts of a fading tradition in which face-to-face communication was crucial. What was once a culture founded in folk tales and contained within clear geographical boundaries has given way to an electronic revolution that respects neither time nor place. The world has been reduced to what Marshall McLuhan (1964) referred to as 'the global village' in which our culture becomes mediated rather than situated:

> **Through [the] networks of direct interpersonal communication we participate in a *situated culture*. We may hear or relay news of recent events in the neighbourhood, likewise rumours, gossip, stories or jokes. We may attend and participate in local events, entertainments, family ceremonies or other rituals. These cultures of situation are primarily oral, by word of mouth relationships and . . . tend to be limited and defined in relation to a particular locale. In certain ways they embody elements of pre-industrial cultures, relatively small-scale forms of social interaction and groupings derived from the immediate, face-to-face environment and its daily experience. Since the mid-nineteenth century, however, we have increasingly learned to live not only in our situated culture, but also in a *culture of mediation*, whereby specialised social agencies – the press, film and cinema, radio and television broadcasting – developed to supply and cultivate larger-scale forms of communication; mediating news and other forms of culture into the situation. 'Our' immediate world co-exists with the mediated 'world out there'.**
>
> ***(O'Sullivan et al. 1994: 12–13)***

The rate and scale of these changes are also important aspects of the mediation of culture; as yesterday's technological miracle becomes today's obsolete gizmo, we begin to grasp how rapidly our lives become transformed by media technologies which we take for granted.

Case Study

## The media in Britain 1945 and 1990

**1945** There was no television. About ten million households had a radio set and most were run off a mains, not off a battery. The compulsory licence-fee was ten-shillings [50p]. You had a choice of two BBC stations. One was 'serious'; the other broadcast light music and entertainment. The nine o'clock evening news had an audience of half the population during the war, but this fell quickly in 1945. You could hear music at home on a wind-up gramophone with ten or twelve-inch 78rpm bakelite records. Most people read one of nine London-edited 'national' morning newspapers. If it was the *Daily Mirror* or *Daily Sketch*, it was tabloid. Local evening papers were smaller, but more numerous. Even more people read a Sunday paper than a daily, often for the sport. The national dailies differed sharply in style between the low-circulation 'qualities' and the mass-circulation 'populars'. All nine were separately owned by press barons, such as Lords Beaverbrook, Kemsley and Rothermere. On the news-stands were several popular illustrated news and feature magazines: *Everybody's, Illustrated* and *Picture Post*. There were numerous general magazines and a growing market in women's weeklies and monthlies. You went to the cinema regularly. Thirty million cinema tickets were sold each week. The short weekly 'newsreels', a mix of news and feature stories, gave a foretaste of TV news. Hollywood films predominated. In addition to the main feature, you saw a shorter, low budget 'B' movie.

**1990** There was no escape from television. Three homes out of five had two sets and one person in six had three. ITV broadcast round the clock. Viewers had a choice of four channels and between them, BBCI, BBC2, ITV and CH4 provided some 450 hours of programmes a week. The licence fee was £71, all of which went to the BBC. ITV was paid for by advertisements, carefully regulated by the Independent Broadcasting Authority. We spent twenty-six hours a week watching TV: news, soaps, films, the House of Commons, endless studio discussion amongst politicians. Snooker was the most popular televised sport with only one team game [football] in the TV top-ten. We spent eight hours a week listening to the radio, but mainly whilst doing something else. The BBC had four national stations and thirty-two locals. There was a commercial station for most people and any number of overseas stations. Stations mostly broadcast music and 'chat'. BBC Radio 4 was news and talk; Radio 3 for classical music. You could listen almost anytime and anywhere, especially with a Walkman headset. Music of high technical quality was available in the home through CD's, cassettes, LP's and pop-videos. Despite TV, most people still read a daily newspaper. Of eleven main dailies, six were tabloids with 80% of the circulation. Your paper had 30–40 pages or more; a large proportion of features, pages of small ads and, increasingly, colour. The Sunday papers came in sections. Fewer people read an evening paper, primarily to see what was on TV. Half of us bought a local weekly paper, and three-quarters received 'free-weeklies'. The national dailies were bunched into eight ownership groups, headed by Murdoch, Maxwell and Rothermere. They had interests as international multimedia organisations; TV, radio, film, video, music and book publishing. Magazines were very popular,

*(box continued)*

*(box continued)*

and station news-stands commonly displayed over 700 titles, including music and hi-fi, computing, body-building, sports and so on. (Seymour-Ure 1992: 1–5)

**Questions**

**There seems to be a world of a difference, yet these developments took place in only forty-five years. Since 1990 you may have noticed media developments which should be added to an update of this snapshot; what would they be? Which have affected your own life most?**

## The press

The early development of the British press occurred at a time of great social unrest and political struggle; the fight for the freedom of the press is often associated with the wider campaigns for individual liberty and workers' rights. In this struggle the newly emerging press was seen as a potential vehicle for political agitation and consequently became a target of government intervention. Using a combination of legal sanctions and covert operations the governments of the late eighteenth and early nineteenth centuries infiltrated, bribed and intimidated newspapers into political obedience. Tough laws of sedition and libel were available to deter political agitation while the infamous Stamp Tax was used to ensure that newspapers were owned and read only by the well off. This 'tax on knowledge' had the opposite effect to that intended and the government's attempts to control the established press simply sparked a proliferation of radical pamphlets and newspapers which were forced to operate as underground and clandestine organizations (samizdat). These papers were owned and written by political activists and they quickly became popular with the new industrial working class for whom they were intended.

In 1826, Cobbett's *Address to Journeymen and Labourers* sold over 200,000 copies, while his *Political Register* sold over 44,000 copies a week compared to the 6,000–7,000 circulation of the London-based *Times* (Hall 1982). In 1831, the *Poor Man's Guardian*, carrying the slogan 'Published in defiance of the Law, to try the power of Might against Right', began a six-year run as the most notorious opponent of government tyranny, at times achieving sales of over 16,000 per copy. By 1836, Curran and Seaton (1991) have estimated, the 'unstamped press' was enjoying a readership of over 2 million in London alone while stamped newspapers really struggled to compete; not surprising when we realize that one copy of *The Times* would have cost the average weekly wage of 7d (3p). The government appeared to accept defeat and eventually abolished the Stamp Tax. This is often hailed as a great achievement in the struggle for democracy and referred to by some as a 'golden age' of British journalism which ushered in a transition from official to popular control (Koss 1973).

This 'liberalization' of the press is challenged by Curran and Seaton (1991) who argue that it is a political myth which disguises the real purpose of the reform: to destroy the popularity of the radical press, to enhance the power (and profitability) of the 'respectable' press, and to ensure that the newly freed newspapers were owned and controlled by 'men of good moral character, of respectability and of capital' (1991: 29). According to this perspective the commercial press did not come into being as a celebration of freedom but as a deliberate attempt at repression and ideological control:

> **The period around the middle of the nineteenth century . . . did not inaugurate a new era of press freedom and liberty: it introduced a new system of press censorship more effective than anything that had gone before. Market forces succeeded where legal repression had failed in conscripting the press to the social order.**
>
> ***(Curran and Seaton 1991: 9)***

By the end of the nineteenth century a newly educated working class provided a mass market which was satisfied by a range of commercial newspapers. The start-up costs were high but so were the returns on investment. Advertising revenue enabled the cover prices to fall dramatically and placed the commercial press in a strong position to see off radical competitors who refused to dilute their political seriousness and as a result were unappealing to readers and advertisers alike. By 1933 the left-wing *Daily Herald* was trading at a loss despite having the largest circulation in the western world, indicating the crucial importance of advertising for newspapers irrespective of their popularity; it closed in 1964 with 8 per cent of market share. New types of newspapers emerged which were aimed at the literate working and lower-middle classes but geared towards entertainment, consensus and patriotism. The *Daily Mail, Daily Express, Daily Mirror* and the *News of the World* all emerged as mass circulation newspapers for the lower-class reader with *The Times* and the *Daily Telegraph* providing serious news for the middle and upper classes.

Behind these ventures were successful businessmen whose power was quickly recognized. As the ownership of the press became concentrated in the hands of four or five press barons and their dynasties, politicians became concerned about the influence of unaccountable proprietors who enjoyed 'power without responsibility'. By 1937, the four major players were Lords Beaverbrook, Rothermere, Camrose and Kemsley who between them owned 50 per cent of national and local dailies and 30 per cent of the Sunday papers, including most of the popular titles. Although often referred to as 'the fourth estate of the realm' because of its independence from party politics and government influence, the British press was now controlled by men with very serious political ambitions. Beaverbrook and Rothermere, for example, used their newspapers to launch the United Empire Party as a challenge to the Conservatives in 1930; for Rothermere, this had turned into outright support of fascism by the end of the decade (Jenkins 1986: 24–5).

After the Second World War a Royal Commission was set up to investigate 'the growth of the monopolistic tendencies in the control of the press'. Despite its conclusion that concentration of ownership did not represent a threat to freedom of expression as long as the public got what it wanted, the issues of monopoly ownership, editorial freedom and political bias have continued to dominate discussion of the relationship between society and 'its' press and been the subject in Britain of two further Royal Commissions.

In the post-war period the great proprietors gradually disappeared from the scene and their 'crumbling palaces' fell into the hands of others amidst intense competition and takeover. The personal fiefdoms of Beaverbrook and Rothermere became corporations run as businesses on behalf of shareholders who were primarily concerned with market share and advertising revenue. Control was seen to pass from powerful and interfering owners into the professional hands of editors and journalists committed to satisfying their customers and running an efficient business (Koss 1973). On the other hand, Curran and Seaton (1991) argue that some of the old barons clung on to their power well into the 1960s by which time a new generation of 'interventionist proprietors' had emerged including one or two members of the old dynasties. While Vere Harmsworth (the third Viscount Rothermere) continued to run Associated Newspapers as a French tax exile, the new breed included Rupert Murdoch (News International), Robert Maxwell (Mirror Group) and Lord Stevens (who replaced Lord Matthews at United Newspapers). Lord Thompson (*The Times*), Tiny Rowlands (the *Observer* ) and Conrad Black ( who purchased the *Telegraph* from Lord Hartwell in 1985) made up the other key players in this shake up.

Curran and Seaton complain that this is not so much a period of 'market democracy' as one of concentration of ownership and corporate takeover resulting in the 'integration [of the press] into the core sectors of financial and industrial capital':

**The ownership of newspapers thus became one strategy by which large business organisations sought to influence the environment in which they operated. This strategy was pursued mainly on the basis of an arm's length relationship between newspapers and conglomerate newspaper companies during the 1960s. But in the more recent period, newspapers campaigned more actively for the general interests of big business, under closer proprietorial supervision. This development signified an important, long-term shift: commercial newspapers became increasingly the instruments of large business conglomerates with political interests rather than an extension of the party system.** ***(Curran and Seaton 1991: 101)***

In the mid-1980s the press world was turned on its head by technological innovations which revolutionized the production process and the relationship of journalists to their work and one another. Computerization made traditional typesetters redundant and dragged the messy business of industrial newspaper production out of Fleet Street and into the shiny new world of Wapping. In theory this reduced production costs and opened up the press to new competition. For the first time in decades new titles were launched which appeared to challenge the monopolistic domination of the established press; *Today*, the *London Daily News*, the *Independent*, *Independent on Sunday*, *Sunday Correspondent*, *News on Sunday* and the *Sunday Sport* hit the streets in a flurry of marketing hype and hard-nosed competition but the costs of breaking into the world of press monopoly were too great and by the mid-1990s only the soft porn *Sunday Sport* and its daily equivalent have survived intact; the *Sunday Correspondent* and *News on Sunday* collapsed within months while *Today* has been forced to close because it was losing so much money and the *Independent* was finally forced to accept a takeover bid from the Mirror Group.

What is interesting in all of this is the way in which a genuinely radical press has become depoliticized, commercialized and integrated into the economic and political core of society; a medium which began its life as a force for political agitation and social change has become part of the entertainment industry.

Economic gains secured by adoption of new technologies for production and printing and the move out to London's Docklands and regional sites have not

**Fig 14.1** Paper mountain: in their desperate battle to retain market share, newspapers are adding more and more supplements. (Photograph by David Hughes, courtesy of Robert Harding Picture Library Ltd.)

stopped newspaper proprietors from seeking new ways to promote their newspapers. The nominal distinction between quality and tabloid format is slowly being squeezed by evermore ingenious attempts to attract new readers by introducing gimmicks, such as fantasy sport, bingo prizes and portfolios, sponsorship of downmarket TV game shows linked to game cards and, during the 1990s, the race to beat the competition through lower prices, for example the price of *The Times* went down to 20p – less than half the price of the *Guardian* at the time.

Advertising revenue, boosted by circulation sales, make newspapers viable so long as they can keep loyal readerships. The popular press is financed by its readers; two-thirds of its income derives from sales, only one-third from advertising. In the quality press – *The Times*, *Guardian* and *Daily Telegraph* – this ratio is reversed. Although 60 per cent of adults read a daily paper, the increasing number of different newspapers and print media forces papers into a desperate battle to retain their market share.

Ironically the 'market democracy' model seems to have led to a decline in journalistic standards and a growing concern over issues such as libel, chequebook journalism and the invasion of privacy. In 1989, the government set up a Committee of Inquiry, chaired by David Calcutt, after public complaints of sleazy tabloid journalism. The committee recommended the creation of a Press Complaints Commission, to replace the voluntary codes of practice within the defunct Press Council. After several further reviews, and the 'odious' press treatment of the former Heritage Secretary, David Mellor, and the Princess of Wales, the final *Review of Press Regulation* came out in January 1993. Its main recommendations were that a statutory tribunal be set up to ensure conduct-code approval by the chief editors of all UK newspapers, to stop publication of offending material, impose fines and award costs and, finally, to create new criminal offences of unauthorized trespass and phone-taps, infringement of privacy and interception of telecommunications (National Heritage Select Committee 1993). The reaction from the editors themselves, however, was highly indignant. Peter Preston, then editor of the *Guardian*, said 'What is now being proposed is an all-purpose Government tribunal enforcing Government guidelines which will sit in judgment on the press year after year, coloured by the views of the Government of the day. That seems to me to be the complete antithesis of press freedom' (leader comment, *Guardian* 11 January 1993).

**Q** Despite the best efforts of government tribunals, individual campaigners, and frequent expressions of public outrage the tabloid press in particular continues to publish sleazy and libellous stories. To what extent do you think a society gets the press it wants and deserves?

### Broadcasting

Since the 1920s technological developments in the electronic and broadcast media have transformed the communications environment and overshadowed the debates about the importance of the press. Although we should not overestimate the power of these new forms of mass communication by falling into the trap of 'technological determinism' (R Williams 1974), it is clear that the instant and immediate nature of telecommunications and broadcasting have played a major role in the modernization of societies; they are essential elements in the creation of mass society and the globalization of culture and for many people represent the most significant link with social reality. In particular the ability of these forms to communicate in sound and images enhances their apparent power over the written word to convey 'how things really are'. This impression is so vital to the broadcasting media that no effort is spared to maintain it. In a *Late Show* review of the CNN coverage of the Gulf War it was revealed that 'live' transmissions from reporters in Baghdad were in fact based on information gained via telephone links to New York and London where foreign correspondents and government officials had much more idea of what was going on (BBC 2, 20 June 1995).

Television and radio broadcasting provision in the UK has undergone some important changes in the post-war period, and particularly so since the arrival of new technologies, such as satellite broadcasting, cable and VCR. In many ways, TV and radio have become essential elements of everyday life so that it is difficult to imagine a time without them but if we turn to the history of these media in Britain it is interesting to note how broadcasting, which began almost by accident, developed within a particular set of cultural, economic and political circumstances. Unlike newspapers, whose early evolution appeared in opposition to the state, broadcasting has always been subject to state regulation and control, primarily through the allocation of scarce channel frequencies. The incorporation of the early BBC under its Royal Charter gave it a degree of licensed independence, but the main paradox lies in the fact that the BBC remains economically dependent on, yet constitutionally separate from the state. The constitution requires that it provides an impartial national service offering a mixed blend of programming 'news, sport, educational, religious and children's programmes' without the need for any advertising support for its production or transmission budgets. It is this commitment to high quality public broadcasting for all which has led to conflict between the BBC and various governments, particularly when the prevailing attitudes are shaped by the enterprise culture and policies of deregulation. This tension between private enterprise and public service runs through the history of British broadcasting.

## Radio

Radio is often overlooked when we talk about the media, yet before the advent of television, it was one of the main sources of news and entertainment in the home. Originally, the BBC was the sole provider of national programming on a public service model. This changed with the arrival of independent radio (IR), and is currently undergoing new changes with the advent of national commercial stations, satellite radio and the growth of community-based stations.

The history and development of UK radio is under-researched at present, although Scannell and Cardiff (1991), Lewis and Booth (1989) and Crisell (1988) offer particular insights into how the arrival of radio created new, even unique, forms of national identity and domestic practices acting through the BBC. Golding (1974) and Curran and Seaton (1991) also offer accounts of the development of radio under the auspices of Lord Reith and the BBC. Beginning life as a 'wireless' version of the telephone, the radio very quickly emerged as a means of mass communication which needed regulation. In Britain this originally involved the British Broadcasting Company, the body set up by the manufacturers of radio sets and licensed by the Post Office to broadcast as a monopoly. The first director of the BBC was John Reith, a strict Calvinist who recognized the importance of the radio to act as 'trustee of the national interest' and to defend middle-class standards of Christian morality. In 1924, Reith wrote in *Broadcast over Britain*:

**As we conceive it, our responsibility is to carry into the greatest possible number of homes everything that is the best in every department of human knowledge, endeavour and achievement, and to avoid the things which are, or may be, hurtful. It is occasionally indicated to us that we are apparently setting out to give the public what they think they need – not what they want. But few know what they want, and very few what they need. In any case, it is better to overestimate the mentality of the public, than to underestimate it.** ***(Reith 1924: 27)***

By 1926 this private company had become a public monopoly (it became the British Broadcasting Corporation) which harnessed the 'initiative of business enterprise' to the 'concept of public service'. This particularly British notion of 'public service broadcasting' has until recently remained at the core of what the BBC stands for and, according to Asa Briggs (1961: 235–9), was based on four key principles:

- Programming was for public good not profit.
- National coverage for an undifferentiated community of the British people.
- Unified control through the 'brute force of monopoly'.
- Maintenance of high moral standards. (Golding 1974: 33)

This model of public service radio broadcasting was how the BBC operated up to and including 1945, at a time when it was crucial to maintain national cohesion. The Home and World Services carried news programmes, while a specially created Forces Programme (comedy shows, big-band music and quizzes) became very popular with the UK listener. Following the war, the Light Programme, Home Service and 'highbrow' Third Programme emerged in recognition of the social class differences which still existed within the 'national' culture. According to Curran and Seaton (1991: 187) these three new radio stations coincided with the tripartite classification of schools to be found in the reformed education system. With some allowance for regional variations, however, the mission of the BBC remained 'to educate, to inform, and to entertain' within a national context:

**Because radio was directed at the home, it was the duty of broadcasters to thread their material into the fabric of family life without warping it; to diffuse ideas, information, music and entertainment without being brashly intrusive . . . for whilst British broadcasters wished to preserve the individuality of their listeners, they recognised that radio had a unique potential for uniting the public to the private sphere of life, and it was for this reason that the programmes of national identity formed the backbone of British broadcasting.** *(Scannell and Cardiff 1991: 14)*

The 1960s brought a breath of sea-spray to the airwaves with the arrival of pirate radio, which was advertising-led and offered a mix of pop music and chat that was immediately popular with young listeners, unlike the middle-class production values of 'Aunty's' middle-of-the-road Light Programme. After pirate broadcasting was outlawed, it was decided to break the existing BBC radio system apart, and in its place to offer programmes geared to particular age and 'taste' groups, through Radios 1 (pop music), 2 (light entertainment), 3 (classical music) and 4 (news/current affairs/drama).

It is very likely that future competition for radio listeners will diversify into increasingly distinctive age and taste groups, with the BBC's national AM and FM services (Radios 1, 2, 3, 4 and 5 Live) being squeezed not only by locally based BBC and IR stations but also by the new national commercial services, such as Atlantic 252, Classic FM, Virgin 1215 and Talk Radio UK. In the battle for the 'pop' audience the BBC saw its Radio 1 figures plummet from 17 million in 1992 to around 11 million in 1995. In order to stem this haemorrhaging of listeners the youthful Chris Evans was recruited from the seriously silly TV show *Don't Forget Your Toothbrush*. Early results showed a return of approximately 1 million listeners but in 1995 the long-term outcome is in doubt. It is certainly a distant cry from the days of Lord Reith when 'the great and the good . . . trooped into studios to educate and inform on every subject from unemployment to the Origin of the Species' (Scannell and Cardiff 1991, quoted in Curran and Seaton 1991: 138).

### *Radio and everyday life*

Radio is, essentially, a user-friendly medium. By its portable and accessible nature, it is so well integrated into everyday routines that it has become a backing soundtrack for many domestic chores or driving the car. For this reason it is often related to 'secondary' or 'tertiary' forms of media consumption which do not require the concentrated activity of 'primary' use. Radio is also relevant to people's daily routines according to different times of day, particularly when there is less demand from other forms of media engagement like newspapers and television.

**Q**

Summarize the listening and viewing patterns illustrated by Figure 14.2.

What does this tell us about how radio and television are used in the domestic context?

Table 14.1 indicates that people listen to the radio for about sixteen hours a week on average, with people in social classes A and B listening to the least amount of radio, but spending longer listening to Radio 4.

Why do you think classes A and B listen to the least amount of radio?

Why do you think the different social class groups exhibit the radio preferences that are shown in Table 14.1?

Fig 14.2 Radio and television audiences throughout the day, 1992 (United Kingdom).

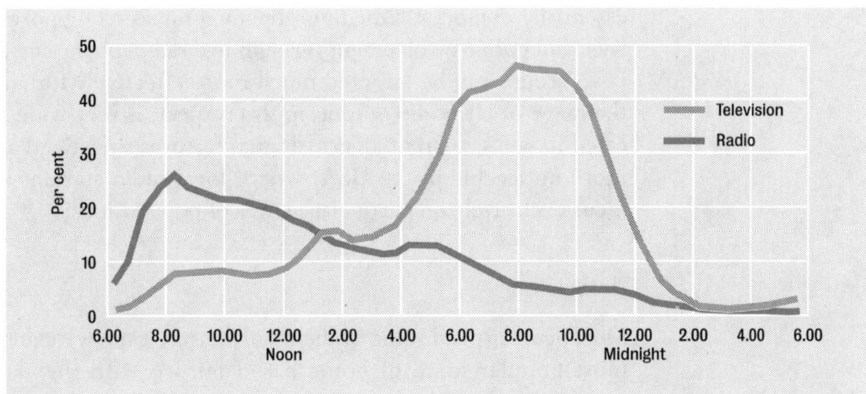


*Notes* : Persons aged 4 or over. Average audience, Quarter 4, 1992

*Source* : *Social Trends 24* 1994: 131
*Original source*: Broadcasters' Audience Research Board; Radio Joint Audience Research; AGB Limited; RSL Limited

Such comparative data are useful in giving us a better idea of radio's popularity in comparison to TV, but they need to be focused within the individual context. In the domestic sphere, where it becomes one of the habits of the daily routine, it enhances personal experience, often meeting the needs of diverse listeners for feelings of companionship and group identity. Baehr and Ryan (1984) apply this familiarity factor to the domestic world of women listeners, but criticize the taken-for-granted nature of radio production, which tends to treat women listeners as solely interested in women-only issues and programme strands. Much the same can be said for the 'typical' listener which Radio 5 Live is aiming to attract, with its programmes heavily centred on rolling news and sport. Radio is also seen as an

Table 14.1 Radio listening: by social class, 1993.

| United Kingdom | Hours and minutes per week | | | | |
|---|---|---|---|---|---|
| | AB | C1 | C2 | DE | All persons |
| Radio 1 | 2:13 | 3:09 | 4:10 | 3:05 | 3:16 |
| Radio 2 | 1:58 | 2:03 | 2:05 | 1:57 | 2:01 |
| Radio 3 | 0:29 | 0:14 | 0:07 | 0:06 | 0:12 |
| Radio 4 | 3:44 | 1:55 | 1:01 | 0:55 | 1:40 |
| Radio 5 | 0:21 | 0:21 | 0:17 | 0:18 | 0:19 |
| BBC local/regional | 1:07 | 1:31 | 1:51 | 1:59 | 1:41 |
| Atlantic 252 | 0:17 | 0:25 | 0:38 | 0:44 | 0:33 |
| Classic FM | 0:46 | 0:31 | 0:18 | 0:18 | 0:26 |
| Virgin 1215 | 0:12 | 0:18 | 0:23 | 0:19 | 0:18 |
| Local commercial | 3:14 | 4:56 | 6:23 | 6:29 | 5:32 |
| Other | 0:20 | 0:28 | 0:30 | 0:34 | 0:29 |
| Total listening time | 14:41 | 15:51 | 17:43 | 16:44 | 16:27 |

*Note:* Persons aged 4 or over

*Source: Social Trends 25* 1995:217
*Original source*: Radio Joint Audience Research: British Broadcasting Corporation

essentially democratic medium, opening up scarce opportunities for listener feedback and public involvement through live radio 'phone-ins'. Different age, class and taste groups can be targeted much more effectively for advertising purposes, and the range of UK radio output, in this respect, is very wide, covering channels dedicated to news, current affairs, drama, features, sport and all types of music. This is more noticeable in the USA, where local radio stations are the norm and often focus exclusively on particular genres of popular music.

## Television

Most people spend some of their daily leisure time watching TV which is, by far, the most popular form of home-based leisure with the average person watching approximately 27 hours of TV every week. In recent years there has been a slight decline but people watched more TV in 1992 than in each of the previous five years. All social groups spend roughly a quarter of their viewing time on information and news, and 40 per cent view light entertainment and light drama, though there is a difference according to social class and gender.

Television viewing always involves mixed audiences, but there does seem to be a higher percentage of women viewers and an increasing scale of TV-watching in the C2 and DE class groups. This is partly a result of an increased use of cable and satellite TV (see pp.568–71). High-rating soap operas, quiz shows and news programmes tend to be watched by a complete cross-section without any skew towards a particular age group, sex or class. According to Barnett (1989), patterns of television viewing do not depend exclusively on the content or quality of the programme. There are many independent and unpredictable variables as well as the more obvious social and cultural ones.

### *Development of television broadcasting*

Currently, British viewers have the choice of four terrestrial channels (BBC 1, BBC 2, ITV and Channel 4) and sixteen regional commercial TV companies, with S4C providing a Welsh-language service. Funding follows from the annual BBC licence fee, while independent TV and radio operate from spot-advertising revenue and programme sponsorship deals. The BBC sees itself as a particularly 'national' service, with regional and cultural variations, while ITV/IR developed from strong regional production bases, but sharing programmes with other companies across the independent network. Recent developments, such as Channel 4 and TV Asia, exist to cater for minority and multicultural interests. There has been a growth in both satellite and cable TV services which offer subscription-only programmes, such as sport, movies, cartoons, 'lifestyle' and MTV (music television); these are commercial enterprises competing with the terrestrial networks for a limited pot of advertising revenue.

Television started life in 1936 as the poor relation of radio at the BBC with a privileged audience of 20,000 Londoners. After the war the experiment resumed but TV licence sales had barely reached 2 million by 1953. The exciting potential of television was being explored and exploited by commercial broadcasters in the USA, but in Britain it remained under the control of an old-fashioned organization which had grown out of radio and tended to treat television as a 'wireless' with pictures. At a time when the disposable income of the 'affluent' working class had increased to the extent that they represented a large consumer market it was dangerous to ignore their tastes, which were becoming heavily influenced by the popular culture of North America (see Tunstall 1977: 100–1)

Independent Television in Britain grew out of the desire in the 1950s to challenge the monopoly of the BBC and to make money out of the advertising potential of television. This was a time of relative economic expansion and, under pressure from the commercial TV lobby, the Conservative government approved legislation for the creation of advertising-funded commercial television under an Independent Television Authority (ITA). Branded at the time by Lord Thompson as 'a licence to print money', the ethos of commercial television, and the later developments incorporated in the Broadcasting Act 1990, had been established.

The new commercial TV companies were allocated eight-year regional franchises and operated a system of 'pooling' programmes for transmission. The existing ITA was soon replaced by the Independent Broadcasting Authority (IBA) which licensed the regional companies and oversaw the transmission facilities. This federal system of local companies having strong regional identities helped to further encourage competition and diversity. However, the IBA held control of advertising. The US system of direct sponsorship was rejected and, in its place, spot advertising at set intervals was permitted to enable programme continuity and flow. Independent TV in this form prospered but grave concerns over the quality of programming resulted in a poor end-of-term report in 1962 from the Pilkington Committee, which complained that the ITV companies had failed to deliver good quality public broadcasting. As a result the BBC were awarded the third channel and BBC 2 expanded into new areas of programme production, particularly with the arrival of colour TV in 1967.

In the 1980s the Conservative government began to explore the opportunities for deregulation and private enterprise in broadcasting which challenged the duopoly of the BBC/ITV networks. As a result of the Broadcasting Act 1981,Channel 4 was created from within the existing TV network. Like BBC 2 it was to provide for minority tastes but was initially subsidized from the advertising profits of the ITV companies in an attempt to provide public service broadcasting via commercial channels. Under the IBA the new channel was required 'to ensure that the programmes contain a suitable proportion of matter calculated to appeal to tastes and interests not generally catered for by Service 1( ITV); to ensure that a suitable proportion of the programmes are of an educational nature; to encourage innovation and experiment in the form and content of programmes, and generally to give Service 2 a distinctive character of its own' (Blanchard and Morley 1982: 22). By mixing popular programmes with the 'risky and challenging', Channel 4 has become a successful alternative to the ITV companies with a 10 per cent share of viewers and taking over £300 million in advertising revenue in its first year as an independent operator (Peak 1994: 101). Whether Channel 4 can retain its distinctive character and remain commercially viable will be important for the development of public service broadcasting in the twenty-first century.

The Peacock Committee considered alternative forms of funding the BBC but direct sponsorship via advertising was ruled out. However, the BBC was heavily criticized for waste and 'red tape' and the Peacock Report (1986) recommended that the Corporation should be opened up to commercial ideas and practices, 'enlarging the freedom of choice of the consumer and the opportunities to programme makers to offer alternative wares to the public.' Under the new regime of Michael Checkland and John Birt the BBC has been drastically reorganized in the hope that a more commercial outfit will win government approval when its charter comes up for renewal in 1996. Apart from internal reforms the BBC contracts out much of its programming, engages in international co-productions and pursues a range of income-generating enterprises, including the launch of its own satellite channel, UK Gold in conjunction with Thames Television. Indications from the Heritage Secretary suggest that the licence fee will be maintained and that the BBC will remain a major provider of national public services although some hints have been dropped about the possibility of popular radio stations attracting advertising. The stage has been set for a battle between 'the fossilized fogeys' of the traditional BBC and 'the thrusting modernizers' of John Birt's new order while writers like Hargreaves (1993) have argued for a complete break with the past and the end of BBC paternalism funded by a licence fee (G Williams 1994: 9)

In 1990 the Broadcasting Act revolutionized the industry and in particular the dominance of the old ITV companies. Under the Act, broadcasting came under the remit of a new Heritage Ministry, committed to the idea of 'typically British' public service broadcasting. Furthermore, the Act obliged both the BBC and the ITV companies to contract out up to 25 per cent of their programmes to independent producers, which has meant a growth in the subcontracting sector, for example Hat Trick, Action Time, Zenith, Witzend and so on. The BBC came through relatively unscathed from the Act's implementation and its function was recognized as a necessary part of national public service programming policies. The Act's main effect was on the ITV companies, which were now to be licensed and regulated by the Independant Television Commission (ITC) whose members are appointed by the Heritage Secretary. The commercial broadcasters were required to bid for the right to operate as regional broadcasters and franchises went to those who tabled the highest bids so long as they satisfied quality requirements. Several existing ITV companies failed to secure their existing franchises while Channel 4 became an independent corporation in its own right, selling its own advertising in place of subsidy from within the ITV operating budget.

**Q** **What assumptions about society lie behind the concept of public service broadcasting? How important is it in a period of rapid commercialization?**

### *Cable and satellite broadcasting*

As more and more homes link up to cable and BSkyB, the market dominance of the old BBC/ITV duopoly is being challenged. Major 'listed' sporting events like Premier League football and the Benson and Hedges cricket final have been bought up to ensure that live coverage is exclusive to those able to receive BSkyB (Whannel and Williams 1993). In the long run the choices offered by 'pay to view' broadcasting and video on demand may take us to a future where all our telecommunications needs arrive through a modem connection to the family PC subsidized by spot advertising and sponsorship deals. In this kind of customer-led marketplace the future of public service broadcasting is open to doubt. As Granville Williams has pointed out:

**We now have two different delivery systems into the home. We can watch BBC, ITV and Channel Four Television free at the point of use, or with the new delivery systems, such as cable, pay-per-view and television-on-demand, payment is made as we view. There is an important issue of public policy in the future relationship between the two systems, and at the heart of it is the continued provision of broadcasting free at the point of use .** *(G Williams 1994: 51)*

Contrary to popular belief, cable broadcasting is not new to the UK. Many homes in the 1950s and 1960s were cabled up to receive radio and paid through subscription for the better quality reception. The cable systems which are being installed across Britain in the mid-1990s were first established in Swindon and Milton Keynes. The go-ahead for cable and satellite services began with two Information Technology Advisory Panel (ITAP) reports in 1982 which led to the creation of the Cable Authority. It was decided that the future for television services would be better served by the market and, in particular, that government policy should be one of introducing and promoting competition so that the industry and the consumer could benefit.

At the same time the first steps towards satellite transmission were taken where again the development in the UK was primarily market-driven, in contrast to other operations such as the Minitel service in France, which offers public access to a wide range of interactive communication services. The early initiative was taken by a consortium of television and publishing interests (the original British Satellite Broadcasting) but they were left at the starting-gate by Murdoch's gamble in creating Sky Television on European-owned transmission facilities. This venture required a great deal of heavy initial investment, partly offset by his profits from other publishing interests. However, the competition for subscribers left both BSB and Sky TV at a disadvantage, and they combined into the single BSkyB with Rupert Murdoch in control. It seems that Murdoch's gamble paid off, and his advertising profits will be used for other international forays into other areas, such as the South-East Asian-based Star TV satellite as well as the development of Digital TV with the French Canal Plus which promises to open up the possibilities of interactive TV for the twenty-first century.

In domestic audience terms, Britain has virtually reached saturation point for broadcast programmes from domestic, cable and satellite companies. Viewers can enjoy a greater range of channels and broadcasting services which provide a wide range of 'thematic' programmes, such as box-office films, sport, lifestyle, cartoons, classic repeats, soaps, and twenty-four-hour news as well as the traditional 'mixed' programming from the BBC and the ITC companies. According to Veljanovski (1991), this is a prime example of viewer sovereignty which the new television marketplace is geared to provide:

**The viewer will no longer be restricted to a few general entertainment channels, but will be able to create his or her own viewing schedule at times which are convenient to them and not the broadcasters. In the absence of government restrictions on the spread of new technologies and programming, viewers will have greater choice, variety and access to more programmes. It follows that British broadcasting should move towards a market system which recognises that viewers and listeners are the best ultimate judges on their own interest, which they can best satisfy if they have the option of purchasing from the broadcasting services from as many alternative sources of supply as possible.** *(Veljanovski 1991: 14)*

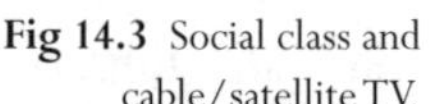

**Fig 14.3** Social class and cable/satellite TV.

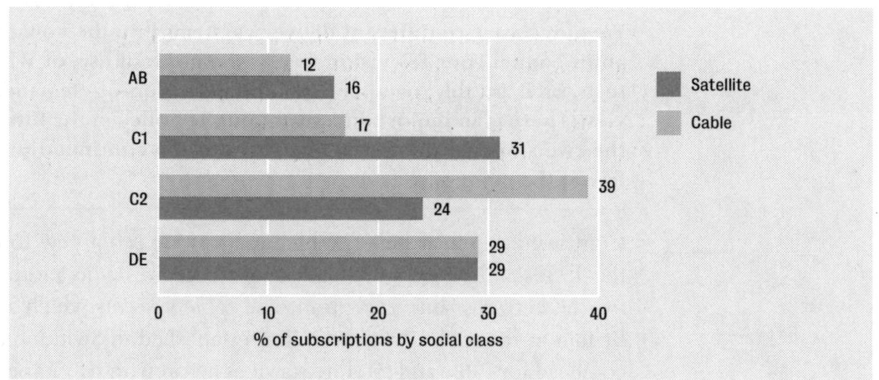


*Source*: Denscombe 1995: 10

By 1995 the penetration of cable and satellite was lower than anticipated, with BSkyB dish sales running at around 3 million and cable links in approximately 700,000 homes. These are unevenly distributed with a greater concentration in working-class homes.

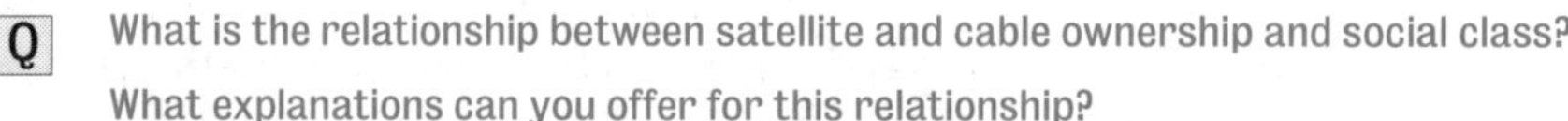

Q What is the relationship between satellite and cable ownership and social class? What explanations can you offer for this relationship?

In the mid-1990s and beyond, technical innovations in UK broadcasting will have important repercussions on the public service and commercial organizations as well as the public at large who will experience great changes in the worlds of work and leisure. Williams (1994) has argued that the developments in fibre optics and digitalization will create a new interactive multimedia environment in which nothing will be the same again:

> **Television, with its limited terrestrial and satellite TV channels, will be transformed into a two-way medium offering a superfluity of information and entertainment: movies-on-demand, video games, databases, educational programming, home shopping, telephone services, telebanking, teleconferencing, and even the complex simulations of 'virtual reality'.** *(G Williams 1994: 12)*

On the consequences of all this for society, opinion is divided between what Curran and Seaton (1990: ch. 14) call the 'neophiliacs' on one hand and the 'cultural pessimists' on the other. In the view of the neophiliacs we are moving towards a bright new post-industrial future (the Information Society) where the whole world is at our fingertips thanks to the Internet and the World Wide Web (WWW). Interactive communications will increase the opportunities for democratic participation and education while authoritarian national governments struggle to control the flow of information. Customer choice becomes paramount as demand is stimulated and satisfied by a range of 'specialised narrowcast channels and services' (see O'Sullivan *et al*. 1994: 276–7). In reply, the cultural pessimists point to the inevitable decline of quality broadcasting and the damage done to cultural standards by the new forms of communication. Concentration of media ownership, the globalization of culture and the distortion of political power represent the unwelcome side of the new, media-saturated order. In the view of Graham Murdock (1990) we run the risk of creating a world where the principle of universal access to information is sacrificed in the interests of diversity of production and consumer choice. The end result may be a divisive fragmentation based on access to the skills required to travel the superhighway. As the poor and ill educated are excluded from these skills they will become 'an unplugged, disenfranchised underclass' falling further behind 'a technological elite' (G Williams 1994: 20). In their review of the impact of satellite TV on sport, Whannel and Williams (1993) come to a similar conclusion:

**In summary, we are well on the road to a two-tier system of television sport. Terrestrial television will continue to feature a wide range of sports. But major events may be increasingly available only on satellite television, to those able to afford the dish, the channel rental and the pay-to-view fee. . . . Television sport from the 1950s to the 1980s could be seen as a form of social cohesion – developing a series of major national and international events and building an audience for them. These events – the FA Cup Final, Wimbledon, the Olympic Games and the World Cup – became major national shared rituals; events that large numbers of people watched simultaneously, and, symbolically, shared. The more recent developments are characterised by fragmentation. . . . As a result, audiences too, will fragment, and sport may no longer provide as many nationally shared rituals.** *(Whannel and Williams 1993: 4–5)*

## The mass media and control

So far we have concentrated on the development of media technologies and institutions. In emphasizing the power and autonomy of media technologies there is a danger of falling into the trap of 'technological determinism'; as Williams warned in 1974 this diminishes the importance of social, economic and political factors in the development and use of the media. By focusing on the idea that media institutions are driven by technological innovation we imply that society merely deals with the consequences of change instead of looking at the ways in which media technologies, society and culture shape one another:

**New technologies are discovered by an essentially internal process which then sets the conditions for social change and progress. Progress, in particular, is the history of these inventions, which 'created the modern world'. The effects of the technologies, whether direct or indirect, foreseen or unforeseen, are as it were the rest of history. The steam engine, the automobile, television, the atomic bomb, have made modern man and the modern conditions.** *(R Williams 1974: 13)*

In the rest of this chapter we shall explore the wider relationship between the media, society, culture and power. The issues raised will include media freedom, censorship, social control, public responsibility and the ethics of media production; in particular, three areas will be emphasized. First, media and control – the extent to which media communicators and audiences are restricted by social, political, economic and organizational determinants of media production and consumption. Second, theories of media freedom and control – an examination of the different theoretical positions which analyse the relationship between the media, the audience and the structure of society. Third, media power – a brief review of the debates over the media's influence on culture and social behaviour, focusing on the relationship between media presentations of violence and violent behaviour.

As we noted when reviewing the history of the press, the issue of media freedom has been seen as crucial to the development of democratic societies. In opposition to 'authoritarian' and 'soviet' models of deliberate media control, McQuail (1994: 126–31) has noted the emergence of 'public service' and 'libertarian' models which emphasize the creative freedom of media personnel and the customer's right to choose. These ideas underpin the liberal and pluralist views of media production (see pp.584–7) that are at the centre of the debate over the relationship between the media and democracy (Keane 1991). In its most idealized form this view exaggerates the investigative and creative freedom of individual journalists and broadcasters who, according to Gans (1974), 'fight to express their personal values and tastes . . . and to be free from control by the audience and media executives' (quoted in Lull 1995: 122). However, as Gans recognizes, media personnel are also trained employees of large organizations as well as members of society. Whether producing hard hitting news, dramatic fiction or alternative comedy there are institutional restraints placed upon what the media professional can and cannot do. As Brian Whitaker (1981) pointed out in his review of the production of 'the news', journalists and editors are not only gatekeepers of news events, but also actively involved in the creation of news through the criteria by which they select 'newsworthy' stories:

> **There is no limit to what might be reported. The number of observable events is infinite. . . . We often fail to realise what a very, very limited selection of events it is that appears on our table at breakfast time.** *(Whitaker 1981: 23)*

The criteria that govern this selection process involve individuals in making decisions, but they are decisions made in the performance of an organizational role which in turn has to be placed in the context of wider social, economic and political factors.

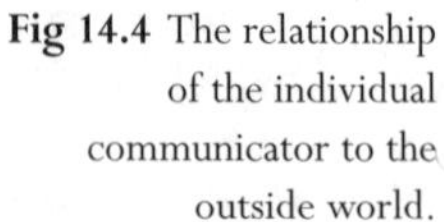
**Fig 14.4** The relationship of the individual communicator to the outside world.

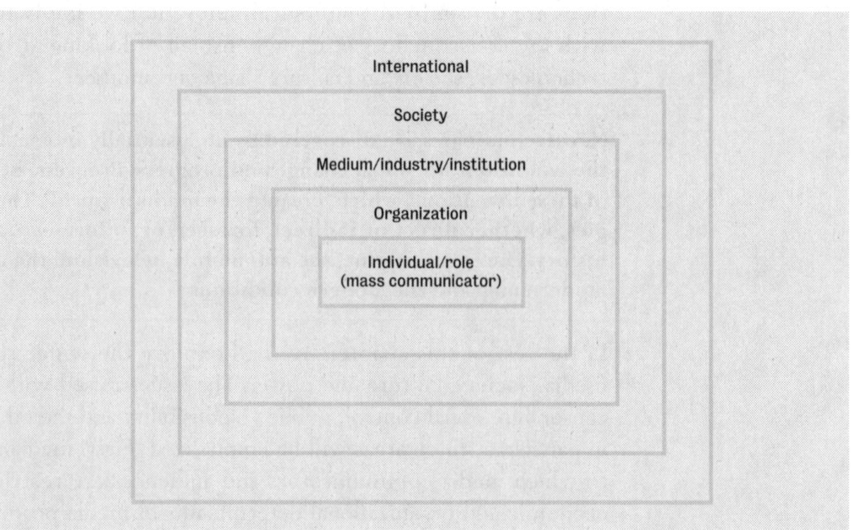


*Source*: McQuail 1994: 189

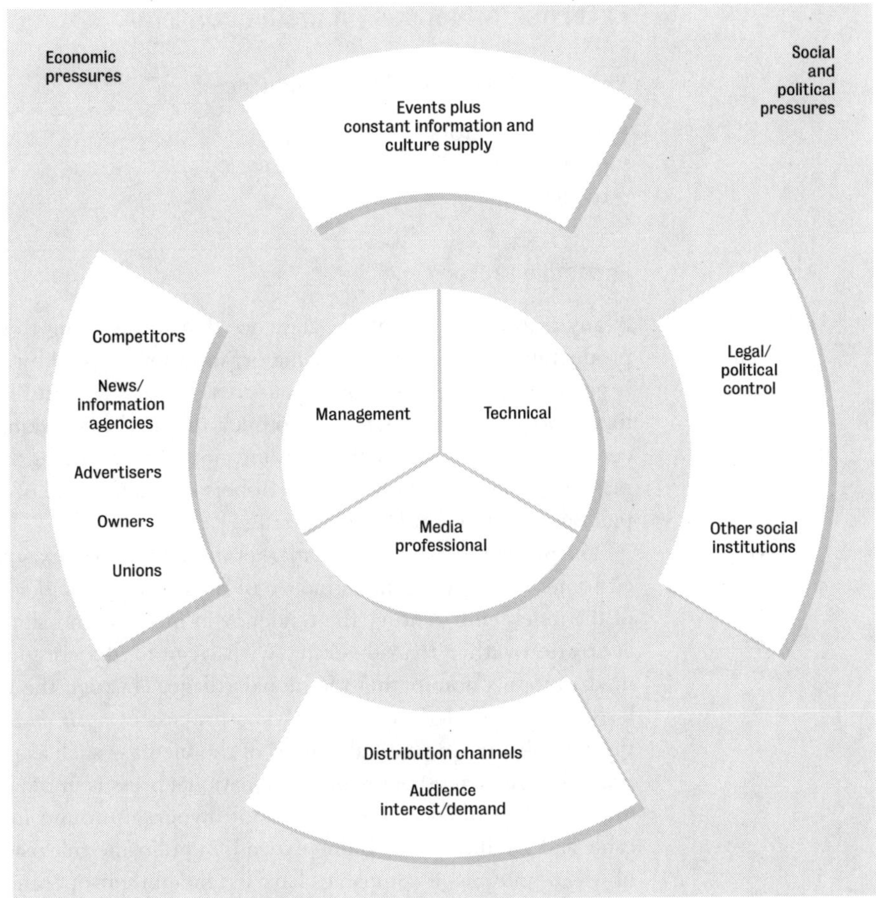


**Fig 14.5** Pressures that journalists have to deal with.

*Source*: McQuail 1994: 191

McQuail (1994) identifies a hierarchy of five levels of analysis for understanding the relationship of the individual communicator to the outside world (see Fig 14.4).

The range of factors or pressures that journalists have to deal with can be expressed in a different way which emphasizes the competing interest groups seeking to influence media decisions (see Fig 14.5).

The various influences on media content can be referred to as 'determinants'. Some of these determinants operate internally and some are external to the media organization. The external influences include economic, political and legal interventions while the internal relate to the constraints inherent in the structure of media organizations.

**Q** Provide examples of the ways in which the work of journalists or broadcasters can be analysed at the five levels given by McQuail.

How might the factors identified in the second model influence news production?

Find some recent examples of media personnel being constrained by these influences.

## External influences on media content

There are three main external influences:

- economic factors
- political control
- regulation

### Economic factors

In any market-led operation, audience demand is going to have a major impact on production. A privately run media organization, owned by a handful of individuals, is good for business because it ensures competition and freedom of choice. Any media organization which tries to buck the market is asking for trouble: 'My concern is to give people what they want, not what improves them. Television does not make the times. It follows them' (Robert Giovalli, Head of Programme Planning at Finninvest, quoted in Keane 1991: 121).

The problem with the basic market model is that it exaggerates the power of the customer and ignores the influence of media owners and advertisers. Since the end of the nineteenth century the tendency in media ownership has been towards concentration rather than diversity with large media conglomerates and powerful media moguls dominating the global village. Through the takeover of their rivals, large companies have expanded via a process of *horizontal integration* to establish their dominance in particular areas of the media – such as publication. By the same process in Britain 90 per cent of the national press is in the hands of five major producers with similar concentrations of ownership found in the local press and, as cable and satellite broadcasting expand, in radio and television. Through the process of *vertical integration* companies have extended their operations into media distribution as well as production. BSkyB, for example, is involved in not only the production of television programmes but also their transmission, while the Japanese electronics giants Sony have bought out software production companies, like Columbia, in order to have greater control over media consumption. This is part of a wider trend towards cross-media ownership on a global scale which is of great concern to media analysts distrustful of the concentration of a variety of media interests in the hands of a few powerful and extremely wealthy operators. In the USA a series of mergers and takeovers since 1993 have seen Paramount going to Viacom for $10 billion, Disney merge with CapCities/ABC for $19 billion and CBS taken over by Westinghouse for $5 billion. In Europe the empires of Murdoch and the Italian media magnate Berlusconi indicate the extent to which national and global conglomerates can dominate the media and entertainment industries.

**We can see that the new generation of media conglomerates encompass much more than the traditional mix of press and television and are now extending their ownership and influence into many related industries such as publishing, radio, film, video, recorded music, telecommunications, computers, advertising, marketing and public relations, cinemas, couriers, hauliers and even postal services. . . . We have a highly concentrated media in the hands of politically partisan owners who use their power to defend and advance their commercial and political influence. Unre-**

**stricted ownership and control will lead to a narrowing of choice and the elimination of diversity in media at a local, regional and national level.**

*(G Williams 1994: 52)*

Although writers such as Veljanovski (1989, 1991) have sought to justify unrestricted cross-media ownership on the grounds that it stimulates competition by 'baling out' ailing newspapers, more critical commentators disagree. While ownership does not automatically imply control, there is much evidence from the history of media institutions and from the biographies of great media moguls such as Beaverbrook that owners have always sought to intervene in media production to further their own commercial and political interests or those of others whom they support (see e.g. Bower 1995; Coleridge 1994; Clarke and Riddell 1992; Jenkins 1986; Shawcross 1992; Tunstall and Palmer 1991).

Case Study

## Newspaper owners and journalists

**The extract below is taken from the letter of resignation that *Times* journalist Peter Kellner wrote in 1986 after *The Times* did not publish a column he wrote on Rupert Murdoch. It illustrates how newspaper owners can exert an influence on newspaper content – indirectly in this case through *Times* sub-editors not wishing to print any criticisms of the paper's owner.**

Dear George

. . . On Sunday I told you of my intention to write my column for tomorrow's *Times* on Rupert Murdoch and the unions. You said that this might cause problems, but that there were no general rules covering this kind of piece and that the article would be judged on its merits. . . .

You told me that there was no way the article could be revised to make it suitable for publication in the *Times*. . . . Your message was clear: legitimate and robust criticism of the *Times'* proprietor is banned from its pages.

I understand your position, but have these comments to make on it:

First, your statement that there was no point even referring my article to Charles Wilson [the editor] demonstrates the oppressive environment in which Murdoch's journalists are now required to work.

Second, your comments about criticisms of proprietors in other papers are wrong. You seem to have forgotten Donald Trelford's public criticisms in *The Observer* of Atlantic Richfield at the time of the paper's sale to Lonrho. . . .

Murdoch is not like any other media boss. He is different, and worse, and has decisively broken the tradition that good journalists and their editors always strive to put the interests of their readers above those of their paymasters. . . . Fine it is his paper. Now we all know where we stand, you can seek and may find columnists willing to write according to these rules. I regret that I cannot be one of them.

(Letter written by Peter Kellner, 11 February 1986, quoted in Seaton and Pimlott 1987: 252–4)

### Questions

**In what ways and to what ends do owners and shareholders attempt to influence the content of 'their' newspapers or radio and television stations?**

**What kinds of constraints are there on this influence? How effective do you think they are?**

On the surface the power of media owners to intervene in media production is itself constrained by a countervailing economic force – the audience. Whatever their personal and political ambitions, owners are in business and have to respond to market pressure. Newspaper cover prices and 'pay per view' television rates are an important source of income but it has often been said that the chief function of the privately owned media is to produce audiences for advertisers.

Advertising is a multibillion dollar business, with independent broadcasters and newspaper companies caught up in an endless battle over ratings. As Carlton TV's Director of Programmes told the *Daily Telegraph*, 'there is no place in prime time television for programmes which cannot achieve ratings of six to eight million' (G Williams 1994: 17). This places advertisers in a strong position to influence programming, production values and even the script: through 'product placement' some shows are thinly disguised commercials. Historical drama is not popular with TV programme makers because the opportunities for product placement or identification are limited. As Peggy Charren, president of Action for Children's TV, has pointed out: 'You can't make Marie Antoinette eat Domino's Pizza' (quoted in G Williams 1994: 18). But this is less of a problem in the UK where product placement is strongly controlled by the Advertising Standards Authority.

In the USA where television has always been a commercial enterprise, even news programmes have to be angled towards dramatic reconstruction of sensational incidents in order to boost audience ratings. K7, the Florida news channel, set a new trend for newscasting in the 1990s when it deliberately shifted towards news as entertainment. Tabloid television is the result providing a diet of human interest and trivia with a heavy emphasis on violent crime. Special effects, background music and trained presenters work together to turn other people's tragedies into prime-time television; in the pursuit of ratings, sensation, excitement and drama replace the quest for serious news coverage (BBC 2 *Late Show* 25 May 1994).

In theory the market-driven media model should guarantee customer choice and satisfy audience needs but as Keane (1991) argues, the outcome ignores the needs and opinions of minority groups (1991: 84). In this relentless pursuit of advertising revenue the media become terrified of controversy and depth and learn to play safe:

> **Advertising works in favour of advertisers and business and against citizens. It privileges corporate speech. Bent on maximising audiences and minimising costs, advertising ensures that material which is of interest to only a small number of citizens will at best be available on a limited scale. Advertising reduces the supply of 'minority interest' programmes, aesthetically and intellectually challenging themes and politically controversial material which fails to achieve top audiences and, hence, does not entice advertisers to open their cheque books.** ***(Keane 1991: 83)***

What examples of 'product placement' (brand name products being seen or mentioned) have you noticed on recent television programmes?

Look at TV programme schedules for one week. List as many 'minority programmes' as you can? When are they scheduled? To what extent does this support the argument about the power of advertisers made above?

## Political control

In the twentieth century the potential of the media for political influence and control has been widely recognized. It is no accident that in times of political upheaval the fiercest battles are often for the control of the radio or television stations as warring factions seek to establish ideological as well as military victory (for example, radio broadcasts whipping up racial hatred played an important role in Rwanda's slide into civil war and genocide in 1994). In periods of political stability the media also play a major role in establishing and maintaining social order and political control. McQuail (1994) describes how the state in totalitarian regimes deliberately suppresses freedom of expression through official censorship while at the same time seeking to establish ideological hegemony through orchestrated propaganda campaigns.

In the 1930s Hitler expressed his opinion on the importance of political propaganda in *Mein Kampf*, identifying two clear objectives in the battle for the hearts and minds of the masses: the silencing of critical intellectuals and the brainwashing of everyone else:

**All propaganda must be popular and its intellectual level must be adjusted to the most limited intelligence among those it is addressed to. Consequently, the greater the mass it is intended to reach, the lower its purely intellectual level will have to be. . . . The art of propaganda lies in understanding the emotional ideas of the great masses and finding . . . the way to the attention and thence to the hearts of the broad masses. . . . The receptivity of the great masses is very limited, their intelligence is small, but their power of forgetting is enormous. [Therefore] all effective propaganda must be limited to a very few points and must harp on these slogans until the last member of the public understands what you want him to understand by your slogan.** ***('War Propaganda', in Hitler 1969)***

In the former Soviet Union the importance of the press for the purposes of agitation, propaganda (agitprop) and organization date from the victory of Lenin in 1917 and the subsequent domination of Soviet society by the Communist Party.

**The press is the strongest instrument with which, day by day, hour by hour, the party speaks to the masses in their own essential language. There is no other means so flexible for establishing spiritual links between the party and the working class.** ***(Stalin, quoted in Whitaker 1981: 45)***

However, such intentions do not always have the desired effect; audiences can react against deliberate attempts at ideological manipulation. Lull (1995) points out that many Chinese people ridicule and resist government propaganda:

**They detest the Communist Party's simple minded self-promotion, its blatantly biased news reports, the laughable TV 'model worker' programmes, the many exaggerated advertising claims about domestic products, and the unavailability of advertised foreign goods.** ***(Lull 1995: 62)***

Case Study

**Television in Iran**

Parliament in Iran, where clerics want to stop people watching television programmes they see as corrupting, yesterday passed the final parts of a bill which bans the private use of satellite television equipment.

The bill, which prohibits the import, distribution and use of satellite dishes, will become law when the guardian council, a parliamentary watchdog, ratifies it in a fortnight. That is considered all but certain.

The legislation empowers the Ministry of Islamic Guidance and Culture 'to safeguard cultural boundaries of the country and of its families against destructive and indecent satellite programmes'.

Iranians watching programmes with dish antennas have a month to dismantle the equipment or risk its confiscation and fines of 1 million to 3 million riyals (£360 –1000).

(*Guardian* 2 January 1995: 9)

In liberal democracies the freedom of the media is a much valued principle but in practice there are still many restrictions imposed by the state. Politically sensitive and morally offensive material is often suppressed; the state also uses the media to transmit information (and misinformation) which serves its interests. This is particularly true in times of political crisis or war. During the First World War, for example, press coverage was tightly controlled and manipulated by the British government (Lovelace 1978). In the 1980s, similar criticisms were made of the news coverage of the Falklands War (Glasgow University Media Group 1985; Morrison and Tumber 1988), while Curtis (1984) is one of many writers to highlight the involvement of British governments in a 'propaganda war' over Northern Ireland.

According to Keane (1991), as the power of the media has grown so the need to curb and control their influence has increased. Since the First World War he notes the growth of 'the democratic leviathan', a range of unaccountable political institutions at all levels of government which combine to further state power at the expense of citizenry. A key element in this process has been the control of the media and Keane highlights the four types of political censorship of the media.

First, the British government can exert direct political censorship on the media. It can vet any sensitive material before it is released; the 'thirty year rule' on Cabinet papers is an example of the automatic 'prior restraint' on information. It can also take legal action against journalists, radio stations and TV companies to prevent the dissemination of material already available or in production. This may include banning, shredding, burning or confiscating material. An example of this direct legal action was the 'Spycatcher' case in 1986 where the British government tried unsuccessfully to stop the publication of a book detailing the memoirs of Peter Wright (1987), a former member of the Secret Services.

Second, state officials have involved themselves in surveillance, infiltration and information management which has 'resulted in a well organised form of permanent political censorship at the heart of state power' (Keane 1991: 99). In 1995 newscaster Jon Snow revealed that in his first days as a journalist, MI5 (the UK Security Service) had tried to recruit him as an agent because of his contacts with the radical student movement.

Third, governments may be 'economical with the truth' or deliberately orchestrate a campaign of disinformation. Tactics can include stage managed briefings, denial of access to official sources and the leaking of misinformation. Those seeking to expose such activities can expect to find their careers destroyed. When in 1985 Clive Ponting, a civil servant, leaked a memo to the Labour MP Tam Dalyell which implied that a Conservative government minister had misled the House of Commons over the sinking of the *Belgrano* during the Falklands War of 1982 he ended up in court, but was found not guilty after a celebrated legal battle. Sarah Tisdall, also a civil servant, had been less fortunate the previous year when she leaked to the *Guardian* government plans for managing public opinion over the siting of US cruise missiles in Britain and received a six-months' prison sentence. The *Guardian* was forced to reveal its source by threat of legal action.

Fourth, governments seek to use the media to influence public opinion: 'All governments seek to manage the news; to trumpet the good, to suppress the bad and to polish up the image of the Prime Minister' (Cockerell *et al.* 1984: 9). Through 'lobby system' briefings, public information campaigns and the manipulation of links with media organizations, governments and politicians use the media to market political policies and careers. Media organizations can scarcely afford to offend such powerful clients, with the result that TV and radio interviews often seem to reflect the demands of the interviewee rather than the interests of the public. Margaret Thatcher, for example, seemed unwillingly to be interviewed by Brian Redhead on Radio 4 but positively enjoyed appearing on the *Jimmy Young Show* on Radio 2. Shortly after coming to power she singled out the editors of the *Sun* and the *Sunday Express* for knighthoods, while Victor Mathews, owner of the *Daily Express*, received a peerage (Shawcross 1992: 212)

As a result of these trends in what might euphemistically be called 'information management,' Keane (1991) suggests that western democracies have become immune from public evaluation and criticism. Government officials have less interest in consulting the public and little belief in their right to know what is going on. The media have had to become part of a strategy of public deceit, or else face the consequences of legally sanctioned intimidation. The Official Secrets Act was extended in 1989 to gag government officials for life and to render it a criminal offence for a journalist to make a 'damaging disclosure'. Simultaneously Clause 28 has ensured that the public promotion of homosexuality by government employees is now an offence. An example of this official censorship was the dubbing of Sinn Fein members' voices between 1988 and 1994 in an attempt 'to starve [them] of the oxygen of publicity' (Gilbert 1992). However, Sinn Fein's leader, Gerry Adams, later commented that the actors assigned to speak his words were rather better at it than Adams himself!

## Regulation

Most state control of the media is exerted through the law and voluntary codes of conduct entered into by media organizations and journalists and broadcasters. While the USA guarantees freedom of expression in its First Amendment and the European Convention on Human Rights does so in Article 10, British governments are not bound by such rights.

As Robertson and Nicol (1992: 3) observe in a 650-page book devoted to legal restrictions on the media, 'Free speech is what is left of speech after the law has had its say'. We shall touch briefly on these legal constraints and identify the more important regulatory bodies and codes or practice.

**Case Study**

## Legal restrictions on the media

### Official Secrets Act

Under the Official Secrets Act 1911 the leaking of official information by civil servants was forbidden and the use of unauthorized material by journalists became a criminal offence. The police were given special powers of arrest, seizure and interrogation in cases where leaks occurred. After the Spycatcher case it was replaced in 1989 with even tighter legislation, which meant that civil servants were bound by 'a lifelong duty of confidentiality'(Burnet 1992: 54) and journalists could be prosecuted for disclosing information 'damaging the security forces or the interest of the United Kingdom' (Robertson and Nicol 1992: 424). That revelations were 'in the public interest' was no longer an admissible defence.

### Blasphemy

In 1950 the crime of blasphemy was defined as any contentious, reviling, scurrilous or ludicrous matter relating to God, Jesus Christ or the Bible, or the formularies of the Church of England. Since 1922 there has been one prosecution as a result of a private action brought by Mary Whitehouse against *Gay News* in 1977. *Gay News* lost the case, were ordered to pay costs and fined and the editor was given a nine-months' jail sentence.

### Obscenity

The Obscene Publication Act 1857 that empowered magistrates to confiscate and destroy immoral books was amended in 1959 to make a distinction between erotic literature of genuine artistic merit and pornography. A number of show trials ensued, the most famous of which concerned *Lady Chatterley's Lover* by D H Lawrence in 1961, the *School Kids' Oz* (1971) and *Inside Linda Lovelace* (1976). Since then the law has largely been used against works glorifying violence and drug abuse, and hard-core pornography, though in 1991 it was invoked against the misogynist lyrics of rap artists N.W.A. Films and videos came within the provisions of the Act in 1977 and 1979, and television and radio were covered by the Broadcasting Act 1990.

### Contempt of court

In Britain there are strict rules governing the media coverage of court cases that are *sub judice* (under consideration). Though cases such as the trial of OJ Simpson 1995 in the USA illustrate how difficult it is to reach a judgment that is fair and *seen* to be fair when there are not strict controls on the media, these controls can sometimes be used to avoid unwelcome publicity.

### Civil law

Civil law covers private litigation relating to breaches of confidence, copyright and libel. At a secret hearing judges are requested to grant an injunction which, once granted, prevents anyone repeating the material covered by it. Where injunctions are not sought or granted and a libel action is successfully prosecuted, the aggrieved party can make a lot of money: Elton John £1 million, Jeffrey Archer £500,000.

### *Regulatory bodies and codes of conduct*

Through statutory laws and voluntary agreement, regulatory bodies have been set up to establish guidelines on 'public taste' and to maintain decent standards of journalism. Pornography, violence, bias and invasions of privacy tend to be the main concerns of such bodies. However, the codes of conduct they try to enforce are seen by Harris (1992) as a minor part of the regulatory framework as journalists and broadcasters are more concerned with the constraints imposed by proprietors, advertisers, public demand and the law.

In Britain there has been some attempt by the press to safguard standards and deal with complaints from the public. Following post-war concerns over the effects of media ownership on free expression, it was suggested that a Press Council be formed which would ensure 'the highest professional standards' in journalism. After threats of government intervention, newspaper proprietors agreed to support the Press Council, which was set up as a voluntary body in 1953. Over the next thirty-five years the Press Council struggled to impose its principles on a press which did not take it seriously. By 1989 agitation and threats of statutory control by MPs of all parties led to the Calcutt Report (1990) which threatened the press with a tribunal possessing legal powers of censorship unless the profession made some attempt to regulate itself. Under threat of government regulation the newspaper prorietors rushed to set up their own Press Complaints Commission (PCC). With a clear code of conduct covering six controversial subjects (accuracy and fairness, privacy, chequebook journalism, race reporting, financial journalism and disclosure of sources) the PCC deals with complaints from the public and publishes a quarterly bulletin of its judgments. However, the PCC has no power to restrain publication or even to insist on prominent public apologies. Robertson and Nicol (1992) are pessimistic about its ability to enforce decent standards of journalism or guarantee the privacy of individuals; they argue that it may be no more than a public relations exercise to avoid government intervention. By comparison the Advertising Standards Authority (which provided the model for the PCC) has more teeth as a self-regulating body to ensure that adverts are 'legal, decent, honest and truthful' because it has the power to hurt advertisers in the pocket by forcing the withdrawal of offensive adverts (Robertson and Nicol 1992: 542–5 and 559–61).

With regard to broadcasting, the power of the spoken word and the moving image has always been considered more deserving of public control than written text. The broadcast media have a captive audience and the normal rules which cover the distribution of magazines and newspapers cannot be applied to radio and television programmes which are beamed into our homes. The power of broadcasters has always been closely tied to government control through the granting of licences and the insistence on clear codes of conduct particularly in relation to accuracy, impartiality and public taste. In Britain there are three major forms of control.

First, the Broadcasting Complaints Commission was set up under the Broadcasting Act 1981 and has the narrow function of investigating complaints of unfair and unjust treatment and the invasion of privacy. Unlike the PCC it has the power to enforce judgments.

Second, the Broadcasting Standards Council (BSC) , established in 1988, has a much wider role which includes the monitoring of sex and violence on television and providing codes of conduct for the portrayal of sensitive and controversial material. Under the Broadcasting Act 1990 these codes were given statutory status. According to Robertson and Nicol this gives the BSC real power to influence programme content and is a far more serious constraint on the freedom of broadcasters:

> **It is another external pressure on broadcasters to bring their professional judgements (about what the public interest requires to be seen) into line with official judgements about what the public does not need to be shown.**
>
> ***(Robertson and Nicol 1992: 606)***

Third, the licensing and censoring of films and videos (but not video games) has a long history of quasi-statutory regulation. The British Board of Film Classification, set up in 1912, has become a means of prior classification of films (U, PG, 15, 18, 18R) and is the chief censor of films shown in cinemas and broadcast on television. Since 1984, the power of classification was extended to video cassettes in the wake of concern over 'video nasties'. The Video Recording Act 1984 requires that all video material, including current affairs, sex education and television drama, receives certification before being sold in cassette format. Films which have already received an 18 or 18R certificate for cinema release do not automatically get approval for transfer to video; the *Evil Dead*, for instance, can be seen on the large screen but cannot be sold legally on cassette. Despite these attempts at prior censorship, it is still possible to bring court action against certified films for obscenity (e.g. *Last Tango in Paris*) or for local authorities to ban any film from cinemas within their jurisdiction (e.g. *The Life of Brian*).

## Internal influences on media content

There are a number of factors that occur within media organizations and influence media production, including the social construction of 'media reality' by journalists and broadcasters working within media organizations. The 'reality' journalists produce has to be accounted for in terms of the practices of those who have the power to determine the experiences of others; these practices have to be placed within the context of media personnel working within bureaucratic organizations.

The organizational structure of the media means that media workers are constrained in two main ways. First, by the hierarchical and paternalistic nature of media organizations. As with any bureaucracy, the lines of authority are clearly marked and the interaction between journalist and editor and between editor and owner are of crucial importance. Second, the journalist relies on sources and contacts within other organizations. The story of journalism 'is the story of the interaction of reporters and officials' (Schudson 1991: 148).

Journalists are members of a profession governed by its own internal regulations (the National Union of Journalists' Code of Conduct). These regulations can be used as a defence against the more unscrupulous editors employed by newspapers. In his study of the BBC, Burns (1977) noted that for many journalists a commitment to professional standards can be a source of conflict with management. John Tusa's criticism in 1995 of John Birt's running of the BBC is a good case in point; Tusa as a foreign correspondent represented the old values of public service broadcasting while Birt was much more market-driven.

The social backgrounds of media personnel are also important because their social and educational backgrounds may simply reinforce the taken-for-granted assumptions underlying organizational definitions of 'newsworthiness' and 'professionalism'. According to US critics such as Lichter *et al.* (1986), the liberally educated 'media elite' in the USA are biased towards 'liberalism' (a dirty word in US politics during the early 1990s) and the Democratic Party. However, the white, male, middle-class profile of most media professionals has led others to provide a different interpretation:

> **Journalists, who are better seen as bureaucrats than buccaneers, begin their work with a stock of plausible, well-defined and largely unconscious assumptions. Part of their job is to translate untidy reality into neat stories with beginnings, middles and denouements. The values which inform the selection of news items usually serve to reinforce conventional opinions and established authority.**
>
> *(Curran and Seaton 1991: 265)*

By definition the experiences and perspectives of those groups who are not part of 'the club' are likely to be undervalued and under-represented. The formal training of journalists through degree programmes may only serve to reinforce this bias by recruiting into the profession those with formal academic qualifications.

Q There are frequent complaints from both Conservative and Labour politicians about bias in the media. What evidence can you find of it in the BBC or ITV?

Would you say that either clearly supports the views of a particular party?

## Perspectives on the mass media

In order to understand the relationship between media personnel, media organizations and social structure it is necessary to examine some of the major theoretical perspectives on the role of the media. The media have to be examined within the context of social interaction and social rules. These rules are formed within the structures of power in society and within this set-up the electronic media have a crucial role to play:

> **The special authority of electronic media, asserting and reinforcing endless streams of ideologically charged information is, without question, an impressive social force. . . . Media help shape and maintain rules and the ideological predispositions underlying them because their unique and powerful technical capabilities and appealing content are the most effective means of information diffusion ever invented. . . . By articulating ideological syntheses that promote certain perspectives and exclude others . . . . the mass media help constitute and regulate social reality by structuring some of their audiences' most common and important experiences. . . . Mass media help break down distance between the macro social and the micro social. They bring public themes into private environments where they enter into and are influenced by local conditions, orientations, authorities and practices.**
>
> *(Lull 1995: 60–1)*

Recognition of this 'special authority' of the media is not a simple acceptance of its social control function; it is the starting-point in an exploration of a range of perspectives which ask us to think about the relationship between the media and society in a variety of ways. These perspectives do not fit neatly under the conventional headings for organizing our ideas on social theory (as, for instance, in Chapter 2); we may wish to compare media perspectives in terms of their emphasis on materialist or culturalist factors. Whether these theories are expressed in optimistic or pessimistic terms is also important. McQuail (1994) has shown how difficult it is to talk about media theories as if they exist in a simple and agreed relationship with one another. The comparison of the *dominant paradigm* with *alternative paradigms*, which is the way in which we categorize different media perspectives below, is therefore only one way of presenting media theories. It may be helpful in providing 'the general structure of thinking about the mass media and society' (McQuail 1994: 93) but it can provide only a limited map of the area.

## The dominant paradigm

Early theories tended to exaggerate the power of the media to influence behaviour and were strongly associated with fears of 'mass society'. In particular fears that developments such as mass education, mass communication and political democracy would lead to the collapse of the old order and elite rule, leading to a fragmented society in which individuals suffer isolation and anomie, and the mob rule. The mass media were seen as part of this 'problem': 'Rather than being viewed as vehicles for enlightenment, popular education and the press are regarded as reducing intelligence to the level of the lowest common denominator' (Bennett 1982: 34). However, precisely because the new mass media dealt in the artefacts of mass culture they could also be seen as a popular means by which the masses could be integrated into the social consensus of the new order:

> **The links between popular mass media and social integration were readily open to conceptualisation in terms both negative and individualistic (more loneliness, crime and immorality), but it was also possible to envisage a positive contribution from modern communications to cohesion and community. Mass media were a potential force for a new kind of cohesion, able to connect scattered individuals in a shared national, city and local experience.** ***(McQuail 1994: 34)***

The dominant paradigm which emerged tended to emphasize a positive view of modern society as liberal, democratic and orderly within which the media play an important role. These ideas found their early expression through the perspectives of functionalism and pluralism.

### *Functionalism*

By responding to human needs, social institutions develop which are said to be functional for society as a whole (see pp.46–7). The mass media can be looked at in this way, with an emphasis on the ways in which they satisfy a range of social needs more effectively than alternative social institutions (e.g. church, family, school). The media according to this model are clearly involved in socialization, integration and the maintenance of social consensus.

**[We are talking of] the ability of the media to bind together disparate and fragmented audiences into a classless community of individuals who feel others to be their equals, with whom they can share news of events, television characters and fictional narratives.** *(Keane 1991: 120)*

Case Study

## The functions of the mass media

From the early work of Lasswell (1948), Wright (1960) and Mendelsohn (1966) a number of writers have identified the essential functions of the mass media. McQuail (1994) provides a summary of these media functions:

**Information**

- providing information about events and conditions in society and the world
- indicating relations of power
- facilitating innovation, adaptation and progress

**Correlation**

- explaining, interpreting and commenting on the meaning of events and information
- providing support for established authority and norms
- consensus building
- setting orders of priority and signalling relative status

**Continuity**

- expressing the dominant culture and recognizing subcultures and new cultural developments
- forging and maintaining common values

**Entertainment**

- providing amusement, diversion and means of relaxation
- reducing social tension

**Mobilization**

- campaigning for societal objectives in the sphere of politics, war, economic development, work and sometimes religion (Adapted from McQuail 1994: 79)

### Question

Give an example of how the television and the national press might fulfil each of the functions listed by McQuail.

### *Pluralism*

Usually associated with theories of power and political participation, the concept of pluralism has been adapted to explain the role played by the media in modern democracies. The pluralist model developed in direct opposition to the negativism of the mass society approach.

In the 1960s and 1970s the fears endemic to the mass society model were attacked by US writers such as Bramson (1961), Dahl (1961), Gans (1974) and Shils (1959), who argued that such distrust of the masses was elitist and undemocratic. Rather than fearing the totalitarian potential of mass society, these writers celebrated its power to liberate 'the cognitive, appreciative and moral capacities of individuals' and the various 'taste cultures' which make up a heterogeneous popular culture (Billington *et al.* 1991: 17). According to this view the media play a key role in the democratic process by providing access to information, stimulating open debate and giving all groups the opportunity to share their beliefs and tastes with others. In exerting political and cultural choices in a democratic society the freedom of the media is crucial.

Case Study

## The liberal model of the mass media

O'Donnell (1981) suggests that this model has five key elements:

- The freedom to set up media ventures ensures that a range of opinions and interests are represented.
- Editorial freedom and professional standards of journalism underpin an effective media.
- Public access to press and broadcasting allows individuals to express their opinions and criticisms – through, for example, letters to the editor, right to reply or phone-ins.
- A commitment to balance which ensures that all groups in society have access to the media and are fairly represented – through programming which reflects minority tastes and interests (Channel 4 was established in part to achieve this – see p. 567).
- Market power enables the audiences to determine in the long run which media prosper and who goes out of business.

(Adapted from O'Donnell 1981: 546)

Whether this represents a normative theory (how things should be) or an actual model of how the media operate is debatable and relates to another key area of debate, how best to deliver a genuinely pluralist media. On the one hand is the belief that the media (and especially broadcasting) are so important to a free and rational society that they must be controlled for the public good. Hence regulations are imposed on ownership, offensive content and political balance. Public service broadcasting derives from this 'top-down' approach, with the BBC an obvious example. On the other hand such 'nannying' of the public by the state is seen as a threat to liberty. According to the liberal, market model, the only means of providing a diverse public with genuine freedom of choice is through a deregulated marketplace. This view was clearly expressed by Rupert Murdoch in his lecture on 'Freedom in Broadcasting' in 1989, which has been summarized by Keane (1991):

**Murdoch insists that market competition is the key condition of press and broadcasting freedom, understood as freedom from state interference, as the right of**

**individuals to communicate their opinions without external restrictions. Market led media ensure competition. Competition lets individual consumers decide what they want to try. It keeps prices low and quality high, forces suppliers to take risks and to innovate continually, lest they lose business to rivals offering better, improved products. A privately controlled press and a multi-channel broadcasting system in the hands of a diversity of owners is a bulwark of freedom.**

*(Keane 1991: 53)*

This confidence in the ability of the market to provide real choice and a genuinely pluralistic media is supported by writers such as Whale (1980) and Veljanovski (1989) but it is rejected by Keane and others who argue that the marketplace fails to provide genuine competition or free access to all media operations when it is dominated by a handful of global monopolies. Keane also rejects the idea that consumer choice and satisfaction are secured by a liberal market; some consumers are excluded by the purchase costs of media technology, others by their membership of minority groups who are not attractive to advertisers. The market becomes led by the demands of advertisers and the caprice of private owners and corporate decision-makers. Choice exists within the confines of commercial viability and this often amounts to broadcasting more of the same in order to satisfy the 'mass audience' which the advertisers demand. In the long run this will lead to the 'Americanization' of the media and an increase in what Keane (1991: 64) terms 'garbage television' and 'satellite slush'.

Although critical of both the public service and liberal market models, Keane retains a belief in the potential of the modern media to provide:

**A radically new public service model which would facilitate a genuine commonwealth of forms of life, tastes and opinions. Communications media . . . should aim to empower a plurality of citizens who are governed neither by undemocratic states nor by undemocratic market forces. The media should be for the public use and enjoyment of all citizens and not for the private gain or profit of political rulers or businesses.** *(Keane 1991: xi–xii)*

## Alternative paradigms

It is difficult to talk about an alternative paradigm as if it comprises a consistent set of ideas and perspectives that constitute a particular school of thought. The challenge to the dominant paradigm includes the work of Marxists, feminists and some strands of post-modernism and cultural theory. There are, then, enough critics who reject the consensus underlying functionalism and the democratic assumptions behind pluralism to talk of an alternative, oppositional paradigm, which McQuail has summarized:

**Most broadly, an 'alternative paradigm' rests on a different view of society, one which does not accept the prevailing liberal-capitalist order as just or inevitable or the best one can hope for in the fallen state of human kind. Nor does it accept the rational-calculative, utilitarian model of social life as at all adequate or desirable. There is an alternative, idealist and sometimes utopianist ideology, but nowhere a worked out model of an ideal social system. Nevertheless, there is sufficient common basis for rejecting the hidden ideology of pluralism and conservative functionalism.** *(McQuail 1994: 46)*

This approach grew out of the concern expressed by radical academics and critical theorists over the emergence of mass society and the rise of popular culture which echo those put forward by conservative thinkers (see p.584). The first attempts to make sense of the media in modern society from a critical perspective were made by the Frankfurt School (and particularly Horkheimer, Adorno and Marcuse: see pp. 91–4) who argued that the media were a conservative force acting to replace working-class aspirations with a false and one-dimensional consciousness dominated by commercialism, individualism and false needs.

This pessimistic view was endorsed in the USA by C Wright Mills (1956), who argued that the media were a powerful instrument for manipulation and control which operated in the interest of the 'power elite'. In Europe similar concerns were expressed through the writings of Althusser (1971), Barthes (1972) and the rediscovered works of Gramsci (1971). As a result Marxists began to develop an interest in the cultural and ideological aspects of social life with an emphasis on the significance of the media and the emergence of popular culture. Although Marxist writers disagree with each other over the importance of ideology and the relationship of the media to the structures of power and ownership, the following six elements of an alternative paradigm of the media can be highlighted:

- the political-economy of the media
- the media as ideological state apparatus
- the media and hegemony
- Glasgow University Media Group
- the threat of technology
- feminism.

### *The political-economy of the media*

This approach derives from the classic 'base-superstructure' model in Marxist thought which focuses on the relationship between the economic base or infrastructure and the ideological superstructure. It emphasizes the power of the economy (through, for instance, owners, advertisers and media markets) to determine media content. This power has been enhanced by the moves toward deregulation and the concentration of ownership on a global scale. Such a view is concerned with the power of owners and advertisers to influence public agendas and media content, and is sometimes known as the manipulative model (Trowler 1988: 33–7). However, the critical political-economy approach also examines the economic forces which may constrain the extent to which influential individuals can meddle in the media.

**Government and business elites do have privileged access to the news; large advertisers do operate as a latter-day licensing authority . . . and media proprietors can determine the editorial line and cultural stance of the papers and broadcast stations they own. [However, they] operate within structures which constrain as well as facilitate.** *(Golding and Murdock 1991: 9)*

Case Study

**The political-economy model**

A number of writers can be placed within the political economy model, including Bagdikian (1988), Collins, Garnham and Locksley (1988) and Miliband (1969). For Golding and Murdock (1991) this approach concentrates on three 'core tasks':

1 *The production of meaning and the exercise of power* emphasizes the increasing control exerted over cultural production by large corporations and the failure of governments to regulate such developments.
2 *Political economy and textual analysis* the selection and promotion of particular cultural forms and discourses are determined by economic rather than cultural factors. The 'Americanization' of British TV, for example, is partly due to the need to fill increasing broadcasting space with cheap and cheerful imports (Tunstall 1977).
3 *Consumption: sovereignty or struggle?* represents an attack on the assumptions behind the liberal market and pluralist approaches which celebrate the free choice of the audience and its ability to impose its own interpretation on cultural texts. As a result the material and cultural barriers to free and equal access are explored.

### *The media as ideological state apparatus*

In the writings of structuralists like Althusser (1969, 1971) and Poulantzas (1973) the state is seen as operating in an almost mechanical manner to reproduce the class relations of a class society. The involvement of individuals in this operation is irrelevant as it is the overall function of the apparatus of the state which is important and not the motivations, interests or activities of its agents. In this process social control is established through physical coercion (repressive state apparatus) or the power to persuade (ideological state apparatus). Along with the school and the church, the media are clearly regarded as having a key role in establishing ideological domination and false consciousness among those classes whose interests are not served by capitalism. In his attack on humanist Marxism and the Frankfurt School, Althusser established a model which saw all aspects of 'civil society' (family, church, media, for example) as extensions of state power so that human consciousness and subjectivity are constituted by external forces created by the structures of society. Althusser (1969, 1971) admits that ideas have some 'relative autonomy' but he insists that in the last instance ideology is determined by the economic structure of society and the agencies of the state. It is against this rigid and mechanistic model that Gramsci's (1971) more flexible concept of hegemony has been adopted by European Marxists.

### *The media and hegemony*

Although the concept of hegemony relates to the general discussion within Marxism about the ways in which dominant ideologies encourage a 'false consciousness' among the lower classes in society, it has also been applied to the role of the media in the transmission of popular culture, consumerism and national identity.

In his original use of the term hegemony, Gramsci (1971) refers to the 'dual perspective' whereby as well as using 'levels of force' those in power will also seek to establish 'moral and philosophical leadership' over the mass of the population by winning their active consent.

**The convictions of people are . . . not something manipulated by capitalists or put into the minds of the masses by them, but rather they flow from the exigencies of everyday life under capitalism. The workers, and others, hold the values and political ideas that they do as a consequence of both trying to survive and of attempting to enjoy themselves, within capitalism. These activities require money . . . mediated by ideological means, for people have to come to desire the goods for sale. Such desires . . . are not natural, not inborn. . . . These desires to consume various products have to be constructed by ideological apparatus, especially in the mass media.**

***(Bocock 1986: 32–3)***

As Lull (1995) has pointed out, such a media-transmitted ideology establishes itself through two processes of mediation – technological and social. *Technological mediation* refers to the power of the media to influence human consciousness on behalf of consumer society. Advertising is a classic example of this:

**Selection of corporate spokespersons, visual logos, audio jingles, catchy slogans, the style and pace of commercials, special technical effects, editing conventions, product packaging, and the welding of print and electronic media campaigns . . . all combine to generate the desired result, selling capitalism's big and bright products and the political-economic-cultural infrastructure that goes along with them.**

***(Lull 1995: 16)***

According to this view, media personnel are not coerced or manipulated into deliberately misrepresenting social reality; they have become socialized into accepting the values and techniques of their profession and to a large degree believe in what they are doing and that they are giving the customers what they want.

*Social mediation* emphasizes the humanism of Gramsci's work by stressing the active involvement of people in the hegemonic process. If we are duped by the system we are partly responsible by virtue of our participation in the language and image systems which have been created by the media. In our everyday interaction with one another we give credibility to and reinforce 'media transmitted ideology' by referring to its content and using its codes and incorporating its messages into our social discourse.

The admission that ordinary people have a part to play in creating and reaffirming their culture raises the possibility that the audience may also reinterpret, resist or reject the preferred messages of those responsible for media production and thus undermine the ideological control of those in power. This 'relative autonomy' in cultural production underpins the work of the Centre for Contemporary Cultural Studies (based at the University of Birmingham: see e.g. Hall and Jefferson 1976). Although they accept the Marxist idea that the media reproduce the relations of class society through the reinforcement of a consensus-based 'common sense', they reject the economic determinism of traditional Marxist models. The meanings of cultural texts are not pre-given but open to interpretation and negotiation and therefore never ideologically fixed.

This cultural flexibility allows writers such as Hall and Jefferson (1976) and Hebdige (1979) to argue that subcultural groups can express their resistance to dominant ideological forms through their cultural practices (for instance, music, fashion, language):

**Style in sub-culture . . . challenges the principle of unity and cohesion [and] contradicts the myth of consensus. . . . It is this alienation . . . which gives the teds, the mods, the punks a truly subterranean style.** *(Hebdige 1979: 118–19)*

It is also possible within the more liberal Marxist model to recognize the relative freedom of journalists and broadcasters to challenge the ideological consensus. In *Channels of Resistance* (Dowmunt 1994), a variety of media analysts reveal the ways that television producers around the world have managed to preserve their local identities against the threat of cultural imperialism and global homogenization. Although the contributors are not necessarily Marxist, their conclusions clearly reflect the dialectical notions of domination and resistance found in the concept of hegemony:

**The fact of [television dominance] does not stop us from imagining, developing and analysing alternatives . . . groups all over the world, in institutional and technological situations not of their own making, have begun to resist this domination in diverse and creative ways. . . . Although the economic and political pressures on the global television system are strong, they are not totally determining. We can dare to imagine, and start to create, something different.** *(Dowmunt 1994: 15)*

### *Glasgow University Media Group*

Although they do not represent a particular element of Marxist theory of the media, the Glasgow University Media Group have provided much empirical evidence to support the view that the media tend to favour conservative representations of reality. In analysing news coverage of industrial disputes, politics and warfare, they have focused on the ways in which political bias affects the structuring of the news, its content and the language used to report it:

**The essential thrust of our critique is not against media workers as such. . . . Rather, it relates to the picture of society that the media construct with such remarkable consistency. We attribute this artificial and one-dimensional picture to the nature of organisations whose basic assumption is that our industrial, economic and social system operates to the benefit of everyone involved . . . unfortunately [this] involves the mass of the 'public' being misrepresented.**

*(Glasgow Universty Media Group 1982: 144–5)*

The Glasgow University Media Group have also become increasingly well known for developing new research methods relating production, content and reception. A recent example of their work applies their innovative approach to representations of mental illness in the media (see Further reading).

### *The threat of technology*

While Marxist writers tend to blame those who control the mass media for cultural decline and political manipulation, other writers have argued that it is the technology itself which threatens cultural and intellectual life. In the 1960s Marshall McLuhan first warned that the new media technologies were transforming our relationships by promoting lazy and irrational attitudes. Whereas a culture based on reading books demands a level of rational concentration, the television has ushered in a 'couch potato' culture for the masses which makes very little demand on the individual other than turning on the TV set (McLuhan1964; McLuhan and Fiore 1967).

In the 1980s, Postman (1987) returned to the debate with a blistering attack on television and the threat it poses to western culture. He argues not that we are being deliberately misled or brainwashed by those in power but that we are conniving in our own cultural and political downfall through our demand for continual entertainment:

**Our politics, religion, news, athletics, education and commerce have been transformed into congenial adjuncts of show business, largely without protest or even much popular notice. . . . The result is that we are a people on the verge of amusing ourselves to death.** *(Postman 1987: 4)*

Television clearly plays a central role in providing this endless stream of amusement but for Postman the real threat is not in the arena of entertainment (which is after all what television was invented for) but in the belief that television can operate as a serious medium for the transmission of culture and political debate:

**When a population becomes distracted by trivia, when cultural life is redefined as a perpetual round of entertainment . . . when, in short, a people become an audience and their public business a vaudeville act, then a nation finds itself at risk; culture-death is a clear possibility.** *(Postman 1987: 161)*

### *Feminism*

If the Marxist tradition tends to focus on the ways in which the media reproduce relationships and ways of thinking that are of benefit to capitalism, feminists concentrate on the ideological work carried out by the media on behalf of men. However, while the importance of gender has long been recognized in the field of cultural studies the feminist perspective has not always been treated as significant by media theorists. Van Zoonen (1991) argues that before the rise of the women's movement, the 'gendered' nature of culture was accepted as natural and consequently the use of gender as a mechanism for analysis was largely ignored by traditional and critical theorists alike. But consequent research such as Meehan's (1983) study of prime-time television revealed that in North American serials women characters were restricted to a limited number of stereotypical roles. However, Radway's (1984) work on romantic novels and Winship's (1986) study of women's magazines suggest a more supportive role in what is still a male-dominated culture. Similarly the work of Geraghty (1991), Hobson (1982) and Kilborn (1992) reveals that strong and positive role models for women exist in soap operas:

**Many of the British soaps . . . are marked by the presence of women – most of them no longer in the prime of youth – who have remained sturdily independent, in spite of sometimes quite strong social or family pressures to be otherwise. As such their judgement is respected and they often operate as confidantes or advisors to the young, vulnerable or inexperienced. Bet Lynch and Rita Fairclough in Coronation Street are good examples of this particular type of strong woman.**

*(Kilborn 1992: 47)*

Although there is much agreement that the media play a crucial role in the gendering of culture there is little evidence of theoretical convergence among feminist writers (see pp. 79–88 on the different strands of feminist theorizing). We shall look briefly at how different feminist approaches have been applied to the media.

*Liberal feminism*

Women have been the victims of prejudice and stereotyping which are at the root of a gendered outlook for women as well as men. The limited role models and negative images that are offered by the media play an active part in reproducing dominant and traditional values and reinforcing the power of men and the absence of opportunities for women. The liberal solution is for women to compete with men for the powerful positions within the media and to educate journalists and broadcasters in the values of non-sexist media production. Janet Street-Porter's criticism (at the Edinburgh Television Festival, August 1995) of the media organization as a male, mediocre, middle-aged and middle-class 'broadcasting boys' club', reveals the extent to which individual women can feel powerless to change the system.

*Radical feminism*

According to this view the media are simply one more institution run by men for the convenience of men in a patriarchal society. As such the media demean women and overlook their concerns while actively encouraging female abuse through pornography and violence. The promotion of individual women within male structures which promote masculine culture is regarded as nothing other than a short-term gain for the individual career women concerned. Radical strategies entail women writers, producers and broadcasters cooperating to create their own alternative media. There have been some successful attempts to create independent publishers – The Women's Press, Virago and Pandora, for example – but Van Zoonen (1991) is pessimistic that this can be achieved without female broadcasters and publishers adopting masculine management styles.

*Socialist feminism*

Adopting elements of the Marxist approach, socialist feminism uses class analysis to examine the economic position of women under patriarchal capitalism. The commercial pressures on the media are clearly recognized in this perspective as important constraints on the media reforms proposed by liberal feminists or the separate developments favoured by radical feminists. Power in the media is related to the economic structures of society and although in support of changes for women, the socialist feminists are also aware that the benefits of reform are most likely to improve the career opportunities of middle-class women.

## Effects of the mass media

The debate over the power of the media to influence attitudes and behaviour goes back to the nineteenth century. It is a controversial area where strength of opinion often outweighs hard evidence; it has therefore become increasingly difficult to talk with any certainty about the power of the media to influence social behaviour. We cannot in this chapter do justice to the range of techniques used to research the effects of the media or to summarize the mountain of research findings amassed since the 1930s, but we can identify the major areas of concern: the media's economic, political, and moral and social influences.

### Areas of concern

#### *Economic influence of the media*

Apart from its potential for making money for itself, the media are thought to possess the power to influence consumer choice. Billions of pounds are spent on advertising every year by companies seeking to improve their market share and customers pay over the odds for the privilege. The *Guardian* (18 September 1992) estimated that for every £1.50 spent in Britain on a top brand of coffee, 12 pence goes in profits and wages to the growers but 57 pence is accounted for by the advertising budget. In 1987 Gold Blend instant coffee launched its successful 'mini-soap' campaign which saw sales rise by 15 per cent over the first year and by 40 per cent after five years (Cashmore 1994: 76). By the same token, companies are terrified of bad publicity and will resort to the law to stifle public complaint. The organizers of the 'What's Wrong with McDonalds?' campaign ended up in court for spreading anti-Mac propaganda.

#### *Political influence of the media*

Since the advent of public education and mass circulation newspapers, the role of the media in the coverage of politics has been regarded as important; however, it is with the introduction of broadcasting that the power of the media to influence opinion has been a key issue in political debate. Some of the earliest content analysis of newspapers was concerned with political bias and propaganda (Krippendorf 1980: 13–20). Original research into media effects concentrated upon the effectiveness of wartime propaganda (Hovland 1949) and the links between election campaigns and voting behaviour (Berelson *et al.* 1954; Katz and Lazarsfeld 1955; Lazarsfeld *et al.* 1944). Despite little evidence that the media can do much more than reinforce existing political attitudes, the media have been heavily involved in election campaigns since the1950s; with strict controls imposed in some societies on the extent to which political parties may have access to broadcasting at election time.

The first politician to take advice on his election campaign from an advertising agency was Dwight D Eisenhower, who paid for TV commercials to get his message across in the defeat of Adlai Stevenson in 1952. In 1960, the first real 'election by television' took place when John F Kennedy and Richard Nixon debated the issues on both television and radio. It is widely held that despite a good performance Nixon came across poorly on television, largely due to his appearance, and that this cost him the election. This success was repeated in the 1964 election when Lyndon Johnson was advised to use a negative advertising campaign against Barry Goldwater which highlighted the Republican's desire to use nuclear weapons in Indo-China. In what has become a classic example of the genre, the 'Daisy Girl' commercial shows a young girl plucking the petals from a flower as we hear the countdown to the launch of a nuclear warhead.

By the 1980s negative campaigns and zappy commercials had replaced the more traditional approaches to electioneering. Political advertising and, to some extent, political discussion became reduced to the wisdom of what works on television. As Kern (1989) has argued, a political broadcast is deemed effective only if it is short, entertaining and capable of provoking a reaction.

These lessons have been learned in Britain where, despite the restrictions on access to the broadcast media, the major parties engage 'spindoctors' to grab the soundbite and advertising agencies to manage the image (Jones 1995). Concern has also been expressed about the potential of television satire to influence political perceptions, with *Spitting Image* grabbing most of the attention; on the eve of the 1987 election the spoof *Election Special*, which included scenes of Thatcherites dressed as Nazis singing 'Tomorrow Belongs To Us', was delayed until after the polling stations had closed. After the election David Steel complained that the repeated trivialization of his SDP by *Spitting Image* had contributed towards undermining its credibility with the electorate. In general, however, the evidence suggests that for all the efforts by politicians to exploit or blame the potential of television, it is still the press which is more likely to influence voters. In his study of the 1987 general election in Britain, William Miller (1991) concludes that once party identification (partisanship) had been taken into account, the press had some influence in the swing back to the Conservatives especially among tabloid readers:

**The influence of the tabloid press was particularly strong on those voters who denied being party 'supporters', even when they had a party preference. They made up half of the electorate. The Conservative lead increased by 50% amongst politically uncommitted Sun/Star readers but not at all amongst politically uncommitted Mirror readers. Since Sun/Star readers as a whole were relatively uncommitted they were relatively easy to influence anyway but, in addition, the tabloids were particularly good at influencing their readers' voting preferences.** *(Miller 1991: 199)*

### *Moral and social influences of the media*

An area that has provoked particular concern has been the effects of media violence and pornography, especially upon children. Historically these fears about juvenile delinquency and the link between mass entertainment and moral degeneration predate the invention of the television set and the 'video nasty' by at least a century. Murdock and McCron (1979) remind us of this when they quote from a concerned observer in 1851, who warns of the corrupting and demoralizing influence of the theatre acting as a 'powerful agent for the depraving of the boyish classes of our towns and cities . . . which are so specially arranged for the attraction and ensnaring of the young' (quoted in Glover 1985: 372). In the 1950s the comic book became the focus of a moral panic in the USA over educational standards and deviant behaviour which ultimately led to the official censorship of horror and crime stories (M Barker 1984). However, it is the issue of violence in the cinema, television and computer games which grabs the headlines in the 1990s.

Levels of screen violence are notoriously difficult to measure and comparisons have to be made with care (Gunter 1985). The SDP MP David Alton claimed in 1994 that by the age of 5 the average child will have witnessed 20,000 murders on television; Mary Whitehouse's National Viewers' and Listeners' Association (1994) monitored the output of the terrestrial channels in the first half of 1994 and concluded that 'broadcasters are promoting a relentless culture of cruelty and violence' (Denscombe 1994: 43). Studies by less partial bodies such as the Henley Centre (1993), the Broadcasting Standards Council (1994) and the Independent Television Commission (1993) all suggest that whatever the relative levels of violence on television, sex, violence and bad language remain an issue for many people with 65 per cent feeling that there is still too much violence on television (Broadcasting Standards Council 1994).

Whether such concerns reflect a real threat or simply represent an imaginary moral panic is difficult to assess, but there is much hearsay evidence that violence on screen is a direct cause of copy-cat behaviour in society. In 1971 *A Clockwork Orange* was withdrawn from British cinemas by its director because of imitative violence by young gangs. In 1987 the Hungerford massacre was said to have been inspired by Michael Ryan's obsession with Rambo films. Three young men were convicted of a murder in Cardiff which followed repeated exposure to the film *Juice,* while the video of *Child's Play 3* was cited in the 1993 murders of James Bulger in Liverpool and Suzanne Capper in Manchester (see Newburn and Hagell 1995).

On a less serious level the antics of cartoon characters such as Tom and Jerry, Ren and Stimpy, Beavis and Butthead and the Simpsons have all been linked to the incitement of violence, vandalism and anti-social behaviour; Mighty Morphin Power Rangers have also been accused of promoting imitative violence in the play-

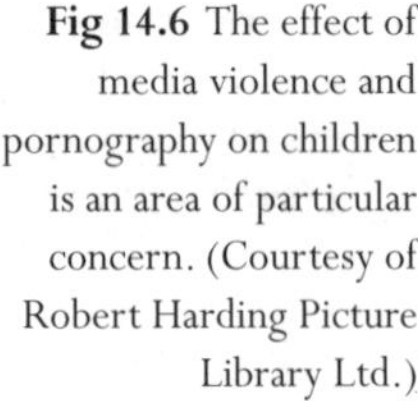

**Fig 14.6** The effect of media violence and pornography on children is an area of particular concern. (Courtesy of Robert Harding Picture Library Ltd.)

ground. Professor Provenzo at Miami University has found that of forty-seven Nintendo games monitored, only seven were not violent; much of the violence was directed at women with 'foreigners'most likely to be portrayed as villains (*Guardian* 4 November 1991). Since the early 1990s the threat of computer pornography has been treated as a serious offence as children gain widespread access to acts of buggery, rape and bestiality through floppy disks available at car boot sales and in the schoolyard. Catherine Itzin has claimed that such extreme pornography distorts the perceptions that boys have of women and can contribute to sexual violence:

**Many studies show that if teenage boys are repeatedly exposed to images where women are reduced to their genitals and presented as sexually voracious, passive and servile it desensitises them and increases callous attitudes towards women. Pornography is often a contributing factor in child sexual abuse, sexual harassment and forced sex.** *(quoted in Bouquet 1994: 2)*

In March 1994, Elizabeth Newson, Professor of Developmental Psychology at the University of Nottingham, claimed that the new levels of mindless violence occurring in society could be explained only by the 'easy availability to children of gross images of violence on video' (Newson 1994: 3). From her summary of research findings she suggested that video violence leads to identification and imitation among the young but Newson's main concern was with the way in which vicious and cruel behaviour was portrayed as entertainment and amusement, encouraging desensitization. She quotes an American writer to emphasize the point:

**Not only do these films suggest that brute force is a prerequisite for manliness, that physical intimidation is irresistibly sexy, and that violence offers an effective solution to all human problems; today's movies also advance the additional appalling idea that the most appropriate response to the suffering of others is sadistic laughter.**
*(Medved 1992, quoted in Newson 1994: 4)*

It is true that many studies, especially those conducted under experimental conditions, support the view that violence on the screen leads to aggressive attitudes and violent behaviour but whether this is the cause or the trigger of such behaviour is another matter. It should not surprise us that young offenders express an interest in films which sensationalize crime or that sex offenders show an interest in pornography, but this does not demonstrate any original cause, it merely suggests an attraction to the behaviour which has got them into trouble in the first place and accepts that the media plays a part in the story. McQuail has summarized this link:

**The balance of evidence supports the view that media *can* lead to violent behaviour and probably have done so; these effects occur mainly as a result of 'triggering' of aggressive acts, imitation, identification with aggressive heroes and 'desensitisation', leading to a higher tolerance for real violence.** *(McQuail 1994: 334)*

Critics of the violent effects model have argued that there is no clear evidence to prove a link between screen violence and social behaviour. After more than 1,000 studies, 'no satisfactory consensus has emerged' with different research techniques tending to produce contradictory results (Newburn and Hagell 1995: 8). The work of Hodge and Tripp (1986) and Gunter and McAleer (1990) have questioned the reliability of studies which show a causal link while Cumberbatch has been a persistent critic of those who too readily accept the pessimistic warnings of media induced violence (Cumberbatch and Howitt 1989). Cumberbatch has pointed out the relatively low levels of violence on British screens, especially in comparison to law-abiding societies like Japan, as well as refuting the evidence that short-term responses to media violence indicate long-term changes in behaviour. These conclusions are to some extent supported by the work of Gauntlett (1995), who suggests that the link between TV and juvenile crime has been exaggerated by a middle-class moral panic over social order which ignores the more obvious part played by unemployement and poverty. Noble (1975) has gone further by suggesting that some forms of television violence may have the cathartic effect of releasing feelings of aggression. This is a point of view also expressed by Yaffe and Nelson (1982) about the use of pornography in sex education and therapy sessions. However, they also point out that pornography can be used in different ways by different people and will have more than one set of consequences. They conclude that apart from the harmful effects of violent pornography on children, especially those who are already disturbed, 'pornography might be offensive, distasteful and a nuisance, but it did not appear to pose a threat to society' (Yaffe and Nelson 1982: xii).

The contradictory evidence and the range of possible responses by different audiences to different stimuli make it difficult to draw firm conclusions. The debate over the effects of the media on children raises important issues about the nature of the society we want them to grow up in and the kind of people we want them to become but the evidence, quite simply, fails to resolve these questions; the remarks of Wilbur Schramm in 1961 are still true today:

> **For *some* children under *some* conditions, some television is harmful. For *other* children under the same conditions, or for the same child under *other* conditions, it may be beneficial. For *most* children under *most* conditions, most television is neither particularly harmful nor particularly beneficial.** *(Schramm et al. 1961: 1)*

## Summary

- The mass media play an ever increasing part in our modern way of life. People depend on the media for information and for their entertainment.
- Technological developments have increased the range and changed the nature of the mass media that are available to people. The diversity of channels and broadcast services available enables consumers virtually to create their own viewing schedules.
- While there have always been attempts by governments to control the mass media, recent developments have led to a greater concern about the power of the media. Restrictions on the media include economic, political and legal controls and regulations.
- There are a number of theoretical perspectives which explore the relationship between the media and society. These perspectives do not fall conveniently under 'conventional' sociological headings. There is a broad distinction between theories that take a generally optimistic view of the media – that emphasize its ability to provide us with more information and a greater choice of material to read, listen to and view – and those that express concern over the negative consequences of the role of the media – highlighting the danger of the media being used as an instrument for manipulation and control.

- The extent to which the media affect attitudes and behaviour is contentious. While it is clear that people will be influenced by what they read, see and hear, evidence on whether the media directly determine specific forms of behaviour – whether watching violence causes children to behave violently, for instance – is inconclusive.

## Further reading

Chippendale, P and Horrie, C (1992) *Stick It Up Your Punter: The Rise and Fall of the Sun*, London: Mandarin.

An inside account of the tabloid culture of the *Sun*. Easy to read and very amusing.

Curran, J and Seaton, J (1991) *Power Without Responsibility: The Press and Broadcasting in Britain*, London: Routledge.

A detailed account of the history and development of the media in Britain that also provides an introduction to the main theories of the media.

Gauntlett, D (1995) *Moving Experiences: Understanding Television's Influences and Effects*, London: John Libbey.

An up-to-date review of the debate on the effects of TV.

Glasgow University Media Group (1996) *The Media and Mental Illness,* London: Longman.

An innovative approach to representations of mental illness in the media.

Keane, J (1991) *The Media and Democracy*, Cambridge: Polity.

An important contribution to the debate over the public service nature of the media and the move towards deregulation.

Lull, J (1995) *Media, Communication and Culture*, Cambridge: Polity.

An up-to-date and readable discussion of the relationship between social order and the ideological power of the media.

McQuail, D (1994) *Mass Communications Theory: An Introduction*, London: Sage.

Now in its third edition, the standard text on the sociology of the media. Its coverage of theories of the media is particularly extensive.

O'Sullivan, T, Dutton, B and Raynor, P (1994) *Studying the Media: An Introduction*, London: Edward Arnold.

A useful introduction to media studies.

Trowler, P (1988) *Investigating the Media*, London: Collins.

A brief and clear introduction to the sociology of the media; it includes sections on deviance and the media, race and the media and women and the media.

Van Zoonen, L (1994) *Feminist Media Studies,* London: Sage.

An introduction to the differing feminist perspectives on the media.

Weymouth, A and Lamizet, B (1996) *Markets and Myths: Forces for Change in the European Media*, London: Longman.

This analyses the impact of media policy and practice on the political, social and cultural life in Britain, France, Germany, Italy and Spain.

Williams, G (1994) *Britain's Media: How They are Related*, London: CPBF.

This brief introduction is packed with information and ideas about media ownership in Britain. It is available from the Campaign for Press and Broadcasting Freedom (8 Cynthia Street, London N1 9JF).

## Activities

### Activity 1 Neophiliacs and cultural pessimists

In looking at the historical development of the media, some of the range of current technological innovations were introduced and discussed. Such a review is almost bound to be out of date as soon as it is committed to print as technological innovation shows little sign of slowing up. However, here are differing views over the effects of these developments for society. The positive view that improved media technologies will benefit society through increasing customer choice and providing greater opportunities education and democratic participation is termed by Curran and Seaton (1991) the **neophiliac approach**. Those adopting a **cultural pessimistic** viewpoint believe that a decline in quality and cultural standards inevitably accompanies new forms of media and communication.

Look at the following list of positive statements about change in the modern media from the 'neophiliac' approach. Give an example of each one.

How might a 'cultural pessimist' respond? Again give an example for each row. The first row has been completed as an illustration. You might find the following chapters useful in completing this task: Curran and Seaton (1991: ch. 14); O'Sullivan *et al.* (1994: ch. 8); G Williams (1994: ch. 1).

| Neophiliacs | Cultural pessimists |
|---|---|
| More services offer more choice | More channels = more of the same |
| End of broadcasting monopoly | |
| Two-way technology is interactive | |
| Access to global information/other cultures | |
| Introduction of new work practices | |
| End of traditional class divisions | |
| New educational opportunities | |
| Political empowerment of individuals | |

### Activity 2 Life without the media

Have you ever considered what life would be like without the media?
Try it out for one day as an experiment – and don't cheat!
No newspapers, no radio, no magazines and no television (even if you have to record your favourite programmes for future viewing).
Make some notes as to how you feel at different times of the day.
Which media did you miss most and for what reasons?
At the end of the experiment consider the questions asked earlier:
How did your life change?
What were the effects on social life and interpersonal communication?

Abbott, P. (1991) 'Feminist perspectives in sociology: the challenge to "mainstream" orthodoxy', in J. Aaron and S. Walby (eds) *Out of the Margins: Women's Studies in the Nineties*, Brighton: Falmer.

Abbott, P. and Wallace, C. (1990) *An Introduction to Sociology: Feminist Perspectives*, London: Routledge.

Abercrombie, N. and Urry, J. (1983) *Capital, Labour and the Middle Classes*, London: Allen & Unwin.

Abercrombie, N. and Warde, A. (eds) (1992) *Social Change in Contemporary Britain*, Cambridge: Polity.

Abercrombie, N. and Warde, A, with Soothill, K, Urry, J. and Walby, S. (1994 [1988]) *Contemporary British Society*, 2nd edn, Cambridge: Polity.

Abrams, M., Gerard, D. and Timms, N. (eds) (1985) *Values and Social Change in Britain*, London: Macmillan.

Abrams, P. (1968) *The Origins of British Sociology*, Chicago, IL: University of Chicago Press.

Acker, S., Barry, K. and Esseveld, J. (1983) 'Objectivity and truth: problems in doing feminist research', *Women's Studies International Forum* 6(4): 423–35.

Acton, H. (1967) *What Marx Really Said*, London: Macdonald.

Acton, J. (1887) Letter to Bishop Mandell Creighton, 3 April, in J. Button (1995) *The Radicalism Handbook*, London: Cassell.

Adams, C. (1990) *The Sexual Politics of Meat*, Cambridge: Polity.

Adkins, L. (1995) *Gendered Work: Sexuality, Family and the Labour Market*, Milton Keynes: Open University Press.

Aldred, C. (1981) *Women at Work*, London: Pan.

Alibhai, Y. (1990) 'Still papering over the cracks', *Guardian* 10 September.

Allen, J. and Massey, D. (1988) *The Economy in Question*, London: Sage.

Allen, S. and Walkowitz, C. (1987) *Homeworking Myths and Realities*, London: Macmillan.

Almond, G. and Verba, S. (1965) *The Civic Culture*, Boston, MA: Little, Brown.

Althusser, L. (1969 [1965]) *For Marx*, London: Allen Lane.

Althusser, L. (1971) *Lenin and Philosophy and Other Essays*, London: New Left Books.

Althusser, L. (1972) 'Ideology and ideological state apparatuses', in B. Cosin (ed.) *Educational Structure and Society*, Harmondsworth: Penguin.

Amos, V. and Parmar, P. (1984) 'Challenging imperial feminism', *Feminist Review* 17 (July): 3–20.

Anderson, C. (1974) *Towards a New Sociology*, Homewood, IL: Dorsey.

Anderson, M. (1971) 'Family, household and the industrial revolution', in M. Anderson (ed.) *The Sociology of the Family*, Harmondsworth: Penguin.

Andreski, S. (ed.) (1971) *Herbert Spencer*, London: Nelson.

Anthias, F. and Yuval-Davis, N. (1993) *Racialized Boundaries: Race, Nation, Gender, Colour, Class and the Anti-Racist Struggle*, London: Routledge.

Anti-Slavery International (1993) *Britain's Secret Slaves*, London: Anti-Slavery International.

Arber, S. and Ginn, J. (1991) *Gender and Later Life*, London: Sage.

Arber, S. and Ginn, J. (1992) 'Gender and resources in later life', *Sociology Review* 2(2): 6–10.

Archard, D. (1993) *Children: Rights and Childhood*, London: Routledge.

Archbishop's Commission on Urban Priority Areas (ACUPA) (1985) *Faith in the City*, London: Church of England.

Aries, P. (1973) *Centuries of Childhood*, Harmondsworth: Penguin.

Armen, J. C. (1974) *Gazelle Boy*, London: Bodley Head.

Arnold, M. (1963 [1869]) *Culture and Anarchy*, Cambridge: Cambridge University Press.

Arnot, M. (1986) *Race, Gender and Educational Policy Making*, Module 4, E333, Milton Keynes: Open University Press.

Arnot, M. (1991) 'Equality and democracy: a decade of struggle over education', *British Journal of Sociology of Education* 12(4).

Askew, M. and Ross, S. (1988) *Boys Don't Cry: Boys and Sexism in Education*, Milton Keynes: Open University Press.

Atkinson, J. (1984) 'Flexibility, uncertainty and manpower management', Institute of Management Studies, Report 89, Brighton: Falmer.

Bachrach, P. (1967) *The Theory of Democratic Elitism*, Boston, MA: Little, Brown.

Baehr, H. and Ryan, M. (1984) *Shut Up and Listen: Women and Local Radio*, London: Comedia.

Bagdikian, B. (1988) *The Media Monopoly*, Boston, MA: Beacon.

Baignent, M, Leigh, R. and Lincoln, H. (1986) *The Messianic Legacy*, London: Corgi.

Ball, S. (1981) *Beachside Comprehensive: A Case Study of*

*Secondary Schooling*, Cambridge: Cambridge University Press.

Ball, S. (1991) *Politics and Policy Making in Education*, London: Routledge.

Ballaster, R, Betham, M. and Hebron, S. (1991) *Women's Worlds: Ideology, Feminism and the Women's Magazine*, London: Macmillan.

Banks, O. (1968) *The Sociology of Education*, London: Batsford.

Banton, M. (1977) *The Idea of Race*, London: Tavistock.

Banton, M. (1987) *Racial Theories*, Cambridge: Cambridge University Press.

Banton, M. and Harwood, J. (1975) *The Race Concept*, Newton Abbot: David & Charles.

Barker, E. (1984) *The Making of a Moonie*, Oxford: Blackwell.

Barker, E. (1989) *New Religious Movements: A Practical Introduction*, London: HMSO.

Barker, M. (1984) *A Haunt of Fears: The Strange History of the British Horror Crimes Campaign*, London: Pluto.

Barker, R. (1992) 'Civil disobedience as persuasion: Dworkin and Greenham Common', *Political Studies* 4(2).

Barley, N. (1986) *The Innocent Anthropologist*, Harmondsworth: Penguin.

Barnett, S. (1989) *The Listener Speaks: The Radio Audience and the Future of Radio*, London: John Libbey.

Barrett, M. (1980) *Women's Oppression Today*, London: Verso.

Barrett, M. and McIntosh, M. (1982) *The Anti-Social Family*, London: Verso.

Barron, P. and Sweezy, P. (1968) *Monopoly Capitalism*, Harmondsworth: Penguin.

Barron, R. D. and Norris, G. M. (1976) 'Sexual divisions and the dual labour market', in L. D. Barker and S. Allen (eds) *Dependence and Exploitation in Work and Marriage*, London: Longman.

Barth, F. (ed.) (1969) *Ethnic Groups and Boundaries: The Social Organization of Culture Difference*, London: Verso.

Barthes, R. (1972) *Mythologies*, London: Jonathan Cape.

Barton, L. and Tomlinson, S. (eds) (1981) *Special Education: Policy, Practices and Social Issues*, London: Harper & Row.

Bartos, A. and Hitchens, C. (1995) *International Territory: The UN 1945–95*, London: Verso.

Barzun, J. (1937) *Race: A Study in Superstition*, New York: Harcourt Brace.

Baudrillard, J. (1990) *Cool Memories*, London: Verso.

Bauman, Z. (1989) *Modernity and the Holocaust*, Oxford: Polity.

Bauman, Z. (1990) *Thinking Sociologically*, Oxford: Blackwell.

Bausinger, H. (1984) 'Media, technology and daily life', *Media, Culture and Society* 6(4).

de Beauvoir, S. (1974) *The Second Sex*, New York: Vintage.

Becker, H. (1932) *Systematic Sociology on the Basis of the Bezeitunglehre and Gebidelehre of Leopold von Wiese*, New York: Wiley.

Becker, H. S. (1963) *Outsiders: Studies in the Sociology of Deviance*, New York: Free Press.

Becker, H. S. (1982) 'Problems of inference and proof in participant observation', in R. McCormick, J. Bynner, P. Clift, M. James and L. M. Brown (eds) *Calling Education to Account*, London: Open University Press/Heinemann.

Beckford, J. (1975) *Religious Organization*, The Hague: Mouton.

Beckford, J. (1985) *Cult Controversies: The Societal Response to the New Religious Movements*, London: Tavistock.

Beechey, V. (1978) 'Women and production: a critical analysis of some sociological theories of women's work', in A. Kuhn and A. M. Wolpe (eds) *Feminism and Marginalism: Women and Modes of Production*, London: Routledge.

Bell, D. (1973) *The Coming of Post-Industrial Society: A Venture in Social Forecasting*, London: Heinemann.

Bellah, R. (1967) 'Civil religion in America', *Daedalus* 96: 1–21.

Bellah, R. (1975) *The Broken Covenant: American Civil Religion in Time of Trial*, New York: Seabury.

Belsey, A. and Chadwick, R. (eds) (1992) *Ethical Issues in Journalism and the Media*, London: Routledge.

Bem, S. (1993) *The Lenses of Gender*, New Haven, CT: Yale University Press.

Bennett, T. (1982) 'Theories of media, theories of society', in M. Gurevitch, T. Bennett, J. Curran and J. Woollacott (eds) *Culture, Society and the Media*, London: Methuen.

Berelson, B., Lazarsfeld, P. and McPhee, W. (1954) *Voting: A Study of Opinion Formation in a Presidential Campaign*, Chicago, IL: University of Chicago Press.

Berger, A. A. (1991) *Media Analysis Techniques*, London: Sage.

Berger, P. L. (1967a) *Invitation to Sociology: A Humanistic Perspective*, Harmondsworth: Penguin.

Berger, P. L. (1967b) *The Social Reality of Religion*, Harmondsworth: Penguin.

Berger, P. L. and Luckmann, T. (1963) 'Sociology of religion and sociology of knowledge', *Sociology and Social Research* 47: 417–27.

Bernstein, B. (1971) 'On the classification and framing of educational knowledge', in M. F. D. Young (ed.) *Knowledge and Control: New Directions in the Sociology of Education*, London: Collier-Macmillan.

Bernstein, B. (1974) 'Sociology and the sociology of education', in J. Rex (ed.) *Approaches to Sociology*, London: Routledge & Kegan Paul.

Beveridge, W. (1942) *Social Insurance and Allied Services*, London: HMSO.

Beynon, H. (1975) *Working for Ford*, London: Allen Lane.

Beynon, H. and Nichols, T. (1977) *Living with Capitalism*, London: Routledge.

Bhabha, H. K. (1990) 'The third space: interview with Homi Bhabha', in J. Rutherford (ed.) *Identity: Community, Culture, Difference*, London: Routledge.

Bhat, A., Carr-Hill, R. and Ohri, S. (eds) (1988) *Britain's Black Population: A New Perspective*, 2nd edn, Aldershot: Gower.

Bhavnani, R. (1993) 'Talking racism and the editing of women's studies', in D. Richardson and V. Robinson (eds) *Introducing Women's Studies*, London: Macmillan.

Bhavnani, R. (1994) *Black Women in the Labour Market: A Research Review*, Organisation Development Centre, City University, Equal Opportunities Commission.

Billington, R., Strawbridge, S., Greensides, L. and Fitzsimons, A. (1991) *Culture and Society*, London: Macmillan.

Bilton, T., Bonnet, K., Jones, P., Sheard, K., Stanworth, M. and Webster, A. (1987) *Introductory Sociology*, 2nd edn, London: Macmillan.

Birke, L. (1992) 'In pursuit of difference', in G. Kirkup and L. Smith-Keller (eds) *Inventing Women*, Cambridge: Polity.

Blackburn, R. and Mann, M. (1981) 'The dual labour market model', in P Braham, E. Rhodes and M. Pearn (eds) *Discrimination and Disadvantage in Employment: The Experience of Black Workers*, London: Harper & Row.

Blanchard, S. and Morley, D. (1982) *What's This Channel Four?*, London: Comedia.

Blau, P. M. (1963) *The Dynamics of Bureaucracy*, Chicago, IL: University of Chicago Press.

Blauner, R. (1972) *Racial Oppression in America*, New York: Harper & Row.

Block, N. and Dworkin, G. (eds) (1977) *The IQ Controversy*, London: Quartet.

Bloomfield, F. (1983) *The Book of Chinese Belief*, London: Arrow.

Bocock, R. (1986) *Hegemony*, London: Tavistock.

Boff, L. (1987) *Feet-on-the-Ground-Theology*, Maryknoll, NY: Orbis.

Bond, J., Coleman, P. and Peace, S. (1993) *Ageing in Society: An Introduction to Gerontology*, London: Sage.

Booth, C. (1889) *Life and Labour of the People in London*, London: Williams & Norgate.

Borstein, K. (1994) *Gender Outlaw: On Men, Women and the Rest of Us*, London: Routledge.

Bottomore, T. B. (1963) *Karl Marx: Early Writings*, London: C. A. Watts.

Bottomore, T. B. (1965) *Classes in Modern Society*, London: Allen & Unwin.

Bottomore, T. B. (1983) *A Dictionary of Marxist Thought*, Oxford: Blackwell.

Bouquet, T. (1994) 'Computer porn, a degrading menace', *Reader's Digest* June.

Bourdieu, P. and Passeron, J. C. (1977) *Reproduction in Education, Society and Culture*, Beverly Hills, CA: Sage.

Bourne, R. (1991) *Lords of Fleet Street*, London: Unwin Hyman.

Bourque, S. and Grossholtz, J. (1984) 'Politics, an unnatural practice: political science looks at female participation', in J. Siltanen and M. Stanworth (eds) *Women in the Public Sphere: A Critique of Sociology and Politics*, London: Hutchinson.

Bowen-Jones, C. (1992) 'Multiple marriage', *Marie Claire* 9 (July).

Bower, T. (1995) *Maxwell the Outsider*, London: Mandarin.

Bowles, S. and Gintis, H. (1976) *Schooling in Capitalist America: Educational Reform and the Contradictions of Economic Life*, London: Routledge & Kegan Paul.

Box, S. (1983) *Power, Crime and Mystification*, London: Tavistock.

Brah, A. (1994) 'Time, places, and others: discourses of race, nation, and ethnicity', *Sociology Review* August: 806.

Braham, P. (ed.) (1992) *Racism and Anti-Racism: Inequalities, Opportunities and Policies*, London: Sage.

Braham, P., Rhodes, E. and Pearn, M. (eds) (1981) *Discrimination and Disadvantage in Employment: The Experience of Black Workers*, London: Harper & Row.

Bramson, L. (1961) *The Political Content of Sociology*, Princeton, NJ: Princeton University Press.

Brannen, J. and Moss, P. (1991) *Managing Mothers: Dual Earner Households after Maternity Leave*, London: Unwin Hyman.

Braverman, H. (1974) *Labour and Monopoly Capital: The Degradation of Work within the Twentieth Century*, New York: Monthly Review.

Briault, E. W. H. (1976) 'A distributed system of educational administration: an international viewpoint', *International Review of Education* 22(4): 429–39.

Brierley, P. and Hiscock, V. (eds) (1993) *UK Christian Handbook 1994–5*, London: Christian Research Association.

Briggs, A. (1961) *The Birth of Broadcasting*, Oxford: Oxford University Press.

Briggs, A. (1967) 'The language of "class" in early-nineteenth-century England', in A. Briggs and J. Saville (eds) *Essays in Labour History*, London: Macmillan.

Brittan, A. (1989) *Masculinity and Power*, New York: Blackwell.

Brittan, L. (1983) *The Role and Limits of Government*, London: Temple Smith.

Broadbridge, A. (1991) 'Images and goods: women in retailing', in A. Redclift and T. Sinclair (eds) *Working Women: International Perspectives on Labour and Gender Ideology*, London: Routledge.

Broadcasting Standards Council (BSC) (1994) *Radio and Audience Attitudes*, London: BSC.

Broadfoot, P. (1988) 'Educational research: two cultures and three estates', *British Educational Research Journal* 14(1).

Brod, H. and Kaufman, M. (1994) *Theorizing Masculinity*, London: Sage.

Broom, L., Selznick, P. and Darroch, D. (1981) *Sociology*, New York: Harper & Row.

Brown, C. (1992) '"Same difference": the persistence of racial disadvantage in the British employment market', in P. Braham (ed.) *Racism and Anti-Racism: Inequalities, Opportunities and Policies*, London: Sage.

Brown, P. (1989) 'Education', in P. Brown and R. Sparks, *Beyond Thatcherism: Social Policy, Politics and Society*, Milton Keynes: Open University Press.

Brown, P. and Scase, R. (eds) (1991) *Poor Work: Disadvantage and the Division of Labour*, Buckingham: Open University Press.

Brown, R. (1992) *Understanding Industrial Organizations*, London: Routledge.

Brownmiller, S. (1976) *Against Our Will: Men, Women and Rape*, Harmondsworth: Penguin.

Bryan, B., Dadzie, S. and Scafe, S. (1987) 'Learning to resist: black women and education', in G. Weiner and M. Arnot (eds) *Gender under Scrutiny*, London: Hutchinson.

Bryson, V. (1992) *Feminist Political Theory: An Introduction*, London: Macmillan.

Buckley, W. F., Jr. (1959) *Up from Liberalism*, New York: McDonnell & Oblensky.

Bunch, C. (1981) 'Not for lesbians only', in The Quest Book Committee, *Building Feminist Theory: Essays from Quest*, London: Longman.

Burawoy, M. (1985) *The Politics of Production*, London: Verso.

Burchill, J. (1985) 'The last sacred cow', *New Society* 20–27 December.

Burnet, D. (1992) 'Freedom of speech, the media and the law', in A. Belsey and R. Chadwick (eds) *Ethical Issues in Journalism and the Media*, London: Routledge.

Burney, E. (1988) *Steps to Racial Equality: Positive Action in a Negative Climate*, London: Runnymede Trust.

Burnham, J. (1945) *The Managerial Revolution*, Harmondsworth: Penguin.

Burns, T. (ed.) (1969) *Industrial Man*, Harmondsworth: Penguin.

Burns, T. (1977) *The BBC: Public Institution and Private World*, London: Macmillan.

Burrows, R. and Loader, B. (eds) (1994) *Towards a Post-Fordist Welfare State?*, London: Routledge.

Burt, C. (1925) *The Young Delinquent*, London: University of London.

Burtonwood, N. (1986) *The Culture Concept of Educational Studies*, Windsor: NFER Nelson.

Butler, D. and Stokes, D. (1974) *Political Change in Britain: The Evolution of Electoral Choice*, 2nd edn, London: Macmillan.

Butler, J. (1990) *Gender Trouble: Feminism and the Subversion of Identity*, London: Routledge.

Button, J. (1995) *The Radicalism Handbook*, London: Cassell.

Byrne, D, Williamson, B. and Fletcher, B. (1975) *The Poverty of Education: A Study of the Politics of Opportunity*, Oxford: Martin Robertson.

Byrne, E. (1978) *Women and Education*, London: Tavistock.

Calcutt (1990) *Report of the Committee on Privacy*, London: HMSO.

Callinicos, A. (1993) *Race and Class*, London: Bookmarks.

Callinicos, A. and Harman, C. (1987) *The Changing Working Class*, London: Bookmarks.

Campbell, C. (1971) *Toward a Sociology of Irreligion*, London: Macmillan.

Carby, H. V. (1982a) 'White women listen! Black feminism and the boundaries of sisterhood', in Centre for Contemporary Cultural Studies, *The Empire Strikes Back*, London: Hutchinson.

Carby, H. V. (1982b) 'Schooling in Babylon', in Centre for Contemporary Cultural Studies, *The Empire Strikes Back*, London: Hutchinson.

Cashmore, E. (1984) *No Future: Youth and Society*, London: Heinemann.

Cashmore, E. (1994) *... and there was Telev!s!on*, London: Routledge.

Cashmore, E. and McLoughlin, E. (eds) (1991) *Out of Order: Policing Black People*, London: Routledge.

Cashmore, E. and Troyna, B. (1990 [1983]) *Introduction to Race Relations*, 2nd edn, London: Falmer.

Castles, S. and Kosak, G. (1972) 'The function of labour immigration in Western European capitalism', in P. Braham, E. Rhodes and M. Pearn (eds) (1981) *Discrimination and Disadvantage in Employment: The Experience of Black Workers*, London: Harper & Row.

Castles, S. and Kosak, G. (1973) *Immigrant Workers and Class Structure in Western Europe*, Oxford: Oxford University Press.

Cavadino, M. and Dignan, J. (1993) *The Penal System: An Introduction*, London: Sage.

Central Advisory Council for Education (CACE) (1954) *Early Leaving*, Gurney-Dixon Report, London: HMSO.

CACE (1959) *15 to 18*, Crowther Report, London: HMSO.

CACE (1963) *Half our Future*, Newsom Report, London: HMSO.

CACE (1967) *Children and their Primary Schools*, Plowden Report, London: HMSO.

Centre for Contemporary Cultural Studies (1981) *Unpopular Education: Schooling and Social Democracy in England since 1944*, London: Hutchinson.

Centre for Contemporary Cultural Studies (1982) *The Empire Strikes Back: Race and Racism in 70s Britain*, London: Hutchinson.

Chapkis, W. (1986) *Beauty Secrets*, London: Women's Press.

Charles, N. and Kerr, M. (1988) *Women, Food and Families*, Manchester: Manchester University Press.

Chesney, K. (1991) *The Victorian Underworld*, Harmondsworth: Penguin.

Chippendale, P. and Horrie, C. (1992) *Stick It Up Your Punter: The Rise and Fall of the Sun*, London: Mandarin.

Chomsky, N. (1972) 'The fallacy of Richard Herrnstein's IQ', *Social Policy* May–June.

Chopp, R. (1986) *The Praxis of Suffering: An Interpretation of Liberation and Political Theories*, Maryknoll, NY: Orbis.

Cicourel, A. V. (1976) *The Social Organization of Juvenile Justice*, London: Heinemann.

Clark, E. (1873) *Sex in Education*, London.

Clarke, H., Chandler, J. and Barry, J. (eds) (1994) *Organizations and Identities*, London: Chapman & Hall.

Clarke, J, Critcher, C., and Johnson, R. (eds) (1979) *Working Class Culture Studies in Theory and History*, London: Hutchinson.

Clarke, N. and Riddell, E. (1992) *The Sky Barons*, London: Methuen.

Clay, J. (1839) 'Criminal statistics of Preston', *Journal of the Statistical Society of London* 2.

Cloward, R. A. and Ohlin, L. E. (1961) *Delinquency and Opportunity*, New York: Free Press.

Coard, B. (1971) *How the West Indian Child is Made Educationally Subnormal in the British School System*, London: New Beacon.

Cockburn, C. (1983) *Brothers: Male Dominance and Technological Change*, London: Pluto.

Cockburn, C. (1985) *Machinery of Dominance*, London: Pluto.

Cockburn, C. (1987) *Women, Trade Unions and Political Parties*, Fabian Research Series 349, London: Fabian Society.

Cockburn, C. (1993) *Gender and Technology in the Making*, London: Sage.

Cockerell, M., Hennessy, P. and Walker, D. (1984) *Sources Close to the Prime Minister*, London: Macmillan.

Coe, T. (1992) *The Key to the Men's Club*, Bristol: IM Books.

Cohen, A. K. (1955) *Delinquent Boys: The Culture of the Gang*, New York: Free Press.

Cohen, R. (1994) *Frontiers of Identity: The British and the Others*, London: Longman.

Cohn, T. (1988) 'Sambo: a study in name calling', in E. Kelly and T. Cohn, *Racism in Schools: New Research Evidence*, Stoke-on-Trent: Trentham.

Cole, B. (1988) *Princess Smartypants*, London: HarperCollins.

Coleman, S., Jemphrey, A., Scraton, P. and Skidmore, P. (1990) *Hillsborough and After: The Liverpool Experience*, Edge Hill: Centre for Studies in Crime and Social Justice.

Coleridge, N. (1994) *Paper Tigers: Latest Greatest Newspaper Tycoons and How They Won the World*, London: Mandarin.

Collier, R. (1992) 'The new man: fact or fad', *Achilles' Heel* 14: 34–8.

Collins, R, Garnham, N. and Locksley, G. (1988) *The Economics of Television: The UK Case*, London: Sage.

Collinson, C., Collinson, D. and Knight, C. (1992) *Managing to Discriminate*, London: Routledge.

Commission for Racial Equality (CRE) (1984) *Race and Council Housing in Hackney: A Report of Formal Investigation*, London: CRE.

CRE (1987a) *Formal Investigation: Chartered Accountancy Training Contracts*, London: CRE.

CRE (1987b) *Employment of Graduates from Ethnic Minorities: A Research Report*, London: CRE.

CRE (1988) *Homelessnesss and Discrimination*, London: CRE.

CRE (1989) *Racial Discrimination in Liverpool City Council: A Report of Formal Investigation in the Housing Department*, London: CRE.

CRE (1990) *Sorry, It's Gone*, London: CRE.

Connell, R. W. (1987) *Gender and Power*, Cambridge: Polity.

Cook, D. (1989) *Rich Law, Poor Law: Different Responses to Tax and Supplementary Benefit Fraud*, Milton Keynes: Open University Press.

Cooper, D. (1972) *The Death of the Family*, Harmondsworth: Penguin.

Cowie, J., Cowie, S. and Slater, E. (1968) *Delinquency in Girls*, London: Hutchinson.

Cox, O. C. (1970) *Caste, Class and Race*, New York: Monthly Review.

Craft, M. and Craft, A. (1983) 'The participation of ethnic minority pupils in further and higher education', *Educational Review* 25(1).

Craib, I. (1992) *Modern Social Theory*, Hemel Hempstead: Harvester Wheatsheaf.

Crewe, I. (1992) 'Why did Labour lose (yet again)?', *Politics Review* 2(1): 2–11.

Crewe, I., with Norris, P., Denver, D. and Broughton, D. (1992) *British Elections and Parties Yearbook 1992*, Hemel Hempstead: Harvester Wheatsheaf.

Crisell, A. (1988) *Understanding Radio*, London: Methuen.

Croall, H. (1992) *White-Collar Crime: Criminal Justice and Criminology*, Buckingham: Open University Press.

Crompton, R. (1989) 'Class theory and gender', *British Journal of Sociology* 40(4): 565–87.

Crompton, R. (1993) *Class and Stratification*, Cambridge: Polity.

Crompton, R. and Jones, G. (1984) *White-Collar Proletariat: Deskilling and Gender in Clerical Work*, London: Macmillan.

Crook, S., Pakulshi, J. and Waters, M. (1992) *Postmodernisation Change in Advanced Societies*, London: Sage.

Crowley, H. and Himmelweit, S. (eds) (1992) *Knowing Women*, Buckingham: Open University Press.

Cuff, E. C., Sharrock, W. W. and Francis, D. W. (1990) *Perspectives in Sociology*, 3rd edn, London: Unwin Hyman.

Cumberbatch, G. and Howitt, D. (1989) *A Measure of Uncertainty: The Effects of the Mass Media*, London: John Libbey.

Curran, J. and Gurevitch, M. (eds) (1991) *Mass Media and Society*, London: Edward Arnold.

Curran, J. and Seaton, J. (1991) *Power Without Responsibility: The Press and Broadcasting in Britain*, London: Routledge.

Curtice, J. (1994) 'Political sociology 1945–92', in J. Obelkevich and R. Catterall (eds) *Understanding Post-War British Society*, London: Routledge.

Curtis, L. (1984) *Ireland: The Propaganda War*, London: Pluto.

Dahl, R. A. (1958) 'A critique of the ruling elite model', in J. Urry and J. Wakeford (eds) (1973) *Power in Britain*, London: Heinemann.

Dahl, R. A. (1961) *Who Governs?*, New Haven, CT: Yale University Press.

Dahrendorf, R. (1959) *Class and Class Conflict in an Industrial Society*, London: Routledge & Kegan Paul.

Dahrendorf, R. (1992) 'Footnotes to the discussion', in D. Smith (ed.) *Understanding the Underclass*, London: Policy Studies Institute.

Dalton, R. and Keuchler, M. (eds) (1990) *Challenging the Political Order: New Social and Political Movements in Western Democracies*, Oxford: Oxford University Press.

Daly, M. (1991) *Beyond God the Father*, London: Women's Press.

Daniel, W. W. (1968) *Racial Discrimination in England*, Harmondsworth: Penguin.

Darwin, C. (1968 [1859]) *On the Origin of Species*, Harmondsworth: Penguin.

Daud, F. (1985) *Minah Karan: The Truth about Malaysian Factory Girls*, Kuala Lumpur: Berita.

David, M. (1993) 'The citizen's voice in education: parents, gender and educational reform', paper presented at International Conference on the Public Sphere, University of Salford, January.

David, T. (1993) *Child Protection and Early Years Teachers*, Buckingham: Open University Press.

Davie, G. (1994) *Religion in Britain since 1945: Believing Without Belonging*, Oxford: Blackwell.

Davis, K. (1949) *Human Society*, London: Macmillan.

Davis, K. and Moore, W. E. (1967) 'Some principles of stratification', in R. Bendix and S. M. Lipset (eds) *Class, Status and Power*, 2nd edn, London: Routledge & Kegan Paul.

Dawkins, R. (1976) *The Selfish Gene*, Oxford: Oxford University Press.

Dawkins, R. (1977) 'Sex and the immortal gene', *Vogue*.

Deem, R. (1978) *Women and Schooling*, London: Routledge & Kegan Paul.

Dennis, N., Henriques, F. and Slaughter, C. (1956) *Coal is our Life*, London: Eyre & Spottiswoode.

Denscombe, M. (ed.) (1995, 1994, 1993, 1992) *Sociology Update*, Leicester: Olympus.

Denver, D. (1989) *Elections and Voting Behaviour in Britain*, London: Philip Allan.

Department of Education and Science (DES) (1965) *The Organization of Secondary Education*, Circular 10/65, London: HMSO.

DES (1988) *Advancing A Levels*, Higginson Report, London: HMSO.

DES (1992) *Statistics of Education: Teachers in Service, England and Wales 1990*, London: HMSO.

Department of Health and Social Security (DHSS) (1988) *Working Together*, London: HMSO.

Department of Social Security (DSS) (1994) *Households Below Average Income*, London: HMSO.

Devine, F. (1994) '"Affluent Workers" revisited', *Sociology Review* 3(3): 6–9.

Dex, S. (1985) *The Sexual Division of Work*, Hemel Hempstead: Harvester.

Disraeli, B. (1835) *Vindication of the English Constitution*, London.

Dizard, W. (1982) *The Coming Information Age: An Overview of Technology, Economics and Politics*, London: Longman.

Donaldson, F. (1976) *Edward VIII*, London: Futura.

Dostoevsky, F. (1962 [1860]) *The House of the Dead*, London: Dent.

Douglas, J. W. B. (1964) *The Home and the School*, London: MacGibbon & Kee.

Dowmunt, A. (ed.) (1994) *Channels of Resistance*, London: British Film Institute.

Dowse, R. E. and Hughes J. A. (1986) *Political Sociology*, 2nd edn, Chichester: Wiley.

Doyal, L., Hunt, G. and Mellor, G. (1981) 'Your life in their hands: migrant workers in the National Health Service', *Critical Social Policy* 1(2): 54–71.

Doyle, L. and Harris, R. (1986) *Empiricism, Explanation and Rationality*, London: Routledge & Kegan Paul.

Draper, A. (1991) 'Liberal studies for life', *Guardian* 13 August.

Drew, D. and Gray, J. (1989) 'The fifth-year examination achievements of black young people in England and Wales', University of Sheffield Research Centre.

Drew, D. and Gray, J. (1991) 'The black–white gap in examination results: a statistical critique of a decade's research', *New Community* 17(2).

Driver, G. (1980) 'How West Indians do better at school', *New Society* 17 January.

Duelli-Klein, R. (1983) 'How to do what we want to do: thoughts about feminist methodology', in G. Bowles and R. Duelli-Klein (eds) *Theories of Women's Studies*, London: Routledge.

Dunleavy, P. (1980) *Urban Political Analysis*, London: Macmillan.

Durkheim, E. (1952 [1897]) *Suicide: A Study in Sociology*, London: Routledge & Kegan Paul.

Durkheim, E. (1956 [1903]) *Education and Sociology*, New York: Free Press.

Durkheim, E. (1960 [1893]) *The Division of Labour in Society*, New York: Free Press.

Durkheim, E. (1964 [1895]) *The Rules of Sociological Method*, New York: Free Press.

Durkheim, E. (1976 [1912]) *The Elementary Forms of the Religious Life*, trans. J. W. Swain, London: Allen & Unwin.

Dworkin, A. (1983) *Pornography: Men Possessing Women*, London: Women's Press.

Easthope, A. (1986) *What's a Man Gotta Do: The Masculine Myth in Popular Culture*, London: Paladin.

Eden, F. M. (1797) *The State of the Poor*, London: Frank Cass.

Edgell, S. (1993) *Class*, London: Routledge.

Edley, N. and Wetherell, M. (1994) *Men in Perspective*, London: Harvester Wheatsheaf.

Edwards, R. (1979) *Contested Terrain*, London: Heinemann.

Edwards, R. (1993) *Mature Women Students*, London: Taylor & Francis.

Edwards, V. (1976) *West Indian Language: Attitudes and the School*, London: National Association for Multiracial Education.

Edwards, V. (1979) *The West Indian Language Issue in British Schools*, London: Routledge & Kegan Paul.

Eggleston, J., Dunn, D. and Anjali, M. (1986) *Education for Some: The Educational and Vocational Experiences of 15–18 Year Old Members of Ethnic Minority Groups*, Stoke-on-Trent: Trentham.

Ehrlich, C. (1976) 'The conditions of feminist research', Research Group One, Report 21, Baltimore, MD.

Elliot, F. R. (1986) *The Family: Change or Continuity*, London: Macmillan.

Elster, J. (1985) *Making Sense of Marx*, Cambridge: Cambridge University Press.

Engels, F. (1958 [1845]) *The Condition of the Working Class in England*, Oxford: Blackwell.

Engels, F. (1972 [1884]) *The Origin of the Family, Private Property and the State*, London: Lawrence & Wishart.

Equal Opportunities Commission (EOC) (1995) *New Earnings Survey*, Manchester: EOC.

Etzioni, A. (1993) *The Spirit of Community*, Washington, DC: Responsive Community.

Ewing, K. D. and Gearty, C. A. (1990) *Freedom under Thatcher: Civil Liberties in Modern Britain*, Oxford: Clarendon.

Eyre, A. (1989) 'After Hillsborough: an ethnographic account of life in Liverpool in the first few weeks', unpublished paper.

Eyre, A. (1995) 'Religion, politics and development in Malaysia', in R. H. Roberts (ed.) *Religion and the Transformations of Capitalism: Comparative Approaches*, London: Routledge.

Eysenck, H. J. (1971) *Race, Intelligence and Education*, London: Temple Smith.

Fairbrother, H. (1983) 'Who's the brightest of them all?', *Radio Times* 19–25 February: 8–9.

Fawcett, H. and Pichaud, D. (1984) *The Unequal Struggle*,

Featherstone, M. (1991a) *Consumer Culture and Post Modernism*, London: Sage.

Featherstone, M. (1991b) *Global Culture: Nationalism, Globalization and Modernity*, London: Sage.

Ferguson, M. (1985) *Forever Feminine: Women's Magazines and the Cult of Femininity*, London: Heinemann.

Festinger, L., Riecken, H. W. and Schachter, S. (1956) *When Prophecy Fails: A Social and Psychological Study of a Modern Group that Predicted the Destruction of the World*, London: Harper & Row.

Feuer, L. S. (ed.) (1969) *Marx and Engels: Basic Writings on Politics and Philosophy*, London: Fontana.

Feuerbach, L. (1957) *The Essence of Christianity*, New York: Harper & Row.

Fevre, R. (1984) *Cheap Labour and Racial Discrimination*, Aldershot: Gower.

Fevre, R. (1992) *The Sociology of Labour Markets*, Hemel Hempstead: Harvester Wheatsheaf.

Field, D. (1992) 'Elderly people in British society', *Sociology Review* April: 16–20.

Field, F. (1989) *Losing Out: The Emergence of Britain's Underclass*, Oxford: Blackwell.

Field, F. and Hankin, P. (1971) *Black Britons*, Oxford: Oxford University Press.

Finch, J. and Groves, D. (1983) *A Labour of Love: Women, Work and Caring*, London: Routledge & Kegan Paul.

Fincham, R. and Rhodes, P. S. (1994) *The Individual, Work and Organization*, Oxford: Oxford University Press.

Fineman, S. (1987) *Unemployment: Personal and Social Consequences*, London: Tavistock.

Firth, R. (1956) *Two Studies of Kinship in London*, London: Athlone.

Fiske, J. and Hartley, J. (1978) *Reading Television*, London: Methuen.

Fletcher, R. (1988) *The Abolitionists: The Family and Marriage under Attack*, London: Routledge.

Fletcher, W. (1992) *A Glittering Haze*, London: NTC.

Flew, A. (1984) *Education, Race and Revolution*, London.

Flude, M. and Ahier, J. (1974) *Educability, Schools and Ideology*, London: Croom Helm.

Fogelson, R. M. (1971) *Violence as Protest: A Study of Riots in Ghettos*, New York: Doubleday.

Foucault, M. (1977 [1975]) *Discipline and Punish: The Birth of the Prison*, London: Allen Lane.

Foucault, M. (1981 [1976]) *The History of Sexuality Volume 1: An Introduction*, Harmondsworth: Penguin.

Fox, A. (1974) *Beyond Contract: Work, Power and Trust Relations*, London: Faber & Faber.

Francis, M. (1988) 'Issues in the fight against the Education Bill', *Race and Class* 29(3).

Frank, A. G. (1967) *Capitalism and Underdevelopment in Latin America*, New York: Monthly Review.

Franklin, B. and Murphy, D. (1991) *What News? The Market, Politics and the Local Press*, London: Routledge.

Fraser, R. (ed.) (1968) *Work: Twenty Personal Accounts*, Harmondsworth: Penguin.

Freire, P. (1972 [1970a]) *Pedagogy of the Oppressed*, Harmondsworth: Penguin.

Freire, P. (1976 [1970b]) 'A. few notions about the word "conscientization"', in Schooling and Society Course Team, *Schooling and Capitalism: A Sociological Reader*, Milton Keynes: Open University Press.

Friedan, B. (1963) *The Feminine Mystique*, London: Norton.

Friedman, A. L. (1979) *Industry and Labour: Class Struggle at Work and Monopoly Capitalism*, London: Macmillan.

Friedman, M. (1962) *Capitalism and Freedom*, Harmondsworth: Penguin.

Frobel, F., Heinrichs, J. and Dreye, O. (1980) *The New International Division of Labour*, Cambridge: Cambridge University Press.

Fromm, E. (1960) *The Fear of Freedom*, London: Routledge & Kegan Paul.

Fryer, P. (1984) *Staying Power: The History of Black People in Britain*, London: Pluto.

Fryer, P. (1991) *Black People in the British Empire*, London: Pluto.

Fukuyama, F. (1989) 'The end of history?', *The National Interest* 16: 3–17.

Fuller, M. (1980) 'Black girls in a London comprehensive school', in R. Deem (ed.) *Schooling for Women's Work*, London: Routledge & Kegan Paul. Also in M. Hammersley and P. Woods (eds) (1984) *Life in Schools: The Sociology of Pupil Culture*, Milton Keynes: Open University Press.

Gainer, B. (1972) *The Alien Invasion: The Origins of the Aliens Act of 1905*, London: Heinemann.

Gaines, J. (1990) 'Introduction: fabricating the female body', in J. Gaines and C. Herzog (eds) *Fabrications: Costume and the Female Body*, London: Routledge.

Galbraith, J. K. (1967) *The New Industrial State*, Harmondsworth: Penguin.

Gallie, D. (ed.) (1989) *Employment in Britain*, Oxford: Blackwell.

Gallie, D., Marsh, C. and Vogler, V. (1993) *Social Change and the Experience of Unemployment*, Oxford: Oxford University Press.

Gamman, L. and Marshment, M. (1988) *The Female Gaze*, London: Women's Press.

Gans, H. (1974) *Popular Culture and High Culture*, New York: Basic Books.

Garaudy, R. (1970) *Marxism in the Twentieth Century*, London: Collins.

Garfinkel, H. (1967) *Studies in Ethnomethodology*, Englewood Cliffs, NJ: Prentice-Hall.

Garland, D. (1990) *Punishment and Modern Society*, Oxford: Clarendon.

Garmarnikov, E., Morgan, D., Purvis, J. and Taylorson, D. (eds) (1983) *Gender, Class and Work*, London: Heinemann.

Garrard, J. (1971) *The English and Immigration 1880–1910*, London: Oxford University Press.

Gauntlett, D. (1995) *Moving Experiences: Understanding Television's Influences and Effects*, London: John Libbey.

Gehrig, G. (1981) 'The American civil religion debate', *Journal for the Scientific Study of Religion* 20(1): 51–63.

Geraghty, C. (1991) *Women and Soap Operas*, Cambridge: Polity.

Gershunny, J. I. and Miles, I. (1983) *The New Service Economy: The Transformation of Employment in Industrial Relations*, London: Frances Pinter.

Gerth, H. H. and Mills, C. W. (eds) (1991 [1970]) *From Max Weber: Essays in Sociology*, London: Routlege.

Gerzina, G. (1995) *Black England*, London: John Murray.

Gibson, C. (1994) *Dissolving Wedlock*, London: Routledge.

Giddens, A. (1972) *Emile Durkheim: Selected Writings*, Cambridge: Cambridge University Press.

Giddens, A. (1973) *The Class Structure of the Advanced Societies*, London: Hutchinson.

Giddens, A. (1986) 'The rich', in M. Williams (ed.) *Society Today*, London: Macmillan.

Giddens, A. (1990) *The Consequences of Modernity*, Cambridge: Polity.

Giddens, A. (ed.) (1992) *Human Societies: An Introductory Reader in Sociology*, Cambridge: Polity.

Giddens, A. (1993a [1989]) *Sociology*, 2nd edn, Cambridge: Polity.

Giddens, A. (1993b) 'Dare to care, conserve and repair', *New Statesman and Society*, 29 October.

Gide, A. (1952) *The Journals of André Gide 1889-1949*, trans. J. O'Brien, New York: Knopf.

Gifford (1989) *Loosen the Shackles: First Report of the Liverpool 8 Inquiry into Race Relations in Liverpool*, London: Karia.

Gilbert, N. (1993) *Researching Social Life*, London: Sage.

Gilbert, P. (1992) 'The oxygen of publicity: terrorism and reporting restrictions', in A. Belsey and R. Chadwick (eds) *Ethical Issues in Journalism and the Media*, London: Routledge.

Gill, D., Mayor, B. and Blair, M. (1992) *Racism and Education: Structures and Strategies*, London: Sage.

Gill, T. (1990) 'Too high a price for excellence?', *Daily Mail* 28 July.

Gilroy, P. (1987) *There Ain't No Black in the Union Jack*, London: Hutchinson.

Gilroy, P. (1993a) *The Black Atlantic: Modernity and Double Consciousness*, London: Verso.

Gilroy, P. (1993b) *Small Acts*, London: Serpent's Tail.

Ginsburg, N. (1992) 'Racism and housing: concepts and reality', in P Braham (ed.) *Racism and Anti-Racism: Inequalities, Opportunities and Policies*, London: Sage.

Gittins, D. (1985) *The Family in Question*, London: Macmillan.

Glasgow University Media Group (1982) *Really Bad News*, London: Writers & Readers.

Glasgow University Media Group (1985) *War and Peace News*, Milton Keynes: Open University Press.

Glasgow University Media Group (1996) *The Media and Mental Illness*, London: Longman.

Glasner, P. (1977) *The Sociology of Secularisation*, London: Routledge & Kegan Paul.

Glendinning, C. and Millar, J. (1992) *Women and Poverty: Women's Poverty in the 1990's*, Hemel Hempstead: Harvester Wheatsheaf.

Glock, C. Y and Stark, R. (1968) 'Dimensions of religious commitment', in R. Robertson (ed.) *Sociology of Religion*, Harmondsworth: Penguin.

Glover, D. (1985) *The Sociology of the Mass Media*, Ormskirk: Causeway.

Goffman, E. (1968) *Asylums: Essays on the Social Situation of Mental Patients and Other Inmates*, Harmondsworth: Penguin.

Goffman, E. (1969) *The Presentation of Self in Everyday Life*, Harmondsworth: Penguin.

Goffman, E. (1971) *Relations in Public*, Harmondsworth: Penguin.

Golding, P. (1974) *The Mass Media*, London: Longman.

Golding, P. and Murdock, G. (1991) 'Culture, communications and political economy', in J. Curran and M. Gurevitch (eds) *Mass Media and Society*, London: Edward Arnold.

Goldthorpe, J. H., Lockwood, D., Bechhofer, F. and Platt, J. (1968) *The Affluent Worker: Industrial Attitudes and Behaviour*, Cambridge: Cambridge University Press.

Goldthorpe, J. H., Lockwood, D., Bechhofer, F. and Platt, J. (1969) *The Affluent Worker in the Class Structure*, Cambridge: Cambridge University Press.

Goldthorpe, J. H., Llewellyn, C. and Payne, C. (1980) *Social Mobility and Class Structure in Modern Britain*, Oxford: Clarendon.

Gorbutt, D. (1972) 'The new sociology of education', *Education for Teaching* 89 (autumn).

Gordon, D. (1988) 'The global economy', *New Left Review* 168.

Gordon, P. (1988) 'The New Right, race and education', *Race and Class* 29(3): 95–103.

Gordon, P. and Newham, A. (1986) *Different World*, London: Runnymede Trust.

Gorz, A. (ed.) (1979) *The Division of Labour*, Brighton: Harvester.

Gorz, A. (1982) *Farewell to the Working Class*, London: Pluto.

Gouldner, A. W. (1954) *Patterns of Industrial Bureaucracy*, New York: Free Press.

Gouldner, A. W. (1971) *The Coming Crisis of Western Sociology*, London: Heinemann.

Gouldner, A. W. (1973) 'Anti-minotaur: the myth of a value free society', in A. W. Gouldner (1975) *For Sociology: Renewal and Critique in Sociology Today*, Harmondsworth: Penguin.

Gouldner, A. W. (1975) *For Sociology: Renewal and Critique in Sociology Today*, Harmondsworth: Penguin.

Grabrucker, M. (1988) *There's a Good Girl: Gender Stereotyping in the First Three Years of Life: A Diary*, London: Women's Press.

Graham, H. (1984a) *Women, Health and the Family*, Brighton: Wheatsheaf.

Graham, H. (1984b) 'Surveying through stories', in C. Bell and H. Roberts (eds) *Social Researching*, London: Routledge & Kegan Paul.

Gramsci, A. (1971) *Selections from Prison Notebooks*, London: Lawrence & Wishart.

Grant, D. (1989) *Learning Relations*, London: Routledge.

Graunt, J. (1973 [1662]) *Natural and Political Observations mentioned in the Following Index and made upon Bills of Mortality*, New York: Arno.

Green, E., Hebron, S. and Woodward, D. (1990) *Women's Leisure, What Leisure?*, London: Macmillan.

Grint, K. (1991) *The Sociology of Work*, Oxford: Blackwell.

Gross, E. (1992) 'What is feminist theory', in H. Crowley and S. Himmelweit (eds) *Knowing Women*, Cambridge: Polity.

Guardian (annually) *Guardian Political Almanac*, London: Fourth Estate.

Gunter, B. (1985) *Dimensions of Television Violence*, Aldershot: Gower.

Gunter, B. and McAleer, J. (1990) *Children and Television: The One Eyed Monster*, London: Routledge.

Gurr, T. (1970) *Why Men Rebel*, Princeton, NJ: Princeton University Press.

Gutierrez, G. (1973) *A Theology of Liberation*, Maryknoll, NY: Orbis.

Gutierrez, G. (1990) *The Truth Shall Set You Free*, Maryknoll, NY: Orbis.

Habermas, J. (1971) *Legitimation Crisis*, London: Heinemann.

Habermas, J. (1976) Adaptation of his Theory of Legitimation Crisis, Open University D209 Unit 23 p. 78 and D102 Unit 15 p. 79, Milton Keynes.

Haines, H. (1988) *Black Radicals and the Civil Rights Mainstream 1954–70*, Knoxville, TN: University of Tennessee Press.

Hakim, C. (1979) *Occupational Segregation: A Comparative Study of the Degree and Patterns of Differentiation between Men's and Women's Work in Britain, the United States and Other Countries*, Research Paper 9, London: Department of Employment.

Hall, S. (1977) 'The "political" and the "economic" in Marx's theory of classes', in A. Hunt (ed.) *Class and Class Structure*, London: Lawrence & Wishart.

Hall, S. (1982) *Culture and the State*, Milton Keynes: Open University Press.

Hall, S. (1992) 'New ethnicities', in J. Donals and A. Rattansi (eds) *Race, Culture and Difference*, London: Sage/Open University Press.

Hall, S. and Jacques, M. (1989) *New Times*, London: Lawrence & Wishart.

Hall, S. and Jefferson, T. (1976) *Resistance through Rituals*, London: Hutchinson.

Hall, S., Critcher, C., Jefferson, T., Clarke, J. and Roberts, B. (1978) *Policing the Crisis: Mugging, the State and Law and Order*, London: Macmillan.

Halsey, A. H., Floud, J. and Anderson, C. A. (1961) *Education, Economy and Society*, New York: Free Press.

Halsey, A. H, Heath, A. F. and Ridge, J. M. (1980) *Origins and Destinations: Family, Class and Education in Modern Britain*, Oxford: Clarendon.

Hammersley, M. (1992) 'Introducing ethnography', *Sociology Review* 2(2): 18–23.

Hammersley, M. and Woods, P. (eds) (1984) *Life in Schools: The Sociology of Pupil Culture*, Milton Keynes: Open University Press.

Hammond, P. (1976) 'The sociology of American civil religion: a biographical essay', *Sociological Analysis* 37(2): 169–82.

Hanmer, J. and Saunders, S. (1984) *Well Founded Fear: A Community Study of Violence to Women*, London: Hutchinson.

Haralambos, M. and Holborn, M. (eds) (1995) *Sociology: Themes and Perspectives*, 4th edn, London: HarperCollins.

Harding, S. (1987) *Feminism and Methodology*, Milton Keynes: Open University Press.

Hargreaves, D. H. (1967) *Social Relations in a Secondary School*, London: Routledge & Kegan Paul.

Hargreaves, D. H. (1978) 'Power and the paracurriculum', in C. Richards (ed.) *Power and the Curriculum: Issues in Curriculum Studies*, Driffield: Nafferton.

Hargreaves, I. (1993) *Sharper Vision*, Demos.

Harris, G. (1988) *The Sociology of Development*, London: Longman.

Harris, N. (1992) 'Codes of conduct for journalists', in A. Belsey and R. Chadwick (eds) *Ethical Issues in Journalism and the Media*, London: Routledge.

Harrison, T. and Madge, C. (1986 [1939]) *Britain by Mass Observation*, London: Hutchinson.

Hart, A. (1991) *Understanding the Media: A Practical Guide*, London: Routledge.

Hart, A. and Wilson, T. (1992) 'The politics of part-time staff', *AUT Bulletin* January.

Hart, J. (1985) 'Why do women commit less crime?', *New Society* 30 August.

Hart, N. (1976) *When Marriage Ends*, London: Tavistock.

Hartmann, H. (1981) 'The unhappy marriage of Marxism and feminism: towards a more progressive union', in L. Sergent (ed.) *Women and Revolution*, New York: Monthly Review.

Harvey, D. (1989) *The Condition of Postmodernity*, Oxford: Blackwell.

Hattersley, R. (1981) Speech 16 July, *Hansard* 18, cols 1407–9.

Hayek, F. (1967) *Studies in Philosophy, Politics and Economics*, London: Routledge & Kegan Paul.

Hayek, F. (1976) *The Constitution of Liberty*, London: Routledge & Kegan Paul.

Hearn, G. (1987) *The Gender of Oppression: Men, Masculinity and the Critique of Marxism*, London: Pluto.

Heath, A. (1992) 'The attitudes of the underclass', in D. J. Smith (ed.) *Understanding the Underclass*, London: Policy Studies Institute.

Hebdige, D. (1979) *Subculture: The Meaning of Style*, London: Methuen.

Hegel, G. W. F. and Knox, T. M. (1952 [1821]) *Hegel's Philosophy of Right*, Oxford: Oxford University Press.

Heidensohn, F. (1989) *Crime and Society*, London: Macmillan.

Henley Centre (1993) *Media Futures* (July), Henley, Oxon.

Hennelly, A. (ed.) (1990) *Liberation Theology: A Documentary History*, Maryknoll, NY: Orbis.

Henry, C. and Hiltel, M. (1977) *Children of the SS*, London: Corgi.

Henwood, M., Rimmer, L. and Wicks, M. (1987) *Inside the Family*, London: Family Policy Studies Centre.

Hermes, J. (1995) *Reading Women's Magazines*, London: Routledge.

Herrnstein, R. and Murray, C. (1994) *The Bell Curve: Intelligence and the Class Structure*, New York: Free Press.

Hester, S. and Eglin, P. (1992) *A Sociology of Crime*, London: Routledge.

Hill-Collins, P. (1990) *Black Feminist Thought: Knowledge, Consciousness, and the Politics of Empowerment*, London: Unwin Hyman.

Hilton, R. H. (1969) *The Decline of Serfdom in Medieval England*, London: Macmillan.

Hinnells, J. (1984) *Dictionary of Religions*, Harmondsworth: Penguin.

Hite, S. (1981) *The Hite Report on Male Sexuality*, London: Macdonald.

Hitler, A. (1969 [1925]) *Mein Kampf*, trans. R. Manheim, London: Hutchinson.

Hobson, D. (1982) *Crossroads: The Drama of Soap Opera*, London: Methuen.

Hodge, B. and Tripp, D. (1986) *Children's Television*, Cambridge: Polity.

Holmes, C. (1979) *Anti-Semitism in British Society 1876–1939*, London: Edward Arnold.

Holmes, C. (1988) *John Bull's Island: Immigration and British Society 1871–1971*, London: Macmillan.

Holt, J. (1969) *How Children Fail*, Harmondsworth: Penguin.

Home Office (1927) *Children as Victims*, London: HMSO.

Honey, J. (1983) *The Language Trap: Race, Class and the 'Standard English' Issue in British Schools*, Kenton, Middlesex.

Honeyford, R. (1984) 'Education and race: an alternative view', *Salisbury Review* winter.

hooks, b (1984) *Feminist Theory: From Margin to Centre*, Boston, MA: South End Press.

hooks, b (1989) *Talking Back: Thinking Feminist, Thinking Black*, Boston, MA: South End Press.

Hough, M. and Mayhew, P. (1993) *The British Crime Survey*, London: HMSO.

Hovland, C. (1949) *Experiments in Mass Communications*, Princeton, NJ: Princeton University Press.

Hughes, J. (1984) 'The concept of class', in R. Anderson and W. Sharrock (eds) *Teaching Papers in Sociology*, London: Longman.

Hughey, M. (1993) *Civil Religion and Moral Order*, Westport, CT: Greenwood.

Hulme, D. (1990) *Sociology and Development: Theories and Practice*, Hemel Hempstead: Harvester Wheatsheaf.

Humm, M. (ed.) (1992) *Feminisms: A Reader*, Hemel Hempstead: Harvester Wheatsheaf.

Humphries, J. and Rubery, J. (eds) (1995) *The Economics of Equal Value*, Manchester: Equal Opportunities Commission.

Hunte, J. (1965) *Nigger Hunting in England?*, London: West Indian Standing Conference.

Huxley, A. (1932) *Brave New World*, Toronto: Clarke Irwin.

Independent Television Commission (ITC) (1993) *Television: The Public's View*, London: ITC/John Libbey.

Information Technology Advisory Panel (ITAP) (1982a) *Inquiry into Cable Expansion and Broadcasting (Hunt Report)*, London: HMSO.

ITAP (1982b) *Report on Cable Systems*, London: HMSO.

Inglehart, R. (1977) *The Silent Revolution: Changing Values and Political Styles among Western Publics*, Princeton, NJ: Princeton University Press.

Institute of Economic Affairs (IEA) (1992) *Equal Opportunities: A Feminist Fallacy*, London: IEA.

Institute of Public Policy Research (IPPR) (1993) *Education: A Different Vision*, London: IPPR.

Itzin, C. (1994) 'A harm-based equality approach to legislating against pornography without censorship', paper presented at Sexualities in Social Context Conference, University of Central Lancashire, Preston, 28–31 March.

Jackson, B. and Marsden, D. (1963) *Education and the Working Class*, London: Routledge & Kegan Paul.

Jackson, D. (1990) *Unmasking Masculinity: A Critical Autobiography*, London: Routledge.

Jackson, D. and Salisbury, J. (1993) 'The playing fields of masculinity', *Achilles' Heel* 14: 12–15.

Jackson, P. (1968) *Life in Classrooms*, New York: Holt, Rinehart & Winston.

Jacobs, B. (1988) *Racism in Britain*, London: Croom Helm.

Jaggar, A. (1983) *Feminist Politics and Human Nature*, New Jersey: Rowman & Allanheld.

James, W. (1890) *Principles of Psychology*, London: Henry Holt.

Jayaratne, T. E. (1993) 'The value of quantitative methodology for feminist research', in M. Hammersley (ed.) *Social Research Philosophy, Politics and Practice*, London: Sage.

Jeffcoate, R. (1979) *Positive Image toward a Multiracial Curriculum*, London: Chameleon.

Jeffreys, S. (1994) *The Lesbian Heresy: A Feminist Perspective on the Lesbian Sexual Revolution*, London: Women's Press.

Jencks, C. (1993) *Culture*, London: Routledge.

Jenkins, J. (1988) *GCSE Religious Studies: Contemporary Moral Issues*, London: Heinemann.

Jenkins, P. (1987) *Mrs Thatcher's Revolution*, London: Jonathan Cape.

Jenkins, S. (1986) *Market for Glory*, London: Faber & Faber.

Jensen, A. R. (1969) 'How much can we boost IQ and scholastic achievement?', *Harvard Educational Review* 39(1).

Jensen, A. R. (1973) *Educational Differences*, London: Methuen.

Johnson, A. G. (1989) *Human Arrangements: An Introduction to Sociology*, 2nd edn, Orlando, FL: Harcourt Brace Jovanovich.

Johnson, N. (ed.) (1985) *Marital Violence*, London: Routledge & Kegan Paul.

Johnson, R. (1983) 'Educational politics: the old and the new', in A. M. Wolpe and J. Donald (eds) *Is There Anyone Here from Education?*, London: Pluto.

Jones, C. and Mahony, P. (1989) *Learning our Lines*, London: Women's Press.

Jones, N. (1995) *Soundbites and Spindoctors*, London: Cassell.

Jones, P. (1993) *Studying Society: Sociological Theories and Research Practices*, London: Collins.

Jones, S. (1991) 'We are all cousins under the skin', *Independent* 12 December.

Jordon, B. (1984) *Invitation to Social Work*, Oxford: Blackwell.

Jowell, R. and Witherspoon, S. (eds) (1985) *British Social Attitudes Survey*, Aldershot: Gower.

Jowell, R., Brook, L., Prior, G. and Taylor, B. (eds) (1992) *British Social Attitudes Survey*, Ninth Annual Report, Aldershot: Dartmouth.

Kamin, L. (1977) 'Heredity, intelligence, politics and psychology', in N. Block and G. Dworkin (eds) *The IQ Controversy*, London: Quartet.

Kanter, R. M. (1977) *Men and Women of the Corporation*, New York: Basic Books.

Karabel, J. and Halsey, A. H. (1977) *Power and Ideology in Education*, Oxford: Oxford University Press.

Karn, V., Kemeny, J. and Williams, P. (1983) 'Race and housing in Britain: the rule of major institutions', in N. Glazer and K. Young (eds) *Ethnic Pluralism and Public Policy*, London: Heinemann.

Katz, E. and Lazarsfeld, P. (1955) *Personal Influence*, New York: Free Press.

Kavanagh, D. (1992) 'Opinion polls, predictions and politics', *Politics Review* 2(2): 6–14.

Keane, J. (1991) *The Media and Democracy*, Cambridge: Polity.

Keddie, N. (ed.) *Tinker, Tailor, ... The Myth of Cultural Deprivation*, Harmondsworth: Penguin.

Kelly, A. (ed.) (1981) *The Missing Half: Girls and Science Education*, Manchester: Manchester University Press.

Kelly, E. (1988) *Surviving Sexual Violence*, Cambridge: Polity.

Kelly, E., Regan, L. and Burton, S. (1992) 'Defending the indefensible: quantitative methods and feminist research', in H. Hinds, A. Phoenix and J. Stacey (eds) *Working Out New Directions for Women's Studies*, Brighton: Falmer.

Kennedy, P. (1993) *Preparing for the 21st Century*, London: Random House.

Kent, R. (1981) *A History of British Empirical Sociology*, Aldershot: Gower.

Kenway, J. and Willis, S. (1990) *Hearts and Minds: Self-Esteem and the Schooling of Girls*, Northern Territory, Australia: Darwin University Press.

Kern, M. (1989) *30 Second Politics: Political Advertising in the Eighties*, New York: Praeger.

Kerr, C., Dunlop, J. T., Harbison, F. H. and Mayers, C. A. (1962) *Industrialism and Industrial Man*, London: Heinemann.

Kerr, M. (1958) *The People of Ship Street*, London: Routledge & Kegan Paul.

Kettle, M. and Hodges, L. (1982) *Uprising! The Police, the People and the Riots in Britain's Cities*, London: Pan.

Keynes, J. M. (1936) *The General Theory of Employment, Interest and Money*, London: Macmillan.

Kilborn, R. (1992) *Television Soaps*, London: Batsford.

Kimmel, M. S. (1990) *Revolution: A Sociological Interpretation*, Cambridge: Polity.

King, A. (1993) 'Mystery and imagination: the case of pornography effects studies', in A. Assiter and C. Avendon (eds) *Bad Girls and Dirty Pictures*, London: Pluto.

Kingdom, J. (1991) *Government and Politics in Britain*, Cambridge: Polity.

Kinsey, A. C., Pomeroy, W. B. and Martin, C. E. (1948) *Sexual Behavior in the Human Male*, Philadelphia, PA: W. B. Saunders.

Kinsey, A. C., Pomeroy, W. B., Martin, C. E. and Gebhard, P. H. (1953) *Sexual Behavior in the Human Female*, Philadelphia, PA: W. B. Saunders.

Klein, J. (1965) *Samples from English Cultures*, vol. 1, London: Routledge & Kegan Paul.

Kogan, M. (1975) *Educational Policy Making*, London: Allen & Unwin.

Koss, S. (1973) *Fleet Street Radical: A G Gardiner and the Daily News*, London: Allen Lane.

Krippendorf, K. (1980) *Content Analysis: An Introduction to its Methodology*, London: Sage.

Kuhn, T. S. (1962) *The Structure of Scientific Revolutions*, Chicago, IL: University of Chicago Press.

Kumar, K. (1978) *Prophecy and Progress: The Sociology of Industrial and Post-Industrial Society*, Harmondsworth: Penguin.

Kumar, K. (1995) *From Post-Industrial to Post-Modern Society*, Oxford: Blackwell.

Labov, W. (1969) 'The logic of non-standard English', in P. P. Giglioli (ed.) (1972) *Language and Social Context*, Harmondsworth: Penguin. Also in N. Keddie (ed.) (1973) *Tinker, Tailor, ... The Myth of Cultural Deprivation*, Harmondsworth: Penguin.

Lacey, C. (1970) *Hightown Grammar: The School as a Social System*, Manchester: Manchester University Press.

Laclau, E. (1977) 'Feudalism and capitalism in Latin America', *New Left Review* 67: 19–38.

Laing, R. D. and Esterson, A. (1970) *Sanity, Madness and the Family*, Harmondsworth: Penguin.

Lambart, A. (1976) 'The sisterhood', in M. Hammersley and P. Woods (eds) *The Process of Schooling*, London: Routledge & Kegan Paul.

Laslett, P. (1972) 'Mean household size in England since the 16th century', in P. Laslett (ed.) *Household and*

*Family in Past Times*, Cambridge: Cambridge University Press.

Lasswell, H. (1948) 'The structure and function of communications in society', in L. Bryson (ed.) *The Communication of Ideas*, London: Harper.

Lather, P. (1988) 'Feminist perspectives on empowering research methodology', *Women's Studies International Forum* 11(9): 569–81.

Lawson, T. (1986) 'In the shadow of science', *Social Studies Review* 2(2): 36–41.

Layder, D. (1994) *Understanding Social Theory*, London: Sage.

Layton Henry, Z (1989) 'Black electoral participation: an analysis of recent trends', in H. Gouldbourne (ed.) (1990) *Black People and British Politics*, Aldershot: Avebury.

Lazarsfeld, P., Berelson, B. and Gauder, H. (1944) *The People's Choice*, New York: Duell, Sloan & Pearce.

Lea, J. and Young, J. (1984) *What's to be Done About Law and Order?*, Harmondsworth: Penguin.

Leach, E. (1967) *A Runaway World?*, London: BBC Publications.

Leadbetter, C. (1987) 'The divided workforce', *Marxism Today* April.

Lee, C. H. (1995) *Scotland and the UK*, Manchester: Manchester University Press.

Lee, D. and Newby, H. (1983) *The Problem of Sociology*, London: Hutchinson.

Lee, D. and Turner, B. S. (1996) *Conflicts about Class: Debating Inequality in Late Industrialism*, London: Longman.

Lee, J. (1989) 'Social class and schooling', in M. Cole (ed.) *The Social Contexts of Schooling*, London: Falmer.

Leeds Revolutionary Feminists Group (1981) 'Political lesbianism: the case against heterosexuality', in Onlywomen (eds) *Love your Enemy? The Debate between Heterosexual Feminism and Political Lesbianism*, London: Onlywomen Press.

Lees, S. (1986) *Losing Out: Sexuality and Adolescent Girls*, London: Hutchinson.

Lees, S. (1993) *Sugar and Spice: Sexuality and Adolescent Girls*, Harmondsworth: Penguin.

Lee-Treweek, G. (1994) 'Bedroom abuse: the hidden work in a nursing home', *Generations Review* 4(1): 2–4.

Lemert, C. (ed.) (1993) *Social Theory: The Multicultural and Classic Readings*, Oxford: Westview.

Lenin, I. V. (1978 [1917]) *Imperialism, the Highest Stage of Capitalism*, London: Progress.

Levin, J. (1993) *Sociological Snapshots*, Newbury Park, CA: Pine Forge Press.

Levitas, R. (ed.) (1986) *The Ideology of the New Right*, Oxford: Polity.

Lewis, O. (1966) *La Vida*, New York: Random House.

Lewis, P. and Booth, J. (1989) *The Invisible Medium: Public, Commercial and Community Radio*, London: Macmillan.

Lichter, S., Rotham, S. and Lichter L. (1986) *The Media Elite: America's New Powerbrokers*, Bethesda, MD: Adler & Adler.

Liebert, R. M. and Baron, R. A. (1972) 'Some immediate effects of televised violence on children's behaviour', *Development Psychology* 6: 469–75.

Lindsey, L. (1990) *Gender Roles: A Sociological Perspective*, London: Sage.

Lion (1988) *The World's Religions: A Lion Handbook*, Oxford: Lion.

Little, A. (1981) 'Education and race relations in the United Kingdom', in J. Megarry, S. Nisbet and E. Hoyle (eds) *World Yearbook of Education*, London: Kogan Page.

Littler, C. R. (1982) *The Development of the Labour Process in Capitalist Societies*, London: Heinemann.

Lobo, E. (1978) *Children of Immigrants to Britain*, London: Hodder & Stoughton.

Lockwood, D. (1989 [1958]) *The Blackcoated Worker*, 2nd edn, Oxford: Oxford University Press.

Lodge, P. and Blackstone, T. (1982) *Educational Policy and Educational Inequality*, Oxford: Martin Robertson.

Lombroso, C. and Ferrero, W. (1895) *The Female Offender*, London: T. Fisher Unwin.

Longman Community Information (1995) *Education Yearbook*, London: Longman.

Lord, D. N. (1992) 'Marriage could become irrelevant', *Independent* 10 February: 2.

Lorenz, K. (1965) *Evolution and Modification of Behaviour*, Chicago, IL: University of Chicago Press.

Lorenz, K. (1973) *Civilised Man's Eight Deadly Sins*, New York: Methuen.

Lovelace, C. (1978) 'British press censorship during the First World War', in G. Boyce (ed.) *Newspaper History: From the Seventeenth Century to the Present Day*, London: Constable.

Lovenduski, J. and Randall, V. (1993) *Feminist Politics*, Oxford: Oxford University Press.

Luckmann, T. (1967) *The Invisible Religion: The Problem of Religion in Modern Society*, New York: Macmillan.

Lull, J. (1991) *China Turned On: Television, Reform and Resistance*, London: Routledge.

Lull, J. (1995) *Media, Communication and Culture*, Cambridge: Polity.

Lyndon, N. (1992) *No More Sex War: The Failures of Feminism*, London: Sinclair-Stevenson.

Lynn, R (1970) 'Comprehensives and quality: the quest for the unattainable', in C. B. Cox and A. E. Dyson (eds) *Black Paper Two: The Critical Survey 1968–70,* London: Critical Quarterly Society.

Lyon, M. (1972) 'Race and ethnicity in pluralistic societies', *New Community* 1: 256–62.

Lyon, M. (1973) 'Ethnic minority problems: an overview of some recent research', *New Community* 2(4): 329–52.

Lyotard, J. (1985) *The Postmodern Condition*, Minneapolis, MN: University of Minneapolis Press.

Mabey, C. (1981) 'Black British literacy', *Educational Research* 23(2).

McClelland, D. (1961) *The Achieving Society*, New York: Van Nostrand.

McCulloch, J. R. (1825) *Principles of Political Economy: With a Sketch of the Rise and Progress of Science*, London.

Macdonald, I. (1983) *Immigration Law and Practice in the UK*, London: Butterworth.

Macdonald, I., Bhavnani, R., Kahn, L., and John, G., (1990) *Murder in the Playground*, London: Longsight.

McGuire, M. (1992) *Religion: The Social Context*, Wadsworth, CA: Belmont.

McIlroy, J. (1995) *Trade Unions in Britain Today*, 2nd edn, Manchester: Manchester University Press.

McIntosh, I. (1991) 'Ford at Trafford Park', unpublished PhD thesis, University of Manchester.

McIntosh, I. (1995) 'It was worse than Alcatraz: working for Ford at Trafford Park', *Manchester Regional History Review* May, 9.

McIntosh, I. and Broderick, J. (1996) 'Neither one thing nor the other: competitive compulsory tendering and Southburch Cleansing Services', *Work, Employment and Society*.

McKenzie, J. (1993) *Education as a Political Issue*, Aldershot: Avebury.

McKie, D., with Bindman, D., (1994) *The Guardian Political Almanac 1994/5*, London: Fourth Estate.

MacKinnon, C. (1982) 'Feminism, Marxism, method and the state: an agenda for theory', *Signs* 7(3): 515–44.

MacKinnon, C. A. (1989) *Towards a Feminist Theory of the State*, Cambridge, MA: Harvard University Press.

Maclean, C. (1977) *The Wolf Children*, London: Allen Lane.

McLuhan, M. (1962) *The Guttenberg Galaxy*, Toronto: Toronto University Press.

McLuhan, M. (1964) *Understanding Media*, London: Routledge & Kegan Paul.

McLuhan, M. and Fiore, Q. (1967) *The Medium is the Message*, Harmondsworth: Penguin.

McNeill, P. (1990) *Research Methods*, 2nd edn, London: Routledge.

McQuail, D. (1994) *Mass Communications Theory: An Introduction*, London: Sage.

McRobbie, A. (1982) 'Jackie: an ideology of adolescent femininity', in B. Waites (ed.) *Popular Culture: Past and Present*, Milton Keynes: Open University Press.

McRobbie, A. (1991) 'The politics of feminist research', in A. McRobbie (ed.) *Feminism and Youth Culture*, London: Macmillan.

Maguire, M. J. and Ashton, D. N. (1981) 'Employers' perceptions and use of educational qualifications', *Educational Analysis* 3(2).

Maguire, M., Morgan, R. and Reiner, R. (eds) (1994) *The Oxford Handbook of Criminology*, Oxford: Clarendon.

Maidment, S. (1985) 'Domestic violence and the law: the 1976 Act and its aftermath', in N. Johnson (ed.) *Marital Violence*, London: Routledge & Kegan Paul.

Malik, R. (1995) 'Young "forced into FE to avoid poverty trap"', *Times Educational Supplement* 21 July.

Malinowski, B, (1926) 'Magic, science and religion', in J. Needham (ed.) *Science, Religion and Reality*, London: Macmillan.

Malson, L, and Itard, J. (1972) *Wolf Children*, London: New Left Books.

Malthus, T. R. (1973) *An Essay on the Principle of Population*, London: Dent.

Mama, A. (1992) 'Black women and the British state: race, class and gender analysis for the 1990s', in P. Braham (ed.) *Racism and Anti-Racism: Inequalities, Opportunities and Policies*, London: Sage.

Manning, P. (1992) *Erving Goffman and Modern Sociology*, Cambridge: Polity.

Mao Tse-Tung (1966) *Quotations from Chairman Mao Tse-Tung*, Beijing.

Marcuse, H. (1964) *One Dimensional Man: Studies in the Ideology of Advanced Industrial Society*, Boston, MA: Beacon.

Mars, G. (1982) *Cheats at Work: An Anthology of Workplace Crime*, London: Allen & Unwin.

Marshall, G., Newby, H., Rose, D. and Vogler, C. (1988) *Social Class in Modern Britain*, London: Hutchinson.

Marshall, T. H. (1992 [1947]) 'Citizenship and social class', in T. H. Marshall and T. Bottomore, *Sociology at the Crossroads*, London: Heinemann.

Martin, J. and Roberts, C. (1984) *Women and Employment: A Lifetime Perspective*, London: HMSO.

Martindale, D. (1960) *The Nature and Types of Sociological Theory*, London: Lowe & Brydon.

Marx, K. (1967 [1867]) *Das Kapital, Volume 1*, London: Lawrence & Wishart.

Marx, K. (1969 [1875]) 'Critique of the Gotha Programme', in L. S. Feuer (ed.) *Marx and Engels: Basic Writings on Politics and Philosophy*, London: Fontana.

Marx, K. (1970 [1845]) *The German Ideology: Students' Edition*, London: Lawrence & Wishart. Also in (1976) *Collected Works*, vol. 5, London: Lawrence & Wishart.

Marx, K. and Engels, F. (1952 [1848]) *The Manifesto of the Communist Party*, Moscow: Progress.

Marx, K. and Engels, F. (1955) *On Religion*, Moscow: Foreign Languages Publishing House.

Marx, K. and Engels, F. (1976) *Collected Works*, 10 vols, London: Lawrence & Wishart.

Maslow, A. H. (1970) *Motivation and Personality*, 2nd edn, New York: Harper & Row.

Mason, H. and Ramsay, T. (1992) *A Parents' A–Z of Education*, London: Chambers.

Massey, D. (1994) *Space, Place and Gender*, Oxford: Polity.

Massey, D. and Allen, J. (1988) *Uneven Re-Development: Cities and Regions in Transition*, London: Hodder & Stoughton.

Masterman, L. (1985) *Teaching About Television*, London: Macmillan.

Masters, W. and Johnson, V. (1966) *Human Sexual Response*, London: Churchill.

Masters, W. and Johnson, V. (1970) *Human Sexual Inadequacy*, London: Churchill.

Matza, D. (1969) *Becoming Deviant*, London: Prentice-Hall.

Mayhew, H. (1949) 'Mayhew's London', in P. Quennell (ed.) *Mayhew's London*, London: Pilot.

Maynard, M. (1990) 'The reshaping of sociology? Trends in the study of gender', *Sociology* 24(2): 269–90.

Maynard, M. and Purvis, J. (eds) (1994) *Researching Women's Lives*, London: Taylor & Francis.

Mays, J. B. (1954) *Growing up in the City*, Liverpool: University of Liverpool Press.

Mead, M. (1935) *Sex and Temperament in Three Primitive Societies*, London: Routledge & Kegan Paul.

Medved, M. (1992) *Hollywood vs America*, New York: HarperCollins.

Meehan, D. (1983) *Ladies of the Evening: Women Characters on Prime Time TV*, Metuchen, NJ: Scarecrow.

Meighan, R. (1986 [1981]) *A Sociology of Educating*, 2nd edn, London: Cassell.

Meighan, R., Shelton, I. and Marks, T. (eds) (1979) *Perspectives on Society*, Sunbury on Thames: Thomas Nelson.

Mendelsohn, H. (1966) *Mass Entertainment*, New Haven, CT: College and University Press.

Mennell, S. (1992) *The Sociology of Food and Eating*, London: Sage.

Mental Health Foundation (MHF) (1993) *Mental Illness: The Fundamental Facts*, London: MHF.

Merton, R. K. (1938) 'Social structure and anomie', *American Sociological Review* 3: 672–82.

Merton, R. K. (1952) 'Bureaucratic structure and personality', in R. K. Merton, *A Reader in Bureaucracy*, New York: Free Press.

Metcalf, M. and Humphries, A. (eds) (1985) *The Sexuality of Men*, London: Pluto.

Meyer, S. (1981) *The Five Dollar Day*, New York: Albany.

Michels, R. (1959) *Political Parties*, New York: Dover.

Mies, M. (1986) *Patriarchy and Accumulation on a World Scale*, London: Zed.

Mihill, C. (1995) 'Public enemy number one', *Guardian* 2 May.

Miles, R. (1982) *Racism and Migrant Labour: A Critical Text*, London: Routledge & Kegan Paul.

Miles, R. (1987) 'Recent Marxist theories of nationalism and the issue of racism', *British Journal of Sociology* 38(1): 24–43.

Miles, R. (1989) *Racism*, London: Routledge.

Miles, R. (1990) 'Racism, ideology and disadvantage', *Social Studies Review* 4 (March): 148–51.

Miles, R. (1993) *Racism after 'Race Relations'*, London: Routledge.

Miles, R. and Phizacklea, A. (1984) *White Man's Country: Racism in British Politics*, London: Pluto.

Milgram, S. (1974) *Obedience to Authority*, London: Harper & Row.

Miliband, R. (1969) *The State in Capitalist Society*, London: Weidenfeld & Nicolson.

Miller, A. (1983) *For Your Own Good: The Roots of Violence in Child-Rearing*, London: Virago.

Miller, H. (1970 [1945]) *The Air-Conditioned Nightmare*, New York: New Directions.

Miller, W. (1991) *Media and Voters*, Oxford: Clarendon.

Miller, W. B. (1958) 'Lower-class culture as a generating milieu of gang delinquency', *Journal of Sociological Issues* 14: 5–19.

Millett, K. (1970) *Sexual Politics*, London: Abacus.

Mills, C. W. (1951) *White Collar: The American Middle Classes*, Oxford: Oxford University Press.

Mills, C. W. (1956) *The Power Elite*, Oxford: Oxford University Press.

Mills, C. W. (1970) *The Sociological Imagination*, Harmondsworth: Penguin.

Milner, D. (1983) *Children and Race Ten Years On*, London: Alan Sutton.

Mintz, S. (1974) *Caribbean Transformation*, Chicago, IL: Aldine.

Mirza, H. (1991) *Young, Female and Black*, London: Routledge.

Mitchell, G. D. (1968) *A Hundred Years of Sociology*, London: Duckworth.

Mohanty, C., Russo, A. and Lourdes, T. (eds) (1991) *Third World Women and the Politics of 'Feminism'*, Bloomington, IN: Indiana University Press.

Moir, A. and Jessel, D. (1989) *Brain Sex: The Real Difference Between the Sexes*, London: Mandarin.

Moore, S. (1988) *Investigating Deviance*, London: Unwin Hyman.

Morgan, D. (1975) *Social Theory and the Family*, London: Routledge & Kegan Paul.

Morgan, D. (1981) 'Men, masculinity and the process of sociological enquiry', in H. Roberts (ed.) *Doing Feminist Research*, London: Routledge & Kegan Paul.

Morgan, D. (1991) *Discovering Men*, London: Routledge.

Morgan, D. (1992) 'Sociology, society and the family', in T. Lawson, J. Scott, H. Westergaard and J. Williams (eds) *Sociology Reviewed*, London: Collins.

Morgan, D. (1994a) 'The family', in M. Haralambos (ed.) *Developments in Sociology*, vol. 10, Ormskirk: Causeway.

Morgan, D. (1994b) 'Theater of war: combat, the military and masculinities', in H. Brod and M. Kaufman (eds) *Theorizing Masculinities*, London: Sage.

Morison, M. (1986) *Methods in Sociology*, London: Longman.

Morris, D. (1968) *The Naked Ape*, London: Corgi.

Morris, D. (1977) *Manwatching: A Field Guide to Human Behaviour*, London: Jonathan Cape.

Morrison, D. and Tumber, H. (1988) *Journalists at War: The Dynamics of News Reporting During the Falklands Conflict*, London: Sage.

Mosca, G. (1939) *The Ruling Class*, New York: McGraw-Hill.

Muggeridge, M. (1978) *Things Past*, London: Collins.

Mullard, C. (1982) 'Multi-racial education in Britain: from assimiliation to cultural pluralism', in J. Tierney (ed.) *Race, Migration and Schooling*, London: Holt.

Muncie, J. and Sparks, R. (eds) (1991) *Imprisonment: European Perspectives*, Hemel Hempstead: Harvester Wheatsheaf.

Murdock, G. (1990) 'Redrawing the map of the communications industries', in M. Ferguson (ed.) *Public Communication*, London: Sage.

Murdock, G. and McCron, R. (1979) 'The broadcasting and delinquency debate', *Screen Education* 30: 51.

Murphy, L. and Livingstone, J. (1985) 'Racism and the limits of radical feminism', *Race and Class* 4 (spring): 61–70.

Murray, C. (ed.) (1990) *The Emerging British Underclass*, London: IEA Health & Welfare Unit.

Musgrave, P. W. (1965) *The Sociology of Education*, London: Methuen.

Nairn, T. (1988) *The Enchanted Glass: Britain and its Monarchy*, London: Hutchinson.

National Association of Citizens' Advice Bureaux (NACAB) (1988) *Homelessness: A National Survey of CAB Clients*, London: NACAB.

National Commission on Education (1993) *Learning to Succeed*, London: HMSO.

National Heritage Select Committee (1993) *Privacy and Media Intrusion*, London: HMSO.

National Society for the Prevention of Cruelty to Children (NSPCC) (1989) *Child Abuse Trends in England and Wales 1983–1987*, London: NSPCC.

National Viewers' and Listeners' Association (NVLA) (1994) *A Culture of Cruelty and Violence*, Colchester: NVLA.

Neibuhr, H. (1957) *The Social Sources of Denominationalism*, Cleveland, OH: World Publishing.

Newburn, T. (1995) *Crime and Criminal Justice Policy*, London: Longman.

Newburn, T. and Hagell, A. (1995) 'Violence on screen: just child's play', *Sociology Review* February: 7–10.

Newson, E. (1994) 'Video violence and the protection of children', Child Development Research Unit, University of Nottingham.

Nichols, T. (1979) 'Social class: official, sociological and Marxist', in J. Irvine, I. Miles and J. Evans (eds) *Demystifying Social Statistics*, London: Pluto.

Nilsen, A. P. (1975) *The Cult of the Apron*.

Nisbet, R. A. (1970) *The Sociological Tradition*, London: Heinemann.

Noble, G. (1975) *Children in Front of the Small Screen*, London: Constable.

Nott, J.C. and Gliddon, G.R. (1854) *Types of Mankind*, Philadelphia, PA.

Oakley, A. (1972) *Sex, Gender and Society*, London: Temple Smith.

Oakley, A. (1974a) *Housewife*, London: Allen Lane.

Oakley, A. (1974b) *The Sociology of Housework*, Oxford: Martin Robertson.

Oakley, A. (1981) 'Interviewing women: a contradiction in terms', in H. Roberts (ed.) *Doing Feminist Research*, London: Routledge & Kegan Paul.

Oakley, A. and Oakley, R. (1981) 'Sexism in official statistics', in J. Irvine, I. Miles and J. Evans (eds) *Demystifying Social Statistics*, London: Pluto.

O'Brien, M. (1981) *The Politics of Reproduction*, London: Routledge & Kegan Paul.

O'Donnell, M. (1981) *A New Introduction to Sociology*, London: Harrap.

O'Donnell, M. (1993) *New Introductory Reader in Sociology*, London: Nelson.

O'Faolain, J. and Martinez, L. (1979) *Not in God's Image*, London: Virago.

Offe, C. (1985) 'New social movements: challenging the boundaries of institutional politics', *Social Research* 52(4): 817–68.

Office of Population Censuses and Surveys (annually) *Social Trends*, London: HMSO.

Oppenheim, C. (1993) *Poverty: The Facts*, London: Child Poverty Action Group.

O'Sullivan, T., Dutton, B. and Raynor, P. (1994) *Studying the Media: An Introduction*, London: Edward Arnold.

O'Toole, R. (1984) *Religion: Classic Sociological Approaches*, Whitby, Ontario: McGraw-Hill.

Ottoway, A. K. C. (1953) *Education and Society*, London: Routledge & Kegan Paul.

Owen, D. (1991) *Ethnic Minority Women and the Labour Market: Analysis of the 1991 Census*, Centre for Research in Ethnic Relations (CRER), University of Warwick, Equal Opportunities Commission.

Pachman, J. (1981) *The Children's Generation*, Oxford: Blackwell.

Pahl, J. (1989) *Money and Marriage*, London: Macmillan.

Pahl, R. E. (1984) *Divisions of Labour*, Oxford: Blackwell.

Pahl, R. E. and Wallace, C. (1988) 'Neither angels in marble nor rebels in red: privatization and working-class consciousness', in D. Rose (ed.) *Social Stratification and Economic Change*, London: Hutchinson.

Pareto, V. F. D. (1935) *The Mind and Society*, 4 vols, London: Jonathan Cape. Also in P. Bachrach (1967) *The Theory of Democratic Elitism*, Boston, MA: Little, Brown.

Park, R. E., Burgess, E. and Mackenzie, R. (1923) *The City*, Chicago, IL: University of Chicago Press.

Parkin, F. (1972) *Class, Inequality and Political Order*, London: Paladin.

Parry, G., Moyser, G. and Day, N. (1989) *Participation and Democracy: Political Activity and Attitudes in Contemporary Britain*, Cambridge: Cambridge University Press.

Parsons, T. (1954) 'The kinship system of the contemporary United States', in T. Parsons, *Essays in Sociological Theory*, New York: Free Press.

Parsons, T. (1959) 'The school class as a social system: some of its functions in American society', *Harvard Educational Review* 29. Also in A. H. Halsey, J. Floud and C. A. Anderson (eds) (1961) *Education, Economy and Society*, New York: Free Press.

Parsons, T. (1966) *Societies: Evolutionary and Comparative Perspectives*, London: Prentice-Hall.

Parsons, T. (1971) 'Belief, unbelief and disbelief', in R. Caporale and A. Grumelli (eds) *The Culture of Unbelief*, Berkeley, CA: University of California Press.

Parsons, T. and Bales, R. F. (1955) *Family, Socialization and Interaction Process*, New York: Free Press.

Partington, G. (1982) Article in *Police* August.

Partington, G. (1986) 'History: re-written to ideological fashion', in D. O'Keeffe (ed.) *The Wayward Curriculum: A Cause for Parents' Concern?*, London: Social Affairs Unit.

Pascall, G. (1995) 'Women on top? Women's careers in the 1990s', *Sociology Review* February: 2–6.

Pascall, G. and Cox, P. (1993) 'Education and domesticity', *Gender and Education* 5(1)

Pateman, C. (1987) 'Feminist critiques of the public/private dichotomy', in A. Phillips (ed.) *Feminism and Equality*, Oxford: Blackwell.

Pawson, R. (1989) 'Methodology', in M. Haralambos (ed.) *Developments in Sociology*, vol. 5, Ormskirk: Causeway.

Peach, C. (1972) *West Indian Migration to Britain*, Oxford: Institute of Race Relations.

Peacock (1986) *Report of the Committee on Financing the BBC*, London: HMSO.

Peak, S. (1994) *The Media Guide 1994*, London: Fourth Estate.

Pearson, G. (1983) *Hooligan: A History of Respectable Fears*, London: Macmillan.

Pearson, J. (1972) *The Profession of Violence: The Rise and Fall of the Kray Twins*, London: Weidenfeld & Nicolson.

Penelope, J. (1986) 'The lesbian perspective', in J. Allen (ed.) *Lesbian Philosophy: Explorations*, Palo Alto, CA: Institute of Lesbian Studies.

Persell, C. H. (1990) *Understanding Society: An Introduction to Sociology*, 3rd edn, New York: Harper & Row.

Peters, T. J. and Austin, N. (1985) *A Passion for Excellence*, New York: Random House.

Peters, T. J. and Waterman, R. H. (1982) *In Search of Excellence: Lessons from America's Best Run Companies*, New York: Harper & Row.

Philips, D. (1986) *What Price Equality? Report on the Allocation of GLC Housing in Tower Hamlets*, London: Greater London Council.

Phillips, A. (1987) *Divided Loyalties: Dilemmas of Sex and Class*, London: Virago.

Phillips, A. (1993) *The Trouble with Boys*, London: Pandora.

Phillips, A. and Taylor, B. (1980) 'Sex and skill: notes toward a feminist economics', *Feminist Review* 6: 79–83.

Pilger, J. (1994) 'Death for sale', *Guardian* 12 November.

Pilkington (1962) *Report of the Committee on Broadcasting*, London: HMSO.

Pines, M. (1981) 'The civilising of Genie', *Psychology Today* 15.

Piore, M. (1973) 'On the technological foundation dualism', MIT Working Paper 112a, Manchester, May.

Piore, M. and Sabel, C. (1984) *The Second Industrial Divide*, New York: Basic Books.

Plint, T. (1851) *Crime in England: Its Relation, Character and Extent, as Developed from 1801 to 1848*, London: Charles Gilpin.

Plowden (1967) *Children and their Primary Schools*, London: HMSO.

Plummer, K. (1978) 'Men in love: observations on male homosexual couples', in M. Corbin (ed.) *The Couple*, Harmondsworth: Penguin.

Policy Studies Institute (PSI) (1983) *The Police and People in London*, London: PSI.

PSI (1994) *Ethnic Minorities and Higher Education: Why are There Different Rates of Entry?*, London: PSI.

Polity (1994) *Polity Reader in Gender Studies*, Cambridge: Polity.

Pollert, A. (1981) *Girls, Wives, Factory Lives*, London: Macmillan.

Pollert, A. (1988a) 'The flexible firm: fact or fiction?', *Work, Employment and Society* 2(3): 281–316.

Pollert, A. (1988b) 'Dismantling flexibility', *Capital and Class* 34: 42–75.

Popham, P. (1992) 'Throwing away the key', *Independent Magazine* 17 October.

Popper, K. (1961) *The Poverty of Historicism*, London: Routledge.

Postman, N. (1987) *Amusing Ourselves to Death*, London: Methuen.

Poulantzas, N. (1973) 'The problems of the capitalist state', in J. Urry and J. Wakeford (eds) *Power in Britain*, London: Heinemann.

Poulantzas, N. (1979) *Class in Contemporary Capitalism*, London: New Left Books.

Powell, E. (1981) Speech to Thurrock Conservative Association, 30 October, reported *Guardian* 9 November.

Propp, V. (1968) *Morphology of Folk Tales*, Austin, TX: University of Texas Press.

Pugh, A. (1990) 'My statistics and feminism: a true story', in L. Stanley (ed.) *Feminist Praxis*, London: Routledge.

Radcliffe-Brown, A. R. (1952) *Structure and Function in Primitive Society*, London: Cohen & West.

Radical Statistics Health Group (RSHG) (1987) *Facing the Figures: What Really is Happening to the National Health Service?*, London: RSHG.

Radway, J. (1984) *Reading the Romance: Women, Patriarchy and Popular Literature*, Chapel Hill, NC: University of North Carolina Press.

Radzinowicz, L. and King, J. (1977) *The Growth of Crime*, London: Hamish Hamilton.

Ramazanoglu, C. (1991a) 'Feminist epistemology and research', in J. Gubbay (ed.) *Teaching Methods of Social Research*, report of a City conference, City University, London, November.

Ramazanoglu, C. (1991b) 'Gender', in M. Haralambos (ed.) *Developments in Sociology*, Ormskirk: Causeway.

Ramdin, R. (1987) *The Making of the Black Working Class in Britain*, Aldershot: Gower.

Rampton (1981) *West Indian Children in Our Schools: Report of the Committee of Inquiry into the Education of Children from Ethnic Minority Groups*, London: HMSO.

Redcliffe Maud (1969) *Report of the Royal Commission on Local Government in England 1966/9*, Cmnd 4040, London: HMSO.

Reid, I. (1978) *Sociological Perspectives on School and Education*, Shepton Mallet: Open Books.

Reid, I. (1989) *Social Class Differences in Britain*, 3rd edn, London: Fontana.

Reid, I. (1993) 'More than a touch of class', in Centre for Ethnic Studies in Education (CESE), *The Education Reform Act and Equal Opportunities: Emerging Patterns*, proceedings of a CESE conference, Manchester, November 1992.

Reinharz, S. (1993) 'The principles of feminist research: a matter of debate', in C. Kramarae and D. Spender (eds) *The Knowledge Explosion: Generations of Feminist Scholarship*, Hemel Hempstead: Harvester Wheatsheaf.

Reith, J. (1924) *Broadcast Over Britain*, London: Hodder & Stoughton.

Rex, J. (1970) *Race Relations in Sociological Theory*, London: Weidenfeld & Nicolson.

Rex, J. (1973) *Race, Colonialism and the City*, London: Routledge & Kegan Paul.

Rex, J. and Mason, D. (eds) (1986) *Theories of Race and Ethnic Relations*, Cambridge: Cambridge University Press.

Rex, J. and Moore, R. (1967) *Race, Community and Conflict: A Study of Sparkbrook*, Oxford: Oxford University Press.

Rex, J. and Tomlinson, S. (1979) *Colonial Immigrants in a British City: A Class Analysis*, London: Routledge & Kegan Paul.

Rey, P. P. (1976) *Las Avanzas de Classes*, Mexico: Giglo.

Rich, A. (1977) *Of Woman Born: Motherhood as Experience and Institution*, London: Virago.

Rich, P. B. (1986) *Race and Empire in British Politics*, Cambridge: Cambridge University Press.

Richardson, D. and Robinson, V. (1993) *Introducing Women's Studies: Feminist Theory and Practice*, London: Macmillan.

Richardson, J. and Lambert, J. (1985) *The Sociology of Race*, Ormskirk: Causeway.

Riessman, F. (1962) *The Culturally Deprived Child*, New York: Harper & Row.

Riley, M. (1988) *Power, Politics and Voting Behaviour: An Introduction to the Sociology of Politics*, Hemel Hempstead: Harvester Wheatsheaf.

Ritzer, G. (1992) *Sociological Theory*, 3rd edn, New York: McGraw-Hill.

Ritzer, G. (1993) *The McDonaldization of Society*, Newbury Park, CA: Pine Forge Press.

Robbins (1963) *Higher Education: Report*, Cmnd 2154, London: HMSO.

Roberts, K., Cook, F. G., Clark, S. C. and Sememeoff, E. (1977) *The Fragmentary Class Structure*, London: Heinemann.

Roberts, R. H. (ed.) (1995) *Religion and the Transformations of Capitalism: Comparative Approaches*, London: Routledge.

Robertson, G. and Nicol, A. (1992) *Media Law: The Rights of Journalists*, Harmondsworth: Penguin.

Robertson, R. (1970) *The Sociological Interpretation of Religion*, Oxford: Blackwell.

Robinson, C. J. (1983) *Black Marxism*, London: Zed.

Roper, M. and Tosh, J. (1991) *Manful Assertions*, London: Routledge.

Rose, D. (ed.) (1988) *Social Stratification and Economic Change*, London: Hutchinson.

Rose, D. and Gershuny, J. (1995) 'Social surveys and social change', *Sociology Review* 4(4): 11–14.

Rose, E. J. B. (1969) *Colour and Citizenship*, Oxford: Institute of Race Relations/Oxford University Press.

Rosenau, J. (1990) *Turbulence in World Politics*, Hemel Hempstead: Harvester Wheatsheaf.

Rosenthal, R. and Jacobson, L. (1968) *Pygmalion in the Classroom*, New York: Holt, Rinehart & Winston.

Rostow, W. W. (1960) *The Stages of Economic Growth: A Non-Communist Manifesto*, Cambridge: Cambridge University Press.

Rousseau, J. J. (1965 [1754]) 'A dissertation on the origin and foundation of the inequality of mankind', in T. B. Bottomore, *Classes in Modern Society*, London: Allen & Unwin.

Rousseau, J. J. (1968 [1762]) *The Social Contract*, trans. M. Cranston, Harmondsworth: Penguin.

Rowbotham, S. (1982) 'The trouble with patriarchy', in M. Evans (ed.) *The Women Question*, London: Fontana.

Rowntree Foundation (1995) *Income and Wealth*, York.

Rowntree, B. S. (1901) *Poverty: A Study of Town Life*, London: Macmillan.

Roy, D. (1954) 'Efficiency and the fix', *American Journal of Sociology* 60: 255–66.

Rubin, G. (1993) 'Misguided, dangerous and wrong: an analysis of anti-pornography of politics', in A. Assirte and C. Avendon (eds) *Bad Girls and Dirty Pictures*, London: Pluto.

Runciman, W. G. (1990) 'How many classes are there in contemporary society?', *Sociology* 24: 377–96.

Rusche, G. (1980 [1933]) 'Labour market and penal sanctions: thoughts on the sociology of punishment', in T. Platt and P. Takagi (eds) *Punishment and Penal Discipline*, Berkeley, CA: University of California Press.

Rusche, G. and Kirchheimer, O. (1968 [1939]) *Punishment and Social Structure*, New York.

Rutherford, J. (1990) 'A place called home: identity and the cultural politics of difference', in J. Rutherford (ed.) *Identity: Community, Culture, Difference*, London: Routledge.

Rutter, M., Maughan, B., Mortimore, P. and Ouston, J. (1979) *Fifteen Hundred Hours: Secondary Schools and their Effects on Children*, Shepton Mallet: Open Books.

Sabel, C. (1982) *Work and Politics*, Cambridge: Cambridge University Press.

Saggar, S. (1992) *Race and Politics in Britain*, Hemel Hempstead: Harvester Wheatsheaf.

Samuel, R. (1982) 'The SDP and the new political class', *New Society* 22 April.

Sarre, P., Philps, D. and Skellington, R. (1989) *Ethnic Minority Housing: Explanations and Policies*, Aldershot: Avebury.

Saunders, P. (1987) *Social Theory and the Urban Question*, London: Unwin Hyman.

Savage, M., Barlow, J., Dickens, A. and Fielding, T. (1992) *Property, Bureaucracy and Culture: Middle Class Formation in Contemporary Britain*, London: Routledge.

Sayer, A. and Walker, R. (1992) *The New Social Economy*, Oxford: Blackwell.

Scannell, P. and Cardiff, D. (1987) 'Broadcasting and national unity', in J. Curran, A. Smith and P. Wingate (eds) *Impacts and Influences: Essays on Media Power in the 20th Century*, London: Methuen.

Scannell, P. and Cardiff, D. (1991) *A Social History of Broadcasting, Volume 1 1922–39*, Oxford: Blackwell.

Scarman (1982) *The Brixton Disorders 10–12 April 1981: Report of an Enquiry by the Rt Hon. Lord Scarman OBE*, Cmnd 8427, London: HMSO.

Scase, R. (1992) *Class*, Milton Keynes: Open University Press.

Schattschnieder, E. E. (1969) *The Semi-Sovereign People*, New York: Holt, Rinehart & Winston.

Schramm, W., Lyle, V. and Parker, E. (1961) *Television in the Lives of our Children*, Stanford, CA: Stanford University Press.

Schudson, M. (1991) 'The sociology of news revisited', in J. Curran and M. Gurevitch (eds) *Mass Media and Society*, London: Edward Arnold.

Schulze, L. (1990) 'On the muscle', in J. Gaines and C. Herzog (eds) *Fabrications: Costume and the Female Body*, London: Routledge.

Schuman, H., Steel, C. and Bobo, L. (1985) *Racial Attitudes in America: Trends and Interpretation*, Cambridge, MA: Harvard University Press.

Schumpeter, J. A. (1976) *Capitalism, Socialism and Democracy*, 5th edn, London: Allen & Unwin.

Scott, J. (1991) *Who Rules Britain?*, Cambridge: Polity.

Scott, J. (1992) *The Upper Classes: Property and Privilege in Britain*, London: Macmillan.

Scott, J. (1994) *Poverty and Wealth: Citizenship, Deprivation and Privilege*, London: Longman.

Seacole, M. (1984[1857]) *The Wonderful Adventures of Mary Seacole in Many Lands*, ed. Z. Alexander and A. Dewjee, New York: Falling Wall Press.

Seaton, J. and Pimlott, B. (1987) *The Media in British Politics*, Aldershot: Avebury.

Segal, L. (1994) *Straight Sex: The Politics of Pleasure*, London: Virago.

Seidler, V. (1989) *Rediscovering Masculinity*, London: Routledge.

Seidler, V. (ed.) (1991) *Men, Sex and Relationships*, London: Routledge.

Seymour-Ure, C. (1992) *The British Press and Broadcasting since 1945*, Oxford: Blackwell.

Sharpe, S. (1994a [1976]) *Just Like a Girl*, 2nd edn, Harmondsworth: Penguin.

Sharpe, S. (1994b) 'Great expectations', *Everywoman* December.

Shawcross, W. (1992) *Murdoch by Shawcross*, London: Chatto & Windus.

Sheeran, Y (1993) 'The role of women and family structure', *Sociology Review* April.

Sheppard, D. (1983) *Bias to the Poor*, London: Hodder & Stoughton.

SHIL (Single Homeless in London) and LHU (London Housing Unit) (1989) *Local Authority Policy and Practice on Single Homelessness Among Black and Other Ethnic Minority People*, London: SHIL/LHU.

Shils, E. (1959) 'Mass society and its culture', in N. Jacobs (ed.) *Culture for the Millions? Mass Media in Modern Society*, London: Van Nostrand.

Shils, E. and Young, M. (1956) 'The meaning of the coronation', *Sociological Review* 1(2): 63–81.

Siltanen, J. and Stanworth, M. (eds) (1984) *Women in the Public Sphere: A Critique of Sociology and Politics*, London: Hutchinson.

Simpson, A. (1981) *Stacking the Decks: A Study of Race, Inequality and Council Housing in Nottingham*, Nottingham Community Relations Council.

Simpson, E. S. (1994) *The Developing World: An Introduction*, 2nd edn, London: Longman.

Sinclair, J. (1974 [1791-9]) *Statistical Account of Scotland drawn up from the Communications of Ministers of the different Parishes*, 21 vols, Edinburgh: William Creech / Witherington & Grant, E. P. Publishing.

Sinclair, M. T. (1991) 'Work, women and skill: economic theories and feminist perspectives', in N. Redclift and M. T. Sinclair (eds) *Working Women: International Perspectives on Labour and gender Ideology*, London: Routledge.

Sivanandan, A. (1982) *A Different Hunger: Writings on Black Resistance*, London: Pluto.

Sivanandan, A. (1990) *Communities of Resistance*, London: Verso.

Skellington, R. (1992) *'Race' in Britain Today*, London: Sage.

Sklair, L. (1991) *Sociology and the Global Process*, Hemel Hempstead: Harvester Wheatsheaf.

Skolnick, R. (1969) *The Politics of Protest*, New York: Simon & Schuster.

Skuse, D. (1984) 'Extreme deprivation in early childhood', *Journal of Child Psychology and Psychiatry* 25(4).

Smart, N. (1978) *The Phenomenon of Religion*, Oxford: Mowbray.

Smith, A. (1964 [1776]) *An Inquiry in the Nature and Causes of the Wealth of Nations*, vol. II, ed. E. Cannon, London: Methuen.

Smith, A. D. (1995) 'The dark side of nationalism: the revival of nationalism in late twentieth-century Europe', in L. Cheles (ed.) *The Far Right in Western and Eastern Europe*, London: Longman.

Smith, B. (1987) *The Everyday World as Problematic: A Feminist Sociology*, Milton Keynes: Open University Press.

Smith, D. (ed.) (1992) *Understanding the Underclass*, London: Policy Studies Institute.

Smith, D. J. and Gray, J. (1983) *Police and People in London IV: The Police in Action*, London: Policy Studies Institute.

Solomos, J. (1989) *Race and Racism in Contemporary Britain*, London: Macmillan.

Solomos, J. and Rackett, T. (1991) 'Policing and urban unrest: problem constitution and policy response', in E. Cashmore and E. McLoughlin (eds) *Out of Order? Policing Black People*, London: Routledge.

Sommerville, J. (1982) *The Rise and Fall of Childhood*, Beverly Hills, CA: Sage.

Southern, R. W. (1988) *The Middle Ages*, Harmondsworth: Penguin.

Spencer, C. (1986) *Colin Spencer's Fish Cookbook*, London: Pan.

Spender, D. (1981) *Men's Studies Modified: The Impact of Feminism on the Academic Disciplines*, Oxford: Pergamon.

Spender, D. and Sarah, E. (1980) *Learning to Lose: Sexism and Education*, London: Women's Press.

Sprott, W. J. H. (1954) *The Social Background of Delinquency*, Nottinghan: Nottingham University Press.

Stacey, J. (1988) 'Can there be a feminist ethnography?', *Women's Studies International Forum* 11(1): 21–7.

Stacey, J. (1993) 'Untangling feminist theory', in D. Richardson and V. Robinson (eds) *Introducing Women's Studies*, London: Macmillan.

Stanko, E. (1992) 'Wife battering: all in the family', in A. Giddens (ed.) *Human Societies*, Cambridge: Polity.

Stanley, L. (ed.) (1990) *Feminist Praxis: Research, Theory and Epistemology in Feminist Sociology*, London: Routledge.

Stanley, L. and Wise, S. (1983) *Breaking Out: Feminist Consciousness and Feminist Research*, London: Routledge & Kegan Paul.

Stanley, L. and Wise, S. (1993) *Breaking Out Again: Feminist Ontology and Epistemology*, London: Routledge.

Stanworth, M. (1983) *Gender and Schooling: A Study of Sexual Division in the Classroom*, London: Women's Research and Resources Centre.

Stanworth, M. (1984) 'Women and class analysis: a reply to John Goldthorpe', *Sociology* 18(2): 159–70.

Stark, E. and Flitcraft, A. (1985) 'Women battering, child abuse and social heredity: what is the relationship?', in N. Johnson (ed.) *Marital Violence*, London: Routledge & Kegan Paul.

Statham, J. (1986) *Daughters and Sons: Experiences of Non-Sexist Childraising*, Oxford: Blackwell.

Statham, J., Mackinnon, D., Cathcart, H. and Hales, M. (1991) *The Education Fact File: A Handbook of Education Information in the UK*, 2nd edn, London: Hodder & Stoughton.

Stevens, P. and Willis, C. (1979) *Race, Crime and Arrests*, London: HMSO.

Stewart, A., Prandy, K. and Blackburn, R. M. (1980) *Social Stratification and Occupations*, London: Macmillan.

Stewart, J. and Stoker, G. (eds) (1989) *The Future of Local Government*, London: Macmillan.

Stirk, P. M. R. and Weigall, D. (1995) *An Introduction to Political Ideas*, London: Cassell.

Stolenberg, J. (1990) *Refusing to be a Man*, London: Fontana.

Stone, M. (1981) *The Education of the Black Child in Britain: The Myth of Multiracial Eduction*, London: Fontana.

Strinati, D. (1992) 'Postmodernism and popular culture', *Sociology Review* 1(4): 2–7.

Swann (1985) *Education for All: Report of Committee of Inquiry into the Education of Children from Ethnic Minority Groups*, Cmnd 9453, London: HMSO.

Swingewood, A. (1991) *A Short History of Sociological Thought*, London: Macmillan.

Sydie, R. (1987) *Natural Women, Cultured Men*, Milton Keynes: Open University Press.

Syer, M. (1982) 'Racism, ways of thinking and school', in J. Tierney (ed.) *Race, Migration and Schooling*, London: Holt Education.

Taking Liberties Collective (1989) *Learning the Hard Way: Women's Oppression in Men's Education*, London: Macmillan.

Tanner, D. M. (1978) *The Lesbian Couple*, Lexington, MA: Lexington Books.

Taylor, F. W. (1967 [1911]) *The Principles of Scientific Management*, New York: W. W. Norton.

Taylor, I., Walton, P. and Young, J. (1973) *The New Criminology*, London: Routledge & Kegan Paul.

Taylor, I., Walton, P. and Young, J. (eds) (1975) *Critical Criminology*, London: Routledge & Kegan Paul.

Taylor, S. (1992) 'Measuring child abuse', *Sociology Review* 1(3): 23–9.

Thane, P. (1982) *The Elderly in Modern Society*, London: Longman.

Thompson, E. P. (1968) *The Making of the English Working Class*, Harmondsworth: Penguin.

Thompson, H. S. (1967) *Hell's Angels*, Harmondsworth: Penguin.

Thompson, I. (1986) *Religion*, London: Longman.

Thompson, K. and Tunstall, J. (eds) (1971) *Sociological Perspectives*, Harmondsworth: Penguin.

Thompson, P. (1983) *The Nature of Work*, London: Macmillan.

Thompson, P. (1990) *Work Organizations: A Critical Introduction*, London: Macmillan.

Tiefer, L. (1995) *Sex is Not a Natural Act*, Oxford: Westview.

Tilly, L. and Scott, J. (1987) *Women, Work and Achievement*, London: Macmillan.

Timperley, C. (1994) 'Bringing home the bacon', *Everywoman* May.

Tinker, A. (1996) *Elderly People in Modern Society*, 4th edn, London: Longman.

Toffler, A. (1970) *Future Shock*, New York: Random House.

Toffler, A. (1980) *The Third Wave*, London: Collins.

Tomlinson, S. (1980) *Educational Subnormality: A Study in Decision Making*, London: Routledge.

Tomlinson, S. (1983) *Ethnic Minorities in British Schools: A Review of the Literature, 1960–1982*, London: Heinemann.

Tonge, J. (1994) 'The anti-poll tax movement: a pressure movement?', *Politics* 14(2): 93–9.

Touraine, A. (1971) *The Post-Industrial Society*, New York: Wildwood House.

Toye, J. (1993) *Dilemmas of Development*, 2nd edn, Oxford: Blackwell.

Trenchard, L. and Warren, H. (1984) *Something To Tell You*, London: Gay Teenage Group.

Trigg, R. (1985) *Understanding Social Science*, Oxford: Blackwell.

Troeltsch, E. (1931) *The Social Teaching of the Christian Churches*, London: Allen & Unwin.

Trowler, P. (1988) *Investigating the Media*, London: Collins.

Tumin, M. M. (1967) 'Some principles of stratification: a critical analysis', in R. Bendix and S. M. Lipset (eds) *Class, Status and Power*, 2nd edn, London: Routledge & Kegan Paul.

Tunstall, J. (1962) *The Fishermen*, London: MacGibbon & Kee.

Tunstall, J. (1977) *The Media are American*, London: Constable.

Tunstall, J. and Palmer, M. (eds) (1991) *Media Moguls*, London: Routledge.

Turner, E. (1965) *The Young Man's Companion*, London: Hugh Evelyn.

Turner, R. (1961) 'Modes of social ascent through education', in A. H. Halsey, J. Floud and C. A. Anderson (eds) *Education, Economy and Society*, New York: Free Press.

Tutt, N. (1974) *Care or Custody: Community Homes and the Treatment of Delinquency*, London: Dartford Longman & Todd.

UN (1984) *World Development Report*, Washington, DC: United Nations.

Unemployment Unit (1995) *Working Brief*, 61, February.

Unesco (1972) *Apartheid*, 2nd edn, Paris: Unesco.

Van Zoonen, L. (1991) 'Feminist perspectives on the media', in J. Curran and M. Gurevitch (eds) *Mass Media and Society*, London: Edward Arnold.

Van Zoonen, L. (1994) *Feminist Media Studies*, London: Sage.

de Vaus, D. A. (1986) *Surveys in Social Research*, London: Allen & Unwin.

Veljanovski, C. (1989) *Freedom in Broadcasting*, London: Institute of Economic Affairs.

Veljanovski, C. (1991) *The Media in Britain Today*, London: News International.

Waddington, D., Jones, K. and Critcher, C. (1989) *Flashpoints: Studies in Public Disorder*, London: Routledge.

Waddington, P. A. J. (1993) *Calling the Police: The Interpretation of, and Response to, Calls for Assistance from the Public*, Aldershot: Avebury.

Wagg, S. (1992) 'I blame the parents: childhood and politics in modern Britain', *Sociology Review* April: 10–15.

Wajcman, J. (1983) *Women in Control*, Milton Keynes: Open University Press.

Walby, S. (1986) *Patriarchy at Work*, Cambridge: Polity.

Walby, S. (1990) *Theorizing Patriarchy*, Oxford: Blackwell.

Walker, A. (1988) *Living by the Word: Selected Writings 1973–87*, London: Women's Press.

Walker, A. (1990) 'Blaming the victim', in C. Murray (ed.) *The Emerging British Underclass*, London: IEA Health & Welfare Unit.

Walker, A. and Walker, C. A. (1987) *The Growing Divide: A Social Audit 1979–87*, London: Child Poverty Action Group.

Walker, N. (1991) *Why Punish*, Oxford: Oxford University Press.

Wallerstein, E. (1979) *The Capitalist World Economy*, Cambridge: Cambridge University Press.

Wallerstein, E. (1983) *Historical Capitalism*, London: Verso.

Wallis, R. (1976) *The Road to Total Freedom: A Sociological Analysis of Scientology*, London: Heinemann.

Walter, N. (1990) *Blasphemy Ancient and Modern*, London: Rationalist Press Association.

Ward, C. (1972) *Work*, Harmondsworth: Penguin.

Warnock (1978) *Special Education Needs: Report of the Committee of Enquiry into the Education of Handicapped Children and Young People*, London: HMSO.

Weber, M. (1949) *The Methodology of the Social Sciences*, New York: Free Press.

Weber, M. (1963 [1920]) *The Sociology of Religion*, Boston, MA: Beacon.

Weber, M. (1964 [1922]) *The Theory of Social and Economic Organization*, Oxford: Oxford University Press.

Weber, M. (1974 [1902]) *The Protestant Ethic and the Spirit of Capitalism*, London: Unwin.

Webster, F. (1995) *Theories of the Information Society*, London: Routledge.

Webster, J. (1996) *Shaping Women's Work: Gender, Employment and Information Technology*, London: Longman.

Weeks, J. (1986) *Sexuality*, London: Tavistock.

Weeks, J. (1990) *Coming Out*, Aylesbury: Hazell.

Weeks, J. (1991) *Against Nature: Essays on History, Sexuality and Identity*, London: Rivers Oram.

Weelock, J. (1990) *Husbands at Home*, London: Routledge.

Weiner, G. (1985) *Just a Bunch of Girls*, Milton Keynes: Open University Press.

Wellings, K., Field, J., Johnson, A. and Wadsworth, J. (1994) *Sexual Behaviour in Britain: The National Survey of Sexual Attitudes and Lifestyles of the British Population*, Harmondsworth: Penguin.

Wellman, D. (1977) *Portraits of White Racism*, Cambridge: Cambridge University Press.

Wells, T. (1993) *The World in Your Kitchen*, Oxford: New Internationalist.

Westergaard, J. (1970) 'The rediscovery of the cash nexus', in R. Miliband and J. Saville (eds) *The Socialist Register*, London: Merlin.

Westergaard, J. and Resler, H. (1976) *Class in a Capitalist Society*, Harmondsworth: Penguin.

Westwood, S. (1983) *All Day and Every Day: Factory and Family in the Making of Women's Lives*, London: Pluto.

Westwood, S. and Bachi, P. (1989) *Enterprising Women: Ethnicity, Economy and Gender*, London: Routledge.

Weymouth, A. and Lamizet, B. (1996) *Markets and Myths: Forces for Change in the European Media*, London: Longman.

Whale, J. (1980) *The Politics of the Media*, London: Fontana.

Whannel, G. and Williams, J. (1993) 'The rise of satellite TV', *Sociology Review* 2(3).

Wheen, F. (1982) 'Having a smashing time', *New Statesman* 22 October.

Whitaker, B. (1981) *News Ltd*, London: Minority.

Whiteside, N. (1991) *Bad Times*, London: Faber & Faber.

Williams, G. (1994) *Britain's Media: How They are Related*, London: Campaign for Press and Broadcasting Freedom.

Williams, K., Cutler, T., Williams, J. and Haslam, C. (1987) 'The end of mass production?', *Economy and Society* 16(3): 405–39.

Williams, M. (1986) *Society Today*, London: Macmillan.

Williams, R. (1958) *Culture and Society: 1780-1850*, Harmondsworth: Penguin.

Williams, R. (1974) *Television, Technology and Cultural Form*, London: Fontana.

Williams, R. (1983) *Towards 2000*, Harmondsworth: Penguin.

Willis, P. (1977) *Learning to Labour: Why Working-Class Kids Get Working-Class Jobs*, Farnborough: Saxon House.

Willmott, P. (1988) 'Urban kinship past and present', *Social Studies Review* November: 44–6.

Wilson, A. (1986) 'The family', in P. McNeill and C. Townley (eds) *Fundamentals of Sociology*, Cheltenham: Stanley Thornes.

Wilson, B. (1963) 'A typology of sects in a dynamic and comparative perspective', *Archives de Sociologie de Religion* 16: 49–63.

Wilson, B. (1969) *Religion in Secular Society*, Harmondsworth: Penguin.

Wilson, B. (1982) *Religion in Sociological Perspective*, Oxford: Oxford University Press.

Wilson, B. and Dobbelaere, K. (1994) *A Time to Chant: The Soka Gakkai Buddhists in Britain*, Oxford: Blackwell.

Wilson, E. (1986) *Adorned in Dreams: Fashion and Modernity*, London: Virago.

Wilson, E. (1989) *The Myth of British Monarchy*, London: Journeyman.

Wilson, E. and Rodgerson, G. (1991) *Pornography and Feminism*, London: Lawrence & Wishart.

Wilton, T. (1993) 'Queer subjects: lesbians, heterosexual women and the academy', in M. Kennedy, C. Lubelska and V. Walsh (eds) *Making Connections*, London: Taylor & Francis.

Winship, J. (1986) *Inside Women's Magazines*, London: Pandora.

Witte, R. (1996) *Racial Violence and the State: A Comparative Analysis of Britain, France, and the Netherlands*, London: Longman.

Wolf, N. (1991) *The Beauty Myth*, London: Vintage.

Wollstonecraft, M. (1982[1792]) *Vindication of the Rights of Woman*, Harmondsworth: Penguin.

Wolpe, H. (1980) 'Capitalism and cheap labour power in South Africa: from segregation to apartheid', in H. Wolpe (ed.) *The Articulation of Modes of Production*, London: Routledge & Kegan Paul.

Wood, S. (ed.) (1982) *The Degradation of Work?*, London: Hutchinson.

Wood, S. (ed.) (1989) *The Transformation of Work?*, London: Unwin Hyman.

Woodhouse, A. (1989) *Fantastic Women*, London: Macmillan.

Woolf, R. (1969) 'Beyond tolerance', in R. Woolf, B. Moore and H. Marcuse, *A Critique of Pure Tolerance*, London: Jonathan Cape.

Worsley, P. (1964) *The Third World*, London: Weidenfeld & Nicolson.

Worsley, P. (1987) *The New Introductory Sociology*, Harmondsworth: Penguin.

Worsley, P. (ed.) (1991) *The New Modern Sociology Readings*, Harmondsworth: Penguin.

Wright, C. R. (1960) 'Functional analysis and mass communication revisited', *Public Opinion Quarterly* 24: 606–20.

Wright, E. O. (1985) *Classes*, London: Verso.

Wright, P. (1987) *Spycatcher: The Candid Autobiography of a Senior Intelligence Officer*, New York: Viking.

Wynne, D. (1990) 'Leisure, lifestyle and the construction of social position', *Leisure Studies* 9: 21–34.

Yaffe, M. and Nelson, E. (1982) *The Influence of Pornography on Behaviour*, London: Academic.

Yinger, J. M. (1946) *Religion in the Struggle for Power*, Durham, NC: Duke University Press.

Young, J. (1992) 'The rising demand for law and order and our Maginot lines of defence against crime', in N. Abercrombie and A. Warde (eds) *Social Change in Contemporary Britain*, Cambridge: Polity.

Young, J. and Mathews, R. (eds) (1992) *Rethinking Criminology: The Realist Debate*, London: Sage.

Young, M. and Willmott, P. (1962 [1957]) *Family and Kinship in East London*, Harmondsworth: Penguin.

Young, M. and Willmott, P. (1975) *The Symmetrical Family*, Harmondsworth: Penguin.

Young, M. F. D. (ed.) (1971) *Knowledge and Control: New Directions in the Sociology of Education*, London: Collier-Macmillan.

Zakaria, R. (1988) *The Struggle within Islam: The Conflict between Religion and Politics*, Harmondsworth: Penguin.

Zeitlin, I. (1989) *The Large Corporation and Contemporary Society*, Cambridge: Polity.

Zimbardo, P. (1972) 'Pathology of imprisonment', *Society* 9: 4–8.

# Index

300 – 315 Gender
358 Race
509 - 552 Crime & D